THE
PEOPLE'S
LOBBY

THE
PEOPLE'S
LOBBY

Organizational Innovation

and the Rise of Interest Group Politics

in the United States, 1890–1925

ELISABETH S. CLEMENS

The University of Chicago Press / Chicago and London

Elisabeth S. Clemens is associate professor in the Department of Sociology at the University of Arizona. She is co-editor, with Walter W. Powell, of *Private Action and the Public Good.*

The University of Chicago Press, Chicago 60637
The University of Chicago Press, Ltd., London
© 1997 by The University of Chicago
All rights reserved. Published 1997
Printed in the United States of America
06 05 04 03 02 01 00 99 98 97   5 4 3 2 1

ISBN (cloth): 0-226-10992-5
ISBN (paper): 0-226-10993-3

Library of Congress Cataloging-in-Publication Data

Clemens, Elisabeth Stephanie, 1958–
    The people's lobby : organizational innovation and the rise
    of interest group politics in the United States, 1890–1925 /
    Elisabeth S. Clemens.
        p.   cm
    Includes bibliographical references and index.
    ISBN 0-226-10992-5. — ISBN 0-226-10993-3 (pbk.)
    1. Lobbying—United States—History.   2. Pressure
groups—United States—History.   3. United States—Politics
and government—1865–1933.   4. Organizational
change—United States—History.   5. Social institutions—
United States—History.   6. Institution building—
History.   I. Title.
JK1118.C49   1997
324'.4'097309034—dc21   97-1339
                                                                    CIP

Contents

Illustrations

Acknowledgments

Books, like political change, are often the product of collective action. For the writing of this one, I am especially indebted to my advisors at the University of Chicago—Wendy Griswold, Edward O. Laumann, and Theda Skocpol—not only for their advice, but for their consistent interest, encouragement, and unceasing demands for clarification. This project grew out of conversations with their work, at times in strange tongues.

Throughout the researching, writing, rewriting, and revising of this project, I have relied on friends who are also the best of colleagues. For all their inspiration, support, and talent for inciting frivolity, I am deeply grateful to Bruce Carruthers, Alfred Darnell, Wendy Espeland, Kelly Moore, Kathy Neckerman, Ann Orloff, Maryjane Osa, and Sunita Parikh. Jim Wooten has been generous with conversation and criticism and an unfailing source of references. Most importantly, however, he once said those two little words—"predatory politics"—that revealed the argument that I wanted to make. David Meyer helped me to think through the intersection of social movements and formal political institutions. Patrick Miller shared his enthusiasm for American history and conviction that the writing of books is difficult but worthwhile.

This book could not have been written without the generosity of my colleagues in the Department of Sociology at the University of Arizona. Woody Powell and Doug McAdam introduced me to the tools that I needed to reformulate my argument—institutional analysis and social-movement theory—and Paula England taught me how to stay sane in the process. Neil Fligstein, Cal Morrill, and Marc Schneiberg all provided incisive criticism, inspired suggestions, and welcome camaraderie, while David Snow was there to warn me whenever I showed signs of "howling determinism." Gordon Abra, Doug Adams, Patrick Ledger, and Kris McIlwaine each provided valuable research assistance and Barb McIntosh helped to wrestle the manuscript into the proper format.

I have benefited from discussions at Columbia University, the University of Michigan, New York University, Rutgers University, and the Social

Movements and Social Organization seminars at the University of Arizona. Edwin Amenta, Nancy Cauthen, Douglas Chalmers, Dan Cress, Mustafa Emirbayer, Jeff Goodwin, Joseph Luders, Howard Lune, and Mayer Zald all provided helpful comments and critical challenges that have helped me to sharpen arguments throughout the book.

At the beginning and the end of this project, predoctoral and postdoctoral fellowships from the Spencer Foundation gave me much-needed, and greatly appreciated, time to think and to write. Portions of the research were supported by a Young Faculty Fellowship from the Project on the Governance of Nonprofit Organizations, supported by the Lilly Endowment, and a grant from the Social and Behavioral Sciences Research Institute at the University of Arizona. Harrison White and all the members of the Center for the Social Sciences at Columbia University provided both a haven for writing and constant encouragement to find more general social theory in the historical details.

To the extent that I have succeeded in making those connections clear, much of the credit is due to Richard Bensel and Frank Dobbin. As reviewers for the University of Chicago Press, both read the manuscript with extraordinary care and insight. Unfortunately, this means that I must take responsibility for any errors that remain.

As always, my greatest debts—too numerous for listing—are to my parents, William and Dorothy Clemens. Finally, the earliest inspirations for a study of the power of association were provided by my late grandparents: Max and Ora Thelen, Vincent and Estella Clemens. From the Lincoln-Roosevelt League and the Commonwealth Club through the PTA, Gamma Phi, Troop 23, the Businessmen's Garden Club, and the AARP, they were part of the story that I have tried to tell.

List of Abbreviations

AFBF   American Farm Bureau Federation
AFL   American Federation of Labor
CIH   Commission of Immigration and Housing (California)
CSFL   California State Federation of Labor
CSG   California State Grange
GFWC   General Federation of Women's Clubs
FTC   Federated Trades Council
IWC   Industrial Welfare Commission
IWW   Industrial Workers of the World
JLC   Joint Legislative Council (Washington State)
NAWSA   National American Woman Suffrage Association
NCF   National Civic Federation
WaSFL   Washington State Federation of Labor
WCTU   Woman's Christian Temperance Union
WiSFL   Wisconsin State Federation of Labor
YWCA   Young Women's Christian Association

Prologue

In 1909, a rumor swept the legislature of California. The "machine," led by the political bureau of the Southern Pacific Railroad in company with "the political agents . . . of the tenderloin, . . . racetrack, and public service monopolies," was alleged to control the votes of numerous legislators, both Republican and Democrat. But this arrangement was threatened by a growing movement for political reform. Word had it that

> certain public-spirited citizens of Los Angeles and San Francisco would maintain at the Capitol during the session a lobby to protect the interests of the people, just as the machine lobby looks after the well-being of machine-protected corporations and individuals.
>
> This rumor caused great distress. It had all sorts of versions. One story was that a corps of Pinkertons would be employed to look for bugs in bills, boodle in sacks, and boodle-itching palms. Another account had it that the supervision was to be carried on by the San Francisco graft prosecution, and the Burns men [private detectives] would be in constant attendance. A report, started early in the session, that a Burns man had secured a job as Assembly clerk almost threw that body into hysterics.[1]

This rumor proved to be no more than that. But the existence of such a tale suggests a more substantial development: the appearance of a new form of political organization. In addition to electoral politics and protest movements, direct involvement in legislative activity was emerging as a model for popular political participation. Guided less by loyalty to party than in the past, voters learned to monitor the legislative process, to intervene in shaping policy, and to hold their representatives accountable at the polls. The new currency of political influence included procedural mastery, technical expertise, and the ability to mobilize public opinion. These new organizational capacities were accompanied by new patterns of political action. In significant numbers, voters replaced the guidelines of partisan loyalty with constructions of group interest; others simply ceased to vote. Consequently, the political accomplishments of the Progressive Era involved not merely a change of attitudes or preferences, but

1

the institutionalization of new means by which organized groups might influence the policy process. These changes laid the foundations of modern interest group politics in the United States.

As used in this argument, *interest group politics* designates political organization mobilized around specific issues or policy demands and sustained not only by financial resources (as were many "lobbies" of the late nineteenth century) but by extrapartisan voting blocs. It is difficult for us to appreciate the novelty of these arrangements—but novel, and controversial, they were. The difficulty is due, in part, to the habit of treating interest groups as a timeless feature of American politics. In *The Governmental Process,* one of the classics of "group theory" first published in 1951, David Truman observes that "group pressures, whatever we may wish to call them, are not new in America." He goes on to provide examples from the Federalist Papers, constitutional ratifying conventions in the states, and the political observations made by Alexis de Tocqueville in the 1830s.[2] Both contemporary common sense and much formal political theory also assume that political behavior is motivated by individual interests and that groups representing the aggregation of such interests will regularly mobilize in order to demand specific policy responses. Consequently, it is difficult to understand why efforts to link policy to organized groups would have been avoided earlier in the nation's history.

But interest group politics entails more than the aggregated actions of self-interested individuals. As Truman recognized, party systems have a history, and new forms of association—including parties—produce "waves of association-building." Consequently, the organization of group pressures also has a history, one that is obscured by the treatment of interest group phenomena as ubiquitous, functional responses to the complexity of social organization.[3] Writing in 1900, the economist John R. Commons observed that "there is no social movement of the past twenty years more quiet nor more potent than the organization of private interests. No other country in the world presents so interesting a spectacle."[4] Manufacturers organized nonpartisan trade associations in both the United States and Europe, but only in the United States did "interest"—rather than party, class, language, or religion—become the primary idiom of popular political life. Under the rubric of "interest," various configurations of citizens made demands upon the political system. Although the "People's Lobby" of California proved to be mere rumor, similarly titled organizations actually were established throughout the nation. The late nineteenth century also saw the multiplication of voluntary associations, many with formal committees dedicated to drafting legislation, lobbying, or cultivating public opinion.

These organizations provided arenas in which individuals reconstituted themselves as political actors, learned to articulate demands for specific policies, and then to monitor the responses of elected officials.

This history reemerges if we attend to controversies over the forms of political organization. Why—to take some examples from agricultural history—would California farmers in 1892 defeat a proposal to publicize the voting records of elected representatives, denouncing such action as a corruption of politics? Why, after the First World War, were farm organizations described as "the return, in an entirely new and menacing form, of one of the outworn dogmas that were overthrown by the French Revolution—the doctrine of privileged classes"? Why, in the 1920s, would Senator Arthur Capper of Kansas assert that "[t]he organization of the agricultural group in the Congress *should not* have been necessary"?[5] For political commentators of the late nineteenth century, the puzzle was how "the people" could employ a model of political organization associated with corrupt corporate lobbying and "class legislation" that, by definition, were opposed to the common good. After all, one knew lobbyists were corrupt not solely by those they represented but by the form of their ties to elected representatives. By pressuring legislators after they had been elected and intervening in the drafting of bills, lobbyists embodied the corruption of American politics. If the people were to pursue the same strategies, to organize themselves as lobbies, surely they would endanger their own claims to political virtue? A transformation of political norms, motives, and practices lay between the nineteenth-century blanket condemnation of the "Interests" and the twentieth-century characterization of political contests as "your interests vs. the 'special interests.'"[6]

To invent a politics of interest required disassembling—at least in part—the politics of party. Large numbers of voters had to unlearn their identities as partisans and learn to behave as voters with interests beyond party, willing to vote for whichever candidate promised more of what they wanted. As John H. Aldrich has observed, the history of American political parties comprises both partisan realignments (significant shifts in voter identification) and changes in partisan institutional form. Between the 1890s and the 1930s, political challengers did not produce a classic realignment. Rather, these challengers secured major changes in the form of government (e.g., primary elections, initiative and referendum, the multiplication of government programs and agencies) that greatly altered the parties' vulnerability to other political challengers and created alternative channels for influencing policy outcomes. In the short term, these changes produced a hybrid regime of party and extrapartisan organizations and, in the long term, created the conditions for the decline of the "party in the electorate."[7] But the puzzle of process remains. How were political rules and institutions transformed such that varied groups of citizens came to feel both able and entitled to promote their explicitly self-interested claims in party conventions, legislatures, and state agencies?

The institutional transformation of late-nineteenth- and early-twentieth-century American politics combined three distinct processes. First, beset by increasing criticism and changing conditions, the system of nationally competitive, mass-mobilization parties oriented toward electoral politics began to decay. Second, in response to growing discontent, Americans developed new organizational models for political participation, generating a repertoire of possible alternatives to the party system. Finally, over the course of three decades of political contestation, these alternative models transformed—and were transformed by—existing political institutions. In the place of a polity centered on the electoral competition of national parties, by the 1920s legislatures, administrative agencies, and public opinion were established as competing foci of American politics.

In the telling of American history, the first of these processes has received the lion's share of attention. Concentrating on the dilemmas faced by party leaders, the actions of elite reformers, and the aggregation of individual attitudes through the ballot box, historians and political scientists have generated rich portraits of the decline of the party system and a vigorous debate over its causes.[8] More recently, scholars have turned to the third process, described by Stephen Skowronek as "building a new American state."[9] But party decline and state formation do not exhaust the story of how we got from there to here. To trace the origins of this new system of interest-based politics, we must turn to the invention of alternatives to the politics of party.[10]

A Paradox of Progressivism

Viewed in terms of pure power politics, periods of reform are puzzling moments when those with less power are able to change the rules by which old elites have prospered. In some cases, the paradox may be only apparent. Challengers may actually possess more of the resources that matter under the prevailing rules, such that "reform" is but a circulation of elites, a realignment of political institutions with social or economic hierarchies. But at other times, no such hidden resources can be located in order to salvage theories that explain political outcomes as the product of interests and advantages of power. The decades surrounding the turn of the last century were one such moment in American politics.

The puzzle appears most clearly when attention is shifted from the general struggle between established elites and reformers to the relative success of different challengers to the political system. In terms of the standard metric of numbers and resources, however approximate, organized labor must be judged one of the most potent groups outside the constellation of contending elites. Boasting a large and largely enfranchised membership mobilized into nationwide organizations integrated through the American Federation of Labor, labor unions nevertheless enjoyed comparatively few successes prior to the New Deal. While European nations were establishing welfare states organized around the needs of working men,[11] labor unions in the United States saw their repertoire of action curtailed by judicial injunctions and their legislative gains limited to the prevention of, and compensation for, injury. The more general threats of unemployment and old age went virtually unremedied.

The fate of agrarian movements is also puzzling. Agrarian groups were from the start in a slightly less advantageous position than labor. With farmers divided among associations with distinct regional bases, any national mobilization of agrarian opinion faced considerable obstacles. But while the momentum of agrarian association was reputedly destroyed in the wake of the Populist defeat in the presidential elections of 1896, some farmers quickly regrouped to become the beneficiaries of one of the earliest components of the American welfare state: the agricultural extension system. The combination of education, regulation, and subsidy pioneered in response to agrarian problems foreshadowed the New Deal's Agricultural Adjustment Administration and, by virtue of its close links to the American Farm Bureau Federation, stands as one of the first examples of the "iron triangles" linking pressure groups, congressional committees, and executive agencies that became symptomatic of the interest group system by midcentury.

Finally, there is the paradox of the woman movement. Formally disenfranchised, women played a large role in the foundation of the distinctively "maternalist" welfare state in the United States. Unlike the social-policy regimes of most European nations, American social policy focused on aiding or regulating women and children, while leaving workingmen to the laissez-faire system of the marketplace. Operating without the vote, women not only won suffrage but helped to deprive voting men of the right to drink. These gains, however, marked the pinnacle of success for organized women. Following the constitutional amendment of 1920 establishing national woman suffrage, the movement fragmented, its political power dissipated.

Scripture, rather than Realpolitik, describes this era of contestation: the last was first, the first last. While the strength of employer opposition might explain the defeats suffered by labor, parallel arguments are less convincing in the other cases. Farmers faced the railroads, finance capital, and commodity exchanges; women threatened the authority of enfranchised men. So we are left with the puzzle of how disenfranchised women and oft-defeated farmers secured their places within the political system.

To unravel this paradox, new theories of political organization and institutional change are required. Institutional position, economic resources, and numbers of votes cannot account for the unexpected accomplishments of organized women nor for the ways in which organized labor was largely shut out of political decision-making. Such accounts are analytically weak, insofar as they treat political process as a black box, shedding no light on the practices and strategies necessary to translate resources and numbers into outcomes. *How* groups organize is as important as what they organize for and the resources they can muster. As Alexis de Tocqueville said of the era that gave rise to the party system:

> In democratic countries knowledge of how to combine is the mother of all other forms of knowledge; on its progress depends that of all the others.
> Among laws controlling human societies there is one more precise and clearer, it seems to me, than all the others. If men are to remain civilized or to become civilized, the art of association must develop and improve among them at the same speed as equality of conditions spreads.[12]

The forms of political association matter as well as preferences and resources. The rumored People's Lobby of California was remarkable, after all, not for its goals but for *how* these reformers were said to pursue them. The shock value of the rumor came from the assertion that, despite their unquestionably different goals, reformers might act and organize *as if* they were a machine lobby. The organizational form itself was not novel; the combination of form, actor, and purpose was. The theoretical insight contained in the rumor stems from the recognition that social movements remake and rearrange organizational forms, thereby changing the rules about who may use them and to what end.

Frustrated by the party system, many organized groups attempted such rearrangements. Partisanship still mattered, but less with each passing decade. Instead, voluntary associations increasingly defined their membership on the basis of specific social roles: what are your interests, not as a citizen or a partisan, but as a worker or a farmer? The constructions of specific interests eventually linked electoral blocs to legislative outcomes. Individual politicians were monitored in new ways, as groups learned to hold them accountable for specific votes. But legislators also gained access to new electoral resources (both votes and organizations) that diminished their dependence on party leadership. These changes in political organization produced new patterns of legislative behavior. In response to demands for workmen's compensation or minimum-wage laws, legislatures set up special commissions, which frequently evolved into standing committees or new state agencies. Thus the articulation of specific interests by voluntary associations was mirrored in the increasingly rationalized, bureaucratic organization of government. While it is wishful thinking to claim that "once upon a time there were no interests" in American politics, the tight linkage of demands articulated by popular associations, legislative responses, and specialized political institutions is a legacy of the turn of the century.[13]

Staking out his claim for a new kind of political science in 1908, Arthur F. Bentley declared,

> If a law is in question, we find that our statement of it in terms of the groups of men it affects . . . is much more complete than any statement in terms of self-interest, theories, or ideals. If it is a plank in a political platform, again we find we can state its actual value in the social process at the given time in terms of the groups of men for whose sake it is there: a group of politicians and a number of groups of voters holding the prominent places.[14]

By asserting that "there is no group without its interest," this new science of politics canonized a development still in process. Through the first decade of this century, *interests* was regularly printed with a capital *I* and uttered in tones of moral outrage.[15] Among philosophers, individual self-interest had long joined—even supplanted—virtue as a political motivation, as Albert O. Hirschman has demonstrated.[16] But as late as the 1920s, in the United States, the organized pursuit of *group interests* was hotly condemned:

> It would indeed have amazed the members of that National Assembly if they could have foreseen a time when, in a democracy still purporting to be based upon this theory of equality before the law, not the noble, but the farmer could raise the plea of privilege, and could say in its courts of justice, when charged with an offense punishable by others, "I am of a privileged class."[17]

In response to such charges, organized farmers—along with organized labor and women—claimed that to the extent they pursued privileges, these were only privileges already granted to business corporations. Furthermore, they argued, the political parties themselves gave "the people" no choice but to harness their associations to political goals.

But this tie was not easily forged. Political campaigns were regularly criticized as bereft of meaningful issues; even when issues appeared to be at stake, state campaigns were often waged as debates over presidential politics. The leaders of popular associations complained that members could not be counted on to vote "in their interest," but instead blindly followed one or the other party. Thus, the linkage of "a group of politicians and a number of groups of voters" did not occur automatically or consistently. Particularly for those groups whose primary resource was the votes of their members, the practices of interest group politics required new capacities for organization and a transformation of the meaning of the vote. Based on penetrating insights into the logic of this emerging system, Bentley's new model of interest group pluralism paid little attention to the historical conditions of its development.[18] By treating ties between politicians and groups of voters as unproblematic, this model glossed over the long struggle to replace the politics of partisanship with an issue-oriented politics.

Interests and Institutions

An adequate account of the origins of interest group politics cannot begin by assuming that aggregated individual self-interest is a transparent explanation of group identity or political outcomes. Even if self-interested behavior by individuals is assumed,[19] the mechanisms that aggregate those interests—that generate collective action—are problematic.[20] Furthermore, the model of a self-interested, rational actor may itself be criticized: first, by recognizing the constraints on rational choice or, second, by developing an alternative model of action. Whichever of these two approaches is taken, the question arises as to what explains patterns of action. And, in both cases, the answer is *institutions*.

The first of these two paths to a renewed concern with institutions is exemplified by the "positive theory of institutions" within political science and the new institutionalism developed by economists and economic historians. Both retain a model of the rational, utility-maximizing actor but recognize that action often takes place in the context of rules or institutions. Within Congress, for example, the actions of individual representatives are constrained by the rules and committees that govern the passage of legislation. Furthermore, actors may choose to impose these constraints upon themselves, to build institutions such as procedural rules or property law to promote stability or ensure public goods.[21] Recognition of additional limitations on utility maximization—information costs, restricted searches, uncertainty—further modifies the image of rational individuals pursuing the maximization of their own interests. In the absence of total information and a foolproof metric for assessing the costs and benefits of different options, actors must find other guides for action.

This path away from an interest-driven model of political action, with its successive levels of constraint, may lead to a theoretical gestalt-switch. Just as ducks are rerecognized as rabbits, action constrained by institutions may reappear as action constituted by institutions. This is the second path, taken by the "new institutionalists" in organizational sociology. Rejecting both the strong assumptions of rationality made by the positive theory of institutions and socialization theory, "with its affectively 'hot' imagery of identification and internalization," these scholars "prefer cooler implicit psychologies: cognitive models in which schemas and scripts lead decision makers to resist new evidence . . . ; learning theories that emphasize how individuals organize information with the assistance of social categories . . . ; and attribution theory where actors infer motives post hoc from menus of legitimate accounts."[22] Rather than requiring a search for exogenous sources of individual preferences, this theory of action calls for an archaeology of schemas, a reconstruction of the scripts available within particular societies at particular times. This approach does not deny that politics may be driven by self-interest but asks how "self-interest" is constructed and under what conditions it becomes the dominant script guiding political action.

For both the positive theory of institutions and the new institutionalists in organizational sociology, the first step of the "institutionalist turn" involves reconceptualizing individual action. Moving from models that attribute political outcomes to the aggregation of choices by rational individuals, proponents of the positive theory of institutions recognize institutions as constraints on choice, and organizational theorists portray action as guided by scripts or standard operating procedures. In the study of organizations, institutional theory has typically been used to explain stability and homogeneity: why do firms resemble one another? why do patterns of organization persist even as environmental conditions are changing? Similarly, the effort to explain the development of enduring policy regimes and the "ordering" institutions of particular societies led political scientists to the banner of institutionalism. But the utility of institutional analysis is not restricted to the explanation of endurance and order. Instead, historically inclined scholars have taken a second step in the institutionalist turn, one toward a theory of change.[23]

Reflecting on their own practices, both organizational and historically inclined political institutionalists agree on what is needed to accommodate an explanation of change: a recognition of heterogeneity. As Roger Friedland and Robert Alford have argued, "[I]nstitutions are potentially contradictory and hence make multiple logics available to individuals and organizations. Individuals and organizations transform the institutional relations of society by exploiting these contradictions." Karen Orren and Stephen Skowronek agree that institutional heterogeneity generates social change: "Separate institutions and institutional arrangements, operating according to distinctive ordering principles, structure the passage of time—the sequences and cycles, the changes and lulls—at varying rates. . . . As institutions congeal time, so to speak, within their spheres, they decrease the probability that politics will coalesce into neatly ordered periods, if only because the institutions that constitute the polity at that time will abrade against each other and, in the process, drive further change."[24]

Both moves in the institutionalist turn—the recognitions that action is shaped by institutions and that the social world consists of multiple, heterogeneous institutions—are compatible with models that assume interests or preferences are fixed and exogenous to political action. But an endogenous account of change can be built if we assume that the scripts that shape action are themselves products of the organization of social life.[25] Given this argument, institutional heterogeneity at the macrosocial level will produce actors guided by *repertoires* of purpose, contention, and organization.[26]

The concept of repertoire entails an indeterminacy of action, implying that institutions and repertoires do not necessarily reinforce one another. While individuals may master the differences between the interactions expected at a business meeting and a dinner among friends, this does not ensure that they will be guided by those expectations. Insofar as they do, institutional reproduction and the preservation of order result. Insofar as they don't, there is a possibility of change. If this failure is intentional, it constitutes a potent strategy for political opposition. "The power of protest," according to Sidney Tarrow, "lies neither in its numbers . . . nor in its level of violence. . . , but in its threat to burst through the boundaries of the accepted limits of social behavior."[27] But social movements are not simply the negation of order; they also invent or refine alternative models of interaction among contenders.[28] These alternatives then become potential elements of a reconstructed social order.

If institutional heterogeneity and repertoire models of action are linked, the contours of a model of institutional change emerge. First, the social world is understood as a congeries of institutions rather than as an integrated social system. These institutions constitute a set of opportunities for, and constraints on, action.[29] Second, the experience of institutional heterogeneity provides individuals with repertoires of action such that they may either follow scripts that "match" a particular institutional setting or rearrange configurations of scripts and institutions. Each of these assumptions corresponds to a distinctive style of institutional analysis: the first to the "historical institutionalism" of political science and sociology, with its image of institutions as systems of constraint; the second to the institutionalism of organization theory, with its attention to the scripts and templates that inform practical action.[30] Institutions both constrain and enable; they set limits on and provide models for action. The task of this book is to combine these two institutionalisms to explain the foundations of a third: the historical production of a political world where individuals follow scripts of self-interested utility maximization and where formal political institutions not only accommodate but elicit such behavior.

Informed by this institutionalist theory of institutional change, the questions raised by the role of interests in politics can be restated. Rather than beginning with an assumption of preferences or interests that are exogenous to politics and asking how these interests are aggregated into political outcomes,[31] we need to ask how people understood their individual preferences and when these preferences were defined as politically salient. Where did they find models for the collective pursuit of those preferences that appeared as legitimately political both to themselves and to the groups with whom they contended? In this view, organized groups are not simply vehicles for the expression of preexisting interests but constitute templates for collective identity or arenas in which preferences and values are discovered.[32] Consequently, the deployment of familiar organizational forms (or scripts for *collective* action) in new settings or the incorporation of new members will typically result in some reconstitution of identities or preferences. Once trade unions were extended to encompass unskilled as well as skilled laborers, the goals of action shifted from the protection of craft monopoly toward the promotion of class solidarity. Once farmers appropriated "business models," they sought to compete in commodity markets rather than to advance populist demands for corporate regulation. Through debates over the advantages and appropriateness of organizational forms and strategies, these changes in identities and purposes can be tracked.

If the novel recombination of familiar scripts and settings generates new political identities and strategies, the question remains as to when such innovations will produce institutional change. Much of the time, after all, novelty is not appreciated in politics but is ignored or suppressed. The more novel the recombination, the more at odds with the established rules of the game, the closer to the centers of power, the more likely that suppression rather than transformation will follow. So rather than resulting from the resistance of the most disempowered, lasting rearrangements of institutional rules are more likely to be produced by the least marginal of the marginalized, the most advantaged of the disadvantaged. To the extent that such groups share repertoires with those in power, they are better able to misapply familiar organizational scripts to new settings. Thus if agrarian or women's associations are reordered by the use of "business methods," the quality of solidarity changes, but so does the standing of those organizations in the eyes of the political or economic actors that they may seek to influence. Rather than appearing as wild-eyed radicals, they reappear as people with whom "we can do business." Through such oblique approaches, the roster of recognized political claimants and claims expands, transforming the relation of state and society.

This argument helps to account for both the overall pattern of reform politics in the United States at the turn of the century and the relative success of different organized challengers. Why did organized labor secure so few policy victories in comparison to its counterparts in Europe? In part, because many workingmen and union leaders were deeply committed to partisan models of political action that obstructed mobilization on the basis of class-based political demands. Why were farmers able to regroup after the seeming disaster of their electoral efforts in 1896? Because their organizational repertoire was not limited to partisan models, many farmers abandoned discredited populist forms of electoral mobilization for "business methods" that facilitated ties to the emerging regulatory state. How were women, denied both the vote and political standing, able to secure both enfranchisement and maternalist social policies and yet lose their political leverage once they gained full standing as citizens? Precisely because women lacked the vote, they were insulated from co-optation by the "predatory" system of party politics and thus enjoyed a greater degree of the organizational and cultural autonomy needed to develop and deploy a nonpartisan model of political mobilization. Finally, the experiments and struggles of these political challengers help to explain the trajectory of institutional transformation in American politics. How did we get from a politics of party to the People's Lobby, and then to a taken-for-granted system of interest group politics?

The answer does not lie in the intentions of these challengers, or at least not entirely. Those who felt disadvantaged, ignored, or oppressed by the parties sought to dismantle the party system in the hope that this would usher in a more responsive, democratic government. In the process, they institutionalized new opportunities for political access and new models for political organization, but they secured a monopoly over neither. Innovation led to imitation, and many onetime insurgents found that they were increasingly defeated in a game whose rules they had helped to invent. The "Interests" became "interests" and learned to prosper under the new rules.

Just as collective action is facilitated by common models for organizing, books profit from an element of familiarity in the plot. But in rejecting both the elite narratives of traditional political history and the accounts of resistance that characterize much of the new social history, I must also forego the plots typically employed in political analysis, stories centered on the coercion of the weak by the strong, the triumph of visionary reformers, or of victories hard-won through resistance. None of these are suited for a story with multiple challengers, diverse tactics, and poorly understood links between actions and outcomes. So to present a process of institutional transformation characterized by uncertainty and indirection, I have resorted to a genre familiar to scholars if less familiar in scholarly writing: detective fiction.[33] Chapter 1 introduces the victim, the party system, and various groups that had reason to wish for that system's demise. If we are to account for both the weakening of mass-mobilization parties and the rise of interest group pluralism, popular associations are likely suspects. With motive established, chapters 2 and 3 turn to the means and opportunities available to popular associations aggrieved by the prevailing political arrangements. By making novel use of familiar organizational forms, popular associations contributed to new patterns of political mobilization. The opportunities for such rearrangements were greatest in the western states, where the party system was weakest. Although eastern states gave the nation many prominent reform politicians and policy intellectuals, they rarely dismantled party systems and created significant new spaces for popular political participation; in the 1990s, after all, the New York State Republican Party still presents formidable obstacles to outsiders seeking a place on the primary ballot. Many westerners presumed that their region was the vanguard of national reform, harboring into the 1920s "a contempt for Easterners who are still in an earlier stage. 'In Montana,' said Senator-elect Wheeler, 'we have bankers who are more progressive than your workingmen in the East.'"[34] For western challengers, the structure of federalism and the networks built by national associations presented possibilities for diffusing innovation, leveraging local changes into a more general institutional transformation.

This theoretical argument necessitates a somewhat unusual comparative design. While the starkest contrast is found between politically progressive western states and the rest of the nation, an adequate account of the process of organizational innovation and institutional change must rely on a closer analysis of variations in the organizational repertoires and political opportunities available to various political challengers. Drawing on materials from three states—California, Washington, and Wisconsin—that were recognized exemplars of political reform, chapters 4, 5, and 6 explore how the distinctive repertoires cultivated by organized workers, farmers, and women shaped their capacity to mobilize outside the framework of the existing party system. Local opportunities informed the selections made from these repertoires in each state and the extent to which effective challenges were translated into enduring institutional change. Chapter 7 examines how different selections from these repertoires crystallized into quite different polities or policy regimes in the three states. Finally, chapter 8 addresses the robustness of these transformations—first, by examining the extent to which Progressive Era reforms survived the political reaction of the 1920s, second by considering how these new repertoires were transposed to national politics.

Reflecting on the independent presidential ticket of Senators Robert La Follette and Burton K. Wheeler in 1924, a social-welfare publication argued,

> However we may regard the Independent-Progressive candidatures as a political innovation . . . we may all find ourselves indebted to this new movement for bringing economic and social considerations, which lie close to the life and labor of the common lot of Americans, clear through into the arena of searching public discussion. These, the older parties with their mixed memberships tended, otherwise, to elide for the sake of party unity.[35]

The La Follette campaign had attempted to engage identities and organizations distinct from the partisanship that had long structured presidential elections. Judged by the standard of victory, the effort failed. The relative success of this hastily organized, poorly funded, third-party effort, however, illuminates far-reaching changes in the nation's political landscape. Economic and social, rather than partisan, concerns increasingly structured political participation and conflict. Of more lasting significance were the steadily multiplying pressure points and the parceling out to distinct governmental units of decisions to be influenced. Organized groups came to define their demands in terms of new programs or agencies; once established, those programs and agencies defined specialized fields of political contest and frameworks for the very calculation of interest in politics.

From partisanship to propaganda, from the lobby to the interest group, the organization of political action had been profoundly changed. But if the identities of the players, the distribution of power, and the potency of various resources had changed, the ability of the powerful to play a disproportionate role in politics had not. Ultimately, the "people's lobbies" helped to institutionalize and legitimate new patterns of political organization. But their role at the founding brought no guarantee that they would either control or benefit from what they had wrought.

ONE

"Partisan Politics: The Evil and the Remedy"

> We plow right through the old parties. We will cultivate
> the political field until we get the farm sufficiently tilled,
> and we know the harvest is assured.
>
> Member of the Walla Walla County [Washington] Farmers'
> Alliance, 1891

As the United States entered the last decades of the nineteenth century, discontent with the political system flourished, but the prospects for change appeared dim. In *The American Commonwealth*, Lord Bryce attributed this situation to the national character: "The Americans surpass all other nations in their power of making the best of bad conditions, getting the largest results out of scanty materials or rough methods." As he traveled through the country in the 1880s, Lord Bryce found widespread agreement with his assessment of the workings of American government, yet this discontent was not channeled into movements for reform:

> Aware that they possess this gift, the Americans are content to leave their political machinery unreformed. Persons who propose comprehensive reforms are suspected as theorists and crotchet-mongers. The national inventiveness, active in the spheres of mechanics and money-making, spends little of its force on the details of governmental methods.[1]

Even the keenest social observers frequently falter when it comes to prediction. In response to growing political dissatisfaction and multiplying demands for legislative remedies, the turn of the century brought with it an expansive discourse on the mechanics of government. Australian ballots (which listed candidates by office rather than by party slate and were printed by the government); initiative, referendum, and recall; commission forms of government; nonpartisanship; direct primaries—the politics of both populism and the Progressive Era were very much a politics of method.

This flurry of political invention produced a new type of regime. The elections of the early 1890s marked the transition from the "third party

17

system" of highly competitive, nationwide stalemate between the Republicans and Democrats to the "fourth party system" with its increasing regionalization of party loyalty and Republican ascendancy at the national level. But the more fundamental shift took place not within the party system, but out of partisan politics into new forms of political action: "The vigor of American electoral politics, rooted in the passionate confrontations between two well-developed and dominant parties, was sapped by what was ultimately an anti-party, and then a nonparty, way of carrying on political activities."[2] In this new politics, organized groups formulated explicit political demands and found channels for bringing pressure to bear directly on legislatures and administrative agencies as well as agitating for the initiative, referendum, and recall.[3] These were no small accomplishments. As illustrated by the passage of Wisconsin's mothers' pension bill through thirty-one different decision points (fig. 1.1), to monitor a legislature was a daunting task, often made still more difficult by corruption and elaborate parliamentary maneuver. Success at direct democracy required extrapartisan organization, agitation, and mobilization throughout a state. Although the development of methods for addressing these challenges represented only a legitimation of the much-maligned "lobby" for some corporations, for a much broader range of social groups these developments constituted new access and new forms of influence. These popular associations did not simply imitate the lobby of the Gilded Age. By linking pressure group tactics to a deep strain of popular antipartisanship, these associations taught their members to vote "their interest" rather than their party.

This new style of politics was a response to the late-nineteenth-century party system and the grievances it engendered. From the elite informants of Lord Bryce to the manifestos of agrarian revolt, the turn away from parties animated political debates and strategies. In lyrics published in 1891 "for the use of Alliances, Grange Debating Clubs and Political Gatherings," condemnation of the party spirit anchored each verse:

> All the way my party led me,
> I was blind and could not see.
> When I hallowed and I shouted
> Over party victory.
> In our victory was defeat,
> As we now can plainly see,
> For we're on the road to slavery,
> And must fight if we'd be free. . . .

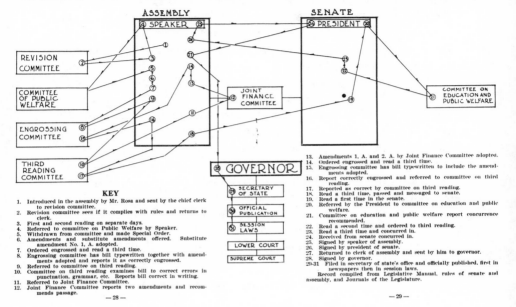

PROCEDURE IN PASSAGE OF MOTHERS' PENSION BILL WISCONSIN LEGISLATURE 1913

Figure 1.1   Procedure in the Passage of Mothers' Pension Bill, Wisconsin Legislature, 1913. (Source: Irma Hochstein, *A Progressive Primer* [Madison: Wisconsin Women's Progressive Association, 1922])

All the way my party led me,
Led me to the fix I'm in;
But I will no longer heed them,
A new life I'll now begin.
O yes, farmers, day is breaking,
Scales now from our eyes do fall;
For we see the great injustice
That's been done to one and all.[4]

This distrust of party formed a sad bookend to a period of American history in which parties had emerged as the vehicle of a more popular politics embodied in Jacksonian democracy, the tool of the people in displacing elite factions in the decades following the Revolution.[5] Well suited to electoral conflicts, parties nevertheless frustrated the expression and remedy of many grievances, particularly those that might split the coalitions carefully built across regions and social groups in order to win national elections.[6] So half a century after its invention, the American party system itself became an object of contention. But organizational arrangements that worked by obscuring social conflicts could not be displaced by the simple voicing of grievances. The organizational logic of the party system and the potency of partisanship as a script guiding individual political action presented formidable obstacles to would-be challengers.

The eventual reorganization of American politics stemmed from distinctive combinations of grievances, opportunities, and repertoires of action. The organizational logic of the party system generated many grievances, but the opportunities to act upon them were uniform neither throughout the nation nor across social groups. Liberal progressive elites presented one set of challenges to the party system; less-privileged activists made novel use of popular associations to pressure, or simply to circumvent, the party system. But if elites were well positioned to secure reforms of state institutions, popular associations with their mass membership of voters (and would-be voters) posed a more direct threat to the patterns of political participation that underpinned the party system.

The Organizational Logic of the Party System

In the first decades of the nineteenth century, the concept of party triumphed over the position that "the representative institutions of republicanism were in themselves sufficient as instruments of government, and any attempt to set up political clubs or societies outside them would be an attempt not to extend but to destroy republican institutions."[7] The invention of something like parties was a direct response to the constitutional design of a decentralized electoral system that both posed "greater obstacles . . . to the concert and accomplishment of the secret wishes of an unjust and interested majority"[8] and established a chief executive elected by all the states. Even later enemies of the party system portrayed its origins as a practical response to the need for political coordination in a developing nation: "With the growth and concentration of population beyond the natural limits of the simple plan for choosing representatives for public office, neighborhood meetings and discussion, some go-betweens to collect the popular will, were indispensable. None was provided. Party assumed the labor. Party organization was thus innocent in its birth, supplying a void in the machinery, essential to any operation of democracy."[9]

Control of political office drove the development of the party system that resulted from a strategic construction of party differences in order to win presidential contests: "The push for parties came out of three streams: the need for institutions to handle mass electorates; the need for coalitions, that is, the coming together of pluralist factions in a bitterly divisive political situation in order to win elections; and the need to find a way to enact specific policies, or to avert the serious public danger that would occur if the wrong policies, people, or groups dominated the nation." [10] Thus parties were an effective organizational response to changing conditions of the nineteenth century. Population growth and the gradual achievement of full manhood suffrage increased the number of individuals who could potentially influence political outcomes. Territorial expansion and industrialization multiplied the number of distinct "interests." Finally, the expansion of both polity and economy, driven by the growth of transportation and communication, left each community increasingly exposed to decisions over which locales had no control. Each of these changes increased the scale of coordination required to win national elections. The expansion of the electorate created a situation in which the direct organization of voters was more effective than reliance on locally based chains of deference and dependence. Thus the nineteenth-century political party represented an organizational innovation that increased electoral control in the context of profound social and technological changes.

Stripped of its political content, this account reads as a gloss of the standard explanation for the growth of the corporation during the nineteenth century. In his classic analysis, *The Visible Hand,* Alfred Chandler argued that "modern business enterprise appeared for the first time in history when the volume of economic activities reached a level that made administrative coordination more efficient and more profitable than market coordination." [11] Chandler's argument was prefigured in an American Federation of Labor pamphlet published for the Paris International Exposition in 1900, which suggested that

> the great improvements in the means of communication and the resultant rapid settlement of vast tracts of fertile land soon opened wider markets, stimulated production on a larger scale, and created the necessity for similar aggregations of capital. This industrial expansion, however, was paralleled by a like expansion of the trade union idea, which, as a natural consequence, resulted not only in the formation of unions of the unions that had previously arisen, but also in the systematic organization of new local unions of the several trades in places where none had before existed. [12]

Driven by expanding markets and new technologies, this increased volume provided an opportunity—perhaps even an ultimatum—for organizational experimentation.

Just as the growth of the corporation gave rise to a new profession—the middle managers—so the growth of the parties created a new occupational class: "In America (Canada as well as the United States) people do not say 'politicians' but 'the politicians,' because the word indicates a class with certain defined characteristics."[13] Like any other sort of class, politicians had distinctive interests that frequently conflicted with others' conceptions of the common good. As one nineteenth-century critic complained of the party:

> It is a conspiracy, often openly avowed, on the part of certain combinations of citizens to seize the offices, honors, and emoluments which pertain to the government service, and distribute them exclusively among the members of the successful party. . . . They are simply political joint stock and mutual benefit associations.[14]

Like their counterparts in business, party organizations were the objects of constant criticism through the second half of the nineteenth century. Frequently, these criticisms flowed directly from the "problem" that party organization had originally solved: the construction of coalitions to win federal, and especially presidential, elections and secure the patronage that came with victory. The goal of winning elections shaped the content—and significant silences—of American politics. Issues that threatened intraparty coalitions (e.g., regional economic differences, woman suffrage, and temperance)—as opposed to those that structured interparty competition (e.g., national finance and imperialism)—were pushed off the party agendas. Substantive questions that might have been addressed at state and local levels were often overwhelmed by the terms of national party competition. Thus Robert La Follette's victorious gubernatorial campaign in 1900 was dominated by charges of imperialism directed against the McKinley administration; his campaign speeches were "notable for the complete lack of discussion of state issues and attacks on corporations and the control of state government."[15] And La Follette, in his time, was renowned as a master of issue-based campaigning. But even when many voters lacked a stake in a party's policy commitments, elections provided an opportunity for spectacle, for parade, for reidentification with an understanding of the common good or ethnoreligious affiliation.[16]

Parties of this type were ill equipped to manage the dilemmas faced by a nation in the midst of territorial expansion and industrial growth precisely because the regional and class bases of the two parties crosscut one another. Republicans gained the loyalty of northern elites and southern freedmen, the Democrats of southern elites and the northern working class.[17] In western states, party identification was further weakened by common interests in economic development that crosscut ethnoreligious identities, straining partisan loyalties and feeding the electoral volatility that would explode with the Populists of the 1890s.[18] Although the Democrats were sometimes the beneficiaries of this discontent, it was at the cost of managing the cultural differences between predominantly Protestant (and often pro-temperance) western agrarians, southern conservatives, and the emerging Democratic base among immigrant, working-class groups in eastern cities. Strains within the parties accumulated and undermined old loyalties and practices as the nineteenth-century party system was stretched to encompass new groups, new demands, and new techniques.

Challenges to Party Organization

For all its power as an instrument of political control, the party system could be threatened by either changes in the social conditions to which it was adapted or the discovery of alternative forms of political organization. As organizations for managing elections, parties were threatened by changes in the composition of the electorate. The midcentury waves of immigration had produced nativist reactions and the brief flourishing of the Know-Nothings and the demise of the Whigs.[19] Following the Civil War, the Republican Party emerged as the vehicle of northern elites and native Protestants, while the Democratic Party, disproportionately represented in Congress by former Confederate officers,[20] became a haven in the North for working-class immigrants and Catholics. This mapping of partisan competition onto cultural conflict intensified the electoral stalemate of the Gilded Age.[21] Were a party to make policy concessions to attract one new constituency, an old set of loyalists would be alienated.

But this was a risk that party leaders increasingly took in order to attract a small but critical swing constituency of "independent" voters. While antebellum political rhetoric had exalted loyalty to *some* party, social and economic elites increasingly strayed from the ideal of regularity. In 1884, "[A] section of the Republican party, more important by the intelligence and social position of the men who composed it than by its voting power, 'bolted' (to use the technical term) from their party."[22] Less than a decade later, this action was repeated in the Democratic Party. Despite often profound differences in values, these disaffected voters also began to elaborate a new style of politics: "[I]n the late 1860s and 1870s . . . liberal, upper-class reformers rejected popular politics and formulated a new, less partisan, and less democratic conception of political life."[23] Independents and reformers used networks of clubs and journals to coordinate their efforts to pressure politicians, exporting models of debate and self-education from elite circles to the political arena. In so doing, they changed the strategies of partisan leaders who sought to maximize their votes in the highly competitive elections of the period.

Party leaders sought to incorporate this liberal "educational style" into campaigns. Samuel Tilden of New York pioneered these methods, founding the Society for the Diffusion of Political Knowledge as an extraparty vehicle for Democratic propaganda during the Civil War and later improving on these techniques during his presidential campaign of 1876. By the early 1890s, the Republicans had fully mimicked this style, funding a Bureau of Information to send literature to voters and refusing funds to state leaders for old-fashioned spectacular events.[24] But for all the strategic innovation and maneuvering of party leaders, independent voters tended to remain independent, and the loyalists grew bored with this new style of electoral campaign. At the edges and at the base, loyalties to both parties were steadily eroded.

The historical parallels between the party and the corporation are telling. In response to shifting markets and regulatory constraints, corporate leaders moved from pools, cartels, and trusts to vertical and horizontal integration, and eventually to the multidivisional firm.[25] Through the 1880s and 1890s, the national parties also centralized control of a changing and increasingly volatile electorate.[26] New patterns of immigration, tensions between industrial and agricultural sectors, and debates over the nation's nascent imperialism all roiled American politics. But if the development of the American corporation can be told as a tale of strategic responses by business leaders, the evolution of political institutions is more complex. While American politics has had its share of visionary party bosses and operators, in a democratic regime there is always a possibility that those outside the inner circle may be a source of change. Indeed, they may well have the greatest stake in changing the rules of the game.

The dilemma for political challengers was whether the major parties could be defeated using the rules of the party system or whether an alternative organizational model for politics was required. The nineteenth century was littered with failed third-party movements. As early as 1828, a workingman's movement in Philadelphia "was not able to keep itself free from the activity of the old party politicians, who used force, flattery, patronage, and the slogans of the workers to break up the following behind it."[27] The co-optation of challengers was all too predictable. Most challengers "emulated their enemies" by adopting the conventions,[28] platforms, and campaign strategies of the major parties. Others were even financed by a major party; Republicans, for example, might calculate that Democrats would lose more by the presence of a third contender.[29] Driven by the logic of party competition, in which many benefits depended on capturing national office, still more political discontent took the form of party faction rather than third party.

Faced with a nationally entrenched, powerfully co-opting party system, political commentators of the later nineteenth century saw little hope for change apart from spirited but often quixotic efforts at municipal reform. Instead, voters attempted to limit the damage that politics could do. At the state level, constitutional revisions and the entry of new states brought a steady narrowing of legislative capacity to form and enact policy: "The peoples of the States have come to distrust their respective legislatures. Hence they desire not only to do a thing forthwith and in their own way rather than leave it to the chance of legislative action, but to narrow as far as they conveniently can (and sometimes farther) the sphere of the legislature."[30] As the century progressed, state constitutions ratified by the voters became longer and more detailed, while legislative sessions were often shortened and called biennially rather than annually. This distrust of legislatures persisted into the Progressive Era. Writing in 1912, Charles Beard and Birl Shultz asserted, "It is incontrovertible that the popular estimate of the ability and common honesty of legislators is by no means high. That the popular judgment is often unjust and based upon an exaggeration of the facts in any particular case will be conceded. It is needless, however, to argue the point as to whether the judgment is altogether just and righteous; it stands nevertheless. And as a psychological fact it must be reckoned with by those who contend that no fundamental alterations should be made in our representative system."[31] Together, the rigidified party system and eroded legislative capacity left the nation incapable of addressing the challenges of rapid industrialization and territorial expansion. Yet despite it all, the party system endured:

> When life leaves an organic body it becomes useless, fetid, pestiferous: it is fit to be cast out or buried from sight. What life is to an organism,

principles are to a party. When they which are its soul have vanished, its body ought to dissolve, and the elements that formed it be regrouped in some new organism. . . .

But a party does not always thus die. . . . Parties go on contending because their members have formed habits of joint action, and have contracted hatreds and prejudices, and also because the leaders find their advantage in using these habits and playing on these prejudices. The American parties now continue to exist, because they have existed. The mill has been constructed, and its machinery goes on turning, even when there is no grist to grind.[32]

Critics of the party system attributed its durability to the sectlike quality of partisan identity (its "habits of joint action"), to the interests of party managers, and to their ability to deliver services to individual constituents in a nonprogrammatic fashion.[33] Reinforced by the rhetoric of militarism in countless "bloody shirt" campaigns,[34] the socialization, celebration, and benefits of partisanship still provided a sure guide for many voters.

Although discontent increased among both Democrats and Republicans, disaffection could not in itself bring about political change. Local and state elections could not be contested strictly on the basis of local issues since these offices served as prizes in the complex system of partisan careers and patronage. But as the demographic composition and economic circumstances of the American electorate changed in the decades after the Civil War, party managers had begun to tinker with established practices in an effort to gain crucial advantages in a highly competitive electoral setting. In these changes lay the roots of the electoral instabilities and political challenges that would transform American politics.

Reorganizing American Politics: Elite Reform and Popular Association

Debates over social and political change in the decades surrounding the turn of the century bear a dismaying resemblance to the discussion of those blind men confronted with an elephant. So much was in flux that accounts differ not only in their explanations but in their assertions of what is to be explained. But just as those blind men might well arrive at some consensus concerning the sound and smell of the beast, so many scholars share a rough understanding of the fundamental transformations surrounding populism and progressivism: they involve changes in the organization of American politics.

This consensus, so sweeping yet still partial, begs—at a minimum—

two other questions: what was it about political organization that changed? Was elite reform or a broader pattern of popular political mobilization the critical factor? Many, if not all, of the answers given to these queries may be captured in five points:

1. *Increased state capacity and the rationalization of state structure:* Unlike many European nations where bureaucratization preceded democracy, the United States was slow to develop state agencies with formal structures and significant mandates. But with the introduction of a civil service and the creation of new federal agencies in the late nineteenth century, the nation moved from being a "state of courts and parties" toward a recognizably modern bureaucracy.[35] As a consequence, "state actors" figure more prominently in the political history of the twentieth century than in that of the nineteenth, at times overshadowing the contributions of both political parties and other organized actors to shape political outcomes.

2. *The alienation of traditional elites from party politics:* Urbanization and repeated waves of new immigrants who eventually became new voters steadily undermined the control of old elites over the party organizations. This losing battle produced an assortment of Mugwumps and Independents who sought both to weaken the parties (through reforms such as civil service and practices such as ticket splitting) and to promote an alternative model of governance based on expertise and professional authority. Within parties, struggles between state and national leaders resulted in a migration of power toward the latter during the late nineteenth century, although state party organizations would reassert themselves in the following decades.[36]

3. *The increased regionalism and regulation of political parties:* Whereas the party system of midcentury was characterized by extremely high levels of voter turnout, spectacular displays, and electoral festivities, by the 1890s turnout began to decline. The competitive balance between Democratic and Republican parties gave way to increasing Republican dominance as well to as a regionalization of party strength. Those who voted, however, appeared more likely to deviate from previous standards of partisan regularity. A series of electoral reforms such as the Australian ballot facilitated ticket splitting and eroded the ability of parties to monitor voters' behavior.[37] The public regulation of parties, however, occurred overwhelmingly at the state level, leaving "America's *national* parties . . . almost as private and 'unknownst to the law' as their counterparts in other Western democracies."[38]

4. *The development of new forms of political participation:* If civil-service and electoral reforms posed one set of challenges to the party system, efforts to introduce forms of direct democracy constituted another. In many states, the introduction of initiative, referendum, and recall gave voters the potential to overrule or supplement legislatures. The introduction of primary elections and the direct election of senators further weakened the control of the parties. As formal political institutions were opened to popular participation, so popular associations increasingly established explicit procedures or committees for ad-

dressing political issues and electoral choices.[39] These innovations went beyond the *electoral* techniques of direct democracy to inspire innumerable variants on the "People's Lobby" designed to facilitate popular intervention in the workings of legislatures and state agencies.

5. *The organization of "group interests" outside the political parties:* While self-interest has long played a role in politics, it has not always been acceptable to acknowledge this motive.[40] In the 1880s, partisan loyalty was far more prominent in the nation's rhetoric of motives. Independents, who might be presumed to follow a model of individual interest rather than partisan loyalty, were castigated as heretics and hermaphrodites. Popular associations even rejected proposals to punish legislators for their votes on specific bills. By the 1890s, however, citizens increasingly overcame these scruples. A host of new associations was founded, many dedicated to securing specific public policies. A wide range of organizations developed new methods for influencing political outcomes. Voters were no longer urged to distinguish between "the People" and "the Interests," but to consider "your interests vs. the 'special interests.'"[41]

Taken together, these five changes represent a sweeping transformation of the organizational forms, institutions, and cultural accounts that shaped political life in the United States. Parties were partially supplanted by alternative forms of political mobilization. Formal institutions became more rational and bureaucratic. Finally, the partisan identities so central to political socialization for much of the century were eroded as group differences and individual interests figured ever more prominently in political discourse. In the place of a system based on partisan loyalties enacted through voting, politics was increasingly structured by "interest" and pursued through propaganda, legislation, and bureaucratic administration. The terrain of political competition also expanded significantly. Where parties had once dominated access to power via the electoral system (although bribery was always a possible second option), now a multitude of associations and movements pursued their goals through initiative drives, independent campaigns, and lobbying efforts directed at party organizations, legislatures, and state agencies.

For some, of course, this new political system only substituted one form of corruption for another. One genteel reformer of the 1890s complained, "All classes of associations who have votes to barter for government aid flock to this national market of reciprocal exchange, eager to interchange. The great corporations, the merchants, the bankers, manufacturers and miners, farmers and labor organizations, and the church even, making to itself friends of the mammon of unrighteousness, bids with others for a share of the spoils." To others, however, these practices gradually took on the coloration of timeless arrangements. "This history of representative government in this country and wherever liberty had advanced among men, has been the record of group action," observed the *New York Globe* in 1921. "The barons who wrested the Magna Carta from King John at Runnymede were a bloc, and an agricultural bloc at that."[42]

Whatever the normative judgment of history, these new forms of political organization and their relation to political institutions did represent a fundamental transformation. Under the political system of the late nineteenth century, individuals or groups were motivated by partisan identities, action was organized around the election of officials, and the purpose of legitimate action was understood to be partisan victory or some "common good."[43] Consequently, the pursuit of special interests was understood to be illegitimate and involved methods or models of organization that were culturally corrupt. American courts declared illegitimate the "employment of an agent who acted as an intermediary within the context of the representational relationship. In other words, a lobbyist . . . was perceived not as a facilitator of communication between citizens and the government they petitioned but, instead, as an inhibitor of a direct relationship between representatives and the represented."[44] Groups were a legitimate object of representation, but collective mobilization to secure that representation—particularly when it entailed private acts of delegation—rendered these same interests illegitimate.

What changed was not the simple presence of interests, factions, or pressure groups, but the identity of those who organized as factions and the character of their relationship to political outcomes. As parties weakened, groups actively sought opportunities for unmediated access to legislative bodies and the growing number of executive agencies. Some citizens learned to "be true to their own interests" and increasingly sought to influence legislators directly and to promote specific bills, using methods understood to be legitimate if not always admirable. Rather than subsuming specific interests under a partisan vision of the common good, organized groups increasingly articulated their demands, presented them as legislative proposals, and sought to bind elected representatives to those positions. This increasing interpenetration of state and society was, however, partial—the large numbers of citizens who were both unorganized and unmotivated to vote were doubly absent.

As state capacity increased, the potential payoff of political victories multiplied. Associations urged their members to participate in parliamentary drills, to monitor their representatives' votes, and to use that voting record as a guide in the next election. Organizations sponsored their own legislative lobbyists, learned to draft bills and to shepherd them safely through the maze of committees and multiple readings. Over time, these formerly questionable innovations became standard practice. By the 1920s, one observer commented:

> The present unionized era of leagues, societies, alliances, clubs, combines and cliques offers confederation for mutual support of almost any interest conceivable except the diversified interests of the humble in the application of general law. With united front the bankers, the brokers, the dairymen, the detectives, the sportsmen, the motorists, the innkeepers, the barbers, the mintgrowers, the Swiss bell ringers *et al.,* may and do present their complaints to the legislature for adjustment.[45]

Much about American politics had changed in the space of a few decades. By why? and how?

The Limits of Elite Theories of Progressive Reform

Most narratives of American politics, and particularly of the Progressive Era, have emphasized the actions of social, economic, and political elites. At least three versions of an elite argument can be identified: status politics, professional rationalization, and economic rationalization. Finding continuities between the Mugwumps, Cleveland Democrats, and the emerging Progressives of the early twentieth century, Richard Hofstadter developed the classic statement of the first account: "Progressivism . . . was to a very considerable extent led by men who suffered from the events of their time not through a shrinkage in their means but through the changed pattern in the distribution of deference and power."[46] This explanation is succinctly captured by the title of Robert Wiebe's classic, *The Search for Order.* Beginning with the evocative claim that "America during the nineteenth century was a society of island communities," Wiebe portrays both populism and progressivism as responses to the breakdown of autonomous communities, efforts that constituted "America's initial experiment in bureaucratic order."[47] In political life, bureaucratic order was to supplant—or at least contain—partisan politics. Confronting waves of immigration that both threatened dominant cultural standards and supported the new breed of bosses and machines, elites sought to reform the nineteenth-century party state through such mechanisms as the Australian ballot, stricter registration laws (designed to exclude immigrant groups blamed for growing political instability), and forms of direct democracy that would allow voters (preferably well educated and informed) to voice their preferences without the mediation of an allegedly corrupt party system. In many places, this purge of political methods was joined with an attack on large corporations that were viewed as fueling the party machines:

> Notwithstanding conflicts among themselves, the middle classes, therefore, viewed their mounting public burdens as the alarming portents of a new democracy, a democracy mobilized around two predatory constituencies. One constituency was composed of "vulgar" hordes of workingmen and immigrants substantially devoid of a real stake in society; the other comprised the corporate rich and their "unproductive" retinues. Both constituencies were believed to be drawing power from the debasement of traditional morality and from the confiscation of established properties. In respectable quarters, moreover, the aggressive agent in the advancement of this destruction was identified with party organization, usually symbolized by bosses, rings, and machine politics.[48]

Throughout these arguments, popular political organization appears as a resource of party bosses, a tool that elite reformers sought to weaken through electoral reforms. Since popular politics is portrayed as part of the problem, its contribution to reform efforts remains unexplored.[49]

In their statement of political consequences, arguments based on status politics resonate with an alternative elite account that has emerged from the new institutionalism in political history. Here the response of political, rather than social, elites to changes in the demography and economy is central. As Stephen Skowronek has argued, the electoral shifts of the 1890s and subsequent Republican ascendance produced a new "strategic universe of official action" that could then be exploited by a political leader such as Theodore Roosevelt: "From a position of electoral strength and political security, the executive-professional reform coalition pursued a course of redistributing institutional powers and prerogatives away from Congress and the courts toward the President and the bureaucracy."[50] Although Congress soon rebelled against this systematic diminution of its powers and prerogatives, the result was a national government that muted the voice of less desirable constituencies. By extension, the power of those elites with access to a professionalized civil service and high government posts was enhanced. Although Skowronek portrays his reformers as strategic actors, rather than as driven by status anxieties, he shares with Hofstadter a view of progressive politics as motivated by a power struggle between old elites and the bosses of the party system.

A third variant of the elite argument focuses on the concerns of the nation's economic leadership. Echoing Max Weber's contention that rational law is one of the prerequisites for capitalist development, the "or-

ganizational synthesis" in American history identifies business elites as
the key actors in both the expansion of state bureaucracies and the ob-
struction of to the untrammeled operation of the party state.[51] While the
continued expansion of the Civil War state was blocked by financial elites
unwilling to trust partisan placemen with the regulation of the economy,[52]
the eventual beginnings of an effective civil service made possible the
emergence of a system in which "the ruling class does not rule" but en-
trusts its interests to the state.[53] In a classic critical statement of this perspective, Gabriel Kolko argued:

> The needs of the economy were such . . . as to demand federal as opposed
> to random state economic regulation. But a crucial factor was the bulwark
> which essentially conservative national regulation provided against state
> regulations that were either haphazard or, what is more important, far more
> responsible to more radical, genuinely progressive local communities. Na-
> tional progressivism, then, becomes the defense of business against the
> democratic ferment that was nascent in the states.[54]

Other scholars viewed progressivism as an essentially benign response by
businessmen to the advent of new technologies.[55] Some describe leading
progressive organizations such as the National Civic Federation (NCF) as
agents of the imposition of a hegemonic political ideology and co-
optation of potential challengers such as organized labor,[56] and still others offer an instrumental interpretation of the "growing interest [among
industrial elites] in a larger and more sustained government involvement
in shaping the economy, a willingness to have the government move in
radically new directions."[57]

Each of these elite accounts—driven by status politics, professionaliz-
ing aspirations, or economic rationality—contributes to our understanding of the first two aspects of the political transformation that began in
the late nineteenth century: the emergence of a stronger, more centralized,
more rationalized bureaucratic state and the new relation of elites to political parties. These accounts also shed light on the declining role of party
organization in political life, but they do not address the remaining aspects of the turn-of-the-century political transformation: the creation of
new linkages between legislative policymaking and electoral behavior,
changes in the dominant model of popular political organization, and the
development of a new discourse and organizational practice of "interest"
in politics.

This shared silence reflects a fundamental agreement on how to ask
the questions of what changes and why. In each case, politics is portrayed

as the product of elites responding to macrosocial changes in the form of industrialization, urbanization, immigration, or improved communication. Popular politics remain offstage, as most of the population is relegated to the passive role of not voting as often as they once did; "a historical sociology of party disengagement" remains underdeveloped.[58] Social movements come and go—Grangers, Knights of Labor, Populists, and suffragists—without leaving any acknowledged mark on formal political institutions. Instead, popular political discontent is treated as a natural disaster or environmental uncertainty to which elites respond. But insofar as the membership of large popular associations represented potential blocs of *votes,* the histories of popular and party politics are more deeply entwined than any model of "protest as exogenous shock" would suggest. Elite theories omit both the efforts by popular associations to find organizational vehicles for their discontent and the fact that novel forms of popular political organization often preceded, provoked, and even prefigured elite responses.[59]

Focusing on the actions of elite men, historians and political scientists have offered a variety of explanations for the decline of party and its replacement by something else, something more bureaucratic, more rationalized, more policy-oriented. Applied to the study of parties, the elite perspective attributes "the demise of a politics that depended so clearly on the visible assent of the governed" to the strategies of party leaders. At least one scholar acknowledges the paradox: "Concerned with the demise of a 'popular' form of politics, I have nonetheless devoted most of the following pages to the political strategies of the rich."[60]

Popular Politics: Expanding the Organizational Synthesis

The examination of whether and how popular politics mattered has been foreclosed by the way in which the question of change has been posed. For all their differences, the arguments reviewed above typically begin by assuming some aspect of "modernization" as a prime mover, then focus on elite responses to change or instability.[61] Popular politics is treated as either a symptom of macrosocial change (as farmers and workers respond to industrialization) or a consequence of elite actions (as voters are demobilized by organizational changes in national parties). With respect to a causal explanation of institutional change, such accounts assume a lack of agency on the part of nonelites;[62] with respect to consequences, they naturalize the appearance of interest group politics, treating the emergence of a new model and discourse of politics as unproblematic.[63]

The records of voluntary associations suggest a different account.

Groups from the Grange to the General Federation of Women's Clubs were experimenting with new political techniques *prior to* the electoral shifts of the 1890s. Among themselves, they practiced forms of politics that prefigured a less partisan political system, encouraging participation and obstructing the consolidation of power. Organizational form and practice were used as signals of political character and intent. In a typical statement, the Wisconsin State Federation of Labor (WiSFL) explained its rules for holding office:

> The Wisconsin State Federation of Labor is known throughout the entire country as one of the most progressive of labor or economic organizations. It was one of the first bodies to entirely do away with the office of a perma- nent presiding officer, thus removing those obstacles which have proven so baneful to organized labor, the one man leadership, the temptation of polit- ical and other schemers to influence, and the fear that at any time some weak or corrupt official might betray the interests of his people. Believing that in conducting the affairs of the country, which is the business of the people, there should be no king, no autocrat, whether elected for life by the grace of God, or for a term of years by the grace of gold. They have carried this principle into their organization, and nearly all bodies affiliated with them have done likewise.[64]

In popular politics, a commitment to reform was signaled not only by ideological content but by organizational practice. State labor officials corresponded about the benefits of adopting initiative and referendum within their own federations;[65] farmers' organizations and fraternal groups sought to purge themselves of all "partisan" practices; leaders of women's organizations warned of the dangers of "wire-pulling" politi- cians.

But nonpartisan was not the same as apolitical. Voluntary associations pioneered the use of expert witnesses, public education, and the profes- sionalization of social services, in numerous cases enjoying victories over corporate elites and machine politicians. These techniques, typically asso- ciated with the interests of professionals and other elite reformers, were prominent in the arsenal of popular associations. The membership of these associations lent political weight to the efforts of investigative jour- nalists and crusading reformers.[66] Labor conditions for women and chil- dren, vice, and social insurance made it onto the political agenda through these new channels. The popular politics of public opinion and expertise was, in effect, muckraking backed by votes.

Such victories were often transient, as these innovations were imitated by state agencies and by corporate interests. To pay the fees of an expert witness was, after all, typically less costly than to bribe a legislature. But the transience of the advantages stemming from organizational innovation does not diminish their significance for the explanation of change. The linkage of anti- or extrapartisan reforms to a mass membership represented the distinctive contribution of popular associations to the weakening of the party system. The elite men who figure prominently in the historiography of progressivism rarely led mass organizations outside the party system, precisely because they were already established as players within that system. So to the extent that the political transformations of turn-of-the-century America involved not only substitutions of elites but also changes in the forms of political organization, we must look to those actors who were not simply on the margins of the party system trying to reform it, but to those who were on the margins of the party system trying to replace it with a different model of political action. Popular politics was more than just a source of instability with which elites had to cope; popular associations also contributed to the emergence, diffusion, and institutionalization of alternative models of mobilization and representation. Since alternatives are more likely to be elaborated by those with little incentive to maintain existing arrangements, our attention must turn to groups at the margins of late-nineteenth-century politics: losers such as organized labor and agrarian associations; women and other uninvited guests.

At the same time that political elites were debating new regulatory arrangements, other Americans were joining associations. Women spoke of the late nineteenth century as a "clubbable age"; farmers noted, "Organization is the watchword of the hour."[67] These new organizations could not occupy all their time with ice cream socials, funerary ritual, and economic boycotts. They were also political organizations—although often reluctantly so. As an agrarian paper in Washington state declared in 1897, "We plow right through the old parties. We will cultivate the political field until we get the farm sufficiently tilled, and we know the harvest is assured."[68]

To attend to these proliferating popular associations requires expanding the organizational synthesis in American history. Grounded in the field of business history, this synthesis flows from the assumption

> that some of the most (if not the single most) important changes which have taken place in modern America have centered about a shift from small-scale, informal, locally or regionally oriented groups to large-scale, national, formal organizations. The new organizations are characterized by a bureaucratic structure of authority. This shift in organization cuts across

the traditional boundaries of political, economic, and social history. Businesses, reform groups, professional and labor organizations—all developed along somewhat similar lines. These organizations could and did conflict, but they nevertheless shared certain modes of orientation, certain values, and certain institutionally defined roles.[69]

Framed in classically Weberian terms, the organizational synthesis locates the content of elite accounts—professionalization, bureaucratization, and rationalization—in a more sweeping narrative of organizational transformation. Yet, as Morton Keller has noted, the argument's sweep is overstated, minimizing the persistence of older institutional forms, the pluralism of responses,[70] and the prolonged process of search and experimentation. In particular, "[T]his attempt at synthesis had a hole where social history should have been. Instead of building popular agency and social dynamics into an account of change over time, it substituted the teleology of a bureaucratic search for order."[71] But to fill this hole, social history must be retold in organizational terms, reintroducing agency, conflict, and diversity into accounts of institutional change.

Shifts in popular political organization were driven by many of the same structural changes that had given rise first to the parties and then to their elite critics: the increasing size of the nation and the development of technologies of transportation and communication. As local systems of production and marketing were broken up by the railways and the factory system, so local systems of control were undermined. As one community was increasingly influenced by the decisions of others to build a road or a canal or a railroad, all were influenced by the actions of the federal government and large corporations.[72]

Just as these developments pushed old elites and rising professionals to embark on a "search for order," they also provoked more broadly based forms of organization and resistance. If the 1830s and 1840s were an era of organization in politics, the post–Civil War era brought a broader flourishing of social organizations and voluntary associations. Fraternal orders multiplied, creating networks of solidarity within which the discussion of politics was, at first, explicitly prohibited.[73] This mania for association extended to agrarian groups such as the Grange and the Farmers Alliance, women's groups including the Woman's Christian Temperance Union and the General Federation of Women's Clubs, issue-specific groups such as the Anti-Saloon League, and organized labor movements. While many of these organizations incorporated elements of bureaucratic structure, they constituted a massive diversification and diffusion of organizational structures, methods, and tactics rather than a cumulative shift toward an ideal type of rational, bureaucratic organization. Instead, the late nineteenth century saw an expansion of the *organizational repertoire*[74] of many Americans, who learned not simply to organize, but to organize in many ways and to assess the strategic and symbolic consequences of their choices among organizational forms.

These organizational capacities increasingly sustained a new politics based in associational life. By the 1890s, the development of new forms of social solidarity in American communities was unmistakable. In theory, these popular associations presented a potential counterweight to the control of politics by either elites or party machines. Whereas the NCF in 1903 boasted a membership including over one hundred corporations capitalized at over $10 million along with the leaders of many major unions, the American Federation of Labor (AFL) had a membership of more than 1.5 million by 1904, most of whom were entitled to vote.[75] The challenge was to harness the resource of mass membership.

While the NCF overshadowed the AFL when it came to the political resources of money and status, mass-membership labor organizations were, at least potentially, the more important school for a new kind of political participation. These organizations served as sites for political reeducation. The Socialist Party, for example,

> instructed its locals to emphasize street-corner speaking, pamphleteering, bookselling, and other educational work on behalf of socialism. Locals were to avoid meeting in saloons, where the atmosphere would repel women members and impede serious discussion, to rotate the chair regularly, "so that no one gets too much power and becomes the 'boss' of the local," and to make themselves experts in all deliberations concerning their own needs. "If we are to rule the world," the instructions advised, "we must train ourselves to think clearly, talk calmly, debate kindly but forcibly, and the training can be obtained in the Socialist Local as nowhere else."[76]

In these efforts at political socialization, organized labor was joined by the Farmers Alliance, which boasted one million members in 1890, the Grange, which grew from 65,000 in 1880 to over 200,000 by 1910,[77] the General Federation of Women's Clubs, which claimed over one million members by 1910,[78] the Woman's Christian Temperance Union, with 150,000 members by the turn of the century,[79] and the fraternal orders to which one out of every five to eight American men belonged in the late nineteenth century.[80] These organizations helped to cultivate new political identities and models of collective action.

Rational-choice analyses provide a useful analytic lens for capturing the interplay of elite and popular politics in the decline of the party system. Building on the claim that party solidarity will vary directly with the dependence of individual legislators on the party, Michael Hechter illuminates how the institutional reforms promoted by elite reformers—for example, attacks on patronage and the substitution of seniority rules for party control of committee assignments—contribute to the weakening of the parties.[81] But this party-centered account misses a second set of dependencies linked to nomination and election that were vulnerable to popular political efforts. Procedural reforms, such as the substitution of primaries for nominating conventions or caucuses, inadvertently created incentives for the development of new organizational capacities for running campaigns and getting out the vote. By decreasing the dependence of legislators on the party, these reforms both prompted the development of "personal organizations" by candidates[82] and increased their need to secure endorsements, financial support, volunteer labor, and votes from extrapartisan associations. This dependence, in turn, provided associations with potential leverage over legislators. Lawmakers, as John Mark Hansen has argued, attend to interest groups when those groups contribute to reelection efforts and "when legislators expect the issues and circumstances that established the competitive advantage to recur."[83] Popular associations both generated issue-specific "competitive advantages" by socializing their members to vote for new reasons and ensured that such issues would reappear from one election to the next. So the puzzle is not why legislators attended to groups of organized voters who demanded specific policy outcomes. The question is how popular associations overcame their members' entrenched partisanship as well as a widespread aversion to "class legislation" and learned to ensure that elected officials would take notice of their demands.

The organizational transformation of American politics was produced by both elite reformers and popular associations, but their influence differed in both kind and circumstance. To return to the five aspects of political change, the interpretive frameworks that have dominated the political history of this era have been best suited to explaining changes in state structure and elite politics. Elite reformers gained leverage by acting as independents within the party system; popular associations were potential sources of extrapartisan solidarity and political coordination. Elite reformers may be credited with the expansion and rationalization of state capacities; the source of shifts in popular political participation and the development of a political culture of "interests" lies in the widespread popular critique of parties and the organizational innovations inspired by this criticism.[84]

Organizational Innovation and the New Politics of Pluralism

In their efforts to change or circumvent the political parties, popular associations copied the practice of lobbying from corporations and gave it new legitimacy, trained voters to hold their representatives responsible for specific decisions, pioneered ways of shaping public opinion, and helped to articulate demands for new social policies and new state agencies. "With the whole world organized and sub-organized for the intermutual protection of the members of numberless associations of differing purposes,"[85] American politics changed profoundly between the 1890s and 1920s. The great irony was that the new methods of social politics eroded traditional forms of graft and partisan patronage, only to be appropriated by the same corporate interests that had once fueled the party machines.

The two chapters that follow introduce the theoretical tools needed to understand this transformation. Chapter 2 draws on organizational theory, particularly its version of a new institutionalism,[86] to link the organizational experiments of popular associations to the possibility of institutional change. These efforts—often innovative, rarely revolutionary or entirely successful—were one eruption of the "democratic wish" that has punctuated American political history, the desire to restore citizen participation.[87] But, to invoke the standards of the criminal courts, not only motive and means but opportunity must be demonstrated. Chapter 3 takes up part of this task, locating the openings for innovation afforded by the "political opportunity structure" of turn-of-the-century American federalism. As figure defines ground, the structure of the party system created "political space" or "opportunities for legitimate mobilization not monopolized by established linkages."[88] These discussions of motive, means, and opportunity establish grounds for taking seriously the grand claims of President Charles R. Case of the Washington State Federation of Labor (WaSFL):

> There has assembled here upon the shores of the mighty Pacific, people, a majority of whom have pioneered westward to escape the ever increasing perplexing social problems of older settled communities. But these same problems are fast overtaking them and they cannot as heretofore move westward and escape them.
>
> They are awakening to a realization that they must be met and dealt with. So with their backs to the west which was once their refuge, they are ready to do battle with the evils they have fled from. Here upon our shores must be solved the issues of social and industrial justice, the westward tide must turn, and eastward the cause of freedom and equality must flow.
>
> Indicative of such course is the adoption by the people of Washington,

Oregon, and California of the necessary fundamental principles in the Initiative, Referendum, Recall and Direct Primary and their utilization as *methods of warfare to accomplish the actual will of a majority of our people*. The shortening of our workday by both organization and legislation has made it possible for men and women to have time and energy to study and solve great problems.

The granting of equal suffrage has quickened the pulse of the people to the needs of better education, morality, protection of youth and home.

We are indeed fortunate in being thus located and in having ambition to set a pace for others.[89]

While events would not turn out precisely as President Case might have hoped, the struggle of myriad popular associations for political influence had lasting consequences for the organization of American politics.

TWO

Organizational Repertoires and Institutional Change

> Organization is the watchword of the hour. All the different businesses, trades and professions are today organized. The farmers are the last to see this necessity.
>
> California State Grange, *Proceedings* 1899

> The ancient Greeks used the word "organization" and defined it as an instrument, engine, machine or tool for making or moving anything. To us as organized workers, organization means or is our instrument for enforcing just dealings, shorter hours of labor, better pay, safe and decent and sanitary conditions of labor. . . . This tool—organization—will yet pry the locks from firetrap factories and even force the courts to a sense of social responsibility.
>
> Wisconsin State Federation of Labor, *Proceedings* 1914

Assume a rational voter, endowed with values and interests that he seeks to maximize through the exercise of the vote. Since our voter is male (and so long as he was not excluded on the basis of race, citizenship, insanity, or prior felonies), we may then imagine him confronting American electoral arrangements circa 1890. Going to the polls, he would be given a ballot, typically printed by a party and designed to facilitate a straight party vote rather than an individual evaluation of the candidates for each office. In an era of caucuses and nominating conventions, our average voter would have played little role in selecting the party's candidates. Obviously, these arrangements militated against the straightforward expression of individual interests through the act of voting. Individual choices were constrained by the parties' ability to determine for whom one could vote.

Although state legislators were elected by a direct vote, this was no guarantee that they would keep campaign promises or attend to the demands of their constituents. One might argue that this is still the case, but as of 1890 our voter lacked the means to monitor and sanction legislative behavior. Roll-call votes were not widely available, legislative language easily obscured intent, and parties controlled nomination and renomination for office. In any case, a single voter could do nothing; effective sanctioning of elected officials required joint effort. But in addition to the usual obstacles that constitute the "collective action problem"—problems of coordination and the propensity of potential beneficiaries to free ride on the efforts of others—our rational voter belonged to a polity socialized to partisan identities and lacking organizational vehicles for the cultivation of other sorts of collective *political* interest. Despite these limitations, the election of state and local officials was a model of democratic representation when compared to the selection of holders of higher office. While members of the House of Representatives were elected by a direct vote, U.S. senators were chosen by state legislatures and the president by the Electoral College. In a classic principal-agent dilemma, our rational voter lacked any mechanism for binding the vote of his representative to these intermediary bodies.

Contemporary critics recognized that parties decoupled legislative outcomes from voters' preferences. "Consider what happens when I want to get a bill through the legislature," argued Mary Parker Follett. "I may feel sure that the bill is good and also that 'the people' want it, but I can work only through party, and at the state house I have to face all the special interests bound up with party, all the thousand and one 'political' considerations, whether I succeed or fail." Such situations pointed to the folly of understanding political outcomes as the simple aggregation of individual preferences: "But of course I recognize the humor of this statement: *I* ought never to try to get a bill through the legislature; special and partial groups have to do this simply because there is at present no other way; there must be some other way, some recognized way. We do not want to circumvent party but to replace party."[1]

In this context, the importance of the politics of method and organization is clear. Reforms such as the Australian ballot or the initiative and referendum were not simply the hobby horses of "goo-goos," as the middle-class good-government types were known. The mechanisms of electoral reform and direct democracy facilitated the linkage of individual votes to policy choices. But if these votes were to produce victories, some means of coordinating voters was also necessary. This formulation, however, still starts from individual voters with preexisting preferences, persons sure of what their government can do for them. Yet for people with much less experience with social policy than with sociability, the questions "What sort of people are we?" and "What do people like us want?"

were as salient as "How do I coordinate with others who share my interests?"

To be effective, procedural reforms required new forms of organization that embodied identities powerful enough to displace partisanship as the primary guide for political action—such mobilization, in fact, was almost always necessary to secure procedural reforms in the first place. As workers, farmers, women, and many others well understood, the ability to organize determined whose voice would be heard. The puzzle is how their exercises in organizational innovation resulted in institutional change. An answer requires a model of political outcomes that recognizes not only the fact but the form of organization as critical.

At the heart of much political analysis lies a simple contest model: whoever has the most (in terms of numbers or resources) wins and, by winning, can impose substantive or procedural preferences on other actors.[2] Based on this argument, we would expect both the magnitude and timing of political victories to vary with the size, legitimacy, and material resources of a challenging group. This model informs the instinctive focus on elites in political history; by definition, elites have power and resources, therefore we expect their actions to have greater consequences than those of the less privileged. This contest model also raises expectations about which challenging groups merit the most attention. Under elitist political regimes, the unequal distribution of resources supports the dominance of a minority; under pluralist regimes, the more who join in a coalition, the higher the probability of political success. Organized labor with its millions of mostly enfranchised, employed members should have been a formidable contender. Through the turn of the century, farmers were still more numerous. Hampered by disenfranchisement, cultural constraints, and lack of economic independence, women could be expected to accomplish little.

But in the United States at the turn of the century, the last was first, at least with respect to the linkage of extrapartisan associations to political outcomes. By 1920, women had secured the right to vote, contributed to the distinctively "maternalist" foundations of the American welfare state, and played a leading role in the movement to deprive all men of the right to drink. (Having gained the vote, however, women not only failed to sustain their influence, but lost much of it.) Organized agriculture followed, recovering from the political implosion of Populism to construct enduring iron triangles composed of legislative committees, agencies, and interest groups at both the state and federal level. For all its numbers and comparatively large resources, not until the depression and New Deal did organized labor secure policies gained by European workers decades before.

Closer attention to the role of organization in politics suggests a solution to this paradox. The key lies in the concepts of organizational form and organizational repertoire. Innovations in form and method can provide political advantages to otherwise disadvantaged groups. Initial advantages may flow from the capacity of new forms of organization to disrupt taken-for-granted procedures or from tactical innovations that exploit new opportunities or help to mobilize new resources.[3] Thus resources provided by associations lessen a candidate's dependence on the party leadership not solely in relation to the quantity of resources but also to the extent that the associations are independent of the party organization. Innovations will "take"—in the sense that they mobilize and sustain action—to the extent that they resonate with familiar but apolitical models of action, with other components of individuals' organizational repertoires. The use of familiar organizational forms helps to resolve collective-action problems both through the minimization of coordination problems among those mobilized and, at least in some cases, by securing a measure of legitimacy in the eyes of the authorities.[4]

But what is the link between mobilization and institutional change? This connection lies in the overlap between the organizational repertoires of challenging groups and the organizational forms embedded in existing institutions and recognized by those in power. Challenging groups frequently make use of familiar, highly legitimate, but conventionally apolitical models when pressing new political demands.[5] Women make claims on the state—whether for child welfare programs or the outlawry of war—in their role as mothers, suggesting that the state should be run as a family. The civil-rights movement made repeated use of religious models of organization and action—the revival, the pilgrimage, the prayer meeting—which both enhanced the legitimacy of their claims and secured some measure of protection from official repression. Such mobilizations result in lasting change insofar as these novel applications of familiar forms are adopted by those in power and embedded in the policies and institutions of the state. But change, it must be remembered, does not necessarily benefit those who initiate it.

This chapter provides a theoretical foundation for these accounts, clarifying the connections between the organization of political challengers and the possibilities of institutional change. The argument is built on four propositions. First, because societies encompass multiple forms of organization, individuals master organizational repertoires that guide but do not fully determine their action. Second, collective action is facilitated in settings where individuals have mastered overlapping organizational repertoires. Third, to the extent that oppositional movements employ familiar organizational forms in ways that violate dominant "logics of appropriateness," institutional change is more likely than if the forms of organization are entirely unfamiliar or illegitimate. Fourth, the forms and strategies employed by oppositional movements reflect both efforts to generate contradictions through the displacement of forms and attempts to secure legitimacy through the appropriation of the forms that dominate a particular field of social action.

This process of institutional challenge and change is evident in women's efforts to secure a greater role in American politics. Lacking the vote and a claim on political standing, some women appropriated the model of the family, in which their designated role was to nurture future citizens and guard morality. Transplanted to the field of public affairs, the resulting model of "municipal housekeeping" or "maternalism" allowed women to make political claims while partially insulating them from charges that they were "unnatural"; the frequent denigration of reformers as "long-haired men and short-haired women" suggests the protective cover afforded by a politics of motherhood. This politics of oblique infiltration, as opposed to direct challenge, eventually produced changes in both the roster of acknowledged political players and the scope of state intervention, while at the same time inscribing women's traditional family role in new social policies and state agencies.

Drawn from organizational analysis, this conceptual vocabulary permits the construction of an alternative to the "numbers and resources" model that has dominated political theorizing. Rather than starting with a contest between elites and challengers, it draws attention to the processes by which the choice of organizational form shapes both oppositional strategies and establishment responses. The cumulative efforts of such challengers transformed the organization of politics in the United States by expanding the roster of regular participants and strengthening the ties between constructions of "group interest" and policy outcomes at the expense of partisan loyalties.

Organization Theory and the Problem of Institutional Change

The concept of institutional change is almost an oxymoron. Institutions, after all, are defined by their endurance and resistance to change.[6] Consequently, institutions are invoked to explain absences of variation,[7] the perseverance of distinctive systems of political and economic organization,[8] or the stability and coherence of political regimes and social systems.[9] But institutional change clearly happens—indeed, classical social theorists portrayed history as a sequence of discrete regimes of social organization: gemeinschaft and gesellschaft; status and contract; feudalism, capitalism, and socialism. American political history has been arrayed on a comparable analytic scaffolding: party systems numbered one through five or a stage sequence of preparty, party, postparty, and nonparty.[10] The transition from one set of institutions to another, however, has often been poorly explained, attributed to some exogenous shock, intolerable contradiction, or inevitable development. As Lynn Hunt observed of explanations of one famous transition, the French Revolution "merely serves as the vehicle of transportation between long-term causes and effects; as a result, the emergence of a revolutionary politics has become a foregone conclusion."[11] What is missing is an account of the practical invention of new political styles and their contribution to institutional transformation. Without this, theories of institutional change are vulnerable to the charges leveled by one trade unionist at socialists in the labor movement:

> The trades union ladder stands against the wall; the socialists' ladder stands at its side. On top of the building there is a beautiful garden, "Success." We desire to obtain it, all of us, even the socialists. Let us examine the ladder. The trades union ladder has rung after rung up to the top. The socialists' has one rung at the bottom where we stand to-day and the other one at the top, and until they stand on us with those celebrated Irish 27 mules' bodies they will be unable to arrive at the top.[12]

For the explanation of changing political institutions, many of the intermediate rungs are constituted by the organization of oppositional politics. But this explanation requires an expansion of the "organizational synthesis" that has informed American history since the 1960s.[13] Above all, organization must be understood as social organization, not equated with business or profession alone. Just as entrepreneurs and governments drew on familial, military, and political models to build their new corporations,[14] corporate models of organization influenced the transformations of schools, churches, and associations. In addition, to explain the migration of forms, organization must be treated as meaningful, not merely instrumental. In 1970, Louis Galambos predicted that "[e]xplicit or formal ideology will receive less attention, as historians employ a McLuhan-esque emphasis on the organizational medium instead of the political message."[15] But the medium *is* part of the message. Therefore, the adoption of new organizational forms is not purely a response to environmental conditions and technological requirements—it is also a political and symbolic act.

Once the scope of organizational analysis is expanded and its symbolic dimensions recognized, a third limitation of the organizational synthesis appears. So long as businessmen are understood to adopt organizational innovations for business reasons, the presence of corporate forms can be taken as evidence that business interests have been served. Yet this conclusion falters when confronted with a California farmer's proclamation, "We must do as the corporations are doing—meet combinations of capital and brains with like combinations," or the claim of the Federated Trades Council of Madison, Wisconsin, that its financial standing "by R. G. Dunn and Co. . . . would be rated A1."[16] In his famous "Cross of Gold" speech of 1896, William Jennings Bryan addressed the "gold delegates" and charged,

> When you . . . come before us and tell us that we are about to disturb your business interests, we reply that you have disturbed our business interests by your course.
> We say to you that you have made the definition of a business man too limited in its application. The man who is employed for wages is as much a business man as his employer; . . . the farmer who goes forth in the morning and toils all day—who begins in the spring and toils all summer—and who by the application of brain and muscle to the natural resources of the country creates wealth, is as much a business man as the man who goes upon the board of trade and bets upon the price of grain. . . . We come to speak for this broader class of business men.[17]

The instrumentalist fallacy is clear. If organizational forms are part of a public discourse, business methods may be used by many actors for many reasons, including opposition to business interests. Fire may be fought with fire.

Just as the organizational synthesis is enriched by incorporating politics, political analysis may be improved by attending to organizational form. In the absence of sustained theoretical attention to the how and when of political organization, we tend to rely on a simple contest model of political action.[18] This basic model can provide robust explanations of outcomes within a particular regime, but it fails to address two fundamental questions of political science and sociology. What are the "rules of the game" that determine the character of political resources, the identities of political actors, and their relative efficacy? Just as important, when and how can political action alter the rules of the game?[19]

Organizational Forms and Repertoires

I begin with a set of assumptions about the organized character of society.[20] Rather than thinking of societies as characterized by a single dominant form of organization—feudal, capitalist, bureaucratic—let us assume that any given society will encompass a heterogeneous set of organizational forms.[21] This heterogeneity may be the product of the coexistence of organizations founded at different times,[22] of conscious borrowing of models from other societies,[23] or of the internal differentiation of social organization that preoccupied nineteenth-century theorists such as Herbert Spencer and Emile Durkheim.

This heterogeneity has a cognitive dimension; depending on personal experience, social location, and cultural transmission, actors master distinctive *repertoires* of organizational forms. As part of our "cultural toolkit,"[24] organizational forms are a type of competence, a set of familiar patterns for ordering social relations and action. Organizational forms are a subset of what Douglass North describes as "subjective models";[25] the interpretation of the world and recipe of action of the latter are linked to an understanding of collective identity or a model for collective action. But the potential for innovation lies in the fact that individuals can master more than one form; they can cultivate an organizational repertoire that will offer alternative scripts for action.[26]

The contents of an individual's repertoire reflect two types of relation to social structure. First, organizational repertoires may be characterized by their empirical distribution across social groups: what sorts of people have mastered what combinations of organizational form? Organizational competence is acquired through direct experience and culturally mediated exposure, both of which are socially structured in observable ways. Faiths may promulgate either hierarchical or congregational models. Cohorts may be marked by distinctive organizational experiences; the Civil War brought unprecedented familiarity with models of large-scale hierarchical coordination via military service for men and relief work for women. Economic and social developments change the frequency with which organizational forms are encountered as well as the normative evaluation of those forms. Masonic orders, once the target of riots and repression, were familiarized with the dramatic growth of fraternalism in the late nineteenth century and informed the organization of groups such as the Patrons of Husbandry and the Knights of Labor. The distribution of organizational repertoires also reflects the systems of cultural transmission through education, popular culture, and mass media. Whereas adult men of the nineteenth century internalized the practices of fraternalism, nineteenth-century students mastered a model more directly relevant to political life:

> [T]he significance of [school] monitors rests with the delegation of powers to pupils who performed official functions, who wielded authority based on coercion as well as persuasion, and who competed for their position. Chosen from the student body because of their achievement and obedience as well as their skill at ingratiation, monitors served as models for their fellows, who could simultaneously aspire to such honorific posts and observe authority exerted by an equal. Even the rewards monitors dispensed were reminiscent of political patronage; certainly the system acquainted young Americans with the repertoire of roles they would meet as citizens, including shared officeholding, rotation in office, and representation by untrained officials.[27]

Girls, it should be noted, were never selected as monitors in coeducational schools. Thus the second relationship between organizational forms and social relations is normative or prescriptive: what are the cultural rules or understandings about who should use what form for what purpose? Opportunities to master organizational forms vary with experience, interaction, and a culture's *logics of appropriateness* that specify who should use what form for what purpose.[28]

To recapitulate, *organizational forms* are templates, scripts, recipes, or models for social interaction. Once routine patterns of organization are articulated in these ways, they become "modular," or transposable from one setting to another. Any individual will be familiar with some set of forms; this set constitutes his or her *organizational repertoire*. An aggregation of all repertoires would track the distribution of forms within a society; the more extensive the systems of communication, the greater the heterogeneity of social interaction, the richer the contents of any individual's likely repertoire. But one may be familiar with an organizational form yet also recognize that it would be inappropriate to make use of it. These norms represent logics of appropriateness that tie shared strategies or forms to claims about when they may, must, or must not be used.[29]

Linked to both repertoires and logics, organizational forms are implicated in two types of political project. Because overlapping organizational repertoires facilitate collective action, there may be struggles over expanding or restricting the range of familiarity with a particular form. Because forms are tied to norms concerning who may use them for what purposes under what conditions, political actors engage in cultural elaboration—or frame alignment, extension, or restriction—to reinforce or undermine the acceptability of a particular organizational form in a particular context.[30] But because these logics are not exhaustive, ambiguities and silences in the rules afford opportunities to forge new combinations.

Solving Collective-Action Problems

Once mastered, organizational forms provide not only guides for individual behavior but scripts for collective action.[31] Insofar as the costs and benefits of cooperation determine the probabilities that individuals will participate to secure collective or public goods,[32] shared mastery of organizational forms facilitates collective action for at least two reasons. First, as a form of cultural competence, mutual knowledge of a given form facilitates cooperation, allowing reliance on tacit understandings rather than explicit instruction. Any skill or expertise developed in connection with a particular form of organization also becomes available as a resource for subsequent collective action, presumably increasing the probability of success. Second, shared mastery of a particular model for organization may also be a source of solidarity or collective identity, "immanent goods" in the sense that they "directly satisfy their members' utility."[33] In this respect, organizational forms may be a source of shared identity. The answer to "who are we?" need not be a quality or a noun; "we are people who do these sorts of things in this particular way" can be equally compelling.

The advantages of grafting a familiar form onto new purposes are amply illustrated by the uses made of fraternal rituals of initiation in the nineteenth century. Joseph Smith, a Freemason who had attained a "sublime degree," used Masonic language and ritual to initiate priests in the Mormon temple; the Sons of Temperance, Sons of Honor, and the Independent Order of Good Templars applied fraternal models to the cause of temperance; and the Order of the Star-Spangled Banner, the Knights of the Golden Circle, the Grand Army of the Republic, and the Ku Klux Klan all made political use of fraternal models.[34] In each case, the mobilization of a new group constituted a collective-action problem; the solution of these problems was facilitated by drawing on a model of organization already familiar to would-be members, already part of their repertoire.

The pervasiveness and potency of fraternal models is illustrated by a 1903 *Manual of Common Procedure* to be used by local and "federal"[35] unions affiliated with the American Federation of Labor. Despite its routine title, it was "desirable that this Manual shall be kept under lock and key in the meeting room and not exposed or submitted to the inspection of any person not a member in good standing." Such precautions were

not simply instrumental in preserving the secrecy of ciphers, but reso-
nated with the fraternal ritual used throughout. The president of the local
could open a meeting once "the Guardian [was] at his post to defend us
against all intruders." New members, having been elected at a regular
meeting, would then go through an initiation ceremony, led by "Brother
Guide": "When the Guide arrives with the candidates at the inside door
he will give the alarm. The members will rise to their feet and when the
door is opened the following ode [set to the tune of "Marching through
Georgia"] may be sung." Once initiated, new members would be told the
password and instructed in the salute to be given to the president upon
entering or leaving a meeting. Even the seating arrangements prescribed
for union meetings mimicked those widely used by fraternal societies (see
fig. 2.1).[36] In fraternal rituals, the American Federation of Labor found
both a ready-made, widely known organizational model and a mechanism for instilling identification and solidarity in its members. In this borrowing of means, the AFL followed a tradition of American organizing in
which "wage earners recast themselves in work-neutral terms, shifting
among the multiple identities that the fraternal networks provided for
white men and acquiring public equality as they did."[37]

Form, Field, and the Possibility of Institutional Change
Mastery of common organizational forms facilitates collective action, but
that action often reproduces existing patterns of social hierarchy and interaction. By mastering the system of rotating school monitors, boys were
socialized to the political practices of their nation; girls were doubly excluded, first from school governance, later from party politics. In selecting
union, party, or army as a model for organization, groups invoke a culturally familiar set of scripts for collective action and thereby shape the expectations and probable reactions of others.

Thus a new use of a familiar form is not necessarily novel, in the sense
of challenging the established logics of appropriateness that link forms,
actors, and purposes. But shared repertoires do not always contribute to
social stability and reproduction. Familiar organizational forms may also
be used in unfamiliar settings or for novel purposes in ways that fundamentally challenge existing social arrangements. Popular organizations,
in particular, are a form of "autonomous folkway" with the capacity to
shelter both innovation and resistance. During the depression of the
1890s, for example, unemployed men organized themselves as largely independent companies of Coxey's Army. Stealing trains in the Pacific
Northwest, floating down the Platte River on rafts, working their way

DIAGRAM OF THE POSITION OF
THE OFFICERS IN THE MEETING ROOM

PRESIDENT.

SECRETARY.   ▬▬▬▬   TREASURER.

TRUSTEES.

M E M B E R S.   . . . .   M E M B E R S.
                 . . . .
                 . . . . .   ✳   . . . . .
                 . . . .
                 . . . .

GUIDE. | VICE-PRESIDENT. | GUARDIAN.
                                             [DOOR]

KEY TO CIPHER FOR PRIVATE
AND CONFIDENTIAL COMMUNICATIONS
ALPHABET.

A	B	C	D	E	F	G	H	I
7	13	74	6	8	17	80	4	32
J	K	L	M	N	O	P	Q	R
9	25	40	83	2	5	12	1	15
S	T	U	V	W	X	Y	Z	&
35	18	3	28	82	68	10	14	23

NUMERALS.

1	2	3	4	5	6	7	8	9	0
At	To	It	If	As	Is	Of	Or	Be	In

Figure 2.1 The Persistence of Fraternal Practices: Seating Diagram and Cipher for
Local and Federal Unions. (Source: American Federation of Labor, *Manual of
Common Procedure for the Use of Local and Federal Labor Unions Affiliated with
the American Federation of Labor* [Washington, D.C.: American Federation of
Labor, 1903])

across Iowa playing exhibition baseball, or joining the main contingent
in Ohio, these men marched toward Washington, D.C. to demand an expanded federal public-works program. By linking military models (where
service was rewarded with pensions) to a program of employment on public improvements, the Coxeyites sought to transform the relation of the
federal government to the labor market. Unfortunately for the Coxeyites,
their use of a military model provoked a military response, and their final
encampment was broken up by federal troops.[38] So beyond recognizing
that common mastery of an organizational form facilitates collective action, an account of institutional change must attend to the relation of
forms to particular actors or fields of action.

Organizational forms are not isolated bits of cultural competence. Each form within a repertoire is associated with more or less elaborated rules about who may use it and for what purposes. There are cultural rules about what sorts of people *should* or *could* master what sorts of organizational competence. These logics of appropriateness are learned along with a particular organizational form and link forms to broader fields[39] of action. We learn not simply "how to behave," but how to behave at school, in church, as part of a protest rally, or with the boys. The deployment of a form, however, is not restricted to the field in which it was initially encountered, nor are logics of appropriateness fully elaborated. Forms learned for one purpose may be used for others. The familiarity developed in one organizational field may facilitate collective action and provide leverage for generating change elsewhere.

Familiarity facilitates the consolidation of novel uses of well-known forms insofar as it links those novel uses to existing practical knowledge of how to organize. This process is analogous to that required to change an invention into an innovation by translating the "visions of isolated discoverers" into enduring shifts in how things get done. For an invention to become an innovation, the novel design must be accompanied by accounts of how much to invest in the innovation, by whom and to what end and for whose benefit; and of how to coordinate the personnel and activities necessary to generate a new product or pattern of organization. Requiring only the invention of a theory of why a familiar form is suited to a new purpose, the recombination of forms and settings greatly eases the task of providing the "complex information and decision system" needed to embed inventions in social practices.[40]

The role of familiar organizational forms in facilitating change may be illustrated by considering the interrelationships of forms, actors, and purposes or spheres of action. Within any given organizational field, actions are most institutionalized when familiar agents use familiar organizational models for familiar purposes. Actions of this type contribute to social reproduction, as when American boys use partisan models to organize the self-governance of their activities. Actions are least institutionalized when unfamiliar agents use unknown or inappropriate models for novel purposes. If nineteenth-century schoolgirls were to set up their own system of rotating monitors in order to supervise some unprecedented enterprise, existing logics of appropriateness and institutionalized gender relations would be more profoundly challenged.

The logic of this process is evident in the uses made of the fraternal order; political and organizational entrepreneurs seeking to mobilize people around a new cause repeatedly made use of a familiar organizational model in order to solve collective-action problems and to trade on a sense of familiarity, perhaps even of legitimacy, for their new endeavor. Thus oppositional groups garner elements of both credibility and insulation when led by ministers, successful businessmen, or celebrities—individuals who can call on some other institution to legitimate their stature. But unlike innovations in economics, political innovations rarely generate long-term advantages within participatory or democratic regimes. Whereas the advantages of new products stem from the ability of the innovator to secure property rights to the innovation, to build exclusive ties to clients in the initial absence of competitors, and to learn how to improve production more rapidly than late-arriving competition,[41] all of these sources of advantage are weakened by the publicity or transparency demanded (if not necessarily realized) in a democratic regime. This is particularly true of innovations that rest on resources that are distinctively public: the votes of a mass-membership organization or the coordinated refusal to buy involved in a consumer boycott. So to the extent that political analyses equate the causal significance of actors with the benefits that they secure, the innovations of popular associations are likely to be overlooked precisely because they are so easily appropriated by other actors pursuing different goals.

But if the rapid diffusion of "public" innovations makes it difficult for the innovators to secure exclusive benefits, this public quality also accounts for the power of organizational experiments to undermine existing rules of the game. For nineteenth-century women seeking to carve out a novel public role, the choice of an unfamiliar form was an explicit signal, distancing them from more traditional women's associations. As Caroline Severance, a prominent early "clubwoman" explained:

> The title of "club" had been chosen after considerable discussion as being broad, significant and novel, and with the hope and the promise to the few objectors, that it would be redeemed from the objectionable features of many of the clubs of men. It was claimed to be an escape from the old special titles used for women's unions, in church and other activities, while inclusive of all these within its membership, and therefore significant of a new departure in fellowship and effort. It was a "woman's club"—an unknown quantity heretofore and therefore novel.[42]

Neither "clubs" nor "women's organizations" were unfamiliar; what was novel was women organizing as clubs. The significance of this innovation may easily escape a modern reader, but it involved a precedent-setting claim by women to appropriate heretofore masculine organizational forms.[43] And once organized as men, would it not be appropriate for them to engage in public affairs and politics? The appropriation of an "inappropriate" organizational form was part of a lengthy campaign for women to gain recognition as public actors and to transform the logics of appropriateness governing political participation. The same logic of displacement appears in the rumor that "certain public-spirited citizens of Los Angeles and San Francisco would maintain at the Capitol during the session a lobby to protect the interests of the people, just as the machine lobby looks after the well-being of machine-protected corporations and individuals."[44] Neither public-spirited citizens nor lobbies were particularly novel; what raised eyebrows was the rumor that public-spirited citizens had decided to organize themselves *as if* they were a lobby. In this way, organizational innovations may undermine the logics of appropriateness linking models to actors and purposes.

In complex societies, people master many more forms than are appropriate for any given circumstance. Consequently, institutional reproduction is always at risk of disruption because actors may "mismatch" forms and settings. While unintended errors in following the logics of appropriateness associated with different organizational forms are one potential source of change, the heterogeneity of social organization and the imperfect match between institutions and organizational fields also establishes the conditions for strategic action.[45] As Roger Friedland and Robert Alford have argued:

> The central institutions of the contemporary capitalist West—capitalist market, bureaucratic state, democracy, nuclear family, and Christian religion—shape individual preferences and organizational interests as well as the repertoire of behaviors by which they may attain them. These institutions are potentially contradictory and hence make multiple logics available to individuals and organizations. Individuals and organizations transform the institutional relations of society by exploiting these contradictions.[46]

Sometimes the "exploitation of contradiction" may be unintentional, but oppositional politics and social movements have often relied on the oblique transgression rather than direct confrontation insofar as it shields them from full retribution by the authorities and provides the foundation, however fleeting, for the construction of alternative social orders.

Strategies of Consistency and Contradiction
The difference between institutional reproduction and change depends on the relation of the invoked form to existing arrangements. Viewed from

the perspective of political challengers, there are two basic strategic options. First, they may organize *as if* they were already legitimate participants or act *as if* politics was governed by different but nevertheless legitimate and familiar rules. In cases where unfamiliar political actors use familiar political forms, existing logics of appropriateness are implicitly challenged, but fundamental institutional arrangements are not. Thus, when a judge recognized organized labor as "capital consisting of brains and muscle,"[47] this challenged the application of property law, but not its fundamental form. Whether institutions accommodate new actors or one institution is extended to govern a new field of action, this strategy generates change by processes of *isomorphism,* or the extension of consistent patterns of organization.

The second strategy seeks to delegitimate social arrangements by dramatizing contradictions in prevailing logics of appropriateness. Drawing on the cultural anthropology of Mary Douglas, one might argue that the selection of an organizational form may function as either a ritual or a joke:

> From the physical to the personal, to the social, to the cosmic, great rituals create unity in experience. They assert hierarchy and order. In doing so, they affirm the value of the symbolic patterning of the universe. Each level of patterning is validated and enriched by association with the rest. But jokes have the opposite effect. They connect widely different fields, but the connection destroys hierarchy and order. Essentially, a joke is an anti-rite.[48]

One of the most basic joke-forms involves playing on double meanings or polysemy to smuggle in a second set of meanings that destabilizes the frame established by the joke's premise. A similar effect can be achieved by transplanting familiar organizational forms or collective-action scripts to unfamiliar settings. Consider the following episode, in which Wisconsin suffragists employed a distinctively feminine form of action to undermine the logics of appropriateness linking gender to political privilege:

> On election day Nov. 6th, some of the members of the Equal Rights Association in Monroe prepared bouquets, carried them to the various polling places, and placed them on the ballot boxes saying that as they were not allowed to purify the inside, they wished to be permitted to beautify the outside.[49]

By juxtaposing an action associated with feminine virtue with a location organized for the expression of citizen virtue through voting, these suffragists sought to dramatize the contradiction of excluding the guardians of a society's moral virtue from the arena of politics. For such "jokes" to work, women had to employ organizational forms and tactics that clearly established their identity as "virtuous women" even as they trespassed in the unfamiliar, indeed for them illegitimate, arena of American politics.

Were suffragists to lose the claims to virtue established by *how* they acted and organized, they would lose a powerful weapon in destabilizing the logics of appropriateness that reserved politics to men. Almost thirty years after those Wisconsin women sought to "beautify" local polling stations, the suffragists of the Congressional Union picketed the White House, dramatizing the contradiction between their privileged moral and economic position—educated women dressed in white—and their secondary status as citizens. But this leverage would be lost if women could not sustain claims to feminine virtue. The dangers were clear to Beulah Amidon as she wrote "in confidence" to Mabel Vernon, criticizing the behavior of some of their colleagues in the National Woman's Party after they were thrown in jail for violating wartime restrictions on speech and assembly:

> We all feel that Miss [Alice] Paul made a grave mistake in pursuing the course of action she did. It seems that the chief inconvenience is bad air. As you probably know, all the suffragists are now being held at the District jail. Instead of asking to have the windows opened, our women refused to go into their cells until the windows were opened, and their threat made the warden stubborn. They were forced into their cells, after a hand to hand encounter with the guards and some of the men prisoners. Their next move was to take their breakfast dishes the following morning, and throw them through the windows, to destroy their knives, forks, and spoons, to break all the electric lights, and to tear some of their bed clothing. They are now held in solitary confinement, given their food on paper plates, without any table ware whatever. . . . It is all a dreadful mess. *The suffragists are so obviously in the wrong that we do not dare to give this story to the papers, or to give the matter any publicity.*[50]

Whether or not these suffragists were "obviously in the wrong," the relevant point is that this shift in tactics foreclosed the strategy of dramatizing the contradiction between the virtues attributed to women within the home and their inferior status with respect to political institutions. For individual activists, a more confrontational style might also erode the resonance between their political commitments and deeply felt feminine identities. Once they resorted to physical confrontation with authorities, the suffragists became unfamiliar political actors using forms of action that were held to be universally inappropriate in the political arena. Rather than destabilizing existing logics of appropriateness for political participation, incidents such as this could be used to confirm women's unsuitability for full citizenship.

Disruption alone, therefore, is no guarantee of enduring change. Although challengers may embody or promote alternatives for political organization, those alternatives must be secured or anchored in some way. There are, however, multiple mechanisms for institutionalizing what was once an alternative.[51] At the level of interaction, shared or taken-for-granted strategies or scripts facilitate cooperation and exchange; shared strategies even channel or focus conflict. Thus, the greater the diffusion of an alternative model, the greater its capacity for coordinating action and the costlier its abandonment. The advantages of sharedness may be enhanced in at least two ways. First, the cultural elaboration of new logics of appropriateness can embed a novel strategy in shared systems of belief about social organization or action. In highlighting their education and propriety, rather than their femininity, the suffragists described above sought to link the cause of woman suffrage to widely held ideals of the rational, informed citizen. Some followed out the policy implications of this cultural elaboration, calling for an educational suffrage requirement, a policy that would have disenfranchised numerous male voters. Whereas challenges may exploit ambiguities in existing logics of appropriateness, the institutionalization of change involves articulating new rules that embed new organizational forms in fields of action. Second, alternative models may be reinforced by legal and material resources. Women's politics became less controversial once women had the right to vote, labor organizing benefited from the formal recognition of a right to organize. And, to the extent that government increasingly funded programs demanded by constituents, the material incentives to organize as a "state-oriented challenger" were enhanced.

Shared strategies, cultural elaboration, and resource linkages all display something of what economists call "increasing returns." Unlike the classic model of supply and demand—where increases in supply decrease marginal returns—under conditions of increasing returns, the more is done, the higher the returns.[52] The more voters demand that legislators honor their campaign privileges, the higher the probable benefit of rewarding or punishing candidates. The more cultural norms against women speaking in public were violated, the lower the costs to each new women's association that decides to champion a political issue. These self-reinforcing features contribute to the robustness of organizational forms that become widely shared, heightening the importance of the order in which alternatives are invented and diffused. Institutionalization is, as they say, "path-dependent." Thus, to return to the process of political change, these arguments provide a guide for searching out the sources of political transformation: look for widely shared strategies or organizational forms that can be transplanted to political action; attend to efforts at cultural disruption and elaboration in which logics of appropriateness are rearranged; watch for new legal or material supports for new models of action.

Reconstructing Organizational Repertoires

In a complex society comprised of multiple models of organization and scripts for action, institutional change is often produced by extension and displacement rather than by revolution. As Lord Bryce observed of the writing of the U.S. Constitution:

> There is wonderfully little genuine inventiveness in the world, and perhaps least of all has been shown in the sphere of political institutions. These men, practical politicians who knew how infinitely difficult a business government is, desired no bold experiments. They preferred, so far as circumstances permitted, to walk in the old paths, to follow methods which experience had tested.[53]

This reliance on the already familiar produced "an experiment in the rule of the multitude, tried on a scale unprecedentedly vast."[54] Even at a moment labeled revolutionary, recombination rather than pure innovation was the source of institutional change. As a first step toward disentangling the complex processes of political transformation, the relevant organizational repertoires must be identified. As used by students of social movements, *repertoire* refers to the set of distinctive forms of action employed by or known to members of a particular group or society.[55] Thus members of nineteenth-century American labor unions generally knew how to picket, to petition, and to rally in public places. The contents of a group's repertoire are not given ab initio but develop as new forms of action and organization are acquired and old ones discredited. Only since the 1930s, for example, has the sit-down strike been part of the repertoire of organized labor in the United States.[56] This model of action built on an earlier addition to labor's organizational repertoire, the industrial union, which was formulated in contrast to the still earlier model of the craft union, which, in turn, drew heavily on the familiar practices of guilds and fraternal orders. To understand the development of a repertoire, therefore, requires an exercise in organizational archaeology, one sensitive to both variation in organizational form and change over time.[57]

While no formal listing of such repertoires exists, the set of culturally available models of organization can be reconstructed from debates that groups conducted over what sort of organization they wanted to be. Caroline Severance's claim that the women's club was "an escape from the old special titles used for women's unions, in church and other activities" illustrates the profoundly *comparative* quality of these discussions. The question was not simply "How shall we organize?" but "Shall we be a union, a party, or a business?" Convention proceedings are a particularly rich source of the alternatives considered by different groups, since any change in organization or strategy usually entailed formal motions complete with statements of the facts (the "Whereas" clauses) and an argument for some alternative model of organization or strategy of action. In an 1894 AFL debate on a resolution whose preamble identified the "Trade Unionists of Great Britain" as a model of, and compelling evidence for, effective independent labor politics, one delegate sought to cut off this line of argument with the observation, "This 'whereas' only points to a model, to a pattern, to something which follows that we should imitate."[58] But when there is uncertainty over how to act or considerable costs of coordination, the ability to "point to a model" is of considerable importance.

A close reading of such proceedings reveals two sets of available models: those already used by group members (or traditionally identified with "this sort of group") and those used by other groups in society. Both are analytically important. First, familiar models were one way in which a group defined its identity, both for its own members and for others. Second, the known but not yet used organizational models were both recipes for innovation and symptoms used to diagnose social problems. Consider this declaration made by the Political Committee of the Whitman County, Washington, Farmers Alliance in 1890:

> Resolved, That farmers, together with all other producers, should exert the political influence of their great numerical strength to thwart the increasing danger to the individual and the public interests which comes from the unrestrained greed of the influential anarchist who defies law, and tramples upon the principles of justice in his methods of acquiring the wealth that others create, and the less influential, less successful, but more demonstrative anarchist who, through speech and dynamite boldly proclaims his contempt for law, order, government, human life, and individual rights.[59]

This passage both invokes a collective identity, using a "producerist" frame shared with many nineteenth-century labor organizations,[60] and makes a claim for appropriateness based on a double contrast with the "influential anarchist" and the "demonstrative anarchist," who were linked not by the *ends* of their actions but by their common rejection of legitimate political methods.

While attacking the *methods* of robber barons and bomb-throwing radicals as equally illegitimate, these farmers participated in a collective effort to develop acceptable vehicles for what the authorities often viewed as unacceptable demands. Thus Coxey's Army of 1893–94, united around demands for federal employment and public-works schemes, presented itself as a "petition in boots," invoking a traditional and deferential form of political action by the dispossessed; the sobriquet "Army," however, sent a mixed message helping to shape the government's eventual repression of the petitioners.[61] Whatever their goals, voluntary associations made use of Robert's Rules of Order as a signal of their qualification for civic life and to differentiate "serious" gatherings from other forms of sociability. Aware that the convention of the Wisconsin Woman Suffrage Association might attract newcomers to the cause, the *Wisconsin Citizen* reminded its readers, "Our annual meeting must be a meeting for business, not merely an occasion of social enjoyment and spiritual refreshing. . . . It is desirable that all should study parliamentary usages. Robert's Rules of Order should be fixed in the memory and used, not to defeat the will of the majority and place the power in the hands of one or two wire-pulling maneuverers, but to secure orderly conduct of business." Like the farmers of Whitman County, these Wisconsin suffragists identified themselves through a set of comparisons with other organizations, both the "social enjoyment and spiritual refreshing" of more traditional ladies' groups and the "wire pulling" of corrupt political organizations.[62]

To reconstruct organizational repertoires, I rely on a combination of primary and secondary sources. By tracking debates over organizational form and strategy as recorded in annual convention proceedings and newspapers, I recreate the changing horizon of possibilities for various groups and map their shifting orientation toward other organized actors and institutions. What organizations are admired or condemned for their practices and strategies? Are resolutions directed toward other associations, state governments, or the national government? What range of organizational forms and methods does the association consider for itself, and which are adopted, which defeated? Throughout these accounts, the extent of awareness and mimicry among groups is clear. Rather than asserting that political innovation was grounded in the distinctive characteristics of individual organizations or states, this argument takes the process of organizational imitation and diffusion as central to an understanding of the institutional changes of the period.

This theoretical perspective entails applying the method of "virtual choice" to the study of oppositional politics.[63] What defined the universe of alternative organizational forms known to political challengers? For the study of American politics, such a universe is not captured by any of the conventional units of analysis: city, state, nation, or movement. Rather it is a universe defined interactionally, by the experiential and cultural knowledge of organizational forms shared by those who struggled together or against one another. At the juncture of state and society, social movements acted as political entrepreneurs, exploiting periods of political discontent or opportunity in order to promote novel combinations of problems and solutions. The challenge, of course, is to identify the circumstances under which social movements are able to promote institutional change, which movements are likely to play such a role, and with what consequences.

Social Movements and Institutional Change

The scholarly division of labor that separates the study of protest politics, popular associations, and party politics has produced partial analyses of the institutional transformation of American politics at the turn of the century. Drawn by the dramatic rise and precipitous decline of the Grange, the Knights of Labor, and the People's Party, the history of social movements thins out as popular organization and political opposition moved into different modalities in the twentieth century.[64] But oppositional politics matters not only as a source of strain or disruption that produces "windows of opportunity" for established political actors.[65] The alternative models of organization elaborated and mastered by challenging groups may also inform the institutional changes that result. To understand many instances of institutional change, we need to look more closely at those organizations that are *both* legitimate and marginal. This argument comes with an important caveat: the resulting change cannot be assumed to be either normatively desirable or directly beneficial to those organizations that cause it.

This model generates propositions about the sources of political change different from either elite or protest politics arguments. In contrast to elite theories, which suggest that the disadvantaged and marginal position of many social movements limits their efficacy, these qualities are precisely those that are needed for significant institutional change. If a familiar political actor adopts familiar models of organization for familiar purposes, institutional reproduction will result. But the opposite combination, one that maximizes unfamiliarity, is likely to elicit repression or rejection. Instead, movements are more likely to succeed in producing some (if rarely radical) institutional change insofar as they employ a combination of familiar and unfamiliar elements. Again, this argument is meant to explain the processes of institutional change, not the success of a movement in terms of the well-being of its constituency.

The possibilities of institutional change are thus determined by the presence of political challengers who differ in some degree from institutionalized political actors. To the extent that challengers possess an organizational repertoire distinct from the dominant political institutions, they are more likely to produce institutional change. To extent that the members of these challenging organizations differ from members of the established polity, they are more likely to be immune to routines of political co-optation and, therefore, more capable of producing significant change. Finally, to produce institutional change, challengers are likely to be marginal, but not too marginal. Change requires that other political actors adopt new models or accept new political actors; to the extent that such demands are too extreme, challengers are likely to be trivialized, marginalized, or suppressed.

This model illuminates the distinctive contribution of popular associations to the transformation of American political institutions in the decades surrounding the turn of the last century. Popular associations, often founded for apolitical reasons, were "an instrument, engine, machine or tool"[66] for constructing new collective identities associated with new collective goals. These organizations generated new resources and networks that were not embedded in existing patterns of partisan loyalty and authority. Finally, the internal life of these associations made manifest an alternative model for the conduct of politics—one that valued informed participation, focused on specific issues rather than overarching ideologies, and utilized a pragmatic discourse of "business methods" and political accountability. The impact of such organizations did not stem solely from the fact that they brought new resources to political contests, but from the linkage of those resources to alternative models of political organization and participation.

By focusing on the organizational logic of nineteenth-century American politics and the organizational repertoires of those who challenged it, these first two chapters lay the foundation for an explanation of the party system's erosion. Political challengers were motivated not simply by particularistic grievances or interests, but by the growing recognition that the party system itself was an obstacle to the expression and resolution of those grievances. Consequently, these challengers not only pursued interests and ideological goals, they sought new ways of organizing political action, methods for evading the suffocating logic of the party system and the organizational materials for constructing an alternative. But motive and means are insufficient for conviction—opportunity must also be established. To that end, recall the double claim of the president of the Washington State Federation of Labor. His claim that "the people" were addressing the social problems of the day was not general but regional:

> So with their backs to the west which was once their refuge, they are ready to do battle with the evils they have fled from. Here upon our shores must be solved the issues of social and industrial justice, the westward tide must turn, and eastward the cause of freedom and equality must flow.[67]

Regional variations in the opportunities for oppositional politics would prove to be the institutional equivalent of a loose thread, capable of unraveling the party system.

THREE

The Experiment Station: Political Innovation and Diffusion among the States

> Wisconsin is doing for America what Germany is doing
> for the world. It is an experiment station in politics, in
> social and industrial legislation, in the democratization
> of science and higher education. It is a state-wide labora-
> tory in which popular government is being tested in its
> reaction on people, on the distribution of wealth, on so-
> cial well-being.
>
> Frederic C. Howe, *Wisconsin: An Experiment in Democracy*
> (1912)

Westerners often used an educational metaphor to explain their contribution to national reform. Describing the relations among states, one Washington reformer explained, "We serve as an experiment station. This
seems to me the mission of the newer states. . . . to lead the older states
in trying out new legislative proposals as solutions for old unsolvable
problems, and thus by actual practice eliminating the false theory from
the true."[1] These publicly funded stations were designed to demonstrate
the application of scientific research, to make modifications in light of
local conditions, and to win converts to new methods—efforts as perti-
nent in politics as in agriculture. With respect to the initiative and referendum, Oregon was both praised as a "political experiment station" that
had transplanted ideas from Switzerland[2] and condemned as an example
of folly that other states should not follow. As the *Denver Republican*
complained: "Cannot the people of Colorado do a little sober thinking
for themselves and on their own account? Must they adopt every new
fangled notion which may be adopted or experimented with in some
other state? Let Oregon be foolish if it wants to, but let Colorado always
be sober and sane."[3]

Whatever the normative judgment passed on policy diffusion, the metaphor of the experiment station captures the practical exercise of comparative politics that oriented states toward one another. Some states

provided opportunities for political experimentation and innovation. Associations with members drawn from multiple states were a medium for the diffusion of both policy solutions and political tactics.

Opportunity for innovation is the final component of an account of institutional change that began with grievances against the party system and the organizational repertoires of political challengers. The organizational logic of the party system generated opposition, from both elites who called for institutional reforms and popular groups who sought alternative channels for political influence. In constructing a new system of political organization, these popular associations also possessed a critical resource for institutional change: the mastery of alternative forms of organization. But intentions and instruments alone are insufficient to generate institutional transformation. Much of the power of the party system lay in its ability to suppress, fragment, or co-opt opposition. So at this point, it is necessary to begin working backward, looking for signs of effective challenge, not merely opposition, to the dominance of partisan politics.

One clue is found in the Washington union leader's boast that westerners were "indeed fortunate in being thus located and in having ambition to set a pace for others."[4] Theoretical accounts of American political development and commentaries from the turn of the century suggest that processes of political innovation were most pronounced in the more recently settled sections of the nation. The record of reform substantiates this claim, revealing distinctive regional patterns of political and social-policy innovations during the Progressive Era. Finally, the organizational developments of this period are consistent with processes of state-level policy diffusion—regardless of the region of origin—and help to account for the explosive waves of policy adoption that characterized progressivism at the state level. Mothers' pensions, for example, took off dramatically: twenty states passed legislation between 1911 and 1913, twenty-one more between 1914 and 1919. In 1911, ten states passed workmen's compensation bills that met the test of constitutionality; twelve states followed in the next two years, and eight more in 1915–16.[5] Causal explanations based on the traits of individual states are ill suited to account for these waves of policy innovation and imitation.

These waves of innovation and diffusion pose two questions: What were the sources of new political strategies and policy solutions? And what were the mechanisms by which these solutions diffused from one political arena to another? As will be argued in this chapter, the answers lie in the practical uses of comparative politics, in the opportunity structure of turn-of-the-century federalism, and in the proliferation of associations active in multiple political arenas. The confluence of these factors drove innovations at the state level, and, as will be discussed in chapter 8, the limitations of state polities eventually pushed challengers to transplant those innovations to national politics. The emergence of a new style of social politics across the nation was the product of both the mutual orientation of states to one another and the efforts of popular associations to translate that mutual orientation into legislative replication.

The Geography of Political Opportunity

The political arrangements of the United States pose problems of narrative. Whose story should be told, which actors should be featured? City, state, and nation all present themselves as possible organizing frameworks, each offering the additional advantage of being a unit of documentation and record keeping. But the presence of these convenient options has left a significant part of American politics untold or, more precisely, marginalized. Focusing on a single city, state, or on the nation as a whole, scholarship has often treated the relations among political units as epiphenomenal,[6] factors to be invoked where they seem important, but not to be explored systematically.[7]

This problem has been exacerbated by regional biases and disciplinary conventions. While the national significance of developments in Massachusetts or New York is often noted, state histories covering the rest of the country are typically limited to state politics.[8] Therefore, the possibility that state-level movements have national consequences has been largely unexplored. The major exception to this omission is found in recent work on the significance of the South for national politics.[9] Studying topics as diverse as national finance, antitrust regulation, old-age pensions, and welfare policy, scholars have noted how southern politicians, both in Congress and in their own states, were able to turn aside strong efforts at national state-building and uniform policy implementation.[10] But these arguments emphasize the negative case, southern states as obstacles or constraints.[11] Yet there are a number of reasons to think that the states were important sites of political innovation and, by extension, that developments in one state might have broader consequences.

Of particular concern for the study of social politics is the constitutional reservation of powers and responsibilities to the states, including the regulation of employment, care of the needy, and much of the organization of political life. In the guise of demands for the eight-hour day and child labor laws, for workmen's compensation and mothers' pensions, for the initiative and referendum, these powers of state governments were a primary target of the new social politics. The early significance of these powers has been obscured by federal expansion during the New Deal and the Second World War. In his *American State Politics,* V. O. Key treated the importance of state government as a recent development, dependent on their new responsibilities for disbursing federal grants and new powers for raising revenues. Attributing the management of important issues to either national or local government, Key asks, "What could be expected of the states on fiscal policy? In employment policy? On public works? On old-age security? On conservation?" Whether or not these could be managed adequately at the state level, state governments were among the first to take responsibility for these issues. Numerous states supported public employment offices as well as old-age pensions prior to the New Deal. Wisconsin even developed a large-scale public-works program as part of a countercyclical employment policy along with the original model for the Civilian Conservation Corps.[12] Within each state, different groups mobilized, different rules for political cooperation developed, and different agencies were created. These innovations then served as precedents for political action elsewhere. As national organizations mobilized to replicate these policies in other states or in federal legislation, local innovation cumulated in national reform. In the absence of either uniform legislation across states or federal standards, state-by-state reform invited "degenerative competition," in which states would undercut each other in order to attract or retain investment.[13] Although many of the policy precedents set during the Progressive Era were overturned or ignored in subsequent decades, the institutionalization of the methods and channels of access used to set those precedents endured.

Plentiful evidence of the practice of comparative politics may be found in the policy discourse of the time. Discussions of what to do and how to do it often revolved around state-specific exemplars. "The Wisconsin Idea" stood for a wide-ranging approach to reform, emphasizing expert-based regulation. The "Iowa Idea" linked tariff reform to a refusal of "shelter to monopoly." The "Missouri Idea" referred to novel uses of law for popular control of corporations; "North Dakota-ism" signaled the state-sponsored economic development championed by the Nonpartisan League.[14] Nor were these isolated instances. Comparative politics was a practical method for political actors at the turn of the century. The first step in redressing a problem was to find out what had been done elsewhere. For example, the Washington State Federation of Labor com-

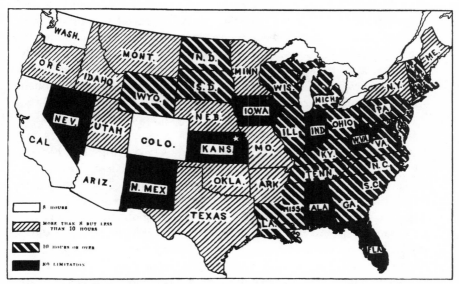

LEGAL LIMITATION OF WORKING HOURS FOR WOMEN IN THE UNITED STATES

The hour limits indicated do not apply to all occupations in which women are employed, but are those which affect a large proportion of female industrial workers.

* In Kansas the industrial welfare commission may fix hours, but up to December 1, 1916, had only placed a limit of 9 hours on work in mercantile establishments.

Figure 3.1   The Map as Comparative Politics: Women's Hours Legislation, 1916.
(Source: *American Labor Legislation Review,* December 1916)

mented on the passage of initiative, referendum, and recall in all the Pacific states, compared their state's workmen's compensation law to others with respect to "first aid," and sent inquiries on the use of referendum elections within unions to thirty-eight other state federations of labor.[15] The significance of state-by-state comparisons was visually reinforced by publications such as the *American Labor Legislation Review.* A map of the American states, shaded according to the passage of a particular law or the number of state factory inspectors, was a dominant mnemonic for tracking the progress of reform (see fig. 3.1).

The prominence of a comparative approach was equally evident once issues moved onto a state's legislative agenda. At this point, the first action was frequently not the passage of legislation but legislative authorization of a study commission. The reports of these commissions have a characteristic form. After a brief preface, asserting the gravity of the problem and the need for a civilized people to address it, the first section is typically devoted to a survey of legislation passed or contemplated in other states or nations.[16] These practices also generated a minor industry of "policy tourism." For example, the Milwaukee Merchants' and Manufacturers' Association followed "the practice of other employer and public groups of the period [and] sent its secretary to England and Germany in 1910 to study the systems of [workmen's] compensation."[17] Reformers and academics put faith in the possibility of "bettering the laws through a study of comparative legislation."[18]

At first glance, this seems an obvious way of approaching the task of legislation. However, there are a number of other possible strategies, some much more characteristic of contemporary policy development. For example, a policy document might begin with a statistical description of the problem. Alternatively, the framework might be provided by a particular model of economic or social behavior: the "domino theory" for foreign policy, Keynesian economics for domestic-spending policy. These alternative strategies suggest two additional reasons for the prevalence of state-to-state influences in policy development: the absence of a national policy bureaucracy and the rudimentary state of statistical methods and empirical social analysis. The absence of methodological expertise was underscored by William Ogburn, one of the most important early advocates of quantitative methods in the social sciences. In his study of the spread of child labor legislation, he frequently stopped to explain such basic matters as the interpretation of averages. As policy expertise grew throughout the country, such methodological issues would soon become tacit. But, in the meantime, political debate was informed by the concrete exemplars provided by other states and nations. The comparative flavor of these arguments is illustrated by a *Report on Old Age Relief* by the Industrial Commission of Wisconsin, one of the nation's more sophisticated and professional public agencies: "There are no such exact records of Wisconsin conditions, for the very reason that no systematic effort has ever been made to deal with old age dependence in this state. That aged pauperism here is less acute than in Europe, or even in Massachusetts needs no proof. But there is less reason to suppose that conditions are better among our people than in New Zealand."[19] Given this practice of comparative politics, local innovation could have national and international consequences.

The comparison of state-level reforms was reinforced by the federal structure of the nation. Both the legislative and judicial branches of American government required practices of comparative politics. As issues became the subject of national legislation, alternatives might bear the names of states. The debate over unemployment insurance, for example, pitted Wisconsin against Ohio.[20] As is evident from the praise and criticism heaped on Oregon for the initiative and referendum, that state played a comparable role as exemplar in debates over direct democracy.

Comparative politics had more immediate consequences as it was practiced by the judiciary.[21] Reacting to state-level decisions on the constitutionality of workmen's compensation legislation, one reform publication crowed, "A Washington 'Yes' to New York's 'No.'"[22] On further appeal, the U.S. Supreme Court upheld the Supreme Court of Washington. During this period, laws upheld by a state supreme court could be appealed to the U.S. Supreme Court, but no appeal was allowed if the highest court in a state ruled that a piece of legislation was unconstitutional.[23] Consequently, friendly state courts were a prerequisite for the U.S. Supreme Court to rule on legislative questions reserved to the states and, when these decisions were favorable, to approve a template for subsequent legislative efforts. For labor reformers and unionists in New York, as well as throughout the nation, the existence of the favorable Washington opinion was of considerable importance.[24]

By maneuvering within the federal system, political actors could foster, attack, and protect policy innovation. Assessing the impact of the U.S. Supreme Court's decision upholding an Oregon law establishing a ten-hour day for men, one reform magazine declared that "the effect of this decision . . . must be to encourage the enactment of laws regulating hours for men, as well as women and children."[25] In the case of women's minimum-wage legislation, the U.S. Supreme Court cast doubt on the constitutionality of such laws in 1923 by overturning a Washington, D.C., statute in the *Adkins* case, effectively halting agitation for further minimum-wage legislation throughout the nation and providing a rationale for the dismantling of already effective laws in states such as Washington and Wisconsin.[26] In a few places, notably California, minimum-wage laws continued in effect, but only through considerable efforts to prevent any legal challenge that might expose the state law to the rulings of the U.S. Supreme Court.[27]

Within American federalism, states could serve as "abeyance structures" in which policy precedents or styles of political action could persist despite changes in the national political climate.[28] Decisions on one state's bill might also restrict the solutions considered by those active in the decisions of another state. For example, Washington unionists refused to compromise on the inclusion of a first-aid amendment to workmen's compensation: "Practically every state that has passed a compensation act has included 'first aid' at the expense of industry. The legislature, dominated as you well know, by 'special interests,' has twice defeated 'first aid.' We

may be pardoned if we are resentful at any further interference by manufacturing interests in legislative halls in the matter of 'first aid.'"[29]

Federalism constituted a distinctive "political opportunity structure,"
a terrain of opportunities and constraints that shaped the possibilities of
strategic action.[30] Within the opportunity structure of turn-of-the-century
federalism, the actions of one state constrained the actions of others.[31] At
a moment when economic activity increasingly spilled over state boundaries, but a national regulatory bureaucracy was still in its infancy, state-
level innovation and imitation were particularly important. Early regulatory efforts, especially in the area of industrial policy, were opposed on
the grounds that capital would flee to other states in order to escape excessive burdens in one locale. In Wisconsin, for example, passage of insurance reform in 1907 prompted twenty-three national firms to cease doing
business in the state. The threat of competitive disadvantage, even when
not acted upon, figured regularly in business opposition to reform: "Any
additional burdens or interference placed on business now, any legislation
further handicapping Wisconsin business in the competitive markets of
the world at this time of extreme competition, may bring about a catastro-
phe of unforeseen violence and scope. Witness North Dakota, where even
some of the torch bearers were engulfed before they had time to make
their getaway."[32] Since the existence of precedents would weaken the
"capital flight" argument, reformers could advance a cause by passing
legislation outside their own states. The success of innovation depended
on diffusion: "The states could act as 'laboratories' of social legislation,
in a later euphemism; but this was only half the story. The states also
acted as competing sellers of jurisprudence in a vast federal bazaar. A
kind of Gresham's law was in operation: easy laws drove out the harsh
ones. Experiments in the 'laboratories' would not work so long as neighbor states refused to go along."[33] But as more and more states adopted a
particular reform, policy laggards were exposed to criticisms as backward, inefficient, or corrupt.

For analytic purposes, these relations among states may be captured by
the application of "garbage-can" models of decision making to political
processes.[34] For political actors in any given state, other states fed the
streams of problems and solutions out of which decisions are ultimately
cobbled together.[35] So what happens in state A is not solely a product of
local conditions, but also of the problem definitions and policy solutions
(or failures) that are known from states B, C, and D. Thus, to the extent
that states constitute exemplars for one another, political diffusion is facilitated by what institutional theorists term "mimetic isomorphism."[36]

These connections among states are strengthened if actors in one state include victory elsewhere in their political objectives and export resources from one arena to another, both common associational practices at the turn of the century. Finally, there may be institutional rules that designate states as precedents for one another. The federal judiciary provides the clearest example of such rule-based diffusion, but the use of a profoundly *comparative* method of political innovation was also widely evident in the reports of legislative commissions and popular associations.

Where Was Innovation Possible?

Recall that the nineteenth-century party system was designed to win elections rather than to address policy issues. Winning elections required suppressing those concerns or contenders that might split the cross-sectional coalitions constructed by each of the major parties. This organizational fact shaped the opportunity structure for political innovation. If parties blocked innovation and absorbed challengers, then the development of novel approaches to policy dilemmas and political mobilization should be most pronounced where the parties were weakest. Given weak parties, the potential for novel outcomes should be greatest where state politics was not dominated by a single economic interest but contested by diverse groups. Taken together, arguments derived from political organization and economic determinism combine to paint a picture of the geography of reform that corresponds to the perceptions of contemporary commentators and the record of political outcomes. All these arguments point west.

Political challenge is both creative and reactive. Popular associations invented new methods of organization and political influence, but the terms of the problem that these groups sought to solve were set in large part by the organizational projects of party leaders. To account for regional variations in party strength, Martin Shefter has argued, "The reason that politicians and local elites found it neither necessary nor especially advantageous to build strong party organizations ultimately concerned the West's peripheral status in both the economic and political systems of late nineteenth century America."[37] Instead, faced with the opposition of entire communities, railroads and other large corporations resorted to buying the votes not only of single legislators but of entire legislatures:

> It is little wonder, then, that the western Progressives regarded political parties as tools of "the interests." Accordingly, they sought to destroy parties

and return government to "the people" by establishing direct primaries and the initiative, referendum, and recall. In time, they were able to overwhelm the prevailing regimes in the western states by pursuing a strategy of mobilization.[38]

As the comparatively stable partisan alignments of the 1880s gave way in the elections of the 1890s, the relative weakness of parties in the West was exacerbated. Democratic fortunes prospered in the early 1890s, nourished by conflicts over cultural issues such as temperance and English-language instruction that attracted immigrant groups to the party. But with the onset of the depression of 1893, economic policies emerged as the new dividing line between parties, a contrast heightened by the success of specific factions within each party. Hoping to stem this development, a Republican delegation from the Northwest argued in 1891 that the "national convention should be held in Minneapolis because 'the doubtful States are now to be found in the West and Northwest, owing to the flocking in of the foreign population and the growth of the Alliance movement.'" Nevertheless, the party concentrated its resources elsewhere in the 1892 elections.[39] Through the 1890s, electoral returns in the Plains states and the West took "the form of a long series of low correlations, indicative of erratic voting patterns, not a sharp and durable realignment."[40] Unlike the eastern states, where the realignment of the 1890s represented "the decisive enlargement of the Republican coalition and the reduction of the Democratic one," politics in the Midwest and West featured a series of third-party efforts, nonpartisan efforts to pledge candidates or shape platforms, and extrapartisan campaigns for direct democracy.[41]

These developments came to a crisis in the presidential election of 1896.[42] Western Democrats secured the nomination of Williams Jennings Bryan, ultimately leading to fusion with the Populists and an identification of the party with the monetarization of silver. But as the Democrats moved in one direction, the Republican Party went in the other: "The Republican victories of 1893–94 altered the balance of power within, as well as between, the major parties. In the Northeast, Republicans hostile to free silver now occupied political positions once held by Democrats of the same persuasion. These Republicans reinforced the sound money forces within their own party. The full implications of this development would become clear at the Republican national convention of 1896, where party managers would make no attempt to placate spokesmen for the silver-producing states of the West." Bryan's defeat threw partisan politics in the West into further disarray. Well into the next century, that region would produce lower electoral turnouts, signaling a weaker party system.[43] So while the fortunes of the two parties fluctuated over the next decades, the context for this volatility varied by region. What was in the East a contest between or against party organizations was, in the West, a competition to organize on terms other than partisanship.

In many states, this competition was stillborn. The presence of a single dominant economic actor or industry—a railroad, mining or lumber companies—encouraged the construction of corporate equivalents to the party organization.[44] Consequently, reform efforts in the western states were often rooted in a struggle against corporate dominance that, not surprisingly, corporations did their best to suppress. As Michael Kazin has argued, such demands for procedural reforms are at odds with traditions of Progressive Era historiography that find no common interest between elite "structural reformers" advocating new city charters and labor groups seeking new sources of political influence. Struggles over the initiative and referendum, which were tools for breaking corporate control over state legislatures, regularly featured an alliance of farmers and organized labor against business interests.[45]

Popular political competition was less easily smothered in states with weak parties *and* mixed economies, a condition met in the early twentieth century by only a few states in the upper Midwest and the states along the Pacific Coast. This diversity created the conditions for political compromise and innovation. Examining the politics of antitrust in light of regional economies, Elizabeth Sanders documents how opposition between states in the industrial core and agricultural periphery generated a polarized debate. But the compromise ultimately informing legislation "as was so often the case, was backed most strongly by congressmen from the economically diverse midwest and Pacific trade areas."[46] Taken together, the arguments by Shefter and Sanders suggest that political innovation was most likely in regions where party organization was weak and local economies were mixed. These considerations direct attention away from the North, the old Midwest, and the South. But in the old Northwest Territory and along the Pacific Slope, the conditions for political innovation were more promising.

These theoretical predictions are supported if we consider three indicators of the emergence of a new political regime centered on legislative and popular politics rather than party organization: policy innovation, political innovation, and legislative activity. An index of policy innovation may be constructed by looking at those states that were among the first (up to and including 1913) to pass central components of the progressive

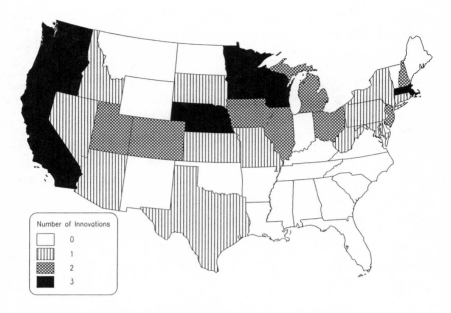

Figure 3.2   Policy Innovation: Workmen's Compensation, Mothers' Pensions,
and Women's Minimum Wage Laws Prior to 1914

social-policy agenda. Given the role of practical comparative politics and
diffusion processes, later adopters may differ significantly from innovators and early adopters.[47] Legislation that reconstituted citizens as (potential) beneficiaries of state programs is of particular significance. As
has been argued by numerous scholars, workmen's compensation and
mothers' pensions were the cornerstones of the two-track, gendered welfare state of this period.[48] Beyond these policies, passage of a women's
minimum-wage law represented a particularly strong commitment to
state regulation of the market. Combining these three types of legislation
produces an index of policy innovation and early adoption (see fig. 3.2).[49]
Of the twenty-eight states that passed at least one of these by 1913, just
eight passed two, and seven passed all three: California, Massachusetts,
Minnesota, Nebraska, Oregon, Washington, and Wisconsin. While Massachusetts is an isolate on the East Coast (and its minimum-wage law was
much weaker, providing only for publicizing the names of firms that paid
less than the recommended minimum), the other six constitute two regional clusters: one in the upper Midwest and one along the Pacific coast.

   But policy innovation was only one aspect of the new form of political regime that developed during this period. Perhaps more fundamental was the displacement of party organizations by both increased possibilities for popular participation and the growing significance of legislatures and state agencies. Like social-policy innovation, political innovation had a distinct regional profile illustrated by the passage of provisions for the initiative, referendum, and woman suffrage, all of which represented a major expansion of the electorate and an attack on party control of legislatures. Urban machines opposed woman suffrage out of fear that new voters would support prohibition, thereby alienating other constituencies, but also out of pragmatic, organizational considerations: "From the beginning the concept of the machine implied authoritarian control, and the smaller and more docile the electorate the better."[50] Direct democracy challenged party control, so it is not surprising that these political innovations appear as the mirror image of party strength. Indeed, the regional pattern evident in political innovation is even clearer than that of policy innovation (see fig. 3.3).[51] Of the seventeen states that adopted the initiative and referendum by 1913,[52] only Maine, Arkansas, and Ohio were east of the Mississippi. Woman suffrage was a purely western phenomenon until 1914, when Illinois adopted presidential and municipal suffrage (the right to vote for state officers required a later constitutional amendment).

A comparison of the distribution of policy and political innovation reveals a marked disjuncture. Policy and political innovation coincide in the Far West. In the upper Midwest, however, social-policy innovations occur in the absence of the progressive reforms most strongly linked to attacks on the party system. At first glance this would seem to undermine the contention that weak parties, new forms of political participation, and state-building were the pillars upon which the emerging regime of interest group politics was built. However, closer inspection reveals that a strain of antipartisanship was also strong in the upper Midwest, but that it took different organizational forms when faced with the more developed parties of this region. Rather than building on nonpartisan lobbying or extrapartisan direct democracy as in the West, criticism of the major parties often fed third-party movements: the Milwaukee Social Democrats and later the Wisconsin Progressive Party, the Farmer-Labor Party in Minnesota, and the Nonpartisan League in North Dakota.[53] In both Nebraska and Wisconsin, insurgent factions captured the Republican Party for at least some part of the progressive period, making even formal third-party organization unnecessary.[54] In these states, challengers transformed the party system so that it no longer obscured pressing social issues but expressed them. Working within the primary system of North

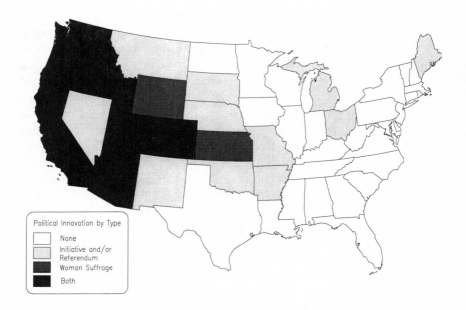

Figure 3.3   Political Innovation: Initiative, Referendum, and Woman Suffrage Laws
Prior to 1914

Dakota, for example, the Nonpartisan League worked to widen "the
scope of conflict between the candidates: it would create broad programmatic differences between two sets of primary candidates." [55] Westerners
were more likely to reject the party as an illegitimate form of political
organization; midwesterners tended to attack Republicans or Democrats
rather than the party form itself. Thus the Far West and the upper Midwest represent different paths beyond the system of party politics dominated by national Democrats and Republicans. Although opportunities
differed from state to state, from the 1890s through the 1920s many political challengers addressed a common project: "[T]he problem was some-
how to turn a system that pivoted on office-holding to one that pivoted
on policy," [56] specifically on those policy issues that were suppressed by
the coalition structure of the national parties.

Social-policy innovation and expanded opportunities for political participation are two traits of an emerging regime defined by interest group
mobilization and legislative politics. They also imply a third: heightened
legislative activity on social-policy issues. As constituent organizations
increasingly took positions on policy issues, the level of legislative activity

concerned with social policy (as opposed to the private bills that proliferated in late-nineteenth-century legislatures) should have increased. Regardless of the specific content of legislation, the amount of social legislation may be taken as a rough indicator of the extent to which all actors in a political arena—business, labor, farmers, reformers, women, and even party politicians—accepted social policy as the appropriate terrain for political competition and the extent to which the political system was open to their efforts.

Throughout the United States, at both state and national levels, legislative activity intensified as the end of the nineteenth century approached. Beginning with the Civil War, westward settlement, immigration, and industrialization all contributed to growing demands on the nation's legislatures.[57] The relationship between these social changes and the level of political activity was not direct, but a simple model linking industrialization to legislative outcomes helps to pinpoint the origins of this new style of political action. Often characterized as a "logic of development" model, this argument suggests that the level of social spending and the scope of welfare state policies will increase as a society becomes more "modern" or industrialized.[58] Extending this rudimentary model to explain the intensity of political decision-making, the extent of legislative activity should vary with the level of industrialization.

The U.S. Census provides a measure of industrialization in the value added by manufacturing in each state in 1909.[59] An estimate of average legislative activity can be constructed from the annual listings of social and labor legislation published by the *American Labor Legislation Review* beginning in 1910.[60] This journal listed all successful social and labor legislation regardless of its content. Thus, the level of legislative activity does not measure the relative strength of organized labor or capital, nor the level of political activity insofar as it failed to produce successful legislation. Instead, it provides a measure of the capacity of state legislatures as arenas for political life and the extent to which issue-oriented politics had become institutionalized.

Not surprisingly, the value added by manufacturing (measured in hundreds of thousands of dollars) is positively and significantly related to the level of social and labor legislation (adjusted $R^2 = .48, p = .0001$).[61] But while the strength of this association might seem to negate the need for further explanatory efforts, adding a variable measuring the openness of the political system improves the model considerably (table 3.1). On this scale, states that by 1913 had adopted all four laws that expanded access or weakened party control (Australian ballot, mandatory direct primary,

Table 3.1   Correlates of Legislative Activity in the States, 1910–1920

Variable	Coefficient	SE	p (two-tail)
Constant	1.748	1.711	0.312
OPEN1913	1.823	0.500	0.001
VALADD09	0.015	0.002	0.000

Note: Adjusted R^2: .589, p = 0.000

initiative and/or referendum, and woman suffrage) received a score of 5; a score of 1 was given to those states that had adopted none of these laws (table 3.2). Value added by manufacturing remains positive and highly significant, but political openness also has a significant positive effect on the level of legislative activity related to social and labor policy.[62] Given a certain level of industrial development, what mattered was not the proportion of the electorate that voted but the institutionalized opportunities for voters—or organized groups of voters—to penetrate the policy process. As advocates of these reforms anticipated, changes in the electoral "rules of the game" altered legislative behavior: "The initiative and referendum also develop legislators by causing them in their deliberations to keep always in mind the interest and viewpoint of the people whose servants they are. This they will do through a realization that, having the power to enact or defeat laws, the people will watch legislative proceedings and hold every legislator accountable for his acts."[63] Later commentators might question both the enforced virtue of legislators and the watchfulness of the people, but the calculus of American politics was changing decisively.

These measures of association among industrialization, political openness, and legislative activity do not constitute a causal explanation of the origins of the new issue-oriented, extrapartisan group politics. But they do suggest where to look for the important causal processes. Furthermore, the regional distribution of increased legislative activity, skewed to the west, had national consequences. The comparative closedness of state polities in the East did not smother reform efforts, but in the absence of space outside the parties the contest over reform took the shape of a factional contest within the parties. As Robert Wiebe argued concerning the Republicans: "The majority which the Republicans acquired during the political revolution of the 1890's remained to curse the party during the progressive era. In 1896 the forces behind McKinley, employing Big Lies mass publicity, so successfully branded the moderate Bryan a woolly-

Table 3.2   Political Openness of the States, 1913

Score[a]	
5	Arizona, California, Colorado, Idaho, Oregon, Washington
4	Kansas, Maine, Missouri, Montana, Nebraska, Nevada, Ohio, Oklahoma, South Dakota, Utah, Wyoming
3	Arkansas, Delaware, Florida, Iowa, Kentucky, Louisiana, Massachusetts, Michigan, Minnesota, New Hampshire, New Jersey, New York, North Dakota, Pennsylvania, Tennessee, Wisconsin
2	Alabama, Connecticut, Illinois, Indiana, Maryland, Mississippi, New Mexico, Rhode Island, Texas, Vermont, Virginia, West Virginia
1	Georgia, North Carolina, South Carolina

Sources: Ida Husted Harper, *The History of Woman Suffrage, 1900–1920,* vol. 6 (New York: J. J. Little and Ives, 1922); Jac. C. Heckelman, "The Effect of the Secret Ballot on Voter Turnout Rates," *Public Choice* 82 (1995): 113, 121; Charles Kettleborough, "Direct Primaries," *Annals of the American Academy of Political and Social Science* 106 (March 1923): 11; Charles Edward Merriam and Louise Overacker, *Primary Elections* (Chicago: University of Chicago Press, 1928), 61–63, 93–94; Austin Ranney, "United States of America," in *Referendums: A Comparative Study of Practice and Theory,* ed. David Butler and Austin Ranney (Washington, D.C.: American Enterprise Institute, 1978), 70; Lisa Reynolds, "Reassessing the Impact of Progressive Era Ballot Reform," Ph.D. diss., University of California at San Diego, 1995.

a. The score indicates how many of the four types of progressive legislation—some form of the Australian ballot, mandatory direct primary, initiative and/or referendum, and woman suffrage—the state had adopted by 1913. States that had adopted all four received a score of 5; states that had adopted none received a score of 1.

headed revolutionary that respectable reformers in the East and Midwest refused even to consider the Democracy a vehicle for national reform." [64] In Congress, a heritage of western progressivism contrasted with the eastern version that dominated the executive branch. Within the federal system, state-level progressivism persisted through the 1920s in the West, preserving political and policy alternatives for the decades that followed.[65] But the consolidation of western progressivism at the national level in the 1920s was grounded in a longer effort to develop an extrapartisan model of political organization, one that would eventually support a bipartisan regional bloc within Congress.

Popular Associations and Policy Diffusion

All politics is local, the saying goes. But to understand the significance of state-level government in American political development, the conditions under which events in one state influence those in another must be appreciated.[66] This acting together can take many forms, not only conscious coordination but also imitation and influence. A few states (or nations in international comparisons) may emerge as policy leaders or innovators; subsequent policy adoption may be driven by diffusion based on either geographical proximity or some sort of hierarchy among different political units.[67]

Diffusion models assume contact among political units, but the extent of such contact is contingent on a variety of historical developments. The establishment of basic channels of transportation and communication is of primary importance; "print languages" and mass publications aid the standardization and diffusion of models or blueprints.[68] In the United States, the construction of trails and roads, canals and railways facilitated the movement of people, carrying with them understandings of political goals and methods.[69] The expansion of the national press in the late nineteenth century also lowered the obstacles to the diffusion of policy debates and proposals. The rapid diffusion of policy innovations could not be expected prior to the last decades of the nineteenth century, since channels for the rapid communication of ideas had not yet been established.

But policies are not like ink blots; they do not spread simply because channels are available. During the decades after the Civil War, however, new vehicles for the diffusion of political problems and solutions developed. New mass organizations spread out along transportation routes, often sponsoring professional organizers who were paid on the basis of how many new members joined or how many new locals were established. Local groups or individuals might also sponsor lecture tours by representatives of national associations; ticket receipts would be split according to some prearranged formula, with the lecturer hoping at least to meet travel costs and, if possible, to bring funds back for the national treasury. These arrangements were frequently the target of critics. After Susan B. Anthony's lecture tour through eastern Washington in 1871, the editor of the *Walla Walla Statesman* complained, "Miss Anthony, in the course of her travels through Oregon and Washington Territory, is reported to have bagged over $5,000. Men, when they go forth on electioneering expeditions usually come out behind; the 'strong-minded' seem to manage these things better."[70] Newspapers and magazines were another channel for the diffusion of organization. The Farmers' Union, centered in the Southeast, arrived in Washington state via a new settler who had kept up his subscription to a southern paper, then wrote for more information, and eventually arranged an invitation to the Union's leader, C. S. Barrett, to come to Washington and begin the organizing work.[71] These networks created by movement organizers were effective channels for the communication of policy goals across state lines.[72]

This expansive mode of social organization helps to explain how new channels of policy diffusion were established but not why groups in one region were willing to subsidize mobilization efforts elsewhere in the country. The answer to that question is found in the economic and political organization of American society, the "opportunity structure" of federalism described above. States were in constant competition with one another, struggling to attract investment, settlers, and manufacturing enterprises. Under these conditions, the costs imposed by a new regulation could cause firms to flee across borders—so, at least, claimed the opponents of such legislation. Consequently, reformers throughout the country could benefit from helping to pass equivalent reforms in competing states. The same logic, of course, applies to their interest in electing sympathetic delegations to Congress or in seeing favorable decisions emanating from the courts of other states.

Due to the opportunities and constraints of American federalism, studies of state-level political development need to attend to the "distinction between community and the social movement: community is a spatial concept, but the social movement goes on quite independently of spatial limitations or relations."[73] The causes and consequences of political action do not necessarily coincide in space, respecting the territorial boundaries of official jurisdictions. So just as the logic of the party system may be understood as a response to the challenge of winning the presidency in a federal system, popular associations developed structures and strategies that allowed them to exploit opportunities for innovation and possibilities of diffusion.

The implications of the organizational logic of associations have not been widely appreciated. Jack Walker did note, "As the American political system has developed, an increasing number of specialized communication systems have been created which cut across traditional regional lines and bring officials from many different regions into contact with each other."[74] But there is an important silence in Walker's remarks, a silence strikingly at odds with the standard model of pressure group politics that has informed endless works of history and policy analysis. While Walker notes that five associations of government officials had been formed by 1900, thirty or so by 1930, and almost one hundred by the late 1960s, these numbers pale in contrast to the ranks of associations at work lobbying state legislatures across the nation. Since the late nineteenth century, labor unions, agrarian and professional associations, women's groups, and many others began to appear regularly at legislative sessions in order to promote specific issues on the political agenda.

In many cases, these groups reproduced the federated structure of national politics in their organizational charts.[75] Local groups formed state associations that then sent delegates to national conventions. State associations frequently reorganized themselves so that their subdivisions mapped onto congressional districts, and urban groups sponsored rural organizing drives in order to gain greater leverage over state legislatures.[76] By promoting the legislative goals of the national association within various states, these organizations were a powerful source of diffusion and coordination in the adoption of social policies and political reforms. Similarly, national associations provided a channel through which innovations in one state could take their place on political agendas elsewhere.

The interplay of political institutions, associational structure, and strategy is evident in the woman suffrage movement, which split into the National Woman Suffrage Association and the American Woman Suffrage Association (NAWSA) in 1869. The former favored an amendment to the federal Constitution; the latter took a states' rights approach to the enfranchisement of women.[77] United as the National American Woman Suffrage Association in 1890, the organization pursued a mixed strategy in which suffragists from one state contributed to campaigns elsewhere in order to set precedents within the federal system. The College Equal Suffrage League of Northern California, for example, reported that one-third of its contributions came from "eastern" as opposed to "local" sources.[78] After winning the vote, California women returned that favor, sending funds and organizers east. Two decades later, a group of veteran feminists from New York City could be found canvasing North Dakota to generate support for a constitutional amendment to outlaw war.[79]

The orientation of the woman suffrage movement to the opportunity structure of federalism was the subject of ongoing strategic concern. The 1893 and 1894 conventions featured extended debates over the organizational and financial implications of different strategies. Organizationally, NAWSA delegates divided on the question of whether the annual convention should always meet in Washington, D.C., or whether in alternate years it should be moved to other cities. This debate elicited two distinct understandings of the political functions of a national association. Long an advocate of a woman suffrage amendment to the Constitution, Susan B. Anthony advocated remaining in the capital:

> The question is, Why do we need a national association since the people in each State must do the work in their own State? There must be an object why we unite in a national body. It is not to educate the people in the school districts of the State. The sole object, it seems to me, of this national organi-

zation is to bring the united influence of all the States combined upon Congress to secure national legislation. The very moment you change the purpose of this great body from national work to district work you have defeated its purpose.[80]

Conventions in the nation's capital, she argued, allowed delegates to testify before congressional committees and to directly petition or lobby their representatives as well as ensured coverage by the national media.

Sharing the conviction that the function of a national organization was to influence Congress, a delegate from Ohio made the case for a "migratory convention":

It seems better to sow the seed of suffrage around through the country by means of our National Conventions. You may give them mass-meetings, and district conventions, and State Conventions, and various other things, but you can never give them anything as good as the National Convention. We must get down to the unit of our civilization, and the unit of civilization is the individual voter or person.[81]

This difference of opinion is critical to the history of political association in the United States. Since the beginning of the republic, groups had sent petitions, lobbied their representatives, and operated as factions within parties. What was novel in the late nineteenth century was the intent *and* organizational technologies to link "lobbying" to significant numbers of voters who would be guided by associational ties rather than partisan loyalty.

At that same convention, others noted the organizational costs of always meeting in Washington, D.C., particularly the absence of delegates from the midwestern and western states: "When we try to organize the Western States they naturally say 'Show the particular advantage to us of working with the National Association.'" Another delegate suggested, "Couldn't the ladies go west as well as a few of us come east and expend so much time and money? I am the only one here from Illinois, except I picked up one lady here and made her a delegate, and I feel that it is a great deal on my shoulders."[82] Under these conditions, the claim of the national organization to represent a nationwide constituency was highly problematic.

This debate resurfaced in 1894 with three significant developments. First, the potential for regional schism was recognized by Carrie Chapman (Catt), future president of NAWSA:

Mrs. *Chapman.* Our conventions meet for two purposes. One is to promote the interests of the organization itself, and the other is to secure legislation. So far as our organization is concerned . . . at least one of those Western states has never sent its per capita tax, partly because it felt it received no benefit from the National and on the other hand it felt it was losing the money at home, and therefore it only paid enough to sustain its auxiliaryship to this association. It is in the interest chiefly of that section that I believe we should have a movable convention. If we should have our convention go further West, as in Cincinnati, we would have a full delegation from those Western states. They will go home with the inspiration that comes from this convention and inaugurate a better work than they have ever done. On the other hand, there has been growing up for a number of years a feeling among those Western workers that if the convention remains in Washington and if the policy of this association remains to be conducted entirely by Eastern people—

The President [Susan B. Anthony]. Never has been.

Mrs. Chapman. There will be a new association formed; that association will not be animated by any feeling against the leaders or against this association—the warmest sympathy and respect will prevail—but it will be organized because they know that the best good for the suffrage cause in their section of the country demands this change.[83]

Carrie Chapman was not alone in charging eastern domination of the association. According to Laura Clay of Kentucky,

We say this is a national body. That is true, but, Madame President, unfortunately our association as it is at present managed is not wholly national. I speak, Madame President, of those on the floor. Let all our forty-four states and territories be represented, and then we will have an influence on the first year of Congress. I wish to speak for the South, for the West. . . . The South has not been represented, the West has not been represented. And why? Because our women know nothing about the National-American. Thousands of people have never heard of the National-American. The way to get them to know us is by taking the convention where they will be compelled to hear us.

Henry Blackwell, formerly of the American Woman Suffrage Association, concurred by noting the precedent set by another women's organization: "The best organizer in this country was a woman, and that woman, Frances Willard [of the Woman's Christian Temperance Union], has adopted the migratory system."[84]

The salience of states outside the Northeast was heightened by a second development, the explicit articulation of alternative strategic responses to the federal system. Henry Blackwell argued that the "party in power," the Democrats, "is a state rights party. The party in power will not listen for a moment to a question involving an amendment to the constitution. The 14th Amendment would never have been granted had

that party been in power. The Solid South to-day is the controlling influence in the administration. Its Representatives, elected by that peculiar
system which I am not here either to justify or condemn, are the longest
headed and shrewdest politicians who sit in that Congress. They can only
be influenced by the Southern constituencies. Therefore, I am in favor of
moving to Atlanta."[85]

Although Blackwell's assessment of the political opportunities confronting the suffrage movement was rendered moot by the onset of two
decades of Republican dominance of national government in 1896, his
recognition of the veto power of state constituencies over national legislation still held. Of more enduring significance was the case made for a
strategy in which state legislation itself was of primary importance. Consistent with the metaphor of the political experiment station, suffragists
argued that victory in one state could improve the prospects for success
elsewhere. There was, however, considerable contention over where an
example could best be set. Lillie Devereaux Blake of New York argued,
"If we carry New York City next fall we will carry the state, and if we
carry the state, Massachusetts and Pennsylvania, Connecticut and New
Jersey will run over each other in their eagerness to pass similar laws. I
am only stating to you facts. I do not think that the effect of a victory in
Kansas will be as great."[86] Laura Johns of Kansas replied that claims for
prominence needed to be modified in light of both the probabilities of
success and the meaning that would be attributed to a particular victory
or defeat:

> Now I hold that success or defeat in Kansas will be far more reaching in its
> effect than success or defeat in New York. In Kansas we have gone a long
> part of the race, we have traveled half way the length of the journey, we are
> half way to the goal; now I ask you, friends, what would be the effect of
> defeat if we failed to make the other half of the journey, the other half of the
> race? Would it not be condemnation? Having the experiment of municipal
> suffrage on trial for seven years in Kansas, if the constitutional amendment
> were now defeated, would not that be condemnation of woman suffrage in
> our state; would not such a defeat as that be far more reaching than any
> other sort of defeat?[87]

Johns returned to this point later in the debate: "You have used Kansas
as an argument, as a leverage; how will you use Kansas in your work, if
Kansas fails now and loses what she has already acquired by hard work
and severe sacrifices?"[88] Besides, another Kansan sniped, "[I]t is about as
much use to try to carry New York for woman suffrage as to try to climb
to the moon."[89] Similar arguments were heard from other sections. Laura

Clay of Kentucky, a member of NAWSA's Southern Committee, argued that "$500 in the South will be worth $5000 in the North in the reflex action of the influence of the South on the North."[90] Echoing Henry Blackwell's sensitivity to party politics, she claimed that "work given in the South is given ten-fold to Kansas and New York, especially to New York. New York is a great Democratic state and let them know that the South is in favor of woman suffrage and it will do more for New York state than anything else."[91]

The intensity of these arguments for regional and state preference reflected a third development in the suffrage movement and in popular associations more generally: increasing reliance on professional organizers and financial contributions, resources easily moved across state lines.[92] The struggle between partisans of Kansas and New York was not solely a matter of pride, but of money. New Yorkers wanted twenty-five thousand dollars for their campaign, had already raised three thousand dollars, and one delegate protested "about the money going out from New York until we get through and I do wish that New Yorkers would hold on to their hearts and purses until after next fall."[93] "From the experience of the former campaigns and from the cost of the great mass of work which we have done," Kansans estimated that they would need more than ten thousand dollars and asked NAWSA for half that "to be paid in installments": "We hope you will cudgel your brains and measure the depths of your pocket books and find the money for the work in Kansas."[94] This business-like language pervaded strategic debates. Arguing for the "migratory convention," Harriet Taylor Upton (the NAWSA treasurer) contended,

> I did not believe in movable conventions until last year, when I determined to vote for the change. When the amendment was brought to vote, I was sitting down by the table below the platform, and as I was about to say yes, I met Aunt Susan's [Susan B. Anthony's] eyes, and such a great lump came in my throat that I never voted at all. To-day that lump is gone, and I shall vote for Cincinnati, because I believe, love or no love, reverence or no reverence, the time has come when we should make a business of organization.[95]

In this shift to movement strategies based on systematic organizational and financial calculations, few suffragists were as skilled as Carrie Chapman Catt. For Catt, the vehicle for "doing business" was the Organization Committee, established in 1895. Born in Wisconsin, Chapman was raised and educated in Iowa, where she began a career as teacher, women's rights activist, and school superintendent before her first husband, a reformist newspaper editor, left for San Francisco when charged with libel by local conservatives. He died of typhoid fever as Chapman was traveling west to meet him, and her subsequent marriage to George Catt, a civil engineer, took her to Seattle and then to New York.[96] This varied exposure to the political opportunities found in different states informed her strategy of combining nationwide mobilization of resources with focused expenditures in individual states. In 1894, she declared,

> I think I never was before placed in quite so embarrassing a position. I am here as a delegate and a representative of the state of New York, but my heart is with Kansas. . . . If all the money that can be raised outside of the state of New York all over this nation can be turned into Kansas, we shall have no more then than they can use and need; and we hope that New York women will grow brave and courageous and go around with their books under their arms, and get all the rich men to donate to this great cause, and let the suffragists of the United States do the work for Kansas.[97]

In the following year, NAWSA allocated $2,570.96 to the Kansas Campaign Committee as well as $68.20 for "Lucy Stone Mite Boxes for Kansas," while only $8.50 went to the New York Campaign Committee. Unfortunately, this contribution did not secure victory in Kansas, a defeat Laura Johns attributed to their mistaken adherence to Colorado's successful strategy of securing major-party endorsements of woman suffrage: "[W]e had been so stimulated by the success in Colorado, where the measure had party endorsement, that endorsement became our shibboleth." The efficacy of exemplars depends on how they are applied to new cases, and when the Kansas Republican League refused an endorsement, "we ought to have taken into consideration the fact that in the Colorado case all the parties had made platform utterance in favor, and when we saw that the strongest party in Kansas would not give us a plank, we ought to have stopped—we ought to have seen that the Colorado plan was not ours to follow further." Ironically, Colorado's earlier request for campaign funds had been denied by NAWSA in favor of the effort in Kansas. Colorado suffragists secured the vote with limited outside resources, including a speaking and organizing tour by the intrepid Carrie Chapman Catt.[98]

Carrie Catt used the Organization Committee to channel national resources into selected campaigns; contributions to the committee were made in addition to regular NAWSA dues and auxiliary fees. In 1897, the Organization Committee received $8,906.57 in pledges from state members (plus another $50 from France), which it used largely for campaigns in Iowa and South Dakota (table 3.3). Although most pledges were only a dollar or two, with more than a few for twenty-five cents, the Organiza-

Table 3.3   National Federations as Fund-Raising Mechanisms

	1897 NAWSA Iowa and South Dakota (%)	1899 NAWSA Oklahoma and Arizona (%)	1906 AFL Political Campaign (%)	1910 AFL McNamara Defense Fund (%)
New England	9.2	28.6	8.0	3.0
Middle Atlantic	21.7	30.6	29.4	11.1
East North Central	16.3	7.1	21.8	62.2
West North Central	44.9	26.4	8.7	5.4
South Atlantic (inc. D.C.)	2.0	2.2	19.9	1.4
East South Central	2.3	1.5	1.5	1.1
West South Central	0.1	0.8	2.3	1.1
Mountain	1.0	0.8	2.3	5.8
Pacific	2.0	2.1	5.0	8.2
Other (Alaska, Canal Zone, Puerto Rico)	0.0	0.0	0.0	0.1
Foreign	0.6	0.0	1.2	0.6
Total Contributions	$8,950.82	$4,471.06	$8,225.94	$236,105.25

Sources: National American Woman Suffrage Association, *Proceedings of the Annual Convention*, 1897, 1899; American Federation of Labor, *Financial Report of the American Federation of Labor, Political Campaign of 1906*, and *Financial Report of the McNamara Defense Fund* (Washington, D.C.: American Federation of Labor, 1912).

tion Committee intensified fund-raising in target states while extracting contributions from states with no hope of a suffrage victory in the near future. By way of comparison, both the California State Grange and the Wisconsin State Federation of Labor reported annual receipts of two to three thousand dollars in the early 1900s. The California State Federation of Labor had receipts of $5,447.02 in 1904 and apportioned $1,014.84 to its organizing account. So by funneling outside contributions into small states, NAWSA could establish a local presence comparable to that of other large associations.[99]

As an opportunity structure, American federalism rewarded interdependence among regions. Just as northern Democrats needed the South and northern Republicans were tied to westward expansion, eastern reformers were offered western possibilities. But if financial resources flowed disproportionately out of the more industrialized states, where party organizations tightly controlled state politics, western states were not passive recipients in a national process of reform. Western states afforded greater opportunities for political innovation, thereby making two critical contributions to nationwide reform movements: experienced organizers and legislative precedents.

Facing few existing lines of division, women's organizations were particularly consistent at exploiting opportunities for regional synergy. Agrarian associations were more likely to succumb to regional divisions along crop lines, while labor's primary organizational template followed divisions of craft and industry rather than political federalism. Among labor and agrarian groups, national contributions more typically consisted of visits by organizers and the movement of national conventions to states where more intensive organization was desired. But, given a sufficiently promising opportunity, similar patterns of cross-regional cooperation appeared. In 1906, for example, the AFL inaugurated the "strike at the ballot box," working (without success in this case) to defeat leaders in the House of Representatives from Maine and Illinois, raising $8,225.94 in contributions throughout the nation (table 3.3). Labor's victories that year, however, were largely the result of local and state-level efforts rather than national strategy.[100] AFL president Samuel Gompers even temporarily overcame his aversion to socialism and visited Los Angeles, urging "unionists to vote for [Job] Harriman; his advocacy caused members of organized labor to believe that the barrier separating the AFL and the Socialist Party would be broken down." Campaigning in the shadow of a trial of the McNamara brothers, two unionists extradited from Indiana and charged with the 1910 bombing of the conservative and ardently open-shop *Los Angeles Times,* Harriman won a plurality of votes in the primary. But in the face of combined antilabor and antisocialist opposition, as well as a confession from the McNamaras, who had benefited from a two-hundred-thousand-dollar defense fund amassed through nationwide contributions, Harriman lost.[101]

In none of these instances were national resources sufficient to guarantee local or state-level success. But neither were political outcomes in a given state solely the product of local resources and organizing efforts. Instead, the linkage of state-level opportunities and imported resources increased the odds of victory; national associations also sought to transform local innovations into national precedents or agenda items. This northern and western axis of popular mobilization skirted the congressional obstacle posed by the southern states. The potential for innovation was concentrated at the peripheries of American politics, where marginalized actors mastered alternative forms and dominant institutions were less firmly established, providing opportunities for experimentation. National associations had the capacity to funnel resources toward those margins and, in time, would help to leverage state-level reforms into national campaigns.

The Peripheries of American Politics

Marginality provides the motives, means, and opportunities for organizations to seek institutional change. Those who are relatively excluded have an incentive to change the rules of the game, which is different from seeking to win within those rules. (Grievances alone, however, do not automatically generate action.) Those who are not fully embedded in a system of action are likely to have mastered an organizational repertoire that includes models for alternative arrangements. Finally, those at the peripheries of the system, where institutions are less consolidated, are more likely to discover opportunities for effective opposition and innovation. So while a contest model predicts that the actor with more power and resources will win in competitions governed by the rules of the game, changes in those rules require a different sort of explanation.

At each step in this argument, however, marginality is defined relative to the existing organization of political action, not in absolute terms. Those who are most oppressed and disadvantaged may well have greater motives for change, but the core truth of the contest model is that resources and numbers do matter. Furthermore, those most unlike established political actors will be less able to mount the oblique challenges that smuggle familiar forms into unfamiliar settings; their social distance from those in power is likely to invite repression and inhibit the consolidation of novel coalitions. Change is more likely to be generated by the marginally marginalized, the most advantaged of the disadvantaged.

The requirement of *relative* marginalization explains the absence of many groups defined by race or ethnicity from this account. Both the political and economic conditions of African-Americans worsened at the end of the nineteenth century with the establishment of Jim Crow and the erosion of political power gained during Reconstruction. Among women, for example, race overrode the moral resources of gender: "At a time when their White peers were riding the wave of moral superiority that sanctioned their activism, Black women were seen as immoral scourges." [102] This heightened marginalization was not limited to blacks in the South. In the West, these decades were marked by periodic political and economic organization against the Chinese and Japanese. In the East, new waves of migrants from southern and eastern Europe raised tensions over Americanization and race suicide, eventually leading to severe restrictions on immigration in the 1920s. For these racial and ethnic minorities, their marginalization was too great to constitute a tactical advantage. Instead, they watched as race was invoked to bolster alliances between organized labor and farmers, to align the concerns of privileged club-ladies and white working men on the Pacific coast.[103]

To the extent that this argument holds, institutional change will be associated with actors who meet three requirements. First, they must be sufficiently excluded that the remedy of their grievances requires a change in the rules of the game rather than a reallocation of resources and outcomes within the existing rules. Second, their organizational repertoire must include forms that are not familiar with respect to politics but are associated with other robust, legitimate social institutions. Finally, challengers will be able to encourage the diffusion of institutional innovation, linking areas of political opportunity to those more fully dominated by existing institutions. Since these requirements are defined relative to a particular political regime and context of social organization, the actors that meet them will change over time. But at the end of the nineteenth century, at least three potentially effective challengers could be identified in the field of American politics: organized labor, farmers, and women.

Three Political Challengers: Labor, Farmers, and Women
Neither organized labor nor agrarian associations were strangers to the party system. Workingmen, whether industrial or agricultural, had the right to vote. Small property-owners, whether artisans or farmers, had interests in questions of taxation and public improvements. But despite these political entitlements, the last decades of the nineteenth century had brought a series of defeats for both groups. Organized labor had been battered by economic depressions, and the dramatic successes of the Knights of Labor had evaporated in the face of the Haymarket Riot of 1886 and the depression of 1893.[104] Farmers had won regulatory victories over the railroads with the "Granger laws" of the 1870s, but these gains withered, while the Grange's efforts to construct marketing organizations collapsed. These failures shadowed subsequent efforts at organizing, particularly the revival of the Grange. As one California Patron complained: "The old Grange had a large membership, nearly every farmer in this vicinity belonged to it. Had there never been a Grange here at all, it would have been much easier to organize and maintain one than it is now."[105] These organizational disappointments would be repeated with

the Populist mobilization of the 1890s and the failed fusion with the Democratic Party in 1896.

But for all these defeats, both organized labor and farmers remained formidable challengers. Both possessed memberships with voting rights and organizational structures that transcended single political units. Both also made potent ideological claims for greater political influence. For organized labor, the tradition of "artisan republicanism" designated skilled workingmen as a repository of political virtue.[106] Sharing this "producerist" political vision, farmers also brought a sense of righteousness linked to the image of the yeoman farmer and the authority of Thomas Jefferson.[107] Finally, both groups demonstrated a capacity for mass mobilization. The AFL grew from forty thousand to 1.5 million members between 1881 and 1903. Recovering from plummeting numbers in the 1890s, the combined membership of general farmers' organizations (the Grange, Alliance, Farmers' Union, and Farm Bureau) increased from a low of approximately 70,000 to almost 500,000 in 1910 and 900,000 by 1920.[108]

Despite their lack of the vote, women's groups also proved to be formidable political challengers. These organizations were in no sense representative of *all* American women; their strength derived from a growing group of middle- and upper-middle-class women with resources of time, education, and money. Over the nineteenth century, the role of the household as a unit of production declined, and new domestic technologies gave women more time for activities outside the home. As norms of female education changed, more women secured secondary and even university degrees, but gender barriers in the labor market made it difficult to apply this learning to economic pursuits. Finally, some women did build careers, while others inherited a share of the growing wealth of an industrializing nation. These socioeconomic changes produced a growing cadre of political actors who founded national associations such as the Woman's Christian Temperance Union (150,000 members by 1900) and the General Federation of Women's Clubs (one million members by 1910).[109] Like workers and farmers, these women also claimed a distinctive political virtue, grounded in the concept of republican motherhood, of women as guardians of citizenship and morality. By drawing analogies between the calls for women's rights and for the abolition of slavery, they further challenged the logics of appropriateness that excluded women from full citizenship rights.[110]

But all three groups were frustrated by the organizational logic of the party system. Organized labor was disadvantaged by districting systems that privileged rural areas and divided by the partisan loyalties of its membership.[111] Farmers found it difficult to translate local political strength into an effective challenge to the national organizations—the railroads and marketers—who controlled their economic well-being. And women lacked the vote. All three had ample motive for pursuing a reorganization of the party system, and all found at least some opportunity at the political peripheries where that system was weakest. But they brought very different organizational repertoires to the task of remedying their grievances.

The comparison among groups, rather than across states, speaks to my first theoretical claim: that the contents of the opposition's organizational repertoire shape both the probability of successful political challenges and the character of the resulting institutional change. The more tightly logics of appropriateness linked a group to the party system, the less likely a sustained political mobilization outside the parties. The more varied the contents of its members' organizational repertoire, the greater the possibilities for a group to mount an oblique challenge to existing political institutions. And, finally, the more robust and legitimate the other institutions to which a challenger can appeal, the more likely that the transplantation of unfamiliar models into the political field will endure. My second claim, that the political opportunity structure allowed local innovation and facilitated the diffusion of reform, is addressed by comparing three important "experiment stations."[112]

Three Paths to Institutional Change: California, Washington, and Wisconsin

To track the changing forms of political organization and the transformation of institutions, these three groups will be followed as they sought, discovered, and attempted to exploit the opportunities available in three states: California, Washington, and Wisconsin. While the West and upper Midwest generally offered opportunity structures more open to political challenges, state-level variations channeled innovation into distinctive political styles. All three states were recognized as politically innovative, but each represents the development of a rather different alternative to the nineteenth-century "state of courts and parties." In Wisconsin, reformers captured the Republican Party and proceeded to construct state agencies with both considerable autonomy and capacity for intervention in the economy. In California, political challengers enjoyed a briefer period of control over the state Republican Party but left a lasting mark in the development of institutions of direct democracy that fundamentally weak-

ened the role of both parties. Finally, Washington's political opposition
failed to make significant inroads in either party and, instead, developed
a coalition style of mobilization that secured important legislative victories but less frequently built the new state capacities that would protect
their achievements. As the following chapters will show, these divergent
outcomes reflected distinctive patterns of oppositional organization by
labor, farmers, and women. These variations across states, rather than
among groups, underscore the significance of political context and opportunity.

While these three cases diverge with respect to political outcomes, in
terms of the standard socioeconomic variables invoked in political analyses, they encompass only a moderate degree of variation. Patterns of employment in the three states resembled the average for the nation as a
whole. All had economies divided between manufacturing and agricultural sectors. In terms of industrialization, none matched the levels of
some of the states in New England or along the Atlantic seaboard. With
respect to the value added by manufactures (1909), Wisconsin ranked
ninth in the nation, California twelfth, and Washington seventeenth.[113]
Judged by the overall composition of its economy, Wisconsin was the
most agricultural of the three but had important heavy manufacturing
centers in the southeastern corner of the state and a large lumber and
wood products industry. Lumbering was also a major component in
Washington's economy, and in all three states mining was an important
industry.

The three states were also roughly comparable with respect to urbanization during this period, although the prominence of agriculture in Wisconsin is reflected in a percentage of urban residents slightly lower than
the U.S. average in 1900.[114] The potential impact of cities on the politics
of the states was more similar than the actual percentages. Each had at
least one major urban center and potentially two. California and Washington experienced strong competition between the dominant city (San
Francisco and Seattle) and an emerging metropolis (Los Angeles and Spokane); in Wisconsin, the conflicts between Milwaukee and Madison were
less those of two cities than of one industrial center and the agricultural
regions that dominated the legislature in Madison.

In terms of ethnic composition, the three present an especially interesting comparison. Wisconsin's social-welfare heritage is frequently explained as the consequence of its large population of German and Scan-
dinavian immigrants. However, Washington's comparatively stronger
legislation was passed in a state that was largely native born (almost half

the males of voting age in 1900 were native-born whites of native parentage). Finally, in both California and Washington, political differences among European immigrant groups were frequently submerged by the shared racial antagonism toward the Chinese and Japanese.

Although these cases are roughly comparable on economic and demographic dimensions, their most important similarities and differences are political. During the Progressive Era, all three states gained reputations as important policy innovators in the field of social welfare. Wisconsin was the first state to implement workmen's compensation; the first state to establish a strong, relatively autonomous Industrial Commission; the first state to pass an income tax; and a leader in recognizing labor's claims on issues ranging from vocational education to occupational safety. California did not lag with respect to policies for the workingman, but women were comparatively privileged in the public policy of the state. California was among the first to pass an eight-hour law for women and a women's minimum-wage law. It led in using the state charities as a source of employment for otherwise dependent women (foreshadowing contemporary Scandinavia). In both of these cases, pioneering legislation was accompanied by expanded legislative and administrative capacity.

Washington presents a rather startling contrast. With respect to individual pieces of legislation, it is one of the forgotten leaders of progressive social reform. The Washington workmen's compensation legislation was among the most favorable to organized labor, and, in 1917, the Supreme Court agreed with Washington and ignored the precedent set by the highest court in New York in finding this type of legislation constitutional.[115] Washington also passed perhaps the strongest women's minimum-wage legislation in the country. Yet in Washington, legislative triumphs were not accompanied by the institutionalization of legislative lobbying as the primary political strategy of organized social groups. As late as 1915, the Washington State Grange passed resolutions in favor of abolishing the state legislature altogether.[116]

Taken together, these three cases provide an opportunity for considering why different groups mobilized effectively and emerged as partners in the progressive reform coalitions of the time. Their common transition to a political system of social-policy expansion allows for the development of a more general model of political transformation. At the same time, the striking variations in the content of these social-policy initiatives help to specify the connections among organizational models, political strategies, and institutional change. Among the most important of the political outcomes of this period in American history was the development of a new system of state agencies tied to new social policies. The comparison of Wisconsin and California with Washington illuminates the conditions under which new forms of political mobilization are translated into the institutionalization of a new organizational field for social politics.

Institutional Change: A Theoretical Reprise

Politics gets in the way of good policy. On this point, nineteenth-century challengers to the party system and contemporary critics of interest group politics would concur. But this agreement obscures a deeper puzzle. If established forms of political organization can block substantive policy outcomes, how can those forms themselves be changed?

The preceding chapters have offered a theoretical framework for addressing this puzzle. The organizational logic of a political regime privileges some groups while marginalizing others. While those who are marginalized lack the resources and formal powers located in political institutions, they may well have mastered other models of organization that can serve as templates for an alternative vision of political life. To the extent that these templates or forms are common to the repertoires of marginalized individuals and groups, the collective-action problems involved in mounting an oppositional challenge are lessened. And to the extent that those forms are linked by logics of appropriateness to other robust and legitimate social institutions, it is more likely that they can be successfully transplanted to the field of politics, thereby altering the existing rules of the game.

Action, however, is constrained by opportunity. The constitutional design of the United States had encouraged the development of national party organizations dependent on cross-regional coalitions, but these parties were weakest in the West, where conflicts over economic development overshadowed the ethnoreligious differences that bolstered party loyalties in the North. Freedom of commerce within national boundaries also facilitated the growth of economic organizations that could escape the regulatory powers of any given state. Consequently, political mobilization around these new economic conflicts—as well as over political institutions and party organization—was most likely where parties were weak, but this mobilization could be supported by outside resources and, subsequently, serve as a precedent for reform elsewhere. The character of American federalism encouraged this association-driven policy diffusion.

The concept of organizational form provides the theoretical discipline necessary for a study that ranges across the regional and social divisions of American historiography. In each of the following chapters, I begin by establishing a group's initial relation to the party system and then trace its efforts to establish alternative forms and channels of political influence. These efforts often revolved around concepts of partisanship; enfranchised unionists and farmers found it difficult to break with a system of "predatory politics" in which the parties engulfed wave after wave of electoral protest. Women, by comparison, were formally disenfranchised, and the feminine domestic sphere was ideologically opposed to the masculine world of politics. Without the vote, they had the greatest incentive to innovate organizationally and the most potential to disrupt the logics of appropriateness that governed political action. But the weakening of the party system and the legitimation of interest group politics were not the outcome of any one of these groups. The roots of institutional transformation lay in the cumulation of change, from local to national arenas, from one group to another.

FOUR

Neither Friends Nor Enemies: Organized Labor and Partisan Politics

> In point of practicability the advice to "strike at the ballot-box" amounts to much the same thing as advice to the man in a storm to seek shelter under the plans of a house.
>
> Walter MacArthur, *Trade Union Epigrams:*
> *Some Reasons for the Faith That Is within Us* (1904)

> Practically every movement for the progress and emancipation of the workers has had its birth in unions. It is true, the progress of modern times has, somehow, invariably taken the form of legislation. But no Legislature, Congress, or Parliament can take sole credit for such progress. The origin of advancement rested at the doors of the workers, through their unions. The people's State and National law-making bodies were but carrying out our ideas, our proposals.
>
> California State Federation of Labor, 1915

Victor Berger, Milwaukee labor leader and the first socialist elected to the U.S. House of Representatives, was not a popular figure at gatherings of the American Federation of Labor. Although Samuel Gompers, the AFL president, had visited Wisconsin repeatedly in the 1890s in support of strikes and the eight-hour-day campaigns,[1] these cordial relations were strained after Social Democrats gained control of Milwaukee's Federated Trades Council and the State Federation of Labor. Nor was conflict with the AFL limited to Wisconsin. In 1914, for example, "Gompers spoke out against general eight-hour laws, infuriating unionists in California, Oregon, and Washington, who had to watch business interests put quotes from Gompers on billboards and on pamphlets distributed during successful efforts to defeat eight-hour laws by popular referenda."[2]

Organized labor was not, and probably has never been, monolithic. State federations of labor, in particular, were sites of resistance to the official AFL policy of promoting economic rather than political organization. This resistance was coupled to alternative models for political action. Berger, for example, frequently attacked the AFL leadership, heaping particular scorn on the nonpartisan "friends and enemies" policy adopted in 1906:

> Your delegate and the progressive element of the [AFL] convention held that the moment a union man votes either the Republican or Democratic ticket he is voting a partisan ticket, only he is voting for partisans of the capitalistic class, which both parties represent, standing for the existing system. In our opinion, if the Federation is to go into politics at all, it should be politics on class lines. A unionist should vote on election day just for the interests of the working class, exactly as he is working for his class in the trades unions, and this would require (since we do not want the trades unions to be used as a political machine) an independent labor party. Gompers' position means that we ought to get promises from the representatives of the old political parties, the congressmen and other officeholders, and to support those on election day who promise most. We declared that before election every capitalistic politician would promise everything, and has promised in the past, but the moment he gets to Washington he is under the control of Joe Cannon on the Republican side, or John Sharp Williams on the Democratic side, both of whom are party whips for the capitalists. The Republican or Democratic congressman could not do anything for labor even if he really tried to. Therefore we told Mr. Gompers that if he only wanted promises he could get all he wanted.[3]

Read as organizational strategy, Berger's diatribe offers a nuanced reading of the opportunities and obstacles faced by the labor movement. A choice of organizational form and strategy made with an eye to workplace conflicts might handicap labor's political efforts. Although only a minority of working people belonged to unions, unionists often presented themselves as representatives of labor. (Approximately one in twenty American workers belonged to a union in 1900, although rates of unionization were considerably higher in parts of the West, where the closed shop prevailed in some industries, and in cities such as Seattle, San Francisco, and Butte, Montana.)[4] However suited to organizing the workplace, trade unions might not facilitate the political mobilization of the working class. Organized labor was endangered by leaders who sought to use unions "as a political machine"; by the absence of any mechanism to bind politicians to their electoral promises; and, finally, by the control exerted by the major parties over elected representatives. Thus the story of American labor, particularly at the state and local levels, includes the search for more effective ways to exploit political opportunities.

In seeking alternatives to partisan regularity, organized labor employed a repertoire of collective action that included economic and fraternal models. But the existence of organizational alternatives proved less significant for organized labor than for groups more marginalized by the political system. Due to the political rights and occasional electoral successes enjoyed by workingmen, a deeply ingrained tradition of "artisan republicanism,"[5] and the restraint exerted by the national AFL leadership, unionists rarely rejected the party system in its entirety. Familiar with politics at the level of the ward and precinct, the model of collective action through the election of major-party candidates was more central to workingmen's repertoires than to those of geographically isolated farmers or formally disenfranchised women.[6] Union leaders often had strong ties to party officials as well. Although discontent fueled discussion of, and experiments with, other models of organization, the costs of abandoning party politics were considerable.

But neither the party system nor the AFL was uniformly entrenched throughout the country. Just as party organization was less developed outside the Northeast and old Midwest, the AFL was dependent on the large unions of the most industrialized states, less able to monitor the activities of its distant affiliates, and, therefore, vulnerable to regional schism.[7] The coincidence of patterns of party organization with the level of AFL control over local unions and state federations produced both greater opportunities for extrapartisan politics and more varied organizational repertoires. The following section traces the efforts that labor "provincials" made to adapt three models of organization drawn from the nineteenth-century repertoire: parties, cooperatives, and craft unions. Each model proved inadequate to the task of harnessing labor organizations to policy outcomes. But in discovering the limits of existing templates, labor organizers began the collective project of elaborating a new model of political action.

Politics and Markets, Community and Nation: Templates for Labor Organizing

Although workers could organize along either economic or political lines, neither option lacked obstacles. On the one hand, they confronted corporations that grew to match national markets, often eluding the restraints of state-level regulation.[8] But without either the fictive personhood of corporations or the liberties of individuals, unions that aspired to this scale of organization were vulnerable to charges of criminal conspiracy. The second path, political action, presented fewer legal restraints but encountered the elaborate machinery of patronage and workers' deeply held partisan identities. Consequently, labor activists and organizers experimented with other political techniques.[9] In convention proceedings, demands for changes in political procedure—the initiative, referendum, recall, direct primary, and Australian ballot[10]—were as prominent as calls for substantive labor legislation. The puzzle, however, was how to secure these changes. The Wisconsin federation was typical in its claim: "While we are opposed to entering any political party as a body, we declare it our duty to use our influence with the law-making power to secure [legislation]."[11] It was equally typical in the lack of detail as to the nature of that influence and the appropriate methods for its deployment.

Workingmen faced two pressing questions: how could workers *collectively* participate in politics, and what were legitimate goals for such participation? Two strategies of political participation had been attempted—cooperation with the major parties and independent third-party efforts. The major parties consistently failed to support labor legislation at the same time that they courted the votes of workingmen. And although labor enjoyed some success in local politics, often under the leadership of the Knights of Labor or a socialist party,[12] these victories rarely produced lasting gains. But politics could not be ignored in favor of pure labor market strategies. So long as employers could call on the police powers of government, labor's ability to act in the "industrial field" was politically circumscribed.

> The employers of labor today realize that we are very powerful and too well organized on the industrial field for them to win a permanent victory; therefore they have changed their tactics and are trying to crush us by legislation and by means of the courts. Having failed in their industrial power, they have changed their tactics to the political power. It is therefore no longer an industrial struggle—it is a political struggle—that is now confronting us as organized workers. It is true, we have an industrial army that knows how to fight on the industrial field, but we have no political army, and we are now in the position of being forced to fight a political battle with no organized force behind us. The politicians at Washington and in Madison laugh at us and ignore us.[13]

Faced with these dilemmas, from the 1890s through the 1920s unionists sought new models of political action. But their searches were heavily influenced by the repertoire of social organization that had brought them to this impasse: political parties, the self-organization of the producing classes, and trade unions.

Political Parties

Deeply committed to partisan identities and attuned to partisan opportunity, most organized workers were reluctant to reject the major parties, even if only as a strategy for holding those parties accountable to the interests of labor. In contrast to workingmen in the rest of the industrializing world, nineteenth-century American men were privileged by their possession of the vote,[14] but they vacillated over the correct form of political action. One answer to the question of how to organize politically has dominated the historiography of the American labor movement: an independent labor party. Workers had been quick to adopt this strategy, establishing a Working Men's Party in Philadelphia in 1828.[15] Labor parties, both socialist and otherwise, continued to appear in local, state, and national contests throughout the remainder of the century. Despite some local successes, these efforts typically failed, and unions reacted by proscribing the third-party model. The collapse of the Greenback-Labor Party in the 1870s led the Knights of Labor to forbid organized electoral activity by their assemblies. Although some Knights did contest elections through loosely linked political clubs, events two decades later seemed to underscore the wisdom of this policy.[16] The defeat of many legislative efforts by the Knights and their affiliation with the failed People's Party in the early 1890s discredited political strategies,[17] leaving unionists uncertain how best to organize. The fusion of the People's Party with the Democrats, and their electoral defeat in 1896, further tainted proposals for independent third-party action. For some workers in a few cities, however, socialist or labor parties brought success and stood as models of union organization.

The lessons of political defeat predominated, however, informing the "voluntarist" ideology promoted by the craft unions that joined to form the Federation of Organized Trades and Labor Unions (later the AFL) in 1881. Based on a guildlike model for controlling the supply of skilled labor, these unions "wished to gain a favorable political context for collective bargaining, not gain political regulation of the labor market." Consequently, "their demands were amenable to *pressure politics exercised through the major parties,* and they resisted the notion of creating a labor party for its own sake, as an expression of working-class solidarity."[18] This antipathy toward independent politics also reflected the web of alliances that had been established between labor leaders and politicians of both parties at local, state, and national levels. These political allies sometimes proved to be traitors to labor. But the motives and opportunities for betrayal varied inversely with the prospects for successful independent mobilization by labor. Faced with strong party organizations in the industrial cities of the North and in national politics, the leadership of the AFL saw little promise in independent politics, deviating from this position only once, in 1924, to endorse the presidential campaign of Wisconsin's Robert La Follette. To protect their ties to *both* parties, national labor leaders repeatedly sought to suppress attempts by workers to mobilize along independent lines.

By the last quarter of the nineteenth century, the organizational consolidation of the party system and the rise of the urban machine had limited the possibilities of either independent politics or effective nonpartisanship.[19] Insofar as union leaders allied with machine politicians, their behavior demonstrated the power of politics to co-opt and corrupt the labor movement. Awareness of this danger informed the practices of labor organizations. Socialists urged their locals "to rotate the chair regularly, 'so that no one gets too much power and becomes the "boss" of the local.'"[20] The first conventions of the California State Federation of Labor (CSFL) divided sharply over a resolution, "No person shall hold office in this Federation who occupies any political position, whether elective or appointive."[21] Despite the possible benefits of an alliance with party politicians, many unionists condemned "the influence of union men who are political pap suckers, and who attend the state conventions as delegates, but who have little or no interest in bettering the conditions of the men and women of labor. These pretended friends and protectors of labor will, if it becomes necessary to maintain their political job, prove ultimately to be the Judas Iscariot of the organized workers."[22]

The major parties were poor friends of labor because they operated to maintain both themselves and the business interests that financed many of their operations, rather than to address social and economic grievances.[23] This symbiosis produced a crisis of representation within the polity not limited to organized labor. In 1902, the CSFL endorsed the claim, "Whereas, In theory we have a representative government, but in practice, owing to the method of electing our representatives the will of the people is constantly thwarted by the representatives of corporate interests and special privilege."[24] This sentiment was echoed in Wisconsin: "Organized capital has not only secured control of the industries and industrial resources of the country, but also of the law-making, law-interpreting and law-enforcing machinery."[25] So if the labor movement was vulnerable to corruption by political machines, and if parties failed to represent "the will of the people" in any case, what was labor to do?

Working through the existing parties, labor was ignored. Organizing as a third party, labor usually lost. Many activists, nevertheless, continued to hold up socialism or, with increasing frequency, the British Trade Union Congress and Labour Party as appropriate exemplars for workers' organization. However, for labor activists who had rejected the independent-party model but were dissatisfied with local alliances to party politicians, there were two basic options: to transform the political system or to quit the field. While much of this chapter addresses the reorganization of labor's political activities at the turn of the century, it is also important to uncover why quitting politics in favor of either cooperative organization or strict workplace unionism was not a viable option.

The Self-Organization of Producers and Consumers

One alternative was to withdraw from both politics and markets. Although this ideal was probably not realizable, the model of self-contained, self-governing economic communities did inform the organizational debates of the nineteenth century. In the face of hard times, workers repeatedly organized themselves into cooperatives and even utopian communities.[26] Although most eventually failed, these efforts provided a lasting alternative model of economic organization and a basis for alliances with other groups.[27]

Of greater importance for the organizational strategies of unionists were efforts to establish worker-owned production companies. Like utopian communities, these companies had a long history rooted in labor disputes and in traditions of self-help. But in the context of strikes, the seemingly benign doctrine of self-organization became a threat. In its struggle for the eight-hour day in all planing mills, the San Francisco Building Trades Council went into business itself in 1900 by establishing "Progressive Planing Mill, Number One." With one hundred workers and one hundred thousand dollars in capital stock, as well as the agreement of union builders to use only union-made wooden fixtures, the Progressive Mill was a force to be reckoned with, and other owners soon gave in to the union's demands.[28] Cooperative enterprises flourished in Seattle, peaking in the years of the first world war, and the Los Angeles movement established cooperatives in their efforts to combat the employers' open-shop drive of the 1920s.[29] Recognizing the threat posed by the self-organization of workers, employers fiercely fought these efforts. In Seattle, for example, the laundry workers' union tried to set up its own laundry since it "had never succeeded in securing more than a very small percentage of the laundry workers of the city as members. To join the Laundry Workers' Union meant discharge." The owners' association responded first by blocking the construction of the building, and then by persuading suppliers to refuse the necessary equipment to the union.[30] Because labor's self-organization deprived other suppliers of potential markets, capitalists used legislation, judicial decisions, and economic collusion to limit workers' ability to exit. The difficulties of self-organization also pointed to the need to confront the power of corporate capital directly, whether in labor markets or legislatures.

A related strategy mobilized workers as consumers rather than producers. The union label worked to harness workers' buying power to union bargaining strength, a technique limited, however, by concerns for propriety. In 1904, the CSFL deemed it impossible to enforce a resolution that "in the future no delegate will be allowed a seat in the convention of the CSFL unless all wearing apparel on his person bears the Union Label."[31] It was also hoped that the union labor would broaden the political constituency of the union movement.[32] But whereas the self-organization of producers was compatible with the craft structure of the AFL, consumer organization—like third-party efforts—invoked identities that undermined established divisions of craft and skill. As Dana Frank has argued compellingly in her study of Seattle, effective mobilization at the "point of consumption" required both cross-craft class solidarity (cooperative organizers spoke of "one big union of consumers") and the support of workingmen's wives, who controlled much of the purchasing power produced by union wages. Consumer cooperatives might also generate solidarity beyond the ranks of the working class. In 1905, a resolution presented to the CSFL argued that the Rochdale system of cooperation could help "to solidify the trade union movement, and in time render it impervious to all assaults of capital as exemplified in the so-called Citizens' Alliance and of bringing to their [the movement's] aid all wage earners, whether susceptible of organization or not, and also to bring the producer and consumer into more permanent, harmonious relations."[33] A decade later, the Seattle Cooperative Food Products Association worked with Grange chapters and the King County Dairymen's Association to market milk "made by organized cows."[34] Short of the institution building represented by cooperatives, boycotts and campaigns to promote the union card, button, or label also depended on the community rather than a particular craft. But, excluded from any role in shaping those goals, the women, whose cooperation was required for success, might choose to direct their energies elsewhere.[35] Just as the ability of capitalists to withhold materials from producers' cooperatives limited the opportunities in one direction, consumption-based strategies were undercut by disjunctures between the repertoires and goals of working-class women and those sanctioned by the AFL. Yet where they succeeded, consumer cooperatives nurtured patterns of solidarity that could sustain political mobilization along lines other than those of either the major party or the AFL. For the most part, however, the union local remained the basic unit of labor organization, so activists worked with the material available in their efforts to generate political influence.

Trade Unions: Local Consolidation and Politicization

Following the ascendance of the AFL in the 1890s and 1900s, the official goal of trade unions moved decisively away from politics toward the control of labor markets and working conditions. Unlike political parties, these unions reflected "the structure of labor markets, because it is the labor market that defines the potential membership of a union and provides it with the most direct channel to improve its members' welfare and job control." [36] But American workers could not escape politics, since relations within labor markets were shot through with politics and law—forms of contract and property, freedom of expression in the use of picketing or boycotts, the assignment of negligence and the content of implied contracts. Increasing repression of union activities, both by Pinkerton detectives and state militias, rendered pure labor market strategies less and less plausible. [37] So even in the best of times, trade unions could rarely afford to ignore the political process. And the late nineteenth century was not the best of times.

This period saw two interrelated developments that increased the political stakes for organized labor. The first flowed directly from the increasing scale and scope of industry. As manufacturing concerns grew to involve multiple plants and diverse products, even a well-organized strike at a single shop became less effective. As the turn of the century approached, labor mounted a series of dramatic, large-scale strikes in an effort to match the growing scale of industry. Employers responded by forming mutual-support associations, protecting one another from the adverse effects of industrial disputes both with direct contributions and by assuming one another's production contracts. Frequently, employers patterned their organization after that of labor. In reaction to the "Great Southwest Strike" against the railroads in 1886, "a secret, extralegal society appeared in the form of the Law and Order League. Mimicking the Knights with its secret passwords, grips, and recognition signs, the league promised to protect railroad property and 'replacement employees.'" The imitation *of* workers *by* employers was one reason offered in early decisions against journeymen's associations. In *Commonwealth v. Hunt* (1840), the judge argued, "Associations of journeymen . . . would beget associations of masters, and together these 'new, secret, and unknown tribunals' would subject citizens 'to varying laws by which their property will be taken from them against their consent and without trial by jury.'"[38] As the mutually reinforcing cycle of organizational growth progressed, labor still won on occasion. But as the organizational resources required for a successful strike increased and the perceived likelihood of a lasting success diminished, there was a clear incentive to seek out alternative models of collective action.

One response by workers was to adopt forms of organization that corresponded more closely to labor markets. This alternative, however, was repeatedly blocked by the entrenched leadership of the craft-oriented unions within the AFL. Even after pure craft principles were displaced by craft-industrial organization in the second decade of the century, the national and international unions remained opposed to the development of united fronts among trades at the local level.[39] With the exception of the building-trades councils, the AFL curbed the power of city centrals both by pressuring locals not to join unaffiliated central bodies and requiring affiliated central federations to deny membership to nonaffiliated locals and to respect the jurisdiction of the international unions.[40] While a few city centrals did manage to coordinate contracts and strikes, the AFL's demand for conformity to the lines of the international unions obstructed the development of effective strategies within communities.[41] Reflecting on the prospects for "amalgamation" or "one big union" in the 1920s, the General Executive Board of the WiSFL observed, "Whenever a change in form has been attempted, opposition has not come in the first instance from the officers of the American Federation of Labor, but from such international unions whose recognized jurisdiction was to be invaded."[42] To return to the theoretical arguments introduced in chapter 2, the organizational models embraced by the international craft unions produced isomorphism with the national industries, but at the cost of a lack of fit with both local economies and political institutions.

Distance, however, lessened the ability of the national and international unions to block local interunion cooperation. Western cities frequently produced coordinated, often political, action in violation of national policy. Milwaukee, for decades, was the jewel of municipal socialism, with officeholders loosely linked to the city's powerful Federated Trades Council. In San Francisco, the building trades were a power in local politics. In open-shop Los Angeles, the central labor council repeat-

edly endorsed successful candidates for city council and other local offices in the 1910s and even celebrated a few victories in the 1920s.[43] In
Washington state, both the Spokane Trades Council and the Seattle Central Labor Council opposed the AFL craft policy. In Seattle, the council
developed a form of organization midway between "simple" craft unions
and politicized industrial unions. Named after a prominent local labor
leader, "Duncanism" entailed the "close cooperation of allied trades in
an industry through the trade councils, cooperation of trade councils, and
their informal allegiance to the Central Labor Council," including efforts
to secure unit bargaining and simultaneous expiration of contracts. These
arrangements concentrated power over local unions in the Central Labor
Council at the expense of the international unions. "Until 1920, Duncanism operated informally in order to avoid giving the AFL Executive Central grounds for punitive action against the Seattle Central." Similar efforts to strengthen the city central were made in Los Angeles, and, as
early as 1907, the CSFL adopted a resolution recommending "to its affiliated unions that where such unions are closely allied, that when they
enter into contracts with employers, such contracts be uniform in regard
to time of expiration."[44]

The consolidation and politicization of city centrals and building-
trades councils exemplifies the process of using familiar organizational
forms for new purposes. Although AFL doctrine endorsed logics of appropriateness that isolated economic from political action and privileged
craft over class identities, local labor movements faced opportunities that
could be exploited only by building solidarity across the jurisdictional
lines of the international craft unions. City federations and building-
trades councils sponsored parades, social events, and the construction of
"Labor Temples" that would foster ties among groups of skilled workers.[45] Rather than creating a new independent-party organization, these
efforts to consolidate local labor movements generated solidarities and
identities that could support pressure group strategies within electoral,
legislative, or administrative settings—as well as within the AFL itself.

But even when successful, local political and economic coordination
was undermined by a secondary effect of the growing wealth of the modern corporation. To the extent that corporations controlled elected politicians, they also controlled legislatures and the police powers of government. The police, the militia, and the courts might all be used against
organized labor during a strike. To preempt these tactics, workers needed
to influence more than labor markets. In almost every state, the labor

movement had evidence confirming the importance of politics; the Knights of Labor argued "that the state had become an appendage of the money power" and worked toward "recapturing government for the people."[46] In Milwaukee, the eight-hour movement had ended in May 1886 with the state militia firing on demonstrators, five deaths, and charges against Robert Schilling, the local leader of the Knights of Labor. By that November, Schilling had organized a successful People's Party, and this "political clout of the Knights was recognized instantly when the newly elected district attorney dropped boycott-related charges against Schilling and the Knights' district officers."[47] In Washington territory, coal companies responded to miners' strikes in 1888 and 1889 by having private guards deputized by the U.S. marshall. This provoked protests from the territorial governor, who rode out to the mining camps himself to arbitrate the disputes,[48] and by 1892 the state platforms of the Populist, Republican, and Democratic parties all included planks either prohibiting or criticizing Pinkertons and other private guards.[49] The same logic drove the politicization of labor further south. In 1901, San Francisco was overwhelmed by one of many strikes on the waterfront. Although eventually settled by a secret pact arranged by the governor, this strike taught an important political lesson. Organized labor attributed its less-than-total success "to the fact that the influence of the city authorities had been used on the side of capital. The coming election furnished another opportunity to show the strength of the labor movement and, at the same time, to weaken the employers by obtaining control of this powerful ally."[50] In that election, candidates of the newly formed Union Labor Party captured the mayor's office and three positions as city supervisors. If the organization of workers prompted association among employers, the growing political power of large corporations drove organized labor to take another look at the possibilities of political action, premised on the consolidation of local labor movements.[51]

Regardless of how insistently the AFL leadership might call for strict business unionism and craft autonomy, the ability of employers to enlist public agencies and the opportunities for electoral participation repeatedly drew local labor movements toward organizational forms that supported greater politicization and consolidation than a pure trades union or even an activist city central. Industry, the militia, the courts—all were organized at state and national levels, so to exert a countervailing influence, workers required forms of collective action that transcended divisions of locality, craft, and even partisan loyalty.

Beyond the Limits of Labor's Repertoire

Were we to recast our average turn-of-the-century voter in the image of
an American workingman, he would appear doubly constrained: first, by
a system of party organization that often suppressed economic conflicts;
second, by a system of occupational organization hostile to alliances that
mapped onto territorially defined constituencies. Organizational innovation was a response to the constraints and opportunities defined by the
intersection of these two systems. Where union membership was concentrated—either territorially or in terms of partisan affiliations—political
access via the parties was facilitated. The conjuncture of concentrated
union membership and electoral districts minimized the need for innovation but potentially conflicted with the national federation's strictures
against partisanship. But where political action required coordination
across locales or party lines, organizational innovation threatened the
principles of craft organization that dominated the AFL. Consequently,
organized labor was faced with the challenge of developing a strategy
of political participation that would alienate neither its often partisan
membership nor the national AFL leadership but would result in the effective coordination of their political actions.

The most important responses to this dilemma were developed neither
in the workplace nor through the national AFL, but in labor organizations formed explicitly for political action: the state federations of labor.[52]
Although state federations had existed since the New York Trades Assembly was established in 1865, the rate of founding accelerated through
the 1890s and 1900s.[53] The rationale for founding a state federation was
usually political. The CSFL proclaimed:

> We declare our purposes to be to devise means for the complete organiza-
> tion of labor in California; to establish better communication between the
> labor unions of the State; to secure united and harmonious action in all
> matters affecting our welfare; to circulate labor literature and promote eco-
> nomic intelligence; to create a public sentiment more favorable to trade
> unions; to prevent unfavorable legislation and make known the enemies of
> organized labor; to collect statistics concerning California labor for the bet-
> ter information of our law-makers; to see to the enforcement of all laws
> calculated to benefit the laboring people.[54]

Although little of this seems revolutionary by contemporary standards,
these resolutions marked an important change in the strategies of social
politics pursued by organized labor.[55] If one compares the resolutions

passed by labor conventions in the late 1880s and the 1910s, many of the substantive policy demands are identical: the eight- (or nine- or ten-) hour day, municipal ownership, curbs on the powers of courts and legislatures to limit union activities. Far more profound differences, both over time and across various sections of organized labor, existed with respect to the methods for securing these ends. In terms of individual strategies, few were absolutely new. But the cumulative reorientation of labor's organizational patterns marked a decisive change.[56]

At both the state and national levels, organized labor faced two questions. Should unions enter politics? If so, how were they to bind elected officials to the demands of their constituencies for specific legislation? The first question was answered, for labor, in the affirmative. Faced with mounting attacks from legislatures and the courts, even Gompers' American Federation of Labor adopted a political strategy of "friends and enemies" in 1906, endorsing and opposing candidates of both parties on the basis of their support for organized labor.[57] But the national organization trailed its affiliates at the state level; the 1906 resolution was based on a plan offered by the state federations of labor of Washington and Missouri. As early as 1902, the language of "friends and enemies" was adopted in the constitution of the CSFL: "Party politics shall positively not be allowed to be discussed in the conventions of this body. This, however, shall not be so construed as to deprive this organization of the right to put its stamp of approval or disapproval upon the friends or enemies of labor, irrespective of party, or measures calculated to affect the welfare of the laboring people."[58]

Yet, as the AFL would soon discover, the simple endorsement of friends and condemnation of enemies meant little in the American political system. If endorsements were to shape legislative outcomes, elected officials would have to be persuaded that their vote on a labor bill could be tied to significant numbers of votes on election day. Entrenched habits of partisan loyalty would have to be undermined and new issue-based guides to electoral behavior put in their place. But the extent of change required depended on the degree of leverage that labor could secure within different states. Where organized workers were geographically concentrated and committed to third-party models, labor could secure some influence by controlling an electoral bloc in the state legislature. In the absence of these conditions, however, political influence required either an effective nonpartisan labor lobby or a resort to the extrapartisan mechanisms of direct democracy.

Electoral Blocs: Loose Linkages
Although labor parties appeared in all three states during the late nineteenth and early twentieth centuries, only in Wisconsin did organized labor establish a reliable and enduring alliance with a third party, the Social
Democrats. The influence of socialism was the most distinctive feature of
Wisconsin's labor movement, but its political orientation reflected a
longer history of electoral activity by the state's workers. Whereas much
of organized labor in the United States oscillated between economic and
political action, Wisconsin's unionists enjoyed repeated political success.
From the mid-1880s, the unions were frequently involved with political
parties, rejecting the arms-length friends-and-enemies approach advocated by Samuel Gompers and the AFL. In Milwaukee, electoral success
came first with the eight-hour movement of the 1880s. The 1890s brought
an alliance among the Federated Trades Council (FTC), Populists, and
socialists.[59] But these ties shattered when the Populists joined with the
Democratic Party in 1896. By 1899, the prospects for coalition with a
major party dimmed as socialists gained control of the FTC. Yet this victory was never made complete. Rather than displacing a trade union
model with a party model, the Milwaukee socialists established a loose
linkage between the two, an arrangement that allowed individuals to use
whichever organizational vehicle would be most useful in a given setting
or for a particular purpose. As the official union paper, *Vorwarts,* declared:

> It is the duty of the Socialists in the Federated Trades Council to use their
> success with wise moderation, and not to forget for a single moment that,
> although a trade-union is a proletarian class organization . . . yet a trade-
> union must never be dragged into purely political struggle. Democrats, Re-
> publicans, Populists and Prohibitionists must all alike belong to the trade-
> union, else the latter fails to fulfill its purpose. However, the seventy trade
> unions affiliated with the Federated Trades Council offer us a broad field
> for our socialistic agitation of the Social-Democratic type of socialism.[60]

The Milwaukee Social Democratic Party pursued a gradual, reformist socialism, with the aim of recruiting from the labor movement. The platform for the Social Democrats' debut as an independent political party in
1890 (prior to the establishment of the national Social Democratic Party,
and Branch One in Milwaukee, in 1897) included planks addressing
public-utility franchises, corporate taxation, public employment for the
unemployed, municipal provision of legal and medical help for the poor,
public baths, slum clearance and park development, free schoolbooks,
public symphony concerts, and half-holidays on election days.[61] While the

insurgent rhetoric of much of the nation condemned parties absolutely, the Social Democrats directed their attack against capitalism and, based on their knowledge of European socialism, viewed parties as useful instruments.[62] Rather than advocating nonpartisanship, the Social Democrats set out to build a party of their own and to protect it from co-optation by either of the major parties.

The geographical distribution of unionization and socialist sentiments shaped the WiSFL's political strategy. As a statewide movement (fig. 4.1; note the Masonic insignia in the background), the WiSFL could not formally ally with the Social Democrats without alienating unionists elsewhere in the state who were loyal to the major parties. Printers in Racine complained, "It is not right to say that trades unions shall go into politics. When you do that you cut the throat of the organization. It is hard enough to convince the laboring man that it is to his own advancement and interest to join the union of his craft, and it would be almost impossible to persuade him that it is necessary for him to change his politics."[63] In 1898, a resolution pledging the WiSFL's support to the Social Democratic Party of America was defeated; the convention resolved "[t]hat party politics whether they be Democratic, Republican, Socialistic, Populistic, Prohibition, or any other, shall have no place in the conventions of the Wisconsin State Federation of Labor."[64] The adoption of this resolution did not end the controversy. In 1900, delegates from the Milwaukee FTC successfully introduced resolutions endorsing working-class support for the socialist party and "international socialism." This provoked a schism, when almost one thousand non-Milwaukee unionists left the state federation, and the WiSFL soon retreated from its identification with the Socialists.

At the same time that the Milwaukee FTC and the WiSFL were searching for an effective—if necessarily loose—linkage of their labor organization to politics, the Milwaukee Social Democrats distanced themselves from reformers in other parties. The misdeeds of public-utility corporations had inspired cross-class reform federations in many Wisconsin cities during the 1890s, but the socialists declined "the honor of being associated with 'these half-baked reformers.'"[65] By keeping their distance, the Social Democrats benefited from revelations of corrupt ties between corporations and major-party politicians. In the spring elections of 1904, Victor Berger received over 25 percent of the votes cast for mayor, and in subsequent city and county elections Social Democratic totals increased steadily. The party's refusal to join a nonpartisan reform league in 1906 left the socialists as the only viable reform option.[66] Just before the munic-

Figure 4.1   Delegates to the 18th Annual Convention of the Wisconsin State
Federation of Labor, 1910. (Source: WiSFL, *Proceedings,* 1910)

ipal election of 1910, the normally Republican *Milwaukee Journal* declared that the Republican, Democratic, and Social Democratic candidates for the mayor's office were all capable and well qualified.[67] Emil
Seidel was elected, marking the beginning of three decades of almost un-
interrupted socialist control of the city government. The combination of
geographical concentration and the centrality of third-party politics in
the repertoire of Milwaukee's labor leaders produced an unusually strong
organizational base for labor politics, insulating organized labor from
predatory co-optation by either the Republicans or Democrats.

This tale of municipal success was not mirrored at the state level. While
the Social Democrats attracted both working-class and reform-oriented
middle-class voters in the city, in state elections these votes often went to
Robert La Follette and the progressive faction of the Wisconsin Republican Party.[68] The WiSFL's commitment to the Social Democratic Party was
contained in a thinly disguised conclusion to the federation platform:

"[A]ll members of this parliament of labor recommend, and ask all affiliated bodies to actively support, with their ballots and otherwise, the political party whose platform is nearest the foregoing declaration of principles." In 1909, there was a resolution to introduce more explicitly socialist language, urging the working class "to actively support, with their ballot and otherwise, the political party engaged in its class struggles," but this motion failed.[69] A large portion of organized labor retained its traditional partisan loyalties, limiting the electoral potential of a socialist party.

The mismatch between the independent-party form and legislative opportunities available to a minority party had devastated populists elsewhere in the 1890s (see chap. 5). The Wisconsin Social Democrats avoided this pitfall through the cultivation of new political techniques. They made up for their relatively weak ties to those workingmen who continued to vote as Republicans and Democrats by fashioning strong controls over elected representatives. The party screened candidates for office, enforced party discipline on votes, and submitted nominees for approval by referendum of the party membership. In return, candidates received campaign funds and, if elected, were provided with a salary supplement (in the form of lecture fees) from the WiSFL.[70]

As this financial arrangement suggests, the socialist legislators served as much as the agents of the state's organized labor movement as the elected representatives of the state's voters. By heightening the dependence of legislators on the party (whose leadership overlapped greatly with the leadership of the WiSFL), the Social Democrats forged an alternative to the AFL's friends-and-enemies strategy. The leadership of the WiSFL also rejected the AFL's "nonpartisan" strategies of questioning and pledging candidates from the major parties as "the same old rot in politics": "the flim-flam cry for the so-called good man policy, which is solely intended to divert the attention of the wage-workers from the fact that they have class interests which can only receive proper care by an organized effort on their own part."[71] The "questioning and pledging of political candidates, irrespective of their political policy, will but prolong the life of the capitalist political vampires, whose sole object is to live and prosper on the life-blood of the working class."[72]

In an era when parties avoided policy commitments on many major issues and the institutional capacities for administrative policy-formation were not yet established, legislative victory was the necessary path to addressing social problems. From its establishment in 1893, the WiSFL had regularly sent delegates to Madison. In 1895, the federation advocated child labor laws, sanitary inspection of factories, modification of employers' liability, repeal of the antiboycott law of 1887, a law against "Pinkertonism," and collective ownership of the means of production.[73] With the exception of the last of these points, these demands did not stray far from the mainstream of American labor politics, nor was the WiSFL unusually successful in achieving its goals during the 1890s.

Because the WiSFL remained committed to a third-party strategy, it failed to develop procedures for monitoring and binding nonsocialist representatives to their campaign pledges: "If the workingmen desire the enactment of protective laws they will have to demand them as the representatives of the working class, from the floor of the legislative bodies, and not whine for them in the committee and ante-rooms."[74] The "old-line, antiquated lobbying system" that many state federations borrowed from their corporate enemies was dismissed as evidence of the primitive state of the labor movement in much of the nation.[75] The year 1913 saw an extensive debate over the creation of legislative committees by city centrals or the establishment of a correspondence bureau by the state federation; a formal legislative lobby was not established until 1915; and labor's first "legislative conference" was not held until 1919. In 1915, the WiSFL defeated a resolution to appoint a paid legislative agent, leaving this work to union leaders and elected Social Democrats. The text of the 1915 resolution illustrates how available models of political organization helped to shape debates over strategy:

> Whereas, The corporations of this state have been particularly active in the past few sessions of our State Legislature in enacting legislation beneficial to their interests and in opposing all legislation proposed by labor, and
> Whereas, The Federation of Labor in our sister and other states is represented by a legislative counsel to further our interests, and
> Whereas, The expense of maintaining a representative at the sessions of our State Legislature would be trivial in comparison to what could be accomplished; therefore be it
> Resolved, That this Convention go on record as favoring such representation at our Legislative sessions and take such steps as are necessary to carry out the provisions of this resolution.

The Committee on Resolutions recommended nonconcurrence in this resolution, and the convention agreed.[76] The WiSFL, however, did publicize legislation itself through an elaborate system of legislative committees within each central body.[77]

But despite these differences, the practices of WiSFL came to resemble those of the more progressive state federations within the AFL. This puzzling outcome was produced by the conjuncture of labor's organizational repertoire and the opportunities afforded by Wisconsin politics. The minority position of the Social Democrats left the WiSFL in a political quandary—all the more so since these state legislators and union officials might be the same people. Prevented by its leadership and official loyalties from making a friends-and-enemies alliance with the dominant Republicans,[78] the federation developed direct relations with both the legislative and administrative branches of state government. Lobbying became more important as the electoral fortunes of the socialists declined after the First World War: "The most important force, both in securing support for labor legislation, and in remaking the gestures of the Socialists into politically acceptable legislation, has been the lobbying of interested groups. . . . The increasing effectiveness of the Federation as a lobbying organization has made organized labor less dependent on their Socialist representatives."[79] Although loyal Social Democrats, the leaders of the WiSFL became increasingly nonpartisan despite their best intentions.

Swing Constituencies and Labor Lobbies

After decades of maneuvering within the political system, the WiSFL arrived at a strategy that had been cultivated much more consistently in
states that lacked a viable third party or solid electoral bloc aligned with
organized labor. Different opportunities elicited different choices among
forms of political mobilization. Limited opportunities reshaped familiar
organizational models. In California, as in Wisconsin, political involvement by organized labor was the norm rather than the exception. But
despite victories at both the local and state level, third-party politics was
never institutionalized to the same degree as the Milwaukee Social
Democrats in Milwaukee; California socialists—more Anglo-American
than German-American—drew more heavily on the deep strain of antipartisanship in nineteenth-century American reform movements. Consequently, labor's forays into independent politics were driven by opportunities rather than a normative commitment to the independent-party model.
In the 1870s, the California branch of the National Labor Union and its
successor, the Workingmen's Party of California, were rallying points for
workers dissatisfied with Chinese immigration, economic conditions, and
the corruption of party politics. As the first platform of the Workingmen's
Party declared in 1877:

> Whereas, The contending political parties of the country having through
> lack of principle or of statesmanship, failed to meet the growing wants of
> this rapidly growing country; . . . then be it
> Resolved, That the workingmen sever all affiliation with existing politi-
> cal parties and do hereby organize for the purpose of good and equitable
> government a new party.

The platform called for "the people to own the offices not the incumbents" and for "[h]olding State and municipal officers to strict accountability for their official acts."[80] The Workingmen's Party elected 51 of 152
delegates to the state Constitutional Convention in 1878, with an additional 78 nonpartisan delegates (including many from the Grange). The
constitution included a law against lobbying, a prohibition of local or
special legislation (which was intended to block corporate interests but
ultimately obstructed protective legislation for labor), and the first constitutional provision for a state railroad commission. The lobbying law declared, "Any member of the Legislature who shall be influenced, in his
vote or action upon any matter pending before the legislature, by any
reward, or promise of future reward, shall be deemed guilty of a felony,
and upon conviction thereof, in addition to such punishment as may be

provided by law, shall be disenfranchised and forever disqualified from holding any office or public trust." This law was not, however, notably effective.[81] Rather than focusing on policies that would benefit organized workers directly, the Workingmen's Party joined a broader effort to implement a model of government that would be insulated from corporations and more capable of regulating the economy.

Despite this support of procedural reform, labor politics in California soon produced the sort of self-serving union bosses against whom the leadership of the Wisconsin movement repeatedly warned: "[W]e do not want the trades unions to be used as a political machine."[82] The Workingmen's Party elected one mayor of San Francisco, who was later impeached for "malfeasance in office."[83] With the victory of the Union Labor Party in the San Francisco municipal elections of 1901, and the ensuing trial of the administration for graft and corruption, state labor leaders had still more evidence of the dangers of mixing unions and partisan politics.[84] In the absence of the rigorous internal checks and constraints devised by the Milwaukee socialists, taking unions into politics undermined both labor policy and workplace organization. To avoid this pitfall, labor activists needed to devise or discover a form of organization that would resist partisan co-optation while effectively harnessing the potential influence of the state's workingmen.

The organization of a state federation provided an alternative channel for political action. The establishment of the California State Federation of Labor in 1901 was tardy, trailing the WiSFL by eight years and the Washington State Labor Congress by three.[85] Within the CSFL, there was considerable support for procedural political reform.[86] But the relation of the new federation to the political parties was a source of serious controversy. From 1904 to 1906, the federation was sharply divided, as a resolution that no elected or appointed public official could serve as an officer pitted the San Francisco Union Labor Party against its critics. The 1904 convention defeated a constitutional amendment that would forbid CSFL officers from holding any elected or appointed "political position." The amendment lost in 1904, debate was closed in 1905, but in 1906 a similar motion was introduced with endorsements from the powerful Sailors' Union of the Pacific Coast, the city centrals of San Francisco, San Diego, and San Pedro (the port of Los Angeles), and thirty-four locals from across the state. After an impressive amount of parliamentary maneuvering, a proposal to submit the motion to a referendum of the membership fell short of the necessary two-thirds majority by 18½ votes out of a total of 23,661.[87] Clearly, a sizable faction within the federation sought to insulate their organization from the party system. Although these efforts were narrowly defeated, the CSFL, like the leadership of the WiSFL, continued the search for an acceptable and effective model of political action.

Commenting on the poor treatment of labor lobbyists in Washington, D.C., the executive council remarked that the "reprimand administered by these government officials has at least raised the curtain of 'no politics in unions,' and brought to the foreground subjects whose consideration urges working men to cease being the slaves of either the Democratic or Republican party and vote with an eye single to their own interest."[88] To this end, the CSFL developed a legislative strategy designed to take advantage of labor's concentrated voting strength in parts of San Francisco (and, until 1910, in Los Angeles) and its more limited leverage as a statewide voting bloc: the leadership identified policy issues directly relevant to workers and then publicized those issues so as to guide their membership's electoral behavior. Proposals to democratize the agenda-setting process by submitting all policy positions to referenda by the membership were diverted or defeated,[89] but the application of the "questioning system" to state candidates in itself represented a considerable threat to the parties. The 1906 *Proceedings* condemned as unconstitutional a statute adopted by the state legislature that outlawed the solicitation of pledges from candidates or demands made "of any candidate for the Legislature, or of any candidate for any legislative body, that he shall vote for any particular bill or specific measure which may come before any such legislative body to which he may be elected; provided always, that this inhibition shall not in any case apply to the pledges exacted of a candidate by the platform or resolutions of any convention by which any such candidate may be nominated."[90]

Despite the best efforts of party stalwarts in the legislature and populist insurgents within the labor federation, the CSFL took a middle way, combining a friends-and-enemies electoral strategy with the development of a formal legislative lobby. Commenting on the AFL's change of policy, the executive council of the California State Federation asserted,

> We have maintained at Sacramento a committee to lobby through labor legislation for the benefit of the Trade Unions, and it is high time that the trade unionists cease bending the knee and begging the Senators and Assemblymen to pass favorable upon such bills as presented, but to the contrary, demanded such legislation and be prepared to back the same up at the ballot box. The cry of "no politics in unions" is beginning to be looked upon with suspicion by the real and genuine trade unionists. We find that

organized capital does not hesitate in promoting its interests and does promote its interests through class legislation. If we propose to fight organized capital we must fight with the same weapons and the same solid front that is used by organized capital.[91]

The combination of electoral and legislative "pressure group" strategies defined a path of organizational development distinct from the more purely electoral path represented by the arms-length alliance of the Wisconsin State Federation of Labor and the Social Democrats. The CSFL's constitution declared it "the duty of the Executive Board to watch legislative matters directly affecting the interests of working people, and to take appropriate steps toward such legislative action as may be necessary," while members were urged to contact their representatives with respect to specific pieces of legislation. Lobbying might even be extended to party conventions, although the hopes of success were slim. The board, however, was not to "endorse or initiate legislation" in the name of the CSFL that had not been approved by a convention or referendum vote. Unlike the conventions of the highly centralized WiSFL, the meetings of the California federation devoted considerable time to legislative proposals from individual unionists or locals, resolutions that often included the entire text of the proposed statute.[92] Whereas the WiSFL leadership hoped to win adherents for the independent labor party model, the CSFL cultivated skills appropriate to legislative policymaking rather than electoral partisanship.

The importance of legislative politics to organized labor was underscored by the creation of a formal lobby in the state capital at Sacramento.[93] The 1904 session was attended by legislative agents of both the San Francisco Labor Council and the CSFL, who paid close attention to the drafting and management of labor legislation so that "they be not permitted to get into the hands of Tom, Dick or Harry and perhaps intrusted to members having no interest in their passage, who will let them die on the files through sheer neglect and inattention."[94] The CSFL stressed the need for clear lines of authority among the representatives of labor and the virtue of cooperation among different labor organizations (even those not affiliated with the AFL). By 1910, a permanent headquarters for the labor lobby had been approved, with the cost to be divided among the different labor organizations involved. Their legislative agent asked the CSFL to "confine its efforts to the passage of a very limited number of bills of primary importance to Labor." The CSFL also hired attorneys to prepare legislation. The CSFL legislative agent repeatedly called for the purchase of a set of the California *Codes*. While this was too great an expense for the federation, a friendly legislator loaned his set to the offices of the labor lobby.[95] The CSFL was well on its way to becoming a focused interest group lobby.[96]

This "professionalization" of the CSFL lobby, however, limited its potential to serve as the keystone of a comprehensive working-class political movement by requiring that its members base their voting decisions on a delimited set of policy issues. As John Mark Hansen has argued with respect to national agricultural lobbies, interest groups gain access to legislators only when legislators expect that electorally significant issues will recur in subsequent contests and that the lobbying organization can provide some electoral advantage.[97] While the first condition could be met by the CSFL's repeated inclusion of specific policies among its legislative priorities, to satisfy the second condition individual workers would have to link their voting behavior to the policy preferences articulated by the state federation. However, "The fact was quite apparent that the endorsement of the State Federation, as such, cut very little figure with the average legislator,"[98] because

> under our present political system it seems almost impossible to arouse a sense of duty in the public mind that will compel *adequate* restrictive legislation. As long as we *will* vote for party candidates as such, regardless of the individual and the influences behind him, it is, perhaps, unbecoming to complain of their shortcomings as officials of state. The voters of California for years have been cognizant of the fact that the machinery of the great political parties is manipulated and controlled almost entirely by corporation influences, and yet with each succeeding election they harken to the pleadings of the political shyster and place in high office individuals who, to all appearances, are mere tools in the hands of their corporation masters.[99]

In order to limit the power of the "corporation masters," the growing labor lobby needed to link legislative behavior to electoral outcomes: "[W]e must weigh carefully the records and character of all candidates for our suffrage before, and not after, election day." Consequently, a system was needed whereby "in the future past records of those seeking support should be accepted for our guidance, rather than mere catch-penny promises."[100] In 1912, the state's leading labor lobbyist, Paul Scharrenberg, attempted to meet this goal by distributing a questionnaire to legislators concerning their position on labor issues, but by the next year Scharrenberg abandoned this tactic for the publication of individual voting records on selected issues. Although this practice is now a commonplace element of a political system in which narrowly defined interests are presumed to drive policy decisions, at the time Californians found the legitimacy of this technique *extremely* questionable: "This method was highly distrusted by legislators who looked upon it as black-listing. Even the San Francisco Labor Council divided over the use of this tactic and dissidents within the Council complained that the end result was a one-man record, referring to the compiler of the statistics, Scharrenberg."[101] Despite these initial objections, the CSFL Committee on Law and Legislation endorsed the "checking up system," arguing that "better results will follow when legislators come to learn that their records on labor legislation will always be an open and interesting book before their labor constituency." The CSFL legislative agent continued to include votes on labor legislation by roll call in his annual report and named those "Senators and Assemblymen who stood ready to work and vote in the interest of the wage earners."[102] These reports were soon published separately as the *Report on Labor Legislation and Labor Record of Senators and Assemblymen*. A parallel effort to coordinate labor's use of direct democracy was made by printing the entire text of many of the forty-eight amendments, initiatives, and referenda put to the voters in 1914, with an X in the recommended yes box or no box.[103]

In the absence of an independent labor party, unionists devised elaborate plans for questioning, nominating, and pledging candidates and promoted the initiative, referendum, recall, and direct primary.[104] Unlike their counterparts in Wisconsin, who condemned "so-called good man policy,"[105] the CSFL embraced the "good man" approach to politics but sought to enforce candidates' pledges with sustained attention to actual votes and to supplement their legislators' efforts with the tools of direct democracy. These efforts aided the passage of key pieces of Progressive Era labor legislation: workmen's compensation, an eight-hour law for women, and laws governing factory inspection and child labor.[106] Although historians have disagreed over the role of labor legislation in establishing the alliance of organized labor and the progressives—some contend that the legislation was an enticement to labor, others that it was the product of labor's own legislative efforts[107]—much of the disparity between these positions may be resolved by recognizing that the organizational project of the CSFL and other labor groups entailed the creation of political identities centered on the evaluation of occupationally defined self-interest rather than the affirmation of partisan identity.[108]

In pursuing both lobbying and electoral accountability, labor was in step with other reform groups in the state. By linking its membership's votes to the subset of legislative decisions directly affecting labor, the

CSFL lobby retained a significant capacity for logrolling on other issues. According to Paul Scharrenberg:

> I learned you could always get a bright young man if you knew or learned to know what his pet bill was. Then you would go to him and say: "I understand that you have such and such a bill." And he would say, "Oh, yes." "Well I'm interested in that bill. Maybe I can help you on it." Before the meeting was over I'd have him all lashed up by a promise that I'd get the San Francisco boys to vote for his bill and he'd vote for mine.[109]

Just as the WiSFL relied on its informal alliance with progressive Republicans to secure labor legislation, the CSFL's successes turned on its ability to cut deals with legislators not directly beholden to labor—but neither could those legislators fear electoral retribution for their support of labor's bills. This dependence on election outcomes was aggravated by a critical difference between the leadership of the California and Wisconsin federations. While the influence of both rested on the electoral organization of their members, the latter also cultivated alliances with experts and state bureaucrats. On occasion, the CSFL did call for increased appropriations for the Commission of Immigration and Housing, Bureau of Labor Statistics, and Industrial Welfare Commission, but convention records include few resolutions directed toward state agencies (in comparison to the numbers directed at the state legislature, the U.S. Congress, or federal agencies, especially the military, that were important employers), few mentions of cooperation with state agencies, and few calls for unionists to work actively in the enforcement of labor laws.[110] In addition, many within the CSFL opposed the establishment of "expert agencies" that would not be accountable to the people.[111]

Within the CSFL, opinion differed on the merits of expert regulation and direct democracy compared to more traditional forms of local control through party politics. In the second decade of the century, the legislative leadership of the CSFL and much of the rest of the federation divided over the desirability of nonpartisan politics. In 1915, the legislative committee declared that the proposed "non-partisan election law, is one of such consequence as to be deserving of particular mention and approbation from the members of organized labor. It is the opinion of [this] committee that the adoption of a non-partisan plan of choosing State officials will result in *bringing to the front humanitarian and social questions which have been denied consideration in the past by reason of the greater attention and consideration given to so-called party issues.*"[112] The convention, however, rejected this recommendation, and their decision was echoed by the electorate, which rejected the progressive-sponsored Non-Partisan Bill by 156,967 to 112,681.[113] The following year, a call for renewed independent political action was rejected by a narrow vote. This proposal came from the Central Labor Council and Building Trades Council of Los Angeles. These groups

> submitted resolutions to the Executive Council [of the CSFL], urging the "State Federation of Labor and the State Building Trades Council of California, to call a convention of delegates from bona fide recognized labor unions in this State to convene at some place and time as may be deemed best for the purpose of devising ways, means and plans for a program that will more effectually further the election of candidates to the Judiciary, the State Legislature and the National Congress, who either are representatives of Labor, or who have pledged themselves to give labor a greater degree of justice than it had been accorded in the past by our courts and our legislative bodies."

The Executive Council polled the state's Labor Councils and "nine in effect rejected the proposal, eight endorsed it, and three failed to reply."[114] The executive council took no further action. Having secured some power as a swing constituency and advocacy group within partisan electoral politics, a majority—however slim—of organized labor in California was unwilling to abandon these strategies. But this strategy worked only so long as parties or party factions were competitive—so that a swing constituency would matter—and other legislators were not sanctioned for supporting labor's political demands. The latter condition was no longer met with the postwar backlash against labor and resurgent conservatism. With neither a party of its own nor an unshakable claim on the loyalties of middle-class progressives and state bureaucrats, labor was vulnerable to the political fortunes of the progressive Republicans and the political sentiments of other reform groups. Once the progressives lost the governorship to a conservative Republican in 1922, appropriations for labor boards were slashed, and the independence of state agencies was undermined.[115]

Direct Democracy

In California, a series of closely divided votes prevented the CSFL from committing itself to the wholesale dismantling of the party system. Yet the very closeness of those votes testifies to the animus of many labor activists toward the parties, a hostility that elsewhere fed directly into extrapartisan political strategies. In political histories of the United States, the struggle against partisan corruption and for procedural reform is typically attributed to middle-class professionals,[116] but labor activists called for similar remedies: the Australian ballot, direct primaries, direct election of United States senators, and the initiative, referendum, and recall.[117] With these procedural reforms, unionists argued, the illegitimate power of corporations and corrupt politicians could be broken. Commenting on electoral outcomes in Ohio in 1913, one California unionist proclaimed: "The 'Interests' thought they could 'fix' the Referendum in the same manner as they had handled Legislatures and City Councils. But it failed to work. The Initiative, Referendum and the Recall are the people's weapons!"[118] Nor were these demands for procedural reform purely strategic. The positive value attributed to models of direct democracy is evident in the many efforts to use these methods to reorganize the state federations themselves.[119]

These developments, however, were opposed wherever organized labor remained committed to a party model, whether in the form of urban political machines or socialist third parties. Wisconsin, for all of organized labor's centrality to the reform coalition, was a laggard with respect to the procedural reforms often associated with the label *progressive*. Although the direct primary was critical for Robert La Follette's election as governor in 1900 and 1904, neither he nor organized labor shared the Far West's effusive enthusiasm for direct democracy, with its opening of the political process to a broad array of extrapartisan organizations.[120] In 1910 Fred Brockhausen, the WiSFL's secretary-treasurer, mildly urged the officers to "promote direct legislation in this state through the state legislature, by such means as from time to time presents itself."[121] A proposal to establish an "indirect initiative," which allowed only that voters could petition for bills defeated in the legislature to be submitted to a popular vote, was defeated in 1915.[122]

The principle of nonpartisanship itself was explicitly opposed by many socialists within organized labor: "[T]rue labor politics can never be nonpartisan." The WiSFL's Brockhausen declared his opposition "to this begging policy of questioning the legislative candidates before election."[123] His counterpart in the CSFL, a federation that would perfect techniques of nonpartisan accountability, observed "what strange bed-fellows politics will make, . . . the two Socialist members [of the state legislature] voted and worked with the most pronounced reactionaries in seeking to defeat the non-partisan election law."[124] Uncommitted to a third-party model, the CSFL exploited the opportunities afforded by the initiative and referendum. Invested in its role in guiding a significant swing constituency, the Californians did not reject partisan politics altogether but combined nonpartisan and extrapartisan forms of political mobilization. Lacking either a durable third party or an ally in the form of a reliably progressive faction within a major party, however, organized labor in Washington sought opportunities beyond the party system altogether.

Thwarted in their efforts at both third-party campaigns and legislative lobbying, labor activists turned toward nonpartisan, and then extrapartisan, strategies. Workers in Washington were fortunate, however, in the models of labor organization that predominated in the Pacific Northwest. Unionists there did not reject the organizational forms that characterized the movements of the 1880s and 1890s. Geographical isolation and the dominant role of large, politically powerful employers contributed to the survival of the Knights of Labor until the turn of the century, a full decade after it had ceased to be the dominant national labor organization. For workers, the Knights—and its quasi reincarnations as the Western Federation of Miners, Western Labor Union, and American Labor Union—perpetuated a commitment to political activism and industrial unionism,[125] tendencies reinforced by the single-tax and nationalist movements.

Despite the efforts of the AFL to foster apolitical craft unionism, from the 1880s onward organized labor in Washington was politically active, often as part of a broader reform coalition. A People's Party in Seattle called on the producing population to oppose the "concubinage of caballers and virtuous dupes," asking if "the people [shall] rule or shall the politicians, lawyers, and other adherents rule by dividing the people on false issues?"[126] Founded in 1888, the Western Central Labor Union attempted to lead workers away from the popular reform parties of the 1880s,[127] but this reversal was short-lived. In 1893, the union met with the Pacific Coast Council of Trades and Labor Federations to consider the establishment of a political farmer-labor alliance, which was carried on by the Populist Party after the Western Central's demise.[128]

Unlike Wisconsin or California, in Washington populism was an electoral success at the state level. Although a broad farmer-labor alliance failed to have provisions for woman suffrage and the single tax incorporated in the constitution of 1889, the constitution did provide that "the legislature shall pass necessary laws for the protection of persons working in mines, factories and other employments dangerous to life or deleterious to health."[129] In 1896, another farmer-labor alliance captured both the legislature and the governor's office; Governor John Rogers was then reelected as a Democrat in 1901. The 1897 legislature established a bureau of labor;[130] the first and second commissioners were union men, who sought the cooperation of unions by requesting both statistical information on organized labor and suggestions for the improvement of the work-ing classes.[131] Observing that "organized labor is taking an active part in the matter of legislation, and is alive to their own interests," William Blackman, the second commissioner and former president of the Wash-ington State Labor Congress and of the WaSFL, published the entire text of resolutions passed by the WaSFL and thereby formally recognized "the sentiments of some fifteen thousand voters of our state."[132] This section of the report disappeared in later years when the administration was less friendly to labor; only "Suggestions from Wage Earners" remained.[133]

Organized labor was not entirely dependent on the goodwill of the commissioner. Following the efforts of a short-lived State Labor Congress in 1893, the Pacific Northwest Labor Congress operated as an organized lobby, promoting legislation and securing the creation of a state labor bureau.[134] The Congress was renamed the Washington State Labor Con-gress in 1898 and, in 1902, reorganized as the Washington State Federa-tion of Labor. After a contested referendum of its member unions, the WaSFL voted to affiliate with the AFL. This was a mixed blessing for the national organization since the WaSFL often opposed Samuel Gompers and the antipolitical policy of the AFL.

The WaSFL differed from the State Labor Congress, which had issued a populist platform that, apart from a few demands for labor legislation, "might just as well have been issued by a farmers' organization."[135] The WaSFL was clearly a labor rather than "producers" organization, but its legislative efforts were blocked by the revival of a corporation-dominated political machine after Governor Rogers's death in 1901. Faced with a series of hostile legislatures, organized labor sought new models of politi-cal action. There were a number of attempts to establish pure "labor par-ties," but none were notably successful. The logical candidate for this ef-fort, the Socialist Party, was plagued by factional infighting, but its presence effectively occupied the political space for an independent labor party.[136] Efforts at independent labor politics were also made at the mu-nicipal level. In Seattle, unionists established the Workingmen's League for Clean Politics, which cooperated with the civic reformers' City Party in 1906 and helped to sponsor a United Labor Party in 1910. The Seattle Central Labor Council refused to support this move into independent-party politics, but even this did not stop efforts at political organization. In 1910, the Bricklayers' Union called for an independent party, and a founding convention was held for the Washington State Labor Party.[137] Faced with apathy on the part of union members, however, the party col-lapsed before the next election. Thus, while third-party politics belonged to the repertoire of political action inherited from the populist movements of the late nineteenth century, the implementation of this model was blocked both by the prior existence of a "legitimate" labor party in the ineffective Socialists and the opposition of the state labor federation.

Efforts to ally unions with a major party were also disappointing. Initially pursuing a friends-and-enemies approach, by the second decade of the century conventions were passing resolutions calling for specific legislation, and an official legislative agent was appointed.[138] Proposed bills, however, were rarely passed by the legislature. In part, these failures stemmed from the greatly diminished strength of the Democratic Party. Unless pressure groups could control the nominating process, threats of opposition at the polls were meaningless and candidates' pledges hollow.[139]

The obstacles created by the entrenched Republican Party were not solely labor's problem. Since labor legislation was blocked by "the growing power of employers' associations and divisions within the ranks of organized labor, the State Federation of Labor resolved at its 1906 convention to seek support from other reform-minded organizations. The Washington State Grange, presided over by ex-socialist C. B. Kegley, quickly endorsed the idea of farmer-labor cooperation."[140] In Olympia, the need for political cooperation fostered political ties among groups seeking various reforms: labor, urban reformers, women's organizations, and agrarian associations. These ties were formalized in a succession of political organizations: the Direct Primary League, the Direct Legislation League, and the Joint Legislative Committee.

These organizations grew out of campaigns for the direct primary, initiative, referendum, and recall. Direct democracy was genuinely popular within organized labor in Washington. In 1904, the WaSFL passed a resolution praising the "Winnetka system for installing the initiative and referendum in cities without waiting for the consent of the party in power in the legislature and without consulting the party machines in the city"; it also endorsed constitutional amendments for initiative and referendum. The federation continued to debate the merits of these models of internal governance and went so far as to contact all other state federations as to their experience with the "referendum method of election."[141] In state government, these goals were achieved by 1912,[142] and the Joint Legislative Committee (JLC) was established as the coordinating body for groups committed to political reform and social-policy legislation. One major activity of the JLC was securing pledges from candidates on specific pieces of legislation and working to bring out the labor vote for important initiatives and referenda.[143] In order to enforce the pledges, the JLC also publicized the voting records of legislators on key bills. Only through such publicity could workers learn to act in their true interests: "[H]ow much more influential [the workers] can be if they will cast aside political partisan domination and use their ballots at all times to protect their rights and promote their own welfare." No matter how elaborate the lobby supported by organized labor, "Men of labor with a voice and vote inside the legislative body are worth a field full of legislative agents on the outside."[144] The importance of these new models of organized political control is evident from the detail in which new methods were described. In 1913, the WaSFL president explained,

> At both the Farmers' Union and State Grange conventions I presented a pencil copy of a proposed tabulated legislative review, so arranged in two colors that any one could tell at a glance whether a legislator voted for or against the people's interests, recording votes on important amendments and final roll calls on Initiative, Referendum and Recall Amendments, Compensation Act and Women's Eight-hour Law. All who saw it expressed the conviction that it was just what was needed to educate the public as to how their senators and representatives voted. With the approval of these organizations and our Executive Committee, this Tabulated Legislative Review was printed and placed in circulation. It proved to be the most influential piece of campaign literature we ever issued, over 100,000 being printed and circulated in response to demands for the same.[145]

Despite these tactical innovations, the WaSFL had little luck electing prolabor representatives, and the legislature remained heavily Republican. Consequently, the JLC promoted a strategy of direct legislation that sought to circumvent the legislature through the sustained use of the initiative and referendum. The WaSFL also called for judicial recall and constitutional amendment by initiative. The secretary of the WaSFL observed that there were disadvantages to this enthusiasm for legislative solutions to labor problems: "A few years ago the business man was panic-stricken when election campaigns began. Not so this year. A few years ago the laborer believed he had to strike that very night to get higher wages. Now he believes he can get them by voting for them. So he wants to count votes after the election before deciding about trade union organization. This makes the organizer's work hard at best."[146] Efforts were also made to reform the system of voter registration so that fewer workers would be taken off the electoral rolls. Among the many pieces of legislation promoted by organized labor were bills that would require the state government to maintain a "Card Index System of Registration as adopted by the State of Oregon, [through which] organized labor was able to defeat certain measures that threatened its very existence" and to pay for printing arguments pro and con with the text of proposed constitutional amendments.[147]

These legislative efforts were matched by some improvement in the ability of organized labor to conduct initiative campaigns.[148] In the 1915 election, the federation succeeded in placing five initiatives on the ballot, but despite the $1,367 that the WaSFL contributed to the JLC for the campaign, only the one banning private employment offices was approved.[149] This defeat was attributed to flaws in the initiative mechanism: "As bad as our Initiative law is, we should put forth every effort to keep it intact, and still further, to try to make it better. In the beginning it was the gift of a reluctant legislature, and during our recent campaign every effort was put forth by the capitalistic press, some state officials and the courts to put Direct Legislation in a bad light."[150] The following year, labor was able to place eight pieces of hostile legislation on the ballot as referenda, and the legislature responded by attempting to gut the constitutional amendments providing for the initiative and referendum. The bills at issue involved broader use of emergency clauses and had been passed by a legislature "determined to 'unhorse' labor from its political influence and turn the tide back towards the despotism of big business control." The WaSFL's legislative agent drew clear parallels with previous political machines: "In many legislative districts the old gang of stand-pat politicians of the notorious railroad lobby days, whose connections with the corrupt practices of those times had caused the voters to place them in the discard, were now returned to the legislature, where they resumed their old practices of legislative bossism in the interests of the big labor exploiters of the state." The governor vetoed these bills, the legislature overturned the vetoes, and, in the end, a decision by the state supreme court saved the direct-democracy laws.[151]

The principle of increasing direct democracy also governed the organizational procedures adopted by the WaSFL. In arguing against holding the convention in the state capital even on alternate years, President Ernest P. Marsh argued that contact with the legislature would become less important than in the past: "[A]s the people become used to direct law-making powers through the initiative and referendum, the legislature becomes less paramount as a feature of government."[152] Organized labor could contribute to this development by promoting initiative measures rather than relying on either the legislature or state agencies to produce new legislation. Labor leaders argued that the fight against legislation hostile to labor

> could best be conducted by offering the people, through the initiative, con-
> structive legislation along progressive lines and in accord with the majority
> of progressive public sentiment. In other words, instead of going before the
> public solely as opponents of proposed laws enacted by the legislature, we
> offer where possible affirmative relief as an antidote for the vile poison that
> the last legislature tried to hypodermically inject into our system.[153]

Frustrated by a recalcitrant legislature and unresponsive parties, Washington unionists—along with their allies in reform—enthusiastically adopted the tools of direct democracy, abjuring the mediation of political parties so far as possible.

To Supplant Party with Interest

Direct democracy was not always successful,[154] in part because it contradicted the central role of partisanship in the existing repertoire of organization. Partisan actions, however, could be modified to serve nonpartisan and extrapartisan ends to the extent that partisan loyalty could be supplanted by "interested" voting guided by candidates' positions on designated issues. Whereas independent labor parties built on an older model in which partisan loyalty was to guide electoral behavior (recall the opposition of socialist parties to the introduction of nonpartisan elections and their comparative coolness toward the mechanisms of direct democracy), when constituted as an electoral bloc in party primaries, as a swing constituency in general elections, or as an extrapartisan legislative pressure group, organized labor needed both a clear delineation of its "interests" and new techniques of accountability. While a solid front could be built on common interests, the recognition of those interests could not be assumed. Instead, union leaders argued that workers had to be taught to perceive their interests correctly and to grasp the connections between legislative actions and individual interests. By combining the collection of preelection pledges with the controversial innovation of published tabulations of roll-call votes, organized labor gained a new capacity for holding legislators accountable on a delimited range of issues identified as of particular interest to working men and women. Both regular elections and the newly acquired tool of the recall (in California and Washington) might be used to punish those who reneged on their campaign promises. Reflecting on the 1913 legislature, the legislative agents of the CSFL observed that this was the first session at which all members had been questioned before election regarding their attitude upon a number of important Labor measures. The replies of all candidates had been compiled in pamphlet form and were freely distributed during the campaign. And we regret to report that quite a few members of the Legislature who had answered our questions in writing with an emphatic "yes," had a change of heart when it came to voting and in some instances actually orated against the very measures which they had promised to support before election. The worst offender in this regard was Senator James C. Owens. . . . And if the "Recall" of a faithless public servant was ever justified it surely is in this case."[155]

As workers tried to hold legislators accountable, "accountable for what?" became a serious question. In the construction of roll-call tables, therefore, scrupulous care was taken to isolate votes that addressed questions of specific concern to organized labor and that provided the most rigorous test of the loyalties of elected representatives. What those specific concerns were depended, in turn, on how labor was organized. In Washington, the WaSFL president included the initiative, referendum, and recall in his legislative table and thereby courted the support of the state Grange and Farmers' Union.[156] In California, interests were defined more narrowly. The CSFL president advised that "there should be no entangling alliances with other labor bodies seeking the advancement of their own pet measures."[157] In 1915, the CSFL executive council elaborated the technique required by this policy:

> [I]f Labor desires to obtain a correct and unvarnished record concerning the attitude of individual legislators, the record must be taken on those legislative propositions which emanate directly from labor and which have no other backing than the principles and influence of organized Labor. When a vote is had on such measures (if it is successful enough to reach that stage) it indicates truthfully and without equivocation each legislator's real attitude toward Labor and its policies.

Votes without opposition or bills sponsored by the administration were explicitly identified as unsuitable for inclusion in such roll calls. Once compiled, voting records revealed that "old-time party designation has no real meaning and is of absolutely no value when it comes to a scrap on a labor bill" and served as an alternative guide for the election decisions of workers: "[T]he 'Comparative Record' . . . enables anyone to see at a glance 'how good' or 'how bad' his Senator and Assemblyman voted upon Labor measures." The CSFL urged trade-unionists to save the *Labor Record* "for future reference. Many of the members of this Legislature will be candidates to succeed themselves, and others will sooner or later aspire for different political honors. . . . So keep informed! Support candidates for the Legislature and for Congress on the basis of actual performances rather than on vague promises!"[158]

Educational strategies and literature were central to this project. Faced with the need to guide the votes of nonsocialist workers outside Milwaukee, even the WiSFL turned to "nonpartisan" methods for constructing political interests. At the 1912 convention, the WiSFL Committee on Education resolved that "the incoming Executive Board make every effort possible to get out such literature as will bring the farmers and wage earners nearer to the goal where they must realize that their interests are identical and that they must fight as a unit to secure industrial freedom." A delegate for the Milwaukee Federated Trades Council echoed this call:

> Whereas, Only through statistics can our fellow workers in different parts of the state find out how deplorable their conditions are and how in many instances the same labor is being paid for at a lower rate of wages, and how the number of working hours differ, and
> Whereas, Statistics are absolutely necessary to determine the facts and to enlighten the workers, therefore be it
> Resolved, That the new incoming Executive Board give this matter its careful consideration and take such steps as will lead to a statistical investigation of the conditions of labor in Wisconsin that confronts [sic] the workers of this state.[159]

These efforts "to determine the facts and to enlighten the workers" were meant to reconstitute their members as informed voters rather than instinctive partisans of the major parties. In this respect, the internal politics of labor organizations document their participation in the broad reaction against the established parties and their contribution to the collective process of innovation that would eventually produce a new calculus for political action.

But for all these innovations, labor participated in these efforts to work around the party system with rather less fervor than other groups. This reluctance to part with older models of organization reflects the central place of partisanship and electoral participation in the repertoire of action mastered by white workingmen in the nineteenth century as well as the organizational and instrumental ties that linked many unionists to the party system. Consequently, the considerable extent to which unionists *did* question the relations between the labor movement and partisan politics testifies to the limitations and inconsistencies of the organizational models inherited from previous eras. The interplay of inherited constraints and unfulfilled demands gave rise to new organizational forms even in the absence of a full critique of partisanship.

If the organizational character of popular reform movements can be traced to a critique of partisan politics, the strength of party organizations influenced the degree to which sweeping changes were sought. In each of these states, organized labor began by adopting models of partisan politics and turned to new strategies only insofar as the established parties proved to be either immune to reform or unbeatable by a third party. This interaction of repertoire and political opportunities produced varied results, ranging from the victory of a labor-based Social Democratic Party in Wisconsin to the radical nonpartisanship of Washington state. In turn, these state-level experiments injected a sometimes destabilizing heterogeneity into national politics, providing exemplars of policy alternatives and challenging the authority of the principles of craft autonomy upon which the AFL rested.

Regional Variation and National Organization

Far from the industrial centers of the northern states, the ability of both political parties and the AFL to enforce organizational conformity diminished. The organizational experiments in western states were fueled by different mixes of opposition—both to the principles of craft unionism and to the system of partisan politics—resulting in distinctive innovations and varied challenges to the organizational orthodoxy of the AFL.

In Wisconsin, organized labor was committed to an independent working-class party, and Milwaukee's Social Democrats were ideologically attuned to the existence of large-scale economic and political institutions and framed their agenda within the context of a state-centered polity. The commitment of the Social Democrats to a party model inhibited innovation at the level of electoral politics, and, consequently, state agencies were left as a possible site for forging new political ties. A model plan promoted by the American Association for Labor Legislation represented a labor commission as an expert-supervised nexus for participation by labor and business as well as for the education of the general public (fig. 4.2). Although the circle of experts centered on the economist John R. Commons has received most of the credit for exporting the "Wisconsin Idea," organized labor was equally anxious to establish the state's labor legislation as an exemplar for the nation. With respect to the workmen's compensation laws, the WiSFL's Committee on Fraternal Relationships remarked, "The Law of Wisconsin being in force, Illinois and Michigan

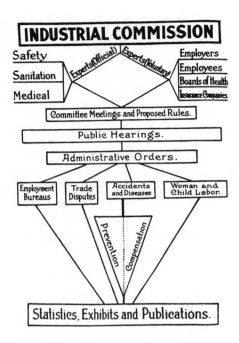

Figure 4.2   Suggestive Outline of a Form of Organization for a State Industrial Commission. (Source: *American Labor Legislation Review,* December 1913)

about to become active, . . . we would have Minnesota, Missouri and all states benefit by the close observation on the laws when they are in force."[160] But since the "Wisconsin Idea," with its quasi-corporatist combination of strong state agencies and advisory boards, presumed that organized labor could make effective demands for policy, unions could not take this path into politics in states where either labor's repertoire or the opportunities for influence differed.

The possibilities of third-party politics were less clear in California. For organized labor, its forays into independent-party politics in the late nineteenth century had produced electoral victories, but less in the way of desired legislation. But the alternative model of the nonpartisan pressure group held little promise so long as legislators of both parties could be swayed by the demands of a few large corporations. Apart from a few logrolling successes of the San Francisco delegation, organized labor secured influence only once a reformist progressive movement made it possible for labor to act as a key voting bloc in factional struggles. The fluidity of party politics in the state, combined with the development of a strong legislative lobby, gave organized labor some political leverage as well as an appreciation for the techniques of direct democracy and roll-call tabulations. So long as political progressives retained control of state government, organized labor proved to be a skillful practitioner of interest-based politics in both legislative and administrative arenas. Yet the outcomes depended on alliances; California's workers lacked either the firm electoral bloc or a dedicated position within major administrative agencies that were enjoyed by their counterparts in Wisconsin.

The impact of political opportunity on the organization and political strategy of unionized labor was particularly striking in Washington. Having joined in the successful effort to elect a Populist governor in 1896, labor was rewarded with the creation of a state Bureau of Labor and the appointment of a leader of the American Railroad Union as its first head.[161] But with the governor's death after his reelection in 1900, a series of conservative and at times corrupt administrations and legislatures relegated labor to the political sidelines. Overwhelmed by the financial power of the railroads and lumber companies, unable to sanction its enemies at the polls, organized labor in Washington was pushed into active cooperation with groups seeking to institutionalize nonpartisan models of direct democracy. Consequently, political struggles in Washington turned explicitly on the nature of political institutions:

> The opponents of our bills were not so gravely concerned as to the merits of the measures as they were over the possible success of popular government. They have too long been the beneficiaries of corrupt legislatures to give up easily. The reactionary forces could see in this success a menace to time-worn institutions, pork-barrel legislation and rank manipulations with the aid of public funds. We have learned much from that campaign. We have learned to what lengths organized greed will go when Direct Legislation is the vital issue. It clearly indicates that what benefits labor gets it must take.[162]

In Washington, the ability of business to control legislatures pushed organized labor into an alliance with agrarian and urban reformers. Unionists subsequently embraced the antistatist models implicit in the mechanisms of direct democracy, with ironic results. Washington repeatedly passed labor legislation more progressive than that of almost all other states, only to see these accomplishments undermined by inadequate administration or reversed by hostile legislators and governors. Faced with these outcomes, labor in Washington was driven further and further from the channels of partisan politics, pushed toward the alternative strategies of extrapartisanship, radical unionism, and cooperative self-governance.

In each state, the organizational repertoires and political opportunities confronting organized labor shaped workers' efforts to fashion collective strategies for harnessing their votes to policy outcomes. As will be seen in the chapters that follow, similar conjunctures constrained the organizational experiments of other political challengers, producing distinctive policy styles and government capacities. Yet the very heterogeneity of organizational strategies within the states had consequences for labor politics nationally; recall that the presence of alternatives will tend to undermine authority, whether of political regimes or associational policies. Within the AFL, state-level innovators attempted to use the existing organization of labor as a channel for the diffusion of innovations, inevitably challenging the interests of existing union leaders. The Milwaukee Social Democrats sought to circumvent the AFL by forging political alliances among city centrals and state federations. In 1902, the Milwaukee FTC invited central bodies of the AFL to join in a National Municipal Labor League, a proposal that the AFL squashed. In 1905, the WiSFL resolved that "the incoming Executive Board be authorized to take steps toward bringing about a National Conference of State Federations for the consideration of uniform labor legislation." The California convention demurred: "While we are in perfect sympathy with the objects herein sought to be attained, we do not believe it advisable at this time to send a delegate to such convention."[163] The WiSFL continued to urge that the delegates of state federations meet separately at the annual AFL convention or use the AFL newsletter as a way of coordinating their actions. Within the upper Midwest, state federations cooperated by exchanging fraternal delegates and holding joint legislative conferences that also included delegates from agricultural organizations, state agencies, and national reform associations.

Far from being isolated experiments, these were part of an ongoing effort to map the organization of labor onto the organization of industry and polity. The challenge was captured in a proposal adopted by the Colorado State Federation of Labor and circulated to other state federations in the form of an invitation to an organizing conference:

> Industrial conditions are rapidly changing in all parts of our country; employers are uniting their forces by joining powerful organizations, whose purpose is to defeat the aims of organized labor, and retard its onward march to the goal of "Justice."
>
> If our unions throughout the land are to successfully cope with the new industrial conditions that confront us it is apparent that some method of

organization should be adopted, so that organized labor's forces can be united to be better able to counteract this new organized opposition that is appearing throughout the land. . . .

The conditions of the wage-earners vary in different localities, and the fact is self-evident that the unions are more familiar with the conditions and needs in their own particular locality, and would therefore be better able to advance their interests, and that of organized labor in general, if given authority to manage their affairs locally, through their State organization, with the assurance that when necessary they would receive the support of neighboring states or all of the states of the Union, if required.

Briefly, then, the purpose is to adopt a system of labor organization through State Federations, making the state organization supreme in the state, and doing mutual business through a National Executive Board, similar in scope and jurisdiction to the United States Congress; this board to be the final court of appeal, with the possible exception of the referendum at the hands of the rank and file of all our organizations.[164]

Although its sponsors claimed that "this system, if adopted, would in no way interfere with the affiliations of unions, either national or international," the AFL leadership was understandably hostile to such proposals. Yet more proposals came, for the same reason that tirades against the party system never ceased; the voting rules within the AFL discriminated against the city and state federations (which received a set number of votes regardless of membership) and advantaged the leadership of international unions (whose votes in convention increased with membership). Consequently, the AFL was unresponsive to insurgent demands for a more aggressively political program.

The CSFL also extended its political experiments to the AFL. As in Wisconsin, Californians frequently criticized the political policy of the AFL, even though one of their own, Andrew Furuseth, was a leading AFL lobbyist in Washington, D.C. But whereas Wisconsin unionists advocated independent-party politics, California's leaders urged the membership to make use of now-familiar methods of electoral accountability. Recognizing that their weakness within the national organization stemmed directly from the great strength of the national and international unions, CSFL secretary Paul Scharrenberg observed that associational and state politics offered much the same opportunities: "[I]t is foolish to complain about standpatters, steam rollers and other things animate and inanimate alleged to have control of the A. F. of L. conventions. The A. F. of L. conventions are dominated by delegates representing national and international unions. Therefore, if we don't like the decisions of the A. F. of L. conventions we should immediately begin to assume a little individual responsibility and investigate how the delegates from our own national or international unions lined up on vital issues." [165]

California unionists sought to transplant nonpartisan techniques of electoral accountability to the governance of the AFL. Organized labor in Washington was more likely to attempt supplanting the AFL, or at least its current leadership, altogether. The enduring influence of the Knights of Labor in the Pacific Northwest, the recurrent farmer-labor alliances, and the strength of the Western Federation of Miners and Western Labor Union all represented threats to the dominance of the American Federation of Labor with its principles of craft unionism. Among the most striking symptoms of the state's deviance from AFL organizational doctrine were the strength and autonomy of its city centrals. Recall that in an effort to protect the autonomy of craft unions in negotiating and upholding contracts, AFL policy forbade city centrals to affiliate with non-AFL associations (such as Knights' assemblies, socialist groups, or political parties) or to coordinate negotiations across trades. The model of "Duncanism" perfected by the Seattle Central Labor Council violated both requirements, supported by an intense localism evident in what was claimed to be the nation's highest rate of affiliation with a city central: even the Industrial Workers of the World (IWW) judged the Seattle labor movement to be affiliated with the AFL more "in form than in spirit." [166]

This opposition to the AFL's political methods was grounded in differences of both organizational repertoires and political opportunities. Ideologically, labor's enduring ties to the Knights, Populists, and nativist agitation left it culturally aligned with groups that were antagonistic to unionists in the industrialized Northeast. Washington's synthesis of unionism and temperance is emblematic of these distinctive cultural legacies: "The association of drinking and loose moral habits with the East and eastern labor served to heighten Seattle's suspicion of Samuel Gompers and his AFL. To local labor Dries, 'booze' was injurious not merely to the workingman but also to his organization." [167]

Opposed to eastern leadership with respect to both values and political style, James Duncan cast the only vote against Gompers in the AFL presidential elections of 1919 and 1920. [168] Wisconsin's delegate to the 1920 AFL convention voted differently but shared these sentiments: "there was no other candidate in opposition to President Gompers, hence there was no opportunity to register a vote against Mr. Gompers." [169] So although organized labor in Washington deviated from AFL policy in particularly dramatic ways, it was not alone in its discontent.

Resistance to the national AFL leadership could also be linked to techniques of direct democracy and programs of worker education. Here again, disagreements with the AFL were framed in terms of the difficulty of linking policy outcomes to member preferences:

> Whereas, Definite instructions to delegates from Central Labor Bodies, Federal Labor Unions, and State Federations of Labor, and National and International Unions as to the choice of the officials for the American Federation of Labor will be of no avail to rectify wrongs and *break the autocracy that now exists* with the president, secretary and members of the executive board of the American Federation of Labor; therefore be it
>
> Resolved, That the delegate from the Wisconsin State Federation of Labor at its annual convention assembled in Denver, in the year of 1921, is hereby directed to introduce into and work for its passage, a resolution embodying an amendment to the constitution of the American Federation of Labor, that all officials and members of the executive board of the American Federation of Labor be *elected by a general referendum vote* of all the organized workers who are affiliated.[170]

Echoing the claim that "here upon our shores must be solved the issues of social and industrial justice, the westward tide must be turned, and eastward the cause of freedom and equality must flow,"[171] the delegates from both Washington and Wisconsin clearly recognized that if federal associations were to be mechanisms for the diffusion of reform, internal reorganization was required. These reforms entailed new organizational models that disrupted the identities and lines of authority embedded in the AFL. And, although the national labor leadership was not toppled, its political policies were set aside during the 1920s, if only temporarily. Faced with a postwar mix of strikes, business reaction, political repression, and judicial injunctions, serious debates over the possibility of forming a new party resurfaced in national labor circles. In 1924, the AFL stopped just short of this step, endorsing Robert La Follette for president but declining to establish the organizational framework for a new party.

Labor's halfhearted insurgency of 1924 reminds us that the heterodox tendencies of organized labor in Washington and other western states should not obscure the inertial force of the logics of appropriateness that anchored workingmen to the party system. Across all three states as well as in national politics, organized labor first turned to partisan politics, in the guise of either electoral alliances or an independent labor party. The hand of the past, acting through an inherited and familiar repertoire of political organization, guided political action toward familiar channels. State federations, then the AFL itself, developed new political strategies as a response to the strength of existing party machines and their level of resistance to labor's agenda. Unionists sought out alternative strategies only to the degree that these familiar channels were blocked.

So for all the organizational experimentation undertaken by workers in Wisconsin, California, and Washington, labor's political efforts remained deeply influenced by models of partisanship. The organizationally conservative character of many unionists' forays into politics will become clearer in comparison to the efforts of organized farmers, who typically embraced a much more intense variant of nonpartisanship. While organized labor continued to invest its energies in elections and legislative politics, farmers gradually turned away from the traditional centers of political activity to forge relations with new state agencies or to construct entirely new channels of decision making using the tools of direct democracy.

FIVE

From Agrarian Protest to Business Politics

> It should be understood that there is a wide diver-
> gence between politics and partisanry. The first I advo-
> cate, the second I will oppose to my dying day.
>
> We have passed, at many conventions, resolutions of
> an iron-clad nature declaring our position on this issue.
> We have made it as much as the membership of a man is
> worth to embark in partisan politics while associated
> with the Union. What we need is to select only those
> men of demonstrated mental and moral fitness.
>
> This is not partisan politics. It is business politics,
> and the plainest sort of self-preservation. Every corpora-
> tion and big business of every description is today in pol-
> itics. You cannot point me to a single industry in this
> country, save that of the farmer, which has not accred-
> ited representatives in Congress and in the large conven-
> tions that meet to determine party nominees every two
> or every four years. You will remember that even our
> organized labor friends sent powerful delegates both to
> the Chicago and Denver conventions last year.
>
> Charles Simon Barrett, *The Mission, History,
> and Times of the Farmers' Union* (1909)

At first glance, American farmers appear to have attempted much but for
long accomplished little. The history of agrarian politics is of moments,
crusades, revolts, and rebellions against the increasing size and centralization of the U.S. economy.[1] These challenges, like those of organized workers, took forms that were inextricably *both* economic and political. The
National Farmers Alliance and Industrial Union, for example, was based
in a system of marketing cooperatives but, in its later appearance as the
People's Party or Populists, "challenged the corporate state and the creed
of progress it put forward. . . . [It] tried through democratic politics to
bring the corporate state under popular control without fully anticipating
the counter-tactics available to the nation's financial and industrial
spokesmen."[2] This dual emphasis on market strategies and democratic

145

politics was woven through the actions and rhetoric of agrarian reformers from the 1870s through the 1890s. But the centrality of populist democratic themes appears jarring in retrospect; by the time of the First World War organized farmers had begun to develop a tight network of relations with state agencies.[3] Agrarian organizations emerged as central components of a project of bureaucratic state-building. To a significantly greater extent than their counterparts in the labor movement, organized farmers secured bureaucratic beachheads and policy initiatives at both state and national levels. The puzzle, then, is to understand how the transition from agrarian democracy to economic corporatism could occur so swiftly.

This transition involved the development of an organizational model that redefined agrarian "interests" and linked them in new ways to political processes and outcomes. Farmers began with much the same organizational repertoire as nineteenth-century workingmen: fraternal orders and political parties. This repertoire was enriched by the popularization of cooperative organizing, inspired in large part by the English Rochdale system. Yet no purely social, political, or economic model was capacious enough to address the wide range of agrarian grievances. Nor, it would prove, were any of these organizational models sufficiently robust to survive being exported to politics. The fraternal order of the Grange foundered in its adventures into electoral politics as well as into cooperative marketing and production. The cooperative-based Farmers Alliance, it was widely concluded, was "killed by politics."[4] Membership figures for major agrarian organizations reveal an episodic pattern as organizations collapsed, leaving farmers to search for another form of association with which to improve their situation (table 5.1). Each success and collapse enriched or discredited the repertoire of organizational models altering the possibilities for future organizing efforts. As the Master of the Salinas California Grange sadly concluded a decade after the collapse of the order's cooperative-marketing plan of the 1870s, "[T]he old Grange had a large membership, nearly every farmer in this vicinity belonged to it. Had there never been a Grange here at all, it would have been much easier to organize and maintain one than it is now."[5] Yet had farmers entirely lacked prior experience with organizing, there would have been little material—either organizing skills or the network ties that constitute social capital—to fuel the explosive waves of agrarian organizing that have punctuated American political history.

The earliest of these waves were informed by a political vision that identified farmers as the essential citizens of the republic, a group that could have no special interests in conflict with the general interest of the

Table 5.1 Membership in Major Agricultural Associations, 1875–1930

	1875	1880	1890	1900	1910	1920	1930
U.S.							
Grange	451,605	65,484	71,295	98,675	223,702	231,416	316,462
Alliance	—	39,473	1.053m	—	—	—	—
Union	—	—	—	—	116,504	131,475[a]	77,953[c]
AFBF	—	—	—	—	—	317,108	321,196
California							
Grange	7,488	2,053	1,380	1,604	1,047	1,368	4,553
Union	—	—	—	—	3,930	438[a]	1,243[c]
AFBF	—	—	—	—	—	5,700	20,240
Washington							
Grange	1,142	—	157	402	5,044	8,770	10,453
Union	—	—	—	—	4,489	2,919	393
AFBF	—	—	—	—	—	1,150[b]	866
Wisconsin							
Grange	9,066	2,739	1,040	330	255	861	1,792
Union	—	—	—	—	—	—	5,486
AFBF	—	—	—	—	—	500	2,586
Equity	—	—	—	—	10,000[d]	40,000	?

Sources: Robert L. Tontz, "Memberships of General Farmers' Organizations, United States, 1874–1960," *Agricultural History* 38, no. 3 (1964); Theodore Saloutos, "The Wisconsin Society of Equity," *Agricultural History* 14, no. 2 (1940).

Note: With the exception of the Wisconsin Society of Equity, all membership figures are for *family*, not individual memberships.

a. Total is for 1919.   b. Total is for 1921.   c. Total is for 1933.   d. Total is for 1907.

nation.[6] Through the nineteenth century, the rhetoric of agrarian democracy exerted a powerful influence over many politically active farmers. The State Master of the Washington Grange called for the support of farmers, arguing, "Where else shall we look but to the farmer to counteract the venality and corruption of the slums of our city population, that seem to be so rapidly increasing by the aggregation of alien voters, anarchists and saloon influences?"[7] This link between the well-being of agriculturalists and the good of the entire nation was also made in 1887 by the Worthy Master of the California State Grange:

> One-half of the voters of the United States, united in a common cause and seeking the triumph of a common principle, are capable of accomplishing anything that is just and right. . . . State and national legislation can be so thoroughly controlled by this powerful army of voters that no unjust or burdensome laws can be enacted. The repeal of those of which they complain can be effected, and the passage of such laws as are necessary to the inauguration of an era of *justice* and *equality* secured.[8]

As late as the 1920s, an Iowa paper argued that "agricultural legislation never will be 'class legislation.' It may be unwise legislation which will not enable the farmers to increase their productivity or their buying power and it may be legislation designed to keep certain politicians in power, without benefiting the farmers. But any legislation which actually does benefit the farmers can not be 'class legislation,' for it will benefit the whole nation as well."[9]

Although this rhetoric linking agrarian demands to the national good was extraordinarily robust, by the turn of the century many farmers had become disillusioned with the organizational vehicles it implied: "people's parties" and "producerist" associations. Like their counterparts among workingmen, farmers searched for the unrealized potential of agrarian organizations and for unrecognized opportunities to influence political and economic institutions. The resulting transformation of the organizational repertoire of agrarian activists began as a choice among strategies that had proven of limited success in the nineteenth century: fraternalism, electoral politics, and economic self-organization. Each of these models implied different paths for the realization of agrarian goals: mutuality, third-party action, or efficient management. Although the history of agrarian activism has been told primarily from the perspective of social movements and third parties, a closer look at the organizational development of agrarian associations suggests that farmers' concern for the business of farming was an equally influential factor. Driven by the interaction of organizational failures and a cultural awareness of organizational alternatives, agrarian activists increasingly invested their energy in the administrative control of markets rather than the political control of trusts, speculators, and other exploitative corporations. It is in the extent to which they adopted "business methods," and eventually business politics, that agrarian associations stand apart from other popular political organizations of the period. Ironically, this turn from politics would prove an indirect path to interest group pluralism.

With respect to their initial organizational repertoire, the nation's farmers resembled the workingmen of the late nineteenth century. Both groups drew on the heritage of fraternalism, both oscillated between political and economic strategies, both experimented with the "business methods" developed by their economic oppressors and sought to turn these new models of organization to their own advantage. But the relations of farmers and workers to the opportunity structure of federalism differed significantly. Whereas both the Knights of Labor and the AFL sought to organize workers on a national or even international scale, agrarian organizations tended to be regional, mapping onto the particular crops or conditions of production. So unlike both the major parties and the AFL, in many agrarian associations there was no entrenched eastern leadership to rein in the political and organizational experiments of insurgents from the Midwest and West. The one national organization in which easterners became dominant—the Grange—was, by the 1920s, riven by a regional schism and the eventual expulsion of some radical members from the Pacific Northwest.

The mapping of organizations onto territory was complicated further by the migratory nature of many agrarian associations. In the 1870s, for example, the center of Grange strength was in the Ohio River Valley; by 1890, membership had declined dramatically, and the center of gravity had shifted east, with over 80 percent of Patrons found in Ohio and states to the northeast.[10] One branch of the Farmers Alliance originated in Texas, moving into the South, Midwest, and West before its demise after the presidential elections of 1896. The Northwestern Alliance began in the old Midwest and spread across the northern tier, occasionally competing directly with the Southern Alliance for members. Following the collapse of the Alliance and People's Party, other associations appeared in the organizational vacuum. Advocating cooperative marketing and purchasing, the American Society of Equity and the Farmers' Union developed strongholds in the north central and Great Lakes states. The latter often "built upon the ruins of the Farmers' Alliance. In thousands of communities the locals of the wrecked Alliance still existed as independent units and when the organizers of the Farmers' Union came along, offered them a state and national affiliation and invited them to join another crusade, they eagerly accepted."[11] Reacting to the diagnosis that politics had undermined the Alliance, the Union focused on cooperation as its organizational base. Other associations, however, spread along channels of political mobilization. The Nonpartisan League of 1915–22 originated in North Dakota and moved out through the northern tier of states.[12] Each of these regional waves left pockets of strength—the Grange in Washington, Equity in Wisconsin—which were overlaid by subsequent organizing efforts.[13] So whereas the federated structure of the AFL linked labor locals into international unions, any effort at organizing farmers confronted regional fragmentation, crop-specific concerns, and competition from other associations representing alternative selections from the organizational repertoire. This geographical fragmentation, however, freed state and local organizations from pressure to conform to a single, national policy. Absent an equivalent to the AFL hierarchy, agrarian associations were freer to experiment with forms of economic and political organization.

Even in the absence of a single unifying association, therefore, agrarian discontent threatened the major parties. To the extent that agricultural and manufacturing interests were at odds over issues such as the tariff, factionalism within parties was aggravated. To the extent that agricultural demands went unmet by either major party, the Midwest and West were fertile ground for third-party movements. And, to the extent that farmers learned to hold their representatives responsible for championing their demands in Congress, an interest-based bipartisanship ensued that threatened party discipline in the national legislature.[14] Whereas the near hegemony of the AFL channeled challengers into internal organizational struggles, the absence of an overarching association allowed agrarian discontent to feed successive waves of organizing that overflowed the limits of voluntarism into business enterprise, independent politics, and the increasingly effective practice of interest group politics.

The Grange, the People's Party, and the Cooperative

The organizational history of the nineteenth century is littered with the remnants of agrarian associations. These efforts were punctuated by forays into independent politics. As early as the 1830s, the Association of Farmers, Mechanics, and Other Workingmen pursued an independent political strategy in Massachusetts[15] and it was soon followed by other independent-party movements, sometimes restricted to farmers, sometimes in alliance with workingmen. Still other groups sought to promote the cooperation of farmers as producers and consumers in a market economy. Some of the most successful, notably the Patrons of Husbandry (the Grange), were fraternal societies that organized farmers for social and economic reasons. These experiments left agrarian activists with a number of important legacies: a recognition of the power of markets over their daily lives, a disillusionment with the possibilities of electoral politics, and a growing familiarity with the practices of modern business. Each of these, in turn, would have important consequences for the transformation of agrarian politics.

Selections from this organizational repertoire were shaped by the distinctive character of agriculture in individual states (table 5.2). Representing an earlier wave of settlement, Wisconsin farms were relatively small,

Table 5.2   Agricultural Productivity and Employment, 1900

	Total Value of Farm Product, 1899	Males Employed in Agriculture, 1900	Product per Employee
United States	$4,739,118,752	9,458,194	$501
California	131,690,606	157,504	893
Washington	34,897,495	59,159	589
Wisconsin	157,445,713	261,450	502

Source: U.S. Bureau of the Census, *Abstract of the Twelfth Census* (Washington, D.C.: Government Printing Office, 1900), 88–89.

labor intensive, and diversified. Consequently, the state's farmers were a diverse group, divided between the relatively prosperous who gathered in the State Agricultural Society or the State Dairymen's Association and a more heterogeneous collection of farmers who would join the Grange and, later, the Society of Equity.[16] California presented a striking contrast to Wisconsin. Despite the large role of agriculture within the state's economy, the early dominance of agribusiness squeezed the smaller farmers who filled the ranks of agrarian associations throughout the rest of the nation; more prosperous farmers gathered in the State Agricultural Society. Federal and state policy tended to preserve large Mexican land grants, and public lands were sold rather than used as homesteads to induce settlement—a superfluous goal in light of the flood of migrants to the state's mining districts. These large holdings were reinforced as their owners subsequently sought monopolies over the water rights necessary for farming in much of the state.[17] California's agricultural sector prospered with economies of scale and capital investment, illustrated by the high value of product per employee. These large concerns wielded proportionate political power, securing laws that favored large over small, ranchers over truck farmers and horticulturalists: "[O]wners of the state's 5,000,000 acres of improved rural land in the 1880s paid taxes at a rate eight to ten times greater than those who owned the 21,000,000 acres of unimproved land. Moreover, the small farmers who held 20 percent of the cultivated land paid 75 percent of the total taxes collected on agricultural real estate."[18] Consequently, smaller farmers sought channels of influence that would take advantage of their relatively limited electoral strength.

Washington presents an intermediate case. The state's initial settlement was motivated largely by agrarian concerns; Washington was the "New Eden,"[19] with its eastern counties dominated by wheat farming. These farmers identified with granger and populist concerns over transportation, credit, and international commodity markets. Various "land-grant" railroads had failed to complete their transcontinental lines in the 1870s, so high rates and the extensive lands granted to the railways generated further agrarian discontent.[20] This discontent was aggravated by the price deflation of the 1880s, which was especially threatening to the heavily mortgaged, cash crop–oriented farmers of Washington. But if the eastern counties resembled the single-crop pattern of the Midwest, which left farmers vulnerable to speculators and fluctuations in commodity markets, the western and southern sections were oriented to dairy and fruit production and therefore bore a closer resemblance to the more prosperous agricultural sectors in Wisconsin and California.

These differences in the character of each state's agricultural sector interacted with successive waves of agrarian organizing to produce distinctive patterns of political and economic mobilization. The selective establishment of organizational models, in turn, gave a characteristic accent to agrarian demands, sometimes social, sometimes economic, sometimes political. But although different associations became dominant in different states, all would confront the shortcomings of the nineteenth-century agrarian repertoire as an instrument for influencing a rapidly modernizing economy and polity.

Fraternalism on the Farms

The first obstacle to organizing farmers was their isolation. Not only was it difficult for farmers to gather regularly, the lack of community also led farmers to view their problems in isolation, as "personal troubles" rather than "public issues."[21] Simply by changing the ways that farmers understood their situation, any form of organization could have political consequences: "The advent of the Grange changed the psychological relationship of the farmer to his environment. Farmers met and compared notes; they discovered that their failure to 'get ahead' could not be an individual matter since it was duplicated by the experience of hundreds of others all around them."[22]

The Patrons of Husbandry used the organizational model provided by fraternal societies, specifically the Masons.[23] Emphasizing ritual and moral community, the Grange was dedicated to overcoming the social isolation that left farmers, like Marx's French peasants, as unorganized as potatoes in a sack. Describing this transformation, Sister Roache of Watsonville, California (see fig. 6.2), argued that the Grange "has rendered the farmer and his family intelligent, reasoning beings who use their brains as well as hands. . . . Has made our young men and women speakers, singers and even orators; taught them that priceless gift, the ability to express themselves in public and to preside at public meetings, giving them the same standing socially as when in other professions, and forever rid them of the stigma, clod-hopper, hayseed and mud-sill, so freely and so patronizingly bestowed during their condition of isolation and ignorance before the advent of the Grange."[24] Throughout the 1870s organizers founded new Granges and recruited existing farmers clubs. Over three hundred charters were issued by August 1873, less than four years after the Grange was founded.[25] But when transplanted to a new setting, some elements of the Masonic organizational model—particularly its rejection of partisanship—appeared at odds with the purposes of the men *and* women who were organized.[26]

Like most fraternal orders, the Grange was founded on explicitly nonpolitical terms. But this principle was soon challenged. These efforts to take the Grange into political campaigns and independent-party politics suggest the shortcomings of fraternalism as an organizational model for agrarian groups. Good fellowship, ritual, and solidarity were insufficient responses to the crises and challengers confronted by farmers. In 1873, the Minnesota Grange provided a launching pad for the political career of Ignatius Donnelly. This campaign resulted in the ouster of the State Master. Iowa Grangers helped to establish an Anti-Monopoly Party in the same year, but the state organization declined to ally officially with its creation. In some midwestern states, Grangers secured passage of new railroad regulations.[27] Forays into independent politics took place in other states where the Grange had become established. California Grangers elected a number of their own as delegates to the constitutional convention of 1878, who then actively cooperated with the state's Workingmen's Party.[28] Despite some initial political victories, the Grange rapidly collapsed under the weight of the economic schemes that had been grafted to its fraternal foundation. Cooperative purchasing, marketing, and production schemes failed; national membership plunged from over 450,000 in 1875 to 65,000 in 1880.

This collapse discredited large-scale economic organizing and shifted the geographical composition of the order so as to block any renewed interest in harnessing the Grange to a political strategy. Subsequent efforts to join insurgent politics were resisted by the National Grange as control passed to farmers from the Republican northeast who were at odds with the populist sentiments articulated by independent candidates or, in 1896, by the Democrat William Jennings Bryan. The National Master that year, J. H. Brigham, was a former Republican member of the Ohio legislature, and Ohio was the home state of Republican candidate William McKinley. Brigham had loudly criticized "free silver," had been charged with "trying to deliver the Grange to the Republicans," and, after McKinley's victory, was named secretary of agriculture.[29] Even before the climactic election of 1896, Grangers in the insurgent western states were left to watch as "our members have run off after strange gods. The Alliance and the People's Party movements have crushed out as by a Juggernaut every Grange on our side of the mountains."[30] Just as the international unions and the AFL leadership suppressed local efforts at independent labor politics, the National Grange limited local and regional efforts to form political alliances. Along with the often devastating electoral defeats of Farmers' Alliances and people's parties in the 1890s, the position of the national leadership discredited third parties as a model for political action by members of the Grange.

In reaction, Grange leaders retreated to the fraternal foundations of their organization. But in a social world increasingly organized around models drawn from modern business and bureaucracy, the fraternal model inherited by agrarian groups seemed out of step. Many Grangers defected to other organizations, viewing them as more effective vehicles for securing remedies for their problems. As early as 1891, the Master of the Elk Grove Lodge in California attacked the principle of passive nonpartisanship and pointed to the success of the Farmers Alliance: the Grange's "founders framed her Constitution wisely and well, as best suited to the times, when therein was placed the clause 'Matters political or politic cannot be discussed in the Grange.' But, brothers and sisters, the times have changed, and as if by magic in response to the necessities of the change has sprung into existence a sister organization, composed of tillers of the soil, many being members of the Grange, under the suggestive name, Farmers' Alliance."[31] To survive, however, the California Grange emphasized its original identity as an agrarian fraternal order, resisting temptations to return to large-scale political participation or economic cooperation.[32] To maintain its identity in the face of ongoing change in the economic and social fabric of agrarian life, the Grange clung to its fraternal rituals to integrate new cohorts into the organization. In 1888, members of the Tulare Grange offered a resolution to shorten the ritual work, contending, "Whereas, While we recognize the beauty and im-

pressiveness of our Ritual, we are at the same time convinced that very valuable time is consumed in conferring the degrees of subordinate Granges
upon initiates, to the exclusion of the due consideration of those purposes
for which the Grange exists." Nearly three decades later, the Master of the
Valley Oaks Grange echoed this complaint: "[T]he number and lengths of
our degrees preclude the Grange from keeping in as close touch with the
times as they would be able to do if the ritualistic work was shorter." [33] But
the rituals were largely retained, providing for organizational continuity
in the face of rapid social and economic change, but at the price of forgo-
ing other possible lines of political action.

In the far northwest, however, one state Grange pursued politics; the
cost of this strategy, however, was the expulsion of the State Master by
the National Grange in 1921.[34] First established in the 1870s, the Washington Grange had disappeared altogether and was reestablished in 1889
by organizers from California and Oregon. Reappearing at the moment
of statehood, the Washington Grange's first resolution was explicitly political: "We are opposed to the constitution as framed by the constitutional convention at Olympia . . . an instrument fraught with so much
peril to the public welfare." Despite this opposition, the constitution was
approved, but the Grange continued to be active as a "state-oriented challenger," securing greater funding of rural schools and participating in debates over tax and railroad reform even as the more politically oriented
members left to join the two competing Farmers Alliances. Among those
who remained in the Grange, no doubt, many cast votes in 1896 that
helped to elect a Populist governor and to carry the state for Bryan. And,
as an organization, the Grange offered an important selective incentive
for its members to stay. The state's permissive insurance laws allowed the
formation of a mutual Fire Insurance Association, and "reports from subordinate Granges during the remainder of the nineties noted repeatedly
the influence exerted by the fire insurance company in maintaining membership in the local groups." [35]

Elsewhere in the nation, political engagement was sharply restricted
by the national leadership of the Grange.[36] Consequently, as the scope of
both agricultural markets and governmental regulation increased, those
organizational forms most conducive to *local* solidarity, such as fraternalism, were judged to be inadequate vehicles for political mobilization at
the state and national levels. Even the capacity of fraternal orders to generate local solidarity was limited, since the religious affiliations of many
immigrant farmers precluded joining "secret societies." [37] Yet for all these

limitations, in much of rural American the Grange was "the mother of organizations,"[38] laying a foundation of organizing skills and activist networks for the associations that followed.

From the Alliance to the People's Party: The Dangers of Party Politics

By 1880, the collapse of the Grange had left an organizational vacuum in much of rural America. In some areas, this void was filled by churches, elsewhere by other fraternal orders. Neither of these organizational forms, however, were sufficient to meet the economic and political challenges that confronted farmers. After the defeat of another round of independent-party efforts in the 1880s, a new wave of agrarian organizing began to crest. By the 1890s, the rapid expansion of railroads and the organizational infrastructure of commercial agriculture had placed many farmers in a common position as producers for international commodity markets and, therefore, vulnerable to exploitation by both purchasing agents and railroads. In the South and Midwest, organizing began in an extensive cooperative marketing movement and built toward political mobilization.[39] From this core, both the Southern and Northwestern Alliances sent organizers out to other states. The Southern Alliance began organizing in California in April 1890 and within six months claimed a membership of thirty thousand, with thirty-four county alliances. The Northwestern Alliance had begun organizing in Washington in 1888; the Southern Alliance appeared two years later.[40] As in other states, agrarian organizing led rapidly to a consideration of political involvement.

For farmers inclined to organization, the appearance of the Alliance represented an opportunity for economic cooperation and political engagement, but this opportunity posed two organizational dilemmas. The first was the familiar fear that economic goals required political struggles, but that politics would destroy the organization itself. Echoing concerns voiced by Grangers in both the 1870s and 1890s, the president of the Washington State Alliance argued,

> The moment the Alliance leaves its present organization and rushes wildly into a new political party, with all the antagonistic elements which are continually crowding to the front of the third party movement, . . . [at] that moment, the Alliance will dissolve in the midst of political discord and fanaticism. The Alliance as it now stands is one of the most perfect agricultural organizations ever devised in this country for the speedy and efficient correction of the monster evils which have crept into American politics.[41]

Deeply distrustful of the major parties, Alliancemen first approached politics indirectly. In both California and Washington, the Alliance ini-

tially coexisted with the major parties, influencing their platforms, push-
ing pieces of legislation rather than "forcing their constituents to choose
between an ancient political allegiance and a new class-group allegiance."[42] Yet the major parties were rarely responsive, and Alliances soon
sponsored distinct but closely linked units of a new People's Party as their
own electoral vehicles. As a Texas leader explained, "There is a way to
take part in politics without having it in the order. Call each neighborhood together and organize anti-monopoly leagues . . . and nominate
candidates for office."[43] In 1890 and 1892, populist governors, congressmen, and state representatives were elected in a number of states, and
the organization enjoyed growing membership. Although the leaders of
California's Alliance initially sought to keep the organization out of politics, the success of Alliances elsewhere in the 1890 elections "boosted
the California Alliance's membership and made it more willing to enter
politics."[44] In both California and Washington, Populists gained seats in
the legislature, and the former sent one member of the party to the U.S.
House of Representatives. The Populist candidate for president, James B.
Weaver, drew almost 10 percent of the vote in California and 22 percent
in Washington.[45]

These initial successes were entwined with a second organizational dilemma. If Alliancemen had sought to preserve their agrarian cooperative
associations by spinning off a separate party structure, the party constituted an opportunity that then attracted other political challengers. In the
mountain West, populism took the form of a politicized antimonopolism that linked agrarian discontent to legislative solutions, an expansive
frame that attracted support from workingmen as well as farmers.[46] The
movement built on a blossoming alliance with industrial workers, who,
like many farmers, had grown suspicious of the intentions of both parties
and resented the concessions granted to the wealthy.[47] In California, the
state's Nationalist clubs (the most numerous in the United States) poured
into the People's Party, bringing along not only urban cooperative reformers but some of the socialists who had sought to ally with the reformers
in the national United Labor Party of 1890.[48] In 1894, this alliance elected
Adolph Sutro as mayor of San Francisco following a contest waged
against the railroads and utility monopolies in terms that bore a greater
resemblance to the urban progressivism of the twentieth century than to
the agrarian populism of the 1890s. Once available in the public repertoire, "People's Party" became a vehicle that could be appropriated by a
wide variety of concerns, thereby introducing greater heterogeneity into
the constituency "represented" by the organization and, potentially, more

sources of division among its membership. By 1897, the California Populist Party changed its name to the Industrial Federation; the convention "was reportedly strongly socialistic."[49]

In Washington, the agrarian character of the People's Party was similarly altered by its electoral adventures. The Northwestern Alliance had initially sought to address the grievances of farmers through a combination of cooperative buying plans (rather than the cooperative production or selling), education, and politics. Rather than the recitations and debates that played a prominent role in the "civic education" of the women's clubs and of the Grange, the Alliance promoted contemporary political literature—the works of Weaver, Peffer, Donnelly, Powderly, and Bellamy.[50] The Alliance urged that farmers train themselves to be effective principals with respect to the elected officials who served as their agents. Reform was brought about

> [b]y the ballot-box, by the farmer and laborer taking more interest in governmental affairs; by reading and thinking; by acting honestly with the ballot, casting it according to their own true convictions, and not simply at the instance of a party, so often managed and controlled by corrupt politicians; by selecting the best men for office, men whose character and uprightness of conduct can be vouched by the community in which they live; not men of one idea, but men of broad liberal views, who from an honest conviction, believe all men are equal before the law, and that legislation is for the many and not the few.[51]

Lacking the commitment to individual mastery of public speaking and parliamentary drill that characterized the educational programs of the Grange and the women's clubs, the Alliance quickly overcame any aversion to partisan activity. As early as 1890, the Whitman County Northwestern Alliance had devised a system whereby members were appointed to promote Alliance interests in the primaries and conventions of both parties. "After the conventions had nominated tickets, the County Alliance met and selected a ticket from the two tickets nominated. Then all knew just what the Alliance ticket was."[52] As in California, the move toward third-party action transformed populism from a predominantly agrarian movement. In July 1891, agrarian and labor groups calling themselves a Confederation of Industrial Organizations met at Yakima.[53] In November, the state convention of the Alliance resolved to "stand independent politically." The Alliance's political demands were taken over by the emerging People's Party, whose constituency extended well beyond the farmers. The 1892 elections reflected this alliance; Populist legislators were elected from counties both rich and poor, urban and rural, agricultural and lumber.[54]

At the state and national levels, the People's Party exposed organized farmers to the pressures of both coalition and institutional politics. In California and Washington, the first process generated a set of demands that shared as much with the institutional-reform movements of the Progressive Era as they did with the nineteenth-century agitation for economic and monetary reform. Party platforms incorporated demands for labor legislation, for the initiative and referendum, and for regulation of utilities.[55] But this coalition politics also set in motion a process that undermined the organizational integrity of the People's Party as a vehicle for this broad-based political challenge.[56] The first fissures appeared, not in the presidential politics of 1896, but in the senatorial selections of 1892. As a minority within the state legislatures that made these selections, Populists were immediately caught between the uncompromising independence that members of their own party demanded as a signal of political integrity and the opportunity to strike bargains with other parties. In state after state, the division between "middle of the road" Populists (those who refused to cooperate with either major party) and the legislative logrollers who would be known as "fusionists" by 1896 erupted in battles over the selection of U.S. senators, discrediting Populist representatives and obstructing passage of the party's legislative agenda. In California, two Populists were expelled from the party "for the failure to observe strict party regularity." In Washington, on the twenty-first ballot three Populists switched from supporting one member of their party to another, allowing the election of a Republican on the twenty-eighth ballot. In Illinois, two years earlier, Herman Taubeneck had been elected to the state legislature with the help of the Farmers Mutual Benefit Society (which later amalgamated with the Northwestern Alliance) and had refused to shift his support to a Gold Democrat as part of a bargain for the Democrats' support of an agrarian reformer for senator from South Dakota. His reputation for incorruptibility would secure his subsequent selection as national chairman of the People's Party.[57]

In linking the agrarian Alliances to the model of independent-party politics, therefore, the Populists created a situation in which the strict regularity required by the party model was incompatible with strategic efforts to harness the leverage of a swing constituency in a winner-take-all electoral system. Within the national movement, California Populists interjected the intense concern over entanglements with party that was the legacy of urban labor and reform politics. The "Cator pledge," introduced to the 1892 Omaha convention by a California delegate, required that "no person holding an office or position of any profit, trust or emolument under the Federal or any state or municipal government, including senators, congressmen, and members of the legislatures, state and national, should be eligible to sit or vote in any convention of this party"— a proposal that prefigured the debates that would threaten to split the infant California State Federation of Labor a few years later.[58] Time and again, agrarian activists encountered the dilemma identified by Robert Michels. The interest of a movement's leaders in winning political office leads to differences with movement membership; leaders will craft compromises with established elites in order to secure their own political careers and economic well-being.[59]

In 1896, the candidacy of William Jennings Bryan as the Democratic nominee for president presented this dilemma to Populist leaders in even starker terms. Following much acrimonious debate, the Populists fused with the Democratic Party in an unsuccessful effort to elect the congressman from Nebraska and to reelect Populists who had won state office in 1892 and 1894 with the combined support of Populists and Democrats: "If the People's Party nominated a Populist ticket against both Bryan and McKinley, Populist officeholders in the West were doomed to defeat by a division of their electorate, and they knew it."[60] Fusion, however, did not forestall defeat. Although victories in some states, including Washington, allowed the party to endure for a few years, the crushing defeat of the Populist campaign of 1896 discredited independent agrarian politics as a viable organizational strategy.[61] Promoters of subsequent agrarian associations were quick to announce, "It is not the object of the society to become a political party," and to acknowledge that "[i]n years past the very word 'politics,' as applied to the farmer as a class, has been enough to set every dog in the country howling."[62]

Despite its political defeat, the People's Party left an important legacy to future agrarian associations. Its failure discredited the independent party as an appropriate model for collective action. But in the years prior to 1896, the Populists had articulated a set of agrarian demands for public programs. As the *Seattle Post-Intelligencer* noted rather disparagingly: "The Populist party howled themselves hoarse against 'class legislation' and yet they never fail to support 'class legislation' which seeks to discriminate in favor of farmers by providing that the government shall loan them money at nominal interest on land or Hubbard squashes."[63] This turn toward government intervention marked an important departure in the rhetoric of agrarian democracy that had equated the farmers' interest with the national good,[64] and it presaged the development of strong ties between agrarian organizations and state agencies. But for this relationship to flourish, two conditions had to be met. First, farmers would have to be persuaded that state expansion did not come disproportionately at their expense as property owners and taxpayers; the relation of political mobilization to state finance will be addressed in chapter 7. Second, farmers would have to select an organizational form that mapped onto government capacities for providing benefits.

Self-Organization and Scientific Management

One organizational component common to both the Grange and the Alliance continued to figure prominently in the work of agrarian associations through the end of the nineteenth century and into the twentieth: cooperation. Cooperative efforts offered a way to survive in a market society while avoiding exploitation by railroads, grain speculators, and bankers.[65] By cutting out the middlemen, farmers could control the disposition of their products and establish direct exchanges with their customers, particularly with urban workers. Agricultural cooperatives were, therefore, both a means for more efficient marketing and a potential source of solidarity among the "producing classes," both rural and urban:

> Co-operation comes to the public as a system of industry and commerce . . . offering dividends to the masses instead of profits to the few. Yet in and above all this is a purpose still larger—to unite the people through their needs, to organize purchasing power and productive energy for the control of industry; to eliminate extortion and excessive wastes and expenses; to benefit labor; to associate men and women—young and old—free and self-reliant, for mutual aid and to reinforce the world wide fraternal upward movements for universal peace and Democracy.[66]

The Grange itself had a rather ambivalent attitude toward its business efforts, wary that they might undermine the organization's social and educational functions:

> While I [State Master W. W. Greer] recognize the importance of our educational features, and the necessity of the thorough cultivation of the social side of man's nature, yet I am thoroughly convinced that the Grange movement in California is lacking in some other cohesive power necessary to keep life and activity in our subordinate Granges. While we do not emphasize our business features, yet that little piece of pasteboard called the trade card is silently doing its work.[67]

Lacking the Grange's formal commitment to a noneconomic fraternalism, other agrarian organizations felt no need to apologize for the importance attributed to marketing arrangements. The Southern Alliance, after all, was based on a system of cooperative marketing developed first in Texas. Organized in 1902, the Farmers' Union symbolized its mission as a triangle: "*Education* is the base. The two sides reaching upward to join at the top are *Cooperation* and *Legislation*. The three are held together by a powerful magnet. That magnet is Organization."[68] Despite the failures of many cooperative marketing and purchasing schemes—in addition to the more ambitious utopian communities—there were enough successes to protect the cooperative model from being discredited. The myriad efforts at cooperative organizing among farmers also left rich deposits of experience and technical knowledge. Any veteran agrarian activist was familiar with the Rochdale model imported from England, the differences between cash and credit systems, as well as those among marketing, purchasing, and production cooperatives. This variety helped to insulate the model from specific failures; it was always possible to argue that the particular arrangements, rather than cooperation in general, had been the problem.

Cooperation took two dominant forms, each with distinct orientations toward other political actors. Producer-consumer co-ops tended to strengthen the ties between organized farmers and organized labor. In their efforts to avoid middlemen and speculators, "[B]oth groups have discovered a *practical interest* which may bind them as firmly as the desire for protection bound the manufacturers of the first half of the Nineteenth Century."[69] Producer-marketing co-ops oriented farmers toward the market and the state agencies that regulated transportation and marketing. Like workers, farmers encountered business opposition to their efforts at cooperation. The Alliance cooperatives had been resisted by merchants and denied credit by bankers.[70] Larger efforts at cooperative marketing were attacked with the Sherman antitrust laws. Yet within states, legislatures sometimes facilitated economic self-organization by farmers. In both California and Washington, Grangers were able to form mutual fire insurance companies; a later California cooperative, the California Fruit Exchange, began insuring packing houses in 1902 and, by 1929, carried $15 million in fire insurance.[71] By the second decade of the century, cooperative marketing was also aided through state legislation and the establishment of state marketing boards.[72] But the form of cooperation that dominated in each state was shaped by the balance between the strength of producer-consumer cooperative alliances with organized labor and the openness of the state to cooperative-marketing arrangements. This balance, in turn, was shaped by the character of the agrarian association that came to predominate in each state: the Society of Equity in Wisconsin, the Grange in Washington, and the American Farm Bureau Federation, along with other large marketing cooperatives, in California.

In Wisconsin, the Grange had steadily declined since the 1870s, and organizers from the Northwest Alliance made little headway in the 1890s. Small farmers later turned to a national organization characterized by its managerial tenor, the American Society of Equity. Built up from local organizations into county and then statewide organizations (fig. 5.1), Equity promoted economic rather than political mobilization among farmers. Equity emphasized collaboration among farmers to limit production and fix prices. In addition to sponsoring producer groups, the Wisconsin Society of Equity promoted a vision of social betterment based on control of market relations rather than on thoroughgoing political purification.[73] Instead of supplanting existing associations, a system of "Industrial Cooperation" would coordinate

> direct exchange between farmers' and laborers' organizations and present industries so that all farm products and "union made" labor products can pass directly into the respective consumer's hands without paying one cent of tribute to any intermediary except necessary transportation charges, hence these two classes and the organizations they compose will be at once interested in this new movement and as women will be accepted on the same terms as men, the possibility of a very large membership is at once apparent.[74]

Wisconsin's farmers discovered that their interest in market regulation provided a basis for cross-class alliances. The initial vision of this alliance was framed in the terms of antimonopolism. This rhetoric provided a link between the agrarian association and the Wisconsin's labor movement:

> The trust is the common foe. It is not the labor union that keeps down the price of farm products. It is the trust. It is not the labor union that robs the farmer by its effort to keep wages up. It is the meat trust, the sugar trust, the railway trust, the elevator trust, the farm machinery trust, etc. . . . It is not the labor union and the farmer who are enemies. They have one common enemy—the trust, the monopoly—the capitalistic system.[75]

Yet these intentions did not translate into a solid alliance. At least two efforts were made to sponsor urban cooperative exchanges along with organized labor, but neither prospered.[76] In the meantime, production and marketing cooperatives flourished. By 1920, Frederic C. Howe (by then executive secretary of the Committee on Banking and Credit of the All-American Farmer-Labor Cooperative Congress) observed, "The farm-

Figure 5.1   Wisconson State Equity: Map of Local and County Unions. (Source: *Wisconsin Equity News,* vol. 4, no. 22 [25 March 1912])

ers of Wisconsin own and operate 2,000 cooperative producers' societies. They own 718 cheese factories, 380 creameries, 437 telephone companies, 214 insurance societies, 150 livestock shipping societies, 4 packing plants, 2 laundries, and 7 fruit exchanges."[77] In Wisconsin, cooperation did not provide a firm foundation for an extrapartisan farmer-labor alliance but increasingly reoriented farmers toward the state agencies charged with economic regulation. Farmers' lack of legislative leverage, however, meant that those agencies were both comparatively weak and often less responsive than the governmental entities charged with overseeing industrial conditions in Wisconsin.

In Washington, by comparison, both marketing co-ops and producer-consumer co-ops prospered, the former being particularly prominent in the eastern, grain-growing counties. The first local of the Farmers' Union was established in Waitsburg on 17 April 1907, and the Washington State

Union was founded in 1908, "the first State organization west of the Rocky Mountains." At this time the delegates claimed to represent seven thousand members (compared to the nine thousand claimed by the state Grange in 1909).[78] The Farmers' Union combined a concern for the business aspects of agriculture—markets, mortgages, credit, and commodity speculation—with a commitment to legislative politics. The Union "insisted that the next session of the State Legislature of Washington repeal the law of 1907, which exempted money and money securities from taxation."[79]

Producer-consumer co-ops, however, were far more central to the popular politics of Washington state. Undergirded by a growing system of cooperative marketing that linked agricultural producers to their customers in the cities, the alliance of farmers and organized labor persisted through the Progressive Era and the First World War. Founded by the Grange in 1911, the short-lived Producers and Consumers' Cooperative Company built on the state's tradition of cooperative and utopian organization and strengthened ties between farmers and urban consumers. Numerous cooperative efforts followed, including the Cooperative Food Products Association, which was first sponsored by the butchers' union, but its board of directors was split evenly between labor and farm representatives. Farmers also bought thirty thousand dollars of the cooperative's stock, investing both as individuals and through the Grange and the King County Dairymen's Association.[80] Cooperative marketing in Washington strengthened the alliance between organized labor and the Grange while blocking the development of the state-centered "business" strategies that characterized agrarian organizing in California.

To the south, the Grange lingered on, but changes in California's agricultural sector diminished the appeal of the next organizing waves of the first two decades of the century: the Society of Equity and the Nonpartisan League. Agrarian radicalism flourished in regions dominated by wheat and subject to fluctuation in global markets and exploitation by middlemen and merchants, but wheat had become far less important as California farmers turned toward crop specialization, including fruits and nuts. This tendency changed the economic basis for agrarian organization, facilitating the development of crop-specific marketing cooperatives, extending the business-like orientation toward farming that had long been represented by the "gentleman farmers" of the State Agricultural Society.[81]

The American Farm Bureau Federation quickly surpassed the influence of the Grange, boasting a membership of over ten thousand families in

1920 and twenty-six thousand at its initial peak in 1926. The growing redefinition of the collective interests of farmers as marketers consolidated the constituency for a new state agency, the office of the State Market Director, to "receive and sell for a commission on a self-supporting basis 'agricultural, fishery, dairy and farm products.'"[82] Established in 1915, the State Marketing Commission was directed by a prominent progressive reformer and businessman, Harris Weinstock, whose half brother David Lubin and brother-in-law Aaron Sapiro were influential exporters of the California cooperative model to other regions. Their efforts would eventually contribute to the success of cooperatives in the southern states and the subsequent growth of agrarian influence on that region's politics and congressional delegations.[83] Within California alone, there was ample evidence of the benefits of alliances between state marketing agencies and crop-specific marketing cooperatives; by 1919–20, the California Fruit Growers Exchange—better known by its brand name Sunkist—had a membership of over ten thousand and was shipping $59 million in fruit with an ultimate value to consumers of $166 million.[84] A parallel trajectory from self-organization to farmer-friendly government regulation was evident in managing agricultural pests; the resulting "regulatory network linked fruit growers to powerful state, federal, and academic institutions that had been weak or non-existent before 1880."[85] These developments were reflected in the shifting fortunes of agrarian associations.

Starting with much the same organizational repertoire as their counterparts in Wisconsin, California's farmers traveled a different path in response to distinctive economic conditions and political opportunities. Whereas a sizable portion of Wisconsin farmers remained vulnerable to market fluctuations and held onto lingering suspicions of state agencies that emphasized increased production, California's agricultural sector was more easily organized around the transportation and marketing of crops. These cooperatives then turned to the state, demanding regulatory support and tariff protection. The use of this business model divided producers from consumers and employers from agricultural laborers.[86] But such potential coalition-partners were irrelevant so long as business-minded, middle-class progressives dominated the state government and its agencies.

Through the 1890s and into the Progressive Era, techniques of market organization redefined the comparison of farmers and capitalists. Rather than denouncing large corporations and monopolies, cooperative associations increasingly demanded to be treated on the same terms as the one-time nemeses of the Grangers and populists. Explaining their demand for federal legislation in 1921, "[T]he cooperative producers' organizations point out that what they demand is *merely the same legality* for interstate transactions which, for instance, the large packing concerns, with their numerous branches throughout the country, already enjoy."[87] Consequently, the practices of market competition began to edge out the old rules of fraternal mutuality. The very emphasis of these plans on business organization linked these agrarian associations to the growing influence of corporations through the themes of efficiency and rationality: "There should be but little difference in the organization, control and management of a co-operative business and a corporate business. But there is often a *big* difference and it is this *big* difference that frequently makes a growing success of one and a dwindling failure of the other . . . if a co-operative business is to succeed control must be lodged in a *competent manager,* just as it is in a corporation."[88]

In pursuing business-like methods, agrarian cooperators also stepped away from pure economic self-organization. Recognizing that their enemies were aided by politicians and state agencies, the development of agricultural cooperatives eventually led back to political action.[89] In California, the move by farmers toward a business model combined with state-centered strategies had consequences at both the state and national levels. Within California, the ascendance of business models of agrarian organization and the predominance of large landholdings removed farmers as potential members of any coalition dedicated to broader transformations of the political system. For these business-minded farmers, antipartisanship took the form of nonpartisan ties to state agencies rather than the experimentation with farmer-labor politics of the upper Midwest or the intense commitment to direct democracy evident in Washington state. At the national level, therefore, California agrarians anticipated the move toward state support of agriculture that would find expression in federal policies of the 1920s and 1930s.

By the end of the nineteenth century, farmers had almost exhausted their inherited options for organization. Fraternalism seemed antiquated. Electoral politics, both partisan and independent, had proved spectacularly unsuccessful. To a greater extent than organized labor, which maintained a close but ambivalent relation to parties and legislative politics, agrarian associations (particularly in the western states) had been disappointed by both independent-party politics and "good man in office" efforts to pledge candidates to support specific policies. Self-organization through cooperatives had often been defeated by internal incompetence and the opposition of commercial interests, but aided by state universities and a trio of new organizations—the Farmers' Union, the Society of Equity, and the American Farm Bureau Federation—cooperation endured as an important component of the agrarian repertoire. To this new foundation of "business methods," farmers would harness novel political techniques.

Inventing the Farm Bloc

As vehicles for harnessing agrarian mobilization to political goals, the fraternal order, the independent party, and economic self-organization all had shortcomings. The fraternal model was limited in its ability to recruit new immigrants and hobbled by the combination of an official nonpartisanship with the deeply held partisan loyalties of the membership. As Alliancemen discovered, however, adopting an independent-party model was equally unsatisfactory. The powerfully co-optative, indeed predatory, character of the American party system ripped apart most efforts to construct an independent electoral coalition. Yet despite these defeats, these waves of agrarian mobilization left three important legacies: new practices or mechanisms of electoral accountability, widespread familiarity with models of cooperative organization, and state laws that facilitated cooperative organizing. As Lawrence Goodwyn contends in his analysis of populism, "[M]ass protest requires a high order not only of cultural education and tactical achievement, it requires a high order of *sequential* achievement." [90] The same may be said of organizational innovation and institutionalization, with the caveat that sequences may extend across pulses of protest and mobilization. Activists themselves were one medium of continuity: Grangers became Alliancemen, former populists joined cooperatives. Laws and state agencies were another: the institutional accomplishments of one movement became opportunities for the next. Over the decades from the 1890s through the 1920s, agrarian organizers constructed a new synthesis of these materials that would burst on the national political scene as the "Agricultural Bloc," a landmark in the emergence of interest group politics.

Techniques of Political Accountability

Faced with unrelenting pressures from both markets and legislatures that often favored railroads and middlemen, organized farmers of the late nineteenth century sought alternatives to third-party politics and to pure fraternalism. In the process, they profoundly reconstituted the character of agrarian association. This transformation began with a selective focus on particular elements of the fraternal model. Reflecting its origin in the 1870s, the organizational ideology of the Grange embraced a nineteenth-century image of the farmer as the ideal democratic citizen, informed yet independent in his actions.[91] Thus nonpartisan strategies were more easily accommodated by the Grange than were party models. In 1873, following what would come to be known as "the good man policy," Wisconsin Patrons "sent out comprehensive questionnaires on railroad controls to every candidate for the state legislature," and their political mobilization around these *issues* rather than parties or candidates contributed to the passage of important regulatory legislation.[92] Yet the legislative successes of state Granges were limited. Without the electoral mobilization of farmers, the Grange had little leverage over political decision-makers. Nor could farmers constitute themselves as an effective voting bloc so long as elections were structured as choices between parties rather than policies. This would require both identifying a limited number of policies as "in the farmers' interest," and resocializing farmers to vote as self-interested nonpartisans keyed to these issues—two developments that would require decades of organized effort.

The deliberate effort to refashion agrarian fraternalism to suit political purposes was evident even in relatively conservative organizations such as the California State Grange. Even prior to the Alliance's rapid growth, the state Grange had sought to change the political system. In 1887, the Legislative Committee concluded that "the Patrons of Husbandry will never influence legislation to any great extent, till they elect to the Legislature men as Patrons of Husbandry, and not as Democrats or as Republicans."[93] But farmers were thought to become capable of voting in accordance with their own interests by virtue of belonging to organizations such as the Grange:

> [T]he influence of the Grange simply loosens the bands that bind men to old parties and makes them feel free to choose their own places. This at least places the balance of power in the hands of the Patrons of Husbandry, and if they will be true to their own interests and see to it that only men who are tried and true receive the support of the farmers, then the Grange will have accomplished one of its missions.[94]

Unlike contemporary theorists who link voting behavior to the calculation of individual interests, the members of the California State Grange recognized interest as a collective phenomenon and described the power needed to realize their interests by analogy to business corporations:

[I]t stands us in hand, as Patrons, to study well the lesson which these great corporations that dominate the country are teaching, not only the farmer, but mankind, viz.: That in unity, in intelligent co-operation, there is strength, there is power; but in divided effort, there is weakness, there is disintegration. . . . We must do as the corporations are doing—meet combinations of capital and brains with like combinations; unite heart and hand in intelligent co-operative effort for the accomplishment of the laudable objects so clearly set forth in our declaration of purposes. The farmers have more votes, and more capital in the aggregate, than any other class in the country. Who doubts, if they were united, as the members of the corporations are, and educated to intelligent co-operation, that they could exercise a controlling influence in this Government to-day?[95]

The strategy of uniting to elect good men proved disappointing; even good men demonstrated a dismaying tendency to follow the dictates of their parties or a surreptitiously lined pocket. One common response to this problem was to extract pledges from candidates on specific issues: "See to it that no man is sent to either House of our State Legislature, who will not pledge himself to vote for a Mutual Insurance law." This strategy, however, also brought disappointing results. As the Legislative Committee reported in 1891:

[P]ledges were prepared and submitted to the candidates for legislative offices in favor of the leading measures that had been approved by this Grange. These pledges received the signatures of enough of the candidates who were elected to have effected the object sought if the officers elected had been faithful to those pledges. But they had been nominated by the political party conventions, and in many cases the exigencies of party or the pecuniary interest of the legislator required a breach of faith with the Grange.

Let us learn from this that we must commit the political parties to our measures rather than their instruments. Let us seek to procure the incorporation of our measures into the party platforms.[96]

Despite this recommendation, proposals to influence party platforms and to transform the Grange into an organization commanding a unified bloc of votes were repeatedly defeated during the 1890s.[97] The annual conventions were willing to sponsor a lobbyist, and to have that lobbyist record legislators' votes, but not to publish those voting records in order to influence Grangers' decisions in subsequent elections.[98]

This reluctance stemmed from a particular theory of political representation: if one elected men of good character, one must allow them to follow the dictates of their conscience and not presume to hold them responsible for protecting the special interests of their constituents.[99] This aversion to coordinated electoral action was reinforced by the organizational culture of nineteenth-century fraternal societies, which defined themselves as fundamentally nonpartisan. While the Grange might solicit pledges from political candidates, efforts to dictate the political choices of its own membership were condemned as violations of the central tenets of fraternal organization. At the 1892 convention, the State Master included the following in his official "suggestions for the good of the order":

> Seventh, have a committee of good men at Sacramento, during the coming session of the Legislature, to give information concerning agriculture, and to urge the passage of certain needed and reform legislation.
>
> Eighth, let this body, at this session, examine the merits of the proposed amendments to the State Constitution, to be voted upon this fall, at the general election, and let such action be taken by this body as will inform the farmers of the State what their interest is in this matter.

The first of these suggestions was routinely approved, but the second was rejected by the Committee on the Good of the Order. The convention sided with the committee and against the Master. Thus, the limits of political activity were placed firmly between gathering information and coordinated bloc voting.[100] Even lobbying was suspect. As State Master C. W. Emery proclaimed in 1901, "[W]e must agitate and educate. No measure that the people clamor for persistently and continuously can fail of legislative enactment. Lobbying will not avail. The intelligent exercise of the elective franchise and an enlightened public opinion are our remedies." Lobbying was deemed not only ineffective but illegitimate, insofar as it represented "special interests":

> The farmers of this country who produce so large a proportion of its material wealth and prosperity are vitally interested in both State and National legislation. They do not, however, demand and the Grange, as the representative farmers' organization, does not desire so-called *special legislation* in their behalf. We insist upon the passage of just and equitable laws that shall safe-guard all *legitimate interests,* preventing one from taking advantage of another and guaranteeing to each an equal opportunity for normal development.[101]

Even when a powerful model of organized political action was available, the Grange was unwilling to pursue this strategy; the model of the lobby was condemned by prevailing logics of appropriateness. Constrained by a distaste for "class legislation," the nonpartisan ideology of fraternalism, and the partisan loyalties of its members,[102] the California

State Grange failed to craft an acceptable organizational strategy for legislative action but turned instead to state agencies. In 1901, the annual session "urgently request[ed] of his Excellency, Hon. Henry T. Gage, that in making appointments to said Board [of the State Agricultural Society] he appoint only men engaged in practical agriculture, representing the various branches, of known sympathy with her producing classes."[103] By securing the appointment of "public-spirited" practical farmers, the Grange hoped to paper over the divide between the legitimate representation of interest and the illegitimate power of special interests. Yet this arrangement left organized farmers dependent on the goodwill and promises of the appointee; it abjured all possibility of using mechanisms of electoral accountability to influence these "farmers in government."

This sequence of political learning was repeated in state after state. With the defeat of efforts at third-party politics and the increasing turn to "business methods" in their routine practices, most general farm organizations increasingly adopted a more thoroughgoing nonpartisanship. Initially the emphasis was placed on "electing good men" rather than legislation or implementation. Agrarian activists attacked party politicians in rhetoric almost identical to that used by leaders of organized labor:

> I have begged, I have plead, I have prayed in local and National Conventions for the delegates to elect the proper men to office. The same qualities of voting for a man because he has an oily grin, or because he comes from your part of the country, of which I have already spoken, operate to boost incompetents, and sometimes scheming rascals, into office. Until we get rid of this vicious habit, all of our enthusiasm is likely to be spent in vain.[104]

The "vicious habit" of partisan politics could be replaced by either extrapartisan direct democracy or nonpartisan lobbying (whether of parties, legislatures, or agencies). Both methods required that groups first define an "interest" or position with respect to specific policies and, second, demonstrate that the demands of the organization represented the preference of a voting constituency. The constellation of organizational and institutional changes implied by this approach are evident in the resolutions adopted by the 1905 convention of the Farmers' Union, then centered in Texas and adjacent states: "the banning of 'partisan' political discussions in Union meetings, the establishment of a lobby at the State capitol, cooperation with trade unions, and promotion of laws for pure food control, an improved State department of agriculture, better facilities for the State agricultural college, and better roads."[105] In these demands, the outlines of interest group politics are clear: the rejection of partisanship; the establishment of ties to the legislature, other pressure groups, and state agencies; and the articulation of specific demands to be met by new laws, public spending, or the strengthening of state agencies. Yet one after another, agrarian organizations provide ample evidence of the "unnaturalness" of interest group politics; voters had to be educated, cajoled, and conditioned to "vote their interest" rather than their party.

The Wisconsin Society of Equity, for example, was hobbled by a postpopulist aversion to political involvement by agrarian associations. Although individual farmer-politicians and farm papers had long made endorsements, association leaders hesitated to commit their organizations to candidates: "In 1908, the *Wisconsin Equity News* commented that, although the organization should not dabble in politics, the members *as individuals* should not hesitate to express their preferences." [106] But, as many other associations had discovered, reticence in mobilizing the membership resulted in political disappointment. Frustrated in 1909 by the failure of the legislature to appropriate the funds needed to complete a state-owned binder-twine plant, Equity moved toward a more active, issue-based engagement with the Republican Party, securing a binder-twine plank in its 1910 platform and sending out a questionnaire to candidates. The progressive governor, Francis McGovern, supported many Equity demands and appointed its members to state commissions. [107] But even this string of successes did not overcome the association's aversion to politics. Offering the reassurance "Politics: Don't Get Frightened," the officers of the Equity evenhandedly published the platforms of all three state parties and urged farmers to "Ask Your Candidate for Congress" where he stood on a series of issues ranging from the parcel post through direct democracy to government ownership of utilities. [108] In a few cases, the Equity paper published a roll call of the vote on bills of essential interest to farmers, but this information was followed with the weak admonition to "keep the above list for future reference." [109] But this advice was not sufficient. As the editor of the *Equity News* observed:

> As is usual, the undesirable legislation emanated from city representatives backed by Big Business, Special Interests and Corrupt Influences. It was they, too, who were able to kill good legislation proposed by others and designed to curb evil or to really benefit and improve the condition of our citizenship. This condition will remain just as long as the voters in the country and the smaller towns permit "the other fellows"—be they brewers, saloon men, sportsmen, businessmen, lumbermen or extensive landowners,—to select your representatives. [110]

Despite their repeated advice to elect "good men," the leaders of Equity failed to mobilize their members as an effective electoral bloc. In 1916, the Equity paper went so far as to print a form under the heading "Who Do You Want for Governor?" Respondents were asked to "record my first and second choice as follows and circulate nomination papers if enough of us can agree upon one man to make it worth while." This request generated little interest, and, seven months later, the political advice of Equity consisted of no more than the statement that "[t]he Editor, personally, knows the following candidates and can vouch for their reliability." More than one candidate for some offices was deemed reliable; other offices had no guaranteed candidates.[111] Whereas labor unions in many states widely publicized the voting records of representatives in order to mobilize voters in direct response to their legislative interests, the *Equity News* cautioned,

> It is not safe to depend upon those out of office, wanting to get in, for your information nor upon newspapers that are recognized as partisan or that are controlled by big business, brewers or the "advertising agent." Official data is available and should be used. A letter of inquiry to any state department should bring a courteous reply with correct information on any question asked.[112]

Although the triumph of Wisconsin progressivism had come and gone by this point, many farmers had yet to find a method for securing legislation. One speaker at the annual Wisconsin Equity convention lamented this failure: "The American farmer, and the Wisconsin farmer in particular, has had very little legislation in comparison with what the other great interests of Wisconsin have received. I sometimes think that we are to blame ourselves, because we have not asked it. There is an old saying—'ask and ye shall receive.'"[113] Because Wisconsin's organized farmers had not learned to define their demands in terms of specific legislation and to press them effectively, their legislative harvest was comparatively meager.

The California State Grange displayed a similar reticence with regard to politics. During the years following 1910, the height of progressivism in California, the convention proceedings say little about electoral or even legislative politics. Instead, reports of the local Grange chapters are filled with mentions of meetings held with county supervisors, school boards, and city councils. The establishment of political relations unmediated by party structures extended to the state government and its institutions, particularly to the University of California and its agricultural experiment

stations.[114] While educational institutions provided an initial target for
the new nonpartisan politics, this strategy was soon extended to other
state agencies and officials. The Sebastopol Grange reported, "At a get-
together meeting, which we held a short time ago, we had our State Senator, also both of our Assemblymen, who all gave us very interesting and
instructive talks." The Tulare Grange fought the university's efforts to
close a local agricultural experiment station in 1905 and won both a
hearing before the regents and an additional four years of operation in
their district.[115]

Among farmers, as among organized labor, Washington state provides
a telling contrast. Parallel to the efforts of other members of the state's
encompassing reform coalition, the Grange developed an issue-oriented
approach to the election of state senators and representatives. The Legislative Committee of the State Grange was to submit a questionnaire to
each candidate that included very specific queries concerning the establishment and powers of a state railroad commission, proposed changes in
the system of taxation (including a mortgage tax law that would shift the
incidence of taxation from the debt-ridden farmers to their creditors), the
administration of state land, woman suffrage, candidates for U.S. Senate,
and the general inquiry: "In any legislation in which the interest of the
farmers and some other interest comes into conflict, which interest would
you favor?" Having distributed this questionnaire, "[T]he Committee
shall have the answers printed and distribute them among Masters of subordinate Granges throughout this jurisdiction."[116] In this friends-and-
enemies strategy, preelection pledges were not initially supplemented with
reports of roll-call votes. Furthermore, the demands were primarily negative: the state government should *stop* taxing the farmers unfairly and
granting unfair privileges to corporations, especially railroads. Into the
second decade of the century, there is little sense that the farmers were
organized as an interest group to demand specific benefits or state services
for themselves. Paradoxically, the Grangers' emphasis on equal treatment
by the state limited farmers' ability to pursue a more equitable system
of taxation and state services: "Grangers' insistence upon equality and
uniformity, while carried to a point which demanded that bonds, mortgages, notes and credits should be treated as personal property, still
seemed to blind them to limitations inherent in the general property tax
and the possibility that other types of taxation might lend themselves to
the equity which they actually endorsed."[117]

The promise of legislative strategies declined markedly after the death
of Governor John Rogers in 1901 and the resurgence of conservatives

within the Republican Party. Direct democracy provided the issue around which farmers, and other reform forces, rallied, and State Master C. B. Kegley "urged cooperation with all reform groups and proposed the establishment of a committee to work with the Washington State Federation of Labor to secure legislation of mutual interest."[118] The Grange had endorsed direct legislation in 1893, and proposals for the direct election of senators, initiative and referendum, and a simplified procedure for constitutional amendments had been introduced in—and defeated by—the 1897 legislature.[119] In 1900, the Grange used nonpartisan methods to work for the initiative and referendum, interviewing candidates and asking them to pledge their support to direct democracy.[120] The first step in this direction, the passage of a direct-primary law in 1907, was led by a reform group that grew out of Seattle municipal politics.[121] But a direct-primary law offered few opportunities for a nonpartisan organization.[122] The results of the first direct primary in 1908 also disappointed reformers, strengthening calls for the initiative and referendum. But bills to establish direct democracy failed in both 1907 and 1909: "Kegley was sure that the 'saloon power' defeated the proposal in 1909, and he urged the Grangers to drive the saloon out of politics and to redouble their efforts to secure the direct legislation amendment."[123] Republican Governor Hay condemned the proposed reforms: "There are those who advocate a return to a system that a race outgrew as it emerged from barbarism. . . . They would have us who are in the midst of a highly organized civilization, full of distractions and requiring the closest application of time and talent to a wide variety of interests, attempt to govern ourselves with a system that met the needs of a simple, pastoral, and barbaric age."[124]

The "barbarism" of the age lay in its refusal to respect the indirection of party-dominated representative government. In Washington state, this refusal was particularly stark, but elsewhere farmers also joined in the effort to construct new channels of political influence that would link popular concerns more directly to policy outcomes. Before agrarian interests could be linked to pressure group strategies, however, one final difficulty had to be overcome. Although national associations such as the Grange and the Alliance had built on the general identity of "farmers" and proceeded as if all farmers shared a set of political concerns, general farm organizations had repeatedly foundered on sectional differences and crop-specific demands. In order to emerge as an effective pressure group, therefore, farmers required associations that either embodied these more specific concerns or were capable of brokering deals among sections and across crops.

Finding a Good Side to State Government

Farmers' embrace of "business" as a model underscores the importance of distinguishing organizational forms from political preferences. In adopting "business methods," agrarian associations were not agreeing with the political preferences of big business but rather promoting their demands in the same manner as businessmen did,[125] demanding specific legislative actions to benefit a constituency defined by its economic position. Indeed, agrarian demands for the expansion of state intervention and regulation were frequently opposed by business. Although in retrospect these reforms may appear as beneficial rationalizations of capitalism, to credit them to industrial rather than agricultural efforts[126] misses the distinctive organizational and strategic innovations made by agrarian activists. Unlike business groups, agrarian "interests" were linked to large constituencies of voters, representing a challenge to the *electoral* bases of politics that far exceeded that of comparable business associations. Thus, the adoption of business methods, combined with the weakening of partisan loyalty among farmers, led eventually to alliances between state agencies and the agrarian pioneers of interest group politics.

These political strategies were complemented by the associational benefits of adopting "business" as a model. The enforcement of regular financial contributions from members both defined a constituency and facilitated the organizational centralization that would allow associations to speak with a single voice on policy issues. Increased organizational capacity also allowed the campaigns of public education and voter mobilization that were needed to persuade legislators to attend to the demands of agrarian pressure groups.[127] The establishment of good management and clear lines of hierarchy was used to explain the success of some agricultural associations and the failure of others. As a supporter of the Farm Bureau reflected on earlier organizations,

> With such an excellent start it is rather difficult to understand just why the Alliance failed so completely within a few years thereafter. One clue is given, however, in the treasurer's report for 1890. The entire gross receipts for the year were $13,530.55 and of this only $11,231.27 were from membership fees. And this at a time when more than a million farmers were in some way or other "affiliated" with the Alliance! At five cents each—the amount set aside for the national organization—this should have amounted

to not less than $50,000.00. The Alliance was not a closely organized, business-like group.[128]

Once cooperatives (and federations of cooperatives) began to edge out general farm organizations, new opportunities for political action came within reach. These opportunities differed from those afforded organized labor and stemmed from agriculture's central place in national policy. The U.S. Department of Agriculture had attained cabinet status in 1889, and between 1900 and 1915 its budget increased over 550 percent (compared to 43 percent for total federal spending).[129] In contrast, organized labor had called for a federal agency since the Civil War, but its demands were met only with the establishment of the Bureau of Labor Statistics in 1888, and a joint Department of Labor and Commerce in 1903; only in 1913 was a separate Department of Labor established.[130] At the level of state government, the presence of land-grant colleges and their extension services represented further opportunities for agrarian groups to secure specific benefits from public agencies.[131] Initially, these opportunities were perceived as a mixed blessing. Although many had benefited from government grants in the form of homesteads, for decades farmers had argued over proposals to invest public funds in the promotion of agricultural productivity. The application of scientific and business techniques to agricultural marketing divided the "gentlemen farmers" from the less affluent remainder who comprised the membership of the Grange, the Alliance, and the Society of Equity. Through the nineteenth century, these two groups could be found opposing one another in many states, gentlemen farmers advocating "scientific farming" to increase production, the rest calling for cooperative marketing, limited production, and the regulation of predatory corporations such as the railroads and grain elevators.[132] Wealthy farmers often belonged to state-subsidized agricultural societies with close ties to the agricultural colleges, while state Granges were often hostile to the public universities, which appeared to have subverted the original purpose of the land-grant colleges.[133]

Grounded in the suspicion that government programs were used to benefit classes other than needy or worthy agriculturalists, this hostility toward the land-grant universities and other state agricultural agencies was exacerbated by farmers' role as taxpayers. In an era when property rather than income was the primary object of taxation,[134] farmers believed that they bore a disproportionate share of the financial burden of government.[135] Consequently, they often opposed any institutional expansion, even if it promised some benefit. California Grangers voiced their complaints in both fiscal and moral terms: "[I]t is an imposition and a fraud to make the people of this State support a State Viticultural Commission, and that the tax we are compelled to pay for that purpose is an extortion forced upon us by the liquor traffic."[136] One California farmer expressed his opposition in verse:

> Oh, dear, what can the matter be,
> Dear, dear, what can the matter be,
> Oh, dear, what can the matter be,
>   That causes taxpayers to swear?
> The candidates promise reduction in taxes,
> And not to help any in grinding their axes,
> But when they're elected the sum of the fact is
>   They still make the taxpayer swear. . . .
>
>   . . . .
>
> Their platform is only a pint of molasses,
> Made up for the purpose of catching the masses
> Who swallow it down like a great lot of asses,
>   And still the taxpayers swear.
> They resolve and resolve that *they* will never do it,
> And resolve if *they* do that *they all* will rue it,
> Drive us to the polls, we the least evil choose it,
>   And still the taxpayers swear.
>
> Now, how will this end, oh, tell me, ye sages,
> You've made it a study for all the past ages,
> Oh when will officials be content with their wages
>   And cease to make taxpayers swear?
> "When you, my kind friend, put a stop to your whining,
> Regardless of party, join forces in finding
> True men to serve whose oath will be binding,
>   Then no more will taxpayers swear."[137]

Recognizing that both a clarification of taxpayers' interests and rejection of party would be required to remedy the situation, this songster captured an important strain of resentment against the state as a fiscal burden rather than as a source of benefits. In 1889, Grangers in Washington used similar arguments to oppose the proposed state constitution:

> First. It provides for more offices than the public service requires, and it also makes provision for the creation of offices by the courts and legislature that are uncalled for and unnecessary.

Second. The salaries are fixed too high, with no provision for a reduction of the same, but in nearly every case it provides for an increase.

Third. This being the case, the result will be an office-seeking class, the most worthless class than can exist. It will also foster machine politics of the most corrupt and offensive character.

Fourth. It is calculated to encourage extravagance in the expenses of the legislative Assembly, and also in all its appropriations, and thus to grievously overburden an overtaxed people.[138]

Following the Populist campaigns of the 1890s, such consistent opposition to the development of state capacities was less frequent. In some states, taxation was shifted at least partially from property to income or business activity. In 1905, California introduced a system in which property taxes supported city and county governments while the state relied on taxes on utility companies; political demands for an equalization of rates between the two systems generated large revenues for the state treasury. Wisconsin introduced personal and corporate income taxes in 1911; with progressive rates and an offset for property taxes, farmers were partially relieved of the costs of state government. In addition, the popular discovery that "business corrupts politics"[139] (or at least received disproportionate benefits from the public purse) weakened farmers' normative objections to "class legislation" for agriculture, putting a broad array of organizations in a position to demand new programs from state agencies and universities. But changing desires are rarely sufficient to produce changes in policy. Those changes would arise from the development of new forms of agricultural organization that facilitated the articulation of blocs of votes with legislative demands.

Trajectories of Agrarian Organization: California, Wisconsin, and Washington

After the collapse of the Grange in the 1880s and the People's Party in the 1890s, agrarian organizing was largely freed from the constraints of a single dominant national organization. Unlike organized labor, where state-level associations had to maneuver within and against the common framework of the AFL and the international unions, agrarian association took a distinctive form in each state, thereby creating different opportunities for political participation and coalition building.

In Washington state, the Grange endured as the dominant agrarian association, providing an organizational bridge between the producerist politics of the nineteenth century and the farmer-labor alliances of the

1920s. This pattern was complemented by the enduring influence of the Knights of Labor and the openness to industrial unionism that characterized the state's labor movement. This model of organization included an antipartisan, at times anti-statist, orientation. Washington's farmers repeatedly went to the polls demanding government by direct democracy rather than party politics. Fighting constant political battles over the basic nature of government institutions, the organized farmers in Washington embraced a broad political agenda, encompassing a reform platform endorsed by many other groups. With the lines of conflict drawn between party politicians on one side and reformers on the other, there was little chance of institutional concessions to farmers that might provide the starting point for an alliance between agrarian activists and state bureaucrats. By the end of the Progressive Era, agrarian associations elsewhere in the nation were more likely to demand new state subsidies and regulations than to call for a thorough revision of the political system. But by developing direct forms of cooperation with labor and consumer groups, the Washington Grange avoided "capture" by state agencies and remained available to join in the state's volatile electoral politics.

In Wisconsin, by contrast, the decline of the Grange and the absence of much populist organizing activity in the 1890s left many farmers available for mobilization through the party system. The emergence of a reform faction within the Republican Party in the 1890s—led first by dairy farmer and governor W. D. Hoard and then by Robert La Follette—provided an alternative to independent agrarian organization.[140] By 1900, the electoral triumphs of progressive Republicans created an opportunity for organized farmers to establish alliances with reformers. But farmers lacked the coordinated electoral strength that allowed unionists to demand the creation of an independent agency responsible for labor policy, the Industrial Commission, and then to forge a strong alliance with the agency's staff. Although farmers became increasingly appreciative of academic reformers and the benefits of the university, they were unable to overcome a tradition of nonpartisanship to mobilize demands for a more favorable agricultural policy on the part of the state. Consequently, agrarian grievances endured to fuel a movement into independent farmer-labor electoral politics in the 1920s.

The break between nineteenth- and twentieth-century models of agrarian organization was sharpest in California. Even in its decline, the state Grange increasingly restricted its electoral demands but looked toward state agencies for solutions. Rather than continuing to claim generalized political power as a "class" with more votes and capital than any other in the country, the California Grange emphasized the self-organization of agriculture through cooperative efforts and adopted a strategy of making specific claims on state agencies and elected officials. These legislative accomplishments prepared the way for the formation of numerous cooperative-marketing associations that soon dwarfed the remnants of general agrarian associations. These crop-specific organizations then made crop-specific demands on elected officials. With the establishment of new agricultural agencies, even staunch opponents of "the interests" could be transformed into champions of "agricultural interests." Campaigning for reelection to the U.S. Senate in 1922, former governor Hiram Johnson was praised (and criticized) "for his services at Washington to the California prune, the California almond, the lemon, the walnut, the peach, the pear, and the bean. . . . One major reason why Johnson will be reelected is his success in getting for California landowners a federal license to raid American breakfast tables and sideboards."[141]

In all three states, agrarian associations illustrate the interorganizational character of political change during this period. Rather than playing itself out within the recognized boundaries of the formal politics, this process of reorganization was a reaction to the spread of a new form of economic organization—the modern corporation—and its establishment of new relations to the existing parties. This relationship had helped to produce the much-maligned political machine, particularly its variant in western states, where corporate funds were a more reliable source of influence than the electoral mobilization of immigrant groups. Frustrated by this turn of events, agrarian groups sought alternatives to the parties as vehicles for political activity and, in the process, drew upon their known repertoire of forms of social organization. As the model of "business methods" for farming became increasingly prominent, the agrarian demands narrowed in scope and called for the same sorts of privileges and regulations that state agencies had long extended toward industrial corporations.

Farmers were not alone in this diminution of political ambition. Labor unions no longer called for a workers' democracy, but for the extension of workmen's compensation to cover occupational diseases. Women did not look for the purification of politics but for the establishment of playgrounds and the passage of child labor laws. Across a wide range of social movements, sweeping demands for social reform were replaced by specific demands for state action. Contrary to the heritage of Populism and other radical agrarian movements, organizers recognized—with pride—that organization could also have profoundly conservative effects:

And this brings me around to the meat in the kernel. If the farmer is permanently organized into helpful bodies he at last becomes conservative. The flames of sudden anger, righteous anger, too, very often, do not come upon him. He works steadily and soberly to right his wrongs, to better his condition, and to accomplish his ends. He realizes that swift and burning anger is a waste, and that it does not always reach the right object. He comes to lean upon the matured and sound judgement of his leaders. His natural suspicion of everything and everybody is allayed. He comes to know that there are other men with wrongs as deep as his, who move slowly, surely, without passion, and inexorably toward definite reforms. Organization becomes his balance wheel, for he knows that the mass can reach what the individual cannot.[142]

But, despite the repeated praise of agricultural cooperation, farmers' associations also learned that self-organization was not enough. For business methods to be successful, a cooperative state government was needed, and this *political* cooperation depended on the effective mobilization of farmers' electoral power in support of their interests. During the Progressive Era, agrarian associations stumbled repeatedly over this requirement. Only in the 1920s would commentators begin to note the proliferation of "blocs," both in Congress and in state legislatures, with the congressional "Agricultural Bloc" leading the way (see chap. 8). The appearance of blocs depended on overcoming the traditional ideological basis for agrarian politics: the equation of the farmers' interests with the common good. But this transformation of the legitimate basis for representation did not come solely from within the agrarian movements. Instead, this revaluation of political participation was largely the work of those traditionally excluded from party politics and hence protected from suspicion of corrupt practices and illegitimate lobbying: women's groups. While the internal development of agrarian organization, with its increased emphasis on business methods, helped to identify the "special interests" of farmers, political mobilization on behalf of these interests depended upon a much broader transformation of the terms of political participation.

SIX

Politics without Party: The Organizational
Accomplishments of Disenfranchised Women

> Amid tense excitement the roll call by States was ordered
> on the minority report. And now something else never
> before seen in a party convention happened. The women
> with the yellow ribbons produced roll-call forms and be-
> gan jotting down each vote as it was cast. Said the New
> York *Times:* "The sight of them had a most unnerving
> effect upon the delegates. It was like the French conven-
> tion of the Revolution, gallery ruled, and the women
> with the roll-call blanks, noting the way they voted, sug-
> gested the knitting women of the Reign of Terror."
>
> Carrie Chapman Catt and Nettie Rogers Shuler,
> *Woman Suffrage and Politics*

If the party system suppressed the grievances of many organized workingmen and farmers, for women it did so doubly. Reforming the parties
or developing nonpartisan techniques meant little so long as women
lacked the primary currency of political life: the vote. But to gain the vote,
women had to displace the profoundly fraternal models upon which the
parties themselves had been constructed. As women sought new models
for organized action, they disrupted the mapping of masculine and feminine onto public and private, onto citizen and dependent, thereby undermining established logics of appropriateness. Consequently, the *New
York Times* correspondent at the Democratic convention of 1916 could
be reminded of the Terror of the French Revolution at the same moment
that he described middle- and upper-class women engaged in the otherwise conventional progressive activity of recording a vote, gathering information to be fed into the genteel machinery of political education and
public opinion. The juxtaposition of images is comic, but the incongruity
should not obscure the puzzle it presents. How were American women
able to secure a place within the formerly masculine political sphere?
How did their actions help to define the emerging rules and techniques

184

of a new style of politics in the United States? What do these efforts tell us more generally about the possibilities and processes of institutional change?

These questions are complicated by the fact that much of the "woman movement" adopted seemingly conservative strategies and organizational models. Describing the successful Washington suffrage campaign of 1910, suffragist Emma Smith DeVoe explained, "We worked for our vote in womanly ways, for we weren't men and we didn't want to be men, therefore, we didn't propose to try to get our vote in the way that men would."[1] The use of organizational forms linked to traditional understandings of feminine virtue allowed women to secure an initial public presence. But by relying on forms that invoked norms of difference between men and women, these strategies also created obstacles for women who sought to establish themselves as regular political actors alongside the representatives of business, labor, and agriculture. To move from public service to political action, the middle- and upper-class women who constituted the woman movement increasingly adopted organizational forms less linked to feminine identities than were the philanthropies and reform associations of the late nineteenth century. By gradually adopting the less feminine but also nonpolitical methods associated with business and education, women activists of the early twentieth century made an oblique entrance into American politics.

Operating from outside the world of electoral politics, the innovations and strategies of women's associations had a more general significance for all those who sought to change the party system. Women attacked the fraternal world of nineteenth-century American politics only to find their extrapartisan strategies adopted by antiparty renegades of the opposite sex. As the clubwomen who organized a San Francisco luncheon and lecture series proudly claimed, "[T]he attendance at these luncheons averages larger than at any series ever given in San Francisco. The fact that the Appellate Court adjourned for the La Follette luncheon, that a group of men came from San Diego and that there are always a great many nonmembers at the luncheons and dinners, shows a widespread interest in the programs."[2] Careful to avoid expressions of partisanship so long as women lacked the vote, women's organizations were far less ambivalent in their commitment to nonpartisan and extrapartisan methods than were contemporary associations of workers, farmers, or male reformers. Lacking the aversion to dependency that informed the political visions of many of their male counterparts, women activists were also more open to state regulation and sustained cooperation with government agencies. Programs such as free kindergartens, juvenile courts, probation officers, and the support of single mothers were often established as experimental programs funded by clubwomen and then taken over by public agencies (whose staff frequently included former volunteers).[3] Laws regulating maximum hours and minimum wages for women paved the way for more active state intervention through economic regulation. Because women had long been excluded from the realm of contract, programs advocated by and for women could set important precedents for government action.

In attacking the explicitly masculine world of partisanship, familiar feminine forms of organizations were regularly criticized: "Philanthropic work is not new to women. The woman's club as a means of recreation, intellectual exercise, and growth is a new feature. It seems best to keep the ideas distinct."[4] Records of women's associations document sustained debates over organizational methods, a collective search for models that could define women's common concerns and effectively articulate them with public and political institutions. Lacking a legitimate model for political participation, women of the late nineteenth century provide a clear example of the impact of available organizational models on the development of strategies and techniques.[5] Women mimicked modern bureaucracies and firms by substituting cash and accounting for personal service while introducing "departmental" forms to provide for the efficient division of labor within clubs that had been seen as intimate communities. They took the extraelectoral paths of legislative influence used by corporations as exemplars for the development of a "lobby" suited to their needs as a disenfranchised group. Lacking access to party organizations, women constructed cooperative ties between their own organizations and newly created state agencies in the provision of social services.

Viewed from this perspective, the enfranchisement of women and the creation of new capacities for state intervention are not separate problems. Both contributed to the elaboration and institutionalization of a new model of political influence. This model combined the deployment of expertise and public opinion,[6] the tactics of legislative lobbying and administrative regulation, as well as the electoral threat of soon-to-be enfranchised women. Out of these processes of organization and counterorganization, a new kind of polity emerged: lobbying was legitimated, the politics of education was perfected and gradually shaped into a recognizably modern politics of public opinion and advertising. In the process, however, the explicitly gendered symbols and practices of nineteenth-century politics faded, and gender became a semicovert category of public order, something to be rediscovered by later generations of feminist scholars.[7]

But the distinctive organizational forms and strategies adopted by women's associations cannot fully account for their comparatively large policy victories and subsequent disappearance as a major political force. If the logics of appropriateness that linked gender to organizational forms distinguished women's groups from organized labor and farmers, so did the political opportunity structure that they confronted. Prevailing logics of appropriateness censured women for acting *as if* they were a party, just as the law barred them from pursuing electoral strategies. This limitation of their organizational repertoire combined with blocked opportunities to mobilize through formal political institutions sharply distinguished the trajectory of women's associations from those of labor and agrarian groups. Whereas the latter spent much energy trying to find alternative vehicles for electoral action, women invented alternatives to electoral politics, if often only as a means of gaining the vote for themselves.

Gender and Political Identity

Since the nation's founding, American women were barred from political participation by a dense web of informal customs and formal laws that allowed the occasional property-holding widow to vote on a local bond or tax issue. Only the passage of the Fourteenth Amendment to the Constitution of the United States after the Civil War codified the vote as the exclusive prerogative of adult men.[8] This formal exclusion was reinforced by a rich network of political organization. Insofar as turn-of-the-century political mobilization built on the fraternal organizations and workplace identities of nineteenth-century America, it perpetuated that period's distinctively male and female political cultures.[9] While some organizations embraced moral issues of concern to women, and occasionally even allowed women to join, in all cases the political organization of men at the end of the nineteenth century powerfully shaped the participation of women.

In some cases, this led women to reject formal organization. Informed by a hostility to organized religion and government inherited from the abolitionist movement,[10] some activists carried "no-organizationism" into other political causes. Among Spiritualists, who included many leading suffragists and reformers, some "compared organizations to Chinese foot binding, and Lucy Stone said she 'had had enough of thumb-screws and soul screws never to wish to be placed under them again.' They all used religious associations as examples of the oppression resulting from organization."[11] Without fully rejecting formal organization, mainstream women's groups also watched for symptoms of the wrong kind of organization. Writing "Helps and Hindrances in the Organized Work of Women," prominent clubwoman Mrs. Croly argued:

> Haste, publicity, personal ambition, and the willingness to use unworthy means to accomplish personal ends, are all foes of club life, but if I were to state what seems to me to be the great hindrance of all to club life and growth, it would be the employment of political methods, of political machinery and wire-pulling to bring about results. Politics can never be purified until its methods are changed, while its introduction into our club life subverts the whole intention and aims of club organization.[12]

The challenge was to devise methods of organization that would appeal to women yet not corrupt or oppress them.

Opening her massive overview of the women's club movement in the United States, "Jennie June" Croly proclaimed, "When the history of the nineteenth century comes to be written, women will appear as organizers, and leaders of great organized movements among their own sex for the first time in the history of the world."[13] In this endeavor, women activists drew on familiar yet nonpolitical models from their organizational repertoire. Women's models of political action derived from their history of public participation: the revivalism of the Jacksonian era was echoed in the fervent calls for reform made by the Woman's Christian Temperance Union; social reformers drew on a legacy of friendly visiting and personal service to the poor.[14] Women also drew on a less public repertoire. "Charity women" staged Thanksgiving dinners for the poor, drawing on domestic rituals to inscribe "their own reading of class relations on public culture."[15] Middle- and upper-class women adopted the models of the parlor meeting and charitable society, gradually adapting them as vehicles for a greater role in public affairs. Finally, women experimented with recognizably political forms, seeking to translate them into feminine imagery and practice.

As was the case for farmers and labor, each component of women's organizational repertoire both enabled and constrained political participation. For the members of a particular organization, their model of association was also an image of collective identity and purpose. Even the clubwomen, now quaint and moderate figures, named themselves in violation of existing logics of appropriateness. The term *club* was rejected by some as a "masculine" label, while more daring groups such as the New England Women's Club "deliberately chose *club* to indicate a break with tradition; it did not want to be associated with good-works societies."[16]

For outsiders, organizational form was a signal of a group's qualities and aims: "'What is the object?' was the first question asked of any organization of women, and if it was not the making of garments, or the collection of funds for a church, or philanthropic purpose, it was considered unworthy of attention, or injurious doubts were thrown upon its motives."[17] By distancing itself from reform associations, political parties, charitable societies and literary academies, the nineteenth-century woman's club was constituted as "absolutely a new thing under the sun."[18]

   In defining itself by what it was not, the women's club movement exemplifies innovation grounded in the materials at hand. In their efforts to gain a larger public role, women organized themselves as parliaments or congresses, as charitable societies, moral-reform associations, and clubs. But these efforts were limited so long as they were not articulated with political institutions. However, women would not gain full political standing so long as they used organizational scripts that invoked an opposition of femininity to politics. Yet explicitly political strategies rarely succeeded; calls for women's parliaments or demands for the vote were viewed as direct assaults on existing institutions and, not surprisingly, met with both derision and suppression. A second set of approaches, by contrast, built on traditionally feminine forms of organization and sought to link these models to new public purposes. These initial forays into the *public* realm served as a forward position from which women could redeploy their organizations for *political* ends.

Parliaments, Congresses, and Votes for Women

One strategy for securing institutional change is to act *as if* existing institutions already apply to formally excluded categories of actors or domains of activity (see chap. 2). In seeking full membership in the American polity, some activists and women's associations began by organizing along explicitly political lines. Sometimes this involved defining women as a separate polity, requiring representative institutions of its own. Following standard procedures for political meetings, the Women's Rights Convention of 1848 at Seneca Falls issued a formal "Declaration of Principles"; Elizabeth Cady Stanton pronounced that "woman herself must do this work; for woman alone can understand the height, the depth, the length, and the breadth of her degradation."[19] By the second half of the century, "Women's Parliaments" were held as forums in which women could debate and publicize their views. In 1892, for example, the Womans Parliament of Southern California met for "the full and free discussion of reforms necessary to the progress of woman's work in the church, home and society."[20] This model of separate polities paralleled the logics of appropriateness embedded in the rhetoric of separate spheres.

By the end of the century, however, the appeal of this form of political organization had faded. Although the National Congress of Mothers, established in 1897, perpetuated the name, its organization resembled an elite pressure group more than a deliberative body of women.[21] By constructing a parallel set of "political" institutions, these female "parliamentarians" had sought to avoid the cultural sanctions against their public activities. But in adopting this dual vision, women's groups were cut off from the allies and resources needed to secure substantive goals such as the relief of poverty, the protection of women and children, and the right to vote. The adoption of conventional political models such as the parliament was also easily linked with woman suffrage,[22] thereby negating much of the ideological insulation gained by conforming to the construct of separate spheres. The women's parliaments or congresses had no mechanism by which to influence policy outcomes. Jane Croly, the founder of one of the first women's clubs, saw "no advantage in waiting, like the enchanted princess in the fairy tale, for a lover, in the shape of a vote, to set us free and transform us into living, breathing, acting women. . . . Two weapons women are free to use—either of them mightier than the ballot—the tongue and the pen. These can keep up a perpetual warfare."[23] But while both tongue and pen might be wielded by individuals, if they were to be used "in the name of women," these weapons would need to be linked to the visible organization of women.

Through the end of the century, therefore, the prospects were poor for a direct assault on the gendered logic of the electoral system. Women did gain the vote in Wyoming and Utah; the first victory reflected an alignment of women with male settlers against the roving men of the frontier and mines, the second was offered as symbolic counterpoint to the alleged degradation of women by Mormon polygamy. In Idaho and Colorado, Populist electoral victories also secured the vote for women. Elsewhere, women continued to organize for the vote through the turn of the century, making innovative use of traveling organizers and fund-raising techniques that would have far-reaching consequences for the woman movement. But the majority of women's associational activity was not linked directly to the demand for enfranchisement or other reforms of political institutions. Most women who joined women's associations during the late nineteenth and early twentieth centuries had rather different motives: alarm over moral decay, a commitment to aid the unfortunate, or a desire for sociability and self-improvement. Pursued collectively, these goals fueled a massive expansion of women's associations in the decades following the Civil War. Whereas agrarian associations tended to expand and collapse, leaving an episodic trace of organizational activity, women's groups cumulated and were knit together by dense patterns of multiple membership. The Woman's Christian Temperance Union, the General Federation of Women's Clubs, and the National Congress of Mothers all built on this groundwork of apolitical association but, in time, had profound political effects.

Moral-Reform Associations

Few images of the nineteenth-century woman movement became so rooted in the popular imagination as the temperance worker, praying outside of saloons and wielding an axe to split open barrels of whiskey. These confrontations also signaled the difficulty of linking the scripts of the moral crusade or revival to the project of women's political organization. The language of moral condemnation exacerbated the very ethnoreligious tensions that party politicians were most anxious to suppress. Popular perceptions of these groups as intolerant, evangelical, or nativist made these moral-reform societies dangerous as coalition partners.

To combat this political isolation, temperance groups drew on varied exemplars of organizational form and strategy.[24] The Woman's Christian Temperance Union (WCTU)—the largest female temperance association and long the largest women's association in the country[25]—initially built upon an existing network of church-based groups and capitalized on the early steps toward organizational independence taken by women's missionary societies during the Civil War. Yet even in this early phase, the WCTU represented a profound break with the organizational repertoire of its female membership:

> It was . . . their first experience with a nonsectarian organization not auxiliary to a specific Protestant denomination, and their first experience with an organization led exclusively by women. These innovations were offset, however, by the conservative implications of the convention's clear connection to Protestant Christianity. *The means were radical but the goals widely accepted.* The convention also showed its conservatism by eschewing politics. No reference was made to woman suffrage in its deliberations. No political party was endorsed, although the Prohibition party had been in existence since 1869.[26]

The WCTU continued to adopt novel means if not goals, engaging in political activity and legislative lobbying well before it formally embraced even the limited "home protection" ballot for women in 1881.[27] Its formal organizational structure combined a "modern" departmental form with traditional feminine concerns. The departments of the national WCTU were initially nonpolitical: in 1882, only three of twenty were devoted to nontemperance issues. This rose to nine of thirty-one by 1883, and, by 1896, twenty-five of thirty-nine were "dealing wholly or in major part with non-temperance issues." [28] This organizational transformation was echoed at the state level. As of 1880, the Northern California WCTU was organized in the following twenty-two departments: Evangelistic, Legislation and Petitions, Scientific Temperance Instruction, Hygiene, Heredity, Song, Prison, Press, Viticulture, Literary Bodies and School Conventions, County Fairs, Religious Bodies, Sunday Schools, Public Lectures, Coffee Houses, Soldiers and Sailors, Free Reading Room, Young Ladies' Unions, Object Lessons, Fruit and Flowers, German Work, and Juvenile Work. [29] This list illustrates how the departmental form facilitated monitoring of a complex social environment, but the substantive topics suggest a lack of orientation to political issues or procedures. The old-fashioned reliance on petition was supplemented in 1882 with the creation of a department of franchise, by the notably divided vote of fifty-four to forty. But even this move toward a more direct articulation with the political process was overridden by the Northern California WCTU's primary commitment to moral reform: "[A]n earnest debate followed on the motion to ask the legislature to grant the ballot to women. This was conceded to be premature, and it was voted to concentrate all forces this year to secure the Temperance Education Law." [30]

Even though the California association did gradually adopt new goals, it could not overcome others' perception of its organizational character. A group's professed interests are not the only determinants of its actions; others' perceptions shape the possibilities of alliance. In 1896, at the time of a promising campaign for woman suffrage, the National WCTU proposed to hold its convention in California. The state's suffrage societies "begged the National Union to call off its Convention, for fear of antagonizing the liquor powers. Letters were received by women prominent in the cause of Suffrage, warning them to keep clear of 'White Ribboners,' and not to be compromised by the Temperance element, but the ladies to whom these appeals were sent were found to be nearly all official members of the W.C.T.U." [31] Suffrage was defeated—110,335 to 137,099— despite the agreement of the WCTU to lay low during a campaign that it supported.

In an era before opinion polls, associational activities provided clues to public opinion and helped to frame political issues. As potential participants in a system of interest group politics, the temperance societies and other moral-reform associations were handicapped. Because the visibility of their organization might mobilize opposing forces, they were frequently shunned as coalition partners, although individual "White Ribboners" were welcome as members of other women's organizations. Thus, while moral reformers and other politically active women might agree on a wide range of goals, their choices of organizational vehicles made cooperation difficult. Even as moral-reform associations became structurally diversified, mirroring the increasing rationalization of charitable groups, the cultural connotations of the form remained. Consequently, many activists looked elsewhere for organizational forms more easily accommodated to political action.

Charitable Societies

While the parliaments or congresses attempted to map formal political models onto the separate spheres, the vast majority of women's organizational efforts involved more incremental extensions of familiar feminine activities. Charities or "benevolent societies" were the first major form of American women's separate engagement with the public sphere, appearing in the eighteenth century and multiplying rapidly thereafter.[32] In large part, these groups grew out of the separate spheres of the nineteenth century, taking "on some of the tasks—the care of dependents and the enforcement of moral norms—that governments had abandoned. . . . Women's positions outside traditionally defined politics and their elevated moral authority took on new importance."[33] Charitable work allowed women to develop their organizational autonomy, and the Civil War provided opportunities to deploy their skills and resources in new arenas.[34]

As cities grew and differences of class, ethnicity, and religion increased the social distance between donors and clients, charities followed paths taken by business corporations in managing national markets and complex production processes: procedures were standardized, lines of authority were formalized.[35] In many cities, the "scientific charity movement" sought to rationalize and professionalize the delivery of relief by creating central registration bureaus and replacing traditional forms of "friendly visiting" and moral oversight with practices from the newly developed field of social work.[36] Existing benevolent societies remade themselves along "scientific" lines. The 1901 *Annual Report* of the Managers of the San Francisco Ladies Protection and Relief Society celebrated

[t]he little band of "praying women," as our President has called them, [who] sowed in 1853 seed that still "shoots after rainless years, bearing bright leaves." In these forty-eight years charity has become less sentimental and more reflective. We are more scientific in methods without being, I hope and believe, less sympathetic with individual suffering and individual joy. Our belief in the germ theory and sanitary science may be entirely compatible with the truest charity.[37]

In making the philanthropic model their own, charitable associations set an important precedent for women's subsequent organizational experiments. To a far greater extent than male-dominated benevolent societies, women allied themselves with the state, seeking public subsidies and state power with which to pursue their goals.[38] Women also claimed superior virtue in the administration of state institutions. "I seriously doubt if women had been on the Board of Commissioners if bribery would have been attempted; where in instances, it has been active in corrupting men serving alone," asserted one Wisconsin suffragist. "Where women control state elementary institutions, they bring them within state appropriations oftener than men; for women have been so long accustomed to small economies within the household they have perfected themselves in making much of small measures."[39] Precisely because logics of appropriateness established the presumption that women were not partisan, they were insulated from charges—and perhaps from practices—of political corruption.[40]

These developments presented particular dilemmas and opportunities to women. So long as charity had taken the form of personal service and friendly visiting, it was compatible with established understandings of feminine domestic and religious duties. The shift from district-based delivery of services to casework distanced the activities of charitable associations from specific communities, and the coordination of efforts among charities attenuated the links of member associations to their religious or ethnic bases.[41] But as the activities of these associations became less personal, charitable work drew women into a public sphere where their activities were hobbled by their lack of political standing. As the *Wisconsin Citizen* queried in 1890, "Are advisory councils merely a 'sop to Cerberus?'"—a bone thrown to active women who might otherwise raise a hue and cry over the conditions in public institutions. The *Citizen* observed that the advisory council "is heard with respect, and if the report is in accordance with the interests of the managers, it is all very well; but if it reflects upon the management, then the women are set aside as incapable of judging public matters." Years of filling advisory roles would lead one Wisconsin suffragist to conclude, "Our boasted 'indirect influence' is found to be of very fluctuating value."[42]

Over the nineteenth century, women adopted the philanthropic model, seeking support from the state and developing internal bureaucratic structures quite distinct from traditional feminine models while facilitating ties to both corporations and state agencies. But this form proved inadequate on at least two counts. First, women's philanthropies frequently depended on state support that was endangered as the patrician order of American politics came under increasing attack. The demands of other social reformers—for state supervision of charities or the expansion of state-run asylums and orphanages—forced private charities to attend to politics where benevolent ladies had little influence. Second, as benevolent women grappled with the problems of industrialization and urbanization, they increasingly pressed the limits of traditional models of feminine virtue and charity. Suffragists argued that philanthropic activities addressed only symptoms, leaving women without time or energy to address the root problem of their own disenfranchisement and social injustice. Rev. Olympia Brown, a prominent suffragist and one of the first women to be ordained, explained:

> In Wisconsin the chief obstacle to organization appears to be that women are already overburdened by a great number of charitable and religious societies, and have not time for anything more, and yet if they could realize how easily these charitable objects could be accomplished when they have the power that the ballot gives, they could give up all other societies and work for woman suffrage.[43]

But for all the complaints of ardent suffragists, in those "other societies" women were developing new techniques of political influence and establishing new public identities that paved the way for a thoroughly extrapartisan politics, a politics without party.

Women's Clubs

The women's club was the most widespread model of women's association at the end of the century and shared an organizational ancestor with the women's parliaments—the literary women's clubs. Although the literary clubs appear in retrospect as thoroughly traditional, to their founders they represented a break from women's charitable activities and a claim for the value of women's discourse independent of their good works. In its constitution of 1869, the first New York club, Sorosis, declared that it aimed "to establish *a kind of freemasonry* among women of similar pursuits, to render them helpful to each other, and to bridge over the barrier which custom and social etiquette place in the way of friendly intercourse."[44] Adopting an organizational model from the male fraternal societies, the early clubwomen sought to create social spaces in which the system of separate spheres would be transformed, at least insofar as women expanded their awareness beyond the boundaries of domestic life. As Croly, the founder of the General Federation of Women's Clubs (GFWC) argued, the attainment of "agreement and equality, where differences and traditions had built up walls of distinction and lines of caste" required a transformation of consciousness, not of action and organization.[45] In a metaphorical attack on women's relegation to childlike dependency, Sorosis celebrated its "majority" in 1890 by calling for the formation of a national organization of women.

Adopting the name of "club" from men's groups, women were initially vague as to what sort of women's organization they had created. At first, this question was answered in the negative: "A club that is narrowed to a clique, a class or a single object is a contradiction in terms. It may be a society or a congregation of societies, but it is not a club. The essence of a club is its many-sided character, its freedom in gathering together and expressing all shades of difference, its equal and independent terms of membership, which puts every one upon the same footing, and enables each one to find or make her own place."[46] At the first biennial convention of the GFWC, Julia Ward Howe declared that the "club is a larger home, and we wish to have the immunities and defenses of home, and therefore we do not wish the public present."[47] Others drew on educational imagery: "The earliest form of the woman's club was the study club, the 'Middle-Aged Woman's University.'" The refusal to respect the logic of appropriateness linking the club form to men, however, led some to attribute radical political goals to the new women's clubs: "In the South religious associations continued to be the dominant form of organization until women there began to realize that 'club' did not necessarily imply suffrage or radical feminism, whereupon black and white women there began to organize literary societies."[48]

By creating a home without adult men, a school not governed by state authorities, the earliest versions of the club form represented a small step toward political action. As one clubwoman explained in 1895: "The literary clubs were the first clubs, but were not enough for all women. They were formed to meet the defects of elder women. College-bred women were well furnished with literature, and demanded something more. Hence civic clubs." By the biennial convention of 1896, only 50 of over

1,200 affiliated clubs were "pursuing purely literary lines of work"; the "department club was evidently in the ascendant."[49] In the years that followed this shift of emphasis the club movement grew rapidly (fig. 6.1). In 1896, 17 California clubs had joined the General Federation; this grew to 192 in 1908 (with 13,000 members) and 373 by 1915 (33,790 members). In Washington, clubs grew from 7 in 1896 to 163 in 1915 (11,428 members); in Wisconsin from 8 to 203 (with approximately 10,000 members). Washington and Wisconsin established state federations in 1896; California followed in 1900. Individual clubs emerged as major civic organizations; by 1922, the Friday Morning Club and Ebell Club of Los Angeles both claimed over 2,000 members, while the San Francisco Center of the California Civic League of Women Voters reported 2,400.[50]

Both literary and department clubs contributed to the development of women's organizational skills.[51] Since a typical club program consisted of one member presenting a paper on which others commented, women were forced both to speak in public and to voice their own opinions on a wide array of topics. Publicity, observed Croly, "was a stumbling block every step of the way. The women who composed club membership were not used to seeing their names in print."[52] But clubs provided a haven in which new skills and dispositions could be cultivated. In 1898, the Tuesday Club of Fort Atkinson, Wisconsin, reported that after examining the political and economic development of Boston and New York City, "We also spent several afternoons in the study of municipal government, cause[s] of municipal mis-government, municipal reform and other topics connected with the government of cities."[53] Although explicit mentions of parliamentary drills, courses of study in political science, and legislative institutes were more common in suffrage publications,[54] clubwomen frequently described their practices as the development of an organizational capacity to be deployed for political ends: "Through the years of disinterested intelligent service as soldiers of the common good, the club women have been proving their fitness for full citizenship, have been aroused to the necessity for their own enfranchisement, have been building up a great and powerful mechanism to be employed in the interests of the public weal."[55] By embedding the practices of formal politics in the more intimate setting of women's clubs, these organizational innovations steadily transformed the relation between the club form and the field of political action: "[C]lub life and club work has been the necessary school of citizenship."[56]

The development of this organizational capacity for political action

Figure 6.1 California State Federation of Women's Clubs in Yosemite Valley.
(Courtesy, The Bancroft Library)

did not address two other questions: what purposes would be served? and how would this capacity be linked to formal political institutions? The answer to the first eventually centered on social reform: "[I]n 1869 we find Mrs. Croly attempting to introduce a measure which commended to the attention of the club, matters connected with public education and reformatory schools, hygienic and sanitary reforms, female labor, and the department of domestic economy, dishonesty in public life, and so forth. The measure was defeated it is true, but its introduction at that time shows conclusively that, even at the outset, the founders of the Woman Club Movement had in mind the organization of a body of social workers, who should make better conditions on every hand."[57] But the initial defeat of this proposal suggests that welding the personal development of the literary clubs to an active public role in the service of "municipal housekeeping" was not automatically accepted by most clubwomen.

Many of the early clubwomen resisted social-service activities precisely because they were viewed as the raison d'être of charitable associations and other traditional women's groups. Philanthropy or social service threatened to invoke a logic of appropriateness that these women had

HALF DOME   GRIZZLY PEAK   LITTLE YOSEMITE

CAMP CURRY, YOSEMITE MAY 24 - 27 1921

UBS IN YOSEMITE VALLEY—MAY 24-28, 1921

rejected in choosing the explicitly masculine form of the club. The clubs'
eventual turn from literary and moral concerns coincided with the depression of 1893 and the recognition of the poor as victims of social problems
rather than as individual moral failures.[58] This reframing of the problem
moved issues of poverty and unemployment beyond the established mandate of traditional charitable societies (and therefore of action motivated
by the presumed superior virtue of women) and made them available to
new forms of intervention or as topics for "courses of study" in politics,
economics, and sociology. In the 1890s, one president of the GFWC
urged, "Departments of civics and social economics should be a part of
all club work and study classes. The clubs which have been organized
within the last two years differ from those at first formed in this: the
membership of the new clubs is very large; some are over a hundred, and
several have started with three or four hundred and a waiting list. Such
clubs naturally divide up into departments, and at once begin municipal
or other work."[59] This development marked a dramatic shift from the
organizational heritage of women's groups, grounded in parlor meetings
and small societies. Increases in scale and scope were managed by the
introduction of internal bureaucratic structure, a borrowing of organizational models from business that reinforced women's claim to a nonparti-

san but nevertheless public role. The growing use of business methods also created new possibilities for linking women's voluntary associations to other established civic actors.

Just as Grangers had found themselves handicapped by the mutuality and ritual of fraternalism, women were limited so long as their organizations relied on the small-scale sociability of the literary clubs and parlor teas. Consequently, clubwomen found that there were advantages to abandoning organizational forms based on personal ties for a greater reliance on bureaucratic relations. Department clubs could expand their activities incrementally; politically active women could work in suffrage or social-economics departments while other members devoted themselves to more traditional literary, musical, or service projects. This organizational innovation allowed groups to avoid specifying on a single "woman's interest," thereby facilitating coalition formation (but, in the long term, contributing to the fragmentation of women's political agenda).[60] Unlike the moral-reform associations, where the cultural connotations of the form overrode internal diversification of goals, individual club departments were rarely constrained by a clear public understanding of what clubwomen should do. The increased size of the clubs also gave public-minded clubwomen the stature of public leaders.

The clubs helped women to cultivate citizenship skills and to make women more visible as a potential political constituency, but they remained aloof from the fraternal world of party politics: "The [California] Federation can have no political affiliations, in the sense of partisanship. We must advocate measures only."[61] By not requiring partisan political commitments from their members, the clubs served as a channel for a wide variety of issues perceived as relevant to women. As Ellen Henrotin, president of the GFWC, argued: "Other organizations of women—of which we have so many—represent each a single cause; the federation represents the sum and the soul of all causes."[62] Conventions of the GFWC were addressed by prominent settlement workers and social reformers; an agrarian crusader for pure-food legislation captured the attention of both the General Federation and the Consumers' League by addressing their meetings at the St. Louis Exposition of 1904. Following in the steps of many reform groups, the Consumers' League raised concern over the plight of sales girls by addressing "women at their club meetings, at their church guild meetings."[63] Some clubs also actively enforced behavior supportive of reforms: "As a result of a discussion following the reading of a paper on the 'Wearing of Bird Plumage' . . . the ladies [of the San Francisco Contemporary Club] decided by a unanimous vote to discontinue the practice, exclusive of ostrich feathers"; "one woman's club after another has adopted the league's slogan of 'Do your Christmas shopping early!' [in order to spare shopgirls from excessive overtime] and at the meeting held the first week in December, the president of the club often calls on all those members present to rise if they have finished their Christmas shopping. No member wishes to hurt the reputation of her club by being delinquent, so the individual members have developed the group conscience."[64] Clubs were mechanisms for generating collective action and mobilizing pressure to bring to bear on either markets or politics.

Although many individual clubs chose to remain as "resting places" and literary circles,[65] the active "civic clubs" carved out a new public identity for organized women's groups. Like the women's parliaments, the clubs embraced a wide variety of causes, but this lack of overall specialization was countered by the developing internal framework of the departments. Yet the clubs still lacked a mechanism for translating their growing numbers and the resources of their membership into political capital. As late as 1916 the chairman of the Industrial Committee of the Washington State Federation of Women's Clubs regretfully reported on efforts to improve industrial conditions in the state:

> Our plan was education among the club women of the state. Clubs have not taken up the subject generally for the reason that it would lead them into that forbidden realm "politics," for causes and cures, and could not be discussed dispassionately, even though our women and children's welfare was at stake.
>
> Since this is the case, little can be done in this department except philanthropic and charity work, relieving distress a little here a little there, quieting our consciences by persuading ourselves that we have done our duty, and leaving the solution of these perplexing problems to those who do the useful work of the world.[66]

Six years after women in Washington had regained the vote, the aversion to linking clubs and politics endured. Working with their inherited organizational repertoire, these civic-minded women found that the exclusionary cultural logic of the electoral system was not to be easily uprooted.

Despite these limitations, the organizational accomplishments of the women's clubs should not be underestimated. Perhaps women had a special charge for the care of women and children; perhaps they had distinctive developmental needs that could only be met by organizations such as clubs. Either way, these organizational forms allowed women (albeit limited largely to the middle and upper middle class) to venture beyond the traditional bounds of the domestic, but still embodied gender-specific logics of appropriateness that limited political participation. To move further into politics, these women's associations would have to reorient themselves, to look to the practices of established actors in the polity.

Limits of the Nineteenth-Century Repertoire

By the closing decades of the nineteenth century, middle- and upper-middle-class American women had developed a varied repertoire of social organization and increasingly sought to turn these organizations toward public activities. Yet establishing a link between women's organizations and active *political* participation was not easy. Such a connection violated nineteenth-century ideas of the distinctiveness of women's work and its exclusion from the fraternal realm of partisan politics. If women were to gain a legitimate role as political participants, this logic of appropriateness had to be undermined.[67] If women were to secure a place in politics, the grounding of their organizational repertoire in the ideology of separate spheres would need to be weakened while new methods of defining collective interest and organizing collective action were devised.

Just as the convention proceedings of labor federations and state Granges were filled with debates over the implications and advantages of different organizational forms, public-minded women were highly aware of the task of organizational innovation that they faced. As one president of the GFWC wrote, her "little book [*The Business of Being a Clubwoman*] does not deal with purposes or programs, but with *ways* of running our affairs. We must learn to avoid our old mistakes and gain our ends by more direct paths. We can learn out of our own past. And no one but ourselves can give us much help. Colleges and social scientists and experts of various kinds can help us in the *matters* upon which we are working, but as to the *ways* of working we have to blaze our own trail."[68] The need to invent new "ways of working" was not a universal condition of American women, but a product of the organizational repertoire that these economically privileged women inherited from the nineteenth century, combined with their double exclusion from male organizations and partisan politics. Faced with these constraints, the clubwomen and their social peers were pushed to innovate.

The distinctive context for these organizational innovations is suggested by a comparison to the experiences of working-class and rural women.[69] Although women rarely had equal standing within the labor movement, within two years of dropping its commitment to secrecy in

1878, the Knights of Labor authorized the initiation of women. The reasons that women could not join the Knights earlier were rooted in cultural beliefs about the feminine character, a logic of appropriateness linking actors and organizational form. The founder of the Knights "was so obsessed with the value of secrecy and with the sexist view that women could not keep secrets that he did not advocate opening membeship to women."[70] In 1882, the second convention of the Federation of Organized Trades and Labor Unions (the forerunner of the AFL) extended an invitation to women. Unlike fraternal societies, these male-dominated organizations did not formally exclude women, but women rarely accounted for more than 10 percent of the membership in the Knights of Labor, and a smaller proportion yet in the AFL.[71] The large nineteenth-century labor unions remained clearly the province of men, unlike the Patrons of Husbandry, who often found themselves claiming "some earnest Grangers and good workers, especially the sisters, who seem to take more interest in the grange than the brothers."[72] The sisters, in turn, felt that their position within the Grange prefigured an enlarged public role for women. As Mrs. A. P. Roache rhymed:

> We would not break our youthful ties,
>   Our love would not be changed,
> If men would only give the rights
>   We have within the Grange.
>
> . . . .
>
> For you alone can never stay
>   The evil of the hour
> So, with your band, but let us stand
>   We'll aid you with our power.[73]

The extensive support for woman suffrage evident in Grange records of the late nineteenth century grew out of decades of experience with an unfamiliar combination of actors and organizational form, of women and a fraternal order. In 1876, the first chaplain of the national Grange had argued that the Grange, as "an extension of the farm home . . . was domestic and so a legitimate part of women's sphere; politics belonged to the rough, male world. Voting in the Grange, therefore, had no more to do with politics than did 'voting for officers or for resolutions in a sewing circle.'"[74] But as women moved out of the offices reserved for them (Flora, Ceres, and Pomona; see fig. 6.2) to serve as masters, chaplains, and lecturers, the first chaplain's distinction between the internal life of the Grange and the "politics [that] belonged to the rough, male world" appeared less and less tenable.

Figure 6.2   Mrs. E. Z. Roache as Pomona, California State Grange, 1887.
(Source: CSG, *Proceedings* 1887)

Confronting logics of appropriateness that excluded women from political life by linking gender to a capacity for organization, working
women engaged in their own search for new organizational forms and
political methods. Direct imitation of their male counterparts was dangerous; working women could not pursue politics without attracting
charges of impropriety. One contemporary researcher concluded that unionized waitresses in San Francisco "as a body and individually exhibit
considerable more interest in municipal politics than do the women of
other trade unions. This gives rise to many rumors that the waitresses
include within their membership women who serve, from time to time, at
least, in the type of cafe and resort which is always a factor in the darker

side of municipal corruption."[75] Any association with elected officials tarnished the waitresses' own reputations and implied a further corruption of politics. The reputation of the waitress union was also attacked because the organization flouted standards of feminine propriety in order to secure the financial basis of a solid union: "The waitresses raise most of their funds for relief and sick benefits from their large annual ball. This ball provokes considerable disapproval. One of the main features is a bar, and from the sale of drinks the receipts are $600 to $800. The sum thus derived goes into the benevolent fund." With these ill-gotten gains, the waitresses provided death benefits, supported a paid staff that was "not customary in other unions," established a minimum wage scale, and "moulded together a class of workers who are notably hard to weld." Despite all these accomplishments, the culturally questionable methods of the waitresses caused "the personnel of the waitresses' union [to receive] more criticism than is accorded to the women in the other unions."[76] But if the world of patronage politics remained taboo for women workers, the same was not true of legislative politics. Faced with defeat at organizing workers, both the Knights of Labor and the AFL had sometimes turned to legislative strategies, and this path was also open, at least potentially, to working women and their more privileged allies.[77]

The potential flexibility of working women's repertoire is illustrated by the wide array of organizing efforts undertaken by wage-earning women and union wives in Seattle, who "combined the women's organizations made available to them within the Seattle labor movement with the feminist discourse of the early 20th century 'Woman Movement' to produce a local movement of their own."[78] Women were first encouraged to join a "Women's Label League" in their roles as "wives, mothers, sisters, and sweethearts" of workingmen. This group, after declining for a number of years (and cutting its ties to the International Label League and Trades Union Assembly in order to focus on local issues), was supplanted by the Seattle Women's Label League, which shared the local labor movement's lack of commitment to the craft unionism of the AFL. "League leaders urged women to abandon trade-union auxiliaries for the League's 'one big organization' of women, proclaiming: 'There are no evidences of 'craft-consciousness' in the Label League—we are for organized labor and all that it demands.'"[79] This move toward an organization of all working-class women in the city facilitated alliances with the politically oriented associations of middle-class women who had organized the King County Legislative Federation in 1913, a few years after the state's women had gained the vote. But recalling the relation of Milwaukee Social Democrats to the state's Republican Party, the leaders of the Seattle Label League kept their allies at arm's length by insisting that working-class women pursue "women's interests" through working-class organization and by rejecting organizational practices strongly associated with middle-class identity, notably formal "educational programs" and "pink teas."[80]

As the contrasting trajectories of middle-class and working-class women's organizations demonstrate, the relationship between gender and politics was mediated by organizational form and capacity. For working-class women, the availability—albeit limited—of exemplars and allies in both the union movement and middle-class women's organizations generated eclectic and flexible syntheses of these two repertoires at the same time that the hardships of their lives lessened the time and resources available for independent organizing. For middle-class women, by comparison, the sharp ideological delineation between the separate spheres pushed them to recognize that "as to the *ways* of working we have to blaze our own trail"[81] and to invent new organizations that would evade the logics of appropriateness that barred women from politics.

From Public Life to Political Power

Starting in the protected spaces of religious congregations and literary clubs, women's associations multiplied through the late nineteenth century. But the puzzle of how to link them to political processes remained. One solution relied on the informal arrangements of "feminine influence" that recognized the inherent virtue of women while denying them recognition as legitimate political actors. Many women who struggled for political access, however, rejected techniques that defined them as less than full members of the polity:

> We repudiate the present system called "Woman's influence." We know *too* well that we have influence and we know just how to use it. We have long been trained to deception, cunning and intrigue; but we are tired of successes that have been obtained at the sacrifice of our self-respect. If our demands are right and just, we want success because it *is* right and not because we have been smart, or cute enough to hoodwink our legal superiors into granting us this or that.[82]

In the place of "influence," women sought legitimate political participation by drawing on formerly nonpolitical *and* nonfeminine models of organization. These new organizational procedures and political strategies weakened the logics of appropriateness that linked women to organizational forms defined as incompatible with politics. By adopting techniques not traditionally associated with feminine activity, women sought to present themselves as legitimate political actors, using novel strategies to redefine their goals and identities in the eyes of other political actors.

Three shifts in organizational procedure were central to the development of a new political strategy for women, a recognizably modern version of voluntaristic interest group politics. The first involved an increasing reliance on cash rather than personal service as the preferred medium for social action and, more generally, the adoption of recognizable corporate forms and business methods. This shift in practices depersonalized women's organizations, rendering them more appropriate for public endeavors. The second stemmed from replacing the deferential politics of petition with campaigns of political education designed to shape public opinion and alter the decisions of legislators. Finally, women turned with greater frequency to state and federal governments, rather than their own communities, as the appropriate arenas for political action. If these three tendencies are taken to an extreme, one arrives at a picture of the modern-day interest or issue group, with its use of literature and expert testimony to secure federal funding for some sort of program. As timeless as this form of political action may now seem, it was an invention of the Progressive Era and played a central role in articulating the relations among constituencies and state agencies that characterize the modern American state.

Business Methods and Women's Work

The multiplication of women's parliaments, benevolent societies, moral-reform associations, and clubs took place during a period now widely recognized as an organizational revolution. Consequently, any analysis of the relations between women's groups and politics must consider the sweeping changes in the broader repertoire of social organization in nineteenth-century America. Of particular importance was the rise of the modern corporation. Although the use of corporate forms had blocked women's participation in the major cultural and philanthropic institutions of the antebellum period,[83] by the end of the century women sought to appropriate the cultural cachet of business methods for their own associations. Clubwomen, temperance activists, and labor reformers instituted increasingly centralized and formal hierarchies.[84] But for women's groups, the adoption of business methods had consequences that were not apparent in the activities of men already immersed in a system of market relations: the reconstitution of action around a cash nexus and the establishment of formal hierarchical relations among women of the same age, ethnicity, or class.

For women's groups, part of becoming a modern organization involved substituting cash exchanges for personal service. Speaking on "Woman's Work in the Church," the Rev. Lila F. Sprague declared, "The woman of to-day is inaugurating an epoch of belief; a belief that it is better in every way, for all concerned, to give five dollars in cash to the needs of the church, rather than ten dollars in poor cake, and poorer pie, which may, with a big crowd and plenty of hard work, yield a net return of one or two dollars."[85] During the Civil War, the women of the Sanitary Commission imitated the festivals and fairs of benevolent and moral-reform groups and "systematized them, tightened their coordination, and heightened their visibility."[86] The monetarization of women's reform work, and the uneasy balance between home and market, remained a theme through the suffrage victory of 1920. The Kansas suffrage campaign of 1900 received "many small donations, a car load of flour from the Kansas Millers' Association, and 200 pounds of butter from the Continental Creamery Co." Wisconsin suffragists "sold washing machines for $3.50 'to make money without begging for it.'"[87] In 1911, the *Milwaukee Journal* proclaimed, "Doughnuts to Win Votes for Women": "Mrs. Belle Case La Follette proposes to transplant the 'doughnut picnic' to Wisconsin and use it in furthering the cause of woman suffrage there as California women have used it on the coast." In a less cosmopolitan vein, the *Oshkosh Northwestern* announced that the local Equal Suffrage League planned a fund-raising poultry sale.[88]

By the turn of the century, these home-based models were augmented by efforts to extract funds on the basis of the more "modern" feminine identity of the consumer. Mainstream suffrage associations sponsored "consumer fasts" in which women promised to forgo cosmetics and other luxuries, sending the money saved to fund the fight for the vote; the New York City Political Equality League went further by pledging its department of hygiene to sponsor a "suffrage temple of beauty."[89] Even the more radical suffragists of the Congressional Union employed womanly subterfuge to obtain the cash necessary to support their political causes: "Some used the 'charging a hat or coat' method to obtain spending money. By this method, women charged an item that a shrewd shopkeeper would bill to the woman's husband, while giving the customer cash instead of the merchandise—for a modest fee."[90]

The use of money was not purely instrumental but also signaled character. The 1898 GFWC biennial convention faced the threat of withdrawal by some of the large clubs, which charged dues of ten to twelve dollars yet balked at paying a few additional dollars for membership in the General and State Federations. Chiding them for shortsightedness, the GFWC president argued,

> As long as a woman will spend $25 or $10 two or three times a year for a bonnet, and stop at $2 for her club for the State Federation, you see how narrow is her view. (*Applause.*) As soon as women get big enough to spend money impersonally, then the story is told. You know Voltaire, or rather Merope in his Life of Voltaire, apologizes for speaking of Voltaire's financial affairs, and he says very gracefully, "the way in which people spend their money is the outward and visible sign of an inward and spiritual grace," and I think that is the attitude you see of the big club.[91]

Fund-raising methods premised on women's traditional role in the domestic economy were widely used but endangered women's claims to full citizenship. In Wisconsin, the leader of the Political Equality League declared that "she will not conduct sales of cookbooks or postcards to raise a campaign fund and further declares that if it is to be that sort of a campaign, she will seek a cool spot near Lake Superior and retire there. Promises, Miss Wagner points out, do not pay the bills and begging for money is humiliating."[92] Underlying this complaint was a recognition that cash was a criterion of citizenship. To the extent that American women had exercised the vote in the eighteenth century, it was by virtue of their status as property holders or taxpayers. (By comparison, women of the late nineteenth century were sometimes granted school suffrage by virtue of their identity as mothers or potential mothers.) The connection between cash and citizenship persisted in debates over the political autonomy of employees and regularly framed women's claims for a legitimate public role. Recounting their contributions to the San Francisco Panama-Pacific Exposition of 1915, the Woman's Board explained the absence of "an accounting of funds drawn from official sources"; "the Woman's Board which helped in the creation of San Francisco's Dream City of 1915 and in bringing it to a picturesque and notable success. This Board has faced no such obligation of stewardship; it financed all its own undertakings as well as those undertakings which it cheerfully assumed at the request of the Exposition directorate." The importance of this claim is underlined by its presence in the second paragraph of the preface, the first substantive claim in a book-length account. The political significance of financial autonomy is explained in the paragraph that follows:

[T]here are in mind the men and women everywhere who may be interested in these achievements not merely for their intrinsic worth, but also for the reason that they bear eloquent witness to the success of a great human cause, for the reason that they are, in some sort, the first fruits of woman's emancipation in a state newly made politically free, a practical thank-offering of woman's pride and woman's patriotism.[93]

By adopting "business practices"—the Woman's Board was financed by over three hundred "stockholders"[94]—these activists diminished the role of distinctively gendered organizational forms in constituting their public identity. The adoption of cash exchanges also potentially undermined the forms of intimacy, solidarity, and community traditionally associated with women's groups of the nineteenth century. In promoting the organization of working women, for example, elite clubs no longer sought to maintain the personal, albeit supervisory, ties of friendly visiting. In San Francisco, the prestigious California Club first sponsored the working-class Porteous Club and then left it to support itself. Once again, business practices and cash resources signaled civic maturity:

That the little club is capable of managing its own affairs in a small way is sufficiently evidenced by the concert it gave in the early part of the year, when it was practically, though not yet nominally, on its own resources. . . . None the less was the affair organized and carried through in all business details by the Porteous members themselves, and so well did they manage that they netted $108.05 as their profit from the entertainment. After such a result none can doubt the business capacity of the baby Porteous.[95]

Such shifts toward business practices displaced the familial models of sisterhood and mother-daughter relations that had shaped the self-image of women's organizations of the nineteenth century. Even divisions among women were expressed in terms drawn from the world of business. In 1911, one woman suffrage group proclaimed its intention to smash "the Wisconsin suffrage trust" and to found an alternative organization "with a commission form of government."[96]

The shift to cash characterized the delivery of services as well as their underwriting. Whereas personal contact between charitable women and their clientele had once been viewed as central to the project of moral uplift, "friendly visiting" was increasingly attacked. From the perspective of scientific charity, this form of aid was inefficient; from the perspective of the disadvantaged and their advocates, it was demeaning. In response to these complaints, volunteers in numerous cities sponsored Women's Industrial Exchanges, where working women could sell homemade items such as baked goods and needlework, while charities joined together as "Charity Organization Societies" seeking to coordinate both fund-raising and the delivery of services.[97] Women's efforts to promote the production and appreciation of art also relied increasingly on mixed models assembled from business and charity rather than on traditional feminine forms of philanthropy.[98]

The move from personalistic ties to cash exchanges was accompanied by the increasing formalization of the division of labor and lines of authority. As clubs grew in size, "[I]t was deemed expedient to subdivide the larger club into smaller departments . . . to act in conjunction with the club proper."[99] Although Roberts Rules of Order had long been the sacred text of associational life, there was an increasing distinction between the membership and a more "professional" activist core in many organizations. Sometimes this might entail no more than specialized training for organizational leadership. In San Francisco, the purpose of the Richelieu Club, "mostly composed of the presidents of other clubs," was "to carry on the drill of parliamentary usage with a view to having a more accurate knowledge of one's rights upon the floor and one's duty in the chair of an assembly." As efforts at coordination among clubs and other organizations grew, additional levels of authority were formalized. In California, Bay Area suffragists formed an "Inter-Association Conference" that "held semi-monthly meetings . . . delegates presiding in turn. . . . The strictest parliamentary forms were observed, and not a moment of our precious time wasted in idle compliment or discussion."[100] Once the vote was won, California women continued to rationalize and reorganize their political work. In 1912, the following notice went out:

> The California Federation of Women's Clubs, through its Chairman of Legislation, invites all State organizations of women to cooperate with it in forming a central committee, or State Legislative Council of Women. . . . The purpose of this body will be to prevent duplication of this work and expense; to bring together experts from each society who can plan mutually for better work than would be possible alone; to decide how much legislation and what, is wise to ask for, and to see that this is being prepared by responsible organizations; also to select a small committee to be in Sacramento during the session of the Legislature to look after all interests involved in such legislation.

By 1922, the Women's Legislative Council of California included delegates from fifty-three women's organizations. As a nonpartisan organization, "Its work is fundamentally educational, but its power lies in its ability to focus as well as enlighten public opinion." One reform-minded journalist proclaimed that the California women had invented "the Scientific Management of Club Influence."[101]

The increasing visibility of hierarchical, bureaucratic forms was driven by two circumstances common to women throughout the country: the rhetorical value of assimilating business methods as a signal of public standing and the growing centralization facilitated by the symbolically significant reliance on cash. The latter was particularly evident in the national associations, large federated structures in which national and local units were linked by either state federations or city centrals. The origins of these structures were diverse; sometimes locals would be established independently and later federate (GFWC); sometimes national associations would pay for organizers to found groups at the state and local levels (NAWSA); and, finally, one federated group might serve as a seedbed for another, replicating across different levels of organization (e.g., the California Federation of Women's Clubs carried on "an educational campaign for the advancement of the work of the Consumers' League").[102] But whatever their origins, these national associations increased their power relative to local groups as cash became more important.

In part, this centralization of resources reflects the simple fact that cash, once given, is less easily controlled than personal service. A volunteer retains the power to quit at any time; once a donation is made, the donor has less control over how it is used. But, on its own, this would not necessarily lead to greater centralization at the national, as opposed to local or state, level[103] were it not for two factors: first, the geographical disjuncture between the resources of women's organizations and the opportunity structure for women's politics; second, the institutional context of federalism. From the eastern seaboard through the older settlements of the Midwest, women's organizations were comparatively large and included many members with disposable incomes and a number with sizable fortunes. However, these states were also controlled by well-developed party organizations, hostile to many social reforms but especially to those that would expand the electorate and make it less easily controllable.[104] To the extent that these women wanted to contribute to the general cause of women's rights, they maximized the chances of success by sending contributions out of state, often by way of the national association.

Such contributions were not purely altruistic. Because of the nature of federalism, political and judicial victories in one state could set precedents for others (see chap. 3). Thus large donors and the national leadership had an important stake in which western campaigns were funded and how they were run. Sometimes they guessed wrong; NAWSA funded the unsuccessful 1896 campaign in Kansas while snubbing Colorado suffragists who would win the vote that year.[105] But regardless of the outcome, the growing importance of the national associations tended to standardize practices and goals across different states and localities. Both the GFWC and NAWSA developed uniform "courses of study" and legislative priorities for each year, although the latter practice was a source of tension with state and local leaders who claimed superior knowledge of political conditions in their own area. Suffrage defeats, far more common than victories, might be blamed on either amateurish local efforts or domineering national leaders. Responding to the criticisms of an Oregon suffrage leader, Susan B. Anthony asserted, "There are not methods that are good for the East that are not equally good for the West. . . . I have been in nearly every state . . . and I have never seen that one place required any different tactics from every other."[106] Western suffragists, however, begged to differ. But, so long as the national leadership controlled the cash, the implementation of standardized methods was likely to prevail. And so long as women lacked the vote—a resource tied to locality—their associations were particularly susceptible to this resource-driven centralization.

To the extent that cash served both as a symbol of citizenship and as a medium of centralization, these developments were more prominent in the suffrage movement than in other women's organizations. But monetary matters also distinguished women's groups from many male-dominated labor and agrarian associations. Whereas full-time suffrage organizers were typically paid a monthly salary and then expected to return all donations and lecture proceeds to the national office,[107] agrarian groups often adopted a more entrepreneurial system where organizers would receive a fee for each local group they established, and dues would be divided among local, county, state, and possibly national levels according to a prearranged formula, typically weighted against the national association.[108] Labor organizers might also be salaried, but transfers of money from one locale to another typically involved extraordinary strike appeals or defense funds rather than routine organizational finance. For women's organizations, and particularly for the most political of them, the pragmatics and symbolics of business methods gradually produced relatively centralized and standardized organizations that could mobilize across electoral districts and levels of federalism.

Out of the Smoke-Filled Room: Legislative Lobbying and Public Opinion

But even as such organizational capacities developed, an important practical challenge remained—how were disenfranchised women to influence elected officials? To address this dilemma, women linked a traditionally feminine rhetoric of education to the disreputable model of the lobby, producing a new form of pressure politics grounded in the cultivation of public opinion. Although the Gilded Age had known a sprinkling of female reformers and even political insiders, the model of the lobby drew extra fire when used by women. Writing in 1886, Ben Perley Poore observed feminine wiles at work in Washington, D.C.:

> [T]he most adroit lobbyists belong to the gentler sex. Some of them are the widows of officers of the army and navy, others the daughters of Congressmen of a past generation, and others have drifted from home localities, where they have found themselves the subject of scandalous comments. . . .
>
> To enable them to do their work well, they have pleasant parlors, with works of art and bric-a-brac donated by admirers. Every evening they receive, and in the winter, their blazing wood fires are often surrounded by a distinguished circle. Some treat favored guests to a game of euchre, and as midnight approaches there is always an adjournment to the dining-room, where a choice supper is served. A cold game pie, broiled oysters, charmingly mixed salad, and one or two light dishes generally constitute the repast, with iced champagne or Burgundy at blood heat. Who can blame a Congressman for leaving the bad cooking of his hotel or boarding house, with the absence of all home comforts, to walk into the parlor web which the cunning spider-lobbyist weaves for him.[109]

In such a deceptively domestic setting, the wine at "blood heat" and even the salad were instruments of illicit political influence. But so long as women were kept from conventional forms of political participation, they continued to forge unexpected—and often culturally illegitimate—connections between private and public in an effort to secure leverage within local, state, and national polities.

Precisely because American women initially pursued their political goals without the benefit of the vote and access to the patronage system, they developed methods of influence distinct from partisan politics. One opening was found in lobbying or petitioning, "a constitutionally guaranteed right of all citizens . . . that nonetheless has no respectability unless it masquerades under euphemistic aliases." Unlike the vote, the right of petition was available to all; "minors, minorities, aliens, women, even idiots have always been able to employ it." Annie Wittenmyer, the first president of the WCTU, felt that memorializing Congress was compatible with the group's identity as a "purely religious movement."[110] Consequently, women faced a dilemma; the form of political action that was "appropriate" for them was also one that positioned them as dependents, lacking leverage over elected officials.

Women worked to rehabilitate petitioning, by associating it with practices and organizational forms that signaled full political standing. Among these was the claim to speak before an elected assembly, rather than to present a petition and be spoken for. State suffrage histories regularly identify the first woman to be granted this privilege, but to speak was not necessarily to be heard. Even as women went to legislatures and "lobbied," they possessed no leverage over elected officials—no votes to be delivered, little money for campaigns, and the possibility of endorsements that might hurt more than they would help. Therefore, in constructing their own "euphemistic alias," one that would distinguish them from aliens, idiots, and others with no claim on citizenship, women drew on the symbolic resources of women's social organization, particularly its overwhelmingly educational style.[111]

Women's organizations used various methods for linking education to political outcomes. The most basic was to work on and through the schools themselves. Recall the decision of the Northern California WCTU to delay asking the legislature for woman suffrage in order "to concentrate all forces this year to secure the Temperance Education Law"; in time, the "Temperance Instruction Law" was the WCTU's first legislative victory in that state. In Washington state, the WCTU promoted the Alcohol Education Act passed by the legislative session of 1885–86.[112] While the immediate object of these bills was to deter students from drinking, to the extent that such education was effective it also produced future constituencies for dry legislation. Hoping to convert the young, women's organizations sponsored school essay contests on subjects ranging from woman suffrage to world peace. And, recognizing a threat when they saw one, politicians fought back. In Nevada, Ann Martin credited opposition to a College Equal Suffrage League essay contest to "George Wingfield, republican 'boss,' ex-gambler, and new millionaire . . . who wishes to restore gambling and make Nevada a wide open state, a sort of 'Men's playground of the western world.' This is why he is fighting equal suffrage and why he had reached out to attack it even through the University, the school system, the boards of county and city park commissioners."[113] As such reactions suggest, women's educational strategies—to a far greater extent than the electoral work of labor and agrarian activists—had the potential to produce long-term shifts in political sentiments.

While the schools were the most obvious target for an educational strategy, the press was another. In an era when cities still boasted multiple newspapers, reformers could often find a sympathetic publisher to print their essays and notices. Even discounting political sympathies, the economics of the newspaper business gave publishers an incentive to accept stories prepared for publication, particularly if they came preset on printing plates. Recognizing this opportunity, activists urged women's organizations at all levels to appoint a press chairman and to distribute regular notices to local papers. Organizing manuals invariably included a section titled "Press Work." The GFWC had both a Bureau of Information and a Press Bureau and sponsored sessions on "the Relation of Women to the Press."[114]

Relations with the press were also shaped by the increasing centralization of national associations. The Northern California branch of the College Equal Suffrage League sent material to four hundred of the state's seven hundred papers: "[W]eekly, or fortnightly or monthly for five years the press matter went out regularly. At first all the material was that published by the National and furnished free to any State association which will distribute it. There was always criticism of the character of the articles from certain local women who knew nothing of the traditions of suffrage and had not been trained under the great leaders. They thought the matter supplied to the local papers should be local in character. . . . I [Mabel Craft Deering] held that what we wanted in the papers was propaganda," news of how suffrage was working in other states and nations.[115] Club manuals included detailed, practical analyses of "making news" and explained how women could work the system: "The word propaganda has fallen into ill repute. As a matter of fact, it is not only legitimate but absolutely necessary to give publicity and push—organized push—to ideas and movements in which we believe. You cannot get such material published as news. How can you get at it? Get someone who has weight to make a statement or get your club to state its position in a resolution or vote. This, with names attached, is often news."[116]

In relying on either people with "weight" or formal organizations as vehicles for public statements, women confronted logics of appropriateness that condemned women who spoke in public. Antebellum female reformers were physically attacked for such behavior; trance speakers were among the first women to speak to large mixed audiences, but then

only as the passive medium for spirit voices. Suffragists, however, sometimes sought to exploit the shock value of women speaking in public to
gather a crowd. Such "street speaking" was the specialty of more radical
and working-class suffragists; the more privileged often spent money to
take meetings indoors to rented halls or engaged in "automobile speaking," which drew regular comment from the press. But these practices
were censured by the more conservative suffragists, who promised "no
parades, no brass bands, no street corner or park speeches, and no automobile rides by our women. We feel confident that the spectacular women
can only amuse, while the intellectual, earnest, home-loving women will
have a message that reaches the heart of all thoughtful men and women
throughout the state." Even when constrained by decorum, however,
women's efforts to shape opinion were influential.[117]

Combined with the greater organizational capacity produced by the
use of business methods, these educational strategies allowed women's
groups to move from the personalistic deployment of "woman's influence" to the systematic cultivation of public opinion:[118] "Formerly we
tried to secure reforms by passing laws, and then letting them become but
dead letters, but we have learned that instead of the sequence of legislation, agitation, and education, better results are obtained by reversing
the order, having education and lots of it precede agitation and needed
legislation." Other groups advocated similar strategies: "The method employed by the Consumers' League to better conditions invariably followed
this rule: obtain facts through investigation, acquaint the public with the
facts, and after educating public opinion, secure legislation."[119]

Education and the cultivation of public opinion gave women the leverage they needed to be convincing as a lobby. Whereas organized labor
could point to a bloc of votes (if union men could be weaned from their
partisan loyalties), women's use of roll-call tabulation and file-card records on individual legislators rang hollow in the absence of a politically
meaningful constituency. But public opinion, however amorphous, mattered to politicians, particularly as they began to take note of partisanship's weakening hold on the electorate. Discouraging the use of public
debates, central to club strategies of civic self-improvement, one California suffragist argued in 1913, "I think we must frankly acknowledge that
people are not all convinced through reason, and that although the proposition that women should vote is seriously and profoundly true, it will,
at first, be established with this class of people much as the virtues of a
breakfast food are established,—by affirmation."[120]

Although the rise of media politics and propaganda has been associated with "the advertising-led consumer prosperity of the 1920s," it was firmly rooted in the politics of education and persuasion developed by reform groups in the preceding decades.[121] Yet the politics of public opinion still ran into difficulty when women attempted to translate research and expertise directly into political influence. Having adapted the model of the lobby and linked it to public opinion, women found that this organizational form could be easily linked to a "logic of inappropriateness." During the debate over California's eight-hour bill for women, Maud Younger, a San Francisco union organizer and "millionaire waitress," encountered this dilemma:

> The rule against lobbying while the houses were in session was strictly enforced. Miss Younger's efforts in behalf of the Eight-Hour Bill had earned her the name of lobbyist. Having business with Senator Caminetti one forenoon, she ventured on the floor of the Senate while that body was in session. Her presence was observed and objection made to lobbyists being permitted on the floor.
> When Caminetti understood that Miss Younger was the "lobbyist" referred to, he became furious even for him. . . .
> "This young woman is assisting me in my work. She is not a lobbyist," she is acting as my clerk. She will not leave my desk."
> Still the objection was made.[122]

The rule against lobbyists on the floor had been passed only two years earlier by antimachine progressives yet was frequently used by machine politicians against reformers. Then, as now, the line between legitimate and illegitimate representation of interests was far from clear. Progressive journalist Franklin Hichborn acknowledged, "The problem of drawing the line between legitimate and reprehensible lobbying has perplexed wiser men than sat in the California Legislature of 1909." Hichborn himself accepted lobbying when one had a "legitimate interest" in a bill, but the criteria for legitimacy remained unclear.[123] But despite these dangers, lobbying was one of the few forms of political influence available to women. The cultural opposition of women's work and politics persisted uneasily in the discourse and practices of women's associations. A year after members advocated "education, agitation, legislation," the Executive Board of the Wisconsin Federation of Women's Clubs declared, with a certain delight:

> True it is that this "many-sided life without the home" tugs at us this way, and pulls us that way, but we are, as yet, only students of the science of good government. We are non-sectarian, non-partisan, non-political. The scope of our work transcends all that, our aim being the higher intellectual,

social and moral conditions. *A wonderful thing it is to belong to a vast organization with no political ties.* While each one of us individually may work for whatsoever or whomsoever we please, as a federation, we do not commit ourselves to parties.[124]

Every move toward more explicitly political action was accompanied by the specter of partisanship. It was not enough for women's groups to pass resolutions favoring social legislation; outcomes depended on developing the means to influence its content and implementation. Resolutions and leaders had to be backed up by leverage stemming from the organization's membership. Yet each of these activities brought women closer to elected officials. Even when working through avowedly nonpartisan organizations, American women continued to find that their choice of political techniques drew comment. As Maud Wood Park of the NAWSA wrote: "The Front Door Lobby was the half-humorous, half-kindly name given to our Congressional Committee in Washington by one of the press-gallery men there, because, as he explained, we never used backstairs methods."[125] But there was always the danger that women would be tempted by the backstairs, that efforts to influence elected officials would lead them to party politics. To avoid this danger, institutional alternatives to legislative lobbying were needed.

From Community to State Agency

While the use of cash promoted civic dignity, women's move away from personal service also stimulated the expansion of state agencies. By adopting business methods, women's groups became increasingly isomorphic to all the other associations, including corporations and state agencies. To the extent that their activities were constructed around a cash nexus, experimental private programs could be more easily sponsored by donors and adopted by state agencies once sufficient public support had been generated.

If the reliance on cash facilitated such transfers, it was not the sole cause. Charitable programs for men had experienced much the same development; indeed, reliance on work-based systems centered on employment exchanges or coal yards was much more frequent for impoverished men. But there was a danger in distributing public monies to poor men, a danger beyond the threat that dependency posed to their moral character. Any such distribution might be easily turned to partisan advantage. In California, it was charged that "the abuse of the system [of outrelief] had established in some of the counties the practice of giving much larger amounts of aid to men of voting age, and of economizing drastically on relief given for women and children." [126] Yet the same was not as obviously true for impoverished women (although aiding the sister, aunt, or destitute mother of a voter was not without consequences). Unable to vote themselves, and unattached to adult men as the very condition of their eligibility for aid, widows and unmarried women could be the targets of public aid without programs inviting attack as politically corrupt. In this respect, the disenfranchised were comparatively acceptable as recipients of public largesse. While the fraternal world of partisanship excluded women, this very exclusion certified them as immune to the corruption of patronage politics.

If the initiation of public spending for women was less fraught with danger, it was also true that public spending in general was less hazardous in the absence of strong, urban-based political machines. As one Eastern reformer noted of the "heterodox" West:

> In the West, the relation between public outdoor relief officials and charity organization societies has on the whole been more cordial than in the East. A comparative freedom in government and a confident resort to governmental agencies instead of private societies characterizes the social development of the West. This has gone so far in places that there has been the danger of a too great readiness to leave the whole social development in the hands of public authorities, forgetting, as has been well said, that "without the experimentation of private agencies and their education of public opinion to better standards, public authorities cannot go a very great distance."

But despite such warnings from advocates of "the sound principles of case work," westerners continued to transfer programs to state agencies, notably in Los Angeles, where the city government both created and funded a municipal charities commission. [127] Women were frequently in the vanguard of this movement. In contrast to the AFL, which sought to address social problems *within* the context of employment contracts, women's groups and voluntary associations freely invited the cooperation of state agencies or, if such agencies did not exist, agitated for their establishment.

State agencies were central to the new politics of interest groups and social programs. In the United States, many women demanded the vote not as a natural right but in order to secure specific reforms—child labor laws, temperance, protective legislation for working women. Frequently, women's groups not only demanded state intervention, but initiated it by providing funds for kindergartens, probation officers, and health inspectors and other services later provided by public agencies. [128] The national

THE CHILDREN'S HEALTH CRUSADE

—*Baltimore Evening Sun*

THIRTY-FOUR states have plans already under way for baby week. The first week of May is the time agreed upon by the General Federation of Women's Clubs, but Nebraska, Massachusetts, California and Pennsylvania will observe it earlier to avoid possible risk of poliomyelitis. The importance of complete birth records has been chosen as their special study by Washington, Illinois, Iowa, New Hampshire and Ohio. Delaware will discuss the prevention of infant paralysis; North Dakota, the needs of children below school age; Kansas, which had last year the largest number of local celebrations, will emphasize birth registration, instructing mothers in infant care, the care of expectant mothers. The federal Children's Bureau at Washington has published a bulletin to assist committees in preparing for baby week. It refers to many agencies from which bulletins, list of exhibit material and other assistance may be had for the asking.

Figure 6.3   The Children's Health Crusade: Women's Associations and Policy Diffusion. (Source: *Survey,* 24 January 1920)

federated organizations coordinated campaigns across states, producing new levels of policy uniformity (see fig. 6.3). Arguing that working women were without the protection of union contracts, women's labor reform groups called for state regulation of women's hours and wages, often drawing criticism from organized labor. These demands for economic regulation and social services mean that women's politics are of particular importance for understanding both the beginnings of the American welfare state and the entrenchment of interest group politics.

The creation of state agencies also had important implications for the future of women's politics in the United States. By shifting to bureaucratic organizations and cash transactions, away from personal service and the creation of community, the adoption of business methods and corporate forms eroded the personal networks and commitments that so often account for the success of a social movement. Yet insofar as women's groups had both created and captured state agencies, a smaller set of reformers and activists could successfully promote a political agenda that once required a mass movement.[129] But in the absence of successful institution-building, the organizational transformations that had secured political access for women also diminished the awareness of a distinctive "women's interest" in public affairs.

Toward a Politics without Parties

Women's influence on the state-building enterprises of the Progressive Era reflected the distinctive cultural and institutional location of their organizing efforts. As an element in the rhetoric of American political reform, women were placed in symbolic opposition to the corrupt mechanisms of late-nineteenth-century politics. As early as 1888, Brother O. F. Alley of the San Jose Grange declared: "We believe that the coming person who shall purify politics, elevate the moral condition of the human race and cultivate and enlarge the spiritual growth, will be a woman, and that this woman will be found in the Grange, a living embodiment of the divine principles of the Patrons of Husbandry."[130] Women's groups reinforced this opposition between women and the existing *partisan* organization of political participation. Claims that these new strategies and models of organization were inappropriate were met with accusations of the vices of political organization among men: "Women are criticized for the methods they pursue to obtain political recognition, also for allowing their impulses rather than their judgment to lead them. Men should remember the beams in their own eyes before pointing out the motes in the eyes of women."[131]

In order to craft new vehicles for political participation, women's groups drew upon forms of organization with which they were already familiar. Thus the central place of education in the women's clubs and moral-reform movements colored the political actions of many women. Prior to gaining the vote, women's groups emphasized civics instruction and discussion of political issues as a means of cultivating informed and independent voters; the same link between education and true citizenship was institutionalized by American farmers, another relatively disenfranchised group. Many women's groups sponsored "civics institutes" prior to the opening of state legislatures or important local elections. This emphasis on the connection of citizenship to education—rather than to party—also informed one of women's most important and enduring contributions to the organizational repertoire of American politics, the nonpartisan forum: "No more amusing or instructive gathering can be imagined than these assemblies of women sitting in judgement while relays of prospective office-holders pass across the stage, explaining each in turn and regardless of his party affiliation, why they should vote for him."[132]

In addition to adopting the practices and imagery of education, women's groups replaced distinctively feminine forms of social organization with organizational models adapted from modern corporations. But while these alternatives muted the opposition of male and female, they heightened that of partisan and nonpartisan. Through a logic of oppositions, where the enemy of my enemy is my friend, these alternatives could be adopted by elite reformers with less experience of popular organizing than their female allies. Thus, at the same time that women drew on forms of economic organization, degendering their associations by imitating the corporations and bureaucracies, they helped to redefine the general terms for political action within the United States.

The organizational and strategic innovations of women's associations were, however, fundamentally limited by their lack of political standing. Without institutionalized opportunities for linking associational resources to public or political goals, women's organizations either stayed with traditional understandings of women's work or explored possible transformations of the domestic sphere or private life. Yet in many states, there were opportunities for organized women to establish a public presence, if only on the margins of the formal polity. Even without the vote, women might establish a public role through their benevolent associations provided that the public sector relied on private associations. Even by 1904, states displayed striking variations in the relations of private organizations and public agencies (table 6.1). In Wisconsin public agencies provided a majority of care; in Washington, ecclesiastical organizations took the lead. In California, by contrast, the prominent place of private benevolent institutions was undergirded by a higher level of public subsidy than was typical of even most western states. For organized women, California's combination of access to public subsidies and the extensive development of what would now be called "the nonprofit sector" offered the greatest opportunity for public engagement.

These variations in resources were overlaid by the strikingly different polities that developed in each state. Most obviously, women secured the vote in Washington in 1910 and California in 1911; in Wisconsin, women had to await the 1920 amendment to the U.S. Constitution. This difference in timing was accentuated by the varied opportunities for political action. In California, the party system was largely dismantled; in California and Washington, early passage of the initiative and referendum left state governments open to nonpartisan and extrapartisan pressure politics. Both developments mapped on to the organizational innovations of the national women's associations. In Wisconsin, however, efforts for political reform were largely contained within the Republican and Social Democratic Parties, a coalition arrangement that required suppressing ethnic and religious differences that would be aggravated by raising issues

Table 6.1   Financing of Benevolent Institutions, 1903

	Public	Private	Ecclesiastical
Percentage of Total Cost of Maintenance Borne, by Type of Supporting Institution			
United States	29.3	43.5	27.3
California	36.2	36.5	27.3
Washington	25.8	24.8	49.5
Wisconsin	57.2	14.2	28.6
Percentage of All Public Funding Received, by Type of Institution Receiving Support			
United States	72.8	16.2	11.0
California	76.6	8.4	14.9
Washington	87.9	6.6	5.5
Wisconsin	99.3	0.3	0.4

Source: U.S. Bureau of the Census, *Benevolent Institutions, 1904* (Washington, D.C.: Government Printing Office, 1905), 19–20.

such as temperance or woman suffrage. Politically much weaker than either organized labor or farmers, the development of women's associations was shaped directly by the opportunities present in different polities.

Wisconsin: The Persistence of Women's Work
The expansion of Wisconsin's social-policy apparatus occurred in the absence of sustained political participation by women's organizations. Their political marginalization was produced by the incompatible organizational forms that structured the public lives of the state's men and women. Unlike Washington with its populist heritage or California where business methods were widely adopted by women's groups, in Wisconsin temperance and moral-reform organizations were among the most visible vehicles available to politically active women who sought to promote issues concerning "domestic" values. A statewide association of charities was organized in the nineteenth century but fell into disarray and was not reorganized until 1917, well after the passage of much of the state's landmark welfare legislation. For the most part, settlement house work was limited to Milwaukee and tended to focus on specific ethnic groups. Even in this city, the settlement houses were not closely linked to one of the few major reform groups in which women were prominent, the Milwaukee Schools Committee. And, unlike its counterparts in other cities, this

committee limited its activities to schools and related issues rather than developing a broader program of social reform.[133]

Even where charities were well established, they were ill suited to serve as an organizational base in the state's politics. The coalition between progressive (often rural) Republicans and Milwaukee socialists survived only insofar as it avoided issues, such as English-language school instruction and temperance, that might split the coalition along ethnoreligious lines. Even if progressive women shared the goals of the temperance movement, they were unable to utilize its organizational resources for the sort of coalition building that was essential for a disenfranchised group to achieve its goals.

The same problems appeared in the state chapter of NAWSA, which was dominated by upper- and middle-class, Protestant, temperance-oriented women. When Meta Berger, wife of the leading Milwaukee socialist, was named president of the state NAWSA affiliate, she declined on the grounds that her political associations might damage the movement.[134] Caught in a particular conjunction of class, ethnoreligious, and gender cleavages, women in Wisconsin repeatedly defined themselves and their interests in terms that were unacceptable to the political coalition promoting progressive reform. Compounding the isolation of conservative women's groups, labor organizations and the Milwaukee Social Democrats discouraged the emergence of women's organizations of the Left. Insofar as the mothers, wives, and daughters of Wisconsin's unionists were organized, they typically formed women's auxiliaries.

Constrained as they were by nativism, dry sentiments, and organizational weakness, some Wisconsin women's groups were still willing to venture into politics. The Milwaukee Consumers' League gave its support to women's hours legislation, although the primary advocates of these bills were the city's Social Democratic legislators. The State Federation of Women's Clubs passed resolutions favoring mothers' pensions and child labor laws, sent officers to testify on bills, and created a Legislative Committee whose members "are finding the work decidedly educational, and are acquiring a knowledge of the methods used to pass or defeat bills never dreamed of in the philosophy of women's clubs."[135] In images of the passage of the mothers' pension law, women are present only as the vulnerable mother or the privileged reactionary. Women organized in support of social legislation are absent; instead, women appear as either objects of, or obstacles to, social reform (fig. 6.4). By the second decade of the century, women's groups in Wisconsin confronted a quasi-corporatist political world tailored to the coalition of progressive Republicans and

Figure 6.4 The Absence of Women's Associations from Reform Politics in Wisconsin. (Source: Irma Hochstein, *A Progressive Primer* [Madison: Wisconsin Women's Progressive Association, 1922])

organized labor. Once these arrangements were in place, women's groups could comment on policy sponsored by other political actors. But the feedback relationship between organized women and state agencies found in California developed in Wisconsin only once women gained the vote.

In 1921, the Wisconsin Women's Progressive Association was founded; its president was a veteran suffragist, and the wives of numerous progressive politicians were listed among the officers. Yet in that same year, activist women were swiftly divided over an ultimately adopted bill giving equal rights to women. Prefiguring the division among women over the Equal Rights Amendment to the U.S. Constitution, numerous suffragists opposed the Wisconsin bill as a threat to protective legislation and, due to its poor drafting, an invitation to the courts to become involved in what should be a legislative decision. Irma Hochstein, a suffragist and employee of the state legislative reference library, explained, "The theory on which Wisconsin bill-drafting has been carried on in the past is to make the working of each law so definite that court constructions will be reduced to the minimum. We have carefully amended the sections of the statutes which we wish to change, striking out the old and inserting new phrases. This requires tedious study, but has its reward in definiteness and a greater degree of safety."[136]

Washington: Integration into the Reform Coalition

In a stark contrast to Wisconsin, women in Washington secured the vote and a reputation for political activism even before statehood. In 1883, Washington Territory passed a woman suffrage bill with farmers providing the margin of victory in the legislature. Unlike the enfranchised women of Wyoming and Utah, the women of Washington rapidly emerged as a significant electoral factor, helping to oust a corrupt administration in Seattle and to pass a series of vice ordinances.[137] In 1887, however, the territorial supreme court declared the 1883 bill unconstitutional. The bill was reenacted and once more overturned, so when Washington became a state in 1890, its women lacked the vote.

This history of political participation helps to explain the absence of a cohesive and enduring suffrage movement between 1888 and 1910, when women regained the vote. Suffrage amendments were debated, but their sponsors were often affiliated with other reform movements; the demand for woman suffrage was part of an eclectic reform agenda promoted by moral-reform groups, voluntary associations, and political parties. Similarly, women's groups embraced a wide variety of substantive issues. By 1903, "They began discussing Marxism, the 'labor question,' and the 'social disease.' And to Olympia they sent a delegation to lobby for laws protecting the interests of female and child wage earners." "These female lobbyists, in the opinion of one legislator, made conservatives look 'like mangy kittens in a tiger fight.'"[138] Once women gained the vote, their lobbying activities were formalized still further: "Suffrage seems to give a certain commanding tone to women's voice," observed a Seattle minister in 1917. "Of the thirty-three measures that women's organizations of the state favored, nine became laws. The women sustained a kind of weather bureau at the capitol, called an 'information bureau,' where the legislators could read the signs in the political sky."[139] Spokesmen for trade unions praised the activist women's lobby. Others criticized it as fundamentally indecent.

The women's clubs, along with the unionized waitresses, worked with the Washington State Federation of Labor in its campaign for workmen's compensation legislation. In turn, the WaSFL—unlike most state labor federations—supported legislation for a women's minimum wage when it was introduced in 1913: "[P]oliticians and businessmen could not afford to antagonize the most aggressive advocates of the minimum wage— the clubwomen."[140] Both in their organization and their policy concerns, "women's politics" were less clearly differentiated in Washington than in other states. The continuing influence of the Grange and the heritage of the Knights, both of which were relatively open to participation by women, contributed to this lack of distinctiveness. These labor and agrarian organizations also shared the moral concerns of many national women's associations. Unlike California, where suffragists reconstituted themselves as well-heeled nonpartisan groups, the women of Washington state imported expansive visions of moral reform into the arena of progressive politics. Three years after gaining the vote in 1910, the cover of a women's newspaper proclaimed:

> The Real Issues Before the People—To Abolish Privilege—Tariff Privilege—Land Monopoly—Money Monopoly—Transportation Monopoly—To Abolish Slavery—Child Slavery—"White" Slavery—"Wage" Slavery—Prison Slavery—Military Slavery—The Slavery of the Sea—To Abolish Government by Injunction—To Banish Poverty, Drunkenness and War—To Destroy All Property in Drugs and Vice—To Abolish Involuntary Idleness—To Abolish Charity—To Insure Personal Liberty and Industrial Freedom—Freedom of Speech—Freedom of Press—Freedom of Thought—Free Land—Free Trade—The Right to Lay Down One's Tools—The Right of Organization—The Ancient Right of Boycott—Some Work, Some Leisure for All.[141]

Populist legacies lessened the incentive to cultivate more organizationally delimited forms of activism; like both labor and farmers in Washington state, women did not form strong alliances with nonpartisan state agencies.[142]

California: A Female Dominion in Politics and Policy

In contrast to both the organizational conservatism of Wisconsin's women's groups and the strength of mixed-sex organizing in Washington,[143] there was a tradition of enduring independent organization among Californian women. The nineteenth century was, as one Los Angeles woman observed, "a clubbable age—particularly among the gentler sex."[144] In Southern California, the women's clubs and literary societies were part of a broader climate of nationalism and urban populism: "[A] middle-class Protestant community which had come to California out of incipiently utopian motivations in the first place found it perfectly natural, once there, to dream of shaping a public polity that would more completely express its collective desire for a better life."[145] The genteel socialism of Pasadena and similar towns resisted recognition of class conflict: "Ideas and possibilities could flow from the far left to the reforming conservatives . . . because the barrier of class and class antagonism, which the California Progressives loathed and feared, was not present."[146] In the more industrialized north, however, the relations between class and gender were less pliable. Among the factors singled out to explain the defeat of a suffrage amendment placed on the ballot in 1896 were "the very wealthy and the very poor in San Francisco and the Bay area; both the Roman Catholic Church and the anti-Catholic American Protective Association; [and] hostile illiterate men who had been able to identify the suffrage amendment because it was last on the ballot."[147] Social cleavages defined in terms of class, ethnicity, and religion reinforced both sides in the conflict over women's appropriate political role.

Despite these unpromising beginnings, California's women not only gained the vote (in 1911) but were active participants in the state's progressive administration and an important element in the coalition that increasingly relied on the votes of urban workers[148]—the very group that had been most opposed to woman suffrage. The transition from fervent opposition to a moderately successful working partnership was facilitated by the distinctive forms of organization adopted by California's socially and politically active women.

The dominant patterns of mobilization among women differed in the two sections of the state. Whereas literary and civic clubs complemented suffrage organizations in the south,[149] the San Francisco Bay area gave rise to reform-oriented service organizations. By the 1890s, loose federations of women's clubs had been established,[150] and, under the impact of the depression of 1893, they turned from literary and artistic concerns to civic projects. In combination with a revived scientific charities movement, the clubs promoted the improvement of education, institutional care for the insane and disabled, and the care of destitute women.[151]

These developments accelerated in the wake of the San Francisco earthquake of 1906. Since the city was then embroiled in a graft prosecution of the Union Labor administration, providers of federal and private relief refused to rely on the municipal government to administer these funds. By default, management of the relief program was entrusted to the Associated Charities of San Francisco, a group in which women had already established a significant presence. While they practiced "scientific charity"—notably the systematic investigation of relief applicants to prevent "double-dipping"—these women also provided "refugee shacks" that were eventually converted into working-class homes on private lots. More surprising was their response to destitute women and children, which one reporter described as "the most important sociological innovation ever made in San Francisco." Continuing an earlier effort to deinstitutionalize the state's orphans, the Associated Charities simply boarded out babies

for $12.50 a month: "[T]he foster mother was a gentle, wholesome look-
ing young woman—a model mother. Deserted by a worthless husband,
she supplemented her slim income by taking a little boy to board, one of
the charges of the Associated Charities."[152] Like the later mothers' pensions, this program provided women with the money to support their own
children. Unlike the mothers' pensions, women earned this money by entering into an explicit employment relationship with a public agency. For
the charity volunteers of San Francisco, the potential of moral suasion or
social control paled in contrast to the power of public spending.

Far more eagerly than either organized workers or farmers, women's
associations supported the expansion of public services. As early as 1889,
Los Angeles clubwomen subsidized the establishment of public kinder-
garten classes by paying part of the assistant's salary as well as some general expenses.[153] In 1905, the Los Angeles clubs were the second district
in the nation to sponsor a "scholarship plan of service," providing "a
small sum, $3.00 a week, which may be paid to the destitute parents of
children, and so enable the children to attend school—a necessity to the
enforcement of the Child Labor and Compulsory Education laws." Clubwomen in San Francisco and Los Angeles also paid for the first probation
officers in their cities, though that responsibility was soon assumed by
state and local governments.[154] In contrast to the language of moral reform and social control that is stereotypically associated with most wom-
en's movements of the period, the women of the charities associations
followed the clubwomen in adopting increasingly bureaucratic *and* political organizational practices. As the system of interest group bargaining
over legislation consolidated, even moral reformers such as the "White
Ribboners" adapted; by 1915, the WCTU helped to create a special
single-issue organization—the California Campaign Federation—in order to promote two bills that would gradually commit the state to prohibition.[155]

The ways in which groups organize and define their interests have significant consequences for the possibilities of forming political coalitions
and passing legislation. Women from the charities movement were given
considerable responsibility within Hiram Johnson's first administration,
even though Johnson had not been a particular supporter of woman suffrage. Unlike the women of Wisconsin, these Californians had been part
of a highly unified woman suffrage campaign that included the state federation of women's clubs, the state WCTU, and a host of other groups.
With their loyalties uncertain and a strong logic of appropriateness linking women's groups to nonpartisan politics, the newly enfranchised voters

were a source of concern to leaders of both parties. While efforts were made to incorporate women in the apparatus of both parties,[156] from 1912 women's associations supported a lobbying effort of their own at the state capital.[157] This standing as an electoral bloc and ability to establish direct relations with state agencies helps to explain the prominent role of women in reorganizing political relations in California.

National Ramifications
As was true with other organized political challengers, women's accomplishments in individual states had far-reaching consequences for American politics. At one level, the simple divergence among state polities expanded the range of "virtual choices" available to political actors in other locales. As women in California and other western states accumulated successful records as civic leaders, state bureaucrats, and even elected officials, the "logics of inappropriateness" that barred women from political life were steadily eroded.

Success also reflected back on the techniques of nonpartisan and extrapartisan pressure politics that were widely associated with women's groups. The long-standing political exclusion of women ensured that their renewed activism would be particularly disruptive to the culture and structure of political life.[158] Rooted in a subculture that had opposed itself to the fraternal world of partisan politics, women's organizations played a special role in the attack on that system:

> Women are surprisingly quick, perhaps because of their experience with naughty boys, to distrust candidates who try to hypnotize the voters with loud oratory and who dodge straight questions from the floor. Their intuitions seem to make them keenly alive to the dangers of machine politics and they are more and more the despair of politicians who wish to enforce party regularity and to herd voters ignorantly to the polls. . . . [I]n their simplicity they demand *clear* issues and when they understand them vote conscientiously; but rather than be befogged into voting wrong they will stay away from the polls.[159]

This profound antipathy for partisan politics aligned women's groups with both populist antiparty movements and more genteel good government groups. But an alliance of the disenfranchised and an idealistic minority did not offer much hope of success, so women's groups directed much of their energy toward discovering new ways of working within a partisan system.

This reinterpretation is clearest in the case of the lobby. In the Gilded Age, the lobby had belonged to the "Interests," said with a sneer and an implication of bribery. Women took the lobby and transformed it into an everyday interest group—just a collection of concerned citizens trying to make their voices heard. This transformation depended on two qualities that the progressive leadership did not share with organized women. As women, they could claim independence from partisan politics; as leaders of a mass movement,[160] they could claim to represent a large and legitimate (potential) constituency. Once they had gained the right to vote, a purification from within could begin. Some women, notably those most active in the suffrage movement, went so far as to imitate the practices of the despised political machines. In their successful campaign for the vote in 1911, California women adopted a system of precinct canvasing and mobilization that their counterparts in New York had borrowed from the infamous Tammany Hall machine.[161]

The combination of symbolic opposition and practical imitation proved unstable. Ironically, woman suffrage threatened the autonomy of women's associations by denying the existence of a distinctly feminine political interest,[162] while allowing the erosion of solidarities based in exclusively female organizations. While women's organizations worked hard to maintain their nonpartisan standing, many individual activists either brought partisan loyalties into their political efforts or developed them in the process of working with elected officials to pass legislation or administer programs. While their official policy declared most women's groups—like fraternal societies—to be nonpartisan, and individuals were sometimes purged for excessive partisanship,[163] increasingly these divisions fractured alliances among women. Anticipating that newly enfranchised women would constitute a formidable electoral bloc, their loyalties were actively courted by both parties (fig. 6.5). Ironically, the very success of women's politics without party helps to account for their failure to articulate a unified political agenda after gaining the national suffrage after the First World War.[164]

Once admitted to electoral competition, women found that the distinctive identities and methods they had cultivated were undermined. Having mobilized around identities and organizational forms defined in opposition to party politics, women activists found it difficult to mobilize as a bloc within the electoral system. The very effort to work within parties appeared at odds with the moral and political rhetorics used to articulate women's distinctive claims upon politics. Arguing that "[w]omen must learn to Play the Game as Men Do," for example, Eleanor Roosevelt urged women to support "women bosses" within the parties rather than pursuing separatist strategies. While "the word 'boss' might 'shock sensi-

"TWO'S COMPANY, THREE'S A CROWD."
—Chapin in the St. Louis *Republic*.

Figure 6.5 Two's Company: Party Politics and the Fragmentation of the Woman Movement. (Source: *Literary Digest*, 28 June 1919, p. 17)

tive ears,'" she asserted that "if women believe they have a right and duty in political life today, they must learn to talk the language of men. They must not only master the phraseology, but also understand the machinery which men have built up through years of practical experience. Against the men bosses there must be women bosses who can talk as equals, with the backing of a coherent organization of women voters behind them."[165] But insofar as women accommodated themselves to existing institutions, their insurgent edge was blunted. Similarly, as their organizational innovations were appropriated by other, often more powerful, groups, the tactical advantages of new forms eroded. Both these developments expose the instrumentalist fallacy. Simply because women's organizations helped to bring about institutional change does not imply that those changes were ultimately to their advantage. But neither can causal significance be measured solely by the ultimate balance of benefits.

In conjunction with the organized challenges from labor and farmers, women's associations contributed to the steady erosion of a political regime centered on elections and structured by partisan loyalties. The lingering effects of older logics of appropriateness were evident in attacks on women's political motives and the persistent taint associated with the form of the lobby. In 1924, an unnamed observer was quoted as charging that

> the American woman in her activities wants, not your way, nor our way, but her own way.
> "Group legislation" we at large have been saying to Labor for some while.
> "Group legislation" we're crying nowadays to the would-be Blocs, the farmer and others.
> "Group legislation" we'll have to cry next to the organized American woman and her lobby, the Women's Joint Congressional Committee. For, of man's political weapons, the American woman has taken for her own the lobby—of all of them the most undemocratic.[166]

Former suffragists and clubwomen who had adopted the lobby might differ with this conclusion, arguing that a party system that excluded women and was unresponsive to much of the male electorate was less democratic still.

In itself, weakening the party system could not produce a new type of political regime. Beyond the erosion of parties, the new models of political organization adopted and adapted by challengers had to be linked into a new system, anchored by ties to legislatures and agencies, sustained by distinctive patterns of resources. The articulation of alternatives and effective disruption of the existing regime were the beginning of institutional change; institutionalization itself was the conclusion.

SEVEN

Challenge and Crystallization: The Institutionalization of Reform in Three States

> The rapid concentration of wealth into the hands of the favored few, the unequal distribution of taxation which burdens the poor and the masses and relieves the rich and the classes are conditions which confront the American people today and demand their attention.
>
> All this, and more, have given rise to organizations amongst the various representations of labor (agriculturalists and wage laborers). A dozen organizations, strong and invincible, have sprung up to do battle against the common foe.
>
> *Colfax Commoner* (Washington), 27 November 1891

> Throughout the West the legislative harvest this year has been more than abundant. Its fruits have left no activity of the human being untouched. . . . During the [California] session's final days they passed laws at the rate of one a minute, and in half a dozen other Western states the bearings of the statute mill smoked with the heat of an equally rapid pace.
>
> *Sunset: The Pacific Monthly,* July 1913

In the decades surrounding the turn of the century, a host of new—if rarely invincible—popular organizations rejected politics as usual and invented strategies of political action that were at least partially independent of the two major parties. These efforts were motivated by the failure of the parties to address the issues that concerned many citizens and by the growing recognition that political outcomes were often more responsive to the demands of large corporations than to popular sentiments. The challenge for organized labor, farmers, and women was to tie policy outcomes to their own concerns. To meet this challenge, much more was required than simply calculating individual interests on election day. First, the party system, which often suppressed policy choices in order to build

235

electoral coalitions, had to be weakened if not dismantled altogether. Second, politically relevant resources—whether votes, money, public opinion, or organizational skills and networks—had to be mobilized in ways that resisted co-optation by the parties. The first effort served to increase the opportunities for extrapartisan political action, to open more space for new forms of organization. The second effort involved the discovery and mastery of these new forms, which, in turn, provided the templates for the enduring rearrangement of institutions or—to use imagery popular in the 1920s, the "crystallization" of a new politics.

Institutional disruption was the first goal of political challengers. Third parties and procedural reforms such as direct democracy and primary elections worked to weaken party organizations. By heightening the dependence of legislators on the goodwill of their constituents, these reforms also diminished (if only temporarily) the control of large corporations and lobbyists over policy outcomes. Corporations were further hobbled by new regulatory agencies and, in Wisconsin and California, by systems of taxation that financed expanded public services with taxes on corporate incomes. All these "opportunity-expanding" reforms were most easily attained where party organizations had never been fully entrenched—in the Midwest and West. Thus the classic reforms of the Progressive Era may be understood as opening up a greater space for new forms of political action and as generating the resources necessary to meet new kinds of political demands.

The consequences of organizational repertoires for political change are most apparent in the degree to which different challengers discovered and adapted organizational forms that were appropriate for political action and yet drew on resources, rhetorics, and networks distinct from the party system. This was a particular challenge for popular associations since their primary political resource—the votes of their members—was intimately bound up with party politics. But to the extent that associations were able to frame political choices in terms other than partisanship (typically by training their members to attend to issues and monitor their representatives' actions) and to muster the organized effort to advance political claims outside the parties, new ties among political actors and institutions could be established. Candidates became less dependent on their party and more dependent on the goodwill *and* election-time assistance of organized constituencies. State agencies, once established, attracted the attention of organizations. Ties between agencies and associations were increasingly independent of both electoral politics and legislative decision-making—although these same constituencies could be most valuable at appropriations time.[1] This process has path-dependent qualities. The strength and character of party organization in a state set the opportunities for challengers. The success or failure of one challenger changed the opportunities for others creating distinctive political configurations.

For workingmen, the degree of dissatisfaction with the party system reflected the extent to which the geographies of politics and industry coincided. Where unionists were geographically concentrated *and* organizationally unified, they could contest elections and constitute a labor "bloc" in the state legislature, a strategy pursued successfully in both Milwaukee and San Francisco. Where this strategy was complemented, as in Wisconsin, by effective coalition partners and state agencies open to influence by organized constituents, there was little incentive to dismantle the party system in favor of a nonpartisan regime of pressure groups and autonomous agencies. In California, organized labor began to move toward extrapartisan, agency-centered models as the state's progressive reformers lost control of elections toward the end of the second decade of the century. Finally, in Washington, organized labor found few openings in the party system. Unionists remained open to both independent-party politics and to expansive visions of self-organization that would also enroll organized farmers.

Like many workingmen, American farmers turned first to partisan politics to address their grievances and found that their demands were largely ignored by the national leadership of both parties. But unlike organized labor, most agrarian associations had no entrenched eastern leadership to restrain them from embarking on the third-party adventures of the 1880s and 1890s. Furthermore, the numerical dominance of farmers, particularly in the Plains states, held out real promise of electoral victory. But despite the scattered Populist victories, the legacy of 1896 was a profound discrediting of independent agrarian politics. In the resulting void, agrarian organizers sought to fashion new political strategies from the remaining components of their repertoire, particularly from the nonpartisan, or friends-and-enemies, pressure group and the cooperative.

In these efforts, however, agrarian organizers were constrained by the opportunities afforded by each state. An effective friends and enemies strategy depended on competitive elections (both primary and general) with candidates taking divergent positions on policies of concern to farmers; in Wisconsin, largely controlled by an alliance of progressive Republicans and Social Democrats, farmers exerted little independent organized influence. An alliance of cooperatives and state agencies required, by definition, that those agencies be established, adequately funded, and relatively free of partisan control and corruption; this situation had been established in California by 1910, leaving organized farmers with considerable control over their own affairs but less general political influence. Finally, if neither major parties nor state agencies afforded openings for agrarian mobilization, the independent party remained an option—particularly in the presence of a like-minded labor movement; this alignment of opportunities and organized challengers prevailed in Washington state. For relatively weak political actors such as farmers in states with mixed economies—short of resources, divided by crop, lacking a national organizing framework—opportunity often dictated which organizational model would prevail.

The weakness of parties and the openness of general organizations to women's participation defined the different opportunity structures confronted by women's associations in the three states. So long as they lacked the vote, women's organizations could pursue policy goals only by cultivating allies among either enfranchised men or sympathetic state officials. Consequently, the opportunity structure for women's politics was not constituted directly by the weakness of parties, but indirectly through the presence of influential popular associations or strong state agencies. But if such allies were too forthcoming, too open to women's participation, the autonomous organizational base for "women's interests" would not develop. In Washington, the persistence of nineteenth-century organizations that were relatively open to women (e.g., the Grange and successors to the Knights of Labor) combined with strong commitments to direct democracy to produce an environment open to women's policy concerns but less likely to foster autonomous women's associations. California, by comparison, combined weak parties with an associational field in which the AFL had displaced "producerist" organizations and nineteenth-century agrarian groups had given way to twentieth-century agribusiness. Strong women's organizations developed in an environment where their organizational resources and political-education campaigns were a significant factor even prior to woman suffrage. Finally, Wisconsin combined an immigrant-dominated labor movement hostile to many of the cultural issues linked to the "woman movement"[2] with a reform effort grounded in partisan insurgency rather than the institutionalization and cultivation of direct democracy. Consequently, only in California were "women's interests" clearly differentiated and institutionalized, affording women's associations leverage within the arena of bureaucratic politics as well as in the politics of elections and public opinion.

Opportunities guided the selection of organizational forms from a group's repertoire and their adaptation for political ends. The possibilities for political action were constrained, however, by the logics of appropriateness attached to forms and actors. The models of the fraternal order and women's club, for example, were widely known but understood to be fundamentally inappropriate for politics. Recall the query in the *Freemason's Repository* in 1880: "Is it not a matter of rejoicing that Masonry knows neither sect nor party, and that the Lodge-room is the one place where men of all opinions can meet in blessed communion?"[3] As late as 1916, a Washington clubwoman bemoaned the failure of her organization to address the improvement of industrial conditions, explaining that the subject "would lead them into that forbidden realm 'politics,' for causes and cures."[4] Even as the obstacles to political involvement were gradually circumvented through the development of new models of collective action, not all popular associations demanded increased government intervention, spending, or provision of services. Workingmen often resisted any taint of dependency on the state; farmers suspected that the expansion of state agencies would come at their expense as property owners and taxpayers. Thus the selection of models for collective action— along with their images of shared identity and logics of appropriateness— might facilitate or inhibit the formation of ties to either legislatures or new agencies. If formed, these ties were strengthened further insofar as they were a source of government programs or resources that could then reinforce the commitment of individuals to organizations and organizations to state-oriented political action. As these new forms became embedded in the habits of the membership, the relations among political figures, and the resources that flowed through policy domains, political inventions became innovations—enduring transformations of political institutions.

The process of institutionalizing reform took a distinctive shape in each state. Political challengers experimented with diverse forms of political mobilization, experienced varying levels of success, and, on these bases, worked to dismantle the party system to a greater or lesser degree. States also differed in the extent to which there developed substitutes for the bonds of partisanship that tied individual voters and associations to the political process. To the extent that challengers valued expertise or "business methods" applied to public service, they might call for the establishment of state agencies and then form close working relations with the newly ensconced state bureaucrats. To the extent that challengers were oriented to economic self-organization and autarky, there were far fewer occasions that elicited ties between popular associations and state agencies.

The availability of resources was a second factor shaping the crystallization of relations among political challengers, elected officials, and state agencies. To the extent that legislatures and agencies were amply endowed with tax revenues, the potential payoffs for effective pressure group politics were higher. Insofar as programs were administered through contracting or subsidies to private groups, the ties between political institutions and public associations were strengthened still further. Even in the absence of significant revenues to distribute, programs that formalized participation by a range of concerned groups in formulating or administering policy also locked in the orientation of popular associations toward state agencies rather than in the direction of self-help or disruptive insurgency.[5]

Regional variations in political resources display a pattern familiar from earlier discussions of political opportunity. While state revenue receipts increased nationally between 1903 and 1913, per capita receipts were highest in states northwest of a line drawn from Arizona to Wisconsin, along with a second cluster of high-revenue states in New England that coincided with the persistence of strong party organizations (fig. 7.1). In the West, there were also robust contrasts among states. From the 1910s through the 1920s, revenues grew, but differences among the three persisted (table 7.1) and, between California and the other two, increased.[6]

A typology of polities is produced by combining variations in the degree of articulation (outside of any party organization) between popular associations and state governments with differences in the level of resources available in a political system (table 7.2). This scheme presumes a minimum level of associational activity as well as a basic framework of democratic rules. Yet within those assumptions, multiple arrangements of state structure and associational politics may develop. Because democratic politics is, above all, a collective enterprise, these emerging patterns of state-society relations tended to be self-reinforcing. If legislators had learned that voters would punish them for violating promises made to associations, it was comparatively easy and advantageous for one more association to extract one more pledge. Had this "lesson" not been learned, efforts to hold candidates to their promises were likely to be both costly and futile.

Since institutionalization is shaped by the extent to which a strategy or model is shared and linked to resources, laws, or cultural norms—

NATIONAL · AND STATE REVENUES AND EXPENDITURES.

MAP 1.—PER CAPITA REVENUE RECEIPTS OF STATES: 1913.

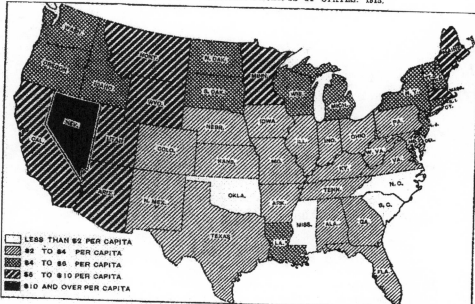

Figure 7.1 State Government Revenues Per Capita, 1913. (Source: U.S. Bureau of the Census, *Wealth, Debt, and Taxation: 1913* [Washington, D.C.: Government Printing Office, 1915])

Table 7.1 Revenues Per Capita from General Property Taxes: 1912, 1922, 1932

	1912	1922	1932
California[a]	$26.36	$52.05	$55.61
Washington	$27.32	$48.84	$46.79
Wisconsin	$15.79	$41.39	$41.37

Sources: U.S. Bureau of the Census, *Financial Statistics of State and Local Governments: 1932* (Washington, D.C.: Government Printing Office, 1935), 200, 1906, 1908; U.S. Bureau of the Census, *Historical Statistics of the United States, Colonial Times to 1970* (Washington, D.C.: Government Printing Office, 1975), 195–209.

Note: Figures are total revenues from the general property tax (state, county, city or town, school district, and other civil divisions) divided by total state population for 1910, 1920, and 1930.

a. In California, no property tax was levied for state purposes. State government was funded by a tax on utility corporations.

Table 7.2 Typology of State Polities: Extrapartisan Associations and State Revenues

State Resources	Extrapartisan Linkages between Associations and State Government	
	Low	High
Low	Associational governance (e.g., Washington)	Participatory governance, (e.g., Wisconsin)
High	Patronage parties	Pluralist spending state, (e.g., California)

rather than by some absolute criterion of efficacy—both initial conditions and sequences of events loom large (see chap. 2). As the previous three chapters have documented, in each of these three states, challengers began with somewhat different organizational repertoires, faced distinctive obstacles or opportunities, and, in consequence, worked with varying intensity and in different directions to invent new models of organization and new mechanisms of political influence.

Wisconsin: Electoral and Regulatory Corporatism

Three organizational accomplishments shaped the trajectory of institutional development in Wisconsin: the success of the La Follette faction of the Republican Party, the consolidation of the socialists in Milwaukee, and the establishment of relatively autonomous and effective state agencies. These accomplishments profoundly shaped state-society relations in Wisconsin. Because a reform faction captured one major party, pressure to dismantle to party system was minimized. La Follette himself championed the direct primary but showed little enthusiasm for the initiative, referendum, and recall. Only in 1911 did the state legislature approve a bill establishing the initiative and referendum—but then only in a modified version that still required proposals to be channeled through the legislature rather than being placed directly on the ballot. Passage by a second session and popular approval at a general election were still required but not soon achieved. Consequently, Wisconsin voters lacked the political access provided by the initiative and referendum well into the 1920s.[7] In contrast to activists in Washington who predicted that direct democracy would soon supplant the role of the legislature, the reformers in Wisconsin did "not [contemplate] that the initiative and referendum will to any considerable extent perform the functions of the legislature. They are looked upon as corrective devices to be invoked when the legislature fails to heed popular demands."[8] The potential terrain for nonpartisan or extrapartisan activity in Wisconsin was narrow.

"Wisconsin progressives," noted one enthusiastic observer, "do not want a new party except in the field of national politics"—nor were they enthusiastic about direct democracy.[9] Although they preferred a different party, much might be said of labor in Wisconsin, perhaps the most influential organized constituency in the state. Many union leaders were committed to the Social Democrats, just as other reformers remained committed to a progressive Republican Party. This alignment was reinforced by a second shared orientation, toward expert administration.[10] In 1915, opposing an attempt by the conservative administration of Emanuel Philipp to dismantle part of the progressive bureaucracy, J. J. Handley of the WiSFL declared the bill "a joke":

> What do you think of a scheme for one board of five members to administer all the laws concerning such related topics as mothers' pensions, bed bugs, maraschino cherries, Asiatic cholera, Limberger cheese, lunatics, peddlers, paupers, the water supply of the state, milk, heating and ventilation of public buildings? . . . Can a board with such a hodge-podge of duties successfully protect you and your families against disease and fraud?[11]

Progressive models of expert administration facilitated labor's participation in policy formation despite the WiSFL's commitment to independent labor politics.[12] With the proper interpretation of expertise, progressive methods might even generate union jobs. With one eye to their own prospects and the other to public safety, a delegate from the Boilermakers and Iron Ship Builders of Superior called for the 1920 convention "to again have drafted a bill providing for boiler inspection, said bill to provide for practical boiler makers of four or more years' experience, to be appointed."[13] In the face of this state-centered model of cooperation, the significance of the federation's commitment to partisanship declined. "The lobbying of interested groups" helped to transform socialist ideology into acceptable policy, "so that the enactment of labor legislation has become increasingly independent of political alliances."[14] Ironically, the presence of a strong, ideologically grounded socialist party—a hallmark of social-welfare politics in Europe—seems to have contributed to the relatively early emergence of a characteristically American political arrangement, the interest group lobby linked to administrative agencies:

> This development of its lobbying power represents a shift in function for the trade unions from the economic, not to the political, but to what might be called the semi-political, a shift that has grown from its successes in this

direction and perhaps from its failure in economic activity, but which has also been created by the state.[15]

This shift from electoral politics to the realm of administrative agencies gave rise to an institutional configuration that appears as the direct ancestor of the iron triangles and policy networks of the contemporary organizational state. A string of legislative victories enhanced the capacities of public agencies as well as of organized labor as a political actor. A bill permitting "the formation of tenant copartnership associations on the English model" allowed the Milwaukee city government to make an initial foray into the public promotion of housing development.[16] The workmen's compensation law was extended to cover occupational diseases in 1919, while the State Federation of Labor secured laws guaranteeing a jury trial "in any case relating to violation of restraining orders of injunctions" and requiring "the registering, licensing and bonding of all private detectives."[17] In 1916 the WiSFL went on record in favor of a state system of health insurance.[18] Seeking to expand the state's role in social-welfare provision still further, throughout the 1920s the state legislature considered bills that would establish unemployment compensation and old-age pensions.[19]

The interaction of a particular configuration of political opportunities and the distinctive organizational repertoire of Milwaukee's Social Democrats generated a new model for linking social groups to policy outcomes: the expert-dominated agency combined with advisory commissions. Pioneered at the level of state politics, this model of administrative-policy formation moved into national politics as an element of the "Wisconsin Idea," an alternative that informed social-policy debates through the 1920s and 1930s.

This articulation of popular associations and state agencies required leverage within electoral politics, an ability to cooperate with expert-run state agencies, and state agencies with which to cooperate. On all three counts, organized labor was advantaged relative to other potential challengers in the state. The socialists' enthusiasm for independent politics was not shared by the state's farmers. During the 1870s, the Wisconsin Grange had its moment of triumph when it helped to pass railroad regulation legislation and then entered into a steady decline.[20] In its place, the dominant agrarian organization in late-nineteenth-century Wisconsin was the state-subsidized Wisconsin State Agricultural Society, which was controlled by comparatively wealthy farmers who condemned the Grange's ritual, asserting that there were "too many secret organizations that pursued special interests, spreading suspicion and fear."[21] Through its alliances with the legislature and university, the State Agricultural Society and the Dairymen's Association addressed the issues of scientific farming, education, and market regulation that were central to the emerging agricultural-service state. Among the experiment stations funded by the U.S. Department of Agriculture, Wisconsin's drew praise for its devotion to "high quality [scientific] investigation in contrast to other stations where nonresearch work and narrowly-conceived applied work occupied excessive time."[22]

For many farmers, however, government efforts to improve agriculture were little more than "agencies or legislation for the aggravation of agricultural problems," intensifying the overproduction that suppressed prices.[23] The comparatively privileged agricultural societies secured state aid for agricultural fairs and research during the 1880s and 1890s, but many poorer farmers lacked an organizational vehicle to consolidate their demands. In Wisconsin, the Populist Party was weak and caught up in alliances with urban and labor reformers. Only a split within the state Republican Party, and the emergence of a reform faction identified with rural areas in the west of the state, provided a political opportunity for organized farmers. But even once La Follette was elected governor in 1900, there was still no independent representative of the less-privileged agrarian interests in the capital at Madison.[24] The alliance of more privileged farmers and state government promoted improved production, neglecting the demands of other farmers for the regulation of both production and marketing. This situation began to change with the establishment of the Wisconsin Society of Equity in 1907. Grounded in a theory of cooperative marketing that urged farmers to withhold crops from the market until a minimum price was reached, Equity sought a form of monopoly control for agricultural producers.[25] In many respects, this orientation complemented the workplace foundation of the state's labor movement. Like organized labor, the Wisconsin Society of Equity faced the question of how to combat the political influence of trusts and corporations. But unlike the organized workers of Milwaukee, Wisconsin's farmers did not have the opportunities and constraints provided by ties to a viable third party.[26] In terms of opportunity, farmers were linked into the La Follette coalition through their local and ethnic allegiances to individual rural legislators.[27]

If the WiSFL remained committed to independent electoral politics, rural Wisconsin remained under the sway of a politics of ethnic solidarity. Even as skilled a campaigner as La Follette repeatedly underestimated the durability of ethnic and religious conflict, as his candidates handpicked for their commitment to political insurgency were defeated by irate Norwegians or anti-Catholics.[28] The publisher of the *Equity News* complained bitterly about the lack of issue-based political involvement among his readers, but neither was cooperation with labor an entirely attractive option. In 1909, one member of the Equity committee charged "that all these union men wanted was to secure the votes of the farmers for their kind of legislation."[29] Two years later, the Wisconsin Equity convention was more sympathetic but still limited itself to assuring "organized labor of our moral support in all progressive labor legislation submitted to the next session of the Wisconsin Legislature."[30]

But if farmers enjoyed comparatively little success as an incipient interest group, as property owners and taxpayers they nevertheless constrained state expansion. Property taxes in Wisconsin were comparatively low.[31] "'High taxes are a good thing' sometimes," declared one agrarian activist. "They make people think. They will make people scrutinize closely all candidates for office and to question them carefully as to where they stand and what they propose to do if elected."[32] Consequently, members of the progressive coalition agreed that if anyone had to pay for state programs, it should be the corporations and the wealthy[33]—not those subject to a general property tax. By 1917 nine states had income taxes; Wisconsin was the only progressive state among them, and, compared to other states in the Great Lakes region, the tax rate on manufacturers was high and more progressive.[34] Organized labor was also well aware of the class implications of an income tax. At the 1905 convention, Fred Brockhausen, the secretary-treasurer, reported: "An attorney for people of large incomes admitted to me that an income tax would be the best method of reaching his clients, and before the committee, in my presence, he expressed satisfaction with the old make-up of the legislature. Referring to the new element in evidence in the legislature, with perhaps more to come, he thought the future operation of the income tax would bring great hardships to the propertied class."[35] While administration of the tax was highly centralized, the state government retained only 10 percent of the revenues, with the remainder returned to the counties and local taxing units. But the efficiency of the state collection system produced a state share of more than double the one-hundred-thousand-dollar administrative costs for the first year, leaving the state government with a restricted but unencumbered source of revenue to support new policy initiatives *and* a broad array of local and county officials committed to protecting the new tax system.[36] This political configuration helped to produce a system of state agencies that took pride in their ability to do much with little. In 1913, the Wisconsin Industrial Commission supported a staff of 53 on an appropriation of $81,000; this compared to 44 staff on $85,000 in New Jersey, 42 staff on $83,500 in Ohio, 41 staff on $79,000 in Indiana, 24 staff on $50,400 in California, and 9 staff on $20,000 in Washington.[37]

Less electorally powerful than organized labor, farm groups were also slower to develop ties to state agencies. Like many agrarian organizations, Equity began as the enemy of state institutions, particularly the university. In 1911, when the progressive Republicans were in control of the state, the *Equity News* announced that "[i]t is time for the rural resident in Wisconsin to decide whether it is best to continue fattening this great institution at Madison or whether it is not time to begin doing something for the common schools." Farmers were urged to "[g]et busy right now and select, and next year elect men pledged to do something for '*lower education.*'"[38] But agrarian hostility toward the university and other state agencies gradually ebbed.[39] In 1913, the *Equity News* bemoaned the defeat of a Market Commission Bill by "Big and Little Business." Publishing a roll call of the votes, the paper urged readers to "[k]eep the above list for future reference. Some of those who voted 'no' will be up for re-election two years hence and that little word '*no*' will re-echo through their campaign and our prediction is they will be *elected to stay at home.*"[40] In 1914, campaigning for farmers' votes and his own reelection, Governor McGovern pointed to the services provided to farmers by the Board of Public Affairs, the university, and the Legislative Reference Library. The Equity leadership agreed that the reference library was "a state sustained institution which enables labor and farmers organization's representatives to provide bills—expertly prepared—that will 'hold water' and escape the decision of 'unconstitutional,' and yet be of real service to the people. *There may be a reason why it is desired to abolish this department.*" Equity leaders also expressed support for the State Board of Public Affairs and, in an effort to develop stronger ties with the government, continued to demand the establishment of a "Market Commission similar to the Railroad Commission and the Industrial Commission to look after and develop the still larger proposition of protecting both producers and consumers from exploitation."[41] Through the 1920s, therefore, the coalition of agencies and pressure groups in favor of state expansion retained some of the momentum of the progressive years, even though facing greater resistance.

Despite their different positions within the state's polity, Wisconsin's farmers and workers occasionally tried to ally on the basis of the shared belief that their problems stemmed from the dominance of large corporations. A resolution passed by the WiSFL called on "all workingmen, including farmers and the masses in general" to study "the aims and principles of the different capitalist parties" and to make "use of their ballot for the emancipation of labor."[42] Farmers concurred in this picture of political conflict. In "The Meaning of Political Terms," the Wisconsin *Equity News* defined "big business" as "Individual, collective or corporate industry or finance that enjoys privileges inimical to the best interests of the community at large—the masses of the people."[43] Running for reelection, Governor McGovern repeated this theme:

> Who oppresses us now? . . . the power of money in industry, and in public life, which, in the latter, debauches government and defiles citizenship; and, in the former destroys the equality of opportunity which was intended to be the heritage of American citizenship everywhere. How are you going to deal with it? *Will each of you meet it single handed and alone, or will you combine against it through the agency of these voluntary co-operative societies? Manifestly, the latter way affords the only hope of obtaining results.*[44]

Despite their agreement on the problem, farmers and organized labor were organized in quite different "voluntary co-operative societies." Through the second decade of the century, the WiSFL maintained its thinly disguised commitment to an independent socialist party and declined to cooperate with farmers on a nonpartisan basis. The WiSFL ignored a 1915 proposal that "the Wisconsin State Union, A. S. of E., the Wisconsin State Grange, the Wisconsin branch of the National Consumers' League be, and they are hereby, invited to take similar action at their next regular conventions or meetings and through their Executive Boards meet with us, assist in the selection of desirable candidates and in the formation and adoption of a platform or declaration of principles for which we shall ask our candidates to stand."[45] The WiSFL's commitment to working-class party politics also overshadowed any enthusiasm for the initiative or referendum.

Organized women possessed far less political influence than either labor or farmers. Women lacked the vote until the passage of the federal amendment, and, even had they been enfranchised, the absence of institutional reforms open to nonpartisan mobilization would have hobbled efforts to shape policy outcomes. Their weakness was also reflected in the state's administrative arrangements. Women's labor law was administered by the Industrial Commission—rather than by a separate agency as in

California—and was pursued less assertively than regulations covering men's employment.[46] One year after the U.S. Supreme Court had upheld the Oregon minimum-wage law for women, the Wisconsin Industrial Commission had not begun to implement the state's own 1913 law: "In May 1918 the Wisconsin Federation of Labor, the Consumers' League of Wisconsin, and the Central Council of Social Agencies of Milwaukee filed a petition asking the commission to proceed to fixing a living wage."[47] By 1919, the minimum weekly wage was set at slightly over eleven dollars, given a nine-hour day and six-day week, well below the minimums in California and Washington, both eight-hour states with minimum weekly wages for women in excess of thirteen dollars.[48] The contrast between industrial and women's programs may be explained, in part, by the nature of the coalitions that did (or did not) support them. Although organized women in Wisconsin had supported protective legislation, they did not control the state agencies charged with its enforcement. Only gradually were close agency-association partnerships established; once the State Conference of Social Work adopted a political program and a permanent staff in 1920, it successfully pushed for the establishment of a Bureau of Juvenile Protection in the State Board of Control (which also gave financial support to the Conference).[49] In a political arena still very much structured by partisanship, however heterodox, "women's issues" were only slowly advanced by nonpartisan methods.[50]

The ideological and organizational heterogeneity of the reform coalition heightened the importance of the unusual institutional setting of Wisconsin politics. The Legislative Reference Library, established in 1905, relieved popular associations of the expense of hiring their own attorneys to draft bills, making regular legislative channels available to a broad range of groups—or at least to those whose demands were formulated as legislation.[51] The creation of agencies capable of "constructive investigation" also consolidated ties between associations and state agencies. The Wisconsin Industrial Commission, established in 1911 to administer workmen's compensation and other labor-related laws, was the center of reform activity and governmental expansion. Numerous committees covering topics such as safety and sanitation were created, with members representing manufacturing, labor, and various academic, technical, or administrative concerns.[52] These arrangements enrolled interested parties in the workings of the Industrial Commission, providing the agency with political insulation beyond the broad delegation of powers established in its enabling legislation.[53] Rather than awaiting legislative action, the Industrial Commission stopped night work for women between 6 P.M. and 6 A.M. (following petitions from the WiSFL, the Wisconsin Consumers' League, and the Wisconsin Council of Social Agencies). In addition to supervising a successful apprenticeship program,[54] the Industrial Commission oversaw a system of public employment offices prior to the war, expanded and elaborated them in cooperation with the wartime federal employment service (adding, for example, specialists in placing disabled workers), and maintained many of these offices after the armistice, with the consequence that "Wisconsin escaped the unemployment problem faced by other states during the early months of 1919, in part probably because of the efficiency of the employment service."[55] The Industrial Commission used its programs and decisions to expand economic regulation and state intervention. The practice of delegating much responsibility for formulating regulations to committees made up of representatives of employers, labor, and "the public" reinforced the highly articulated character of the state polity in the area of economic regulation. The persistence of a sharp distinction between public and private agencies in the area of social spending, however, foreclosed opportunities for the formation of ties between state agencies and other associations, notably women's associations interested in social service issues.

California: The Spending State

In California, the corruption and intransigence of the major parties loomed much larger than in Wisconsin. Railroads, utilities, and development interests were able to sway the votes of legislators from both parties as well as to shape party platforms. Consequently, reformers in California sought not just to capture a party but to dismantle the party system while instituting direct democracy as an alternative channel for policy formation. Unlike Wisconsin, where the consolidation of an electoral bloc was the basis for making policy demands, the sweeping procedural reforms of California progressivism produced a far more open space for nonpartisan mobilization—and the revenues generated by a state tax on utilities provided an incentive. In a political climate of intense antipartisanship, organized labor's history of independent political victories (and subsequent corruption) caused an initial rift between union activists and middle-class reformers. In a state dominated by large landholdings, organized farmers remained weak. Women, by contrast, were advantaged by the logics of appropriateness that bound them to nonpartisan strategies and by the development of an extensive network of charitable and social-service agencies subsidized by state funds. This configuration of opportunities and constituencies produced a precocious social-spending state.[56]

The unifying framework of progressive reform in California was narrow, built predominantly on a common opposition to the political domination of the Southern Pacific Railroad and on support for institutional reforms such as direct democracy and public ownership of utilities. This first track of California progressivism aimed to disassemble not only the party structures that had dominated state politics but also the large corporations that financed the parties. Reformers dealt near fatal blows to the parties, which were saved by the continuing relevance of partisanship for federal elections. The initiative and referendum enjoyed immediate popularity and frequent use; an average of more than twenty-two measures (including constitutional amendments, initiatives, and referenda) appeared on each general-election ballot between 1912 and 1936.[57] The 1911 legislature also introduced a "divided session" to give representatives time to publicize proposed legislation and to consult with interested groups; following Wisconsin, a State Legislative Reference Library was created to aid legislators in formulating bills and, upon the written request of at least twenty-five voters, to aid proponents in the preparation of initiative measures.[58]

Yet the parties were not entirely dismantled; although the legislature approved a system of nonpartisan direct primaries for all state offices and the removal of all party symbols from the ballot, these measures were overturned by referenda in 1915.[59] County and judicial elections were put on a nonpartisan basis, however, and the introduction of "cross-filing" undermined any semblance of party control over the nominating process.[60] Both parties were split between conservative and progressive factions—among Republicans, some progressives left to form a third party from 1913 to 1916. These divisions gave Democrats occasional victories in a state that was increasingly Republican and meant that important redirections in policy were frequently determined in primaries where candidates were particularly dependent upon their personal networks and the organizational machinery provided by alliances with established associations. Against this free-for-all of faction and issue-oriented organizations, the heterogeneous reform coalition in Wisconsin appears a model of electoral discipline. Whereas in Wisconsin a limited number of actors and associations—notably the two Republican factions and organized labor—controlled which issues would be allowed onto the agenda,[61] the extreme weakness of parties in California allowed a proliferation of political issues and interested groups. The efforts of these groups to give shape to public policy constituted the second track of California progressivism.

Policy outcomes typically reflected balances of power among different political contenders. With a terminological awkwardness that bespoke the incomplete transition from populist insurgency to interest group pluralism, V. O. Key and Winston Crouch explained that "measures referred from legislative action to the electorate usually concern disputes between two or more 'partial' interests rather than a dramatic clearcut issue between the 'interests' and the 'people.'"[62] These "partial interests" (a term that encompassed popular associations, professional groups, and business organizations) were advantaged insofar as they could effectively contest issues in both the legislature and popular elections. The former required influence over elected representatives, the latter the organizational and financial machinery for mobilizing a majority of voters in the state's large and rapidly growing electorate. Given its hybrid of electoral blocs from labor strongholds such as San Francisco and a statewide organization oriented to the politics of initiative and referendum, the CSFL (along with its allies in the centralized labor lobby in Sacramento) was a powerful force. As was discussed in chapter 4, organized labor secured numerous pieces of important labor legislation in the second decade of the century and, as will be described in chapter 8, mobilized impressively to fight the open-shop and "Better America" movements after the war.

Farmers in California had an indirect but important influence on these developments. Many of their own policy concerns languished; even with the revival of the Grange in the 1920s and the establishment of the California Farm Bureau Federation in 1919, the divergent sensibilities of the two groups fragmented the political pressure that might be exerted on agrarian issues.[63] But despite their secondary status as both advocates and beneficiaries of policy expansion, farmers were inextricably linked to the fortunes of progressive reform by way of the state's system of taxation. Throughout the 1890s, agrarian associations had agitated against the existing system of taxation based on real property, which fell most heavily on small farmers: "The holdings of the small property owners are in sight, and, down to the last chicken, go on the assessment roll."[64] Large corporations, whose property took the invisible forms of financial assets, could evade the tax assessors. In 1905, farmers received some relief as real-property taxation was reserved to the counties, while state government was funded by taxes on the receipts of railroads and public utilities and on the capital stock of banks. The power of organized labor within the progressive coalition helped to protect manufacturers from increases in taxes on corporate income. California unionists were aware of the benefits that they derived from their regionally limited labor market and unwilling to expose employers to costs that might intensify open-shop sentiments.[65] This solution broke the tie by which popular politics restrains state spending and expenditures were driven by a political logic instead. Controlled by the railroads, which sought franchises and regulatory favors rather than budget items, government spending was used for political favors and, consequently, soared. This new tax system was being implemented at the time of the progressives' 1910 victory, producing a fiscal arrangement that made it relatively easy to respond to group pressures with new government programs.[66]

A second institutional reform removed policy decisions still further from electoral politics and opened them to extrapartisan pressure. First used in 1912, the budget process drove a wedge between electoral and administrative politics. As the chairman of the State Board of Control explained:

> The accepted method of securing appropriations under old conditions in California as elsewhere was particularly vicious. Under the old system the legislature met and simultaneously the heads of departments and institutions left their posts and traveled to Sacramento. Here they stayed throughout the legislative session, begging, wheedling and whining for money enough to properly transact the public business. Of course they promised jobs to friends of legislators in return for votes; of course they promised to aid some constituent of a senator who happened to be in the flour or coal business; of course they neglected their work for three months or as much longer as the legislature lasted.

After the new budget procedures were instituted, department heads typically spent a single day in Sacramento answering questions concerning the budget recommendations and then returned to work: "No promises of jobs or of anything else were made for the simple reason that the governor and Board of Control had assumed responsibility for the entire budget and the heads of departments and institutions realized that the securing of proper appropriations was no longer a contest of trickery and ward heeling strategy."[67]

The combination of ample government revenues with a polity open to nonpartisan political influence was particularly hospitable to women's organizations. With their established orientation to cash-supported, expert-managed programs, women's groups called on the state to fund or administer a variety of new policies, including inspection of institutions and the replacement of an extensive state system of foster child care by "widow's pensions" that "considered the widow an employee, rather than an object of charity, who was paid for a service that she could best render."[68] California also passed an eight-hour day for women in 1911 and a women's minimum-wage law in 1913 (ratified by referendum in 1914).[69] The women's eight-hour law was promoted by the CSFL as a way of shortening the workday for everyone; only one prominent suffragist, herself connected with the waitresses' union, was mentioned in connection with this agitation.[70] The women's minimum-wage law, by contrast, was almost entirely the pet project of suffragists and clubwomen; both organized labor and the state's employers opposed the legislation.[71] Yet the clubwomen won. As organized labor grew less ambivalent over the benefits of labor legislation, unionists and clubwomen joined to promote protective legislation.[72] Organized women also pursued a broader agenda through the Women's Legislative Council of California. By the early 1920s, "the results of the idea of co-operation in legislative work" included

> (1) Industrial Welfare Commission; (2) State Training School for Girls; (3) Birth Registration; (4) Mothers' Pension Law; (5) Teachers' Pension Act; (6) Raising the Age of Consent; (7) Home Teacher's Bill; (8) Red Light Abatement Law; Registration of Trained Nurses; (9) Making Mother Equal Guardian with Father of Minor Children; (10) Law Making Father of Illigitimate [sic] Child Liable for its support; (11) Requiring Wife's Signature to legalize assignment of Husband's wages; (12) Amendment to Juvenile Court Law, separating dependents from delinquents; (13) Safeguarding Educational rights and hours of labor for children; (14) Establishing Civic Centers in Public School Buildings; (15) Making women eligible to Jury Service; (16) Farm for Delinquent Women; (17) Moron Colony for Southern California; (18) Increase in School Funds; (19) Exempting Wife's half of Community Property from Inheritance Tax; (20) Making Provision for Special Education for Crippled Children.[73]

This list of accomplishments tracks the shifting relationship of the state's government to its citizens. First, the extent of government regulation was extended much further into family relations at the same time that aspects of women's second-class citizenship status (often grounded in claims of the wife's dependence on her husband) were steadily removed. Second, the number of institutionalized points of contact between the state government and women's associations multiplied: the Industrial Welfare Commission was a new arena for policy formation; the new schools, farms, and colonies were both objects of policy debate and possible opportunities for public employment of women in the social services. Finally, increases in funding not only raised the stakes of political success, they strengthened the system of financial ties generated by public subsidies to private or religious agencies. Robust contrasts across states in the funding of what would now be called the nonprofit sector are documented by data on spending on child welfare (table 7.3). Whereas public funding was a minuscule component of the budgets of private associations in Wisconsin, estimates for California place the public contribution anywhere from one-third to over half of total funding of private (but not for-profit) welfare agencies. As striking is the disparity in the proportion of private and religious agencies receiving some public funding; in California this proportion was consistently estimated at over 80 percent. To the extent that the child welfare sector was representative of other policy domains, California's polity presents an image of a dense and elaborated web of political decision points, state agencies, and private associations of many stripes.

Access to state funding or institutional support was typically the product of organized demand. Consequently, the uneven strength and shifting composition of the reform coalition was reflected in the patterns of state-building that emerged in California. Government expansion was vigorous but fragmented. The Industrial Accident Commission, the Industrial Welfare Commission, and the Commission of Immigration and Housing (CIH), all created in 1913 "in the common interest of the working groups of the State, . . . made no attempt whatever to coordinate their several activities."[74] Within each of these agencies, representatives of organized groups competed for influence and control. This process is most evident in one of the state's most unusual experiments in government; the CIH was praised by social workers nationally as "without parallel in the United States. It has set a gage of social statesmanship which in the national interest other states should match."[75] Founded in reaction to the Wheatlands riot—a violent encounter between migrant farmworkers and law officers in which the IWW was implicated—the CIH began its work by investigating sanitary conditions in labor camps and then enforced housing standards not only in the camps but in some municipalities as well. Its mandate for the welfare of immigrants supported an expansive agenda. The CIH investigated the extent of land monopoly in the state, supporting both the imposition of a tax on speculative profits from land (designed to break up large holdings, essentially a "single tax") and a state colonization program to transform landless laborers into small farmers. It addressed the problems of women and children in the camps,

Table 7.3   Organizational Composition of and Public Subsidies to the Child Welfare Sector

	Type of Institution			Public Funding of Nonpublic Institutions			
	Public	Religious	Private	Institutions Receiving	Proportion of Total Budget[a]	Public/ Total Spending[b]	Total Budget ($)
California							
1904	2.3%	45.4%	52.3%	83.7%	55.5%	55.8%	485,622
	(1)	(20)	(23)	(36/43)			
1910	4.1%	40.8%	55.1%	85.1%	39.6%	40.2%	843,533
	(2)	(20)	(27)	(40/47)			
1913	16.9%	38.2%	44.9%	82.4%	38.0%	54.2%	1,899,811
	(15)	(34)	(40)	(61/74)			
Washington							
1904	11%	44%	44%	62.5%	18.7%	38.0%	29,543
	(1)	(4)	(4)	(5/8)			
1910	20%	40%	40%	50%	12.7%	35.1%	104,740
	(2)	(4)	(4)	(4/8)			
Wisconsin							
1904	14.3%	71.4%	14.3%	16.7%	1.9%	48.0%	126,130
	(2)	(10)	(2)	(2/12)			
1910	13.7%	50.0%	36.4%	31.5%	2.3%	42.6%	295,858
	(3)	(11)	(8)	(6/19)			

Sources: For 1904, U.S. Bureau of the Census, *Benevolent Institutions, 1904* (Washington, D.C.: Government Printing Office, 1905), table 1; for 1910, U.S. Bureau of the Census, *Benevolent Institutions, 1910* (Washington, D.C.: Government Printing Office, 1913), tables 1 and 2 (on differences from classification system used in 1904, see p. 12; on problems with comparing absolute size of budgets, see p. 22); for 1913, William H. Slingerland, *Child Welfare Work in California: A Study of Agencies and Institutions* (New York: Russell Sage Foundation, 1915), tables 1–6. Of the public institutions covered in the latter study, five were founded after 1910, but many were older, including three founded in the 1880s, each with budgets over $150,000 in 1913. Two organizations that were clearly for-profit were excluded from the totals.

a. Public funds received by private and ecclesiastical institutions as a percentage of the total budget of those institutions.

b. Public funds received by public, private, and religious institutions as a percentage of the total spending in the child welfare sector.

initiating home teacher and "Americanization" programs.[76] During the war, the CIH aided in managing labor in both agriculture and timber, drawing praise as an exemplar of future possibilities in labor relations:

> Were there no other result of the camp sanitation work, this peace-in-war experience would in itself have justified the creation of the commission. And it is most significant that the very work which the state of California has been doing as a normal function began long before there were even

rumors of war, had to be done by the federal government in the Pacific Northwest as a war measure under military direction.[77]

The expansiveness of the CIH's activities was widely supported. The commission was established following a letter-writing campaign by the Young Men's and Women's Christian Associations and the Daughters of the American Revolution.[78] The CSFL eventually won a seat on the new CIH for its secretary, Paul Scharrenberg, and tempered its initial opposition to the new agency. This opposition had flowed from a suspicion of government expansion:

> Labor's objection to this bill is not against the object sought to be accomplished, but only to the indefinite nature of the bill and its interference with the scope of other governmental agencies. If a good personnel is appointed, the bill may accomplish its purpose, but it would have been more proper, to our notion, to limit the sphere of the commission's activities to the definite subject of caring for immigrants proper instead of the larger contingent of alien born resident and immigration population. As the bill reads, it permits the board to dissipate its energies in the fields of research, statistics, etc., where it may do something for the scholarly investigators of social problems, but will have little left to do real good. Its resources are not so great that it can afford to spread out over territory already covered by other governmental agencies"[79]

Clearly, labor no longer automatically resisted any state expansion; the CSFL's own experience working with state agencies is reflected in the focused critique of the CIH's mission in relation to its resources.

The CIH created a governmental niche for many key actors in the state's associational network. In addition to Scharrenberg, who served as secretary, in 1919 the membership of the commission included Simon J. Lubin (a prominent Sacramento reformer) and Mary Gibson (a leading suffragist and clubwoman in the state).[80] These personal ties aided the coordination of agency initiatives and associational efforts. In 1920, the California Federation of Women's Clubs "unanimously voted to focus the attention of all its departments upon Americanization," a central concern of the commission: "This assures the active interest of more than 500 clubs and 50,000 women of California in the most ambitious program of Americanization work yet attempted by any State club organization."[81] At least in its own eyes, the CIH used these networks among reformers and agencies to coordinate what might appear to be an uncontrolled proliferation of new state enterprises.

Nor was the CIH an isolated experiment in state expansion; in many fields, California displayed a distinctive proclivity for shifting activities into the public realm. Along with the clubwomen and organized labor, the state's social workers elected a more explicitly political form, voting in 1919 to establish both a permanent executive secretary and a standing committee on social legislation.[82] At local and county levels, private welfare agencies and associations consolidated with one another[83] and entered into formal partnerships with state agencies.[84] A number of these arrangements explicitly envisioned the transfer of programs from private to public auspices. The "2 × 5" county relief plan set up boards consisting of two officials and five "representative men and women":

> The policy, briefly stated, is to socialize public relief by putting into its administration the methods which have been tried out and found most successful in the best private relief organizations. Instead of burdening a small percentage of the citizens to supplement the shortcomings of public relief, it has been possible in many localities to raise the standards of public charity to a plane of adequacy. An advantage which public aid has over that administered by private agencies lies in the possibilities of wider outlook and ability better to correlate the community needs with the community resources.[85]

These experiments generated momentum for further state expansion and intervention. In 1917, the state commission on health insurance (the first in the nation) reported in favor of universal health insurance for workers, and, the next year, the legislature adopted a constitutional amendment to be submitted to voters.[86] In 1917 a new law established a $350 payment from employers of workers killed without dependents; the receipts would go to the state vocational-rehabilitation fund.[87] In San Francisco, the police department oversaw a team of women supervisors in the public dance halls, their $75 monthly salaries paid by the dance hall proprietors.[88] In 1921, "California, alone, took a forward step in enacting a law for long time advance planning of public works by the state to help in preventing unemployment."[89] Four years later, the legislature passed an old-age pension bill.[90] In the administration of workmen's compensation insurance, the state fund played an ever larger role; the premiums received increased from five hundred thousand dollars in 1914 to $5 million by 1922,[91] as the portion of business going to private insurers shrank steadily (see fig. 7.2). According to one estimate, the state budget increased by approximately 171 percent from 1919–21 to 1927–29; over the same period, the state's population grew by roughly 63 percent.[92] To a far greater extent than in Wisconsin, therefore, California's dismantling of the party system and extraction of new tax revenues allowed the

Growth of California State Fund

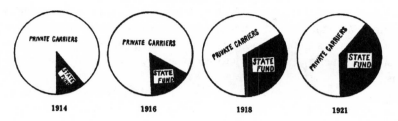

1914   1916   1918   1921

Proportion of Premiums Paid to State Fund and Private Carriers

THE California State Fund, which in its first year wrote only 11 per cent of the workmen's compensation insurance in the state, has grown steadily and in 1921 it was writing 39 per cent.

Figure 7.2   Growth of the California State Fund. (Source: *American Labor Legislation Review*, September 1922)

establishment of a distinctively postpartisan, state-centered political regime.

Washington: Reform without Institutions

With the exception of its reputation for labor radicalism, Washington state is a forgotten pioneer in the history of insurgent politics and social reform in the United States. Upon achieving statehood in 1890, its new constitution gave the government greater-than-usual powers to promote the well-being of its citizens. Washington Populists also diverged significantly from the national party with respect to outcomes. They won. Populists were represented in the state legislature from 1893 to 1901, and their gubernatorial candidate, John R. Rogers, was elected on a fusion ticket of Populists, Democrats, and Silver Republicans in 1896 and then re-elected as a Democrat in 1900.[93] So although the collapse of the national People's Party took the state organization with it, populist victories at the state level left a more favorable memory of independent politics, a state supreme court sympathetic to reform, and a less developed anti-partisanship than prevailed in California. But the forces that created these expanded opportunities for insurgent politics were uninformed by either the state-building models of the Wisconsin Social Democrats or the exemplars of autonomous public agencies valued by the nonpartisan associations that flourished in California. Building on nineteenth-century models of producerist associations, Washington's insurgents combined antistatism and a commitment to direct democracy with an unusual organizational capacity for the private provision of public services. Consequently, political victories generated reform without institutions.

Progressivism in Washington took the form of party faction and insurgency; repeated efforts to circumvent rather than to dismantle the major parties. Building on an enduring regional split between the more conservative western counties and the populist heritage of the eastern half of the state, a group of politicians centered in Spokane and inspired by Theodore Roosevelt steadily built strength within the Republican Party and in 1908 secured a seat in the House of Representatives for Miles Poindexter, who joined the "Insurgent" bloc committed to the removal of Speaker Joseph G. Cannon as well as to reforms of House rules. Through his first term, Poindexter was sympathetic to progressive causes, including those of organized labor, and somewhat reluctantly joined others from the West and the plains states in leaving the Republicans to form the Progressive Party behind Theodore Roosevelt in 1912.[94] At the state level, the significance of the Democratic Party declined, leaving one governor to declare himself "somewhat at a loss to know whether the day of political parties has passed and the day of individualism is what we are coming to."[95]

In many respects, therefore, the political configuration in Washington resembled that in Wisconsin and California. An increasingly dominant Republican Party was divided between progressives on the one hand and "Stalwarts" or the "Old Guard" on the other—for the first decades of the century, these factions traded control of all three state governments. All three states sent prominent insurgents to Congress, each of whom harbored presidential ambitions. Yet for all these similarities, the situation in Washington state differed in two critical respects: the relation of party politicians to various constituencies and the organizational repertoires that popular associations employed to gain political leverage and shape policy outcomes. First, as an entrepreneurial faction within the Republican Party, Washington's progressives did not rest on a specific organized constituency.[96] Just as elected progressives were not tightly bound to constituents, citizens shifted their votes from candidate to candidate—as well as party to party to third party—in a version of California's fluidity with that state's thoroughgoing nonpartisanship muted by a more conventional set of electoral institutions.

The second dimension of Washington's distinctiveness lay in the organizational repertoires mastered by popular associations in the state. If organized groups in California—whether of workers, farmers, or women—pointed toward the future with their cultivation of business methods and nonpartisan practices, Washington reform politics inherited a vision of organizational possibilities from the Grange and the Knights of Labor. Unlike the pressure groups of California, popular associations in Washington were more likely to support third-party efforts, less likely to empower state agencies or experts, and more likely to rely on strategies of cooperation in which state government played little or no role.

In both the impressive extension of direct democracy and the inability to follow pathbreaking legislation with the establishment of effective and autonomous agencies, the development of labor politics in Washington illuminates the influence of inherited organizational repertoires as well as the dense interconnections between the forms of popular political participation and the institutions of the modern state. This persistence of nineteenth-century political styles was reinforced by the lack of opportunities to use the lobbying strategies developed in Wisconsin and California. Faced with hostile legislatures and conservative progressives, organized labor had little chance to be organizationally co-opted by legislative institutions. Consequently, the dominant strategy of popular political association was defined by the point of intersection of the repertoires of good-government reformers, labor insurgents, and politicized farmers: direct democracy. Even with its state-building agenda of labor legislation and old-age pensions, organized labor became committed to fundamentally antistatist strategies.

Unlike either Wisconsin or California, the Grange endured as the dominant agrarian organization in Washington state throughout the Progressive Era. Revived during the 1890s, the Grange was well suited to the community-based, antirailroad agitation that arose as the state faced a great wave of settlement prior to the turn of the century. In the early 1890s, the Grange developed an antistatist political orientation that colored its activities for decades. This hostility toward excessive state offices and budgets was exacerbated by the major parties; the first legislature abolished limitations on state, county, and municipal indebtedness and redefined taxable personal property so that "credits or money at interest" were excluded while improvements upon mortgaged land were included.[97] In comparison, the Populist legislature of 1897 passed legislation protecting debtors, easing the tax burden on farmers, aiding rural education, and allowing widows to administer the estates of their husbands.[98]

In the course of their struggle for the initiative and referendum, Washington reform groups developed the organizational model for political action that is associated with many of the major progressive achievements in that state: the extrapartisan coalition of interest groups,[99] which grew out of the Direct Legislation League, established at a conference of farmers from the western counties, trade unionists, and other progressives called by a former state lecturer of the Grange.[100] Rebuffed by the state's dominant party, in 1911 groups committed to direct legislation—including the Direct Legislation League, the Grange, the Farmers' Union, and the State Federation of Labor—showed up in Olympia to lobby. These lobbyists then formed the Temporary Joint Legislative Committee to advocate the initiative, referendum and other measures. The no-longer temporary Joint Legislative Committee (JLC) managed campaigns for a number of important reforms prior to the First World War. This enduring alliance also countered the crop-specific concerns characteristic of California's agrarian organizations. The extrapartisan organizational arrangements of the JLC helped preserve farmer-labor or "producerist" identities in Washington politics.[101] The alliance of the Grange and organized labor perpetuated the mixed occupational-political models of the nineteenth century, even as associations elsewhere increasingly adopted "business" templates for agrarian organization.

Given the antipathy of both the Grange and the Farmers' Union to regular party politics, it is not surprising that, even by 1913, the reform forces could not manage to elect a legislature responsive to their demands. It was not sufficient to reject the model of regular party organization; a viable alternative template for political cooperation was needed. One possibility lay in radical versions of direct democracy. Following the dismal and reactionary results of the legislative session of 1913, the state Grange voted, by a margin of eight to one,

> in favor of the abolition of the legislature and the substitution of a commission composed of three representatives from each congressional district to meet every other month. The resolution adopted by the Grange declared that, "The people are now convinced that our present legislative machinery no longer serves the best interests of the people and the time is ripe for a more business-like method of conducting that branch of government."[102]

This judgment was reinforced two years later, when the Republican-dominated legislature attacked the farmer-labor coalition further with a series of bills that would have enforced party regularity by severely weakening the direct-primary law in favor of party conventions; disallowed absentee voting despite the strong support of the railroad brotherhoods; severely limited the ability to collect signatures on initiative, referendum, and recall petitions; disenfranchised numerous farmers by requiring voter registration in rural districts; and limited the political power of tenants and the lower working class with the passage of a constitutional amendment "which provided that only owners of property who paid taxes thereon might vote on any proposition to incur or not to incur debt on obligation of the state or any municipal corporation, city, town, or district in the state."[103] These bills were passed over the veto of Governor Lister but were subjected to referenda on the basis of petitions signed by approximately equal numbers of farmers and laborers,[104] and all were overturned, preserving direct democracy.

Although cooperation with labor was the price of influence over state politics, many farmers were unenthusiastic about cooperating with the WaSFL's positions on wages, hours, and working conditions.[105] C. B. Kegley, Master of the State Grange, "believed that the universal eight-hour law, which had been framed by the legislature of 1913, was inserted into the campaign for no other purpose than to divide the ranks of the farmer-labor forces, since the farmers were opposed to the measure as it was drawn."[106] The producerist identity that underlay the farm-labor alliance inevitably restricted the political demands that either could pursue without endangering the coalition. As Seattle labor became more politically and economically aggressive during and after the war, the strains embedded in this producerist coalition grew.

For organized labor, the importance of direct democracy and farmer-labor alliances reflected the recalcitrance of those who controlled both the legislative and administrative arms of state government. Often hostile to labor's policy demands, the legislature also limited the power of the Bureau of Labor; "the appropriation in this state, is less than in any other in which the office has been created," complained one commissioner. "The very small expense appropriation for the maintenance of the office, has made it impossible to employ clerical help; this has made it impossible to undertake every necessary line of investigation, and has caused some things to remain undone."[107] This financial weakness was compounded by a lack of autonomy. The position of commissioner of the Bureau of

Labor was a political football. When held by someone sympathetic to labor, the laws were enforced and the bureau regularly presented recommendations to the legislature for the improvement of labor policy. The WaSFL responded favorably to these efforts, endorsing "in behalf of the 15,000 members of organized labor and citizens of this state" the retention of former unionist William Blackman as commissioner of labor following the death of the Populist-Democratic governor, John Rogers. Blackman lasted until 1905, when he was replaced by a locomotive engineer from Tacoma, who was rewarded "for services rendered during the gubernatorial campaign" and then regularly criticized by the WaSFL for his weak enforcement of the laws.[108] Consequently, labor sought to ensure its control of these agencies through (unsuccessful) proposals such as the resolution that the state mine inspector be "nominated by mining counties and elected by popular vote of the voters of the state" or, more generally, that organized labor select its own representatives on state boards and commissions.[109] Within labor strongholds such as Seattle and Tacoma, this strategy met with some success, notably in the union's influence over the federal employment office in the shipyards during the war.[110] But for the most part, labor's political fortunes shifted with the state's political tides.

When the governor was hostile to labor, labor laws were frequently evaded. After the passage of the eight-hour day for women, for example, unionists complained, "It seems that this law has been enacted and placed upon the statutes of the state, and organized labor to prevent flagrant violations are compelled to employ people to assist in securing evidence to prosecute the offenders, where it is the duty of the Labor Commissioner to look into these matters."[111] Even when there were sympathetic appointees,[112] labor policy was not insulated from the concerns of other political actors. The dangers of embedding labor legislation in Populist reform ideology were illustrated by the fate of one of the original members of the Industrial Welfare Commission, an agency established to administer the eight-hour law for women and children and to investigate the need for a minimum wage. Teresa McMahon—professor of economics, former student of John Commons, and Hull House worker—stressed that the minimum wage would ensure the economic security of women workers.[113] The Spokane Chamber of Commerce, however, charged that the Industrial Welfare Commission (IWC) proceeded "not as an impartial body but as the representatives exclusively of the employees," and the agency was embroiled in battles over the economic and moral well-being of women workers. McMahon and another commissioner were re-placed,[114] their fate documenting the extent to which the implementation of labor legislation was constrained by the broader reform coalition responsible for its initial passage. Unlike Wisconsin, where traditions of scientific socialism and public-service academics created insulated arenas in which labor representatives participated as practical experts, their counterparts in Washington found no comparable shelter in state institutions. Rather than gradually embedding themselves in an increasingly institutionalized pluralist polity, political challengers in Washington repeatedly sought to throw the incumbents out.

In their support of third-party efforts, Washington's voters were more reliably insurgent than most. Rogers left a legacy of appointments to the state's courts after his death in 1901. Running on the Progressive ticket, Theodore Roosevelt carried the state in 1912 with 35 percent of the vote; combined with 27 percent for Wilson and a strong vote for Socialist Eugene Debs, the extensive reform sentiment overshadowed the 22 percent that went to the conservative incumbent Republican, William Howard Taft. Wilson carried the state for the Democrats in 1916, showing particular strength in the eastern counties where reform voting was traditionally strongest.[115] Faced with a choice between Republican and Democratic conservatives in 1920, Washington gave a victory to the former—Warren G. Harding—but cast 19 percent for the Farmer-Labor Party (supported by an alliance of the State Federation of Labor, the railroad brotherhoods, and the state Grange), only 2 percent less than was given to the Democrats. Whereas reformers in California struggled through the 1920s to retain control of the nominating machinery of the parties (since they had failed to make all state offices nonpartisan), in Washington reform efforts and insurgent politics had less impact on the conservative control of the Republican Party: "The Washington primaries showed no tendency to make the Republican Party itself an agency of progressivism." Senator Poindexter was first sent to the Senate as a progressive; "he was renominated as one of the staunchest of Republican wheel-horses in the face of the bitter opposition of the forces for whom and to whom the Seattle *Union Record* speaks."[116] In the 1922 elections, Washington state contributed to a widespread Democratic resurgence, sending C. C. Dill, the insurgent representative from 1914 to 1918 of an eastern congressional district, to the Senate in place of the discredited former progressive, Miles Poindexter.[117] In 1924, almost 36 percent of the presidential vote went to La Follette. With Wisconsin, Washington led the nation in casting an average of more than 15 percent of its presidential vote for economic-protest candidates between 1904 and 1924. (Nine other western and plains states, including California, cast an average of 10 to 14.9 percent of their presidential vote for economic-protest candidates during this period.)[118] The critical difference between the two states stemmed from what lay between these presidential campaigns and individual protest votes: in Wisconsin, cohesive and enduring organizations in the form of the La Follette "machine" and the not-quite-an-alliance of the Social Democratic Party and the Wisconsin State Federation of Labor; in Washington, a more volatile and shifting congeries of labor, agrarian, and urban-reform associations that lacked a dominant leader, particularly after Senator Poindexter shifted to the right during and after the world war.[119]

When combined with antistatist sentiments, insurgent voting obstructed the translation of electoral victories into institutional achievements. In 1897, the Populist-dominated legislature failed to pass a railroad commission bill; Populists who were convinced that any commission would soon be controlled by the railroads joined with conservative Republicans to defeat the legislation.[120] Well into the Progressive Era, groups in Washington state continued to employ a rhetoric of corporations versus the people that implicitly submerged differences among farmers, workers, and small merchants into a common identity as "the producing classes." The antistatist sentiments that informed the financial concerns of taxpaying farmers also strangled the revenue sources that might have financed the expansion of agencies and programs; unlike both California and Wisconsin, Washington did not establish new forms of personal and corporate income tax. In the absence of a constitutional limit on the property tax rate, popular antipathy toward state government tended to increase in direct proportion to the growth of state government.[121] Instead, the desires for a minimalist state and extraparty politics found their voice in the movement toward ever more direct forms of democracy. To a much greater extent than any social-reform agenda, it was this concern for a more democratic political process that provided a unifying theme for Washington's reform politics between 1890 and 1915.

But to a greater degree than in California, the reform coalition in Washington shared substantive as well as procedural concerns. Reform politics in Washington were organized around a series of morally defined coalitions; given a labor movement with a great deal of dry sentiment, this strategy did not pose as great a danger as it did in other states. Instead, antiparty and temperance rhetorics reinforced one another. Liquor was portrayed as the medium of partisan corruption:

> Behind each bar within the state
> Stands a bruiser sleek and fat;
> Who is a true Republican
> Or a trusted Democrat.[122]

Many farmers and workers shared the moral concerns typically attributed to women reformers. Whereas the Wisconsin legislature granted women extensive *political* equality once they had the vote, Washington's women secured new forms of *moral* equality. In the 1917 legislative session,

A law was passed establishing a single standard of morals. Hereafter what is adultery for women is likewise for men. Legislation was also provided for free kindergartens throughout the state. Hereafter, also, when the law refers to an unlawful death it applies to a mother as well as a father. A bone-dry prohibition law was passed, without reference to the people. The legislature refused to restore capital punishment or to provide for military training in high schools, although each of these measures passed one branch. There was no reaction in labor legislation, but a slight advancement.[123]

This mix of moral regulation, labor legislation, and the expansion of state funding for education did not reflect trade-offs among contending pressure groups as much as a broader consensus on the nature of a good society. This moral orientation facilitated the inclusion of women who cultivated the same sort of extraparty coalition politics that characterized the activities of other reform groups in the state. Whereas Wisconsin leaned toward corporatist solutions and California toward the strong state/weak party arrangement that facilitates pressure group politics, social politics in Washington exhibited both an aversion to expert-led, autonomous agencies and a capacity for cooperative reform efforts that spilled over the boundaries of formal politics. Washington was notable for both the exceptional success of reform issues and the striking weakness of the institutions that might perpetuate those accomplishments. The state did not delegate rule-making authority to the industrial commission until 1919, and then only for safety, not for hours rules.[124] In contrast to the detailed negotiations over workmen's compensation that took place in Wisconsin, Washington's version of dialogue consisted of an open meeting which, having attracted over one hundred businessmen, was delayed for a day until labor could call together a delegation of comparable size. This meeting requested the governor to appoint an Employers' Liability Commission, which was composed of a lumberman, a coal miner and an attorney. The bill drafted by this commission was then sponsored by a freshman assemblyman, who had been forced to run as a Republican in 1910 when he was informed that the Populist Party no longer existed.[125]

Although Washington was quick to pass strong laws in the areas of workmen's compensation and safety,[126] the administration of the law was plagued with conflict, corruption, and the constant opposition of the state legislature to active enforcement of labor legislation. The exclusion of the reform coalition from governance was reflected in the weak and disarrayed state agencies entrusted with Washington's pioneering legislation. The fragile character of this coalition was evident both in the specifics of the initial legislation and in subsequent efforts to amend it. By allying with labor, these industries were able to impose a compulsory bill on other employers, thereby precluding competition from firms that might try to undercut firm-specific welfare policies. But rather than entrusting the program to the union-oriented Bureau of Labor, a separate Industrial Insurance Department was established, and financing was organized through forty-seven separate industry pools. Under this system, a given firm might belong to several different pools, firms within a pool were pitted against one another insofar as larger and more safety-conscious firms were forced to underwrite their competitors, and workmen's compensation operated in relative isolation from other labor legislation. Rather than coordinating constituencies for a nascent welfare state, the character of Washington's legislation and its implementation fragmented political alliances.

A similar fate befell the women's minimum-wage policy. Administrative autonomy was hobbled by requirements for consultation with labor and employees. Consequently, the law could be hamstrung by the noncooperation of either group. In 1920, at a conference held in response to petitions from employers in hotels, restaurants, and manufacturing, employers generally refused to discuss the questions at issue: "At the end of their two days' executive session the conferees adjourned with no wage recommendation—for the first time in the six years of the commission's existence." A second conference fared little better: "Again the employers filled the Senate chamber in silence. When one employer did break silence, his companions voiced disapproval among themselves." Retreating into executive session, the conference recommended an eighteen-dollar minimum wage by a five-to-four vote, but this recommendation failed to secure approval from the Industrial Welfare Commission, whose personnel changed between the conference and the end of a series of protest hearings:

> One member resigned. A second was superceded by a new member despite the fact that the women of the state had petitioned the governor to reappoint her. The vote found the labor commissioner, the one salaried member, and the newly appointed member voting against and the other two voting for the recommendations of the conference, with the fifth member not appointed. The additional member is not to be appointed; so the girls find the consideration of their well-being laid aside until after the fall elections.[127]

The shortcomings of implementation eroded the coalitions that initially supported the law. Whereas the organized waitresses and other working women had actively supported minimum-wage legislation in 1913, by 1923 a leader of the Seattle waitresses argued that "laws were poorly written, rarely enforced, and flagrantly violated by employers." Consequently, "actual wages remained below the legislative standards . . . [but] by giving women the illusion of protection, minimum wage inhibited organizational impulses and weakened unions."[128] Since appointments to agencies and commissions were driven by partisan politician concerns (recall the inability of women's groups to secure reappointment of an IWC member), electoral success did not generate steady bureaucratic expansion. In the absence of a bureaucratic interest group to defend these programs and agencies, the reform accomplishments of the Progressive Era were left vulnerable to conservative retrenchment during the 1920s.

Patterns of Politics and Policy

The reforms of the Progressive Era, many historians have contended, were the responses of political and economic elites to the dilemmas of a rapidly growing economy and a society transformed by immigration and technological change. Such accounts, however, pay insufficient attention to the variations within this process—in the organization of challengers, the dismantling of one set of political institutions, and the establishment of new political configurations. When these three states are compared to one another, a similar story emerges with respect to the passage of policy. As strongly progressive states during the heyday of national reform prior to the world war, all three tended to pass strong social and labor legislation at the moment that a particular issue was on the agenda of national reformers and agitators. But similarities at the level of policy outcomes masked important differences at the levels of political mobilization and state-building. The real struggle was to create or capture state agencies that could protect those policy achievements, administer programs, and serve as the basis for policy expansion in the future. On this level, the contrasts among Wisconsin, California, and Washington are striking.

An explanation for these differences is found in the patterns of political organization in each state in the years after 1890. Variations in the models of organization adapted by different groups, as well as in the rules governing the emerging reform coalitions, produced variations in policy, institutions, and, as importantly, in the complex feedback processes by which state agencies come to create and maintain their own constituencies. Where such feedback loops were established between agencies and interest groups, the true beginnings of modern interest group politics were evident.

The critical mechanism behind the persistent differences among these states lay in the distinctive links that were (or were not) created between popular associations and legislative or agency decision making. As vehicles for socializing voters to attend to the issue content of politics, even at the cost of traditional partisan loyalties, popular associations were a crucial medium for connecting individual voters to the issues that proliferated in party platforms and candidates' promises, to the growing social policy agendas of state legislatures, and to the implementation and enforcement of those policies by state agencies, often newly created. The form of these connections, however, reflected the distinctive organizational repertoires that prevailed in each state and the forms of action around which reform coalitions had crystallized.

In Wisconsin, neither organized labor nor farmers abandoned the party as the appropriate model for mobilization; consequently, reform in Wisconsin involved choreographing electoral constituencies and legislative blocs. The institutional reforms most conducive to a politics without parties—initiative, referendum, and recall—were adopted comparatively late for a state famed for its progressivism, and, even once adopted, were used with far less frequency and enthusiasm than on the Pacific coast. Although Wisconsin's urban reformers and farmers often supported direct democracy, this enthusiasm for nonpartisan methods was shared by neither the leadership of organized labor nor by La Follette himself, who "could not understand why [Wisconsin's insurgents] wanted to give power directly to voters to make laws through the initiative and referendum process. He practices representative, not direct, democracy."[129]

In California, by contrast, antipartisanship was the dominant note of

reform, and nonpartisan organizational vehicles came to structure political mobilization across the ideological spectrum. This progressivism of
political institutions and processes was at the core of Hiram Johnson's
commitment to reform. Crediting the senator with "a political progressivism, a humanitarian progressivism, and not an economic progressivism,"
The Nation argued that the former governor, now a leading isolationist
and vocal opponent of the League of Nations, was not guilty of changing
his political tune: "Johnson thought—and thinks—that the electorate
should be permitted (through such devices as direct primaries) to express
its will freely and fully and directly in affairs of government and affairs
of party. He thought—and thinks—that a railroad company . . . should
be a railroad and not a government."[130] Johnson and the prewar progressives dismantled much of the party apparatus, supplanting it with fluid
electoral arrangements and permissive forms of direct democracy. But institutional opportunities alone did not produce the fiercely issue-oriented
and nonpartisan political contests that convulsed the state in the 1920s.
The same associations that mobilized to support Johnson and his allies
in the first waves of California progressivism embodied a combination of
nonpartisan business methods and issue-oriented "educational" (or propaganda) politics. Regardless of a group's political goals, it was this *form*
that prevailed in the struggles of the 1920s over whether the state should
embrace an economic as well as political progressivism.

Like organized labor in Wisconsin, both the Washington Grange and
the State Federation of Labor were initially unenthusiastic about nonpartisan techniques, preferring third-party strategies as the alternative to regular partisanship. But thwarted in the arena of formal politics, a broad
range of organizations became fervent supporters of direct democracy. In
addition, the popular associations of Washington demonstrated a consistent capacity to use private associations to perform functions elsewhere
allocated to state agencies.

A policy map of public employment agencies captures the important
differences between the states with respect to popular organization and
state capacity (fig. 7.3). In Wisconsin, there was a state law establishing
such exchanges, and only state exchanges existed. In California, there
was a state law and state agencies, but city governments (typically in collaboration with labor federations or employer associations) also sponsored employment offices. In Washington, there was no state law, but six
municipal employment offices were in place as of 1915, almost always
operating with close ties to labor organizations. In each case, organized

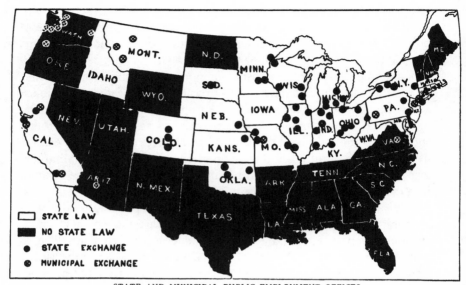

STATE AND MUNICIPAL PUBLIC EMPLOYMENT OFFICES

IN THE UNITED STATES, OCTOBER 1, 1915, 23 STATE SYSTEMS OF PUBLIC EMPLOYMENT BUREAUS OPERATED 64 OFFICES, AND THERE WERE OVER 20 MUNICIPAL BUREAUS

Figure 7.3   State and Municipal Employment Offices. (Source: *American Labor Legislation Review,* November 1915)

groups helped to *structure demand* for specific public services; in each case, the configuration of popular organization shaped state capacity and the ways in which services were delivered.

In each state, a distinctive reform style crystallized as popular selections from organizational repertoires reshaped the rules and institutions of governance. These organizational preferences set the terms for the co-evolution of parties, pressure groups, and state agencies. To the extent that reformers successfully embedded these rearranged organizational fields in reliable flows of votes and financial resources, the innovations of the progressive years were more likely to persist despite the ideological reaction and fiscal conservatism of the 1920s—challenges that increasingly borrowed the nonpartisan methods pioneered by political challengers themselves.

EIGHT

"The Menace of New Privilege"

> An imposing setting was given this conference on the
> state of industry. The hall of the Americas in the Pan-
> American building, a beautiful structure (paid for in part
> by money earned in the steel industry and donated by
> Andrew Carnegie) was the chosen assembly room. In the
> large court fountains played and brightly colored tropi-
> cal birds perched in the palm trees. The marble stair-
> cases, regal in width, gave the dignity of the King's Rob-
> ing Room to this meeting of the representatives of the
> work-a-day world. . . . In this setting the conference rep-
> resenting the public, the employing interest, and orga-
> nized labor convened. The three groups were separated
> and by the rules were compelled to vote as units. Labor
> sat at the left, the public in the center, and the employers
> at the right—thereby producing for the first time on this
> side of the water the divisions so characteristic of the
> legislative chambers of the European capitals. The three
> groups by their emphasis were made to symbolize three
> classes, tangible if less distinct than those so frankly rec-
> ognized in the France of the revolutionary days. The
> President's Industrial Conference had the courage, or the
> indiscretion, to recognize and segregate them along the
> boundaries of their supposed interests. This is a new
> phenomenon in the United States, but perhaps typical
> of the present grasping at the realities of life however
> seriously those realities may seem to challenge the tradi-
> tion of the American Republic.
>
> "The President's Industrial Conference,"
> *The Survey,* 25 October 1919

As much as the struggles of the previous two decades had changed the
political landscape of the United States, it was the First World War that
left many citizens feeling as though they now lived in a different country.
Wartime measures had intensified the centralization and bureaucratization of state agencies as well as of the voluntary associations and corpora-

273

tions on whose cooperation they depended.[1] The lifting of wartime restrictions on organized labor rapidly confirmed the dangers of the increased scale of economic organization. A wave of strikes swept the nation: a general strike in Seattle, an industry-wide organizing strike in steel, the police strike in Boston, and strikes in the printing trades that manifested themselves in the crude typography that suddenly appeared in the same national magazines that carried word of still more unrest (fig. 8.1). Prices and wages spiraled upward, as the "H.C.L." (high cost of living) became a featured player in the news. Under these conditions, it is scarcely surprising that some observers spotted the twin specters of privilege and revolution lurking in the halls of Washington, D.C.

But those invited to President Wilson's industrial conference were not those most involved in the unrest and disquiet that was so widely perceived. On the initial list of fifteen nominated to serve as the "public group," farmers were represented by the president of the Ohio Farm Bureau Federation, an agricultural editor from Iowa, and an unaffiliated farmer from Colorado. No women were included on the first list, although three were quickly added. As with the radical farmers, representatives of the large women's associations that had left their mark on state and national politics were strikingly absent. Appointment of the labor group was given to Samuel Gompers; the resulting delegation of fifteen included nine of eleven members of the AFL executive board, as well as one woman and one "outstanding non-conformist . . . Paul Scharrenberg, secretary of the California State Federation, who is a member of the more liberal wing of the federation." The railroad brotherhoods were entirely absent, but they denounced the delegation and "President Gompers personally for recognizing only one element of labor."[2] As one observer concluded:

> The absence of any spokesman from the more radical groups—whether of workers or farmers—who for better or worse have expressed the unrest that gave occasion for this conference—is, however, the outstanding limitation of the meeting as a gathering representative of the forces at work today in industrial America. It is like an eighteenth-century religious conference with the non-conformists left out![3]

By systematically excluding those most drawn to insurgent politics, the Industrial Conference called by President Wilson in 1919 uncannily reproduced much of the logic of the nineteenth-century party system, albeit in a new organizational form. Once again, an effort to strike a bargain among national actors generated a ring of discontent that included west-

THE WAY IT STRIKES THE PUBLIC.
—Morris for the George Matthew Adams Service.

AT THE PLACE OF DECISION
----McCay in the New York American

Figure 8.1 The Postwar Labor Crisis. (Source: *Literary Digest*, 6 September 1919 and 25 October 1919)

ern labor, reformist women, and aggrieved farmers, who murmured that "the Populist movement and the Progressive revolt will appear to have been a summer's breeze in comparison with the storm now brewing."[4]

The shadows cast by the party system still delineated the geography of political insurgency, selectively magnifying or suppressing economic, cultural, religious, and racial divisions. Without a significant presence in the South, argued Walter Lippmann, "the Republican party is a sectional party" in which

> [t]he West fights alone and in such a contest it has no chance. It is easily overridden by the Eastern politicians whenever they are not engaged, as they were in 1912, in a factional quarrel which leads one faction to form a temporary alliance with the insurgent West. That is why the sectional conflict which prevails as truly in the Republican as in the Democratic Party came to nothing at [the national convention at] Cleveland but an hour of jeering at the Wisconsin delegates.[5]

But if the pattern of discontent was familiar, the means available for its expression had changed significantly since the Populist insurgency of the 1890s and the Progressive Party of 1912. The parties no longer monopolized the institutionalized openings for political mobilization: direct democracy provided alternative channels for lawmaking in many states, and multiplying agencies provided alternative targets for mobilization. Even within the parties, primaries and the direct election of senators eroded the control of party leaders while enhancing the influence of extrapartisan associations: "It is going to be harder for a Senator of independence in the future to hold to a course that does not square with the opinion of the day, for his chance of reelection will be largely determined not by whether his acts have been wise but by whether they have been popular."[6]

These new opportunities for political action corresponded to—and were often the product of—new patterns of organization. The new organizational forms of popular politics had done more than substitute a lens of "interest" for that of partisan loyalty or common good. They also produced a reorganization of government, as new policies, new programs, and new agencies came to be taken as the signs that group interest had been recognized. Organize, politicize, bureaucratize—this sequence recurs from the Progressive Era through the 1920s, blurring distinctions between social movements and formal institutions. Social workers exemplify this pattern. State conferences organized early in the second decade of the century hired full-time executive directors and a few years later voted to engage in legislative politics; by the 1920s they found themselves fighting to protect these new agencies from political reaction and fiscal frugality.[7]

The counterattack was carried out on many fronts. A new open-shop campaign threatened long-term union bastions such as San Francisco and Seattle; wartime censorship laws and the "red scare" were turned against a broad array of progressive organizations, as even the "Sunshine Society" of benevolent ladies was portrayed as caught up in a "Spider Web" of reds. There were repeated efforts to repeal procedural innovations such as the direct primary.[8] Three years after the war, the *American Labor Legislation Review* could still strike a hopeful note: "Despite the persistence of reaction throughout the year and the consequence paucity of constructive measures in the 1921 output of new labor laws, there have been some conspicuous advances in legislation for the protection of the safety and health of the workers." Four years later, the outlook was far bleaker: "Legislative sessions of 1925 show that the recent mass attack by opposition propaganda has resulted in a reactionary attitude which if only temporary is nevertheless acute. This year, for the first time since workmen's compensation became an accepted American principle, it has been necessary to resist organized attempts to weaken the laws."[9] And, at least with respect to methods, "the opposition" was not so different from what the reformers described as "our counter-propaganda—what *we* call our campaigns of education."[10]

Carefully nurtured in countless struggles, the nonpartisan and educational strategies pioneered by challengers had become public knowledge, or "modular"—portable from cause to cause, from setting to setting, from proponent to opponent.[11] In the presidential campaign of 1920, "[T]he Republicans took a leaf out of the campaign procedure of the Progressive Party under Roosevelt and instituted a bureau . . . which made serious studies of the issues . . . and which, during the campaign, collated material and opinion in an effort to lift party discussion to a new and competently informed stage."[12] Overlaid on a common organizational framework defined by business methods and mechanisms of electoral accountability, the increasingly shared techniques of educational campaigns and "propaganda" constituted a new style of politics in which constituent groups forged a direct connection between their demands and policy outcomes. By the 1920s, a stylistically nonpartisan and state-oriented understanding of politics was evident on multiple sides of many issues.[13]

So disheartening as it was for progressives and reformers to watch their policies reversed and their agencies dismantled, this period of political reaction is analytically useful. If the organizational innovations of the decades before the war established a new kind of political field, the years following the armistice tested the extent to which these new patterns had become entrenched in individual behavior, in resource flows or formal agencies, and in the calculations and commitments of organized political actors. As with technical novelties, in order to endure political innovations must be embedded in understandings of action, resources both fiscal and human, and connections to constituencies and elites.[14] Consequently, the selective survival of inventions provides a window on the final moment of institutional change: institutionalization itself.[15]

Just as inventors do not necessarily profit from successful innovations, participation in the process of institutional change did not guarantee any benefit. Control over new forms of organization and state intervention was decided through contests, at both state and national levels. This chapter examines three moments of contestation over the substantive outcomes of this new extrapartisan politics. First, in California, Washington, and Wisconsin, the changed political climate of the postwar years fueled efforts to dismantle the beachheads that reformers had established in new policies and state agencies. The outcomes of these struggles depended in large part on the distinctive organizational configurations that characterized the reform coalitions in each state. Second, frustrated political challengers sought to alter both the formal and informal structures of American politics: to amend the Constitution and to establish a third party grounded in the discontent of farmers and workers. Finally, the opportunity structure of federalism drew the efforts of political challengers from state to national arenas. On the one hand, wartime expansion set a precedent for federal funding of public projects in the states. On the other, as the legislative victories of the progressive years made their way up through the process of judicial review, the power of the Supreme Court to stifle the experiments of "laboratory states" became all too evident. While both efforts failed in the short run, they left a legacy of discontent and a capacity for extrapartisan political pressure that would help to shape American politics from the New Deal onward.[16]

The Limits of Laboratories: Challenging Reform in the States

The strength of the partisan culture of the late nineteenth century lay in its power to teach individuals to understand their preferences or interests through the lens of party loyalty. In theoretical terms, this may be described as individual rationality operating under uncertainty and high information costs or as evidence of institutionalized scripts shaping political behavior. Either way, the available interpretive schemas and models relating causes to effects are crucially important.[17] As party loyalty was subjected to sustained criticism, "group interest" did not automatically appear as an alternative framework for political calculation and organization. Instead, the taken-for-granted character of appeals to group interest was the product of decades of organizational activity in which Americans learned a language of interest, a calculus for its determination, and methods for subjecting elected officials and state agencies to the discipline of constituent demands.

The institution building that took place between 1890 and 1920 rested on this reorganization of social politics. Confronted by the rise of modern corporations and centralized parties, groups throughout American society sought out new channels of political influence, alternatives to a party system that did not respond to the desires of "the People." Farmers became a fraternal order and then transformed themselves into businessmen. Unionists were also rooted in fraternalism, then toyed with the models of partisan politics and economic self-organization, and finally emerged as a powerful legislative lobby. Women's groups, formally outside the party system of the Gilded Age, went furthest in reconstituting themselves in the previously illegitimate form of the lobby.

These new forms of popular politics often prompted the expansion of the capacity and autonomy of state agencies. Groups defined their demands in terms of delimited "interests," then sought the establishment of state agencies dedicated to those goals.[18] But state expansion had not been an inevitable outcome of the reorganization of popular politics. In Wisconsin, organized labor was markedly more successful in embedding its "interests" in new, relatively autonomous state agencies than were other popular political contenders: the Industrial Commission was held up as an exemplar to the nation, but working women's issues were handled by a department within the commission, and agrarian activists bemoaned their failure to establish a marketing agency of their own until 1919. Yet the limits of state revenues shaped the form of these new institutions: autonomous but restricted to limited policy mandates, working through regulation and quasi-corporatist consultation rather than expanded government spending. In California, numerous state agencies were established, often generously financed by taxes on utility corporations. But the very autonomy they secured in an era of budgetary largesse left these agencies vulnerable to the fiscal conservatism of the 1920s. Once again, however, the atypical outcomes in Washington state most clearly illustrate the links between the organizational form of popular politics and the shape of political institutions. Having built a formidable coalition on populist models that valued direct democracy and cooperative organization over state expansion and expert regulation, the state's progressive workers, farmers, and women united to pass landmark social legislation but provided neither the fiscal support nor the institutional havens that could shelter these policy achievements from conservative electoral successes. Instead, the 1920s saw labor, farmers, and business redirect their energies into private governance, self-organization, and third-party efforts. Once a leader in social reform, Washington recedes in the chronicles of these efforts after the war.

In each of these states, the identities and organizational practices adopted by challenging groups set the terms for the construction of new state institutions. Three issues had been crucial: the extent to which parties were dismantled in favor of direct democracy; the relations established between associations and state agencies; and the fiscal arrangements made to support new agencies and programs. The new state institutions, in turn, served as loci for embedding new policies in networks of allies, resources, and constituencies. Where such networks had been established, reforms and reformist bureaucrats had better prospects for surviving once the methods of propaganda and nonpartisan issue politics were turned against them.

Wisconsin

Although the wartime suppression of dissent and reaction to the wave of labor unrest in 1919–20 fractured reform coalitions in many states, the very extent of the hostile reaction to Wisconsin politics and politicians helped to solidify at least some bases of support. Senator La Follette vocally resisted both wartime profiteering by corporations and suppression of civil liberties by the increasingly conservative Wilson administration, thereby earning the loyalty of the liberal, German-American, and pacifist constituencies while deeply alienating others.[19] In Milwaukee, voters in the Fifth Congressional District elected socialist Victor Berger in 1918 and then reelected him at a special election called later that year when the House of Representatives refused to seat him.[20] In 1920, the city reelected Social Democratic mayor Daniel Hoan but did not give that party a majority on the city council.[21] Despite war and reaction, therefore, Wisconsin voters reproduced the constellation of varied but cohesive power blocs, a configuration in which state agencies remained the crucial locus of decision making. But the organizational identities of those power blocs shifted subtly and steadily under the pressure of ongoing grievances, new opportunities, and political reaction.

The alliance of the WiSFL and the Social Democrats was strained but not broken by the First World War, which set socialist pacifists against prowar, projob unionists. Although organized labor continued its financial support of socialist legislators and publications after the war, the Milwaukee leadership increasingly turned from the socialist model of independent-party politics to an educational model that stressed the need to teach individual voters to perceive their interests correctly.[22] Appearing before the 1920 WiSFL convention to urge withdrawal of a resolution in support of his candidacy, the Socialist nominee for governor argued that

> it is not desirable for the convention of the Federation to indorse any political party, or any candidate for an elective or appointive political office, for the reason that such indorsements will not redown [sic] to the welfare of labor, until such time that the rank and file of labor are educated to the necessity of using their ballots intelligently along class lines, in a class conscious manner, and when the workers have once attained that state of intelligence and class consciousness, it will be unnecessary for any labor body to indorse any political party, or a candidate for elective or appointive positions.[23]

Into the 1920s, the loose but durable ties of the WiSFL to the Social Democratic Party continued to generate controversy. Replaying organizational battles of the 1890s and 1900s, the leadership fought off efforts to place the WiSFL on a nonpartisan basis, resisting resolutions to replace the directive that "all members of this parliament of labor recommend, and ask all affiliated bodies to actively support, with their ballots and otherwise, the *political party* whose platform is nearest to the foregoing declaration of principles." Defeated resolutions asked "all affiliated bodies to maintain an active legislative committee, and elect trade unionists to office and advance them on every possible occasion by *independent voting outside party lines*"; "to actively support, with their ballots and otherwise, *candidates for public office* whose platform embodies, and comes nearest to the foregoing declaration of principles"; or that the WiSFL "create a state Non-Partisan Political Committee, and urge all Central Bodies to form a local Non-Partisan Political Committee, and ask all local unions to appoint a committee to co-operate with the state, central bodies and national committee."[24] But although the arms-length alliance with the Social Democrats was successfully defended, there were small accommodations to the increasing presence of nonpartisan practices in Wisconsin politics. In 1923, the federation allowed that affiliated bodies might support "*the political party or individual* whose platform is nearest the foregoing declaration of principles."[25] Even in a stronghold of socialist third-party politics, therefore, the outlines of the interest-motivated, candidate-centered, nonpartisan voter were emerging.

This reorientation of organized labor created new possibilities for coalition politics outside the framework provided by the state's Republican Party. By the 1920s, agrarian groups no longer had to be urged to attend to politics. But as their demands for legislation and administrative action increased, their inability to control elected representatives grew evermore troubling. After repeated efforts to deploy "good man" strategies, the members of Equity still charged that in the legislature "the usual forces and factions are plotting and planning to 'hold up' or to 'get through' the usual grist of measures of various kinds and on almost every conceivable question." Equity, in contrast, had "learned not to 'tear our shirts' nor 'pull our hair'; 'waste our powder' nor 'blow our bugles' unless there is something in sight worthy of such disturbance."[26] But this disciplined focus on specific issues did not produce much in the absence of a reliable bloc in the legislature. As J. B. Houston, the state Equity secretary, explained to the 1920 WiSFL convention, "[T]he big manufacturing interests had fought the Society of Equity marketing measure, even influenced Equity members in the legislature last session to such a degree that they voted against genuine farmers' measures."[27] Only insofar as an association could alter a candidate's electoral calculus would organizational demands be translated into legislative votes.

As state federations of labor had learned, the restriction and specification of demands was only one element of an effective pressure group; the other was pressure. Lacking the leverage of reliable votes in the state legislature, some farmers began to advocate an independent party just at the time that the WiSFL tentatively moved in the opposite direction. Some farmers flirted with the Nonpartisan League, which had spread out of North Dakota. The Farmers' Co-operative Packing Co. of Wausau declared,

> Whereas, We find that the other big interests who are making large fortunes, often at the expense of the farms, are, and always have been, nonpartisan or bi-partisan, and we believe it is folly for the farmers to continue to be partisan and to divide their voting strength among different political parties; and
>
> Whereas, We believe the time has come when the farmers of Wisconsin should cease to vote for politician parties and commence to vote for themselves, their wives and children; and

Whereas, The success of the Farmers' Non-partisan League in North Dakota shows what the farmers can and should do for their own mutual protection and welfare; now, therefore, be it

Resolved, That we, the stockholders of the Farmers' Co-operative Packing Company of Wausau, in annual meeting assembled, do hereby recommend that a farmers' convention be called in the city of Marshfield, Wis., on the twenty-second day of March, 1917, for the purpose of organizing the farmers of Wisconsin into a non-partisan league, in order that the farmers of our state may obtain control of our state government and our delegation in congress at the next election.[28]

This resolution bears the hallmarks of a by-now familiar process of organizational innovation. These Wausau farmers sought to appropriate a recognizable strategy of action ("the bi-partisanship" of corporations) for their own purposes; the precedent for this appropriation was provided by actors in another state (North Dakota, where the Nonpartisan League worked through the primaries of both parties to secure acceptable nominees); and the goal was to construct an alternative to the party system, a mechanism for tying representatives to farmers by teaching farmers to "vote for themselves." Familiar too, were the reasons for the failure of this particular attempt. The Wisconsin Equity declined to actively support the effort, citing its own organizational character: "The A. S. of E. is non-political and hence cannot consistently advance any political movement no matter how meritorious it may be." With its own resources stretched thin, the Nonpartisan League announced that it would not attempt to organize Wisconsin until the 1920 elections. In addition, party politics was already available as an alternative course of action; in 1918, J. N. Tittemore, president of the Wisconsin Society of Equity, headed a complete, although not victorious, slate in the state's Republican primaries.[29]

Embedded in this congeries of interested associations, all to some degree committed to the exercise of *practical* expertise, state agencies helped to reproduce an essentially corporatist style of policy expansion within the state even as momentum gathered among farmers and organized labor for another effort at independent-party politics on a national level. The state Board of Control, charged with supervising state institutions and welfare programs, was subjected in 1921 to a reorganization "with emphasis on business administration," but this effort drew strenuous criticism. The would-be reorganizers "either ignored or curtly refused" advice and "overtures on the part of social work groups, civic bodies and citizens of the state." This reorganization produced "a general demand from all parts of the state, and particularly from Wisconsin women, that immediate action be taken to remedy the situation. So important had the question become that it threatened to take on serious political aspects." The governor, progressive J. J. Blaine, averted this crisis by appointing a new head of the board from among the administrators of state institutions, healing the breach between the organized social workers and the state agency.[30] To the extent that such networks of mobilized constituents and state agencies had been established, neither the postwar reaction nor the scalpel of "efficiency" proved enough to disrupt them.

California

The regulatory style of Wisconsin progressivism worked by enrolling the representatives of associations—organized labor, employers, social workers—into advisory groups charged with the formulation of specific policies. In California, by contrast, nonpartisan pressure groups secured the establishment of state agencies that, amply funded by tax revenues and often managed by appointees from those very associations, then sought to supervise a wide range of social and economic activities. The Commission of Immigration and Housing exemplifies the rapid accumulation of power by state agencies:

> There was, in the beginning, no legal authority behind the duties given to the commission. . . . So the inspectors went out into the field merely as advisers, knowing that lasting results could be obtained only through the education of the public in general and camp operators in particular. . . .
>
> And when the commission had been in the field some eight months a new law was drafted, no longer dealing in generalities but giving specific requirements and regulations. This law was passed by the legislature of 1915, and its enforcement placed directly in the hands of the commission. . . .
>
> The method of disposing of the cases after conviction also contains an interesting feature. For no fine is exacted from the offending camp operator. Instead, a suspended sentence is given, with instructions from the court to comply with the rules of the commission, failure to comply meaning contempt of court. In this way the commission has a perpetual legal check on the conduct of the camp owner.[31]

Not surprisingly, when political reaction developed, it took the form of a protest against the intrusion of government into private life. In some cases, proponents of state regulation turned back these assaults, making masterful use of educational politics and alliances among associations in which all traces of partisanship appeared had vanished. In 1920, social workers allied not only with organized doctors but with the Metropolitan

Life Insurance Company (which "went into the state at the request and invitation of the California State Board of Health") to circulate literature and visit as many as 125,000 homes in order to defeat a bill that would have abolished compulsory vaccination of schoolchildren as well as the power to keep contagious children and teachers out of the schools.[32] Other groups met with less success. Governor Richardson reduced the appropriation for the Sonoma Home for Delinquent Women dramatically—$365,000 for its first two years to under $43,000:

> The women's clubs concentrated their efforts on saving the institution, and the legislature raised the allowance to $80,000. Meanwhile the main building burned down, and the governor vetoed the increase and cut down his own estimate to a beggarly $4,000, on the ground that without this building the home could get along with a much smaller operating expense! The press was not slow in suggesting that more fires might help the governor to economize in other directions.[33]

Political reaction also took its toll on the very associations that had made such campaigns possible. The "Better America Federation" attacked the Los Angeles YWCA for encouraging working women to organize and called for the abolition of the CIH, which it accused of being "a friend of the I.W.W."[34] With more success, the Better America Federation, in alliance with the State Taxpayers League, advocated a bill that consolidated "the State Labor Commission, the Minimum Wage Commission, and the State Housing and Immigration Commission."[35] The Federation also practiced an explicitly educational politics, publishing "two pamphlets, one entitled Fill the Jails—recommending that liberals be so disposed of—and the other, Making Socialists Out of College Students, A Story of Professors and Other Collegians Who Hobnob With Radicals."[36] An officer of the Associated Charities in the East Bay spent time in jail under the criminal-syndicalism law, and Paul Scharrenberg was dismissed from the CIH for "using his position as a state official to influence legislation."[37]

This vulnerability of reformers stemmed from their inability to control elections in a world of cross-filing and ingrained nonpartisanship. As governor, Hiram Johnson had led progressives out of the Republican Party into the Progressive Party and then back again. Johnson left Sacramento for the U.S. Senate in 1917; his successor, William D. Stephens, was reelected once but then defeated in the Republican primary by conservative Friend Richardson, the force behind the budget-driven efforts to dismantle progressive programs and state agencies during the 1920s. These campaigns were funded in large part by the utility companies, the major source of state tax revenues. Herbert Hoover lingered at the edges of state politics, first leaving both Democrats and Republicans in doubt over his party label, then, by the mid-1920s, splitting Johnson's following of progressive Republicans while attracting many votes from the Democrats. In 1923, some reformers regrouped as the Progressive Voters League and, by 1926, won back the governor's office for C. C. Young, but lost the Republican primary for the Senate to the incumbent conservative.[38] Without Wisconsin's insulating web of delegates from labor and industry, California's agencies were left vulnerable to the oscillating fortunes of different factions within state politics.

Reaction against the expansion of state programs, attacks on associations linked to progressive reform, and the extraordinary weakness of the parties in postprogressive California[39] combined to generate the volatile political profile that has characterized the state's role in national politics since the second decade of the century. Like La Follette, Hiram Johnson sought to export the state's political program through senatorial and presidential politics—to "Californianize the nation."[40] As Theodore Roosevelt's vice presidential nominee on the Bull Moose Progressive ticket of 1912, as a rumored or actual candidate for presidential and vice presidential slots in 1920 and 1924, Johnson (again like La Follette) foundered in his efforts to use party slates as vehicles for nationalizing the state's reform projects of the prewar years.

Associational politics was a second medium for perpetuating and expanding the impact of state-level efforts. Widespread mobilization for new forms of state spending and intervention shaped California politics through the 1920s, when struggles centered on public ownership of utilities,[41] into the 1930s, producing widespread support of Democrat Upton Sinclair's EPIC ("End Poverty in California") program and demands for old-age pensions that fed into the Townsend movement (an electoral threat of national significance that contributed to the Social Security Act). Thus issue-based popular volatility, along with a state legislature that came to be dominated by lobbyists, was the legacy of a period of organizational innovation in which parties were dismantled. Individuals as well as associations came to determine their political choices candidate by candidate and program by program.[42] To a far greater extent than the substance of progressive social policy, therefore, the methods of nonpartisan issue-oriented electoral politics were institutionalized in California and made available to political contenders of all stripes. In the favorable political climate before the war, these institutional changes facilitated a remarkably direct mapping of organized pressure groups onto the state in the form of new programs and agencies. But once the critics of these programs struck back using both the "educational politics" and the centralized budget machinery perfected by the reformers,[43] the very weakness of the parties (or some equivalent form of electoral coordination) left those agencies without the bulwark of organized and coordinated constituencies that protected programs in Wisconsin from similar efforts to impose "efficiency."

Washington

The nationwide conservative reaction was particularly intense in Washington—a direct effect of the organizational strength of those who challenged the economic and political order. As in other states, wartime mobilization had intensified the scale of economic activities and enhanced the organizational capacities of those involved in managing this heightened production. In the shipyards of Puget Sound, the Metal Trades Councils (and by extension the city centrals of Seattle and Tacoma) enjoyed more members, higher wages, and new formal privileges of labor market control. Union strength in these skilled trades facilitated the organization of service industries such as hotels and restaurants; by the end of the war, 20 percent of the residents of Seattle belonged to the AFL.[44] The increased scale of the Seattle labor movement inspired efforts to change its form; the shop steward system of electing union representatives plant by plant, a proposal (defeated) to establish cross-city "federated unions," and the "Duncan Plan" for restructuring the AFL itself all pointed toward a vision of a more politically cohesive union movement that would map more directly onto both communities and industries.[45] Although the proposals for a formal restructuring of the AFL were easily turned back, locally unionists built ever denser networks of cooperation both in and out of the workplace:

> It was a new-found sense of union that brought about that surprising coordination of the working forces of Seattle which produced what is still known as the Seattle Revolution. A "revolution" in the sense of intending any bodily harm to anybody it was not. The actual conduct of it was as orderly as a Quaker Quarterly Meeting. It was revolutionary only in the sense that it revealed to a startled public, including the workers themselves, the unrealized dependence of a modern community upon the least and

poorest of the workers, and showed what the economic power of workers means once they move and act with a common purpose.[46]

Part of the surprise lay in the degree to which the general strike of 1919 revealed the capacity of labor's own organizations to substitute for the regular political and economic infrastructure of the city. Order was maintained, emergency kitchens fed union and nonunion workers, milk was delivered for babies and hospitals. In the wake of the general strike, these organizational capacities fueled a wave of cooperative activity, elaborating on prewar efforts while also strengthening ties with the organized farmers, who shared both suspicion of state regulation and support for cooperative organizing with Seattle's labor movement.

Elsewhere in the state, the war also left a legacy of new models of cooperation among organized groups. Building on the precedent of worker assessments for the Red Cross and Liberty bonds, the town of Aberdeen attempted to transfer this model to peacetime civic purposes:

> Organized labor, under this division of work, virtually undertakes to support the social service of the community, on the understanding that organized business will look out for the general prosperity. In other words, home service, visiting nursing, boys' and girls' clubs, community service and the like, instead of being supported, as is the more common practice, by those whose incomes are from profits or the professions, are to be taken care of by wage-earners; while harbor improvements, the location of new industries, and other matters which affect the industrial prosperity of the community and keep Aberdeen on the map, economically and financially, are to be taken care of by the proprietors of the sawmills and logging camps, bankers, merchants, and others ordinarily represented in the Chamber of Commerce. Labor is to look out for philanthropy, thus leaving capital free to insure the continuance of the industrial prosperity on which wages depend.[47]

A report on public-health programs across the state found a similar dependence on existing forms of community organization. Whereas state agencies would frequently take the lead in Wisconsin, and subsume or at least oversee private welfare efforts in California, Washington's programs evidenced a community-level heterogeneity of form: "There was always some organization which took the lead in the community. This proved to be, in one place, the Elks Club or the Knights of Pythias; in another, the Ladies' Aid, the Parent-Teachers' Association, the Red Cross Chapter, the Grange, and so on." The link between existing organizations and the task of launching new programs was explicitly noted: "To get the people to work in terms of their former successes in organization, according to their own methods, not forgetting they had launched on a new undertaking, usually insured success."[48] Farmers also found new forms of organized self-reliance; the Washington Wheat Growers' Association invented a new form of commodity bond backed by the *organization's* promise to deliver grain.[49]

Accelerated by the war and the strike, the use of such nonpolitical organizational forms for public purposes was also prompted by the increasing attacks on those active in politics. As in California, public officials were ejected for their political allegiances.[50] Reform leaders were imprisoned under criminal-syndicalism laws, the leader of the Washington State Grange was both ejected from the national organization and subjected to federal prosecution, and the AFL threatened to revoke the charter of the Seattle Central. The alliance between the Grange and organized labor finally found a partisan expression following the armistice in the Farmer-Labor Party. The party grew out of the "Triple Alliance" of the Grange, AFL unions, and the railroad brotherhoods in cooperation with the state's Nonpartisan League and the Railwaymen's Political Club. Compared to the rest of the nation, this was a spectacular success. The Farmer-Labor Party won a larger share of votes in Washington than in any other state, with some local candidates winning 40 percent of the vote in 1920. The party came in second in the gubernatorial election, but the voting results revealed that the Farmer-Labor Party was much more labor than farmer.[51]

Across organized labor, farmers, and civic associations, the combination of postwar radicalism and reaction split onetime alliances, and comparatively conservative factions gained control over many of the state's large membership associations. Whereas the nexus of organized pressure groups and either legislatures or state agencies provided an element of continuity through the 1920s in Wisconsin, and to a lesser extent in California, in Washington the enduring capacity for organization lay more fully outside both major-party and bureaucratic politics.[52] So even as the political commitments of the leadership shifted over the decade, the organizational skills cultivated through years of cooperative effort endured. Given a new opportunity for mobilization, in this case the crisis of the depression, familiar forms reappeared. Demonstrating extensive self-help (including organized barter with farmers), the Unemployed Citizens' League of Seattle impressed one visitor from the Russell Sage Foundation: "I can't imagine that I shall run across, elsewhere in my travels, so interesting a social experiment or one so balanced between the possibilities for good and evil as the relationship worked out here in Seattle between the social agencies, government, and the organized unemployed."[53] Resentful of "social welfare" methods, members of the Unemployed Citizens' League took over much of the work of vetting applicants and distributing relief. Before long, this cooperative organization was drawn into political contests—although some of the leadership fought to keep that participation on a formally nonpartisan basis. Although a number of candidates endorsed by the league were elected to the state legislature, here again the imprint of the past appeared: "Observers at the Legislature were impressed with the lack of solidarity on the part of the unemployed members. There were no indications of a 'Unemployed Citizens' League bloc.' Many of the other legislators were also inexperienced. The King county [Seattle] delegation was not as strongly organized as usual."[54] Lacking the habits of bloc politics and mastery of parliamentary procedure of the labor representatives from Wisconsin or of the union politicians from San Francisco, Seattle's organized (albeit unemployed) workers once again were unable to articulate cooperative, community-based organization with demands for specific legislative remedies.[55]

From States to Nation
In each of these states, the war and its aftermath brought reactions against the innovations and reforms of the preceding decade. Reforms that had not been embedded in either associational practices or bureaucratic beachheads were more easily swept away. Leaving a core of institutional changes often closely linked to the organizational capacities of mobilized constituencies, state polities served as enclaves (or abeyance structures) of prewar reform. In Wisconsin, consultative methods of policy formation linked both employer and labor organizations to state agencies in robust networks that endured the conservative political reaction of the 1920s as well as organized labor's tentative movements away from the informal legislative cooperation of Social Democrats and progressive Republicans toward a third-party alliance of farmers and workers. In California, ties between associations and agencies were grounded in financial subsidies to a greater extent than were the policy consultations that characterized industrial regulation in Wisconsin. Consequently, conservative demands for fiscal retrenchment during the 1920s not only limited the capacity of state agencies but eroded their connections to popular associations. Policy continuity was maintained less by networks linking associations and agencies than by the associations themselves, which repeatedly sought to use both direct democracy and the unstructured electoral politics of the state to return their programs to the state agenda. But if the reaction of the 1920s pushed these associations away from state agencies

to the terrain of extrapartisan politics in California, in the less-institutionalized setting of Washington state, popular associations away began the decade with far weaker ties to state agencies. Faced with the political and economic turmoil that followed the war, many organized groups turned from politics and, instead, took matters into their own hands, providing social services and economic organization without extensive support from either legislative programs or administrative agencies. In each of these states, therefore, the survival of policy initiatives was selective, determined by the organizational and institutional foundations constructed in the preceding decades.

These legacies of prewar political innovation were threatened, however, by the very structure of federalism that had allowed the emergence of "laboratory states." Although federalism has been discussed as a system of opportunities (see chap. 3), it is also a structure of constraints. As state legislation wended its way through the system of judicial review, many local experiments were declared unconstitutional. Even where state programs survived or evaded review, the shortcomings of state-by-state reform quickly appeared. Finally, the capture of the presidential nomination of both major parties by conservatives in 1920 destroyed the responsiveness to reformers that had defused some of the potential for realignment in the previous decade.[56] With these developments, the displacement of new political methods from the states to national politics was overdetermined.

The war's legacy of centralization and its demonstration of the power of the federal government redirected both protest and reform efforts. If the states had been the "laboratories" of the progressive period, after the war experimentation shifted to the division of powers between state and federal governments—as well as among the branches of the latter. Proposals for constitutional amendments, attacks on the Supreme Court, and demands for new cabinet-level departments vied for attention with the shop committees and corporate welfare plans that have led the decade to be characterized in terms of political complacency and new forms of private economic governance.[57] To focus solely on the corporate liberal trajectory that led to Herbert Hoover's "associational state"[58] is to miss the split personality of American politics in the 1920s. Behind the facade of the Harding, Coolidge, and Hoover administrations, marginalized and discontented political actors continued to adopt new organizational practices and to probe for new political opportunities.

They faced circumstances that were, to a considerable extent, of their own making. The major parties had failed to contain the discontent of groups outside the core industrial states of the North; these discontented groups responded by agitating for increased regulation of parties, by introducing direct democracy so that voters could circumvent the parties, and by using popular associations as media for constructing new political identities. Particularly in the western states, the number of initiatives and referenda on ballots grew, and party labels faded as reliable guides to electoral choice (some candidates avoided them entirely). In California, cross-filing allowed candidates to run in the primaries of multiple parties. While undermining the parties, these challengers often encouraged the proliferation of Industrial Accident Boards, Industrial Welfare Commissions, and State Marketing Commissions. These actions then provoked reactions. Proponents of expanded state regulation of public welfare were accused of bolshevist tendencies.[59] Weakened parties, a struggle over government centralization (at both state and federal levels), and heightened repression of political challengers defined the political context in the decade that followed the war.

But for all these changes in political opportunity, there were important continuities that extended across the war years to ground the conflicts of the 1920s in the organizational and strategic innovations of the preceding thirty years. First, comparisons across states continued to inform political debate. As exemplars of novel configurations of associational power and state capacity, "progressive" states such as California, Washington, and Wisconsin were sites of extensive and often heated struggles to dismantle the administrative and policy legacies of the prewar years. While many reforms were lost in the process, some escaped this winnowing to persist in the abeyance structures of state government.[60]

Second, organizational forms and practices developed in struggles with state parties, legislatures, and agencies were increasingly transferred to the federal government. Commenting on the rise of the "new lobby" during the 1920s, Pendleton Herring observed, "In little more than a decade this descent of Washington representatives of national associations upon the capital has been witnessed."[61] But the features that distinguished the "new lobby" from the old are all too familiar from the histories of labor, agrarian, and women's associations traced in the preceding chapters:

> [T]he first trait which marks these groups as factors of power is that of organization. They are organized to a degree never possible before in the history of the world. Technological processes have made this possible. In the second place, these groups are ably and intelligently directed. They know their way about. In the third place, they have all the strength of a unity and cohesion which is the result of a definite program and a common

aim. Let it be emphasized again that the presence of these groups means that a systematized and integrated organization for the representation of diverse group interests is now functioning at Washington.[62]

Mastery of "educational politics" and propaganda, the development of internal hierarchy and bureaucratic arrangements, the strict delimitation of issues—all these developments had precedents in "the Scientific Management of Club Influence" attributed to the California State Federation of Women's Clubs as well as in the practices of state labor lobbies and agrarian associations. No doubt one reason that the "new lobby" made such a striking first impression on the old hands in Washington, D.C., was that many of its representatives were already veteran practitioners.

Finally, the reform movements of the late progressive period had provided dramatic evidence of the possibilities of linking state, congressional, and constitutional politics. The Eighteenth and Nineteenth Amendments stood as monuments to these new strategies. In pursuit of prohibition, temperance advocates built political machines that utilized "the organized churches as a political battering ram."[63] The key to this strategy was an innovation now at the core of many models of legislative behavior:

> A politician who has no interest in reëlection or no fear of defeat can tell the organized minorities which seek to control his vote, to "go to." Had the Anti-Saloon League not demonstrated its ability to elect and defeat candidates for public office, it is probable that the Eighteenth Amendment would still be a chafing word-symbol in the mind of some political ideologist. Had the League been confined to moral appeals, it would have accomplished no more in the realm of practical legislation than Christian missionaries could accomplish in a well-fed heathen land. But with the strong appeal of bread to starving heathens, and with the appeal of reëlection to aspiring politicians, converts are readily made. It should be kept in mind that whatever power or influence the League developed in legislative lobbies is attributable to the votes of the people back home who take their political advice from the League. It has little money for bribes, even if it admitted such a method of influence. Its single weapon was its actual or assumed control of votes.[64]

The control of votes by a nonpartisan organization was, of course, most easily accomplished where the hold of partisan identity was weak. Thus "the editors of some of our great metropolitan newspapers" wondered at the "almost intemperate speed" of the ratification process in the state legislatures,[65] clearly not having heeded the warning of a prohibitionist two years before: "What the West and South want, they get (witness Wilson as President)."[66]

The "drys" were not alone in their cultivation of regional leverage over national politics. Borrowing the technique of punishing the "party in power" from the British suffragettes, the Congressional Union urged women in the enfranchised states of the West to hold their elected representatives accountable for not supporting the suffrage amendment (fig. 8.2).[67] Linking state-by-state organization to the fight for ratification of the Nineteenth Amendment, the National American Woman Suffrage Association exemplified a homegrown style of pressure politics.

> The suffrage fight served to develop the methods of the lobbyist of the present day and to impress upon the women and upon the public generally the efficacy of organized agitation. Of course, previous to this time, efforts had been made by labor to rouse the working-class vote, and agricultural organizations had at times tried to marshall the farmers, but there was nothing to compare with the systematic campaign of the women directed from the Washington headquarters and extending over a wide number of states. When the women finally found the victory was theirs, they felt that their methods were vindicated. In large measure, they blazed the way for the lobbying organizations in the capital at the present time.[68]

Based in organizations outside the party system, focused on the divisive issues that leaders of both parties had long suppressed (see chap. 1), the successful campaigns for the Eighteenth and Nineteenth Amendments represented the nationalization of a new style of popular politics worked out in state-level struggles over direct democracy, workmen's compensation, child labor laws, and the licensing of agricultural cooperatives. The pragmatics of coalition building pushed challengers toward the forms common to their otherwise diverse repertoires. Although many organizational models contended to supplant parties as the framework for popular political practices, it was the template of group interest that emerged from the fray as a plausible organizational mechanism for identifying the preferences of voters and linking them to electoral outcomes and policy decisions.[69]

Nationalizing the Politics of Interest

Just as the First World War changed the political climate within the states, the experience of national military mobilization also transformed perceptions of the role (both actual and desired) of the states as the dominant units for governing social and economic life. On the one hand, wartime mobilization highlighted the power of the federal government and the

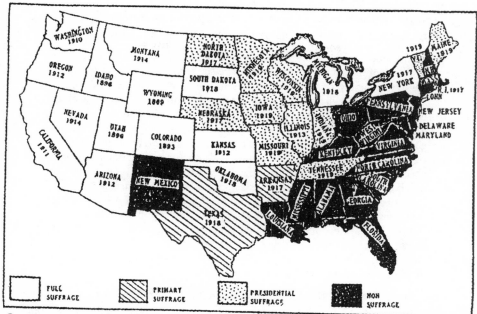

From the New York "Tribune."

PRESENT STATUS OF WOMAN SUFFRAGE.

Figure 8.2 The Present Status of Woman Suffrage (1919). (Source: *Literary Digest*, 21 June 1919)

potential for cooperation with either state governments or voluntary associations ranging from industrial groups to women's clubs. The "soldier vote" set the pace; as "a vote *against* anybody who opposes soldier legislation," this electoral threat secured federal aid for pensions, rehabilitation, and civil-service preferment. Clubwomen were charged with creating a new form of paternalism: "Is it that she sees in the central government what the primitive woman saw in her lord and master? That she seeks her legislative ends through the Federal arm as she from the beginning has sought her personal ends through the strong arm of the individual man, and its power to defend, ensure, and enforce?"[70]

The power of federal intervention also produced a backlash, a desire to retreat to smaller government and less regulation. This reaction was reinforced by the nation's experience with Prohibition and the failure to enforce it effectively. When used sparingly, the power of the federal government had seemed clear. But the failed enforcement of Prohibition, despite the controversial expansion of federal power, brought

> a profound change in the attitude of the public. A very few years ago the response of the average man to any criticism of local administration of the law was to apply to the Federal Government to take charge. Federal efficiency was everywhere contrasted in the public mind with state and local inefficiency. . . . Now, this impression has largely vanished. Not only the great object lesson of the failure on the part of the Federal Government to enforce the prohibition law, even to a reasonable extent, in the great centers of population, but their extraordinary inability for long periods of time to check smuggling, and to enforce the restraints on immigration, the breakdown of the policy of curbing trusts and monopolies, the frequent exhibitions of inefficiency in such long established and peculiarly proper Federal functions as the Post Office, the Navy, the Army, the public lands, and last, but not least, in the administration of the income tax with its aggravating burden of "red tape" and delays—all these experiences have produced in the average citizen a revulsion of feeling. No longer does he think that Washington is the center of efficient government.[71]

But effective or not, the war provided what nineteenth-century reformers would have termed an "object lesson" in the potential benefits of federal programs.

If the efficiency of federal intervention were no longer unquestioned, the shortcomings of state policy remedies were all too obvious. First, policy innovations in the states were vulnerable to review in the federal courts. In the spring of 1923, the U.S. Supreme Court threw out the District of Columbia women's minimum-wage law; in the next two years, state laws were challenged in both California and Wisconsin, with an injunction against the law's enforcement following in the latter case.[72] Later in 1923, the Court ruled against the Kansas Industrial Court, a state-run system of compulsory arbitration asserting that the law rested on an excessively broad definition of industries "imbued with public interest."[73] So even if the federal government's ability to intervene effectively was in question, the obstacles to state-level reform embedded in the U.S. Constitution provided another incentive for challengers to shift their attention from state to national politics.

Just as state politics provided multiple options for political mobilization, there was more than one path from the states to national politics. The most familiar road for political challengers led through the electoral system, particularly the campaign for the presidency. The 1912 campaign brought forth two versions of this approach—the success of progressives within the Democratic Party in nominating Woodrow Wilson and the independent Bull Moose campaign of the former president Theodore Roosevelt and his running mate, Hiram Johnson. As conservatives regained control of the nominating process of both parties in the 1920s, however, the first path was blocked and western reformers once again turned to the option of an independent campaign.

If the third-party model had a long history in American politics, the more innovative strategies available to challengers involved turning from partisanship. This turn came in degrees. First, voters might elect partisan politicians willing to break with their party on occasion; the congressional "Insurgents" of 1909–10, motivated by their opposition to Republican Speaker Joseph Cannon, represent the translation of regional discontent into this mildly nonpartisan form.[74] The agricultural bloc of the early 1920s was another unexpectedly successful instance of this strategy, although much more closely tied to organized, issue-specific constituencies than were the "Insurgents" of the 1910s. But since partisan irregulars were subject to the cross-pressures of party discipline[75] and organized constituents—and were unavailable if unelected—associations moved from electing candidates with a general commitment to reform to efforts aimed at shaping the preferences of a broader set of representatives on a narrower array of issues. The very framework of the federal government might be altered to facilitate the links between organized constituencies, legislation, and agencies that defined the emerging style of interest group politics.

The Possibility of a Party of Interests

The straightest path from the organization of constituents with specific policy demands to policy outcomes was through presidential politics. Just as popular associations had begun their odyssey toward interest group politics by seeking the promises and pledges of party politicians, by the 1920s party politicians were increasingly aware that a broad array of quite specific policy promises might be used to woo voters. New agencies and spending policies were increasingly offered to voters as electoral incentives. In a 1920 campaign speech to "a delegation of women," Senator and soon-to-be President Warren Harding "pledged himself 'to support with all that is in me whatever practical policy of social welfare and social justice can be brought forward by the combined wisdom of all Americans'" and conveyed "his definite proposal that these existing and proposed activities shall be grouped in a single department of public welfare."[76] By structuring the choices offered by politicians, extrapartisan constituent groups sought to map their concerns directly on to the framework of government.

Not surprisingly, the strategies of securing pledges from candidates and planks in party platforms proved as disappointing at the national level as they had in state politics for so many years. Noting that "between the campaign promises of the party in power and fulfillment, there's fallen an unkind breach," *The Survey* enumerated how four years of legislation had failed to deliver on the Republican Party's pledge of 1920:

> The supreme duty of the nation is the conservation of human resources through an enlightened measure of social and industrial justice. Although the federal jurisdiction is limited, they affect the welfare and interest of the nation as a whole. We pledge the Republican Party to the solution of these problems through national and state legislation in accordance with the best progressive thought of the country.[77]

Faced with such unresponsiveness, popular associations did what they had long done in state politics. First, they worked through the primaries and hoped that a major party would nominate an acceptable candidate. But, at the level of national politics, this strategy was severely handicapped since primaries were best established in the West and Midwest; the delegates chosen in these states were outnumbered by those from eastern states, in which party organizations continued to exert much more powerful control over delegate selection. Recognizing that the New York Democratic organization would never support his presidential ambitions, William Gibbs McAdoo moved permanently to Los Angeles in 1922.[78] As a cabinet member in the Wilson administration, McAdoo had gathered a following among organized labor for his role in the nationalization of the railroads (although he was also tainted by his role as a legal counsel to the oil companies involved in Teapot Dome); in a convention held in New York in 1924, McAdoo and the state's governor, Al Smith, battled to gridlock for the nomination, which eventually went to a third candidate. It is hardly necessary to mention that insurgent Republicans met with little success in trying to secure their party's 1924 nomination for La Follette over the incumbent Calvin Coolidge (who took office after Harding's death).

With opportunities blocked in both major parties, many large associations turned with greater seriousness to the efforts to organize a third party that had been under way since after the war. Unlike the Republicans who bolted to the Progressive Party in 1912, those involved in these efforts had established credentials as leaders of large popular associations.

In some cases, these associations had even captured state parties, making them reluctant to abandon efforts to control the national parties as well. At the 1922 meeting of the Conference for Progressive Political Action, a "North Dakota farmer drawled that 'Wall Street would control the old parties just as long as you leave them in Wall Street's hands. The thing to do is to take the parties away from them. Now take our case,' he said. 'I'm a delegate to this conference. I'm also the chairman of the Republican Party of North Dakota.' Whereupon the conference roared with laughter and cheered."[79] But for the most part, the congressional insurgents—including La Follette—kept at arms length from these efforts, which were grounded in the discontent of more radical farm and labor organizations.

In the strike-ridden years of 1919 and 1920, periodicals monitored the political horizons for the appearance of new electoral configurations of farmers and/or organized labor. In 1919, the Brotherhood of Locomotive Firemen and Enginemen as well as the coal miners' union, endorsed the creation of an independent labor party.[80] That November, a founding convention for a national labor party was held in Chicago. Standing as a *labor organization* was the prerequisite for participation:

> Non-labor groups, made up of farmers, middle-class liberals, single-taxers, etc. are excluded from the convention, except as they may decide to send fraternal delegates. Unorganized brain workers or other individuals subscribing to labor party principles may have a voice in the proceedings only through membership in local labor parties, which are open to all "workers with hand or brain."[81]

Progress toward political success was slow, since "[t]rade unions as such are hardly more adapted to political work than are churches or fraternal organizations";[82] in December 1919, the AFL established a nonpartisan political campaign committee but did not endorse the concept of a labor party.[83] The next year, the All-American Farmer-Labor Cooperative Congress met in Chicago but restricted its efforts to the formation of alternative cooperative systems of banking and marketing.[84] By 1922, the Conference for Progressive Political Action brought together organized labor, agrarian associations, prewar progressives and American socialists to influence congressional elections. The victories they secured descended directly from the prewar efforts to erode partisan loyalties and to control nominating processes: "Never in any such contest was there a greater or more intelligent splitting of tickets, or greater evidence of thought on the part of the voters."[85] As *The Nation* crowed:

The impossible has happened. The farmers and labor have got together, and a new party has been born. It does not matter that La Follette, Brookhart, and Howell, in Wisconsin, Iowa, and Nebraska, keep the name "Republican," that Governor-elect Sweet of Colorado and Governor-elect Hunt of Arizona, like Dill and Wheeler, the new Senators from Washington and Montana, call themselves "Democrats." These men stand for the same things and they know it; the same forces elected them regardless of the label; they will work together against the things for which both old party machines stand, and whether or not the forces which elected them frankly take the name "Farmer-Labor Party" as did the forces which elected that stalwart six-foot-two son of the Vikings, Henrik Shipstead, Senator from Minnesota, they are a farmer-labor party. The fusion has been effected, and henceforth the farmer-labor alliance of the producing forces of the country in the middle West is a political fact.[86]

But, to underscore a point made many times before, discontent alone was not sufficient to transform the party system. Some alternative vehicle around which to organize was needed if the disruption of party lines was to result in the institutionalization of new political configurations. A month after the heady victories of November 1922, even *The Nation* had become more cautious about the prospects for political change:

The ice is breaking. American politics is losing its rigidity. But politics never stay long in flux. If these men dally too long politics will crystallize again, and there will once more be two dummy parties, Tweedledum and Tweedledee, neither one with an economic program and neither with any real interest in the producers. If La Follette and the railroadmen wait until after the Republican primaries [of 1924] to crystallize their forces, they may discover that the bricks have been stolen while they were meditating what to build.[87]

On this point, *The Nation* proved prescient.

Two years later, the electorate saw "the first formal alliance of organized labor in America with farmers and Socialists" in support of the presidential ticket of Senators Robert La Follette (Republican of Wisconsin) and Burton K. Wheeler (Democrat of Montana).[88] Securing almost five million votes in the election, the campaign's 17 percent share of the total vote obscures the regional appeal of the ticket. Winning only in Wisconsin, La Follette and Wheeler placed second in California, Idaho, Iowa, Minnesota, Montana, Nevada, North Dakota, Oregon, South Dakota, Washington, and Wyoming—almost all of the states northwest of a line drawn from the California-Arizona border to Milwaukee (fig. 8.3). The regional antipartisanship evident in the organizational challenges within states such as California, Washington, and Wisconsin appeared now as a structural feature of national politics, a reliable source of electoral volatil-

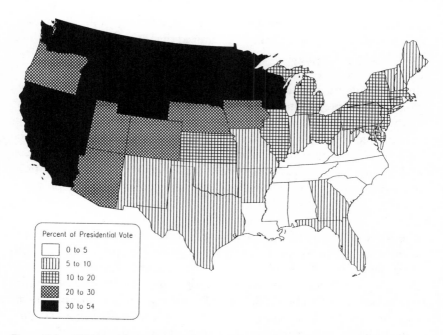

Figure 8.3   1924 Presidential Vote for Robert La Follette and Burton K. Wheeler

ity and issue-based insurgency. As one historian of the 1924 campaign concluded: "The voting behavior of these Western voters in 1924 suggests that the Democratic party members in the West are not nearly so anchored to their moorings as the Democrats of the South and East. Westerners have utilized the Democratic party as a vehicle through which to register their protest. When a more forceful instrument of protest is available, they have no hesitancy in deserting the party."[89]

Viewed from the perspective of party politics, the turbulence of the early 1920s—the farmer-labor parties, the Conference for Progressive Political Action, and the independent ticket of La Follette and Wheeler—represent only a stillborn realignment.[90] But in organizational terms, it is a most revealing failure. Inspired by the victory of the Labour Party in Britain as well as by the efforts of labor and agrarian parties in Canada, the insurgent party-building efforts of the early 1920s began with delegates of the already organized: of labor unions, agrarian associations, and leagues of liberals.[91] But over the previous decades, developments within these organizations had been in the direction of specifying distinctive political demands with targeted legislative remedies while avoiding "entangling alliances" with other reform groups. In reflecting on the disappointing returns, the La Follette camp recognized that "the campaign had tried to unite competing interest groups,"[92] some of which (notably organized labor) felt free to withdraw promised support as the campaign proceeded. But the same organizational developments that made it difficult to forge a party out of preexisting associations rendered those associations all the more effective when they turned to influence national legislation. Commanding considerable resources and professional staff, speaking in the name of their numerous members (if not actually dictating their votes), and pursuing a delimited set of goals, these associations and federations of associations were ideally suited to exert pressure on elected representatives.

The Nationalization of Organizational Repertoires
While disillusioning many citizens, the growth of federal intervention altered the organizational preferences of the popular associations behind the policy expansion of the second decade of the century. Of those voluntary associations that had collaborated in the wartime mobilization, many went into the 1920s with new demands for federal legislation and regulation. Federal programs initiated to support the military effort demonstrated how the national government could be harnessed to the social and economic problems that had motivated political challengers prior to the war. But in order to transfer policy agendas from the states to the national arena, two practical problems had to be solved. First, how could popular associations gain leverage over national politics without the instruments of the direct primary, initiative, and referendum that had proved so important in many of the western states? Second, if national politics could be swayed, what precisely could the federal government do that would support the expansion of social policy and state intervention in the economy?

The nationalization of organizational repertoires began with the weakening of that logic of inappropriateness which had dismissed government intervention as undesirable. The change of heart was most evident on the part of organized labor. Led by the railroad brotherhoods, who thought that labor relations had improved once the government took over for the duration of the war, the AFL reversed course in 1920—over the objections of Samuel Gompers—to endorse government ownership.[93] But proposals well short of nationalization also heightened the politicization of labor. The Railway Labor Board, an arbitration system proposed by the Wilson administration, threatened to make unions more vulnerable to appointments made by the party in power: "As more and more the control of industrial conditions becomes the prize of governmental leadership, inevitably the labor movement will drift into politics."[94] By 1921, an AFL vice-president was calling for the repeal of antitrust laws, preferring to acknowledge the existence of monopolies and to subject them to government regulation.[95] This drift was accelerated as the courts deprived unions of many of the advantages of more purely economic models of organization. Widespread use of the injunction crippled the viability of the strike and, in the *Coronado* decision of 1922, the Supreme Court held that since unions looked like, walked like, and talked like corporations, they could be held legally liable like corporations. Even prior to this decision, "[M]ore than a dozen states [already had] statutes making voluntary associations liable for damages."[96] At its 1922 convention, the AFL reiterated its support for government ownership of the railroads and its nonpartisan campaign committee. These positions were far from "business unionism, pure and simple"—internal organizational developments and changed circumstances provoked a reconsideration of the elements in labor's repertoire.

For agrarian organizations, wartime mobilization left much the same legacy. The federal government figured much more prominently in both the grievances lodged and the solutions sought by farm associations. In 1919, the Grange moved its national offices to Washington. But the more aggressive lobbying was done by a relative newcomer, the American Farm Bureau Federation:

> When a 1921 bill to retool the Muscle Shoals dam for the production of fertilizer lost on a voice vote . . . it asked representatives to report how they voted to Federation lobbyist Gray Silver. That impertinence caused Silver and president James R. Howard to be hauled up before the House Banking and Currency Committee, where a litany of Farm Bureau crimes was recited.

In the wake of this uproar, the federation switched tactics, seeking to link its three hundred thousand members more directly to their representatives.[97] The perfection of lobbying techniques was "a new era" for farmers, who had "profited by their mistakes" and no longer sought "political remedies as they did in the seventies and eighties." The forms of organization had changed—with community-based associations and independent-party politics far less important—along with the primary target of political action. By the late 1920s,

> [S]tate organizations still look to their respective legislatures, [but] it is upon the Congress that attention is chiefly focused. The futility of any solid

accomplishment through the formation of a minority party has been thoroughly recognized and other methods have been adopted and successfully tried. The successful party of farmers to-day is the national organization with a widely distributed and alert membership, self-interested, and prepared to pass on national questions from their point of view. The other requisites are a hierarchy of units reaching from the county and the district to the state and culminating in the national association, a staff of trained officers and experts, and a substantial bank account. Last and by no means of least importance is a suite of offices in the capital.[98]

With presidential progressivism in eclipse, the 1920s brought further experiments with congressional strategies. Particularly striking was the consolidation of the agricultural bloc, a bipartisan alliance of legislators from midwestern farm states that, in the opinion of Secretary of War Weeks,

> has had a tendency to weaken effective government, has resulted in irresponsible legislation, prevented both parties from carrying out the pledges made in their platforms, and in time will divide the legislative branch of the Government into groups, each group championing a special cause, and we will see one group combining with another to bring about a control of legislative action in the interests of a particular faction.[99]

Others argued that this proliferation of groups had already occurred; the farm bloc differed only in its openness: "There has been for some time a labor *bloc* in Congress, more or less under cover. There has been the waterways group. . . . There are the irrigationists, the natural-resource reservationists, and the West Coast members whose *bête noire* is Japan. The open action of the agrarians will encourage the others to a closer and franker organization."[100] The consequence of this proliferation of blocs, as Secretary Weeks understood, would be a weakening of party discipline (fig. 8.4). With narrow majorities, a bloc such as the Senate progressives could "form a sort of 'third party' in between the regular Republicans and the Democrats."[101] But even after the agricultural bloc dissipated— helped along by La Follette's defeat in 1924—agricultural groups demonstrated their worth as allies in the 1925 elections, and, consequently, farm relief measures remained on the congressional agenda. In 1927, even the controversial McNary-Haugen agricultural price support act finally passed both houses.[102]

To create such a shadow "third party," constituencies had to decide congressional elections—a real possibility only for farmers, aided by the overrepresentation of rural districts and the equal power of less-populous

RATHER DIFFICULT DRIVING.

—Pease in the Newark *News.*

Figure 8.4 Rather Difficult Driving: The Farm Bloc as an Obstacle to Party Politics. (Source: *Literary Digest,* 24 December 1921)

states in the Senate. Commentators recognized that these developments as signs of a remapping of politics onto social categories:

> In the forthcoming Congress the Farmer-Labor Party achieves official existence. This, at least, is an attempt to fit classification to actual conditions, and incidentally illustrates how far the Senate has strayed from the path marked out for it by the constitutional fathers. Its members are no longer ambassadors of states, spokesmen of lesser sovereignties which once overshadowed the Federal existence, but representatives of a class.[103]

Informed by the enduring centrality of electoral models in the repertoires of workingmen, organized labor continued to seek leverage by injecting endorsements and resources into congressional campaigns.[104] But, not putting all its eggs in one basket, organized labor also matched farmers' associations in establishing a well-heeled Washington lobby. *The Survey* described a traveler to Washington, D.C., who was amazed to find a group of union leaders in the office of the secretary of labor while owners of the packing houses waited in the hall. "This new influence" worked in two ways: first by the "calling of labor leaders into consultation with government officials over matters of importance"; second through "constructive policies" worked out in new bureaus and agencies devoted to labor issues.[105] Lacking farmers' reliable allies in Congress, however, labor's lobbying efforts had rather less consequence.

If the organizational repertoires of American men kept both farmers and workers partially anchored in electoral politics, for women's associations party politics was unfamiliar terrain. Acknowledged as pioneers of nonpartisan lobbying, organized women found that the 1920s brought both policy successes and greatly heightened divisions among themselves. Their organizational commitments were to nonpartisan models: "The number of their associations is second only to the number of organizations representing the various industries of the United States."[106] As more associations sent representatives to the capital, women's organizations added more innovations to the roster of nonpartisan methods, including the Women's Joint Congressional Committee, which provided

> the machinery whereby national associations that find themselves taking the same standpoint on a legislative measure regarding women's interests may combine their influence and pool their resources to the attaining of a common aim. No member organization is pledged to any policy by joining the body, and the Committee itself, as a committee, does not endorse specific matters of legislation. It provides the ready medium through which the members may consult and coöperate.[107]

Once eight or more member associations endorsed a measure, they formed a subcommittee and planned the campaign in support of some piece of legislation. Reminiscent of the departmental structure of the large women's clubs established in the 1890s, this arrangement preserved an encompassing political identity—women—while accommodating differences of interest and ideology. Just as the large membership of those clubs had given their leaders public standing, the legislative alliance among women's organizations gave them standing as a bloc. As the Harding campaign of 1920 recognized, it was possible to court such a would-be bloc with specific policy promises: the establishment of a Department of Public Welfare or the lifting of the ban on sending contraceptive information through the U.S. mails. In Congress, the 1918 introduction of a maternal and child health bill and its passage three years later as the Sheppard-Towner Act was a tribute not least to the anticipated influence of the "women's vote" on national elections. "The significance of the passage of the act, even in an emasculated form," explained *The Survey*, "is that this is the first articulation in national legislation of the enfranchisement of the womanhood of the country. Women of every creed and clan with the backing of over fifteen women's national organizations, have demanded as the first concrete expression of their new freedom a bill protecting mothers and their babies, and the measure has been jammed through the short session with its congested calendar, and in the face of truculent opposition."[108] As in so many campaigns in so many states, group endorsement was taken as a signal of public opinion. Sheppard-Towner's precedent-setting connection of federal funding to social programs administered by the states was backed by a wide range of women's associations, including the National League of Women Voters (the postsuffrage reincarnation of NAWSA), the National Congress of Mothers, and the Daughters of the American Revolution: "There are few instances where any type of national legislation has received the endorsement of so many groups of citizens."[109]

Constructed of preorganized associations, like the La Follette campaign, the Women's Joint Congressional Committee had the potential to coordinate a broad range of opinion but was vulnerable to schisms among those associations. In the wake of the passage of the Nineteenth Amendment, precisely such divisions appeared. Although there was broad consensus on Sheppard-Towner, which was opposed only by antisuffragists among the women's groups, sharp divisions emerged over the best way to use the political process to improve the condition of American women. One camp sought to link women's new power as voters to the expansion of protective regulation and social-welfare programs established over the previous three decades. The other camp argued for passage of an equal-rights amendment to the Constitution, which, the first camp worried, would undercut the entire body of women's protective regulation.[110] Yet behind this split over strategy and goals lay decades of organizational development away from the loose-knit and encompassing models of the department clubs and the WCTU—with its motto, Do Everything!—to more specialized associations with distinctive and delimited agendas.[111]

Thus the disagreements among women's organizations that surfaced in the 1920s were grounded in the centralization and specialization produced by the application of business methods to nonpartisan politics. By the early 1920s, the labor, farm, and women's lobbies had arrived at roughly the same place in national politics, although they were traveling along different trajectories. All had established formal lobbying organizations with professional staffs, yet the leverage of these lobbies was divided among multiple associations, any one of which might disagree with— or at least fail to support—proposed legislation. For farm groups, this represented improved coordination among regional and crop associations; for labor, the AFL continued to contain differences among its member unions while seeking some basis for coordination with the railroad brotherhoods; for women's associations, the exceptional (although far from total) unity of the struggle for the Nineteenth Amendment had given way to greater uncertainty and division over the methods and goals of ongoing political mobilization. All threatened, if not actually achieved, some linkage of legislative lobbying to issue-based voting on the part of sizable constituencies. In terms of strategy and organizational form, the "new lobby" of the 1920s exhibited clear continuities with the long-standing efforts by popular associations to invent an issue-oriented, nonpartisan alternative to the party system. But with respect to its effects, the translation of state-level innovations to the national arena had the potential to bring about a significant institutional change: the reordering of relations between state and federal governments as well as among the branches of the latter.

The Nationalization of Policy Solutions
On first inspection, the demands made by pressure groups upon the federal agendas differed as little from state-level reform agendas as did the organizational forms and tactics that these groups adopted. But the apparent constancy of goals—new regulatory powers, new spending programs, new agencies—masks a discontinuity of great import: these programs seemed to fall under the activities reserved to the states by the federal Constitution. Yet it was all too apparent that state legislation was either incapable of regulating *national* problems or vulnerable to dismissal by the U.S. Supreme Court.

Given these obstacles, the nationalization of interest group politics involved more than a simple transposition of organizational models from the states to national government. While this transposition accounts for the sudden appearance of the full-fledged "new lobby" in the 1920s, it neglects how the opportunity structure of federalism undercut the efficacy of such extensions of mobilization and pressure politics with the consequence of producing widespread calls for far-reaching rearrangements of the constitutional framework of American government. These calls took three basic forms: the extension of congressional powers with respect to the states; the redistribution of powers among branches of the federal government; and federal incentives for state-level programs. Although each of these efforts provoked a reaction against increasing the power of federal intervention, the nationalizing experiments of the 1920s pointed toward future expansions of the national government.

The division of powers between state and national governments was brought into question by a policy concern that flowed directly from prewar progressive reforms: child labor legislation.[112] Although laws had been passed in all but a handful of states prior to the war, the failure of some southern states to pass comparable limits on the hours, industries, and ages at which children could be employed placed firms in other states at a competitive disadvantage and left this item on the agendas of many national reform associations. State laws were, as one cartoonist observed, "a good sign—but a poor fence" (fig. 8.5). The first federal child labor law, passed in 1917, made use of the interstate commerce clause (following the precedent of the federal pure food law) to ban the employment of children under fourteen "in mills, factories, and workshops" and "in mines and quarries before the sixteenth birthday." Children between fourteen and sixteen were limited to an eight-hour day. Enforcement of the law was supported by national efforts on the part of two alliances of federal agencies and voluntary associations: the Children's Bureau and the General Federation of Women's Clubs promoted comprehensive birth registration, while the Woman's Committee of the Council of National Defense requested member organizations to inquire whether "all children between 6 and 14 in your town, county or school district [are] in school? How do you know? Are any children in need of scholarships in order to attend school?"[113] This law was overturned by the U.S. Supreme Court in June 1918; a second law, which imposed "a tax of 10 percent on the products of establishments that employed children of the ages specified in the earlier law," was passed in February 1919 and overturned by the Supreme Court in May 1922.[114] During the years that the federal law was in effect, the standards of state legislation improved; Alabama went from among the worst to among the best, West Virginia passed stronger legislation, and "the state officials of thirty-one states . . . approved this amendment on the ground that it would be beneficial to the states."[115]

Pressure groups mobilized in support of the proposed constitutional amendment; the AFL, the National Consumers' League, and the Women's

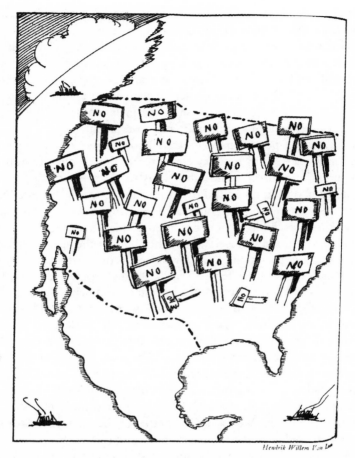

Hendrik Willem Van Loon

Figure 8.5 "A Good Sign—but a Poor Fence": The Limits of State-Level Legislation. (Source: *Survey,* 1 January 1925)

Trade Union League joined to form the Permanent Conference for the Abolition of Child Labor.[116] "[T]he proposed Twentieth Amendment was passed [in 1924] by a Republican Congress at the behest of a Republican President and with the approval of the leaders of all three political parties which contested the subsequent presidential election."[117] The amendment would give Congress the "power to limit, regulate and prohibit the labor of persons under eighteen years of age," but declared that "the power of the several states is unimpaired by this article, except that the operation of state laws shall be suspended to the extent necessary to give effect to legislation enacted by Congress." But despite the speedy passage of the first two federal laws and the amendment itself, ratification foundered on the postwar conservative reaction that also threatened state-level social policies and agencies.

> The enactment of the Volstead law following the adoption of the prohibition amendment has engendered a wide-spread distaste for federal interference. The farmers, too, who have hitherto been immune from child labor laws, are beginning to look askance at the possibility of national regulation. War time interference with business and private affairs has left many people cold to any extension of national control.
>
> The great difference, however, between the debate over the proposed Twentieth Amendment and the earlier child labor laws adopted by the Congress and by the state legislatures is found in the amazing growth of what is literally a "hangover" from the orgy of post-war propaganda. Thus the national protection of American children from harmful industrial processes is being identified by some of its opponents with alleged Russian plans for the nationalization of youth. . . .
>
> But for the *habit of propaganda* acquired during the World War it is hardly conceivable that any group of Americans would have had the effrontery so completely to misrepresent the realities of what is actually a very simple question.[118]

The "educational politics" of the opposition took their toll. By the end of January 1925, only Arkansas, Arizona, and California had voted to ratify, and six states had defeated the amendment; by March, Wisconsin had ratified, but Arkansas was reconsidering. Although the amendment made some progress in other states, the option of addressing social problems through the constitutional expansion of congressional powers appeared to be foreclosed for the time being.[119]

A second line of agitation sought greater freedom for state legislatures and Congress from the federal courts. As the U.S. Supreme Court overturned federal child labor laws, the District of Columbia women's minimum-wage law, the Kansas Industrial Court, the Pennsylvania Old Age Pension Act, and other state-level policy experiments (as well as issuing a series of decisions unfavorable to organized labor), the AFL called for a constitutional amendment allowing Congress to overrule by a two-thirds majority any Supreme Court decision declaring a law unconstitutional. John Commons and John B. Andrews, secretary of the American Association for Labor Legislation, concurred while noting that a three-quarters majority might be preferable.[120] The director of the Department of Social Action of the National Catholic Welfare Council suggested that the votes of eight of the nine justices be required to annul a law and argued that Congress already had the power to alter the Supreme Court's appellate jurisdiction.[121] In February 1923, Senator Borah of Idaho introduced "a bill which would require at least seven members of the United States Supreme Court to concur before pronouncing a federal law unconstitutional. Senator Borah found a strong sentiment among lawyers that the present practice under which a law of Congress may be held unconstitutional by a five-to-four decision should be changed."[122] But, with respect to the Supreme Court as with the powers of Congress, the Constitution proved unalterable during the 1920s. The Court represented a powerful institutional constraint on the legislative methods and openings created by political challengers at both the state and national level over the preceding decades. Yet working within the constraints of the constitution, challengers discovered a third method that enhanced congressional power over the substance of state governments and successfully embedded the new configurations of agencies and pressure groups in the ample resources of the federal treasury.

The invention of the so-called "federal cooperative method" initially appeared inconsequential.[123] First developed to promote agricultural-extension programs and road improvements, the "method" was appropriated by both popular associations and state-level bureaucrats who sought to translate some of the new federal wartime activities to peacetime purposes. These efforts succeeded in the case of funding for the vocational rehabilitation of cripples (industrial as well as military) but were defeated in the case of ongoing federal sponsorship of public employment agencies. By the end of 1920, six federal programs had been initiated using this funding mechanism: agricultural-extension work (Smith-Lever Act of 1914); the Good Roads Act of 1916; vocational education (Smith-Hughes Act of 1917); the 1918 Chamberlain-Kahn Act for the prevention of venereal disease among civilians; and the Kenyon Americanization and Vocational Rehabilitation Acts of 1920. Excluding the Americanization Act, total federal aid under these programs was projected to grow from $600,000 in 1915–16 to a peak of over $109 million in 1920–21 (the last year of the highway program) and then to drop to the range of $9–11 million until 1926.[124] But the 1920s saw the passage of additional "state aid" programs, notably the Sheppard-Towner Maternal Health program, so the funding channel that ran from the federal treasury to state governments remained open.

All of these programs linked national and state bureaus through a system of matching appropriations. In the case of vocational education:

> [T]he Industrial Rehabilitation Act is authorized to allot $750,000 this year and for the year ending June 30, 1922, and $1,000,000 for the next two years among the states in proportion to population on condition that each state appropriate an equal amount for vocational rehabilitation. To qualify for its allotment each state must accept this act, empower its state board for vocational education to cooperate with the federal board, arrange for cooperation between its state board and its workmen's compensation commission, provide for courses of vocational rehabilitation and appoint the state treasurer as custodian of funds. Each state board for vocation rehabilitation must submit its plans to the federal board for approval, open its courses to disabled federal employees and report annually.[125]

Although there were precedents for distributing federal funds to the states, these programs were novel in two respects: first, in "the supervision by the federal government of the expenditure by the state of these federal grants and the power vested in federal authorities to discontinue such grants if a proper standard of efficiency is not maintained," and, second, in the requirement that state governments match most federal funding dollar for dollar. Yet these programs were not strictly a top-down imposition by the federal government. Instead, they built on existing models provided by state aid to localities for education and highway construction: "There was, therefore, being created in the United States a grant-in-aid system within the states. The farmers' organizations, the advocates of industrial education and of good roads, and the legislators, were afforded with a model to study and examine at close range."[126] In an iterative process, pressure groups had demanded legislation creating agencies such as workmen's compensation commissions in the states; subsequently, organized constituents called for federal legislation that would rely on the cooperation of these state-level agencies while rewarding this cooperation with federal funding.[127]

While the precedent set by the postwar vocational rehabilitation program has been largely overlooked, the use of the "federal cooperative method" by the Sheppard-Towner maternal and child health bill is more generally recognized as an important precursor of the social-spending programs of the New Deal.[128] As with the vocational-rehabilitation program, most states rapidly accepted the provisions of Sheppard-Towner; only eight states were not cooperating by 30 June 1923. One of these eight, Massachusetts, challenged the constitutionality of the law, but it was upheld in the Washington, D.C., District Supreme Court in February 1923, and this ruling was affirmed by the U.S. Supreme Court in June. Justice Sutherland declared that "the powers of the state are not invaded since the statute imposes no obligation but simply extends an option which the state is free to accept or reject. . . . If Congress enacted it with the ulterior purpose of tempting them (the states) to yield, that purpose may be effectively frustrated by the simple expedient of not yielding." [129]

The "simple expedient of not yielding" was undermined, however, by the lure of federal monies. [130] The administration sought to staunch the flow of funds. President Coolidge argued, "The federal-cooperative method . . . must not be expanded. Partly as a result of this 'cold water' application the legislation urgently needed to authorize and continue congressional appropriations for rehabilitation of industrial cripples beyond the end of the first four-year period ending June 30, 1924, was delayed." [131] But with the organizational basis and legal precedents for a federal spending state in place, Coolidge's attempt at thrift was necessarily a rearguard action. Too many organized constituencies were in place to demand policies. Commentators began to note the proliferation of blocs, both in Congress and in state legislatures:

> Within recent months, New York newspapers have acquainted their readers with a "Farm" bloc, a "Labor" bloc, "Progressive," "Liberal," "Radical" and "People's" blocs, "New England," "New York," "Western," "Middle Western," "Southern" and "Wisconsin" blocs, "Wet," "Dry," "Bonus" and "Mothers" blocs, "Wall Street," "Sugar" and "Oil" blocs, a "Rivers and Harbors" bloc, a "subsidy" bloc, and even a "Henry Ford" bloc. [132]

Organized pressure groups, specific policy demands, the government capacity to meet those demands, and a new language of political contention in which "Your interests" and "the Special Interests" were no longer different in kind—at this point, the components of modern interest group politics were in place.

The Institutionalization of Interest Group Politics

Surveying the political turmoil of 1924, Walter Lippmann was hopeful that the organizational logic of the party system would prove to be self-correcting. Although the Democratic Party had been riven by sectionalism—and both the Republican Party and the La Follette convention were sectional, not national, entities, lacking representation from the South and, in the latter case, from the East as well—all confronted the same institutional challenge that had prompted the invention of parties a century before: presidential victories and congressional majorities required national electoral efforts. "[S]o long as one party remains national in scope, the other cannot long remain divided . . . as long as one party bids for votes in every part of the country, the other party must do the same." Lippmann recognized, but accepted, the costs of this arrangement for the "representativeness" of American politics: "And in the need to make a diverse appeal, *though it means much ambiguity and hypocrisy*, lies also the necessity of tolerance and moderation. And on the will to live and let live depends the ultimate safety of a varied commonwealth."[133]

For many political challengers, however, the "ambiguity and hypocrisy" required to hold together national party coalitions was too high a price; they had spent decades inventing, improving, and institutionalizing systems of electoral clarity and accountability. No such system was perfect, of course. Many, indeed, proved ineffective or vulnerable to co-optation by a new breed of "party bosses" (a sure sign of "modularity"). But for all the flaws and disappointments of political reform, some undeniable changes had occurred. In the place of a single choice among parties—a choice that was forced to carry many diverse preferences—voters in many states faced both primaries and general elections rather than all-or-nothing elections. This resulted in greater diversity within parties, leaving voters longing for "a day when parties would be moderately cohesive—when 'Republican' for instance, would mean either Mr. Lodge or Mr. Hearst or Mr. Pinchot, but not all three of them at once" and undermining long-established practices for maintaining party balance, such as the "general pair" in the Senate where the absence of a Senator from one party would be offset by the voluntary absence of a Senator from the other.[134] In addition to exerting greater leverage over the nomination of candidates, voters might decide on numerous specific issues presented in the form of initiatives, referenda, and constitutional amendments. Between elections, individuals or, better yet, representatives of associations could lobby legislatures (backed by the threat of electoral retribution) or the growing number of state agencies charged with formulating and implementing public policy. As the capacity for government intervention increased in the first decades of the new century, government institutions also become more porous. "Veto points" multiplied;[135] both government control over social and economic decisions and associational influence over legislative and administrative outcomes increased.

None of these changes occurred automatically. Within each state, "procedural" reforms were hotly contested precisely because they shifted the balance of power. In 1904, the California state legislature had sought to outlaw the pledging of candidates except by party nominating conventions. In state after state, there were intense struggles to secure the direct primary and direct democracy; once secured, in state after state there were efforts to restrict or entirely dismantle these new channels of political influence. Similar battles raged over the creation and funding of administrative agencies, which represented additional points of access to policy formation. Across states, these accomplishments survived the political reaction of the 1920s only insofar as changes in formal political institutions had been embedded in the shared strategies of organized constituencies (e.g., direct democracy was defended by groups that had learned to make effective use of the initiative and referendum), in networks among agencies and constituencies (e.g., the consultative policymaking of the Wisconsin Industrial Commission), or in resources that enhanced the benefits of state-oriented action.

The shared strategies invented and adapted by political challengers across the nation increasingly became "modular"—blueprints for political action that could be transported from arena to arena, adopted by groups of different political orientations. The organizations described in the preceding chapters—organized labor, farmers, and women—were central players in this process of collective innovation, but they were not alone. Temperance advocates, monetary reformers, Americanizers, anti-immigrant leagues—all were aware of and contributed to this collective process of political experimentation, rendering any claim for priority on the part of one or another group problematic. But, once available, all of these groups and more extended these techniques to national politics as they encountered the limits of state polities. In 1924, these insurgents were defeated in their primary goal—the displacement of the two major parties with a third party based on organized interests rather than traditional partisan identities. Yet this defeat should not obscure the extensive, albeit partial, transformation of American politics that proceeded along lines other than presidential elections. Suffragists and prohibitionists opened up constitutional change as an opportunity for popular politics. Within the U.S. Congress, the lobbying efforts of organized farmers, workers, women, and many others steadily eroded party discipline as congressmen looked to their own reelection chances. The stakes entailed in these efforts also increased, as the "federal-cooperative" method linked national revenues to an increasing range of policy decisions. And, as the stakes increased, the intensity of political contests did too. As Walter Lippmann warned, the tendency of "La Follette's progressivism" is to increase the managing activity of government by entrusting it with a leading rôle in the solution of economic questions. That *was* the hopeful course ten years ago. Is it so today?

For to do that is to make the control of government a prize of such enormous consequence that men will contend for it fiercely. Is that desirable? Ten years ago we should have said that in such contention democracies are educated. To-day, with our experience of how the mind of the mass of men can be moved, with our enormously increased electorate and our greatly complicated life, we should be less certain that we wish to accentuate the fierceness of the struggle for power.[136]

Such warnings, however, came far too late. By the 1920s, new models for political organization were well established, and the expectations of benefits accruing to such mobilization were entrenched.[137] The cultural elaboration of new logics of appropriateness had begun, albeit not in the normative language of American politics where "bloc, like 'spit,' has come to be a horrid word."[138] The politics of interest was naturalized in the theorizing of political scientists, inspired by the claim of Arthur F. Bentley:

If a law is in question, we find that our statement of it in terms of the groups of men it affects . . . is much more complete than any statement in terms of self-interest, theories, or ideals. If it is a plank in a political platform, again we find we can state its actual value in the social process at the given time in terms of the groups of men for whose sake it is there: a group of politicians and a number of groups of voters holding the prominent places.[139]

Decades of effort by popular associations to make politicians and agencies responsible to constituent demands would render this statement truer than Bentley had reason to expect.

Coda: In Practice, in Theory

> People are not discontented because they are theorizing;
> they are theorizing because they are discontented.
>
> Henry Jones Ford, Professor of Politics, Princeton University,
> "Direct Legislation and the Recall" (1912)

> To tell what they did in the way of direct, practical action
> and to relate their applications of technical experience
> to special problems, would be useless without some ref-
> erence to the intensely American character of the group,
> their lingo of speech and jazz of manner, their Lin-
> colnian solemnity and involution of thought in handling
> the complexities of an immediate situation, the low per-
> centage of loose and aimless talk, the peculiar touch of
> gravity, the sense of the inevitable, of history, that hung
> over the occasion. They talked hardly at all about the
> wrongs of humanity. They looked tired and stirred un-
> easily if a speaker stayed too long on the subject of hu-
> man wrongs. They were there to consider how to get out
> from under, ways out.
>
> Carl Sandburg, "The Farmer-Labor Congress,"

For the farmers and workers who gathered at Chicago in 1920, the challenge was not to know what they wanted, but to discover *how* "to get
out from under, ways out." In a system of political parties that elided
many of the social and economic problems "close to the life and labor of
the common lot of Americans . . . for the sake of party unity,"[1] preferences—even when articulated—were not easily translated into political
outcomes. Such a translation required citizens to develop means-ends
schemas in which their grievances were understood to have political solutions—as opposed to an economic, religious, or other remedy. In addition, interests could inform policy only if the political system offered
choices that were meaningful. Parties may "structure the vote," but citizens may not care for the choices with which they are presented. That
was the case in 1892, when the Populist platform charged that the Repub-

licans and Democrats "have agreed together to ignore, in the coming campaign, every issue but one. They propose to drown the outcries of a plun-
dered people with the uproar of a sham battle over the tariff."[2] It was still
the case in 1924, at least for a sizable portion of the electorate. But, in
the meantime, much about American politics had changed.

Above all, the parties were not what they once were, particularly west
of the Mississippi. Direct primaries challenged party control over nomi-
nations; the initiative and referendum permitted popular intervention in
the legislative process; and the multiplication of new bureaus and commissions greatly expanded the political world of state bureaucrats and
constituents, a world in which party played little role so long as the civil-
service regulations were respected. Each of these developments made it
easier to link policy outcomes to political action in the form of voting,
lobbying, or protest. "Men and women," observed political scientist
Charles Merriam, "are beginning to discover that they can influence governmental action without the agency of parties. The associations of commerce, the labor unions, the farmers' organizations, vocational and professional groups of all kinds, are tending to pass the party by."[3] Changes
in associational strategy then altered the behavior of party politicians. In
close contests, party candidates tailored their positions to the demands
of organized groups among the voters. Some commentators celebrated
the erosion of party responsibility. Senator George Norris of Nebraska, a
leading insurgent, rejoiced, "The direct primary will lower party responsibility. In its stead it establishes individual responsibility. . . . It takes away
the power of the party leader or boss and places the responsibility for
control upon the individual. It lessens party spirit and decreases partisanship."[4] Others condemned the diminution of party control. Secretary of
War Weeks saw "in the new bloc system a real menace to our institutions.
Eastern newspapers and business organs generally are inclined to agree."[5]
But many popular associations disagreed, instead mobilizing to lobby legislatures and to advocate the establishment of new state agencies with
which they sought to form strong working relationships.

Neither the evolution of the party system nor the growth of government are independent of the history of popular associations in the United
States. The burden of the preceding chapters has been to demonstrate that
these connections were particularly intimate in the decades surrounding
the turn of the last century. In contrast to recent scholarship that has
emphasized the role of corporate elites and state actors in these institutional changes, I have argued that popular associations were of critical
importance due to their dual identity as organized interests and as size-

able collections of individual voters. It was not a matter of "Your Interests vs. 'the Special Interests,'" as that Wisconsin farmers' paper had claimed; increasingly "your interests" were special or "partial" interests, and, therefore, the "special interests" were no longer quite so easily identified.

The argument's central empirical claim is that many of the innovations of American politics in the 1920s and 1930s may be traced to decades of effort by popular associations to link policy outcomes to citizen concerns. These organizations moved from making diffuse calls for reform to presenting demands for specific legislation in a limited policy domain. They developed the capacity to monitor the behavior of elected representatives and to socialize their membership to attend to this information when they decided how to vote. In their efforts to harness public opinion, political challengers were discussing the virtues of propaganda well before the First World War and practicing the politics of advertising years prior to the consumerism of the 1920s. Recall the contention of the California suffragist who asserted in 1913, "I think we must frankly acknowledge that people are not all convinced through reason, and that although the proposition that women should vote is seriously and profoundly true, it will, at first, be established with this class of people much as the virtues of a breakfast food are established—by affirmation."[6]

By failing to connect the concerns of many voters to policy outcomes, the nineteenth-century party system had created an opportunity for political challengers. By selectively magnifying and suppressing issues in order to construct national coalitions, the parties produced those who would aspire to be their gravediggers. Political challengers, riled by the perceived unresponsiveness of their parties, began by locating opportunities within the party system itself: third parties, pledging of candidates, and efforts to shape the content of party platforms. Repeatedly frustrated in these attempts to link associational goals to political outcomes, challengers increasingly demanded changes in formal political institutions that would create both new opportunities for popular political participation and new "veto points" over the policy process.[7] The direct primary opened the party system to candidate-centered politics, often based on associational endorsements and active support. Driven by their own hopes for reelection, politicians increasingly abandoned party loyalty in order to tend to the demands of organized constituencies. The initiative, referendum, and recall provided still further opportunities for popular associations to circumvent the party system. Finally, successful demands for the establishment of new state agencies created entirely new arenas for group-based associational politics. By securing the appointment of members to commissions and boards, by participating in formal systems of consultation, and by lobbying and testifying at administrative hearings, popular associations used extrapartisan techniques to secure a measure of influence over policy formation and implementation. Less dramatic than the wildfire of prairie insurgency, but of tremendous and enduring significance, was the unlocking of the national treasury by social reformers. Initiated in small programs for special cases—the rehabilitation of industrial cripples, the promotion of maternal and child health—the so-called federal cooperative method established one of the most important precedents for the growth of the American state.

Organized workers, farmers, and women were not alone—nor necessarily the first—to seize this opportunity. The significance of these large popular associations for the transformation of political institutions does not rest on a claim for invention but for innovation—the embedding of novel practices in durable social networks and resource flows. Because popular associations were a source of identities that were not partisan identities and networks that were not party networks, they were a potential alternative to the party system. For such challenges to materialize, popular associations first had to agree that particular grievances had a political remedy and then to discover techniques for articulating novel forms of organization with the political system.

These novel linkages between popular associations built on organizational innovations common to a wide range of political challengers. These associations promulgated delimited collective identities: worker, farmer, or mother rather than the more encompassing frameworks of partisanship and producerism. These identities were then tied to group-specific policy demands—workmen's compensation, cooperative marketing, women's hours-and-wages laws—and supported with new organizational techniques for gathering resources and coordinating political action. Activists and organizers discovered new methods of fund-raising and appeals for new members; they appropriated templates of internal authority from the corporations and created an organizational framework that could financially sustain professional activists; they invented educational and publicity techniques for guiding the electoral behavior of their members as well as of other sympathetic voters. NAWSA's Organization Committee learned to accumulate donations nationally and then to target them on a single campaign, shifting the balance of power within a given state. The Nonpartisan League also discovered that new organizational techniques could produce new revenues where once there appeared to be only a scattering of money too small to attract the attention of any campaign finance committee: "[T]he key to the sudden growth of the Nonpartisan League lay in the large-scale application of intensive book-agent or oil-stock-selling technique, supported by a not less carefully worked out literature." The result, concluded *The Nation,* "was the unique spectacle in American national life of a political party financed, and adequately financed, by the rank and file, instead of from the top down." [8]

Forms of organization and opportunities for political access constructed by one set of political actors were not, however, easily monopolized. They could be exploited by others, even the innovators' opponents. As one proponent of direct democracy, rather more farsighted than most, predicted in 1912, the initiative and referendum would probably

> have a permanently wholesome influence on the agents of "special privilege," variously denominated in reformatory nomenclature as "bosses," "lobbyists," "minions of predatory wealth," etc. They will not go to the expense of securing by their peculiar methods legislation that may be vetoed by the people. These "bosses" and "minions" will not, however, be removed from the arena of political activities. They will next go to the sources of power, the people themselves, and make the effort to manipulate them as they have already done, in some instances, through the direct primaries. [9]

Agents of change, recall, are never guaranteed to benefit from what they have brought about.

In Theory

How do institutions change? This account of American political development suggests that the answer must come in two parts. The first involves processes of challenge, destabilization, or deinstitutionalization. The organizational histories of labor, agrarian, and women's groups provide ample support for the two assumptions on which this model is based: complex societies comprise multiple organizational forms, and each form is associated with more or less articulated rules concerning who may use it and for what purposes. The degree of resistance encountered by challengers varies with the extent to which these conventions are violated. Consequently, it will often be advantageous to organize challengers around familiar forms deployed in unfamiliar ways; an oblique attack may succeed where a frontal assault would invite repression.

Power figures in this account of destabilization not only in the final moment when challenges are or are not repressed. The capacity for challenge itself is shaped by the extent to which the disadvantaged or discontented possess the organizational resources or private spaces for cultivating new collective identities and techniques of collective action. The power of employers, for example, extends beyond their control over individual wages and working conditions. In the nineteenth-century United States, "Wage cuts, long hours, industrial accidents, and child labor made it difficult for indigenous forms of association, such as guilds, craft and industrial unions, and ethnic and religious groups, to survive and protest. They disappeared, fell silent, or were absorbed by the corporations." [10] Novel forms of organization by utopian reformers and women were met with hostility and ridicule: "long-haired men and short-haired women." After the First World War, the specter of bolshevism was raised against a wide range of political challengers; members were persecuted, leaders were imprisoned, potential allies were scared away. All such repressive actions restrict the range of "virtual choice." As Arthur Stinchcombe has argued, "An institution has authority when it is regarded as inevitable. . . . it may be fragile in the face of a revolutionary process that throws up alternative possibilities, but it is not subject to challenge so long as it is inevitable." [11] Repression, like the more subtle workings of hegemony, limits the alternatives that are thinkable as well as workable.

If, however, political challengers and innovators are able to articulate alternatives, the second part of the puzzle of institutional change must be confronted. How do alternatives become new institutions? This argument assumes, in Foucault's language, a "rationality of power . . . characterized by tactics that are often quite explicit at the restricted level where they are inscribed. . . , tactics which, becoming connected to one another, attracting and propagating one another, but finding their base of support and their condition elsewhere, end by forming comprehensive systems: the logic is perfectly clear, the aims decipherable, and yet it is often the case that no one is there to have invented them, and few who can be said to have formulated them." [12] In the various institutionalisms in the social sciences, similar processes of bottom-up consolidation or crystallization are captured in vocabularies of "logics," "lock in," or "stickiness."

This imagery of institutional theory invokes multiple mechanisms for the consolidation of patterns of social life: cultural elaboration, increasing returns, and shared strategies. In the development of interest group politics, all of these processes were evident, but they did not operate in parallel. Among individuals, and then among organizations, the invention and diffusion of shared strategies created new capacities for mobilization outside the party system. Yet with respect to cultural elaboration, these efforts remained highly contested; clubwomen, agrarian activists, and labor politicians made claims for the legitimacy of their efforts while they were attacked as subversive, un-American, and dangerous. These cultural attacks on interest group politics persisted, even as the weakening of party discipline, electoral reforms, and new methods of federal funding steadily lessened the costs and increased the returns to mobilizing as a "partial interest." But if the normative attack on interest group politics persists, even to the present, this form of political organization has become thoroughly taken for granted in other respects. Political analyses routinely begin by identifying the "interests" of contenders; public programs are implemented with formal provisions for participation by all "stakeholders."

The disjunctures between various dimensions of institutionalization underscore another important point. While institutions may be defined by their "self-reproducing" qualities, they are not self-initiating. Institutions are made—if not always intended—and, therefore, may vary in their robustness. Part of the challenge for those who would build institutions is to coordinate the various mechanisms of institutionalization such that logics of appropriateness, shared strategies, and increasing returns reinforce one another; for those who would change institutions, the challenge is to disrupt that same coordination. The political challengers described in this volume worked all the angles, simultaneously seeking to link shared strategies or organizational forms to greater returns for the membership, to construct new logics of appropriateness to legitimate their adoption of new forms of action, and to diffuse their organizational innovations so as to expand the scope of potentially shared political mobilization. Precisely because of the *collective* character of these efforts, however, the innovations and advantages secured by one set of political actors were not easily monopolized. Challengers copied elites, elites copied challengers as soon as they secured some margin of political advantage. What new institutionalists have called mimetic isomorphism is not only a reaction to uncertainty—it may also be fundamentally *agonistic*. Recall the words of that California Granger:

> We must do as the corporations are doing—meet combinations of capital and brains with like combinations; unite heart and hand in intelligent cooperative effort for the accomplishment of the laudable objects so clearly set forth in our declaration of purposes. The farmers have more votes, and more capital in the aggregate, than any other class in the country. Who doubts, if they were united, as the members of the corporations are, and educated to intelligent co-operation, that they could exercise a controlling influence in this Government to-day?[13]

In the process of such competitive, combative—and ultimately innovative—imitation, the meaning of what it meant to be a corporation changed, as did the meaning of organizing as a party, as a partial interest, and as a women's club. In the place of a contest between "the People" and "the Interests," American politics was rearranged as a contest of ever-multiplying "partial interests" making demands on the state. Political challengers had helped to dismantle the party system of the nineteenth century to a considerable extent; whether they were pleased with the results is, of course, another question.

Notes

Prologue

1. Franklin Hichborn, *Story of the Session of the California Legislature of 1909* (San Francisco: Press of the James H. Barry Co., 1909), 216, 290.

2. David B. Truman, *The Governmental Process: Political Interests and Public Opinion,* 2d ed. (Berkeley, Calif.: Institute of Governmental Studies, 1993), 4–7.

3. Truman, *The Governmental Process,* 59.

4. John R. Commons, *Proportional Representation,* 2d ed. (New York: Augustus M. Kelley, 1967), 359. As Philip J. Ethington has argued, progressivism marked "the arrival of a politics of social groups and their needs." *The Public City: The Political Construction of Urban Life in San Francisco, 1850–1900* (New York: Cambridge University Press, 1994), 41.

5. California State Grange (CSG), *Proceedings of the Annual Convention 1892,* 10–11, 59; George W. Alger, "The Menace of New Privilege," *Atlantic,* February 1921, 145 (this article supplies the title of chapter 8); Arthur Capper, *The Agricultural Bloc* (New York: Harcourt, Brace and Co., 1922), 5, emphasis added.

6. Daniel Rodgers, *Contested Truths: Keywords in American Politics since Independence* (New York: Basic Books, 1987), chap. 6; Democratic State Central Committee advertisement, *Wisconsin Equity News,* 11 November 1916.

7. John H. Aldrich, *Why Parties? The Origin and Transformation of Party Politics in America* (Chicago: University of Chicago Press, 1995), 278–87.

8. See Walter Dean Burnham, *The Current Crisis in American Politics* (New York: Oxford University Press, 1982), part 1; Richard L. McCormick, *The Party Period and Public Policy: American Politics from the Age of Jackson to the Progressive Era* (New York: Oxford University Press, 1986); Michael McGerr, *The Decline of Popular Politics: The American North, 1865–1928* (New York: Oxford University Press, 1986); and Martin Shefter, *Political Parties and the State: The American Historical Experience* (Princeton, N.J.: Princeton University Press, 1994).

9. Stephen Skowronek, *Building a New American State: The Expansion of National Administrative Capacities, 1877–1920* (New York: Cambridge University Press, 1982). See also Alan Dawley, *Struggles for Justice: Social Responsibility and the Liberal State* (Cambridge, Mass.: Harvard University Press, Belknap Press, 1991); Morton Keller, *Regulating a New Economy: Public Policy and Eco-*

nomic Change in America, 1900–1933 (Cambridge, Mass.: Harvard University Press, 1990); Robyn Muncy, *Creating a Female Dominion in American Reform, 1890–1935* (New York: Oxford University Press, 1991); Martin Sklar, *The Corporate Reconstruction of American Capitalism, 1890–1916: The Market, the Law, and Politics* (New York: Cambridge University Press, 1988); and Theda Skocpol, *Protecting Soldiers and Mothers: The Political Origins of Social Policy in the United States* (Cambridge, Mass.: Harvard University Press, Belknap Press, 1992).

10. On the role of alternative possibilities in the decay of institutional authority, see Arthur L. Stinchcombe, *Theoretical Methods in Social History* (New York: Academic Press, 1978), 37–41.

11. Germany, for example, adopted both compulsory sickness insurance and pension insurance for some workers in the 1880s; the United Kingdom established a national pension plan in 1908. See Peter Flora and Jens Alber, "Modernization, Democratization, and the Development of Welfare States in Western Europe," in *The Development of Welfare States in Europe and America,* ed. Peter Flora and Arnold Heidenheimer (New Brunswick, N.J.: Transaction, 1981).

12. Alexis de Tocqueville, *Democracy in America,* ed. J. P. Mayer, trans. George Lawrence (New York: Anchor Books, 1969), 517.

13. The increasing articulation of policy domains also facilitated—and was facilitated by—the emerging symbiosis between experts and government agencies. While this coevolution has led many scholars to emphasize the contributions of "a powerful alliance between experts and the Federal government in the Progressive Era," Brian Balogh has argued "that the partnership had just barely begun at that time. . . , since both Federal administrative capacity and professionalization were in their infancy." "Reorganizing the Organizational Synthesis: Federal-Professional Relations in Modern America," *Studies in American Political Development* 5 (1991): 121. At the least, such questions of timing suggest the importance of reexamining the contributions of other actors to the reorganization of American politics.

14. Arthur F. Bentley, *The Process of Government: A Study of Social Pressures* (Chicago: University of Chicago Press, 1908), 204.

15. For a rich discussion of the changing meanings of *interest,* see Rodgers, *Contested Truths,* chap. 6. See also Bentley, *The Process of Government,* 211.

16. Albert O. Hirschman, *The Passions and the Interests: Political Arguments for Capitalism before Its Triumph* (Princeton, N.J.: Princeton University Press, 1977).

17. Alger, "Menace of New Privilege," 146. In characterizing American politics during the early 1920s, prerevolutionary and revolutionary France were frequently invoked by commentators across the political spectrum.

18. Contemporary observers typically referred to "pressure groups" or "the lobby." In order to emphasize the broader significance of these changes for interpretations of political behavior, I will use the term *interest group,* reserving the former labels to refer to specific exemplars in the political discourse of turn-of-the-century America. For historical background on the formation of interest groups in Europe, see Reinhard Bendix, *Nation-Building and Citizenship* (Berke-

ley and Los Angeles: University of California Press, 1964), 155–65; and Charles S. Maier, "'Fictitious Bonds . . . of Wealth and Law': On the Theory and Practice of Interest Representation," in *Organizing Interests in Western Europe: Pluralism, Corporatism, and the Transformation of Politics,* ed. Suzanne Berger (New York: Cambridge University Press, 1981).

19. The framers of the U.S. Constitution displaced the classical assumption that republics required citizens possessed of exceptional virtue. Instead they argued that all free governments, regardless of constitutional form, required virtuous citizens, but that republics rested on a particular distribution of self-interest, or, in the words of Noah Webster, on "[a]n equality of property, with a necessity of alienation constantly operating to destroy combinations of powerful families." The interested character of individual action is of less concern than the institutions that shape the interplay of interested actions and organized interests. Bernard Bailyn, *The Ideological Origins of the American Revolution,* enlarged ed. (Cambridge, Mass.: Harvard University Press, Belknap Press, 1992), 373–74; Samuel H. Beer, *To Make a Nation: The Rediscovery of American Federalism* (Cambridge, Mass.: Harvard University Press, Belknap Press, 1994), 258–61.

20. Mancur Olson, *The Logic of Collective Action* (Cambridge, Mass.: Harvard University Press, 1967).

21. Among political scientists, see Kenneth A. Shepsle and Barry R. Weingast, "Structure-Induced Equilibrium and Legislative Choice," *Public Choice* 37 (1981): 503–19; John H. Aldrich, "Rational Choice Theory and the Study of American Politics," in *The Dynamics of American Politics,* ed. Lawrence C. Dodd and Calvin Jillson (Boulder, Colo.: Westview Press, 1994); for critical discussions, Rogers M. Smith, "If Politics Matters: Implications for a 'New Institutionalism,'" *Studies in American Political Development* 6 (1992): 12–30; Kathleen Thelen and Sven Steinmo, "Historical Institutionalism in Comparative Politics," in *Structuring Politics: Historical Institutionalism in Comparative Analysis,* ed. Sven Steinmo, Kathleen Thelen, and Frank Longstreth (New York: Cambridge University Press, 1992), 6–10. Among economists, see Douglass C. North, *Institutions, Institutional Change and Economic Performance* (New York: Cambridge University Press, 1990); and Oliver Williamson, *The Economic Institutions of Capitalism* (New York: Free Press, 1985).

22. Paul J. DiMaggio and Walter W. Powell, "Introduction," in *The New Institutionalism in Organizational Analysis,* ed. Powell and DiMaggio (Chicago: University of Chicago Press, 1991), 15.

23. On the limitations of various "institutionalisms," see Karen Orren and Stephen Skowronek, "Beyond the Iconography of Order: Notes for a 'New Institutionalism,'" in Dodd and Jillson, *Dynamics of American Politics,* 314–20; Walter W. Powell, "Expanding the Scope of Institutional Analysis," in Powell and DiMaggio, *New Institutionalism,* 194–200; and Thelen and Steinmo, "Historical Institutionalism," 14–26.

24. Roger Friedland and Robert Alford, "Bringing Society Back In: Symbols, Practices, and Institutional Contradictions," in Powell and DiMaggio, *New Institutionalism,* 232; Orren and Skowronek, "Beyond Iconography," 320–21.

25. Aaron Wildavsky, "Choosing Preferences by Constructing Institutions: A Cultural Theory of Preference Formation," *American Political Science Review* 81, no. 1 (1987): 4. In contrast to the themes of abrasion and contradiction central to institutionalist images of change, Wildavsky asserts that there are only a limited number of viable combinations of values and social relations. For a nondeterminist account of how institutions shape preferences, see Jane J. Mansbridge, "A Deliberative Theory of Interest Representation," in *The Politics of Interests,* ed. Mark Petracca (Boulder, Colo.: Westview Press, 1992).

26. In the study of social movements, Charles Tilly has developed the concept of a repertoire of contention; others have kept the concept of repertoire while shifting its reference to either forms of social organization or meaningful "frames," not restricted to moments of contention. See Elisabeth S. Clemens, "Organizational Repertoires and Institutional Change: Women's Groups and the Transformation of U.S. Politics, 1890–1920," *American Journal of Sociology* 98, no. 4 (1993): 757–63; David A. Snow et al. "Frame Alignment Processes, Micromobilization, and Movement Participation," *American Sociological Review* 51 (1986): 477; Charles Tilly, *From Mobilization to Revolution* (Englewood Cliffs, N.J.: Prentice-Hall, 1978), chap. 5.

27. Sidney Tarrow, *Struggle, Politics, and Reform: Collective Action, Social Movements, and Cycles of Protest* (Ithaca, N.Y.: Cornell University Center for International Studies, 1989), 7. See also James C. Scott, *Domination and the Arts of Resistance* (New Haven: Yale University Press, 1990), 6–10.

28. Charles Tilly, "Contentious Repertoires in Great Britain, 1758–1834," *Social Science History,* 17, no. 2 (1993): 253–80.

29. An "opportunity structure" in the language of social movement theory. See William A. Gamson and David S. Meyer, "Framing Political Opportunity," in *Comparative Perspectives on Social Movements: Political Opportunities, Mobilizing Structures, and Cultural Framings,* ed. Doug McAdam, John D. McCarthy, and Mayer N. Zald (New York: Cambridge University Press, 1996); Doug McAdam, *Political Process and the Development of Black Insurgency, 1930–70* (Chicago: University of Chicago Press, 1982).

30. John L. Campbell, "Institutional Analysis and the Role of Ideas in Political Economy," photocopy, Harvard University, 1995.

31. For a critical discussion of such models, see David Levine, "The Transformation of Interests and the State," in *Changes in the State: Causes and Consequences,* ed. Edward S. Greenberg and Thomas F. Mayer (Newbury Park, Calif.: Sage, 1990).

32. Mansbridge, "Deliberative Theory."

33. See R. G. Collingwood on criminal investigation as a model for historical inquiry. *The Idea of History* (Oxford: Clarendon Press, 1946), 266–82. The template of detective fiction also underscores an important point about intentions and consequences; whereas murderers may intend to murder, they rarely intend to get caught.

34. "The Bricks of the New Party," *Nation,* 27 December 1922, 707.

35. "Editorials," *Survey,* 1 October 1924, 49.

Chapter One

1. James Bryce, *The American Commonwealth*, 3d ed., vol. 1, *The National Government—the State Governments* (New York: Macmillan, 1893), 173.

2. Joel H. Silbey, *The American Political Nation, 1838–1893* (Stanford, Calif.: Stanford University Press, 1991), 238. On the concept of party systems in American history, see Paul Kleppner, *The Third Electoral System, 1853–1892: Parties, Voters, and Political Cultures* (Chapel Hill: University of North Carolina Press, 1979), and *Continuity and Change in Electoral Politics, 1893–1928* (New York: Greenwood Press, 1987).

3. These changes represented a multiplication of the potential "veto points" at which extrapartisan groups could block or exert leverage over policy. See Ellen M. Immergut, "The Rules of the Game: The Logic of Health Policy-Making in France, Switzerland, and Sweden," in Thelen, Steinmo, and Longstreth, *Structuring Politics*, 63–68.

4. Leopold Vincent, *The Alliance and Labor Songster: A Collection of Labor and Comic Songs for the use of Alliances, Grange Debating Clubs and Political Gatherings* (Indianapolis: Vincent Bros., 1891; reprint, New York: Arno Press, 1975), 62–63.

5. On the party system prior to the Civil War, see Richard Hofstadter, *The Idea of a Party System: The Rise of Legitimate Opposition in the United States, 1780–1840* (Berkeley and Los Angeles: University of California Press, 1969); and Richard L. McCormick, *The Second American Party System: Party Formation in the Jacksonian Era* (Chapel Hill: University of North Carolina Press, 1966); and Silbey, *American Political Nation*.

6. On parties as mechanisms for managing such cleavages, see Aldrich, *Why Parties?* esp. chap. 5.

7. Hofstadter, *Idea*, 95.

8. James Madison, "No. 10," *The Federalist Papers* (New York: New American Library, 1961), 84.

9. Charles C. P. Clark. *The "Machine" Abolished and the People Restored to Power by the Organization of All the People on the Lines of Party Organization* (New York: G. P. Putnam's Sons, 1925), xiii–xiv. Like James Sayles Brown, in *Partisan Politics: The Evil and the Remedy* (Philadelphia: J. B. Lippincott Co., 1897) (the source of the title of my chapter), Clark was a party "abolitionist": "They all believed that the Republic was in mortal danger from the party warfare and corruption that bedeviled American affairs after Appomattox." Austin Ranney, *Curing the Mischief of Faction: Party Reform in America* (Berkeley and Los Angeles: University of California Press, 1975), 35. For a similar assertion of the innocent origins of the party system, see Mary Parker Follett, *The New State: Group Organization—the Solution of Popular Government* (New York: Longmans, Green and Co., 1918), 162–67.

10. Silbey, *American Political Nation*, 27. See also McCormick, *Second American Party System*, 13; Ranney, *Curing the Mischief*, 12–14. Some recent studies disagree with this conclusion for the period prior to the Civil War, arguing that local and state campaigns often included significant programmatic content. For

the postwar period, such programmatic campaigns were largely the province of third parties. For a summary of this literature, see Victoria C. Hattam, *Labor Visions and State Power: The Origins of Business Unionism in the United States* (Princeton, N.J.: Princeton University Press, 1993), 25–26.

11. Alfred D. Chandler Jr., *The Visible Hand: The Managerial Revolution in American Business* (Cambridge, Mass.: Harvard University Press, Belknap Press, 1977), 8. On the parallels between economic and political organization in the late nineteenth century, see C. K. Yearley, *The Money Machines: The Breakdown and Reform of Governmental and Party Finance in the North, 1860–1920* (Albany: State University of New York Press, 1970), 106–7.

12. American Federation of Labor, *A Sketch of the American Labor Federation—It's* [sic] *Origin and Progress,* 4. For an extended discussion of the consequences of national markets for union structure, see Lloyd Ulman, *The Rise of the National Trade Union: The Development and Significance of Its Structure, Governing Institutions, and Economic Policies* (Cambridge, Mass.: Harvard University Press, 1955), part 1.

13. James Bryce, *The American Commonwealth,* 3d ed., vol. 2, *The Party System, Public Opinion, Illustrations and Reflections, Social Institutions* (New York: Macmillan, 1895), 55. On the rise of a class of managers, see Olivier Zunz, *Making America Corporate, 1870–1920* (Chicago: University of Chicago Press, 1990).

14. Brown, *Partisan Politics,* 15. Arguing that no reform could contain the corrupting tendencies of parties, Brown proposed a law to the effect that any candidate who accepted a party's nomination for office would be declared ineligible for that office. Ranney, *Curing the Mischief,* 35–37.

15. Allen Fraser Lovejoy, *La Follette and the Establishment of the Direct Primary in Wisconsin, 1890–1904* (New Haven, Conn.: Yale University Press, 1941), 54. For other examples of the disjuncture between popular political concerns and national party doctrine, see Lawrence Goodwyn, *The Populist Moment: A Short History of the Agrarian Revolt in America* (New York: Oxford University Press, 1978), 3–8; R. Hal Williams, *The Democratic Party and California Politics, 1880–1896* (Stanford, Calif.: Stanford University Press, 1973), chap. 8.

16. Jean H. Baker, *Affairs of Party: The Political Culture of Northern Democrats in the Mid–Nineteenth Century* (Ithaca, N.Y.: Cornell University Press, 1983); Alan Dawley and Paul Faler, "Working-Class Culture and Politics in the Industrial Revolution: Sources of Loyalism and Rebellion," *Journal of Social History* 9, no. 4 (1976): 466–80; McGerr, *Decline of Popular Politics.*

17. For a discussion of the role of racist ideologies in constituting these cross-class, cross-sectional alliances, see Alexander Saxton, *The Rise and Fall of the White Republic: Class Politics and Mass Culture in Nineteenth-Century America* (New York: Verso, 1990), chaps. 6, 10, and 11.

18. Within the Republican Party, a policy of southern-subsidized territorial expansion muted tensions between the financial centers of the East and western states dependent on mortgage and investment capital, as well as railroads. Richard Franklin Bensel, *Yankee Leviathan: The Origins of Central State Authority in*

America, 1859–1877 (New York: Cambridge University Press, 1990), 418–32; Paul Kleppner, *Who Voted? The Dynamics of Electoral Turnout, 1870–1980* (New York: Praeger, 1982), 48–49.

19. Samuel T. McSeveney, *The Politics of Depression: Political Behavior in the Northeast, 1893–1896* (New York: Oxford University Press, 1972), 12; Silbey, *American Political Nation,* 171.

20. Bensel, *Yankee Leviathan,* 408.

21. Migration could also tip the balance between competitive parties, as in California, where the movement of predominantly Republican midwesterners into Southern California during the 1880s and 1890s helped to undermine the state's Democrats. Williams, *Democratic Party and California,* 89–92.

22. Bryce, *American Commonwealth,* 2:45; McSeveney, *The Politics of Depression,* 14.

23. McGerr, *Decline of Popular Politics,* 9.

24. McGerr, *Decline of Popular Politics,* 70–71, 93–99.

25. Neil Fligstein, *The Transformation of Corporate Control* (Cambridge, Mass.: Harvard University Press, 1990).

26. Robert D. Marcus, *Grand Old Party: Political Structure in the Gilded Age, 1880–1896* (New York: Oxford University Press, 1971); McGerr, *Decline of Popular Politics,* chaps. 4–6.

27. Nathan Fine, *Labor and Farmer Parties in the United States, 1828–1928* (New York: Rand School of Social Science, 1928), 15; see also Kim Voss, *The Making of American Exceptionalism: The Knights of Labor and Class Formation in the Nineteenth Century* (Ithaca, N.Y.: Cornell University Press, 1994), 121–22.

28. The national nominating convention was first used in 1830 by the Anti-Masonic Party and was then imitated by the National Republicans in 1831 to nominate Henry Clay to run against the incumbent, Andrew Jackson. Ranney, *Curing the Mischief,* 16.

29. Silbey, *American Political Nation,* 206; Marcus, *Grand Old Party,* 88–89.

30. Bryce, *American Commonwealth,* 1:444; Williams, *Democratic Party and California,* 167; Paul L Beckett and Walfred H. Peterson, "The Constitutional Framework," in *Political Life in Washington: Governing the Evergreen State,* ed. Thor Swanson et al. (Pullman: Washington State University Press, 1985), 23.

31. Charles Beard and Birl Shultz, *Documents on the State-Wide Initiative, Referendum, and Recall* (New York: Macmillan, 1912), 9; see also S. Gale Lowrie, "The Wisconsin Plan for the Initiative and Referendum," *Annals of the American Academy of Political and Social Science* 43 (September 1912): 180.

32. Bryce, *American Commonwealth,* 2:23–24; see also Brown, *Partisan Politics,* 8.

33. These considerations have been central to scholarship on urban political machines. See Steven Erie, *Rainbow's End: Irish-Americans and the Dilemmas of Urban Machine Politics, 1840–1985* (Berkeley and Los Angeles: University of California Press, 1988); Harold F. Gosnell, *Machine Politics: Chicago Model* (Chicago: University of Chicago Press, 1937); and Robert K. Merton, *Social Theory and Social Structure* (Glencoe, Ill.: Free Press, 1957), 72–82. For a review of

criticisms of this argument, see Kenneth Finegold, *Experts and Politicians: Reform Challenges to Machine Politics in New York, Cleveland, and Chicago* (Princeton, N.J.: Princeton University Press, 1995), 10–12.

34. Silbey, *American Political Nation,* 90–108.

35. In comparative analyses, the United States has typically been characterized as a weak state, lacking the centralized, relatively autonomous bureaucracy of many European governments. Various arguments have been advanced to explain this comparative weakness, including the sequence of democratization and bureaucratization, the persistence of premodern political forms, and the nation's liberal political culture. E. g., Bendix, *Nation-Building and Citizenship;* Louis Hartz, *The Liberal Tradition in America: An Interpretation of American Political Thought since the Revolution* (New York: Harcourt Brace Jovanovich, 1955); Samuel Huntington, *Political Order in Changing Societies* (New Haven, Conn.: Yale University Press, 1968), chap. 2. More recent scholarship has explored historical variations in the American state, paying particular attention to the "state-building" enterprises of the Progressive Era and the New Deal. In this literature, Stephen Skowronek's *Building the New American State* has been particularly influential in setting the terms of debate. For other contributions, see Bensel, *Yankee Leviathan;* Barry Karl, *The Uneasy State: The United States from 1915 to 1945* (Chicago: University of Chicago Press, 1983); Muncy, *Creating a Female Dominion;* Skocpol, *Protecting Soldiers and Mothers;* Theda Skocpol and Kenneth Finegold, "State Capacity and Economic Intervention in the Early New Deal," *Political Science Quarterly* 97, no. 2 (1982): 255–78. For a review of this literature, see David Brian Robertson, "The Return to History and the New Institutionalism in American Political Science," *Social Science History* 17, no. 1 (1993): 1–36. A related literature, on the growth of state capacity for economic regulation, will be discussed in chapter 2.

36. The struggle between old and new elites over political control is a central theme in the historiography of the Progressive Era. Among the classic works exploring this topic are Richard Hofstadter, *The Age of Reform* (New York: Vintage, 1955); and George E. Mowry, *The California Progressives* (1951; reprint, Chicago: Quadrangle Books, 1963). For the consequences of these struggles for party organization, see Marcus, *Grand Old Party,* 152–53; and McGerr, *Decline of Popular Politics,* chap. 3. Skowronek's *Building a New American State* echoes this theme in the context of bureaucratization. For a review of the literature on urban progressivism, see Finegold, *Experts and Politicians.* For the enduring effects of Progressive Era party changes, see David Mayhew, *Placing Parties in American Politics: Organization, Electoral Settings, and Government Activity in the Twentieth Century* (Princeton, N.J.: Princeton University Press, 1986), chap. 11.

37. The "realignment synthesis" has been one of the most influential frameworks for historical analysis within political science, producing a large body of work based on the quantitative analysis of voting records. In this debate, the foundational works include V. O. Key, "A Theory of Critical Elections," *Journal of*

Politics 17, no. 3 (1955): 3–18; and Walter Dean Burnham, *Critical Elections and the Mainsprings of American Politics* (New York: Norton, 1970). For recent reviews of this debate, see Walter Dean Burnham, "Pattern Recognition and 'Doing' Political History: Art, Science, or Bootless Enterprise?" in Dodd and Jillson, *Dynamics of American Politics;* and Byron E. Shafer, ed. *The End of Realignment? Interpreting American Political Eras* (Madison: University of Wisconsin Press, 1991). For discussions of electoral reforms, see Peter H. Argersinger, "The Value of the Vote: Political Representation in the Gilded Age," *Journal of American History* 76, no. 1 (1989): 59–90; L. E. Fredman, *The Australian Ballot: The Story of an American Reform* (East Lansing: Michigan State University Press, 1968); Jac. C. Heckelman, "The Effect of the Secret Ballot on Voter Turnout Rates," *Public Choice* 82 (1995): 107–24; Lisa Reynolds, "Reassessing the Impact of Progressive Era Ballot Reform," Ph.D. diss., University of California at San Diego, 1995.

38. Ranney, *Curing the Mischief,* 82.

39. Beard and Shultz, *Documents;* William Bennett Munro, *The Initiative, Referendum, and Recall* (New York: D. Appleton and Co., 1916); Ellis Paxson Oberholtzer, *The Referendum in America* (New York: Charles Scribner's Sons, 1912); Edith M. Phelps, ed., *Selected Articles on the Initiative and Referendum* (New York: H. W. Wilson, 1914). For more recent assessments of these reforms, see David Butler and Austin Ranney, eds. *Referendums: A Comparative Study of Practice and Theory* (Washington, D.C.: American Enterprise Institute for Public Policy Research, 1978), chaps. 4 and 5; Thomas E. Cronin, *Direct Democracy: The Politics of Initiative, Referendum, and Recall* (Cambridge, Mass.: Harvard University Press, 1989); and V. O. Key and Winston W. Crouch, *The Initiative and the Referendum in California* (Berkeley and Los Angeles: University of California Press, 1939).

40. My argument is *not* that individuals were assumed to be altruistic political actors, but that there were organizational and ideological obstacles to the explicit and effective expression of *shared but limited* interests in politics. As Philip J. Ethington has argued, "The crucial development across the long haul of the nineteenth century was the legitimation of policy goods intended to benefit less than the whole people. . . . The project for political activists now became one of proving that one represented a legitimate interest group and that exclusion of one's interest group from ruling coalitions would seriously hurt the 'common interest.'" *The Public City,* 415.

41. *Wisconsin Equity News,* 1 November 1916, 596.

42. Brown, *Partisan Politics,* 93; "The Farm Bloc—a Peril or a Hope?" *Literary Digest,* 14 December 1921, 10.

43. Debates over representation in American political theory recognized that interests would motivate individual political action but argued that the design of the political system could contain those interests rather than translating them directly into policy outcomes. Hanna Fenichel Pitkin, *The Concept of Representation* (Berkeley and Los Angeles: University of California Press, 1967), 196. See

also Bailyn, *Ideological Origins*, 161–75, 366–75; and John Philip Reid, *The Concept of Representation in the Age of the American Revolution* (Chicago: University of Chicago Press, 1989).

44. Margaret Susan Thompson, *The "Spider Web": Congress and Lobbying in the Age of Grant* (Ithaca, N.Y.: Cornell University Press, 1985), 61.

45. Otto G. Wismer, "Legal Aid Organizations: 'Lobbyists for the Poor,'" *Annals of the American Academy of Political and Social Science* 136 (March 1928): 172.

46. Hofstadter, *The Age of Reform*, 135.

47. Robert H. Wiebe, *The Search for Order, 1877–1920* (New York: Hill and Wang, 1967), xiii–xiv.

48. Yearley, *The Money Machines*, xv; see also Mowry, *The California Progressives*.

49. In his comparative analysis of urban reform, however, Kenneth Finegold distinguishes among three varieties of reform: traditional or elite old-stock reform; municipal populism, which often built on working- and middle-class as well as immigrant constituencies; and urban progressivism, which represented a coalition of the first two types. *Experts and Politicians*, 15–26.

50. Skowronek, *Building New American State*, 169, 172.

51. Louis Galambos, "The Emerging Organizational Synthesis in Modern American History," *Business History Review* 44 (1970): 279–90. See also Fligstein, *Transformation of Corporate Control*; R. Jeffrey Lustig, *Corporate Liberalism: The Origins of Modern American Political Theory, 1890–1920* (Berkeley and Los Angeles: University of California Press, 1982); Sklar, *Corporate Reconstruction*.

52. Bensel, *Yankee Leviathan*, chap. 5.

53. Fred Block, "The Ruling Class Does Not Rule," *Socialist Revolution* 33 (1977): 6–28.

54. Gabriel Kolko, *The Triumph of Conservatism: A Reinterpretation of American History* (New York: Free Press, 1963), 6.

55. Robert H. Wiebe, *Businessmen and Reform: A Study of the Progressive Movement* (1962; reprint, Chicago: Quadrangle Books, 1968).

56. James Weinstein, *The Corporate Ideal in the Liberal State, 1900–1918* (Boston: Beacon, 1968).

57. Silbey, *American Political Nation*, 226.

58. Daniel T. Rodgers, "In Search of Progressivism," *Reviews in American History* 10, no. 4 (1982): 117.

59. Business associations often formed as a response to labor organization. E. g., Gilman M. Ostrander, *The Prohibition Movement in California, 1848–1933*, University of California Publications in History 57 (1957), 83, 98–101; Truman, *The Governmental Process*, 67–69; Gertrude Schmidt, "History of Labor Legislation in Wisconsin," Ph.D. diss., University of Wisconsin, 1933, 34–41.

60. McGerr, *Decline of Popular Politics*, 6, 10–11.

61. For a related critique of the role of exogenous disruptions in the equilib-

rium models developed in political science, see Orren and Skowronek, "Beyond Iconography," 314–15.

62. On conceptions of the public as politically reactive or proactive, see Burnham, "Pattern Recognition," 71–74.

63. The scholarly neglect of the origin of interest group politics is linked to the prominence of pluralism (or "group theory") in both American political science and political rhetoric. As Mancur Olson noted of one of the founders of this tradition, "For all his emphasis on the importance and beneficence of group pressures, [Arthur] Bentley said very little about *why* the needs of the different groups in society would tend to be reflected in politically or economically effective pressure. Nor did he consider carefully what it is that causes groups to organize and act effectively. Or why some groups are important in some societies and other groups important in other societies and periods." *Logic of Collective Action,* 122.

64. Wisconsin State Federation of Labor, *Official Directory* 1896–97, 11.

65. Initiatives and referenda had been used within national trade unions at least since 1880. Ulman, *Rise,* 271–74. The Australian ballot was also adopted for labor federation elections, e.g., California State Federation of Labor, *Proceedings of the Annual Convention* 1904, 56–57.

66. While there is a rich literature on the development of political theory during the Progressive Era, this often takes the form of close readings of the work of elite intellectuals without a sustained consideration of the mechanisms by which their work might have come to matter in practical political terms, implicitly assuming a diffusion or trickle-down model. For example, see James T. Kloppenberg, *Uncertain Victory: Social Democracy and Progressivism in European and American Thought, 1870–1920* (New York: Oxford University Press, 1986); and Lustig, *Corporate Liberalism.*

67. Mrs. M. Burton Williamson, "Ladies' Clubs and Societies in Los Angeles in 1892," reported for the Historical Society of Southern California (1892; reprint, Los Angeles: Misses Lillian A. and Estella M. Williamson, 1925), 11; CSG, *Proceedings* 1899, 22.

68. Originally appeared in the *Columbia Chronicle,* 7 March 1891. Quoted in Fred R. Yoder, "The Farmers' Alliance in Washington—Prelude to Populism," *Research Studies of the State College of Washington* 16, nos. 3–4 (1948): 161.

69. Galambos, "Emerging Organizational Synthesis," 280.

70. Keller, *Regulating a New Economy,* 3. See also Balogh, "Reorganizing the Organizational Synthesis," 120–22; Karen Orren, *Belated Feudalism: Labor, the Law, and Liberal Development in the United States* (New York: Cambridge University Press), chaps. 2–3.

71. Dawley, *Struggles for Justice,* 8; see also Rogers M. Smith, "Beyond Tocqueville, Myrdal, and Hartz," *American Political Science Review* 87, no. 3 (1992): 549–66. But in studies of institutional change, attention to diversity may need to be tempered by an appreciation of the continued significance of raw power. Consequently, this study does not address the maximum variety of political organization but, instead, concentrates on *relatively* disadvantaged groups,

those among the marginalized who were comparatively powerful and, therefore, more likely to succeed as challengers to established political institutions.

72. Russell B. Nye, *Midwestern Progressive Politics: A Historical Study of Its Origins and Development, 1870–1950* (East Lansing: Michigan State University Press, 1951), 7–28; Norman Pollack, *The Populist Response to Industrial America: Midwestern Populist Thought* (New York: Norton, 1962)

73. For rich discussions of the spread of fraternalism in nineteenth and early twentieth centuries, see Mark C. Carnes, *Secret Ritual and Manhood in Victorian America* (New Haven, Conn.: Yale University Press, 1989); Mary Ann Clawson, *Constructing Brotherhood: Class, Gender, and Fraternalism* (Princeton, N.J.: Princeton University Press, 1989); and Lynn Dumenil, *Freemasonry and American Culture, 1880–1939* (Princeton, N.J.: Princeton University Press, 1984).

74. Clemens, "Organizational Repertoires," 755–63.

75. For membership figures, see Weinstein, *Corporate Elite*, 8; and John R. Commons et al., *History of Labour in the United States*, vol. 2 (New York: Macmillan, 1918), 522. By comparison, the elite American Association for Labor Legislation grew from 165 members in 1906 to 3,348 in 1913. *American Labor Legislation Review*, March 1914, 146.

76. David Montgomery, *The Fall of the House of Labor: The Workplace, the State, and American Labor Activism, 1865–1925* (New York: Cambridge University Press, 1987), 287; see also Robert W. Ozanne, *The Labor Movement in Wisconsin: A History* (Madison, Wis.: State Historical Society of Wisconsin, 1984), 35–36. The Knights of Labor reached a peak membership of over 700,000, and perhaps 3 million persons were members at some point during its history. For a review of the literature on membership, see Voss, *Making of American Exceptionalism*, 2–3.

77. Robert L. Tontz, "Memberships of General Farmers' Organizations, United States, 1874–1960," *Agricultural History* 38, no. 3 (1964): 147.

78. Margaret Gibbons Wilson, *The American Woman in Transition: The Urban Influence, 1870–1920* (Westport, Conn.: Greenwood, 1979), 100–101; Mary I. Wood, *The History of the General Federation of Women's Clubs: For the First Twenty-Two Years of Its Organization* (New York: General Federation of Women's Clubs, 1912), 131, 154.

79. Ruth Bordin, *Woman and Temperance: The Quest for Power and Liberty, 1873–1900* (Philadelphia: Temple University Press, 1981), 3–4.

80. Carnes, *Secret Ritual*, 1.

81. Michael Hechter, *Principles of Group Solidarity* (Berkeley and Los Angeles: University of California Press, 1987), chap. 5. For an overview of the "ambition theory" of party affiliation, see Aldrich, *Why Parties?* 51–57.

82. Frank J. Sorauf, "Extra-legal Political Parties in Wisconsin," *American Political Science Review* 48, no. 3 (1954): 692–704; Jeanne Jordan Kirkpatrick, *Dismantling the Parties: Reflections on Party Reform and Party Decomposition* (Washington, D.C.: American Enterprise Institute, 1978), 6–7, 10–11.

83. John Mark Hansen, *Gaining Access: Congress and the Farm Lobby, 1919–1981* (Chicago: University of Chicago Press, 1991), 5.

84. The silences in political history are illuminated by a widely acclaimed essay by Daniel T. Rodgers. Working through historiographical debates of the 1970s that proclaimed the demise of "progressivism" as an organizing concept, he asked, "[W]hy then did so many issue-oriented groups demanding so many novel changes burst on the scene at once? That, clearly, was the critical question." With the decline of the party, Americans had begun "their long twentieth-century slide toward political inactivity," but the "result was to spring open the political arena to extra-party pressure groups of all sorts: manufacturers' organizations, labor lobbies, civic leagues, trade associations, women's clubs, professional associations, and issue-oriented lobbies, all trying directly to shape policy." "In Search of Progressivism," 115–16.

Two troubling assumptions inform this account. The first concerns mechanism. Parties decline, generating a political vacuum into which rush "issue-oriented lobbies." The possibility that such lobbies might have contributed to the weakening of parties is not considered, nor are the origins of the associations explained, effectively naturalizing the phenomenon of interest group pluralism. The second problematic assumption emerges if one compares the list above with the associations mentioned in the remainder of the essay. Of this initial encompassing list, women's clubs and labor lobbies disappear, while civic leagues make an appearance only in their most elite manifestations, such as the National Civic Federation. Thus, the political history of this period is effectively an elite history, leavened only by the inclusion of privileged outsiders such as professionals and policy intellectuals.

85. Wismer, "Legal Aid Organizations," 172.

86. See Powell and DiMaggio, *New Institutionalism*, chap. 1.

87. James A. Morone, *The Democratic Wish: Popular Participation and the Limits of American Government* (New York: Basic Books, 1990).

88. David S. Meyer, *A Winter of Discontent: The Nuclear Freeze and American Politics* (New York: Praeger, 1990), 8.

89. WaSFL, *Proceedings of the Annual Convention* 1913, 34; emphasis added.

Chapter Two

1. Follett, *The New State*, 232–33.

2. Pluralist theories tend to assume that power and resources will be dispersed such that "different people have different kinds of power in different issue arenas." For an overview, see Mark P. Petracca, "The Rediscovery of Interest Group Politics," in Petracca, *The Politics of Interests*, 5. Critical accounts retain the contest model while assuming that power and resources are concentrated, typically in the hands of economic elites. For a critique of the contest model, see Frank Dobbin, *Forging Industrial Policy: The United States, Britain, and France in the Railway Age* (New York: Cambridge University Press, 1994), 218–22.

3. Doug McAdam, "Tactical Innovation and the Pace of Insurgency," *American Sociological Review* 48 (1983): 735–54; Tarrow, *Struggle, Politics, and Reform*.

4. Reviewing centuries of protest activity in France, Charles Tilly makes the

point that "[e]ven government officials and industrial managers of our own time generally behave as though they preferred demonstrations and strikes to utterly unconventional forms of collective action." *The Contentious French* (Cambridge, Mass.: Harvard University Press, 1986), 391.

5. David S. Meyer and Nancy Whittier, "Social Movement Spillover," *Social Problems* 41, no. 2 (1994): 277–98.

6. Ronald Jepperson provides a useful definition of institutions as "those social patterns that, when chronically reproduced, owe their survival to relatively self-activating social processes." "Institutions, Institutional Effects, and Institutionalism," in Powell and DiMaggio, *New Institutionalism,* 145.

7. E.g., Paul J. DiMaggio and Walter W. Powell, "The Iron Cage Revisited: Institutional Isomorphism and Collective Rationality in Organizational Fields," *American Sociological Review* 48 (1983): 147–60. As John Meyer and his colleagues observe, if "institutions were simply the products of competing interests and political negotiation, there should be much less uniformity in these dimensions across national societies. The source of that uniformity lies in an institutional environment common to organizations in national societies throughout the world system." George M. Thomas et al., *Institutional Structure: Constituting State, Society, and the Individual* (Beverly Hills, Calif.: Sage, 1987), 19.

8. Dobbin, *Forging Industrial Policy.*

9. For a critical discussion of the equation of institutions with order in political theory, see Orren and Skowronek, "Beyond Iconography."

10. Joel H. Silbey, "The Rise and Fall of American Political Parties, 1790–1990," in *The Parties Respond: Changes in the American Party System,* ed. L. Sandy Maisel (Boulder, Colo.: Westview Press, 1990), 3–4.

11. Lynn Hunt, *Politics, Culture, and Class in the French Revolution* (Berkeley and Los Angeles: University of California Press, 1984), 3.

12. American Federation of Labor, *An Interesting Discussion on a Political Programme at the Denver Convention of the American Federation of Labor* (Washington, D.C.: American Federation of Labor, 1894), 48.

13. Galambos, "Emerging Organizational Synthesis," 279–90. For examples, see Fligstein, *Transformation of Corporate Control;* Keller, *Regulating a New Economy;* Sklar, *Corporate Reconstruction.*

14. On the use of models of republican government in early American corporations, see Gerald Berk, *Alternative Tracks: The Constitution of American Industrial Order, 1865–1917* (Baltimore: Johns Hopkins University Press, 1994), chap. 4; Robert W. Gordon, "Legal Thought and Legal Practice in the Age of American Enterprise, 1870–1920," in *Professions and Professional Ideologies in America,* ed. Gerald L. Geison (Chapel Hill: University of North Carolina Press, 1983); and James A. Ward, "Power and Accountability on the Pennsylvania Railroad, 1846–1878," *Business History Review* 49 (1975): 37–59. I am grateful to William Roy for these examples.

15. Galambos, "Emerging Organizational Synthesis," 289.

16. CSG, *Proceedings* 1889, 43; Trades Council and Labor Union Directory of Madison, Wis. (Madison, Wis.: Federated Trades Council, 1894), 18. In an

unusual 1894 decision preserving union contracts when a railroad was put into receivership, the judge argued, "While a corporation was 'capital consisting of money and property,' organized labor was 'capital consisting of brains and muscle.' . . . 'If it is lawful for the stockholders and officers of a corporation to associate and confer for the purpose of reducing the wages of its employees . . . it is equally lawful for organized labor to associate, consult and confer with a view to maintain or increase wages.'" Quoted in David Brundage, *The Making of Western Labor Radicalism: Denver's Organized Workers, 1878–1905* (Urbana: University of Illinois Press, 1994), 116.

17. Quoted in Genevieve Forbes Herrick and John Origen Herrick, *The Life of William Jennings Bryan* (Chicago: Buxton, 1925), 117.

18. In Stephen D. Krasner's words, "Pure interest group versions of pluralism" conceive of government "as a cash register that totals up and then averages the preferences and political power of societal actors." "Approaches to the State: Alternative Conceptions and Historical Dynamics," *Comparative Politics* 16, no. 2 (1984): 227.

19. For a discussion of the distinction between "constitutive politics and the politics of power," see Berk, *Alternative Tracks*, 11.

20. The tools for this analysis are drawn primarily from organization theory in sociology. In contrast to arguments that emphasize either economic rationality or technological determinism, sociologists address the embeddedness of organizations in populations, networks, or organizational fields. For a review of this literature, see DiMaggio and Powell, "Introduction."

21. Proponents of the "organizational synthesis" in American history typically begin by making the opposite assumption: "the organizational historians who use the Weberian model have a tendency to stress the universal, not the particular, qualities of their subject." Galambos, "Emerging Organizational Synthesis," 280.

22. Orren, *Belated Feudalism*; on founding effects, see Arthur L. Stinchcombe, "Social Structure and Organizations," in *Handbook of Organizations*, ed. James G. March (Chicago: Rand-McNally, 1965).

23. For examples, see Peter J. Coleman, *Progressivism and the World of Reform: New Zealand and the Origins of the American Welfare State* (Lawrence: University of Kansas Press, 1987); D. Eleanor Westney, *Imitation and Innovation: The Transfer of Western Organizational Patterns to Meiji Japan* (Cambridge, Mass.: Harvard University Press, 1987).

24. Ann Swidler, "Culture in Action: Symbols and Strategies," *American Sociological Review* 51 (1986): 273–86. For an important discussion of the relation of agency to structural heterogeneity and transposable models or schemas, see William H. Sewell Jr., "A Theory of Structure: Duality, Agency, and Transformation," *American Journal of Sociology* 98, no. 1 (1992): 1–29.

25. North, *Institutions*, 17, 108, 111.

26. The reconstruction of organizational repertoires exemplified "the method of analyzing virtual choices." Understood as ideal typical representations of possible organizational forms, these constructions "have the properties of being psychologically and socially real alternatives to the people involved and of exhausting

the relevant part of social reality, in the sense that no other choices are likely to be causally effective or made by large numbers of people." Stinchcombe, *Theoretical Methods,* 62–63. A similar process is captured by the application of Claude Lévi-Strauss's concept of bricolage to the explanation of institutional change. See John L. Campbell, "Mechanisms of Evolutionary Change in Economic Governance: Interaction, Interpretation, and Bricolage," forthcoming in *Evolutionary Economics and Path Dependency,* ed. Lars Magnusson and Jan Ottossun (Aldershot, U.K.: Edward Elgar); Elisabeth S. Clemens, "Organizational Form as Frame: Collective Identity and Political Strategy in the American Labor Movement," in *Comparative Perspectives on Social Movements: Opportunities, Mobilizing Structures, and Cultural Framings,* ed. Doug McAdam, John D. McCarthy, and Mayer Zald (New York: Cambridge University Press, 1996).

27. Baker, *Affairs of Party,* 94.

28. James G. March and Johan P. Olsen, *Rediscovering Institutions: The Organizational Basis of Politics* (New York: Free Press, 1989), 23–24.

29. Sue E. S. Crawford and Elinor Ostrom, "A Grammar of Institutions," *American Political Science Review* 89 (1995): 583–86.

30. Margaret S. Archer, *Culture and Agency: The Place of Culture in Social Theory* (New York: Cambridge University Press, 1988), chap. 8; Snow et al. "Frame Alignment Processes," 467–76.

31. The "blueprint" conception of organizational form has been criticized on the methodological grounds that "blueprints for organizations are not observable." Michael T. Hannan and John Freeman, "Where Do Organizational Forms Come From?" *Sociological Forum* 1, no. 1 (1986): 56. While this is true if one takes *blueprint* in a genetic sense, as the code determining organizational form, it does not hold for a "blueprint" understood architecturally, as a model that is discursively available to all participants in a collective-action project. While such models often achieve a taken-for-granted status in everyday social life, they become the objects of discussion and contention under conditions of uncertainty.

32. Olson, *Logic of Collective Action,* 2.

33. Hechter, *Principles of Group Solidarity,* 42. Prominent in recent work on "new social movements," *collective identity* is understood as "a social construct linking the individual, the cultural system, and, in some cases, the organizational carrier of the movement." Aldon D. Morris and Carol McClurg Mueller, eds. *Frontiers in Social Movement Theory* (New Haven, Conn.: Yale University Press, 1992), 15–16.

34. Carnes, *Secret Ritual,* 6–8. For other connections between fraternal orders and popular associations, see O. Fritiof Ander, "The Immigrant Church and the Patrons of Husbandry," *Agricultural History* 8 (October 1934): 154–65; David P. Thelen, *Paths of Resistance: Tradition and Dignity in Industrializing Missouri* (New York: Oxford University Press, 1986), 92, 166–71; Voss, *Making of American Exceptionalism,* 74.

35. Unions with members from many crafts. Federal unions were formed when there were insufficient numbers in a community to create separate craft locals; they were directly affiliated with the AFL.

36. American Federation of Labor, *Manual of Common Procedure for the Use of Local and Federal Labor Unions Affiliated with the American Federation of Labor* (Washington, D.C.: American Federation of Labor, 1903), 1–6. Note how the choice of tune invokes a second powerful collective identity that, no doubt, did not aid organizing efforts in the southern states.

37. Robert H. Wiebe, *Self-Rule: A Cultural History of American Democracy* (Chicago: University of Chicago Press, 1995), 95–96; on the incorporation of military and religious models into lodge life, 73–74.

38. Carlos A. Schwantes, *Coxey's Army: An American Odyssey* (Lincoln: University of Nebraska Press, 1985). Despite this defeat, the "army of the unemployed" was established as an element in the repertoire of American workers. In Los Angeles during 1914, for example, "Under the leadership of 'General' Morris Rose, a group of less prosperous winter tourists who arrived via freight trains established what he chose to call an army, numbering about 400 men." When harassed by the police, the leader of the "Army Unemployed–Los Angeles" retaliated with the organizational equivalent of code switching, "threatening to seize the industrial community of Vernon, register all his men as voters, call an election, and take over the government. He would then raise taxes so high in Vernon that property would be confiscated and his men thus provided with homes." Louis B. Perry and Richard S. Perry, *A History of the Los Angeles Labor Movement, 1911–1941* (Berkeley and Los Angeles: University of California Press, 1963), 14–15.

39. "Organizational fields" are established by the "mutual recognition of actors" based on relations of dependence, competition, cooperation, and legitimation: "[T]hese actors share a similar conception of legitimate action and the place of each organization in that field. The effect of forming organizational fields is, first and foremost, to promote stability." Fligstein, *Transformation of Corporate Control*, 6.

40. Arthur L. Stinchcombe, *Information and Organizations* (Berkeley and Los Angeles: University of California Press, 1990), chap. 5.

41. On the sources of advantage, see Stinchcombe, *Information and Organization*, chap. 5.

42. Ella Giles Ruddy, ed. *The Mother of Clubs, Caroline M. Seymour Severance: An Estimate and Appreciation* (Los Angeles: Baumgardt Publishing, 1906), 24. This concern for the consequences of names was not limited to women. In the 1890s, the Rocky Mountain Social League considered merging with the Socialist Labor Party, but "as a condition of unification . . . the League demanded that the SLP drop the word 'party' from its name, changing its name to the 'Socialist League' or the 'Socialist Association.' These terms were suggestive of the loose and democratic structure emphasized by syndicalists, as well as of their rejection of electoral activity." Brundage, *Western Labor Radicalism*, 108.

43. This organizational form was available to women through direct observation as well as cultural representations. Caroline Severance explained, "I cannot say confidently, after this lapse of time, and in the absence of data, whether this idea of the possibilities and gains of club life for women came to me from the fact of the existence of men's clubs, or whether I was then aware, through the 'English

Woman's Journal,' edited by Emily Faithful, of the formation of clubs for women in England." Ruddy, *Mother of Clubs,* 22.

44. Hichborn, *California Legislature of 1909,* 216. For further discussion of this rumor, see the prologue.

45. Organizational fields are defined by the mutual recognition of actors, institutions by the "self-activating" quality of their own reproduction, a persistence that may be buttressed by formal rules, cultural legitimacy, disproportionate resources, or a monopolization of the means of violence. Jepperson, "Institutions," 145. Rather than a one-to-one relationship existing between organizational field and institution, an organizational field may encompass more than one institution. Reinforcement from those institutions, both rhetorical and material, constitutes an important resource for members of the field. Alternatively, members of a field may construct institutions—formal codes and systems of governance—to stabilize their own system of relations. See Paul J. DiMaggio, "Constructing an Organizational Field as a Professional Project: U.S. Art Museums, 1920–1940," in Powell and DiMaggio, *New Institutionalism;* DiMaggio and Powell, "The Iron Cage Revisited."

46. Friedland and Alford, "Bringing Society Back In," 232. See also Elisabeth S. Clemens, "Continuity and Coherence: Periodization and the Problem of Change," in *Social Time and Social Change,* ed. Ragnvald Kalleberg and Fredrik Engelstad (Oslo: Norwegian University Press, 1997).

47. Brundage, *Western Labor Radicalism,* 116.

48. Mary Douglas, "Jokes," in *Rethinking Popular Culture: Contemporary Perspectives in Cultural Studies,* ed. Chandra Mukerji and Michael Schudson (Berkeley and Los Angeles: University of California Press, 1991), 301.

49. *Wisconsin Citizen,* December 1894, 3. The *Citizen* was a woman suffrage paper, established in 1887.

50. Beulah Amidon to Mabel Vernon, 27 October 1917, Box 1, Mabel Vernon Correspondence, Bancroft Library, University of California at Berkeley; emphasis added.

51. This typology draws on Crawford and Ostrom, "A Grammar of Institutions."

52. North, *Institutions,* 94–97.

53. Bryce, *American Commonwealth,* 1:34.

54. Bryce, *American Commonwealth,* 1:1.

55. As Charles Tilly has argued, "Real people do not get together and Act Collectively. . . . First, collective action generally involves interaction with specific other groups, including governments. . . . Second, collective action usually takes well-defined forms already familiar to participants, in the same sense that most of an era's art takes on a small number of established forms." *From Mobilization to Revolution,* 143.

56. Sidney Fine, *Sit-Down: The General Motors Strike of 1936–37* (Ann Arbor: University of Michigan Press, 1969), 122–23.

57. This has been a weakness of the "new institutionalism" in economics, which interprets institutions and rules as efficient responses to problems such as

information and control in market situations. As Douglass North explains, "While most of the elements of a theory of institutional change are developed, there is no neat supply function of new institutional arrangements specified in the framework. What determines the menu of organizational forms that a society devises in response to changing relative prices?" *Structure and Change in Economic History* (New York: Norton, 1981), 68.

58. American Federation of Labor, *Interesting Discussion,* 12.

59. Quoted in Yoder, "Farmers' Alliance," 143.

60. For discussions of the political significance of this producerist vision in the Knights of Labor, see Hattam, *Labor Visions,* chap. 3; and Voss, *Making of American Exceptionalism,* 86. As will be seen in chapter 4, the Knights had an enduring influence on a wide range of oppositional politics in the Pacific Northwest, contributing to a pattern of farmer-labor alliances in Washington state.

61. Schwantes, *Coxey's Army.*

62. July 1888, 3. The use of mastery of procedure to signal civic competence was not limited to women's groups. In his study of midwestern voluntary associations, Don Doyle has argued that these groups "filled a void the family was unsuited to fill by serving as schools to teach a variety of new skills, values, and a new social discipline demanded by modern society. A major part of this unconscious curriculum was directed toward imparting organizational skills to potential business, social, and political leaders. Here the very process of creating new lodges, literary clubs, reform societies, or fire companies gave dozens of men within the community first-hand experience in drafting constitutions, recruiting members, presiding over meetings and resolving conflicts." "The Social Functions of Voluntary Associations in a Nineteenth-Century Town," *Social Science History* 1, no. 3 (1977): 348–49.

63. Stinchcombe, *Theoretical Methods,* 70–75.

64. For recent efforts to trace the continuities between nineteenth- and twentieth-century labor organization and protest, see Brundage, *Western Labor Radicalism;* Dorothy Sue Cobble, *Dishing It Out: Waitresses and Their Unions in the Twentieth Century* (Urbana: University of Illinois Press, 1991), chap. 3; and Michael Kazin, *Barons of Labor: The San Francisco Building Trades and Union Power in the Progressive Era* (Urbana: University of Illinois Press, 1987). A profound caesura between the centuries is evident in studies of agrarian organization, while analyses of the "woman movement" treat the first decade of the twentieth century as a moment of quiescence and transition between generations of activists.

65. John W. Kingdon, *Agendas, Alternatives, and Public Policies* (Boston: Little, Brown, 1984), chap. 8. "Windows" and "opportunities" are, however, difficult to define, being products both of actors' perceptions of possibility and the organization of power and resources that they confront. For a useful specification of "opportunity structure," see Gamson and Meyer, "Framing Political Opportunity."

66. Wisconsin State Federation of Labor (WiSFL), *Proceedings of the Annual Convention* 1914, 19.

67. WaSFL, *Proceedings* 1913, 34.

Chapter Three

1. Quoted in Joseph F. Tripp, "Progressive Labor Laws in Washington State (1900–1924)," Ph.D. diss., University of Washington, 1973, 13.

2. *Review of Reviews* (August 1906), reprinted in Edith M. Phelps, ed., *Selected Articles on the Initiative and Referendum* (New York: H. W. Wilson, 1914), 159; William E. Rappard, "The Initiative, Referendum, and Recall in Switzerland," *Annals of the American Academy of Political and Social Science* 43 (September 1912): 124–25.

3. Quoted in Cronin, *Direct Democracy*, 52.

4. WaSFL, *Proceedings* 1913, 34.

5. Mark H. Leff, "Consensus for Reform: The Mothers' Pension Movement in the Progressive Era," *Social Service Review* 47, no. 3 (1973): 397–417; Elizabeth Brandeis, "Labor Legislation," in *History of Labor in the United States, 1896–1932*, ed. John R. Commons, vol. 3 (New York: Macmillan, 1935), 571–76; Eliza K. Pavalko, "State Timing of Policy Adoption: Workmen's Compensation in the United States, 1909–29," *American Journal of Sociology* 95, no. 3 (1989): 592–615.

6. For a discussion of policy diffusion and the influence of national political learning on urban reform, see Finegold, *Experts and Politicians*, 6–9.

7. This lack of attention to action that crosses boundaries and diffusion across units is equally evident in studies of social movements. Organized around substantive topics—labor history, agrarian history, and women's history, for example—these studies rarely explore the commonalities across groups or the processes of coalition and diffusion that linked diverse political organizations.

8. Regional biases are also evident in the histories of popular politics and organization. For one discussion of this problem, see Dana Frank, *Purchasing Power: Consumer Organizing, Gender, and the Seattle Labor Movement, 1919–1929* (New York: Cambridge University Press, 1994), 10–11. In his study of the building trades in San Francisco, Michael Kazin repeatedly notes how differences in geography, ethnic composition, and the trajectory of economic development produced distinctive opportunities for the consolidation of union power in this western city. Different opportunities, in turn, generated a different type of labor organization that worked as a private governance system controlling relations at the workplace. *Barons of Labor*, 14–19, 102.

9. For a comprehensive assessment of the role of regionalism in American politics, see Richard Franklin Bensel, *Sectionalism and American Political Development, 1880–1980* (Madison: University of Wisconsin Press, 1984).

10. Bensel, *Yankee Leviathan*, chap. 7; Frances Fox Piven and Richard A. Cloward, *Regulating the Poor: The Functions of Public Welfare* (New York: Vintage, 1971), 115, 130–45; Jill Quadagno, *The Transformation of Old Age Security: Class and Politics in the American Welfare State* (Chicago: University of Chicago Press, 1988), 186–88; Elizabeth Sanders, "Industrial Concentration, Sectional Competition, and Antitrust Politics in America, 1880–1980," *Studies in American Political Development* 1 (1986): 142–214. Looking beyond both the South and the Northeast, Eileen McDonagh has lucidly demonstrated both the

heterogeneity of progressivism within states and the linkages between policy outcomes at the state and national levels. "The 'Welfare Rights State' and the 'Civil Rights State': Policy Paradox and State Building in the Progressive Era," *Studies in American Political Development* 7 (1993): 225–74.

11. The ability of southern states to shape policy within the Republican Party was limited by 1916 reforms that introduced the "bonus vote" system, in which votes were distributed not only in relation to population but to the number of Republican votes cast in earlier national elections. The Democrats did not adopt a comparable system until 1940. Ranney, *Curing the Mischief,* 110.

12. V. O. Key, *American State Politics* (New York: Knopf, 1956), 5. See Abraham Epstein, "The American State Old Age Pension System in Operation," *Annals of the American Academy of Political and Social Science* 170 (November 1933): 107–11; Don D. Lescohier and Florence Peterson, *The Alleviation of Unemployment in Wisconsin* (Madison: Industrial Commission of Wisconsin, 1931), 54–90.

13. See David A. Moss, "Kindling a Flame under Federalism: Progressive Reformers, Corporate Elites, and the Phosphorus Match Campaign of 1909–1912," *Business History Review* 68, no. 2 (1994): 244–75.

14. Frederick C. Howe, *Wisconsin: An Experiment in Democracy* (New York: Charles Scribner's Sons, 1912); John D. Hicks, "The Legacy of Populism in the Western Middle West," *Agricultural History* 23, no. 4 (1949): 231; Thelen, *Paths of Resistance,* 217–65; "'North Dakota-ism's' Victory," *Literary Digest,* 19 July 1919, 15–16.

15. WaSFL, *Proceedings* 1913, 34; 1915, 4, 22.

16. This format was particularly important in the 1890s and early 1900s, when Americans had little experience with either the description of social problems or the administration of social policies. Soon, however, policy reports began to take on the forms more familiar today; beginning with a statistical description of the problem, they proceeded to outline policies in terms of technical efficacy and, as almost an aside, to mention the opinions of different groups with an interest in the policy. For examples, see California State Commission of Immigration and Housing, *Report on Unemployment* (1914), 9–11 and appendix H; Industrial Commission of Wisconsin (ICW), *Report on Old Age Relief* (1915), 12–18. In contrast, a later ICW report devotes the entire first chapter to quantitative descriptions of trends in state population, industry, and employment and makes very little reference to developments outside the state. Lescohier and Peterson, *Alleviation of Unemployment.*

17. Schmidt, "History of Labor Legislation," 36.

18. William F. Ogburn, *Progress and Uniformity in Child-Labor Legislation: A Study in Statistical Measurement* (1912; reprint, New York: AMS Press, 1968), 19.

19. Industrial Commission of Wisconsin, *Old Age Relief,* 7. For discussions of international diffusion of social-welfare policy, see Coleman, *World of Reform;* Kloppenberg, *Uncertain Victory,* chap. 9.

20. Edwin Amenta et al., "The Political Origins of Unemployment Insurance

in Five American States," *Studies of American Political Development* 2 (1987): 137–82; Daniel Nelson, *Unemployment Insurance: The American Experience, 1915–1935* (Madison: University of Wisconsin Press, 1969), chaps. 6 and 8.

21. The logic of these comparisons varied by time and region. Courts in new states might borrow heavily from other bodies of law, but "[e]ach state built up its own body of laws, and as time went on, needed to pay less and less attention to its neighbors; and hardly any at all to mother England." This legal autarky was moderated by patterns of regional imitation by both legislatures and courts; California was a model for western states, Massachusetts for New England. Lawrence M. Friedman, *A History of American Law* (New York: Simon and Schuster, 1973), 353, 357.

22. *Survey,* 21 October 1911, 1015; see also *Survey,* 4 November 1911, 1091–92.

23. The perception that the courts were unduly obstructing progressive legislation provoked both demand for the "recall of judicial decisions" and more defensive calls for reform of the Federal Judiciary Act "so as to provide that an appeal may be taken to the United States Supreme Court on a decision of a State highest court denying the constitutionality of a State statute[;] the people of this country can, by that very slight change enacted by Congress, be fully protected against any reactionary State courts (if such exist)." Charles Warren, "The Progressiveness of the United States Supreme Court," *Columbia Law Review* 13, no. 4 (1913): 296.

24. Tripp, "Progressive Labor Laws," 73–75.

25. The federal judiciary had direct jurisdiction over the District of Columbia. "The Law of the Land: Minimum Wages for Women and Shorter Hours for Men," *Survey,* 14 April 1917, 33. On the "counter-claims" made by state courts against the U.S. Supreme Court, see Harry N. Scheiber, "Federalism and the American Economic Order, 1789–1910," *Law and Society Review* 10, no. 1 (1975): 68–69.

26. Joseph F. Tripp, "Toward an Efficient and Moral Society: Washington State Minimum-Wage Law, 1913–1925," *Pacific Northwest Quarterly* 67, no. 3 (1976): 97–112. The General Executive Board of the WiSFL reported that "cheap labor employers hailed the Supreme Court's decision with elation. Immediately the attorneys of the Milwaukee Employers' Council . . . are reported as preparing to petition the court to nullify the Wisconsin Minimum Wage law." WiSFL, *Proceedings* 1923, 56.

27. Brandeis, "Labor Legislation," 514–15; Norris C. Hundley Jr., "Katherine Philips Edson and the Fight for the California Minimum Wage," *Pacific Historical Review* 29 (1960): 285.

28. For a discussion of "abeyance structures" in the field of social movements, see Verta Taylor, "Social Movement Continuity: The Women's Movement in Abeyance," *American Sociological Review* 54 (1989): 761–75.

29. WaSFL, *Proceedings* 1915, 25–26.

30. The concept of opportunity structures draws attention to factors such as institutional rules, divisions among elites, and political climate that shape the opportunities available to challenging groups. See Hanspeter Kriesi et al., "New

Social Movements and Political Opportunities in Western Europe," *European Journal of Political Research* 22 (1992): 219–44; William A. Gamson and David S. Meyer, "Framing Political Opportunity," in McAdam, McCarthy, and Zald, *Comparative Perspectives;* McAdam, *Political Process,* 40–43; Dominique Wisler and Marco G. Giugni, "Institutional Selectivity and Social Movements," *Sociological Perspectives* 39, no. 1 (1996): 85–109.

31. For a discussion of "federal effects" and the strategic possibilities of federalism, see Scheiber, "Federalism," 97–99, 115–17.

32. Albert Erlebacher, "The Wisconsin Life Insurance Reform of 1907," *Wisconsin Magazine of History* 55, no. 3 (1972): 228; *Milwaukee: A Magazine for Her Business Leaders,* January 1923, 10. For overviews of this problem, see William Graebner, "Federalism in the Progressive Era: A Structural Interpretation of Reform," *Journal of American History* 64, no. 2 (1977): 331–57; Moss, "Kindling a Flame"; David Brian Robertson, "The Bias of American Federalism: The Limits of Welfare-State Development in the Progressive Era," *Journal of Policy History* 1, no. 3 (1989): 261–91; Scheiber, "Federalism"; and Raymond T. Zillner, "State Laws: Survival of the Unfit," *University of Pennsylvania Law Review* 62 (1914): 509–24.

33. Friedman, *History of American Law,* 357.

34. Michael Cohen, James March, and Johan Olsen, "A Garbage Can Model of Organizational Choice," *Administrative Science Quarterly* 17 (March 1972): 1–15; Kingdon, *Agendas.*

35. Elisabeth S. Clemens, "Secondhand Laws: Patterns of Political Learning among State Governments and Interest Groups," paper presented at the annual meeting of the American Political Science Association, San Francisco, 1990. Outcomes in other states or nations function in politics as famous experiments do in science, as "exemplars" that provide practical models for action. Thomas Kuhn, *The Essential Tension: Selected Studies in Scientific Tradition and Change* (Chicago: University of Chicago Press, 1977), 306–7.

36. DiMaggio and Powell, "The Iron Cage Revisited," 151–52.

37. Martin Shefter, "Regional Receptivity to Reform: The Legacy of the Progressive Era," *Political Science Quarterly* 98, no. 3 (1983): 469.

38. Shefter, "Regional Receptivity to Reform," 471. For a comparison of electoral volatility and partisan identification in the West and North, see Paul Kleppner, "Voters and Parties in the Western States, 1876–1900," *Western Historical Quarterly* 14, no. 1 (1983): 49–68.

39. Marcus, *Grand Old Party,* 160, 188. The 1880s were a period of close but relatively stable competition between the two parties; only five states (Connecticut, New York, Indiana, Nevada, and California) shifted party camps more than once. McSeveney, *The Politics of Depression,* 6; Williams, *Democratic Party and California,* chap. 7.

40. Jerome M. Clubb, William H. Flanigan, and Nancy H. Zingale, *Partisan Realignment: Voters, Parties, and Government in American History* (Beverly Hills, Calif.: Sage, 1980), 72; Richard M. Valelly, *Radicalism in the States: The Minnesota Farmer-Labor Party and the American Political Economy* (Chicago:

University of Chicago Press, 1989), 11–16. For a critique of the correlational analysis used by Clubb et al., see Burnham, "Pattern Recognition," 70–72. Burnham argues that the 1890s brought a much clearer electoral realignment.

41. McSeveney, *The Politics of Depression*, 228. For a fine-grained demonstration of how state-level party organization influenced the outcomes of oppositional movements, see Jeffrey Ostler, *Prairie Populism: The Fate of Agrarian Radicalism in Kansas, Nebraska, and Iowa, 1880–1892* (Lawrence: University Press of Kansas, 1993).

42. In his study of California politics, R. Hal Williams argues that the "crisis" of 1896 should not be mistaken for the cause of the decline of the state's Democrats. Describing how Grover Cleveland's actions exacerbated regional tensions within the party and alienated state party leaders during the 1880s and 1890s, Williams contends that the "party was deeply fractured at least two years before 1896, and Bryan's candidacy only formalized a process that had begun as early as 1893. It was Grover Cleveland, not Bryan, who compelled Democrats to commit themselves in the 1890's." *Democratic Party and California*, 203.

43. McSeveney, *The Politics of Depression*, 135; Howard W. Allen and Erik W. Austin, "From the Populist Era to the New Deal: A Study of Partisan Realignment in Washington State, 1889–1950," *Social Science History* 3, no. 2 (1979): 123.

44. The combination of federalism and localized economic power produced "enclave states." Harry Scheiber argues that this effect was the obverse side of the states as laboratories, "celebrated by Justice Brandeis as enclaves where liberal social and governmental experiments could be conducted, whatever the dominant political orientation of the national legislature. "Federalism," 112–13.

45. Kazin, *Barons of Labor*, 44. See also N. D. Houghton, "Arizona's Experience with the Initiative and Referendum," *New Mexico Historical Review* 29, no. 3 (1954): 184–90; Claudius O. Johnson, "The Adoption of the Initiative and Referendum in Washington," *Pacific Northwest Quarterly* 35, no. 4 (1944): 292, 295; Nye, *Midwestern Progressive Politics*, 194.

46. Sanders, "Industrial Concentration,147, 167; see also Elizabeth Sanders, "Farmers and the State in the Progressive Era," in *Changes in the State: Causes and Consequences*, ed. Edward S. Greenberg and Thomas F. Mayer (Newbury Park, Calif.: Sage, 1990), 197–98. Criticizing Sanders's attribution of sectional "interests" on the basis of "an uncertain geographic division of labor," Gerald Berk interprets this episode as a struggle between "constitutive visions" of economic development: one favoring regional development, the other national markets. While the geographical contours of political conflict are consistent with both arguments, Berk's emphasis on the role of "constitutive visions" in shaping enduring institutional configurations is more clearly related to my argument that organizational models provide scripts for collective action. See *Alternative Tracks*, 80.

47. David Knoke, "The Spread of Municipal Reform: Temporal, Spatial, and Social Dynamics," *American Journal of Sociology* 87, no. 6 (1982): 1314–39.

48. Barbara J. Nelson, "The Origins of the Two-Channel Welfare State: Workmen's Compensation and Mothers' Aid," in *Women, the State and Welfare*, ed.

Linda Gordon (Madison: University of Wisconsin Press, 1990); Skocpol, *Protecting Mothers and Soldiers,* chaps. 5 and 8.

49. For women's minimum wage and workmen's compensation, see Brandeis, "Labor Legislation," 502–3, 571–76. The workmen's compensation index excludes three bills that were found unconstitutional (Maryland 1902, Montana 1909, and New York 1910) and the federal legislation of 1908. For mothers' pensions, see Leff, "Consensus for Reform," 401.

50. John D. Buenker, "The Urban Political Machine and Woman Suffrage: A Study in Political Adaptability," *Historian* 33, no. 2 (1971): 265.

51. In a study of state-level party radicalism, Richard Valelly similarly argued that indices of electoral volatility and support for third-party presidential candidates were concentrated in the north central and northwestern states. *Radicalism in the States,* 5–6. But whereas he traced the displacement of major parties by third parties, the central concern of this analysis is with the substitution of extrapartisan methods for party politics.

52. The list includes Nevada and New Mexico, which adopted only the referendum.

53. Thomas W. Gavett, *Development of the Labor Movement in Milwaukee* (Madison: University of Wisconsin Press, 1965); Valelly, *Radicalism in the States.*

54. Robert W. Cherny, *Populism, Progressivism, and the Transformation of Nebraska Politics, 1885–1915* (Lincoln: University of Nebraska Press, 1981); Robert S. Maxwell, *La Follette and the Rise of the Progressives in Wisconsin* (Madison: State Historical Society of Wisconsin, 1956). On the sources of Republican factionalism in the Midwest, see Kleppner, *Who Voted?* 49.

55. Valelly, *Radicalism in the States,* 19.

56. Thelen, *Paths of Resistance,* 207.

57. Thompson, *The "Spider Web,"* 43.

58. Harold Wilensky, *The Welfare State and Equality: Structural and Ideological Roots of Public Expenditures* (Berkeley and Los Angeles: University of California Press, 1975). For critical discussions, see Amenta et al., "Political Origins," 140–41; Quadagno, *Old Age Security,* 3–4.

59. *Abstract of the Thirteenth Census, 1910* (Washington, D.C.: Government Printing Office, 1920), 445. The rank ordering of the states does not change significantly when mining products are added to the value of manufactured products. This measure captures the absolute size of the manufacturing sector, whereas per capita value-added (which is not significant) would reflect the product of manufacturing relative to that of mining and agriculture.

60. The ranking of states reflects the average number of bills passed per session from 1910 to 1920. Most states met every other year. The exceptions were Massachusetts, New York, New Jersey, and Georgia, which met annually, and the Alabama legislature, which met every fourth year.

61. In the growing literatures on state formation and welfare state expansion, some version of economic determinism is frequently used as a foil for more politically oriented arguments. For examples, see Edwin Amenta and Bruce G. Carruthers, "The Formative Years of U.S. Social Spending Policies: Theories of the

Welfare State and the American States during the Great Depression," *American Sociological Review* 53, no. 5 (1988): 661–78; Quadagno, *Old Age Security*, 3–4.

62. The correlation between party strength and the level of legislative activity is consistent with developments in individual states. The legislatures that bracketed the 1910 victory of California's progressive reformers provide a striking contrast in legislative styles. Between the 1909 and 1913 legislatures, the number of bills introduced increased by 45 percent (from 2,705 to 3,922), the introduction of constitutional amendments by 106 percent (from 82 to 169). Over the same period, the number of bills passed by the legislature increased by 23 percent (from 878 to 1,078). CSFL, *Report on Labor Legislation and Labor Record of Senators and Assemblymen, 1913* (San Francisco: CSFL, 1913), 4; Walter V. Woehlke, "Wanted: Law Breakers," *Sunset: The Pacific Monthly*, July 1913,168.

63. Jonathan Bourne Jr. (U.S. senator from Oregon), "Functions of the Initiative, Referendum, and Recall," *Annals of the American Academy of Political and Social Science* 43 (September 1912): 13. Average turnout in the presidential elections of 1912 and 1916 was not significantly related to legislative intensity; what mattered was not the numbers who voted but the ease of access to legislative proceedings—even for a minority of citizens.

64. Wiebe, *Businessmen and Reform*, 101.

65. LeRoy Ashby, *The Spearless Leader: Senator Borah and the Progressive Movement in the 1920s* (Urbana: University of Illinois Press, 1972), chap. 8; Wiebe, *The Search for Order*, 176–80. For an extended discussion of this point, see chapter 7.

66. Virginia Gray, "Innovation in the States: A Diffusion Study," and "Rejoinder to 'Comment' by Jack L. Walker," *American Political Science Review* 67, no. 4 (1973): 1174–85, 1192–93; Edgar C. McVoy, "Patterns of Diffusion in the United States," *American Sociological Review* 5, no. 2 (1940): 219–27; Jack L. Walker, "The Diffusion of Innovations among the American States," *American Political Science Review* 63, no. 3 (1969): 880–99.

67. David Collier and Richard E. Messick, "Prerequisites versus Diffusion: Testing Alternative Explanations of Social Security Adoption," *American Political Science Review* 69, no. 4 (1975): 1299–1315; Knoke, "Spread of Municipal Reform."

68. Benedict Anderson, *Imagined Communities: Reflections on the Origins and Spread of Nationalism* (New York, Verso, 1983), 77–78.

69. Daniel J. Elazar, *American Federalism: A View from the States* (New York: Crowell, 1972).

70. Quoted in G. Thomas Edwards, *Sowing Good Seeds: The Northwest Suffrage Campaigns of Susan B. Anthony* (Portland: Oregon Historical Society Press, 1990), 68. For another example of this financial arrangement, see Scott G. McNall, *The Road to Rebellion: Class Formation and Kansas Populism, 1865–1900* (Chicago: University of Chicago Press, 1988), 232.

71. Charles Simon Barrett, *The Mission, History, and Times of the Farmers' Union* (Nashville, Tenn.: Marshall and Bruce, 1909), 245.

72. Consequently, one would predict that the pattern and intensity of policy

diffusion would vary with the degree to which a particular social group was organized through multiple associations. Despite its internal disagreements, for example, the American Federation of Labor was in a better position to nurture a uniform policy agenda for workers than were the Grange, the Society of Equity, the Farmers' Union, and other agricultural associations that divided farmers along regional lines.

73. Ada J. Davis, "The Evolution of the Institution of Mothers' Pensions in the United States," *American Journal of Sociology* 35, no. 4 (1930): 581.

74. Walker, "Diffusion of Innovations," 894.

75. Organized labor is a partial, and very important, exception to this pattern of federation (see chap. 4).

76. As the Wisconsin State Conference of Social Work noted on holding its convention in the small town of Platteville, until that point it had "failed to see that one section of a state pays for the neglect of another section by submitting to the anti-social votes of its representatives in the legislature." "A Rural Conference," *Survey*, 12 March 1921, 863.

77. William L. O'Neill, *Everyone Was Brave: A History of Feminism in America* (1969; reprint, Chicago: Quadrangle Books, 1971), 18–19.

78. College Equal Suffrage League of Northern California, *Winning Equal Suffrage in California* (National College Equal Suffrage League, 1913), 118.

79. Harriet Hyman Alonso, *The Women's Peace Union and the Outlawry of War, 1921–1942* (Knoxville: University of Tennessee Press, 1989).

80. National American Woman Suffrage Association (NAWSA), *Proceedings of the Annual Convention 1893*, 50.

81. NAWSA, *Proceedings 1893*, 44.

82. NAWSA, *Proceedings 1893*, 45–46.

83. NAWSA, *Proceedings 1894*, 98–99.

84. NAWSA, *Proceedings 1894*, 101, 105.

85. NAWSA, *Proceedings 1894*, 105. In "The Legislative Influence of Unenfranchised Women," published two decades later, Mary R. Beard observed that "in the South, where neither woman suffrage nor campaign states, in the strict sense of the term, exist, congressmen are beginning to find themselves in a dilemma owing to the growing support of the [Bristow-Mondell suffrage] amendment among women of their district and the additional and more potent fact that the women voters of the North are questioning the attitude of the Democratic party toward the amendment." *Annals of the American Academy of Political and Social Science* 56 (November 1914): 56.

86. NAWSA, *Proceedings 1894*, 19.

87. NAWSA, *Proceedings 1894*, 21.

88. NAWSA, *Proceedings 1894*, 149. To this line of argument, Susan B. Anthony replied, "[R]eflex influence from Arkansas or from Louisiana is not the thing we are after. We are after the direct votes" (1894, 52).

89. Annie Diggs. NAWSA, *Proceedings 1894*, 23.

90. NAWSA, *Proceedings 1894*, 48.

91. NAWSA, *Proceedings 1894*, 51.

92. For a discussion of the use of "business methods" by women's organizations, see chapter 6.

93. NAWSA, *Proceedings* 1894, 51.

94. NAWSA, *Proceedings* 1894, 148–49.

95. NAWSA, *Proceedings* 1894, 102. On the first ballot, Washington received 39 votes, Cincinnati 57, and Atlanta 67. Subsequent votes produced a majority for Atlanta, 109–110.

96. Jacqueline Van Voris, *Carrie Chapman Catt: A Public Life* (New York: Feminist Press at the City University of New York, 1987).

97. NAWSA, *Proceedings* 1894, 24–25.

98. NAWSA, *Proceedings* 1895, 104, 1894, 32; Van Voris, *Carrie Chapman Catt,* 33–34.

99. CSFL, *Proceedings* 1906, 84

100. Note that the AFL leadership targeted its most powerful enemies rather than concentrating resources in districts were the opportunities for labor victories were greatest. Julia Greene, "'The Strike at the Ballot Box': The American Federation of Labor's Entrance into Election Politics, 1906–1909," *Labor History* 32, no. 2 (1991): 165–91; Stephen J. Scheinberg, "Theodore Roosevelt and the A. F. of L.'s Entry into Politics, 1906–1908," *Labor History* 3, no. 2 (1962): 131–37.

101. Grace Heilman Stimson, *Rise of the Labor Movement in Los Angeles* (Berkeley and Los Angeles: University of California Press, 1955), 364; American Federation of Labor, *Financial Report of the McNamara Defense Fund: Being a True Account of All Moneys Received and Expended* (Washington, D.C.: American Federation of Labor, 1912).

102. Paula Giddings, *When and Where I Enter: The Impact of Black Women on Race and Sex in America* (New York: Bantam, 1984), 82.

103. Giddings, *Where and When,* 82. See also McAdam, *Political Process,* 66–73; McDonagh, "Welfare Rights State"; and Jacqueline A. Rouse, "Atlanta's African-American Women's Attack on Segregation, 1900–1920," in *Gender, Class, Race, and Reform in the Progressive Era,* ed. Noralee Frankel and Nancy S. Dye (Lexington: University of Kentucky Press, 1991); Saxton, *Rise and Fall,* chap. 13.

104. Leon Fink, *Workingmen's Democracy: The Knights of Labor and American Politics* (Urbana: University of Illinois Press, 1983); Voss, *Making of American Exceptionalism.*

105. CSG, *Proceedings* 1889, 173.

106. Hattam, *Labor Visions,* chap. 3; Sean Wilentz, *Chants Democratic: New York City and the Rise of the American Working Class, 1788–1850* (New York: Oxford University Press, 1984).

107. Grant McConnell, *The Decline of Agrarian Democracy* (Berkeley and Los Angeles: University of California Press, 1953), chap. 1; Michael Kazin, *The Populist Persuasion: An American History* (New York: Basic Books, 1995), chaps. 1 and 2.

108. American Federation of Labor, *St. Louis Exposition, Catalogue of Exhibits* (Washington, D.C.: American Federation of Labor, 1904), 7; Tontz, "Member-

ships," 145. The potential political leverage of farm organizations was magnified by the comparatively low total population in agricultural states. In addition to the so-called general farm organizations, farmers joined cooperatives and commodity organizations; see Louis Bernard Schmidt, "The Role and Techniques of Agrarian Pressure Groups," *Agricultural History* 30, no. 2 (1956): 49. Resembling corporate lobbies, these groups did not pose the same challenge to the party system as did general farm organizations, which enrolled farmers as a constituency of voting citizens.

109. Wood, *History,* 131, 154; Bordin, *Woman and Temperance,* 3–4.

110. Linda K. Kerber, *Women of the Republic: Intellect and Ideology in Revolutionary America* (Chapel Hill: University of North Carolina Press, 1980); Aileen Kraditor, *The Ideas of the Woman Suffrage Movement, 1899–1929* (Garden City, N.Y.: Anchor/Doubleday, 1971).

111. Amy Bridges notes that legislative districting at both state and national levels tended to intensify the minority status of a largely urban population of industrial wage workers, while giving disproportionate political weight to rural areas. "Becoming American: The Working Classes in the United States before the Civil War," in *Working-Class Formation: Nineteenth-Century Patterns in Western Europe and the United States,* ed. Ira Katznelson and Aristide Zolberg (Princeton, N.J.: Princeton University Press, 1986), 160–61.

112. These should not be understood as comparative case studies, since states were not independent units but were embedded in broader networks of policy diffusion and political organization. Instead, the examination of three challengers in three states represents a triangulated approach to the transformation of organizational repertoires and political institutions that were not restricted to particular geographical units.

113. U.S. Bureau of the Census, *Statistical Abstract: 1910* (Washington, D.C.: Government Printing Office, 1920), 445.

114. When urban is defined as communities of 2,500 or more, the percentage of population living in cities in the entire United States in 1900 was 40.2 percent; for California, 52.4 percent; for Washington, 40.8 percent; for Wisconsin, 38.2 percent. If one uses a standard of 25,000 or more, the percentage of the population living in urban areas was 25.9 percent for the United States; 36.5 percent for California; 30 percent for Washington; and 19.5 percent for Wisconsin (U.S. Census 1900, 37).

115. Brandeis, "Labor Legislation," 579, 590.

116. Harriet Ann Crawford, *The Washington State Grange, 1889–1924: A Romance of Democracy* (Portland, Ore.: Binfords and Mort, 1940), 173.

Chapter Four

1. Ozanne, *Labor Movement in Wisconsin,* 20, 26.

2. Skocpol, *Protecting Soldiers and Mothers,* 211.

3. WiSFL, *Proceedings* 1907, 59.

4. Gary Marks, *Unions in Politics: Britain, Germany, and the United States in*

the Nineteenth and Early Twentieth Centuries (Princeton, N.J.: Princeton University Press, 1989), 11.

5. Wilentz, *Chants Democratic*.

6. Many immigrants could vote simply by declaring their intention to become a citizen. John Higham, *Strangers in the Land: Patterns of American Nativism, 1860–1925,* 2d ed. (New Brunswick, N.J.: Rutgers University Press, 1988), 97–98; Gwendolyn Mink, *Old Labor and New Immigrants in American Political Development: Union, Party, and State, 1875–1920* (Ithaca, N.Y.: Cornell University Press, 1986), 137.

7. On "western traditions of inclusive unionism," see Cobble, *Dishing It Out,* 72. Recent case studies of western cities document both the willingness and frequent ability of strong city centrals and building trades councils to enforce quasi-industrial coalitions among craft locals in defiance of the international unions' requirement of craft autonomy. See Brundage, *Western Labor Radicalism,* 139–49; Frank, *Purchasing Power,* chap. 1; Robert L. Friedheim, *The Seattle General Strike* (Seattle: University of Washington Press, 1964), 48–49; and Kazin, *Barons of Labor.*

8. Chandler, *The Visible Hand;* Christopher L. Tomlins, *The State and the Unions: Labor Relations, Law, and the Organized Labor Movement in America, 1880–1960* (New York: Cambridge University Press, 1985), 28.

9. Nationally, labor history after the 1890s has been ordered around three organizational options: the business unionism of the AFL, socialism, and the revolutionary syndicalism of the Industrial Workers of the World. Sean Wilentz, "Against Exceptionalism: Class Consciousness and the American Labor Movement, 1790–1920," *International Labor and Working Class History* 26 (fall 1984): 15. However these tendencies were less clearly opposed to one another in many western cities and states where labor activists often cooperated across ideological divisions, frequently inviting censure from the AFL leadership.

10. In California, organized labor was widely credited with the adoption of the Australian ballot in the 1890s. Franklin Hichborn, *Story of the Session of the California Legislature of 1911* (San Francisco: Press of the James H. Barry Co., 1911), 85–86.

11. WiSFL, *Official Directory* 1896–97, 17.

12. Fink, *Workingmen's Democracy;* Montgomery, *Fall,* 352.

13. WiSFL, *Proceedings* 1909, 41–42.

14. This fact has been used to explain the "exceptionalism" of the American case, its lack of either a labor party or an independent bureaucracy. Marks, *Unions in Politics,* 221–22. In Europe, by comparison, working-class struggles for extensions of the franchise forged labor parties, while the absence of universal suffrage limited the use of state bureaucracies as a source of party patronage. Bendix, *Nation-Building and Citizenship,* 96–105. Kim Voss, however, traces the emergence of American exceptionalism to the second half of the nineteenth century and labor's contrasting experiences of organizational defeat and state intervention in support of employers. *Making of American Exceptionalism.*

15. Marc Karson, *American Labor Unions and Politics, 1900–1918* (Carbondale: Southern Illinois University Press, 1958), 3.

16. The Knights did, however, develop a legislative lobbying strategy at the national and state level and "had some success in having state conventions of the political parties incorporate demands of the Knights in their platform." Fink, *Workingmen's Democracy*, 24; Karson, *American Labor Unions*, 15.

17. Karson, *American Labor Unions*,13–19. On labor's interpretations of its defeats, see Kim Voss, "The Collapse of a Social Movement: The Interplay of Mobilizing Structures, Framing, and Political Opportunities in the Knights of Labor," in McAdam, McCarthy, and Zald, *Comparative Perspectives*.

18. Marks, *Unions in Politics*, 224–25, emphasis added; Michael Paul Rogin, "Voluntarism: The Political Functions of an Antipolitical Doctrine," *Industrial and Labor Relations Review* 15, no. 4 (1962): 521–35.

19. McGerr, *Decline of Popular Politics*; Erie, *Rainbow's End*, 25–66; Mink, *Old Labor*, 49; Martin Shefter, "Trade Unions and Political Machines: The Organization and Disorganization of the American Working Class in the Late Nineteenth Century," in Katznelson and Zolberg, *Working-Class Formation*; Wilentz, *Chants Democratic*, 71–74.

20. Montgomery, *Fall*, 287. This concern led the WiSFL to adopt an organizational structure similar to that of the Milwaukee FTC. As of 1895, the position of state president was replaced by that of state organizer. The organizer was chosen, and held responsible, by an executive board. In this way, it was hoped that the power of the organization would be protected from capture by ambitious individuals. WiSFL, *Official Directory* 1896–97, 11; Ozanne, *Labor Movement in Wisconsin*, 36–39.

21. CSFL, *Proceedings* 1904, 17; 1906, 20–21, 31–35, 38–41. These debates coincided with the rise and fall of the Union Labor Party machine in San Francisco. For leaders of the WiSFL, this episode captured the folly of the AFL's policy of supporting friends of labor within anything other than a pure labor party. This policy had elected "the musical mayor of San Francisco, but yet out of harmony with the interests of the wage-working class." WiSFL, *Proceedings* 1907, 24.

22. WiSFL, *Proceedings* 1913, 98.

23. Skowronek, *Building New American State*, 39; on businessmen's suspicion of party politics, see Yearley, *The Money Machines*, 130–33.

24. This resolution went on to call for the introduction of proportional representation as a method for securing the political representation of the working people. CSFL, *Proceedings* 1902, 70.

25. WiSFL, *Proceedings* 1908, 45.

26. H. Roger Grant, *Self-Help in the 1890s Depression* (Ames: Iowa State University Press, 1983), 113; Ralph Edwards Shaffer, "Radicalism in California, 1869–1929," Ph.D. diss., University of California at Berkeley, 1962, chap. 3; Carlos A. Schwantes, *Radical Heritage: Labor, Socialism, and Reform in Washington and British Columbia, 1885–1917* (Seattle: University of Washington Press, 1979), 87–89.

27. "Cooperation" was an important point of contact between agrarian and labor associations. When farmers struggled to control their own production, they turned to workers as a sympathetic market. See, for example, CSG, *Proceedings* 1899, 99; Crawford, *Washington State Grange;* Philip Taft, *Labor Politics American Style: The California State Federation of Labor* (Cambridge, Mass.: Harvard University Press, 1968), 52; WaSFL, *Proceedings* 1917, 58, 70. Among women, cooperation also served as a basis for alliances as various "Women's Industrial Exchanges" helped to bridge class barriers.

28. Kazin, *Barons of Labor,* 47–50.

29. Frank, *Purchasing Power,* chap. 2; Perry and Perry, *Los Angeles Labor,* 202–3.

30. WaSFL, *Proceedings* 1916, 75–76.

31. CSFL, *Proceedings* 1904, 23.

32. In commenting on their allies in rural areas, Wisconsin unionists were explicit about the need to educate the farmers: "Once we are able to get the American farmer educated to the real meaning of the union label, get him to demanding it upon all the things he buys, we shall have done a work that will thoroughly organize more trades, build more union factories, and do more for labor's general upbuilding than has any previous thing we have accomplished. And I need not tell you the possibilities within our grasp when the time shall have arrived in which the workers of field and factory shall vote as a unit." WiSFL, *Proceedings* 1908, 37, 79–80; 1910, 27. In this view of political process, cooperation leads to coalition rather than simply building upon it.

33. Recognized as a potential threat to the craft-based organization of the labor movement, this resolution was superseded by a blander recommendation that unionists study cooperation. CSFL, *Proceedings* 1905, 15–16, 37–38.

34. Frank, *Purchasing Power,* 41, 50. Plans for similar cooperatives linking the Milwaukee Federated Trades Council and the Wisconsin Society of Equity were put forward in 1908 and 1920. Nothing materialized from the first attempt, but in 1921 a cooperative store was opened in Milwaukee. Gavett, *Labor Movement in Milwaukee,* 116, 143.

35. Members of the Card and Label League in postwar Seattle "worked on behalf of Tom Mooney, for the release of political prisoners, against capital punishment, and for the reduction of judges' salaries" as well as pressuring the state legislature for women's protective labor legislation and the WaSFL for the appointment of a woman organizer. Frank, *Purchasing Power,* 122–24. In their support for legislative remedies and alliances with government agencies, working-class women often resembled more privileged women to a greater extent than they did male trade unionists. See chapter 6 and Cobble, *Dishing It Out,* 80–85.

36. Marks, *Unions in Politics,* 5.

37. Montgomery, *Fall,* 5.

38. Fink, *Workingmen's Democracy,* 122; Tomlins, *State and Unions,* 41.

39. Tomlins, *State and Unions,* 68–69.

40. Kazin, *Barons of Labor,* 100; Schwantes, *Radical Heritage,* 138. For an excellent description of the relations among the AFL, the national unions, and

the city and state federations, see Ulman, *Rise*, 378–422. Philip Taft paints a more benign picture of the relation between the international unions and local politics, arguing that "like the AFL, the international unions normally followed a 'hands-off' policy in political matters." This assessment underestimates the structural disadvantages imposed on state and local bodies by the AFL constitution. Furthermore, the state-national conflicts suggest that the limits of a hands-off policy were quite narrow from the perspective of some state federations. *Organized Labor in American History* (New York: Harper and Row, 1964), 237.

41. "The Convention of the American Federation of Labor," *Survey*, 15 July 1919, 516.

42. WiSFL, *Proceedings 1923*, 59.

43. Perry and Perry, *Los Angeles Labor*, 116–20, 201–2.

44. Friedheim, *The Seattle General Strike*, 48–49; Stimson, *Rise of Labor Movement*, 199, 276; CSFL, *Proceedings 1907*, 36.

45. On the cultivation of a "movement culture" within the Denver labor movement, see Brundage, *Western Labor Radicalism*, chaps. 2–3; on Seattle, see Frank, *Purchasing Power*, chap. 2. On labor temples and union halls, see Frank, *Purchasing Power*, 70–71; Kazin, *Barons of Labor*, 101–2; Perry and Perry, *Los Angeles Labor*, 49–50, 111–16.

46. Fink, *Workingmen's Democracy*, 33.

47. Fink, *Workingmen's Democracy*, 185–98.

48. "Trouble in the Coal Mines, 1889: Documents of an Incident at Newcastle, W.T.," *Pacific Northwest Quarterly* 37, no. 3 (1946): 231–32.

49. David Burke Griffiths, "Populism in the Far West, 1890–1900," Ph.D. diss., University of Washington, 1967, 153–55.

50. Lucile Eaves, *A History of California Labor Legislation, with an Introductory Sketch of the San Francisco Labor Movement*, University of California Publications in Economics, 2 (Berkeley: University of California, 1910), 77.

51. The role of state repression and, especially, court injunctions in politicizing the labor movement has been established in numerous studies. See Eaves, *California Labor Legislation*, 394–438; Marks, *Unions in Politics*, 51–75; Mink, *Old Labor*, 35–36.

52. Although studies of American political development have paid increasing attention to the activities of the state federations, these organizations have been comparatively ignored in labor history. As Philip Taft argued at the opening of his study of the California State Federation of Labor, "The failure of European and American writers to recognize the significance of the state federation of labor as a political institution is perhaps the chief reason for their inability to understand American labor's political behavior." *Labor Politics American Style*, 5; for recent work that acknowledges the significance of state federations, see Amenta et al., "Political Origins"; Ann Shola Orloff, "The Political Origins of America's Belated Welfare State," in *The Politics of Social Policy in the United States*, ed. Margaret Weir, Ann Shola Orloff, and Theda Skocpol (Princeton, N.J.: Princeton University Press, 1988), 55–56.

53. The Wisconsin State Federation dates from 1893, the California Federa-

tion from 1901, and the Washington State Federation of Labor from 1902. These dates refer to the founding of federations affiliated with the AFL. In some cases, there had been earlier state-level labor organizations.

54. CSFL, *Proceedings* 1901, 3.

55. Karen Orren, "Organized Labor and the Invention of Modern Liberalism in the United States," *Studies in American Political Development* 2 (1987): 317–36.

56. Montgomery, *Fall,* 172–73.

57. Scheinberg, "Theodore Roosevelt," 131–37.

58. Gary M. Fink, *Labor's Search for Political Order: The Political Behavior of the Missouri Labor Movement, 1890–1940* (Columbia: University of Missouri Press, 1973), 14; Tripp, "Progressive Labor Laws," 15; CSFL, *Proceedings* 1902, 11.

59. These alliances were a major source of controversy within both the Milwaukee Federated Trades Council and the Wisconsin State Federation of Labor. These controversies, in turn, help to explain the rather low level of union participation in the state as a whole and, especially, the disproportionately low levels outside of Milwaukee, where loyalty to the Republican and Democratic Parties was a much more significant factor.

60. Quoted in Gavett, *Labor Movement in Milwaukee,* 95–96.

61. Marvin Wachman, *History of the Social-Democratic Party of Milwaukee, 1897–1910* (Urbana: University of Illinois Press, 1945), 21–22; Roderick Nash, "Victor L. Berger: Making Marx Respectable," *Wisconsin Magazine of History* 47, no. 4 (1964): 301–8.

62. Wachman, *Social-Democratic Party,* 16.

63. Quoted in Ozanne, *Labor Movement in Wisconsin,* 37–38.

64. Ozanne, *Labor Movement in Wisconsin,* 38.

65. David P. Thelen, *The New Citizenship: Origins of Progressivism in Wisconsin, 1885–1900* (Columbia: University of Missouri Press, 1972), 150–52; Wachman, *Social-Democratic Party,* 46–48.

66. In 1906, a group of reform-minded businessmen formed a Voters' League to contest the April elections on a nonpartisan basis. Despite the League's endorsement of some Social Democratic candidates, the party remained aloof from this new nonpartisan organization. Wachman, *Social-Democratic Party,* 57.

67. Wachman, *Social-Democratic Party,* 70.

68. Nash, "Victor L. Berger," 303. The strength of labor within the state was also reflected in the strong labor stance taken by Wisconsin Republicans within the national party. See Scheinberg, "Theodore Roosevelt," 145.

69. WiSFL, *Proceedings* 1907, 7; 1909, 47–48; see also 1908, 25; 1913, 7.

70. Frederick I. Olson, "The Socialist Party and the Union in Milwaukee, 1900–1912," *Wisconsin Magazine of History* 44, no. 2 (1960–61): 12. The WiSFL also supported higher pay for state legislators. *Proceedings* 1913, 107.

71. WiSFL, *Proceedings* 1908, 38; 1907, 24. The reliance of farmers' organizations on the "good man policy" was identified as an obstacle to effective political cooperation with labor. WiSFL, *Proceedings* 1909, 36, 42; 1907, 59.

72. WiSFL, *Proceedings* 1911, 30.

73. Schmidt, "History of Labor Legislation," 30. Other labor-related proposals introduced by the WiSFL included "abolition of child labor (1893), enactment of safety and sanitation laws in mills, mines, and railways (1893), the eight-hour day (1893), worker compensation (1894), government work relief for the unemployed (1894), wages in cash (1896), and abolition of the company store (1896)." Ozanne, *Labor Movement in Wisconsin*, 123.

74. WiSFL, *Proceedings* 1910, 39. The WiSFL pursued this strategy during campaigns and sought to allow more unionists to serve both by supporting an amendment to raise legislators' salaries from "$500 per term to $600 per annum" (the legislature met regularly every other year) and by providing a subsidy "not to exceed $125 per month, for each month that the Legislature shall be in session in excess of five months" to union members elected to the legislature. WiSFL, *Proceedings* 1913, 107; 1915, 95.

75. WiSFL, *Proceedings* 1912, 82.

76. WiSFL, *Proceedings* 1915, 96.

77. WiSFL, *Proceedings* 1913, 129–32; 1914, 144–48.

78. Ozanne, *Labor Movement in Wisconsin*, 124. In California, the Socialist Party also refused to cooperate with "progressive" legislators. But with only two Socialists elected to the 1915 session, this was little more than a gesture of principle. Shaffer, "Radicalism in California," 189.

79. WiSFL, *Proceedings* 1913, 130–32; Gertrude Schmidt, "History of Labor Legislation," 31–32, 407–8.

80. Quoted in Eaves, *California Labor Legislation*, 30.

81. Spencer C. Olin Jr., *California Politics, 1846–1920: The Emerging Corporate State* (San Francisco: Boyd and Fraser, 1981), 38; Eaves, *California Labor Legislation*, 38; Alexander Saxton, *The Indispensable Enemy: Labor and the Anti-Chinese Movement in California* (Berkeley and Los Angeles: University of California Press, 1971), 127–32; Williams, *Democratic Party and California*, 15–17.

82. WiSFL, *Proceedings* 1907, 59.

83. Saxton, *The Indispensable Enemy*, 140–51.

84. This controversy was revived with the election of the leader of the San Francisco Building Trades Council, Patrick H. McCarthy, as mayor in 1909. Although McCarthy pursued a course similar to the Milwaukee Social Democrats—seeking to broaden his electoral base by supporting public ownership of utilities and antivice campaigns—his 1911 reelection effort was defeated by a fusion organization of Republicans and Democrats in the city's first nonpartisan election. Kazin, *Barons of Labor*, 185–202. The growing political strength of the Socialists in Los Angeles seems to have been less troubling to the state's labor leadership. This tolerance was not limited to California; even Samuel Gompers urged unionists to elect the Socialist candidate, Job Harriman, as mayor of Los Angeles in 1911, a campaign derailed when labor activists from the Midwest confessed to the 1910 bombing of the *Los Angeles Times,* owned by labor's enemy, Harrison Gray Otis. Stimson, *Rise of Labor Movement,* 346–99.

85. The Washington State Labor Congress was reorganized as the Washington State Federation of Labor and affiliated with the AFL in 1902. Philip Taft has argued that the immediate incentive for founding the CSFL was the threat posed by the Western Federation of Miners' efforts to establish the Western Labor Union, a regional labor movement outside the AFL. *Labor Politics American Style,* 17–18. In 1901, the San Francisco Building Trades Council sponsored a parallel effort at statewide organization. The California State Building Trades Council attempted to extend San Francisco's centralized control over construction sites to other cities but met with relatively little success. Kazin, *Barons of Labor,* 106–7.

86. CSFL, *Proceedings* 1902, 9; 1904, 56. There were limits, however, to this enthusiasm for reform. A 1904 resolution requiring that "any delegate found guilty of lobbying or caucusing, or trading his vote or the votes of constituents" forfeit his seat and "be dishonorably retired" from the convention was tabled. CSFL, *Proceedings* 1904, 56.

87. CSFL, *Proceedings* 1904, 17, 27–28; 1905, 17; 1906, 17, 20–24, 32–33, 38–39, 46, 51.

88. CSFL, *Proceedings* 1907, 65.

89. CSFL, *Proceedings* 1904, 20.

90. CSFL, *Proceedings* 1906, 26–27.

91. CSFL, *Proceedings* 1907, 65.

92. CSFL, *Proceedings* 1901, 9, 45; 1902, 37–40; 1904, 19, 58; 1907, 17–21; 1908, 44. By the 1920s, similar resolutions appeared more frequently in the WiSFL *Proceedings.*

93. In adopting a model of political action associated with corporations, however, unionists sought to avoid any taint of corruption. Instructions to the legislative agent were frequently accompanied by demands for propriety: for example, a request that "our representative to the State Legislature endeavor by every honorable means to ask for the favorable consideration of the legislative matters placed in the hands of this convention." CSFL, *Proceedings* 1907, 42; 1910, 8.

94. CSFL, *Proceedings* 1904, 70.

95. CSFL, *Proceedings* 1906, 92; 1907, 79.

96. CSFL, *Proceedings* 1907, 79; 1908, 11, 56; 1910, 8, 27; 1911, 92; 1916, 42; CSFL, *Report on Labor Legislation* 1911, 3–4; 1913, 5; Taft, *Labor Politics American Style,* 24, 41–42; Mary Ann Mason, "Neither Friends Nor Foes: Organized Labor and the California Progressives," in *California Progressivism Revisited,* ed. William Deverell and Tom Sitton (Berkeley and Los Angeles: University of California Press, 1994), 64; see also Mary Ann Mason Burki, "The California Progressives: Labor's Point of View," *Labor History* 17, no. 1 (1976): 26–31.

97. Hansen, *Gaining Access,* 11–22.

98. CSFL, *Proceedings* 1904, 70–71.

99. CSFL, *Proceedings* 1908, 55.

100. CSFL, *Proceedings* 1908, 33, 94–97.

101. Burki, "The California Progressives," 27.

102. CSFL, *Proceedings* 1915, 38–39.

103. CSFL, *Proceedings* 1914, 75–77.

104. CSFL, *Proceedings* 1904, 20, 43, 48; 1906, 30; 1907, 21; 1908, 28; 1910, 28; 1911, 39; 1914, 73. The "divided session" was one of the more interesting procedural reforms in California. The thirty-day recess in the middle of the legislative session was intended to "give the people of the State an opportunity to examine the measures that will be acted upon the Legislature and enable the members of that body to obtain the opinion and instructions of their constituencies." The CSFL supported the measure, noting that it would also be helpful to its own legislative agent. CSFL, *Proceedings* 1911, 27; CSFL, *Report on Labor Legislation* 1913, 3–4.

105. WiSFL, *Proceedings* 1907, 24.

106. Earl C. Crockett, "The History of California Labor Legislation, 1910–1930," Ph.D. diss., University of California at Berkeley, 1931.

107. Michael Paul Rogin, "Progressivism and the California Electorate," *Journal of American History* 55, no. 2 (1968): 313. See also Rogin and John L. Shover, *Political Change in California: Critical Elections and Social Movements, 1890–1966* (Westport, Conn.: Greenwood Press, 1970), chaps. 2 and 3. It should be noted, however, that Johnson's competition in 1914 was an antilabor Republican from Los Angeles. On labor's role in these legislative accomplishments, see Mason, "Neither Friends Nor Foes," 60; Burki, "The California Progressives," 26. See also Gerald D. Nash, "The Influence of Labor on State Policy, 1860–1920: The Experience of California," *California Historical Society Quarterly* 42, no. 3 (1963): 241–57.

108. This interpretation is consistent with the "polity-centered" model developed by Theda Skocpol to explain the politics of social policy during the late nineteenth and early twentieth centuries but draws particular attention to the cultural and organizational conditions that support an interest-based feedback cycle. *Protecting Soldiers and Mothers,* 41–60.

109. Paul Scharrenberg, "Reminiscences," taped interview, Bancroft Library, University of California, Berkeley, 1955. Quoted in Burki, "The California Progressives," 31.

110. CSFL, *Proceedings* 1915, 40. As in Wisconsin, regulations were formulated by inviting representatives of both employees and employers to participate in the formulation of the general rules that would govern the administration of workmen's compensation and the associated "Safety First" program. CSFL, *Proceedings* 1915, 80–81. But in California, this appears to be an isolated instance of cooperation between the state federation of labor and labor agencies in the state government. The convention proceedings rarely publicized the work of state agencies or reported on the number of violations of labor laws.

111. CSFL, *Proceedings* 1911, 28, 45–47.

112. CSFL, *Proceedings* 1915, 40; emphasis added.

113. Robert J. Pitchell, "The Electoral System and Voting Behavior: The Case of California's Cross-Filing," *Western Political Quarterly* 12, no. 2 (1959): 461.

114. CSFL, *Proceedings* 1916, 82.

115. Russell M. Posner, "The Progressive Voters League, 1923–26," *California Historical Society Quarterly* 36, no. 3 (1957): 251–61.

116. Labor was often less enthusiastic about civil-service reform. California unionists dismissed civil service as a "closed shop for college graduates." CSFL, *Proceedings* 1915, 80. Wisconsin unionists, however, were urged to take advantage of the new system, and their "greater knowledge of conditions in shops and factories," by taking "the civil service examination that will enable them to get appointments as state factory inspectors." WiSFL, *Proceedings* 1913, 129.

117. Labor differed with most middle-class reformers, however, in its support of judicial recall and other controls on the courts: "The decisions of our judges actually endanger our American institutions, because they serve to generate among the people, a suspicion, as to whether we are ceasing to be a government by the people and gradually developing into a government by judges." WiSFL, *Proceedings* 1911, 21. California progressives were deeply divided over this issue. But in the middle of the 1911 legislative session, the state supreme court granted a rehearing to Abe Ruef, the Union Labor boss of San Francisco, and even some conservative progressives came to support judicial recall (Hichborn, *California Legislature of 1911*, 102–22). Governor Hiram Johnson, however, did apparently engineer the defeat of an anti-injunction bill favored by the state's labor federation. Burki, "The California Progressives," 33–34.

118. CSFL, *Proceedings* 1913, 70.

119. CSFL, *Proceedings* 1904, 56; 1906, 51; WaSFL, *Proceedings* 1915, 5, 117. The WiSFL, whose leaders adopted a third-party model, repeatedly called for the introduction of the referendum for the election of officers in the AFL but continued to govern itself by more conventional methods. WiSFL, *Proceedings* 1912, 99.

120. In 1908, the Milwaukee Social Democrats endorsed the initiative, referendum, and recall, along with home rule for cities, as part of their effort to build a broader reform coalition. Schmidt, "History of Labor Legislation," 23. The WiSFL endorsed direct legislation in its platform, first calling for the referendum only and later expanding its demands to include the initiative and recall. WiSFL, *Proceedings* 1906, 4; 1909, 46; 1910, 6, 24. Yet the WiSFL expressed skepticism over a proposal to elect AFL officers by referendum rather than the "convention system"; an amendment to the state constitution providing for initiative, referendum, and recall was submitted to the voters for ratification in 1914 but was not approved, so that the model of extrapartisan direct democracy was far less salient in Wisconsin than in either California or Washington. WiSFL, *Proceedings* 1913, 16; 1914, 30.

121. WiSFL, *Proceedings* 1910, 24.

122. Lowrie, "Wisconsin Plan," 186–87; Chester C. Platt, *What La Follette's State Is Doing: Some Battles Waged for More Freedom* (Batavia, N.Y.: Batavia Times Press, 1924), 74.

123. WiSFL, *Proceedings* 1910, 75; 1911, 29.

124. CSFL, *Report on Labor Legislation* 1915, 6. In the end, however, the

CSFL did not support its progressive faction's endorsement of thoroughly nonpartisan state elections.

125. The latter was strengthened by the prominence of large, geographically isolated workplaces in the mining and lumber industries. Schwantes, *Radical Heritage*, 20.

126. Quoted in Robert Donald Saltvig, "The Progressive Movement in Washington," Ph.D. diss., University of Washington, 1966, 7.

127. Saltvig, "Progressive Movement in Washington," 18; Schwantes, *Radical Heritage*, 50.

128. The agricultural movements born in the South and Midwest provided an organizational model complete with national affiliations—the People's Party—that was captured by organized labor in the state of Washington. Populism was also "captured" by urban reformers and labor in California (see Shaffer, "Radicalism in California," chaps. 3 and 4). This model of diffusion and capture must be modified, however, by acknowledging that "people's parties" had been formed as indigenous vehicles for reform coalitions in the previous decade.

129. Quoted in Tripp, "Progressive Labor Laws," 12–13.

130. This was an isolated instance of state-building. As the Labor Commissioner noted in his second report, "This State has no board of agriculture, bureau of mines, railway commission or board of commerce." *Report of the Labor Commissioner of the State of Washington, 1899–1900* (1901), 5.

131. State of Washington, Bureau of Labor, *Report of the Bureau of Labor of the State of Washington, 1897–98* 1899, 77–79; *Report . . . 1899–1900* 1901, 13–16; *Report . . . 1901–1902* 1903, 85–109, 317–18; *Report . . . 1903–1904* 1905, 135–57, 164–72, 295–99; *Report . . . 1905–1906,* 1907, 11–24, 87–105; *Report . . . 1907–1908,* 1909, 11–21, 109–42.

132. State of Washington, Bureau of Labor, *Report, 1901–1902* 1903, 21–24, 109; *Report, 1903–1904* 1905, 20–23; *Report, 1914–1915* 1916, 100.

133. During this period, the Washington Bureau of Labor foreshadowed the role played by the Wisconsin Industrial Commission as a promoter of new labor legislation within the executive branch.

134. Saltvig, "Progressive Movement in Washington," 19; Schwantes, *Radical Heritage,* 135.

135. Schwantes, *Radical Heritage,* 136.

136. Schwantes, *Radical Heritage,* 156.

137. Saltvig, "Progressive Movement in Washington," 404; Schwantes, *Radical Heritage,* 160.

138. WaSFL, *Proceedings* 1913, 34.

139. Saltvig, "Progressive Movement in Washington," 409.

140. Schwantes, *Radical Heritage,* 160. In Washington, the organization of a politicized farmer-labor alliance would eventually produce schisms within the ranks of both as agriculturalists and workers favoring more conservative forms split from the progressives.

141. State of Washington, Bureau of Labor, *Report, 1903–1904* 1905, 21–22; WaSFL, *Proceedings* 1915, 5, 117.

142. C. B. Galbreath, "Provisions for State-Wide Initiative and Referendum," *Annals of the American Academy of Political and Social Science* 43 (September 1912): 86.

143. WaSFL, *Proceedings* 1913, 38, 76, 78, 82.

144. WaSFL, *Proceedings* 1913, 76; 1916, 87.

145. WaSFL, *Proceedings* 1913, 37.

146. WaSFL, *Proceedings* 1913, 62; see also Tripp, "Progressive Labor Laws," 14.

147. WaSFL, *Proceedings* 1913, 27–28, 46; 1915, 120; 1916, 23, 29, 69.

148. WaSFL, *Proceedings* 1916, 65.

149. WaSFL, *Proceedings* 1915, 16–17, 40, 61, 67, 69.

150. WaSFL, *Proceedings* 1915, 58.

151. WaSFL, *Proceedings* 1916, 26–27, 82, 94–100.

152. WaSFL, *Proceedings* 1915, 7, 123; see also 1916, 57.

153. WaSFL, *Proceedings* 1916, 146–47.

154. WaSFL, *Proceedings* 1916, 138–39.

155. The central labor councils and building-trades councils of Owens's district in Contra Costa and Marin Counties did succeed in calling a recall election, but Owens was reelected. CSFL, *Proceedings* 1913, 32–33, 70, 91; 1914, 78.

156. WaSFL, *Proceedings* 1913, 37.

157. CSFL, *Proceedings* 1910, 46.

158. CSFL, *Report on Labor Legislation* 1915, 5–6, 15; 1921, 7.

159. WiSFL, *Proceedings* 1912, 20.

160. WiSFL, *Proceedings* 1912, 25.

161. By 1896, however, Washington's Populists had dropped many of their demands for labor legislation as part of their successful effort to attract an electoral majority. Schwantes, *Radical Heritage,* 60–66.

162. WaSFL, *Proceedings* 1915, 58.

163. Gavett, *Labor Movement in Milwaukee;* WiSFL, *Proceedings* 1905, 36; 1906, 18, 24, 61; CSFL, *Proceedings* 1906, 24–25.

164. John C. Sullivan and Harry B. Waters (president and secretary-treasurer, Colorado State Federation of Labor) to CSFL, October 26, 1903. Reprinted in CSFL, *Proceedings* 1904, 34. From its founding in 1895, the Colorado federation had been strongly sympathetic to industrial unionism and, in 1897, refused to join the AFL, citing the "unnecessary expense." Brundage, *Western Labor Radicalism,* 122.

165. CSFL, *Proceedings* 1915, 78. California's conflicts with the AFL resembled Wisconsin's on a second point: their maintenance of "a friendly working relationship with the Socialists" and, before the 1920s, of a "sympathetic" attitude toward the IWW and other labor radicals. See Burki, "The California Progressives," 27.

166. Quoted in Friedheim, *The Seattle General Strike,* 26–27. Seattle was only one of a number of such examples throughout the state. The Spokane Trades Council was not initially affiliated with either the AFL or the Western Labor Union but was closely tied to both the Knights and the Populists during the 1890s,

until the AFL actively campaigned for dominance during the early 1900s. Schwantes, *Radical Heritage*, 118–21, 137–40.

167. Friedheim, *The Seattle General Strike*, 36. See also "Booze and Bolshevism," *Literary Digest*, 29 November 1919, 16.

168. Friedheim, *The Seattle General Strike*, 27. On divisions within the AFL over wartime prohibition, see "No Beer, No Work?" *Survey*, 21 June 1919, 458, 463.

169. WiSFL, *Proceedings* 1920, 40.

170. WiSFL, *Proceedings* 1920, 71–72, emphasis added.

171. WaSFL, *Proceedings* 1913, 34.

Chapter Five

1. For example, Solon J. Buck, *The Agrarian Crusade: A Chronicle of the Farmer in Politics* (New Haven, Conn.: Yale University Press, 1921); Goodwyn, *The Populist Moment*; McNall, *The Road to Rebellion*; and Norman Pollack, *The Just Polity: Populism, Law, and Human Welfare* (Urbana: University of Illinois Press, 1987).

2. Goodwyn, *The Populist Moment*, xxi–xxii.

3. Orloff, "Political Origins"; Skocpol and Finegold, "State Capacity."

4. Orville Merton Kile, *The Farm Bureau through Three Decades* (Baltimore: Waverly Press, 1948), 10–18; Goodwyn, *The Populist Moment*, 285.

5. CSG, *Proceedings* 1889, 173; Clarke A. Chambers, *California Farm Organizations: A Historical Study of the Grange, the Farm Bureau, and the Associated Farmers, 1929–1941* (Berkeley and Los Angeles: University of California Press, 1952), 10; Gerald L. Prescott, "Farm Gentry vs. the Grangers: Conflict in Rural America," *California Historical Quarterly* 56, no. 4 (1977–78): 330.

6. McConnell, *Decline of Agrarian Democracy*, 6–9.

7. Quoted in Crawford, *Washington State Grange*, 76. Not all agriculturalists subscribed to this vision, of course. "Gentlemen farmers," committed to scientific farming, frequently argued that "[a]griculture . . . although an important and honorable occupation, had no monopoly on virtuousness." Gerald L. Prescott, "Gentlemen Farmers in the Gilded Age," *Wisconsin Magazine of History* 55, no. 3 (1972): 201.

8. CSG, *Proceedings* 1887, 33–34.

9. Quoted in "'Subsidizing' the Farmer," *Literary Digest*, 17 September 1921, 14.

10. D. Sven Nordin, *Rich Harvest: A History of the Grange, 1867–1900* (Jackson: University Press of Mississippi, 1974), 31, 41.

11. Kile, *Farm Bureau through Three Decades*, 18.

12. Although many of these organizations originated in the southern states, they rarely maintained their strength in this region, leaving a vacuum that complemented the dominance of local elites. Hansen, *Gaining Access*, 61–64. On party organization in the south, see V. O. Key, *Southern Politics in State and Nation* (New York: Knopf, 1949).

13. Theodore Saloutos and John D. Hicks, *Agrarian Discontent in the Middle West, 1900–1939* (Madison: University of Wisconsin Press, 1951).

14. Hansen, *Gaining Access,* 31–37; Saloutos and Hicks, *Agrarian Discontent,* chap. 11.

15. Fine, *Labor and Farmer Parties,* 16.

16. Gerald L. Prescott, "Wisconsin Farm Leaders in the Gilded Age," *Agricultural History* 44, no. 2 (1970): 183–200; Theodore Saloutos, "The Wisconsin Society of Equity," *Agricultural History* 14, no. 2 (1940): 78–95.

17. Prescott, "Farm Gentry"; Donald J. Pisani, "Land Monopoly in Nineteenth-Century California," *Agricultural History* 65, no. 4 (1991): 15–37; see also Paul W. Gates, *Land and Law in California* (Ames: Iowa State University Press, 1991).

18. Pisani, "Land Monopoly," 22.

19. Dorothy O. Johansen, "A Working Hypothesis for the Study of Migrations," *Pacific Historical Review* 36 (1967): 1–12; Schwantes, *Radical Heritage,* 7.

20. Keith Alexander Murray, "Republican Party Politics in Washington during the Progressive Era," Ph.D diss., University of Washington, 1946, 4. On the sectional pattern of support for reform in the state, see Howard W. Allen, *Poindexter of Washington: A Study in Progressive Politics* (Carbondale: Southern Illinois University Press, 1981), 21–22.

21. C. Wright Mills, *The Sociological Imagination* (New York: Oxford University Press, 1959), 8.

22. Crawford, *Washington State Grange,* 84. See also Nordin, *Rich Harvest,* chap. 6.

23. Buck, *The Agrarian Crusade,* 3; Nordin, *Rich Harvest,* 9–11. See the discussion of fraternalism in chapter 2.

24. CSG, *Proceedings* 1889, 47. For a discussion of the Grange as a locus for political learning see Crawford, *Washington State Grange,* 130. For a related discussion of the Southern Farmers' Alliance, see Theodore Mitchell, *Political Education in the Southern Farmers' Alliance, 1887–1900* (Madison: University of Wisconsin Press, 1987). A similar argument concerning the relation of organizations to political empowerment may be found in many accounts of the women's club movement; see chapter 6.

25. Nordin, *Rich Harvest,* 21–22.

26. By opening the Grange to full participation by women from the start, the founders greatly enhanced the capacity of the fraternal model to function as a community organization.

27. Ostler, *Prairie Populism,* 38–39.

28. Orville Merton Kile, *The Farm Bureau Movement* (New York: Macmillan, 1921), 8; Ostler, *Prairie Populism,* 38–40, 72–73. For California, see Eaves, *California Labor Legislation,* 38; Nordin, *Rich Harvest,* 168–82; Prescott, "Farm Gentry," 329.

29. Kile, *Farm Bureau through Three Decades,* 10.

30. CSG, *Proceedings* 1892, 68–69; see also *Proceedings* 1891, 39, 124, 127; 1892, 51, 53, 68; Crawford, *Washington State Grange,* 85.

31. CSG, *Proceedings* 1891, 118.

32. On survival as the Grange's organizational goal, see McConnell, *Decline of Agrarian Democracy,* 39–40.

33. CSG, *Proceedings* 1888, 38; 1915, 84.

34. Crawford, *Washington State Grange,* 285; Carlos A. Schwantes, "The Ordeal of William Morley Bouck, 1918–1919: Limits to the Federal Suppression of Agrarian Dissidents," *Agricultural History* 59, no. 3 (1985): 427.

35. Crawford, *Washington State Grange,* 15, 46–47, 85, 213.

36. Although the Grange would endure as an agrarian association with national membership, in most states it retained little of its role as the primary vehicle of agrarian dissent. Its peak membership of almost half a million families in the 1870s was not matched until after the Second World War. Tontz, "Memberships," 146.

37. Ander, "Immigrant Church," 157.

38. Crawford, *Washington State Grange,* 84.

39. Goodwyn, *The Populist Moment.*

40. Griffiths, "Populism in Far West," 17; Yoder, "Farmers' Alliance," 124–29.

41. Quoted in Yoder, "Farmers' Alliance," 168.

42. Donald F. Warner, "The Farmers' Alliance and the Farmers' Union: An American-Canadian Parallelism," *Agricultural History* 23, no. 1 (1949): 12; Griffiths, "Populism in Far West," 154–55.

43. S. O. Daws, quoted in Goodwyn, *The Populist Moment,* 43; see also 179–80 on "brokerage politics." Note how this organizational solution resembles the "shadow" political clubs set up by the Knights of Labor.

44. Williams, *Democratic Party and California,* 138.

45. Griffiths, "Populism in Far West," 30–34, 158–61.

46. William F. Holmes, "Populism: In Search of Context," *Agricultural History* 64, no. 4 (1990): 30–31.

47. Kile, *The Farm Bureau Movement,* 26–28; McConnell, *Decline of Agrarian Democracy,* 37–39; McNall, *The Road to Rebellion,* 52–53.

48. Griffiths, "Populism in Far West," 11–16, 22–23; Shaffer, "Radicalism in California," 90–123.

49. Shaffer, "Radicalism in California," 122; Griffiths, "Populism in Far West," 52–60; Michael Kazin, "Barons of Labor: The San Francisco Building Trades, 1895–1922," Ph.D. diss., Stanford University, 1982, 76–77. The Gatekeeper of the California Grange emphasized the dangers of diversity: "If we admit manufacturers, bankers, members from the ranks of the legal fraternity, and kindred professions who have no direct interest with us, it would create strife and dissension and destroy the usefulness of the Grange." CSG, *Proceedings* 1899, 36–37.

50. Yoder, "Farmers' Alliance," 160.

51. 17 February 1888; quoted in Yoder, "Farmers' Alliance," 148.

52. Quoted in Yoder, "Farmers' Alliance," 164.

53. Yoder, "Farmers' Alliance," 171.

54. Griffiths, "Populism in Far West," 161.

55. Populist alliances in the West, therefore, provide a partial counter to Lawrence Goodwyn's claim that the failure of Populism reflected a disjuncture in the timing between peaks of labor and agrarian organizing. *The Populist Moment,* 297. For example, the 1892 platform of the California People's Party included "resolutions for municipal ownership of water, light, and street railways, free public baths, free employment offices, and proposals for the initiative and referendum. It contained a plank on schools that warned about diverting any public moneys for the benefit of any religious group, an anti-boss and anti-bribery resolution, a resolution against the Southern Pacific, and a plank for the 'suppression of the dives.' It contained a welfare proposal for city housing in which the city would build homes to be rented at cost on a non-profit basis." Griffiths, "Populism in Far West," 29-30.

56. See Holmes, "Populism," 48-49, on increasing heterogeneity within movement and on increasing distance between political platform and the party's organizational base. Williams, *Democratic Party and California,* 240-45.

57. Griffiths, "Populism in Far West," 38-41, 166; Goodwyn, *The Populist Moment,* 240-41; Roy V. Scott, *The Agrarian Movement in Illinois, 1880-1896* (Urbana: University of Illinois Press, 1962), 103-14.

58. Quoted in Griffiths, "Populism in Far West," 26-27. After their "betrayal" in the senatorial selection of 1892, Illinois agrarians had similarly tried to sever all ties to the major parties: "[I]ndicating a tendency to bar the door after the horse was stolen, the McLean County Grange asked that all politicians be expelled from agricultural organizations." Scott, *Agrarian Movement in Illinois,* 114.

59. Robert Michels, *Political Parties: A Sociological Study of the Oligarchic Tendencies of Modern Democracy* (New York: Free Press, 1962). On the closely related "ambition theory" of political parties, see Aldrich, *Why Parties?* 51-57.

60. Goodwyn, *The Populist Moment,* 256.

61. Nor did the third-party vehicle of the Socialists hold much appeal for farmers. The 1898 convention of the newly founded Social Democratic Party refused to include in its platform the "Demands for Farmers" proposed by Victor Berger of Wisconsin; a 1901 "Unity Convention" rejected an agriculturalist plank and instead created a "study committee on agriculture"; and in 1908 the Socialist Party convention rejected the majority report of the Committee on Farmers' Programs, which foreswore the appropriation of land occupied and worked by farmers, adopting instead the minority conclusion "that 'anything but a complete socialization of the industries of the nation' [including agriculture] would be 'unsocialistic.'" Donald B. Marti, "Answering the Agrarian Question: Socialists, Farmers, and Algie Martin Simons," *Agricultural History* 65, no. 3 (1991): 56-57, 60-61, 65-66. Only in 1912 did the Socialist Party embrace an agricultural platform endorsing "Social ownership of transportation and storage facilities, no more alienation of public land, development of cooperative farms, promotion of

purchasing and marketing cooperatives, acceptance of land ownership by people who worked their farms" (68).

62. J. A. Everitt, *The Third Power: Farmers to the Front*, 4th ed. (Indianapolis: J. A. Everitt reprint, New York: Arno Press, 1975), 143; Barrett, *Mission, History, and Times*, 45; see also William P. Tucker, "Populism Up-to-Date: The Story of the Farmers' Union," *Agricultural History* 21, no. 4 (1947): 199.

63. Quoted in Crawford, *Washington State Grange*, 90; see also Goodwyn, *The Populist Moment*, 47.

64. Pollack, *The Just Polity*, 171–73; Saloutos and Hicks, *Agricultural Agrarian Discontent*, 32–34.

65. Grant, *Self-Help*. This vision was not unique to farmers but ran through many reform traditions in the late nineteenth century. See, for example, Edward Bellamy, *Looking Backward, 2000–1887* (New York: Signet, 1960), 82–83.

66. *Wisconsin Equity News*, 10 May 1913, 7.

67. CSG, *Proceedings* 1897, 22.

68. Gladys Talbott Edwards, *The Farmers' Union Triangle*, rev. ed. (Jamestown, N.D.: Farmers Union Educational Service, 1941), 12; Tucker, "Populism Up-to-Date, 199. But the mechanisms that could link these three into an effective economic and political organization were not yet developed. On the increasing political activity by the Farmers' Union as its strength shifted to northern states, see Schmidt, "Role and Techniques," 51.

69. "Labor and Cooperation," *Survey*, 9 October 1920, 57.

70. Goodwyn, *The Populist Moment*, 29–30, 77.

71. Chambers, *California Farm Organizations*, 10; Crawford, *Washington State Grange*, 213–14; California Fruit Growers Exchange, *Annual Report of the General Manager 1928–29*, 23.

72. Saloutos, "Wisconsin Society of Equity," 89.

73. Robert H. Bahmer, "The American Society of Equity," *Agricultural History* 14, no. 1 (1940): 36; Saloutos, "Wisconsin Society of Equity," 90.

74. M. Wes Tubbs, "The American Society of Equity Should Lead in Organization for Industrial Co-operation," *Wisconsin Equity News*, 10 July 1912, 2.

75. WiSFL, "Farmers and City Wage Workers (revised)," supplement to *Wisconsin Equity News*, 25 October 1912, 2.

76. Gavett, *Labor Movement in Milwaukee*, 116, 143; "Jottings," *Survey*, 19 April 1919, 128.

77. Quoted in "Labor and Cooperation," *Survey*, 9 October 1920, 58.

78. Much of the activity of the State Union seems to have involved the establishment of grain warehouses (which gave farmers the ability to wait to sell until prices were higher than at harvest time) and to secure sites for these warehouses along railroad lines and at terminal points from the State Railway Commission. Other cooperative endeavors involved planning for a mutual fire insurance company for Union members only, buying grain bags direct from importers, and securing freight reductions for carload (e.g., pooled) shipments. Barrett, *Mission, History, and Times*, 245–46, 410–14.

79. Barrett, *Mission, History, and Times*, 98–101, 245–46.

80. Crawford, *Washington State Grange* 220–27; Frank, *Purchasing Power,* 41–51; WaSFL, *Proceedings* 1917, 58, 70.

81. H. E. Erdman, "The Development and Significance of California Cooperatives, 1900–1915," *Agricultural History* 32, no. 3 (1958): 179–86; Grace Larsen, "A Progressive in Agriculture: Harris Weinstock," *Agricultural History* 32, no. 3 (1958): 187–95; Prescott, "Farm Gentry."

82. Larsen, "A Progressive in Agriculture," 191–93.

83. Sapiro would also come to be a divisive force in the American Farm Bureau Federation as it sought to turn from reliance on cooperative marketing to demands for government programs to export agricultural surplus in the 1920s. Kile, *Farm Bureau through Three Decades,* 117–19; Saloutos and Hicks, *Agrarian Discontent,* 275–77; Hansen, *Gaining Access,* 63–64.

84. California Fruit Growers Exchange, *Annual Report* 1919–20, 6.

85. Howard Seftel, "Government Regulation and the Rise of the California Fruit Industry: The Entrepreneurial Attack on Fruit Pests, 1880–1920," *Business History Review* 59 (1985): 402.

86. To the extent that agricultural laborers organized at all, it was under the auspices of labor organizations: the IWW in the 1910s, then a communist union, and the AFL in the 1930s. Chambers, *California Farm Organizations,* 33–35. None of these efforts produced lasting organizations, but the problem of agricultural labor prompted the establishment of California's Commission of Immigration and Housing; the California Fruit Growers Exchange reported working on the labor problem with both public agencies and the state university, "not only for present efficiency but for future protection against labor unrest and labor shortage." *Annual Report* 1920–21, 20.

87. "In Restraint of Cooperation," *Survey,* 19 February 1921, 718, emphasis added; see also "Collective Marketing," *Survey,* 17 January 1920, 418.

88. *Wisconsin Equity News,* 1 November 1915, 201.

89. At other times, farmers called for state agencies to cease aiding their enemies. In 1915, the National Convention of the American Society of Equity agreed, "*Whereas,* It is generally believed that the publication of government crop reports and agricultural statistics tends to make easier and increase the volume of future trading and market price manipulation and has resulted in the loss of millions of dollars to the farmers through price depression, *Therefore Be It Resolved,* That we condemn such reports as in the interest of the class that fattens through exploitation of the farmers of these United States." *Wisconsin Equity News,* 1 January 1916, 270.

90. Goodwyn, *The Populist Moment,* xvii.

91. McConnell, *Decline of Agrarian Democracy,* 6.

92. Graham A. Cosmas, "The Democracy in Search of Issues: The Wisconsin Reform Party, 1873–1877," *Wisconsin Magazine of History* 46, no. 2 (1962–63): 97, 101; Nordin, *Rich Harvest,* 175.

93. CSG, *Proceedings* 1887, 16–17.

94. CSG, *Proceedings* 1887, 33. Addressing the failure of "The Farmers Alli-

ance" of 1870s Texas to lead its members into the Greenback Party, Lawrence Goodwyn underscores the importance of "political resocialization": "[T]oo many of the poor had strong cultural memories that yoked them to traditional modes of political thought and behavior. Some means would have to be found to cut such ties before any kind of genuine people's politics was possible." *The Populist Moment*, 26.

95. CSG, *Proceedings* 1889, 43.

96. CSG, *Proceedings* 1891, 11, 79–80.

97. But despite these failures to secure approval of the Grange, the "machine forces" in California were sufficiently threatened to pass a law forbidding the solicitation of pledges from candidates by any group other than a party convention. See CSFL, *Proceedings* 1906, 26.

98. CSG, *Proceedings* 1892, 10–11, 47, 59, 69.

99. CSG, *Proceedings* 1893, 73.

100. CSG, *Proceedings* 1892, 11, 59.

101. CSG, *Proceedings* 1901, 12; 1902, 18, emphasis added.

102. Grangers tended to ally informally with some progressive Republicans and the Democratic Party, which went into decline in both state and national following the 1896 election. By comparison, the American Farm Bureau Federation, which would develop as the dominant agricultural association in the southern counties, was aligned with conservative Republicans (and some conservative Democrats by the 1930s), who dominated the state government. Chambers, *California Farm Organizations*, 180–81.

103. CSG, *Proceedings* 1901, 52–53.

104. Barrett, *Mission, History, and Times*, 415.

105. Tucker, "Populism Up-to-Date," 200.

106. Saloutos, "Wisconsin Society of Equity," 86.

107. Saloutos, "Wisconsin Society of Equity," 86–90.

108. *Wisconsin Equity News*, 25 April 1912, 8; 10 August 1912, 1.

109. *Wisconsin Equity News*, 25 June 1911, 4; 10 June 1913, 41.

110. *Wisconsin Equity News*, 10 August 1913, 104.

111. *Wisconsin Equity News*, 25 December 1913, 246; 10 January 1914, 259; 1 January 1916, 183–84; 1 August 1916, 512.

112. *Wisconsin Equity News*, 15 July 1914, 450.

113. *Wisconsin Equity News*, 15 January 1915, 665.

114. Ronald L. Nye, "Federal vs. State Agricultural Research Policy: The Case of California's Tulare Experiment Station, 1888–1909," *Agricultural History* 57, no. 4 (1983): 437–38.

115. CSG, *Proceedings* 1913, 51; Nye, "Federal vs. State," 445–47.

116. Quoted in Crawford, *Washington State Grange*, 16.

117. Crawford, *Washington State Grange*, 46–47. This model of legitimate fiscal relations also fueled the growth of the single-tax movement in Washington. See Arthur N. Young, *The Single Tax Movement in the United States* (Princeton, N.J.: Princeton University Press, 1916), 184–91.

118. Schwantes, *Radical Heritage*, 161.

119. Carroll H. Wooddy, "Populism in Washington: A Study of the Legislature of 1897," *Washington Historical Quarterly* 21, no. 2 (1930): 112–15.

120. Crawford, *Washington State Grange*, 161; Johnson, "Adoption," 295–96.

121. Murray, "Republican Party Politics," 66.

122. Not all state Granges made the same decision. The Michigan State Grange, for example, endorsed candidates, not just issues. Crawford, *Washington State Grange*, 164–65.

123. Johnson, "Adoption," 297.

124. Quoted in Johnson, "Adoption," 299.

125. Saloutos and Hicks, *Agrarian Discontent*, 331–32.

126. For a related critique, see Sanders, "Farmers and the State," 183–84.

127. Hansen, *Gaining Access*, 16–17, 45–61.

128. Kile, *The Farm Bureau Movement*, 28.

129. Sanders, "Farmers and the State," 199.

130. Philip S. Foner, *History of the Labor Movement in the United States*, vol. 5 (New York: International Publishers, 1980), 120; Sklar, *Corporate Reconstruction*, 294.

131. The Office of Experiment Stations had to urge agency scientists continually to devote their efforts to questions of scientific significance rather than responding to the demands of local farmers. Lou Ferleger, "Uplifting American Agriculture: Experiment Station Scientists and the Office of Experiment Stations in the Early Years after the Hatch Act," *Agricultural History* 64, no. 2 (1990): 5–23.

132. Prescott, "Wisconsin Farm Leaders," "Farm Gentry."

133. CSG, *Proceedings* 1891, 37; Saloutos, "Wisconsin Society of Equity," 85.

134. This issue was at the base of one of the enduring disagreements between organized labor and agrarian reforms: the question of convict labor. Whereas unionists felt convict labor was a source of unfair competition that would lower wage rates, farmers disagreed. One California Granger argued that "the farmers who pay the taxes necessary to meet the expense of erecting and maintaining our penal institutions, should speak out on the subject" and demanded "that the convicts in our public prisons be kept at work at some useful labor, for the double purpose of making those institutions as nearly self-sustaining as possible and qualifying the convicts to be self-sustaining members of society when their terms of imprisonment shall expire." CSG, *Proceedings* 1888, 37. Similarly, Wisconsin farmers viewed the establishment of a Binder Twine plant at the state prison as a great victory, simultaneously lowering the tax burden and striking a blow at the hated "Twine Trust." *Wisconsin Equity News*, 25 August 1912, 8; 1 February 1916, 305.

135. Tax experts often agreed. In 1897, the report of the Wisconsin Tax Commission "dwelt in particular upon the discrimination against the farmer, who seldom has anything that can be concealed from the assessor, and nearly all of whose property is taxed." Raymond Vincent Phelan, "The Financial History of Wiscon-

sin," *Bulletin of the University of Wisconsin*, 193, Economics and Political Science Series, 2, no. 2 (Madison: University of Wisconsin Press, 1908), 340.

136. CSG, *Proceedings* 1887, 47.

137. CSG, *Proceedings* 1893, 59–60; to be sung to the tune of "Oh, Dear, What Can the Matter Be?"

138. Quoted in Crawford, *Washington State Grange*, 15.

139. McCormick, *Party Period*.

140. George William Rankin, *William Dempster Hoard* (Fort Atkinson, Wis.: W. D. Hoard and Sons, 1925).

141. "Hiram Johnson after Twelve Years," *Nation*, 9 August 1922, 142–43.

142. Barrett, *Mission, History, and Times*, 44.

Chapter Six

1. *Milwaukee Free Press*, 7 July 1911.

2. California Civic League, *San Francisco Center: Annual Report* (1912), 3. The San Francisco Center of the League was founded by the College Equal Suffrage League after women gained the vote in 1911. The Center claimed 1100 members in 1912, gave 17 luncheons and sponsored 33 lectures. *Constitution of the San Francisco Center of the California Civic League* (1913).

3. Mary S. Gibson, *A Record of Twenty-five Years of the California Federation of Women's Clubs* (California Federation of Women's Clubs, 1927), 214–16; Mrs. M. Burton, "Ladies' Clubs and Societies in Los Angeles in 1892," reported for the Historical Society of Southern California (Los Angeles: Misses Lillian A. and Estella M. Williamson, 1925), 40.

4. Mrs. J. C. Croly, *The History of the Women's Club Movement in America* (New York: Henry G. Allen and Co., 1898), 125.

5. Because of their comparatively privileged status and acceptability, mainstream groups were in a good position to introduce feminine organizational forms to the taken-for-granted repertoires of turn-of-the-century American culture. This emphasis, however, does not exclude either the existence or the significance of variations in repertoires by ethnicity, class, or region. For discussions of such differences, see Paula Baker, *The Moral Frameworks of Public Life: Gender, Politics, and the State in Rural New York, 1870–1930* (New York: Oxford University Press, 1991), xvi; Debra Campbell, "Reformers and Activists," in *American Catholic Women: A Historical Explanation*, ed. Karen Kennely, CSJ (New York: Macmillan, 1989); Clemens, "Organizational Repertoires," 786–91; Frankel and Dye, *Gender, Class, Race*; Sherry Katz, "Frances Nacke Noel and 'Sister Movements': Socialism, Feminism, and Trade Unionism in Los Angeles, 1909–1916," *California History* 67, no. 3 (1988): 180–90.

6. Women activists viewed public opinion as a particularly fruitful channel of political influence: "Women are the creators of public opinion, and those federated women are using their influence from sea to sea, and the lakes to the gulf." Mrs. A. O. Granger, "The Work of the General Federation of Women's Clubs

against Child Labor," *Annals of the American Academy of Political and Social Science* 25 (1905): 107.

7. Nelson, "Two-Channel Welfare State"; Virginia Sapiro, "The Gender Basis of American Social Policy," *Political Science Quarterly* 101, no. 2 (1986): 221–38; Skocpol, *Protecting Soldiers and Mothers*, chaps. 6–9.

8. Carrie Chapman Catt and Nettie Rogers Shuler, *Woman Suffrage and Politics: The Inner Story of a Movement* (New York: Scribner's, 1926), 32–45.

9. Paula Baker, "The Domestication of Politics: Women and American Political Society, 1780–1920," *American Historical Review* 89, no. 3 (1984): 620–47; Mary Ann Clawson, "Fraternal Orders and Class Formation in the Nineteenth-Century United States," *Comparative Studies in Society and History* 27, no. 4 (1985): 672–95, and *Constructing Brotherhood*.

10. Lewis Perry, *Radical Abolitionism: Anarchy and the Government of God in Antislavery Thought* (Ithaca, N.Y.: Cornell University Press, 1973), 57–92, 113–17.

11. Ann Braude, *Radical Spirits: Spiritualism and Women's Rights in Nineteenth-Century America* (Boston: Beacon, 1989), 164.

12. Croly, *History*, 128.

13. Croly, *History*, 1; Anne Firor Scott, *Natural Allies: Women's Associations in American History* (Urbana: University of Illinois Press, 1991).

14. Bordin, *Woman and Temperance*; Barbara Leslie Epstein, *The Politics of Domesticity: Women, Evangelism, and Temperance in Nineteenth Century America* (Middletown, Conn.: Wesleyan University Press, 1981); Kathleen McCarthy, *Noblesse Oblige: Charity and Cultural Philanthropy in Chicago, 1849–1929* (Chicago: University of Chicago Press, 1982), 3–24; Carroll Smith-Rosenberg, *Disorderly Conduct: Visions of Gender in Victorian America* (New York: Oxford University Press, 1985), 129–64.

15. Mary P. Ryan, *Women in Public: Between Banners and Ballots, 1825–1880* (Baltimore: Johns Hopkins University Press, 1990), 40.

16. Theodora Penny Martin, *The Sound of Our Own Voices: Women's Study Clubs, 1860–1910* (Boston: Beacon, 1987), 63; Ruddy, *Mother of Clubs*, 24. For a discussion of the theoretical significance of this choice of form, see chapter 2.

17. Croly, *History*, 9.

18. Sarah S. Platt Decker, quoted in Wood, *History*, 188.

19. Quoted in Eleanor Flexner, *Century of Struggle: The Woman's Rights Movement in the United States* (New York: Atheneum, 1970), 77.

20. Womans Parliament of Southern California, Proceedings (1892), 1. Bancroft Library, University of California at Berkeley. State Granges also typically had a committee devoted to "women's work."

21. Nor did the women's parliaments of the preceding decades provide an organizational precedent for the National Congress of Mothers. The founder was inspired after moving to Washington and observing "the great number of conventions and assemblages of all kinds and for all purposes held at the national capital." Skocpol, *Protecting Soldiers and Mothers*, 333–40.

22. Women's congresses were frequently used as recruiting grounds for suffrage activists. Edwards, *Sowing Good Seeds*, 159, 190; Gibson, *Record*, 5.

23. Quoted in Karen J. Blair, *The Clubwoman as Feminist: True Womanhood Redefined, 1868–1914* (New York: Holmes and Meier, 1980), 40.

24. Some, notably the male-led Anti-Saloon League, established in Ohio in 1893, drew freely on the forms and tactics of the modern corporation. K. Austin Kerr, "Organizing for Reform: The Anti-Saloon League and Innovation in Politics," *American Quarterly* 32, no. 1 (1980): 38. The ASL differed from many women's associations in that its organization was not intended to display the membership's capacity for democratic citizenship. As representatives of the brewery industry observed, "The scheme of organization might well excite the envious approval of an oriental despot." Quoted in Peter H. Odegard, *Pressure Politics: The Story of the Anti-Saloon League* (New York: Columbia University Press, 1928), 15.

25. As of 1892, the WCTU had nearly 150,000 paid members, compared to 20,000 in the GFWC and 13,000 in the NAWSA. Bordin, *Woman and Temperance*, 4.

26. Bordin, *Woman and Temperance*, 41, emphasis added.

27. Bordin, *Woman and Temperance*, 55, 118–19.

28. Bordin, *Woman and Temperance*, 97–98.

29. Mrs. Dorcas James Spencer, *A History of the Woman's Christian Temperance Union of Northern and Central California* (Oakland, Calif.: West Coast Printing Company, [1913?]), 30.

30. Spencer, *History*, 38.

31. Spencer, *History*, 66–67.

32. Scott, *Natural Allies*, 11–15.

33. Baker, "The Domestication of Politics," 630.

34. Croly, *History*, 8; Scott, *Natural Allies*, 58–83. See also Gloria Ricci Lothrop, "Strength Made Stronger: The Role of Women in Southern California Philanthropy," *Southern California Quarterly* 71, nos. 2–3 (1989): 143–94.

35. Chandler, *The Visible Hand*.

36. James Leiby, "State Welfare Administration in California, 1879–1929," *Pacific Historical Review* 41 (1972): 171–74; Frank Dekker Watson, *The Charity Organization Movement in the United States: A Study in American Philanthropy* (New York: Macmillan, 1922), 90–91.

37. San Francisco Ladies' Protection and Relief Society, *Forty-Eighth and Forty-Ninth Annual Reports* [1901–2] (San Francisco: C. A. Murdock and Co., 1903), 7.

38. Baker, *Moral Frameworks*, 57; Ryan, *Women in Public*, 123–25. The rate of public subsidy of benevolent institutions was low to nonexistent throughout the Midwest and West; only California (11.03 percent of total expenditures) and Arizona (12.2 percent) topped the national average of 10.9 percent. In Washington, the rate was 3.5 percent; in Wisconsin 0.4 percent. In some eastern states, however, public subsidy of charities developed as a component of the party pa-

tronage system, with rates of subsidy topping 20 percent in New York, Maryland, and the District of Columbia. U.S. Bureau of the Census, *Benevolent Institutions* (Washington, D.C.: Government Printing Office, 1904), 12.

39. *Wisconsin Citizen,* September 1887, 1.

40. One politically active newspaper publisher from Oregon was converted to the cause of woman suffrage when she recognized that she would never receive the political spoils doled out to male publishers for their editorial support of candidates. Ruth Barnes Moynihan, *Rebel for Rights: Abigail Scott Duniway* (New Haven, Conn.: Yale University Press, 1983), 174.

41. Watson, *Charity Organization Movement,* 182.

42. *Wisconsin Citizen,* June 1890, 2; Mrs. Henry M. Youmans, "Club Women and Suffrage," 1912, no newspaper identified, Wisconsin Woman Suffrage Scrapbooks, Wisconsin State Historical Society.

43. *Wisconsin Citizen,* August 1890, 2.

44. Quoted in Blair, *The Clubwoman as Feminist,* 23, emphasis added.

45. Quoted in Wood, *History,* 22.

46. Wood, *History,* 21. In 1896, the GFWC gave the following requirements for club affiliation with the federation: "clubs applying for membership in the General Federation must show that no sectarian or political test is required and that while distinctly humanitarian movements may be recognized, their chief purpose is not philanthropic or technical but social, literary, artistic or scientific culture." Wood, *History,* 46. In actuality, of course, these cleavages were frequently reinforced by the establishment of clubs with socially homogeneous memberships. Nevertheless, the assertion that women had a common public identity, transcending familial or denominational ties, was an important contribution to the redefinition of women's role in politics. See Steven M. Buechler, *The Transformation of the Woman Suffrage Movement: The Case of Illinois, 1850–1920* (New Brunswick, N.J.: Rutgers University Press, 1986).

47. Wood, *History,* 47.

48. Wood, *History,* 26; Scott, *Natural Allies,* 118.

49. Croly, *History,* 160; General Federation of Women's Clubs, *Official Proceedings of the Biennial Convention 1896,* 30; 1898, 18. It is probable, however, that many purely literary clubs chose not to affiliate with the GFWC, thereby saving the extra expense of federal dues and insulating themselves from an increasingly broad range of activity and debate.

50. Croly, *History,* 166; Helen M. Winslow, ed., *Official Register and Directory of Women's Clubs in America,* vols. 10, 17 (Boston, 1908, 1915); Louis S. Lyons, ed., *Who's Who among the Women of California* (San Francisco: Security Publishing Co., 1922), 119, 159.

51. Scott, *Natural Allies,* 81; Wood, *History,* 99–103.

52. Croly, *History,* 114.

53. Wisconsin State Federation of Women's Clubs, *Proceedings of the Annual Convention 1898,* 18.

54. E.g., *Western Woman Voter,* February 1911, 7; *Wisconsin Citizen,* July 1888, 3, September 1896, 1; but see *Club Life,* December 1902, 4, April 1903, 8.

55. *Federation Courier,* November 1911, 4.

56. Gibson, *Record,* 67.

57. Wood, *History,* 27.

58. Leiby, "State Welfare Administration," 173–74; Thelen, *The New Citizenship,* 55.

59. Quoted in Wood, *History,* 71.

60. Nancy F. Cott, *The Grounding of Modern Feminism* (New Haven, Conn.: Yale University Press, 1987), 86–87.

61. Gibson, *Record,* 112.

62. Quoted in Croly, *History,* 148.

63. R. James Kane, "Populism, Progressivism, and Pure Food," *Agricultural History* 38, no. 3 (1964): 164; Maud Nathan, *The Story of an Epoch-Making Movement* (Garden City, N.J.: Doubleday, Page and Co., 1926), 42.

64. *Club Life,* April 1903, 3; Nathan, *Story,* 113.

65. See Martin, *Sound of Own Voices.*

66. Washington State Federation of Women's Clubs, *Annual Report 1915–16,* 85.

67. One rhetorical strategy for legitimizing women's activities was to claim that this ideological division of labor had already been breached by social and economic changes. For example, Frances Willard argued that "our brethren have encroached upon the sphere of woman. They have very definitely marked out that sphere, and then they have proceeded with their incursion by the power of invention. They have taken away the loom and the spinning-jenny and they have obliged Jenny to seek her occupation somewhere else, to an extent. They have set even the tune of the old knitting-needle to humming by steam. So that we women, full of desire to be active and useful and to react upon the world around us, finding our occupation industrially largely gone, have been obliged to seek out a new territory and to pre-empt from the sphere of our brothers." *Wisconsin Citizen,* October 1888, 3. See also Margaret J. Evans in *The Woman Citizen's Library,* ed. Shailer Mathews, vol. 12, *The Woman Citizen and the Home* (Chicago: Civics Society, 1914), 2947.

68. Alice Ames Winter, *The Business of Being a Clubwoman* (New York: Century Co., 1925), vi.

69. Clemens, "Organizational Repertoires," 786–91.

70. Philip S. Foner, *Women and the American Labor Movement: From Colonial Times to the Eve of World War I* (New York: Free Press, 1979), 185, 186–87; Ruth Delzell, *The Early History of Women Trade Unionists of America* (Chicago: National Women's Trade Union League of America, 1919), 10; Susan Levine, "Labor's True Woman: Domesticity and Equal Rights in the Knights of Labor," *Journal of American History* 70, no. 2 (1983): 324–25.

71. Clawson, *Constructing Brotherhood,* 180–87; Foner, *Women and Labor Movement,* 188; Levine, "Labor's True Woman," 325.

72. CSG, *Proceedings 1887,* 110; Donald B. Marti, "Sisters of the Grange: Rural Feminism in the Late Nineteenth Century," *Agricultural History* 58, no. 3 (1984): 247–61.

73. CSG, *Proceedings* 1887, 144–45.

74. Marti, "Sisters of the Grange," 251.

75. Lillian R. Matthews, "Women in Trade Unions in San Francisco." *University of California Publications in Economics* 3, no. 1 (1913): 81.

76. Matthews, "Women in Trade Unions," 78–81.

77. Montgomery, *Fall*, 164–69; Nancy Schrom Dye, *As Equals and as Sisters: Feminism, the Labor Movement, and the Women's Trade Union League of New York* (Columbia: University of Missouri Press, 1980).

78. Kathryn J. Oberdeck, "'Not Pink Teas': The Seattle Working-Class Women's Organization, 1905–1918," *Labor History* 32, no. 2 (1991): 193.

79. Oberdeck, "Not Pink Teas," 211.

80. On Seattle working-class women's organizations, see Cobble, *Dishing It Out*, 80–81, 135; Frank, *Purchasing Power*, 56–69, 122–28.

81. Winter, *Business of Being Clubwoman*, vi.

82. *Wisconsin Citizen*, December 1895, 4.

83. Kathleen McCarthy, *Women's Culture: American Philanthropy and Art, 1830–1930* (Chicago: University of Chicago Press, 1991), xiv. Although most women lacked independent legal standing, some antebellum charitable institutions, such as orphan asylums, did model themselves on financial corporations and secure articles of incorporation despite the *femmes couvertes* legal status of the boards of managers. Susan L. Porter, "Benevolent Women at Work: Cultural Exchange in Female Charitable Institutions, 1800–1850," paper presented at the annual meeting of the Social Science History Association, Chicago, 1989, 7.

84. For other examples of the increasing formalization of organization among women's groups, see Bordin, *Woman and Temperance*, chap. 4; Nathan, *Epoch-Making Movement*; Watson, *Charity Organization Movement*.

85. Womans [sic] Parliament of Southern California, *Proceedings*, 8.

86. McCarthy, *Women's Culture*, 40.

87. Ida Husted Harper, *The History of Woman Suffrage, 1900–1920*, vol. 6 (New York: J. J. Little and Ives, 1922), 193; Genevieve G. McBride, "Theodora Youmans and the Wisconsin Woman Movement," *Wisconsin Magazine of History* 71, no. 4 (1988): 255.

88. *Milwaukee Journal*, [?] July 1911; *Oshkosh Northwestern*, 14 September 1911.

89. *Milwaukee Journal*, 28 September 1911; see also *Monroe Times*, 22 July 1911. At times, these efforts to capitalize on women's traditional social identities were humiliating. For all the progressive intentions of the Political Equality League of Wisconsin, its members "found where their strength lay Monday night when they attempted to sell their state publication. The picture of Gov. McGovern as the cover design proved a poor selling card, but when Mrs. Henrietta C. Lyman explained that there were pictures of pretty suffrage workers inside an instant demand was created." *Milwaukee Morning Sentinel*, 8 August 1911.

90. Christine A. Lunardini, *From Equal Suffrage to Equal Rights: Alice Paul and the National Woman's Party, 1910–1928* (New York: New York University Press, 1986), 39.

91. General Federation of Woman's Clubs, *Proceedings* 1898, 140–41.

92. *Racine News,* 11 July 1911.

93. Anna Pratt Simpson, *Problems Women Solved. Being the Story of the Woman's Board of the Panama-Pacific International Exposition. What Vision, Enthusiasm, Work, and Co-operation Accomplished* (San Francisco: Woman's Board, 1915), ix–x.

94. Simpson, *Problems Women Solved,* 165.

95. *Club Life,* May 1902, 4. Even after the First World War, the willingness of California clubwomen to irrigate orange orchards, sell hogs, and save egg money in order to attend their state convention drew comment in the national press. "Jottings," *Survey,* 19 July 1919, 614.

96. *Milwaukee Evening Wisconsin,* 10 October 1911. Presumably, the adoption of a progressive organizational reform signaled their progressive intentions. On family imagery in the suffrage movement, see Ellen C. Dubois, "Harriot Stanton Blatch and the Transformation of Class Relations among Woman Suffragists," in Frankel and Dye, *Gender, Class, Race.*

97. Miscellaneous clipping, September 1911, Wisconsin Woman Suffrage Scrapbooks, Wisconsin State Historical Society; Blair, *The Clubwoman as Feminist,* 73–91; Watson, *Charity Organization Movement.*

98. McCarthy, *Women's Culture,* 61–63.

99. *Club Life,* October 1902, 11.

100. *Club Life,* October 1902, 3; Selina Solomons, *How We Won the Vote in California* (San Francisco: New Woman Publishing Co., [1912?]), 33.

101. Gibson, *Report,* 185; Lyons, *Who's Who,* 116; William Hard in Gibson, *Report,* 188.

102. *Club Life,* October 1902, 1.

103. Cash donations could also strengthen local organizations that acted as brokers between donors and recipients. For example, the relief funds raised in response to the Chicago fire of 1871 had the unintended consequence of entrenching the Chicago Relief Association that disbursed them. Dominated by financiers and manufacturers, the CRA used the funds to gain control over a wide variety of charitable establishments in the city, contributing to the marginalization of women and their subsequent reorganization around the settlement houses. Following the San Francisco earthquake of 1906, relief funds flowed through the woman-dominated Associated Charities, strengthening its role in local affairs. For Chicago, see McCarthy, *Noblesse Oblige;* for San Francisco, Anna Pratt Simpson, "Story of the Associated Charities since the Fire of 1906," reprinted from the *San Francisco Call* (1909), available in the Bancroft Library, University of California at Berkeley.

104. Buenker, "Urban Political Machine"; Shefter, "Regional Receptivity to Reform."

105. Van Voris, *Carrie Chapman Catt,* 33–34.

106. Quoted in Edwards, *Sowing Good Seeds,* 205.

107. For detailed discussions of the financial arrangements with organizers and campaign workers, see the correspondence between Ann Martin and Laura

Gregg Cannon as well as between Mabel Vernon and Katherine Fisher, Ann Martin Papers and Correspondence, Bancroft Library, University of California at Berkeley.

108. McNall, *The Road to Rebellion*, 232.

109. Quoted in Pendleton Herring, *Group Representation before Congress* (New York: Russell and Russell, 1967), 36.

110. Thompson, *The "Spider Web,"* 27. Petition campaigns were central to the early activities of many women's groups. Even as late as 1910, petitions were important in political arenas where women had no institutionalized presence; a petition with 404,000 signatures was presented to Congress in support of a federal woman suffrage amendment. Bordin, *Woman and Temperance*, 50; Catt and Shuler, *Woman Suffrage and Politics*, 235–36.

111. Women did not immediately recognize education as a strategy of political influence. As of the First Biennial of the General Federation of Women's Clubs in 1892, "the educating of public opinion as the only permanent basis for welfare work seems not at the time to have become a part of the inner consciousness of the average General Federation worker." Wood, *History*, 50.

112. Spencer, *History*, 38, 44; Norman H. Clark, *The Dry Years: Prohibition and Social Change in Washington* (Seattle: University of Washington Press, 1965), 35.

113. Ann Martin to Agnes Ryan, 5 May 1914, Box 8, Ann Martin Correspondence and Papers, Bancroft Library, University of California at Berkeley.

114. General Federation of Women's Clubs, *Proceedings 1896*, 5–6; Wood, *History*, 103.

115. College Equal Suffrage League of Northern California, *Winning Equal Suffrage*, 18.

116. Winter, *Business of Being Clubwoman*, 171–72.

117. Braude, *Radical Spirits;* Dubois, "Harriot Stanton Blatch," 173; *Milwaukee Daily News*, 7 July 1911; see also College Equal Suffrage League of Northern California, *Winning Equal Suffrage*, 61–62, 113–14; *Milwaukee Daily News*, 3 July 1911.

118. Some suffragists abandoned the cause of full woman suffrage for the alternative of an "educational" suffrage based on literacy tests. This strategy, which would enfranchise educated women while simultaneously excluding many male members of the new immigrant groups, was strongly opposed by mainstream woman suffrage organizations. *Wisconsin Citizen*, April 1897, 1.

119. Wisconsin State Federation of Women's Clubs, *Proceedings 1913*, 33; Nathan, *Epoch-Making Movement*, 78.

120. College Equal Suffrage League of Northern California, *Winning Equal Suffrage*, 11; see also Wisconsin State Federation of Women's Clubs, *Proceedings 1915*, 34. Note the use of comparative politics as well as the invocation of "propaganda" years before the outbreak of the First World War, which is usually credited with the introduction of "propaganda methods" to American politics.

121. Rodgers, *Contested Truths*, 198. Michael McGerr traces this style to the presidential election of 1896, which provoked Theodore Roosevelt to declare of

the Republican campaign chairman Mark Hanna, "He has advertised McKinley as if he were a patent medicine!" Quoted in *Decline of Popular Politics,* 145.

122. Hichborn, *California Legislature of 1911,* 246–47. Maud Younger later served as legislative chairman of the National Woman's Party. Joan G. Zimmerman, "The Jurisprudence of Equality: The Women's Minimum Wage, the First Equal Rights Amendment, and *Adkins v. Children's Hospital,* 1905–1923," *Journal of American History* 78, no. 1 (1991): 204.

123. Hichborn, *California State Legislature of 1909,* 226.

124. Wisconsin State Federation of Women's Clubs, *Proceedings* 1912, 7–8, emphasis added.

125. Maud Wood Park, *Front Door Lobby* (Boston: Beacon, 1960), 1.

126. Frances Cahn and Valeska Bary, *Welfare Activities of Federal, State, and Local Governments in California, 1850–1934,* (Berkeley and Los Angeles: University of California Press, 1936), 175.

127. Watson, *Charity Organization Movement,* 361–62, 404.

128. Gibson, *Story,* 214–16; Williamson, "Ladies' Clubs," 40.

129. Muncy, *Creating a Female Dominion.*

130. CSG, *Proceedings* 1888, 112.

131. *Wisconsin Citizen,* January 1888, 1.

132. Mary Roberts Coolidge, *What the Women of California Have Done with the Ballot* (San Francisco: n.p., 1916), 4.

133. *Survey,* 11 November 1917, 1179; William J. Reese, *Power and the Promise of School Reform: Grass-Roots Movements during the Progressive Era* (Boston: Routledge and Kegan Paul, 1986).

134. Mari Jo Buhle, *Women and American Socialism, 1870–1920* (Urbana: University of Illinois Press, 1981), 231.

135. Schmidt, "History of Labor Legislation," 187–88; Wisconsin State Federation of Women's Clubs, *Proceedings* 1909, 83.

136. Platt, *La Follette's State,* 149, 159–60, 244. The low level of political skill among the majority of the state's women is suggested by Hochstein's *A Progressive Primer,* which "points out the interdependence between the business of getting a living and the business of politics. We hope that it will awaken in women, a realization of the necessity of making themselves count through the ballot, through holding office, through initiating legislation, and through participation in the enforcement of laws." (Madison: Wisconsin Women's Progressive Association, 1922), iv.

137. T. A. Larson, "The Woman Suffrage Movement in Washington," *Pacific Northwest Quarterly* 67, no. 2 (1976): 49–53.

138. Tripp, "Toward Efficient Society," 101–2, "Progressive Labor Laws," 85–86.

139. "Social Legislation," *Survey,* 19 May 1917, 182.

140. Tripp, "Progressive Labor Laws," 85–86.

141. *Western Woman Voter,* January 1913.

142. For examples of this process, see Vivien Hart, "Feminism and Bureaucracy: The Minimum Wage Experiment in the District of Columbia," *Journal of*

American Studies 26, no. 1 (1992): 1–22; and Muncy, *Creating a Female Dominion.*

143. On the construction of a policy domain dominated by women at the federal level, see Muncy, *Creating a Female Dominion.*

144. Williamson, "Ladies Clubs," 11.

145. Kevin Starr, *Inventing the Dream: California through the Progressive Era* (New York: Oxford University Press, 1985), 208.

146. Starr, *Inventing the Dream,* 218.

147. Ronald Schaffer, "The Problem of Consciousness in the Woman Suffrage Movement: A California Perspective," *Pacific Historical Review* 45 (1976): 470.

148. Rogin, "Progressivism and California Electorate"; Roger E. Wyman, "Middle-Class Voters and Progressive Reform: The Conflict of Class and Culture," *American Political Science Review* 68, no. 2 (1974): 488–50.

149. Williamson, "Ladies' Clubs."

150. Gibson, *Record,* 4.

151. Leiby, "State Welfare Administration"; for accounts of the development of women's social philanthropy in Southern California, see John E. Baur, "Private Philanthropy in Nineteenth-Century Southern California," *Southern California Quarterly* 71, nos. 2–3 (1989): 119–42; Lothrop, "Strength Made Stronger"; and Raymond Starr, "Philanthropy in San Diego, 1900–1929," *Southern California Quarterly* 71, nos. 2–3 (1989): 227–73.

152. Simpson, "Story of Associated Charities, 21–22."

153. Williamson, "Ladies' Clubs," 40; Cahn and Bary, *Welfare Activities,* 14.

154. Gibson, *Record,* 214–17.

155. Ostrander, *Prohibition Movement,* 127.

156. The state's Democrats were particularly attentive to women. In 1912, there was concern that the state party would be punished for the failure of the national party platform to support a constitutional amendment for woman suffrage; in 1916, the Democrats were hopeful that President Wilson's claim that "he kept us out of war" would appeal disproportionately to women. Robert E. Hennings, *James D. Phelan and the Wilson Progressives of California* (New York: Garland, 1985), 78–79, 136–38.

157. Gibson, *Record,* 181–88.

158. Symbolically, women had a place in party politics by way of the increasing use of feminine imagery in the "spectacular" campaigns of the late nineteenth century. McGerr, *Decline of Popular Politics,* 208. This changing symbolism corresponded to a reorganization of political solidarities: "Femininity was inducted into politics hand in hand with the ethnic partition of the public sphere, which was manifested both in partisan rivalries and in violent civil strife. . . . Gender rose to the surface of political groups within the population, identified as much by their ethnicity and religion as by their opinions on specific questions of public policy." Ryan, *Women in Public,* 140. Thus women were not alone in exporting models of family and kinship into the field of politics.

159. Coolidge, *What Women Have Done,* 4.

160. In California, for example, one paper claimed that "one hundred thou-

sand women in California have, through organizations to which they belong, endorsed the suffrage amendment." The State Federation of Women's Clubs alone claimed a membership of thirty-five thousand. *Western Woman Voter*, September 1911, 8.

161. Schaffer, "Problem of Consciousness"; College Equal Suffrage League of Northern California, *Winning Equal Suffrage*, 107.

162. Baker, "The Domestication of Politics," 634.

163. Clemens, "From Clubwoman to Committeewoman."

164. Estelle Freedman, "Separatism as Strategy: Female Institution Building and American Feminism, 1870–1930," *Feminist Studies* 5 (fall 1979): 524; see also Cott, *Grounding of Modern Feminism*; Kathryn Kish Sklar, "Hull House in the 1890s: A Community of Women Reformers," *Signs* 10 (1985): 658–77.

165. *Redbook*, April 1928, quoted in Blanche Wiesen Cook, *Eleanor Roosevelt*, vol. 1, *1884–1933* (New York: Viking, 1992), 366–68.

166. George Madden Martin, "American Women and Paternalism," *Atlantic*, June 1924, 751. George Madden Martin was the pen name of a female author.

Chapter Seven

1. Synthesizing work in interest group theory, Andrew McFarland has argued that the presence of "countervailing" organizations (in contrast to organized economic producers) enhances the autonomy of state agencies. "Interest Groups and Theories of Power in America," *British Journal of Political Science* 17 (April 1987): 129–47.

2. On differences between German and Anglo-American socialism with respect to gender, see Buhle, *Women and American Socialism*, xvi, 21–23, 90–94.

3. Quoted in Dumenil, *Freemasonry*, 102.

4. Washington State Federation of Women's Clubs, *Annual Report* 1915–16, 85.

5. These processes of "political crystallization" are *path dependent*. Variations in initial conditions and the strategic choices of actors in relation to one another establish distinctive patterns of interaction and trajectories of development. North, *Institutions*, 93–98.

6. In each state, the general property tax accounted for between 47.4 percent (Wisconsin) and 50.7 percent (Washington) of total government revenues (including county, municipal, school districts and other civil divisions) in 1932. Total government revenues per capita (1932) were $106.85 in California, $91.05 in Washington, and $86.35 in Wisconsin. U.S. Bureau of the Census. *Financial Statistics of State and Local Governments: 1932* (Washington, D.C.: Government Printing Office, 1935), 161, 200, 1881, 1906, 1945, 1988.

7. Lowrie, "Wisconsin Plan," 188; Platt, *La Follette's State*, iv, 74–75.

8. Lowrie, "Wisconsin Plan," 188.

9. Platt, *La Follette's State*, 21.

10. In 1910, the newly elected Social Democrats established the Milwaukee Bureau of Economy and Efficiency, which was organized by Commons. The bureau was dismantled in 1912, when conservatives temporarily recaptured the

mayor's office, but even its brief existence testified to a new and shared organizational model for government. Vernon Carstensen, "The Origin and Early Development of the Wisconsin Idea," *Wisconsin Magazine of History* 39, no. 3 (1956): 181–88.

11. WiSFL, *Proceedings* 1915, 106.

12. This cooperative model of policy formation was epitomized by the structure of the Wisconsin Industrial Commission itself. The specific rules for factory safety were drafted by an advisory committee "composed of representatives of the Wisconsin State Federation of Labor, the Milwaukee Merchants and Manufacturers Association, the Wisconsin Manufacturers Association, the Milwaukee Health Department, workmen's compensation insurance companies, and the commission itself." Arthur J. Altmeyer, *The Industrial Commission of Wisconsin: A Case Study in Labor Law Administration,* University of Wisconsin Studies in the Social Sciences and History, vol. 17 (Madison: University of Wisconsin, 1932), 124; see also Maxwell, *La Follette,* 159–62.

13. WiSFL, *Proceedings* 1920, 63.

14. Schmidt, "History of Labor Legislation," 407.

15. Schmidt, "History of Labor Legislation," 411.

16. "Milwaukee Housing Projects," *Survey* 19 June 1920, 412.

17. "Report of Work 1919," *American Labor Legislation Review,* March 1920, 73; "Legislative Notes," *American Labor Legislation Review,* June 1923, 104, December 1925, 283.

18. "Prominent Labor Organizations Already on Record for Health Insurance," *American Labor Legislation Review,* December 1918, 319.

19. "Legislative Notes," *American Labor Legislation Review,* September 1921, 183; June 1923, 102; September 1923, 174; March 1925, 9; June 1924, 77, 81; September 1925, 181.

20. Cosmas, "Democracy."

21. Prescott, "Gentlemen Farmers," 201, 206.

22. Ferleger, "Uplifting American Agriculture," 19.

23. Glenn W. Birkett, "A Farmer Speaks Out," *Atlantic,* December 1924, 762.

24. A number of farmers were prominent members of the La Follette faction, however, including Albert R. Hall, the nephew of Oliver Kelley, the founder of the Grange. One of the state's most prominent dairymen, former governor William Dempster Hoard, was also allied with the reformers within the Republican Party. See Rankin, *William Dempster Hoard;* David P. Thelen, *Robert M. La Follette and the Insurgent Spirit* (Madison: University of Wisconsin Press, 1985), 333.

25. Bahmer, "American Society of Equity," 35.

26. Victor Berger had urged the national Social Democratic Party to adopt an agricultural plank in 1898, but Berger's pragmatic recognition of the necessary role of farmers in statewide coalition politics lost out to the dominant socialist conception of farmers as small capitalists destined to join the ranks of either landless workers or agribusiness. Marti, "Answering the Agrarian Question," 56–57.

27. Saloutos, "Wisconsin Society of Equity," 79–80.

28. Thelen, *La Follette,* 48, 62, 119.

29. WiSFL, *Proceedings* 1909, 19.

30. WiSFL, *Proceedings* 1911, 37.

31. See table 7.1; George Leland Leffler, "Wisconsin Industry and the Wisconsin Tax System," 2d ed., *Bulletin of the University of Wisconsin Bureau of Business and Economic Research* 3 (1931): 63–79.

32. *Wisconsin Equity News*, 1 June 1914, 411.

33. Even once an income tax was passed to provide state revenues, the administration of property taxes raised problems at the county level. One farmer complained: "Farm machinery is now exempt except wagons and buggies. The poor farmer gets along with little farm machinery—the well-to-do farmer escapes taxation on his mowers, binders, corn harvesters, gasoline engines, etc. amounting to a thousand or more dollars in value." *Wisconsin Equity News*, 15 June 1914, 424. See also Zona Gale, "Wisconsin: A Voice from the Middle Border," *Nation*, 18 October 1922, 406.

34. Mowry, *The California Progressives*, 317; W. Elliot Brownlee Jr., "Income Taxation and the Political Economy of Wisconsin, 1890–1930," *Wisconsin Magazine of History* 59, no. 4 (1976): 299–324; Leffler, "Wisconsin Industry," 110. The Wisconsin Society of Equity reciprocated by opposing efforts to weaken the tax commission, "which has by its administration of the tax laws, compelled the larger business interests of the state to pay their proportionate share of the tax burden." *Wisconsin Equity News*, 15 August 1916, 526.

35. WiSFL, *Proceedings* 1905, 31. Labor did approve of retaining land taxes "where only the small properties of the producers ought to be exempt." WiSFL, *Proceedings* 1906, 67. The demand for a graduated income and inheritance tax was formally incorporated in the federation's political platform in 1909. WiSFL, *Proceedings* 1909, 7; see also *Wisconsin Equity News*, 25 March 1912, 3.

36. Kossuth Kent Kennan, "The Wisconsin Income Tax," *Annals of the American Academy of Political and Social Science* 58 (March 1915): 65–76.

37. "Duties and Organization of State Labor Departments," *American Labor Legislation Review*, December 1913, 485–511.

38. *Wisconsin Equity News*, 25 May 1911, 5; 25 July 1911, 2.

39. In the meantime, however, these efforts in agricultural extension had an important influence on the consolidation of Wisconsin progressivism around a few of the university's graduates: Robert La Follette and Charles Van Hise, who became the university's president. Defining "the Wisconsin Idea" as "experimental reform based upon detailed research, the extensive use of academic and other experts in government, agriculture and industry, and an enlightened electorate," Vernon Carstensen argues that the university's agricultural extension work in the 1880s and 1890s provided a crucial model for progressive reformers when they later went to design new state agencies and programs. "Origin of Wisconsin Idea," 182–83; "The Genesis of an Agricultural Experiment Station," *Agricultural History* 34, no. 1 (1960): 13–20.

40. *Wisconsin Equity News*, 10 June 1913, 41.

41. *Wisconsin Equity News*, 10 March 1914, 323; 15 August 1914, 497; 1 October 1914, 545.

42. WiSFL, *Proceedings* 1905, 65.

43. *Wisconsin Equity News*, 25 August 1912, 10.

44. *Wisconsin Equity News*, 10 March 1914, 325. Entire passage emphasized in original.

45. WiSFL, *Proceedings* 1915, 92.

46. The *American Labor Legislation Review*, published by an organization closely linked to John Commons and other reformers at the University of Wisconsin, printed only a few brief articles on women's labor legislation in that state while devoting a great deal of space to other accomplishments of the Industrial Commission.

47. Altmeyer, *Industrial Commission of Wisconsin*, 196–97.

48. "Jottings," *Survey*, 16 July 1919, 638; "Minima for Women," *Survey*, 26 July 1919, 635.

49. "Wisconsin Social Work," *Survey*, 13 November 1920, 260; "The State Conference," *Survey*, 15 January 1921, 575–77; "Child Welfare in Wisconsin," *Survey*, 15 June 1922, 405. This new bureau was headed by Dr. Maybelle Park, who, although a graduate of the University of Wisconsin, had been active as a social worker in Seattle.

50. Once women had the vote, however, they gained not only social-policy concessions but an "Equal Rights Law" giving women "the same rights and privileges under the law as men in the exercise of suffrage, freedom of contract, choice of residence for voting purposes, jury service, holding office, holding and conveying property, care and custody of children, and in all other respects." Zona Gale, "What Women Won in Wisconsin," *Nation*, 23 August 1922, 184; see also "Wisconsin, Where Women Are People," *Literary Digest*, 30 July 1921, 10.

51. Edwin E. Witte, "A Law Making Laboratory," *State Government* 3, no. 1 (1930): 3–11.

52. John R. Commons, "Constructive Investigation and the Industrial Commission of Wisconsin," *Survey*, 4 January 1913, 444–45. The distinctive political style of Wisconsin progressivism is nicely illustrated by the passage and subsequent development of workmen's compensation legislation. This legislation had been nurtured by the WiSFL working in collaboration with elected Social Democrats and other progressive leaders, with administrators and academics at the Legislative Reference Library and at the University of Wisconsin, and with the Merchants and Manufacturers Association of Milwaukee. Robert Asher, "The 1911 Wisconsin Workmen's Compensation Law: A Study in Conservative Reform," *Wisconsin Magazine of History* 57, no. 2 (1973–74): 126; Ozanne, *Labor Movement in Wisconsin*. It was noncompulsory (except for state, county, and municipal employees), with benefit levels comparable to those in progressive states such as California and New York. "Main Provisions of Existing State Laws Relative to Workmen's Compensation and Insurance," *American Labor Legislation Review*, October 1912, 478–79.

53. Both Wisconsin and Washington, along with a handful of other states, established "institutional departments and the control exercised by the board is one of lay and business rather than professional, management. In few, if any, cases

is there definite provision for professional representation on the boards. This type of organization has, on the whole been very successful. Whether it is as effective in the largest states with the most complicated welfare problems, as it is in the smaller ones, is open to considerable doubt." Robert Moses, "Reconstruction of State Welfare Agencies," *Survey,* 10 April 1920, 74. The political processes behind this "lay and business" system are evident in the WiSFL resolutions that repeatedly called for the appointment of skilled men with practical experience to state inspection positions and the calls for legislation establishing state licensing procedures for various trades (e.g., WiSFL, *Proceedings* 1920, 63; 1922, 47, 48–49, 52). On business opposition to expanded economic regulation, see "The 1923 Legislature and What It Expects to Do," *Milwaukee: A Magazine for Her Business Leaders,* January 1923, 10.

54. "Apprenticeship in Wisconsin," *Survey,* 19 March 1921, 890.

55. "Placing Men in Wisconsin," *Survey,* 26 February 1921, 765. From July 1919 through June 1920, the state offices made 123,726 referrals and placed 94,770. On the provisions made for the placement of disabled workers, see Irene Sylvester Chubb, "Some Problems of the Partially Disabled, in War and Industry," *American Labor Legislation Review,* December 1918, 301.

56. On the characterization of the nineteenth-century United States as a precocious spending state, see Skocpol, *Protecting Soldiers and Mothers.*

57. Key and Crouch, *Initiative and Referendum,* 423–34, 527. In November 1920, voters decided on twenty different ballot propositions (including ten by initiative or referendum and five constitutional amendments), approving among others an antialien land law (passed overwhelmingly), an "extension of the state mothers' pension law to families in which the father is incapacitated for gainful work or is suffering from tuberculosis," and allowing raises for teachers, the reorganization of irrigation districts, and tax-free status for orphanages. Community property and prohibition enforcement were among the twelve defeated measures. "California: 1920," *Survey,* 27 November 1920, 326.

58. CSFL, *Proceedings* 1911, 27; Franklin Hichborn, *Story of the Session of the California Legislature of 1913* (San Francisco: Press of the James H. Barry Co., 1913), 359; *The Book of the States,* vol. 1 (Chicago: Council of State Governments and the American Legislators' Association, 1935), 213.

59. Key and Crouch, *Initiative and Referendum,* 494–96.

60. In 1918, for example, the Republican mayor of San Francisco won the Democratic primary for the governor's office, but since he lost the Republican primary to the incumbent (and since "a candidate had to win his own party's nomination in order to win that of any other party"), the Democrats were left without a candidate. Hennings, *Phelan,* 166–67; see Pitchell, "Electoral System."

61. Robert La Follette, for example, broke with an older style of politics in insisting on a commitment to issues rather than the distribution of patronage as the basis of party solidarity, but he also restricted campaigns to a very few issues, resisting constituent demands to promote a broader range of reforms. Thelen, *La Follette,* 32–51.

62. Key and Crouch, *Initiative and Referendum,* 505.

63. By the late 1920s, however, farm groups had risen to be among the most powerful lobbies in the state. Reapportionment in 1928 increased the influence of rural counties in the state senate, and farm organizations frequently drafted their own legislation without relying on the platforms of either party. Chambers, *California Farm Organizations,* 174–77.

64. Hichborn, *California Legislature of 1909,* 229. On the history of California farmers' efforts to limit their tax liability, see Yearley, *The Money Machines,* 57–59.

65. Mowry, *The California Progressives,* 218; W. Elliot Brownlee Jr. *Progressivism and Economic Growth: The Wisconsin Income Tax, 1911–1929* (Port Washington, N.Y.: Kennikat, 1974), 123. But the exemption of publicly owned (and therefore predominantly urban) utilities from taxation left rural residents bearing a disproportionate share of the tax burden through higher rates for water and power. Chambers, *California Farm Organizations,* 151.

66. Noting that California spent proportionately more on the care of dependent children than any state except New York, one social worker explained that "[s]ubsidies are often used to aid political intrigues on a large scale; outdoor relief is as frequently the instrumentality for city and county crookedness, and is used to win votes and gain partisan advantage." But even once these programs were rid of most corrupt practices, the price tag remained high. William H. Slingerland, *Child Welfare Work in California: A Study of Agencies and Institutions* (New York: Russell Sage, 1915), 27, 149, 226.

67. John Francis Neylan, "California's State Budget," *Annals of the American Academy of Political and Social Science* 62 (November 1915): 70–71.

68. Leiby, "State Welfare Administration," 181.

69. Brandeis, "Labor Legislation," 475, 515.

70. Brandeis, "Labor Legislation," 476.

71. Hundley, "Katherine Philips Edson."

72. A bill proposing greater regulation of children in the "street trades," such as newspaper boys, was promoted by "the Juvenile Protection Association of San Francisco, California State Federation of Labor, Civic Section California Club (San Francisco), Public Welfare Commission of the County of Los Angeles, Child's Welfare League of Alameda, many of the social organizations and a score of prominent women's clubs." "One Point Where California Lags Behind," *Survey,* 7 April 1917, 29.

73. Lyons, *Who's Who,* 116.

74. Cahn and Bary, *Welfare Activities,* xix. For differing opinions on this assessment, see Caroline Frances Kennedy, "Did California Loop Her Own Noose?" *Survey,* 15 June 1923, 33; Simon J. Lubin, "Overlapping or Dovetailing?" *Survey,* 15 July 1923, 460.

75. Robert W. Bruere, "Do Americans Want Americanization?" *Survey,* 15 April 1923, 75.

76. "Land Settlement in California," *Survey,* 4 August 1917, 408; "Landless," *Survey,* 3 May 1919, 200; "Feudalism in California," *Survey,* 24 May 1919, 310–11. The Home Teacher Act was promoted by the California Federation of Wom-

en's Clubs and the Women's Legislative Council of California in an effort led by Mary Gibson, a prominent clubwoman and member of the CIH. Judith Raftery, "Los Angeles Clubwomen and Progressive Reform," in *California Progressivism Revisited*, ed. William Deverall and Tom Sitton (Berkeley and Los Angeles: University of California Press, 1994), 154–57.

77. Christina Krysto, "California's Labor Camps," *Survey*, 8 November 1919, 77. See also "For Better—or Worse?" *Survey*, 12 February 1921, 688.

78. California Immigration and Housing Bulletin, September 1920, 3; Samuel Edgerton Wood, "The California State Commission of Immigration and Housing: A Study of Administrative Organization and the Growth of Function," Ph.D. diss., University of California at Berkeley, 1942, 99–104.

79. CSFL, *Report on Labor Legislation* 1913, 10; Wood, "California State Commission," 99.

80. "Feudalism in California," *Survey*, 24 May 1919, 310.

81. California Immigration and Housing Bulletin November 1920, 9.

82. "Getting into Politics," *Survey*, 20 December 1919, 256–57. The political strategy of the California Conference of Social Work continued as a source of controversy within the association. See "California Social Agencies," *Survey*, 12 June 1920, 388; "Jottings," *Survey*, 19 February 1921, 740.

83. "Jottings," *Survey*, 26 July 1919, 636; "Personals," *Survey*, 3 January 1920, 375; "Jottings," *Survey*, 15 April 1923, 68.

84. "A Health Outpost by the Pacific," *Survey*, 27 September 1919, 904; "Fresno's Community Plan," *Survey*, 27 March 1920, 800; "Los Angeles City Plan," *Survey*, 30 October 1920, 148.

85. "2 × 5 County Relief," *Survey*, 19 July 1919, 604; Leiby, "State Welfare Administration," 178–79.

86. "Problems and Methods of Legislative Investigating Committees," *American Labor Legislation Review*, March 1918, 86.

87. Five years later, this law was declared unconstitutional by the state supreme court. "Legislative Notes," *American Labor Legislation Review*, June 1922, 87. See also "For Those Injured in Industry," *Survey*, 13 September 1919, 851.

88. "San Francisco Dance Halls," *Survey*, 17 July 1920, 522–23.

89. This plan required cooperation among the Bureau of Labor Statistics, the CIH, and the Industrial Welfare Commission. "State Legislation to Plan Public Works against Employment," *American Labor Legislation Review*, September 1921, 220; "Introductory Note," *American Labor Legislation Review*, December 1921, 287.

90. "Legislative Notes," *American Labor Legislation Review*, June 1925, 77.

91. "Legislative Notes," *American Labor Legislation Review*, March 1923, 6.

92. Jackson K. Putnam, "The Persistence of Progressivism in the 1920s: The Case of California," *Pacific Historical Review* 35 (1966): 402.

93. Woody, "Populism in Washington," 103–19.

94. Allen, *Poindexter of Washington*, 21–34, 59–80.

95. Governor Marion Hay to C. B. Kegley, Master of the Washington State

Grange, September 1910, quoted in Crawford, *Washington State Grange,* 160. Kegley responded, "It is a mistake to suppose that the people do not know what they want. They do know what they want—it is the elimination of the party boss and legislation for special privilege interests. The hatred of the political grafter and the legislator who betrays the people is intense, and the people are united in their determination to secure full control over all their public servants."

96. Perceived as independent of the "big interests" such as the railroads, individual politicians such as Poindexter found themselves caught between multiple smaller constituencies—the Grange favoring rural parcel post service, for example, and small businessmen opposing it. Allen, *Poindexter of Washington,* 28–29.

97. Crawford, *Washington State Grange,* 71–74.

98. Crawford, *Washington State Grange,* 108–9.

99. Christopher Horr of the Direct Primary League became executive secretary of the Direct Legislation League.

100. Johnson, "Adoption," 297.

101. In 1908, the state Grange endorsed the employer liability law and eight-hour days for both women and miners and urged farmers to buy union-made farm implements whenever possible. Crawford, *Washington State Grange,* 162.

102. Crawford, *Washington State Grange,* 173.

103. Crawford, *Washington State Grange,* 182; Murray, "Republican Party Politics," 235–37.

104. Crawford, *Washington State Grange,* 187.

105. Schwantes, *Radical Heritage,* 162.

106. Crawford, *Washington State Grange,* 180.

107. State of Washington, Bureau of Labor, *Report, 1901–1902* 1903, 7; see also *Report, 1903–1904* 1905, 9–10.

108. Tripp, "Progressive Labor Laws," 18, 20; State of Washington, Bureau of Labor, *Report, 1901–1902* 1903, 22.

109. WaSFL, *Proceedings* 1913, 32; 1915, 135.

110. William J. Breen, "Administrative Politics and Labor Policy in the First World War: The U.S. Employment Service and the Seattle Labor Market Experiment," *Business History Review* 61 (1987): 582–605.

111. WaSFL, *Proceedings* 1913, 80.

112. For example, Edward W. Olson held the post of commissioner from 1913 until 1916 when he was appointed head of the Industrial Insurance Commission and subsequently assassinated by a workman unhappy with his compensation for injury. He praised the role of the WaSFL in promoting the conditions of labor: "[O]rganized labor demonstrated its influence as a factor in the industrial and political affairs of this state, but, as the Bureau sees it, what is has done toward the improvement of working conditions is of the greater importance, for it has not only brought about the improvement sought directly by organized labor but its attainment in that respect has tended to improve the situation outside its own ranks and so has been instrumental in bringing about better conditions for all working people." Bureau of Labor Statistics and Factory Inspection, *Ninth Bien-*

nial Report, 1913–1914 (Olympia, Wash.: Frank M. Lamborn, Public Printer, 1914), 99.

113. Saltvig, "Progressive Movement in Washington," 321–24. See also Tripp, "Toward Efficient Society," 103. On the tensions between middle-class women's reform efforts and working-class women's organizations, see chapter 6 and Oberdeck, "Not Pink Teas."

114. Tripp, "Progressive Labor Laws," 97, "Toward Efficient Society," 104.

115. Allen, *Poindexter of Washington*, 83, 168.

116. Allen, *Poindexter of Washington*, 225; "The People's Voices," *Nation*, 27 September 1922, 297–98.

117. "Election by Disgust Again," *Nation* 22 November 1922, 540; "The Third Party Is Born," *Nation*, 22 November 1922, 541; Allen, *Poindexter of Washington*, 246–52.

118. Valelly, *Radicalism in the States*, 14.

119. Electoral politics at the local level was also volatile. Elected mayor of Seattle in 1910, Hiram C. Gill was recalled in 1911 due to his laxness in regulating the city's vice district; Gill was then reelected in 1914. Warren B. Johnson, "Muckraking in the Northwest: Joe Smith and Seattle Reform," *Pacific Historical Review* 40 (1971): 478–500. On labor leader James A. Duncan's unsuccessful bid for mayor in 1920, see "Duncan's Defeat," *Survey*, 13 March 1920, 732. Duncan won a place in the general election but was defeated by the chosen successor of Mayor Ole Hanson, Hugh Caldwell, a one-time progressive who went on to build a national speaking career as the "hero" who suppressed the Seattle general strike. Caldwell was "known as a liberal" and campaigned on the slogan "Public Service, Not Politics."

120. Saltvig, "Progressive Movement in Washington," 29.

121. Donald R. Burrows and Don C. Taylor, "Public Finance in Washington: The Role of Taxation," in *Political Life in Washington: Governing the Evergreen State,* ed. Thor Swanson et al. (Pullman: Washington State University Press, 1985), 182–83.

122. Quoted in Clark, *The Dry Years*, 50. Fearing for their own party organizations, however, politicians suppressed the issue following a bitter controversy in 1909. Consequently, temperance advocates followed other Washington reformers in demanding direct democracy.

123. "Social Legislation," *Survey*, 19 May 1917, 182–83.

124. Brandeis, "Labor Legislation," 482–83.

125. Joseph F. Tripp, "An Instance of Labor and Business Cooperation: Workmen's Compensation in Washington State (1911)," *Labor History* 17, no. 4 (1976): 541–43.

126. The *American Labor Legislation Review* identified Washington as one of "the six leading states" on workmen's compensation, along with California, Massachusetts, New York, Ohio, and Wisconsin. "Progressive Tendencies," March 1915, 30. At this time, Washington ranked approximately seventeenth in the nation in terms of the value of its manufactured products

127. "Minimum Wage in Washington," *Survey,* 9 October 1920, 66–67.

128. In California, by comparison, waitresses initially opposed the law (which was passed by referendum in 1913) but eventually broke with male unionists to support the Industrial Welfare Commission, finding that minimum-wage declarations and the enforcement mechanisms actually strengthened their bargaining position with respect to employers. Cobble, *Dishing It Out,* 82–84.

129. Thelen, *La Follette,* 50.

130. William Hard, "How Many Hirams?" *Nation,* 12 December 1923, 685.

Chapter Eight

1. Grant McConnell, *Private Power and American Democracy* (New York: Knopf, 1966), 60–64.

2. "The President's Labor Conference," *Survey,* 4 October 1919, 18–20; "The President's Industrial Conference: The First Fortnight," *Survey,* 25 October 1919, 35–37.

3. "The President's Labor Conference," *Survey,* 4 October 1919, 20.

4. "The Farmer's Crisis," *Survey,* 18 December 1920, 314; Bernard M. Baruch, "Some Aspects of the Farmers' Problems," *Atlantic,* July 1921, 111–20.

5. Walter Lippmann, "The Setting for John W. Davis," *Atlantic,* October 1924, 530.

6. George H. Haynes, "The Senate: New Style," *Atlantic,* August 1924 , 258.

7. State social work conferences had adopted political programs in at least fourteen states by 1921, including California, Washington, and Wisconsin. "The State Conference," *Survey,* 15 January 1921, 575–77. See also "The State-Wide Drive in Oregon," *Survey,* 19 August 1919, 709–10; on California, "Getting into Politics," *Survey,* 20 December 1919, 256–57; "California Social Agencies," *Survey,* 12 June 1920, 338; "Does California Care?" *Survey,* 15 April 1923, 69–70; on Wisconsin, "An All-the-Year Conference," *Survey,* 15 May 1920, 231–32; "Wisconsin Social Work," *Survey,* 13 November 1920, 260; "Child Welfare in Wisconsin," *Survey,* 15 June 1922, 405.

8. H. W. Dodds, "Removable Obstacles to the Success of the Direct Primary," *Annals of the American Academy of Political and Social Science* 106 (March 1923): 18.

9. "Introductory Note," *American Labor Legislation Review,* December 1921, 287; "A State of Mind Is a Fact," *American Labor Legislation Review,* June 1925, 75.

10. Robert W. Bruere, "Propaganda Methods of Opponents of Protective Labor Legislation," *American Labor Legislation Review,* June 1925, 106. As Edward W. Macy, the director of public information for the National Child Labor Committee, noted later in the symposium: "While we have at our disposal the maturing technique of scientific research, induction, and education, it is also true that certain large manufacturing interests throughout the country are to-day employing scientific investigators and educators for the very purpose of presenting their arguments against social legislation." "Propaganda Methods," 111.

11. Anderson, *Imagined Communities,* 77–79; Sidney Tarrow, *Power in Movement* (New York: Cambridge University Press, 1994), 33–45.

12. "The Republican Victory," *Survey,* 13 November 1920, 247.

13. As Michael McGerr has demonstrated, an "educational style" was evident in elite, independent circles of the nineteenth century. The contribution of popular political associations was to use these techniques to resocialize large numbers of hitherto partisan voters. *Decline of Popular Politics.*

14. For an extended statement of this argument, see Stinchcombe, *Information and Organizations,* chap. 5.

15. Theodore Lowi makes a similar point about the policy continuities from the Johnson administration to the Nixon administration: "The test of institutionalization is succession. If successors repeat and imitate the practices of their predecessors, the patterns are being reinforced in the habits and thoughts of the successors." *The End of Liberalism: The Second Republic of the United States,* 2d ed. (New York: Norton, 1979), 278.

16. For an excellent discussion of three of the most prominent extrapartisan pressure groups of the 1930s—the Townsend Movement, Huey Long's "Share Our Wealth" organization, and the followers of Father Coughlin—see Alan Brinkley, *Voices of Protest: Huey Long, Father Coughlin, and the Great Depression* (New York: Random House, 1982).

17. In his study of industrial regulation in Britain, France, and the United States, Frank Dobbin argues that political institutions both served as models of the mechanisms for economic governance and legitimated the ends of regulatory policies. *Forging Industrial Policy.* My argument is in the same spirit but runs in the opposite direction; popular politics was a mechanism by which some aspects of social and economic organization were used to leverage changes in political institutions.

18. On the importance of expert-led agencies in cementing progressive coalitions at the municipal level, see Finegold, *Experts and Politicians,* 22–32, 178–84.

19. Thelen, *La Follette,* 134–49. On the increased socialist vote as a protest against "extortionist" fund-raising by the business-dominated Councils of Defense, see Charles D. Stewart, "Prussianizing Wisconsin," *Atlantic,* January 1919, 99–105.

20. WiSFL, *Proceedings* 1920, 77. Berger was, however, defeated in the congressional elections of 1920. "The Republican Victory," *Survey,* 13 November 1920, 247.

21. "Wisconsin: 1920," *Survey,* 1 May 1920, 184.

22. Gavett, *Labor Movement in Milwaukee,* 129–30; on the inverse relation between socialist strength and the WiSFL's reliance on lobbying, see chapter 4.

23. WiSFL, *Proceedings* 1920, 49, 70–71.

24. WiSFL, *Proceedings* 1920, 4, emphasis added; 1921, 43, emphasis added; 1924, 54, emphasis added; 1924, 47.

25. WiSFL, *Proceedings* 1923, 48, emphasis added.

26. *Wisconsin Equity News,* 1 March 1917, 720.

27. WiSFL, *Proceedings* 1920, 23.

28. *Wisconsin Equity News,* 1 March 1917, 726.

29. *Wisconsin Equity News,* 15 March 1917, 737; Theodore Saloutos and

John D. Hicks, *Agrarian Discontent,* 189; Herbert F. Margulies, "The La Follette-Philipp Alliance of 1918," *Wisconsin Magazine of History,* 38, no. 4 (1955): 248-49.

30. "Wisconsin Wakes," *Survey,* 15 April 1924, 70.

31. Christina Krysto, "California's Labor Camps," *Survey,* 8 November 1919, 72-73.

32. "Kill the Bill or Kill the Babies," *Survey,* 20 November 1920, 270-71.

33. "California Marches Backward," *Survey,* 1 June 1923, 319. For a sense of the scale of social spending in California, recall that the state share of the Wisconsin income tax in its first year of operation was two hundred thousand dollars, of which half went for the costs of administering the tax. Kennan, "The Wisconsin Income Tax."

34. "The Attack on the Los Angeles Y.W.C.A.," *Survey,* 16 August 1920, 611-13; "California under Attack," *Survey,* 16 October 1920, 185; Edwin Layton, "The Better American Foundation: A Case Study of Superpatriotism," *Pacific Historical Review* 30 (1961): 137-47.

35. "For Better—or Worse?" *Survey,* 12 February 1921, 687-88.

36. "America Is Calling," *Survey,* 12 February 1921, 687; "For Better—or Worse?" *Survey,* 12 February 1921, 687-88.

37. "Charlotte Anita Whitney," *Survey,* 29 May 1920, 296; "California Marches Backward," *Survey,* 1 June 1923, 319.

38. Richard Coke Lower, *A Bloc of One: The Political Career of Hiram W. Johnson* (Stanford, Calif.: Stanford University Press, 1993), chaps. 2 and 6.

39. There were, however, limits to this nonpartisanship. In 1915, voters rejected a proposal that would have made *all* state officers (not just municipal and county) nonpartisan. Lower, *A Bloc of One,* 67. For Paul Scharrenberg's argument as to why organized labor should support this proposal, see CSFL, *Proceedings* 1915, 40.

40. Quoted in Lower, *A Bloc of One,* 158; see also 79-86.

41. In the Senate, Johnson championed federal funding of a dam on the Colorado with the provision that municipalities have priority over private companies in purchasing hydroelectric power. Defeated repeatedly in the 1920s, the bill finally passed in 1928 following revelations that utility associations had made payments to many politicians and lobbyists opposed to the bill and "Additional revelations continued to undermine the opposition by calling into question the reasons for their dissent." Lower, *A Bloc of One,* 235. Even in the late 1920s, the use of educational or propaganda politics by pressure groups elicited serious charges of impropriety. On the congressional investigations of the efforts of utilities to co-opt educators to promote private ownership, see McConnell, *Private Power,* 18-20.

42. The nonpartisan character of state politics diminished as first the Republicans (in the late 1930s) and then the Democrats (in the late 1940s and 1950s) organized "party clubs" similar to those established earlier in Wisconsin in response to Progressive Era regulation of party organization and responsibilities. In 1952, an initiative to abolish cross-filing was defeated, but a proposal to include

candidate's party affiliation on the ballot was passed. Francis Carney, *The Rise of the Democratic Clubs in California* (Henry Holt, 1958); see also Sorauf, "Extra-Legal Parties."

43. Neylan, California's State Budget," 70–71.

44. Frank, *Purchasing Power*, 15.

45. Frank, *Purchasing Power*, 91–92.

46. Robert Whitaker, "Washington: The Dawn of a Tomorrow," *Nation*, 19 December 1923, 709.

47. "Aberdeen's Unique Plan," *Survey*, 22 November 1919, 156.

48. "Rousing Interest in Health," *Survey*, 13 March 1920, 742.

49. Aaron Sapiro, "New Financing of Food Production," *Survey*, 12 March 1921, 857.

50. "Economic Views and Public Office," *Survey*, 16 October 1920, 85–86.

51. Allen and Austin, "Populist Era," 120; Hamilton Cravens, "The Emergence of the Farmer-Labor Party in Washington Politics, 1919–20," *Pacific Northwest Quarterly* 57, no. 4 (1966): 151–57; Frank, *Purchasing Power*, 110–11.

52. Between 1919 and 1925, very few notices of policy accomplishments in Washington appeared in the pages of either the *American Labor Legislation Review* or *The Survey*. In 1925, for example, many of the issues that the WaSFL hoped to put before the Washington legislature had already been decided in either California or Wisconsin: "Leading measures on the immediate legislative program of the Washington state federation of labor include vocational rehabilitation of industrial cripples, inclusion of occupational diseases under the workmen's compensation act, jury trial in injunction cases, statewide old age pensions, ratification of child labor constitutional amendment, and one day of rest in eight for street railway men." "Legislative Notes," *American Labor Legislation Review*, December 1925, 282. See also WaSFL, "Present Legislative Program," in *History of the Washington State Federation of Labor* (Seattle: Washington State Federation of Labor, 1924), 15–16.

53. Quoted in Arthur Hillman, "The Unemployed Citizens' League of Seattle," *University of Washington Publications in the Social Sciences* 5, no. 3 (1934): 198.

54. Hillman, "Unemployed Citizens' League," 214.

55. This commitment to insurgent partisanship endured; in 1936, the so-called Washington Commonwealth Federation captured the state Democratic Party. James L. Sundquist, *Dynamics of the Party System: Alignment and Realignment of Political Parties in the United States* (Washington, D.C.: Brookings Institution, 1973), 197.

56. Sundquist, *Dynamics of Party System*, chap. 8.

57. Ellis Hawley, *The New Deal and the Problem of Monopoly* (Princeton, N.J.: Princeton University Press, 1966), 10–12.

58. Hawley, *The New Deal*, 36–39.

59. "Second Wind," *Survey*, 7 February 1920, 549.

60. See chap. 3; also Taylor, "Social Movement Continuity," 761–75.

61. Herring, *Group Representation before Congress*, 21.

62. Herring, *Group Representation before Congress*, 18.

63. Odegard, *Pressure Politics,* 5

64. Odegard, *Pressure Politics,* 105.

65. "Why the Nation Went Dry," *Literary Digest,* 25 January 1919, 9.

66. Elizabeth Tilton, "The Wets—and the West," *Survey,* 21 July 1917, 9.

67. The Democratic candidate for U.S. Senate from California responded by paying extra attention to the registration and recruitment of women voters. Hennings, *Phelan,* 90–92.

68. Herring, *Group Representation before Congress,* 194–95.

69. On the contrast of "job-oriented" pressure groups with the broader identity of consumer-taxpayer that characterized prewar progressive insurgency, see Thelen, *La Follette,* 99–124.

70. Willard Cooper, "The Soldier Vote," *Atlantic,* September 1924, 387–88; "Government by and for Special Interests," *Nation,* 30 August 1922, 201; George Madden Martin, "American Women and Paternalism," *Atlantic,* June 1924, 744.

71. Thomas F. Cadwalader, "The Defeat of the Twentieth Amendment," *Annals of the American Academy of Political and Social Science* 129 (January 1927): 67. Cadwalader was president of the Sentinels of the Republic, but for similar assessments of the tarnished reputation of federal intervention, see Lincoln C. Andrews (assistant secretary of the Treasury), "Prohibition Enforcement as a Phase of Federal versus State Jurisdiction in American Life," *Annals of the American Academy of Political and Social Science* 129 (January 1927): 82–83; Felix Adler, "The Child Labor Panic," *Survey,* 15 February 1925, 566. For similar lessons drawn from the war mobilization, see William Leavitt Stoddard, "Too Much Federalism," *Survey,* 17 January 1920, 430.

72. "The Common Welfare," *Survey,* 15 February 1925, 572–73; "Legislative Notes," *American Labor Legislation Review,* September 1924, 200. See also Hart, "Feminism and Bureaucracy"; Zimmerman, "The Jurisprudence of Equality." Washington and Wisconsin were among the states that asked "to assist in the oral argument for the law." "Legislative Notes," *American Labor Legislation Review,* March 1923, 7.

73. "Editorials," *Survey,* 1 July 1923, 406.

74. Of the sixteen insurgents in the House, all but La Follette came from districts west of the Mississippi. Allen, *Poindexter of Washington,* 34–36.

75. In the 1920s, President Harding denied patronage appointments to La Follette, and the Republican National Committee sought to block his renomination in 1922. Thelen, *La Follette,* 171. Robert W. Bruere remarked, "The attitude of the Republican nominating convention toward the Wisconsin delegation has been widely interpreted as notice that continued insubordination will mean eviction from the party." "The Non-Partisan Third Party," *Survey,* 15 July 1924, 445. In the wake of the 1924 election, the Republican leadership did strip La Follette, along with Senators Brookhart, Frazier, and Ladd, of their seniority. Hansen, *Gaining Access,* 55.

76. The reporter commented that "unlike the more general program, this proposal does not seem to emanate from the Republican National Advisory Commit-

tee, whose valuable and interesting reports have been published from time to time. It appears to be rather a somewhat impromptu and, it must be admitted, rather shrewd attempt to evade some practical difficulties which have arisen in connection with previous attempts to secure new federal departments." Harding's opponent, Governor Cox of Ohio, responded by endorsing both "the idea of housecleaning our government departments" and "giving education and health equal consideration with labor, instead of dumping all social questions again into another grab-bag, ill-defined department." "Social Justice and the Government," *Survey,* 23 October 1920, 119–20.

77. "'The Supreme Duty' Undone," *Survey,* 15 July 1924, 455–56. In this context, the strategic value of Calvin Coolidge's famed silence became clear: "The President's very reticence in the campaign, for which he was roundly and no doubt rightly berated—although as a canny piece of tactics it worked—has this clear advantage: it leaves him largely uncommitted in facing issues as they come up." "The Common Welfare," *Survey,* 15 November 1924, 182.

78. Hennings, *Phelan,* 207.

79. "The Bricks of a New Party," *Nation,* 27 December 1922, 707.

80. "Jottings," *Survey,* 26 July 1919, 636; "Coal Miners in Convention," *Survey,* 4 October 1919, 25.

81. "Labor in Politics," *Survey,* 30 August 1919, 782.

82. "The A. F. of L. in Politics," *Survey,* 14 February 1920, 568.

83. "A 'Rope of Sand' and Gompers," *Survey,* 26 June 1920, 435.

84. The conference attracted "200 delegates coming from more than 4,000,000 active organization memberships or about 20,000,000 consumers." The extent and character of support for the movement was reflected in the permanent commission created at the Congress: "The chairman is C. H. Gustafson, president Nebraska Farmers' Union; general treasurer, Warren S. Stone, grand chief Brotherhood of Locomotive Engineers; general secretary, Oscar H. McGill, of the Western Cooperative Timber Mills; vice-chairmen, L. E. Sheppard, president, Order of Railroad Conductors; Herbert F. Baker, president, Farmers' National Council; Dalton T. Clarke, president National Cooperative Association; J. W. Kline, president International Brotherhood of Blacksmiths and Helpers; E. O. F. Ames; president Pacific Cooperative League; J. M. Anderson, president Equity Cooperative Exchange; the commission, George P. Hampton, managing director Farmers' National Council; Duncan McDonald, former president Illinois Federation of Labor; Allen E. Barker, president United Brotherhood of Maintenance of Way and Railway Shop Laborers; J. Weller Long, secretary Farmers' Federation; Frank Rust, secretary-manager Seattle Labor Bank; Grant H. Slocum, president National Federation of Gleaners; William Bouck, master Washington State Grange; Bert M. Jewell, acting president Railway Employe's Department, American Federation of Labor." "The Farmer-Labor Congress," *Survey,* 21 February 1920, 605.

85. "Election by Disgust Again," *Nation,* 22 November 1922, 540.

86. "The Third Party Is Born," *Nation* 22 November 1922, 541.

87. "The Bricks of the New Party," *Nation*, 27 December 1922, 707.

88. Kenneth Campbell MacKay, *The Progressive Movement of 1924* (New York: Columbia University Press, 1947), 9.

89. MacKay, *Progressive Movement of 1924*, 224.

90. James Sundquist argues, however, that as "protests against economic hardship . . . much of the rearrangement of political patterns in the 1920s can therefore be considered a precursor of—perhaps not improperly seen as an integral part of—the political revolution precipitated by Wall Street's 'Black Thursday.'" *Dynamics of Party System*, 182.

91. Women, meanwhile, had their own debate over the role and viability of the National Women's Party: "The decision of the women not to form a party of their own and their determination not to line up with the old parties as regulars have made it possible for them to select a plan of action based on unpolitical considerations." "National League of Women Voters," *Survey*, 4 December 1920, 371; see also Park, *Front Door Lobby;* Taylor, "Social Movement Continuity."

92. Thelen, *La Follette*, 192. This was not an unintended outcome but was central to the organizational model borrowed from the British Labour Party: "English experience clearly suggests the strategic procedure for an American political labor movement: a federation in which various organizations retain their entity and principles, uniting in the support of common candidates at elections." "The Coming Political Cleavage," *Nation*, 1 November 1922, 455.

93. "A 'Rope of Sand' and Gompers," *Survey*, 26 June 1920, 435.

94. "Labor and the Railroad," *Survey*, 28 February 1920, 640.

95. "Labor and Monopolies," *Survey*, 26 February 1921, 749.

96. F. Lauriston Bullard, "A Programme for Labor Unions," *Atlantic*, January 1924, 86. This decision illustrates one of the dangers of transposing familiar forms to new purposes: a group may become subject to new logics of appropriateness. As *The Survey* explained, "[W]hether the common law chooses to recognize the fact or not, unincorporated groups do exist and act as entities; they buy and sell, own property, transact business and even possess distinctive individualities. As Chief Justice Taft said in regard to the transactions carried on by labor unions, 'An extensive financial business is carried on, money is borrowed, notes are given to banks, and in every way the union acts as a business entity distinct from its members.' If such a group has the privileges of legal entity, why should it not be subject to corresponding responsibilities?" "The Coronado Decision," *Survey*, 15 June 1922, 385–86.

97. Hansen, *Gaining Access*, 29–30.

98. Herring, *Group Representation before Congress*, 112–13.

99. Quoted in "The Farm Bloc—a Peril or a Hope?" *Literary Digest*, 24 December 1921, 10–11. The article also noted that "Secretary Weeks has never evinced any alarm over the business bloc, which is active. His dismay arises from the fact that a new political power threatens the sway of his own group."

100. From the *Washington Herald*, quoted in "The 'Farmers Party' in Congress," *Literary Digest*, 2 July 1921, 14; Charles Merz, "Progressivism, Old and New," *Atlantic*, July 1923, 103–7. Merz identified the new structure of American

politics: "It might almost be said, in fact, that the lines of conflict are really drawn in the field of economics, and not of politics at all. Organized labor confronts organized capital in the workshops. Cooperative societies struggle with commission men and speculators for control of crops. Labor banks and cooperative loan associations compete with trust companies and commercial banks for credit. The economic rivalry that lagged behind political insurgency is coming to the front" (107).

101. "The Progressives Progress," *Nation,* 19 December 1923, 712; Elmer Murphy, "Government at the Crossroads," *Atlantic,* October 1923, 439.

102. Hansen, *Gaining Access,* 56–60.

103. Elmer Murphy, "Government at the Crossroads," *Atlantic,* October 1923, 444.

104. Ordway Tead, "The New Place of Labor," *Atlantic,* August 1918, 575–76.

105. "How Workingmen Fare at Washington," *Survey,* 23 February 1918, 575.

106. Herring, *Group Representation before Congress,* 186; see also W. L. George, "Women in Politics," *Harper's,* June 1919, 85–87.

107. Herring, *Group Representation before Congress,* 189.

108. "Muskets or Babies," *Survey,* 25 December 1920, 446. For a critical assessment of the political power of women's organizations, see George Madden Martin, "American Women and Paternalism," *Atlantic,* June 1924, 748–50, and "American Women and Public Affairs," *Atlantic,* February 1924, 169–71.

109. "The First Year of the Sheppard-Towner Act," *Survey,* 15 April 1924, 89; Molly Ladd-Taylor, *Raising a Baby the Government Way: Mothers' Letters to the Children's Bureau, 1915–1932* (New Brunswick, N.J.: Rutgers University Press, 1986), 24.

110. Zimmerman, "The Jurisprudence of Equality."

111. The affiliations of successive cohorts of suffragists illustrate the gradual fragmentation of the "woman movement" well before the passage of the Nineteenth Amendment. Of a sample of suffrage activists born in the 1840s, over 90 percent were officers of NAWSA, over 80 percent of the WCTU, and over 15 percent of the GFWC (the sample included all women mentioned in at least four state histories collected in Susan B. Anthony and Ida Husted Harper, *The History of Woman Suffrage, 1883–1900,* vol. 4 [Indianapolis: Hollenbeck, 1902], and Harper, *History of Woman Suffrage,* vol. 6). This overlapping leadership network helped to consolidate the movement. For the cohort born in the 1860s, the relative importance of the WCTU and GFWC as allies of the suffrage movement had reversed: over 20 percent of the activists sampled were WCTU officers, and over 70 percent held leadership positions in the GFWC. But both proportions declined for subsequent cohorts; of the suffrage activists in the sample born in the 1880s, *none* held offices in either the WCTU or the GFWC. Clemens, "From Clubwoman to Committeewoman."

112. For a more general call for an expanded federal role, see "Social Reconstruction," *Survey,* 7 June 1919, 403. For the corresponding concern for the pres-

ervation of states' rights against federal encroachment, see George Madden Martin, "American Women and Paternalism," *Atlantic,* June 1924, 748–50.

113. Florence Kelley, "The Federal Child Labor Law," *Survey,* 1 September 1917, 484–86. Recall that the provision of elementary school scholarships had been used by clubwomen since the 1900s (see chap. 6).

114. William L. Chenery, "Child Labor—the New Alignment," *Survey,* 1 January 1925, 380. The precedent for using federal taxation for the protection of labor was set by the American Association for Labor Legislation's campaign to outlaw the manufacture of phosphorus matches, which caused "phossy jaw" in workers. "Report of Work 1918," *American Labor Legislation Review,* March 1919, 169; see Moss, "Kindling a Flame."

115. Felix Adler, "The Child Labor Panic," *Survey,* 15 February 1925, 566. To enforce the first law, the federal Children's Bureau "enlisted state factory inspectors and labor bureaus as deputies of the federal agency. No state refused cooperation. This kept the federal staff down to a flying squadron." Florence Kelley, "The Federal Child Labor Amendment: Ten Answers to Ten Questions," *Survey,* 15 October 1924.

116. "Working Children," *Survey,* 15 June 1922, 381.

117. William L. Chenery, "Child Labor—the New Alignment," *Survey,* 1 January 1925, 380.

118. William L. Chenery, "Child Labor—the New Alignment," *Survey,* 1 January 1925, 379, emphasis added. But recall that woman suffrage groups in particular were enamored with the techniques of propaganda before the war. The amendment strategy was not limited to child labor. Publisher William Allen White had called for "giving Congress unlimited power over commerce and industry, and under that amendment I should establish a minimum wage commission with full powers, and would provide for federal employment agents who would take up the slack in our labor situation, thus securing so far as possible regular employment for people in the seasonal industries. This would soon wipe out the revolutionary ideals of labor." "A Constitutional Amendment," *Survey,* 20 December 1919, 276.

119. "The Common Welfare," *Survey,* 15 February 1925, 572; 15 March 1925, 740.

120. "Retro-Progress," *Survey,* 15 July 1922, 501; "The Minimum Wage—What Next?" *Survey,* 15 May 1923, 221, 261–63.

121. John A. Ryan, "Our Self-Amending Constitution," *Survey,* 1 August 1923, 481–82.

122. "Legislative Notes," *American Labor Legislation Review,* March 1923, 11. These decisions were particularly damaging to workers: "Twenty-one times during forty years the United States Supreme Court has decided cases affecting labor by four-to-five or four-to-four decisions, and nearly two-thirds of these closely divided opinions have been handed down during the past ten years." John B. Andrews, "Progress of American Labor Legislation," *American Labor Legislation Review,* June 1923, 122. See also Francis Bacon Sayre, "The Minimum Wage Decision: How the Supreme Court Becomes Virtually a House of Lords," *Survey,*

1 May 1923, 150–51. Both Wisconsin and Washington were among the states that asked to assist in the oral argument in support of the District of Columbia minimum-wage legislation. *American Labor Legislation Review,* March 1923, 7.

123. Aware of the difficulty of controlling federal spending on both military pensions and river and harbor improvements (a source of "fat pork" distributed in its "haphazard, wire-pulling, wasteful manner"), Walter W. Woehlke did query, "Is it wise, at this particular time of unsettled revenue conditions, to drill another hole into the federal barrel?" "Federal Money for Local Roads," *Sunset: The Pacific Monthly,* April 1913, 424.

124. Paul H. Douglas, "A System of Federal Grants-in-Aid I," *Political Science Quarterly* 35 (June 1920): 255; "A System of Federal Grants-in-Aid II," *Political Science Quarterly* 35 (December 1920): 522–23.

125. Frederick MacKenzie, "Bill Proposed for Cooperation by All States under the New Federal Law for the Rehabilitation of Industrial Cripples," *American Labor Legislation Review,* December 1920, 246–47; on the appropriation, *American Labor Legislation Review,* September 1920, 198; for similar arrangements proposed for employment service, see John B. Andrews, "A Federal-State Employment Service Advanced in Congress," *American Labor Legislation Review,* June 1920, 121–22.

126. Douglas, "Grants-in-Aid I," 256–58.

127. The American Association for Labor Legislation, AFL, and National Association of Manufacturers appeared at congressional hearings to support the vocational rehabilitation bill. "Vocational Rehabilitation for Industrial Cripples," *American Labor Legislation Review,* June 1919, 199.

128. Skocpol, *Protecting Mothers and Soldiers,* 494–522; on the federal oversight and matching fund provisions, see "The First Year of the Sheppard-Towner Act," *Survey,* 15 April 1924, 89.

129. "Legislative Notes," *American Labor Legislation Review,* March 1923, 7; Irene Osgood Andrews, "Maternity and Infancy Act Stands," *American Labor Legislation Review,* September 1923, 194. See also Thomas Reed Powell, "Umpiring the Federal System, 1922–24," *Political Science Quarterly* 40 (1925): 101–26.

130. Social reformers were not alone in seeking to tap these funds, although they were more attached to federal-state cooperation. President Harding promoted a "ship-subsidy bill," while Senator Norris of Nebraska sponsored a bill that would appropriate $100 million to purchase capital stock in a new Farmers and Consumers Financing Corporation. "Senator Norris's 'Socialism,'" *Nation,* 24 January 1923, 85.

131. "'The Supreme Duty' Undone," *Survey,* 15 July 1924, 455.

132. Stuart A. Rice, *Farmers and Workers in American Politics* (New York: Columbia University Press, 1924), 28–29.

133. Walter Lippmann, "The Setting for John W. Davis," *Atlantic,* October 1924, 532; emphasis added.

134. Charles Merz, "Progressivism, Old and New," *Atlantic,* July 1923, 102; George H. Haynes, "The Senate: New Style," *Atlantic,* August 1924, 258–59. The

practice of securing a "general pair" dated from the 1840s but made little sense as the Senate increasingly faced complex but not clearly partisan decisions.

135. Immergut, "Rules of the Game," 63–68.

136. Walter Lippmann, "The Setting for John W. Davis," *Atlantic,* October 1924, 534.

137. As one Wisconsin farmer explained, his neighbor "has noticed that unions and teachers' organizations seem to have been successful in forcing the government to guarantee financial security of their members. He has seen them set aside for a time the workings of supply and demand. So he ought not to be censured for assuming that a paternalistic government and a benevolent president—toward farmers—could assure prosperity." Glenn W. Birkett, "A Farmer Speaks Out," *Atlantic,* December 1924, 765.

138. Wesley McCune, *The Farm Bloc* (Garden City, N.Y.: Doubleday, Doran, 1943), v.

139. Bentley, *The Process of Government,* 204.

Coda

1. "Editorials," *Survey,* 1 October 1924, 49.

2. Quoted in Murray S. Stedman Jr. and Susan W. Stedman, *Discontent at the Polls: A Study of Farmer and Labor Parties, 1827–1948* (New York: Columbia University Press, 1950), 27.

3. Charles Merriam, "Nominating Systems," *Annals of the American Academy of Political and Social Science* 106 (March 1923): 6.

4. George Norris, "Why I Believe in the Direct Primary," *Annals of the American Academy of Political and Social Science* 106 (March 1923): 23.

5. Quoted in "The Farm Bloc—a Peril or a Hope?" *Literary Digest,* 24 December 1921, 10.

6. College Equal Suffrage League of Northern California, *Winning Equal Suffrage,* 11.

7. On the concept of "veto points," see Immergut, "Rules of the Game," 63–68.

8. "Minnesota, the Nonpartisan League, and the Future," *Nation,* 1 August 1923, 102.

9. Galbreath, "Provisions," 109.

10. Charles Perrow, "A Society of Organizations," *Theory and Society* 20 (1991): 739; Scott, *Domination,* 120–24.

11. Stinchcombe, *Theoretical Methods,* 40.

12. Michel Foucault, *The History of Sexuality,* vol. 1, *An Introduction,* trans. Robert Hurley (New York: Vintage, 1990), 95.

13. CSG, *Proceedings* 1889, 43.

References

Primary Documents

American Federation of Labor. *An Interesting Discussion on a Political Programme at the Denver Convention of the American Federation of Labor.* Washington, D.C.: American Federation of Labor, 1894.

———. *A Sketch of the American Labor Federation—It's [sic] Origin and Progress.* Published by the AFL for the Paris International Exposition, 1900.

———. *Manual of Common Procedure for the Use of Local and Federal Labor Unions Affiliated with the American Federation of Labor.* Washington, D.C.: American Federation of Labor, 1903.

———. *Financial Report of the American Federation of Labor, Political Campaign of 1906. 1906.*

———. *Financial Report of the McNamara Defense Fund.* Washington, D.C.: American Federation of Labor, 1912.

———. *St. Louis Exposition, Catalogue of Exhibits.* Washington, D.C.: American Federation of Labor, 1904.

California Civic League. *San Francisco Center: Annual Report.* 1912.

———.*Constitution of the San Francisco Center of the California Civic League.* 1913.

California Fruit Growers Exchange. *Annual Report of the General Manager.* 1919–29.

California State Commission of Immigration and Housing. *Report on Unemployment.* 1914.

California State Federation of Labor (CSFL). *Proceedings of the Annual Convention.* 1901–16.

———. *Report on Labor Legislation and Labor Record of Senators and Assemblymen.* 1911–21.

California State Grange (CSG). *Proceedings of the Annual Convention.* 1887–1915.

College Equal Suffrage League of Northern California. *Winning Equal Suffrage in California.* National College Equal Suffrage League, 1913.

General Federation of Women's Clubs. *Official Proceedings of the Biennial Convention.* 1896–98.

Industrial Commission of Wisconsin. *Report on Old Age Relief.* 1915.

Madison Federated Trades Council. *Trades Council and Labor Union Directory of Madison, Wis.* Madison, Wis.: Federated Trades Council, 1894.

National American Woman Suffrage Association (NAWSA). *Proceedings of the Annual Convention.* 1893–99.

San Francisco Ladies' Protection and Relief Society. *Forty-Eighth and Forty-Ninth Annual Reports* [1901–2]. San Francisco: C. A. Murdock and Co., 1903.

U.S. Bureau of the Census. *Abstract of the Thirteenth Census, 1910.* Washington, D.C.: Government Printing Office, 1920.

———. *Abstract of the Twelfth Census.* Washington, D.C.: Government Printing Office, 1900.

———. *Benevolent Institutions 1904.* Washington, D.C.: Government Printing Office, 1905.

———. *Benevolent Institutions 1910.* Washington, D.C.: Government Printing Office, 1913.

———. *Compendium of the Eleventh Census: 1890.* Washington, D.C.: Government Printing Office.

———. *Financial Statistics of State and Local Governments, 1932.* Washington, D.C.: Government Printing Office, 1935.

———. *Wealth, Debt, and Taxation: 1913.* Washington, D.C.: Government Printing Office, 1915.

Washington, State of. Bureau of Labor. *Report of the Bureau of Labor of the State of Washington.* 1901–16.

Washington, State of. Bureau of Labor Statistics and Factory Inspection. *Ninth Biennial Report, 1913–1914.* Olympia: Frank M. Lamborn, Public Printer, 1914.

Washington, State of. Labor Commissioner. *Report of the Labor Commissioner of the State of Washington, 1899–1900.* 1901.

Washington State Federation of Labor (WaSFL). *History of the Washington State Federation of Labor.* Seattle: Washington State Federation of Labor, 1924.

———. *Proceedings of the Annual Convention.* 1913–17.

Washington State Federation of Women's Clubs. *Annual Report.* 1915–16.

Winslow, Helen M., ed. *Official Register and Directory of Women's Clubs in America.* Vols. 10, 17. Boston, 1908, 1915.

Wisconsin State Federation of Labor (WiSFL). *Official Directory.* 1896–97.

———. *Proceedings of the Annual Convention.* 1905–24.

Wisconsin State Federation of Women's Clubs. *Proceedings of the Annual Convention.* 1898–1913.

Wisconsin Woman Suffrage Scrapbooks. Wisconsin State Historical Society.

Womans Parliament of Southern California. *Proceedings.* 1892. Bancroft Library, University of California at Berkeley.

Periodicals

American Labor Legislation Review. October 1912–December 1925.

Atlantic Monthly. August 1918–December 1924.

California Immigration and Housing Bulletin. September–November 1920. Bancroft Library, University of California at Berkeley.

Club Life (San Francisco). May 1902–April 1903. Library of Congress.

Federation Courier (joint publication of the California, Utah, and Nevada Federations of Women's Clubs). November 1911. Bancroft Library, University of California at Berkeley.

Harper's Monthly Magazine. June 1919.

Literary Digest. 25 January 1919–24 December 1921.

Milwaukee: A Magazine for Her Business Leaders. January 1923. University of Chicago Library.

Milwaukee Daily News. 3 July–7 July 1911. Wisconsin Woman Suffrage Notebooks, Wisconsin State Historical Society.

Milwaukee Evening Wisconsin. 10 October 1911. Wisconsin Woman Suffrage Notebooks, Wisconsin State Historical Society.

Milwaukee Free Press. 7 July 1911. Wisconsin Woman Suffrage Scrapbooks, Wisconsin State Historical Society.

Milwaukee Journal. [?] July–28 September 1911. Wisconsin Woman Suffrage Scrapbooks, Wisconsin State Historical Society.

Milwaukee Morning Sentinel. 8 August 1911. Wisconsin Woman Suffrage Scrapbooks, Wisconsin State Historical Society.

Monroe Times. 22 July 1911. Wisconsin Woman Suffrage Scrapbooks, Wisconsin State Historical Society.

The Nation. 9 August 1922–19 December 1923.

Oshkosh Northwestern. 14 September 1911. Wisconsin Woman Suffrage Scrapbooks, Wisconsin State Historical Society.

Racine News. 11 July 1911. Wisconsin Woman Suffrage Scrapbooks, Wisconsin State Historical Society.

Sunset: The Pacific Monthly. April–July 1913.

The Survey. 21 October 1911–15 May 1925.

Western Woman Voter (Seattle). February 1911–January 1913. Microfilm, Bancroft Library, University of California at Berkeley.

Wisconsin Citizen. August 1887–April 1897. Wisconsin State Historical Society.

Wisconsin Equity News. 25 June 1911–15 March 1917.

Books, Journal Articles, and Dissertations

Abrams, Philip. *Historical Sociology.* Ithaca, N.Y.: Cornell University Press, 1982.

Aldrich, John H. "Rational Choice Theory and the Study of American Politics." In *The Dynamics of American Politics,* ed. Lawrence C. Dodd and Calvin Jillson. Boulder, Colo.: Westview Press, 1994.

———. *Why Parties? The Origin and Transformation of Party Politics in America.* Chicago: University of Chicago Press, 1995.

Allen, Howard W. *Poindexter of Washington: A Study in Progressive Politics.* Carbondale: Southern Illinois University Press, 1981.

Allen, Howard W., and Erik W. Austin. "From the Populist Era to the New Deal: A Study of Partisan Realignment in Washington State, 1889–1950." *Social Science History* 3, no. 2 (1979): 115–43.

Alonso, Harriet Hyman. *The Women's Peace Union and the Outlawry of War, 1921–1942.* Knoxville: University of Tennessee Press, 1989.

Altmeyer, Arthur J. *The Industrial Commission of Wisconsin: A Case Study in Labor Law Administration.* University of Wisconsin Studies in the Social Sciences and History, vol. 17. Madison: University of Wisconsin Press, 1932.

Amenta, Edwin, and Bruce G. Carruthers. "The Formative Years of U.S. Social Spending Policies: Theories of the Welfare State and the American States during the Great Depression." *American Sociological Review* 53, no. 5 (1988): 661–78.

Amenta, Edwin, Elisabeth S. Clemens, Jefren Olsen, Sunita Parikh, and Theda Skocpol. "The Political Origins of Unemployment Insurance in Five American States." *Studies of American Political Development* 2 (1987): 137–82.

Ander, O. Fritiof. "The Immigrant Church and the Patrons of Husbandry." *Agricultural History* 8 (October 1934): 154–65.

Anderson, Benedict. *Imagined Communities: Reflections on the Origins and Spread of Nationalism.* New York: Verso, 1983.

Andrews, Irene Osgood. *Minimum Wage Legislation.* Appendix 3 of the Third Report of the New York State Factory Investigating Commission. Reprint, Albany, N.Y.: J. B. Lyon, 1914.

Andrews, Lincoln C. "Prohibition Enforcement as a Phase of Federal versus State Jurisdiction in American Life." *Annals of the American Academy of Political and Social Science* 129 (January 1927): 77–87.

Anthony, Susan B., and Ida Husted Harper. *The History of Woman Suffrage, 1883–1900.* Vol. 4. Indianapolis: Hollenbeck, 1902.

Archer, Margaret S. *Culture and Agency: The Place of Culture in Social Theory.* New York: Cambridge University Press, 1988.

Argersinger, Peter H. "The Value of the Vote: Political Representation in the Gilded Age." *Journal of American History* 76, no. 1 (1989): 59–90.

Ashby, LeRoy. *The Spearless Leader: Senator Borah and the Progressive Movement in the 1920s.* Urbana: University of Illinois Press, 1972.

Asher, Robert. "The 1911 Wisconsin Workmen's Compensation Law: A Study in Conservative Reform." *Wisconsin Magazine of History* 57, no. 2 (1973–74): 123–40.

Bahmer, Robert H. "The American Society of Equity." *Agricultural History* 14, no. 1 (1940): 33–63.

Bailyn, Bernard. *The Ideological Origins of the American Revolution.* Enlarged ed. Cambridge, Mass.: Harvard University Press, Belknap Press, 1992.

Baker, Jean H. *Affairs of Party: The Political Culture of Northern Democrats in the Mid–Nineteenth Century.* Ithaca, N.Y.: Cornell University Press, 1983.

Baker, Paula. "The Domestication of Politics: Women and American Political Society, 1780–1920." *American Historical Review* 89, no. 3 (1984): 620–47.

———. *The Moral Frameworks of Public Life: Gender, Politics, and the State in Rural New York, 1870–1930.* New York: Oxford University Press, 1991.

Balogh, Brian. "Reorganizing the Organizational Synthesis: Federal-Professional Relations in Modern America." *Studies in American Political Development* 5 (1991): 119–72.

Barrett, Charles Simon. *The Mission, History, and Times of the Farmers' Union.* Nashville, Tenn.: Marshall and Bruce, 1909.

Baumgartner, Frank R., and Bryan D. Jones. "Agenda Dynamics and Policy Subsystems." *Journal of Politics* 53, no. 4 (1991): 1044–74.

Baur, John E. "Private Philanthropy in Nineteenth-Century Southern California." *Southern California Quarterly* 71, nos. 2–3 (1989): 119–42.

Beard, Charles, and Birl Schultz. *Documents on the State-Wide Initiative, Referendum, and Recall.* New York: Macmillan, 1912.

Beard, Mary R. "The Legislative Influence of Unenfranchised Women." *Annals of the American Academy of Political and Social Science* 56 (November 1914): 54–61.

Beckett, Paul L., and Walfred H. Peterson. "The Constitutional Framework." In *Political Life in Washington: Governing the Evergreen State,* ed. Thor Swanson, William F. Mullen, John C. Pierce, and Charles H. Sheldon. Pullman: Washington State University Press, 1985.

Beer, Samuel H. *To Make a Nation: The Rediscovery of American Federalism.* Cambridge, Mass.: Harvard University Press, Belknap Press, 1994.

Bellamy, Edward. *Looking Backward, 2000–1887.* New York: Signet, 1960.

Bendix, Reinhard. *Nation-Building and Citizenship.* Berkeley and Los Angeles: University of California Press, 1964.

Bensel, Richard Franklin. *Sectionalism and American Political Development, 1880–1980.* Madison: University of Wisconsin Press, 1984.

———. *Yankee Leviathan: The Origins of Central State Authority in America, 1859–1877.* New York: Cambridge University Press, 1990.

Bentley, Arthur F. *The Process of Government: A Study of Social Pressures.* Chicago: University of Chicago Press, 1908.

Bercuson, David Jay. "The One Big Union in Washington." *Pacific Northwest Quarterly* 69, no. 3 (1978): 127–34.

Berk, Gerald. *Alternative Tracks: The Constitution of American Industrial Order, 1865–1917.* Baltimore: Johns Hopkins University Press, 1994.

Berkowitz, Edward, and Kim McQuaid. *Creating the Welfare State: The Political Economy of Twentieth-Century Reform.* New York: Praeger, 1980.

Berman, Harold J. *Law and Revolution: The Formation of the Western Legal Tradition.* Cambridge, Mass.: Harvard University Press, 1983.

Blair, Karen J. *The Clubwoman as Feminist: True Womanhood Redefined, 1868–1914.* New York: Holmes and Meier, 1980.

Bledstein, Burton J. *The Culture of Professionalism: The Middle Class and the Development of Higher Education in America.* New York: Norton, 1976.

Block, Fred. "The Ruling Class Does Not Rule." *Socialist Revolution* 33 (1977): 6–28.

The Book of the States. Vol. 1. Chicago: Council of State Governments and the American Legislators' Association, 1935.

Bordin, Ruth. *Woman and Temperance: The Quest for Power and Liberty, 1873–1900.* Philadelphia: Temple University Press, 1981.

Bourdieu, Pierre. *Outline of a Theory of Practice.* Trans. Richard Nice. New York: Cambridge University Press, 1977.

Bourne, Jonathan, Jr. "Functions of the Initiative, Referendum, and Recall." *Annals of the American Academy of Political and Social Science 43 (September 1912): 3–16.

Brandeis, Elizabeth. "Labor Legislation." In History of Labour in the United States, 1896–1932, ed. John R. Commons, vol. 3. New York: Macmillan, 1935.

Braude, Ann. Radical Spirits: Spiritualism and Women's Rights in Nineteenth-Century America. Boston: Beacon, 1989.

Breen, William J. "Administrative Politics and Labor Policy in the First World War: The U.S. Employment Service and the Seattle Labor Market Experiment." Business History Review 61 (1987): 582–605.

Bridges, Amy. "Becoming American: The Working Classes in the United States before the Civil War." In Working-Class Formation: Nineteenth-Century Patterns in Western Europe and the United States, ed. Ira Katznelson and Aristide Zolberg. Princeton, N.J.: Princeton University Press, 1986.

Brinkley, Alan. Voices of Protest: Huey Long, Father Coughlin, and the Great Depression. New York: Random House, 1982.

Brown, James Sayles. Partisan Politics: The Evil and the Remedy. Philadelphia: J. B. Lippincott Co., 1897.

Brownlee, W. Elliot, Jr. "Income Taxation and the Political Economy of Wisconsin, 1890–1930." Wisconsin Magazine of History 59, no. 4 (1976): 299–324.

———. Progressivism and Economic Growth: The Wisconsin Income Tax, 1911–1929. Port Washington, N.Y.: Kennikat, 1974.

Brundage, David. The Making of Western Labor Radicalism: Denver's Organized Workers, 1878–1905. Urbana: University of Illinois Press, 1994.

Bryce, James. The American Commonwealth. 3d ed. 2 vols. New York: Macmillan, 1895.

Buck, Solon J. The Agrarian Crusade: A Chronicle of the Farmer in Politics. New Haven, Conn.: Yale University Press, 1921.

Buechler, Steven M. The Transformation of the Woman Suffrage Movement: The Case of Illinois, 1850–1920. New Brunswick, N.J.: Rutgers University Press, 1986.

Buenker, John D. "The Politics of Mutual Frustration: Socialists and Suffragists in New York and Wisconsin." In Flawed Liberation: Socialism and Feminism, ed. Sally M. Miller. Westport, Conn.: Greenwood Press, 1981.

———. "The Urban Political Machine and Woman Suffrage: A Study in Political Adaptability." Historian 33, no. 2 (1971): 264–79.

Buhle, Mari Jo. Women and American Socialism, 1870–1920. Urbana: University of Illinois Press, 1981.

Burki, Mary Ann Mason. "The California Progressives: Labor's Point of View." Labor History 17, no. 1 (1976): 24–37.

Burnham, Walter Dean. Critical Elections and the Mainsprings of American Politics. New York: Norton, 1970.

———. The Current Crisis in American Politics. New York: Oxford University Press, 1982.

———. "Pattern Recognition and 'Doing' Political History: Art, Science, or Bootless Enterprise?" In *The Dynamics of American Politics: Approaches and Interpretations,* ed. Lawrence C. Dodd and Calvin Jillson. Boulder, Colo.: Westview Press, 1994.

Burrows, Donald R., and Don C. Taylor. "Public Finance in Washington: The Role of Taxation." In *Political Life in Washington: Governing the Evergreen State,* ed. Thor Swanson, William F. Mullen, John C. Pierce, and Charles H. Sheldon. Pullman: Washington State University Press, 1985.

Butler, David, and Austin Ranney, eds. *Referendums: A Comparative Study of Practice and Theory.* Washington, D.C.: American Enterprise Institute, 1978.

Cadwalader, Thomas F. "The Defeat of the Twentieth Amendment." *Annals of the American Academy of Political and Social Science* 129 (January 1927): 65–69.

Cahn, Frances, and Valeska Bary. *Welfare Activities of Federal, State, and Local Governments in California, 1850–1934.* Berkeley and Los Angeles: University of California Press, 1936.

Campbell, Debra. "Reformers and Activists." In *American Catholic Women: A Historical Explanation,* ed. Karen Kennely, CSJ. New York: Macmillan, 1989.

Campbell, John L. "Institutional Analysis and the Role of Ideas in Political Economy." Photocopy. Harvard University, 1995.

———. "Mechanisms of Evolutionary Change in Economic Governance: Interaction, Interpretation, and Bricolage." In *Evolutionary Economics and Path Dependence,* ed. Lars Magnusson and Jan Ottoson. Aldershot, U.K.: Edward Elgar. Forthcoming.

Campion, Frank D. *The AMA and U.S. Health Policy since 1940.* Chicago: Chicago Review Press, 1984.

Capper, Arthur. *The Agricultural Bloc.* New York: Harcourt, Brace and Co., 1922.

Carnes, Mark C. *Secret Ritual and Manhood in Victorian America.* New Haven, Conn.: Yale University Press, 1989.

Carney, Francis. *The Rise of the Democratic Clubs in California.* New York: Henry Holt, 1958.

Carstensen, Vernon. "The Genesis of an Agricultural Experiment Station." *Agricultural History* 34, no. 1 (1960): 13–20.

———. "The Origin and Early Development of the Wisconsin Idea." *Wisconsin Magazine of History* 39, no. 3 (1956): 181–88.

Catt, Carrie Chapman, and Nettie Rogers Shuler. *Woman Suffrage and Politics: The Inner Story of the Suffrage Movement.* New York: Scribner's, 1926.

Chambers, Clarke A. *California Farm Organizations: A Historical Study of the Grange, the Farm Bureau, and the Associated Farmers, 1929–1941.* Berkeley and Los Angeles: University of California Press, 1952.

Chandler, Alfred D., Jr. *The Visible Hand: The Managerial Revolution in American Business.* Cambridge, Mass.: Harvard University Press, Belknap Press, 1977.

Cherny, Robert W. *Populism, Progressivism, and the Transformation of Nebraska Politics, 1885–1915.* Lincoln: University of Nebraska Press, 1981.

Clark, Charles C. P. *The "Machine" Abolished and the People Restored to Power by the Organization of All the People on the Lines of Party Organization.* New York: G. P. Putnam's Sons, [1900] 1925.

Clark, Norman H. *The Dry Years: Prohibition and Social Change in Washington.* Seattle: University of Washington Press, 1965.

Clawson, Mary Ann. *Constructing Brotherhood: Class, Gender, and Fraternalism.* Princeton, N.J.: Princeton University Press, 1989.

———. "Fraternal Orders and Class Formation in the Nineteenth-Century United States." *Comparative Studies in Society and History* 27, no. 4 (1985): 672–95.

Clemens, Elisabeth S. "Continuity and Coherence: Periodization and the Problem of Change." In *Social Time and Social Change,* ed. Ragnvald Kalleberg and Fredrik Engelstad. Oslo: Norwegian University Press, 1997.

——— "From Clubwoman to Committeewoman: Activist Networks and Movement Decline." Paper presented at the annual meeting of the American Sociological Association, Miami, 1993.

———. "Organizational Form as Frame: Collective Identity and Political Strategy in the American Labor Movement." In *Comparative Perspectives on Social Movements: Opportunities, Mobilizing Structures, and Cultural Framings,* ed. Doug McAdam, John D. McCarthy, and Mayer Zald. New York: Cambridge University Press, 1996.

———. "Organizational Repertoires and Institutional Change: Women's Groups and the Transformation of U.S. Politics, 1890–1920." *American Journal of Sociology* 98, no. 4 (1993): 755–98.

———. "Secondhand Laws: Patterns of Political Learning among State Governments and Interest Groups." Paper presented at the annual meeting of the American Political Science Association, San Francisco, 1990.

Clemens, Elisabeth S., and Patrick Ledger. "Institutional Contradiction and Careers of Activism in the Woman Suffrage Movement." Photocopy. University of Arizona, 1993.

Clubb, Jerome M., William H. Flanigan, and Nancy H. Zingale. *Partisan Realignment: Voters, Parties, and Government in American History.* Beverly Hills, Calif.: Sage, 1980.

Cobble, Dorothy Sue. *Dishing It Out: Waitresses and Their Unions in the Twentieth Century.* Urbana: University of Illinois Press, 1991.

Cohen, Michael, James March, and Johan Olsen. "A Garbage Can Model of Organizational Choice." *Administrative Science Quarterly* 17 (March 1972): 1–15.

Coleman, Peter J. *Progressivism and the World of Reform: New Zealand and the Origins of the American Welfare State.* Lawrence: University of Kansas Press, 1987.

Collier, David, and Richard E. Messick. "Prerequisites versus Diffusion: Testing Alternative Explanations of Social Security Adoption." *American Political Science Review* 69 (1975): 1299–1315.

Collingwood, R. G. *The Idea of History.* Oxford: Clarendon Press, 1946.

Commons, John R. *Myself*. New York: Macmillan, 1934.

———. *Proportional Representation*. 2d ed. New York: Thomas Y. Crowell, 1907. Reprint, New York: Augustus M. Kelley, 1967.

Commons, John R., et al. *History of Labour in the United States*. Vol. 2. New York: Macmillan, 1918.

Cook, Blanche Weisen. *Eleanor Roosevelt*, vol. 1, *1884–1933*. New York: Viking, 1992.

Coolidge, Mary Roberts. *What the Women of California Have Done with the Ballot*. San Francisco: n. p., 1916.

Cosmas, Graham A. "The Democracy in Search of Issues: The Wisconsin Reform Party, 1873–1877." *Wisconsin Magazine of History* 46, no. 2 (1962–63): 93–108.

Cott, Nancy F. *The Grounding of Modern Feminism*. New Haven, Conn.: Yale University Press, 1987.

Cravens, Hamilton. "The Emergence of the Farmer-Labor Party in Washington Politics, 1919–20." *Pacific Northwest Quarterly* 57, no. 4 (1966): 148–57.

Crawford, Harriet Ann. *The Washington State Grange, 1889–1924: A Romance of Democracy*. Portland, Ore.: Binfords and Mort, 1940.

Crawford, Kenneth G. *The Pressure Boys: The Inside Story of Lobbying in America*. New York: Julian Messner, 1939.

Crawford, Sue E. S., and Elinor Ostrom. "A Grammar of Institutions." *American Political Science Review* 89 (1995): 582–600.

Crockett, Earl C. "The History of California Labor Legislation, 1910–1930." Ph.D. diss., University of California at Berkeley, 1931.

Croly, Mrs. J. C. *The History of the Women's Club Movement in America*. New York: Henry G. Allen and Co., 1898.

Cronin, Thomas E. *Direct Democracy: The Politics of Initiative, Referendum, and Recall*. Cambridge, Mass.: Harvard University Press, 1989.

Daniels, Doris. "Building a Winning Coalition: The Suffrage Fight in New York State." *New York History* 60, no. 1 (1979): 59–88.

Davis, Ada J. "The Evolution of the Institution of Mothers' Pensions in the United States." *American Journal of Sociology* 35, no. 4 (1930): 573–87.

Dawley, Alan. *Struggles for Justice: Social Responsibility and the Liberal State*. Cambridge, Mass.: Harvard University Press, Belknap Press, 1991.

Dawley, Alan, and Paul Faler. *Democracy in America*. New York: Anchor Books, 1969.

———. "Working-Class Culture and Politics in the Industrial Revolution: Sources of Loyalism and Rebellion." *Journal of Social History* 9, no. 4 (1976): 466–80.

Deegan, Mary Jo. *Jane Addams and the Men of the Chicago School, 1892–1918*. New Brunswick, N.J.: Transaction, 1988.

Delzell, Ruth. *The Early History of Women Trade Unionists of America*. Chicago: National Women's Trade Union League of America, 1919.

DiMaggio, Paul J. "Constructing an Organizational Field as a Professional Project: U.S. Art Museums, 1920–1940." In *The New Institutionalism in Organiza-*

tional Analysis, ed. Walter W. Powell and Paul J. DiMaggio. Chicago: University of Chicago Press, 1991.

DiMaggio, Paul J., and Walter W. Powell. "The Iron Cage Revisited: Institutional Isomorphism and Collective Rationality in Organizational Fields." *American Sociological Review* 48 (1983): 147–60.

Dobbin, Frank. *Forging Industrial Policy: The United States, Britain, and France in the Railway Age.* New York: Cambridge University Press, 1994.

Dodds, H. W. "Removable Obstacles to the Success of the Direct Primary." *Annals of the American Academy of Political and Social Science* 106 (March 1923): 18–21.

Douglas, Mary. "Jokes." In *Rethinking Popular Culture: Contemporary Perspectives in Cultural Studies,* ed. Chandra Mukerji and Michael Schudson. Berkeley and Los Angeles: University of California Press, 1991.

Douglas, Paul H. "A System of Federal Grants-in-Aid I." *Political Science Quarterly* 35, no. 2 (1920): 255–71.

———. "A System of Federal Grants-in-Aid II." *Political Science Quarterly* 35, no. 4 (1920): 522–44.

Doyle, Don H. "The Social Functions of Voluntary Associations in a Nineteenth-Century American Town." *Social Science History* 1, no. 3 (1977): 333–55.

Dubois, Ellen C. "Harriot Stanton Blatch and the Transformation of Class Relations among Woman Suffragists." In *Gender, Class, Race, and Reform in the Progressive Era.* Lexington: University Press of Kentucky, 1991.

Dumenil, Lynn. *Freemasonry and American Culture, 1880–1939.* Princeton, N.J.: Princeton University Press, 1984.

Dye, Nancy Schrom. *As Equals and as Sisters: Feminism, the Labor Movement, and the Women's Trade Union League of New York.* Columbia: University of Missouri Press, 1980.

Eaves, Lucile. *A History of California Labor Legislation, with an Introductory Sketch of the San Francisco Labor Movement.* University of California Publications in Economics, 2. Berkeley: University of California, 1910.

Edwards, G. Thomas. *Sowing Good Seeds: The Northwest Suffrage Campaigns of Susan B. Anthony.* Portland: Oregon Historical Society Press, 1990.

Edwards, Gladys Talbott. *The Farmers Union Triangle.* Rev. ed. Jamestown, N.D.: Farmers Union Educational Service, 1941.

Elazar, Daniel J. *American Federalism: A View from the States.* New York: Crowell, 1972.

Englander, Susan. *Class Conflict and Coalition in the California Woman Suffrage Movement, 1907–1912: San Francisco Wage Earners' Suffrage League.* Lewiston, N.Y.: Edwin Mellen, 1992.

Epstein, Abraham. "The American State Old Age Pension System in Operation." *Annals of the American Academy of Political and Social Science* 170 (November 1933): 107–11.

Epstein, Barbara Leslie. *The Politics of Domesticity: Women, Evangelism, and Temperance in Nineteenth Century America.* Middletown, Conn.: Wesleyan University Press, 1981.

Erdman, H. E. "The Development and Significance of California Cooperatives, 1900–1915." *Agricultural History* 32, no. 3 (1958): 179–86.
Erie, Steven P. *Rainbow's End: Irish-Americans and the Dilemmas of Urban Machine Politics, 1840–1985.* Berkeley and Los Angeles: University of California Press, 1988.
Erlebacher, Albert. "The Wisconsin Life Insurance Reform of 1907." *Wisconsin Magazine of History* 55, no. 3 (1972): 213–30.
Esping-Andersen, Gøsta. *Politics against Markets: The Social Democratic Road to Power.* Princeton, N.J.: Princeton University Press, 1985.
Ethington, Philip J. *The Public City: The Political Construction of Urban Life in San Francisco, 1850–1900.* New York: Cambridge University Press, 1994.
Everitt, J. A. *The Third Power: Farmers to the Front.* 4th ed. Indianapolis: J. A. Everitt, 1907. Reprint, New York: Arno Press, 1975.
Ferleger, Lou. "Uplifting American Agriculture: Experiment Station Scientists and the Office of Experiment Stations in the Early Years after the Hatch Act." *Agricultural History* 64, no. 2 (1990): 5–23.
Festinger, L. *A Theory of Cognitive Dissonance.* Palo Alto, Calif.: Stanford University Press, 1957.
Fine, Nathan. *Labor and Farmer Parties in the United States, 1828–1928.* New York: Rand School of Social Science, 1928.
Fine, Sidney. *Sit-Down: The General Motors Strike of 1936–37.* Ann Arbor: University of Michigan Press, 1969.
Finegold, Kenneth. *Experts and Politicians: Reform Challenges to Machine Politics in New York, Cleveland, and Chicago.* Princeton, N.J.: Princeton University Press, 1995.
Fink, Gary M. *Labor's Search for Political Order: The Political Behavior of the Missouri Labor Movement, 1890–1940.* Columbia: University of Missouri Press, 1973.
Fink, Leon. *Workingmen's Democracy: The Knights of Labor and American Politics.* Urbana: University of Illinois Press, 1983.
Finn, J. F. "AF of L Leaders and the Question of Politics in the Early 1890s." *Journal of American Studies* 7, no. 3 (1973): 243–65.
Flexner, Eleanor. *Century of Struggle: The Woman's Rights Movement in the United States.* New York: Atheneum, 1970.
Fligstein, Neil. "The Structural Transformation of American Industry: An Institutional Account of the Causes of Diversification in the Largest Firms, 1919–1979." In *The New Institutionalism in Organizational Analysis,* ed. Walter W. Powell and Paul J. DiMaggio. Chicago: University of Chicago Press, 1991.
———. *The Transformation of Corporate Control.* Cambridge, Mass.: Harvard University Press, 1990.
Flora, Peter, and Jens Alber. "Modernization, Democratization, and the Development of Welfare States in Western Europe." In *The Development of Welfare States in Europe and America,* ed. Peter Flora and Arnold Heidenheimer. New Brunswick, N.J.: Transaction, 1981.

Follett, Mary Parker. *The New State: Group Organization—the Solution of Popular Government.* New York: Longmans, Green and Co., 1918.

Foner, Philip S. *History of the Labor Movement in the United States.* Vol. 5. New York: International Publishers, 1980.

———. *Women and the American Labor Movement: From Colonial Times to the Eve of World War I.* New York: Free Press, 1979.

Ford, Henry Jones. "Direct Legislation and the Recall." *Annals of the American Academy of Political and Social Science* 43 (September 1912): 65–99.

Foucault, Michel. *Discipline and Punish: The Birth of the Prison.* Trans. Alan Sheridan. New York: Pantheon, 1977.

———. *The History of Sexuality.* Vol. 1, *An Introduction.* Trans. Robert Hurley. New York: Vintage, 1990.

Frank, Dana. *Purchasing Power: Consumer Organizing, Gender, and the Seattle Labor Movement, 1919–1929.* New York: Cambridge University Press, 1994.

Frankel, Noralee, and Nancy S. Dye, eds. *Gender, Class, Race, and Reform in the Progressive Era.* Lexington: University Press of Kentucky, 1991.

Frankfurter, Felix, Mary Dewson, and John R. Commons. *State Minimum Wage Laws in Practice.* New York: National Consumers' League, 1924.

Fredman, L. E. *The Australian Ballot: The Story of an American Reform.* East Lansing: Michigan State University Press, 1968.

Freedman, Estelle. "Separatism as Strategy: Female Institution Building and American Feminism, 1870–1930." *Feminist Studies* 5 (fall 1979): 512–29.

Friedheim, Robert L. *The Seattle General Strike.* Seattle: University of Washington Press, 1964.

Friedland, Roger, and Robert Alford. "Bringing Society Back In: Symbols, Practices, and Institutional Contradictions." In *The New Institutionalism in Organizational Analysis,* ed. Walter W. Powell and Paul J. DiMaggio. Chicago: University of Chicago Press, 1991.

Friedman, Lawrence M. *A History of American Law.* New York: Simon and Schuster, 1973.

Fuller, Wayne E. "The Populists and the Post Office." *Agricultural History* 65, no. 1 (1991): 1–16.

Galambos, Louis. "The Emerging Organizational Synthesis in Modern American History." *Business History Review* 44 (1970): 279–90.

Galbreath, C. B. "Provisions for State-Wide Initiative and Referendum." *Annals of the American Academy of Political and Social Science* 43 (September 1912): 81–109.

Gamson, William A., and David S. Meyer. "Framing Political Opportunity." In *Comparative Perspectives on Social Movements: Political Opportunities, Mobilizing Structures, and Cultural Framings,* ed. Doug McAdam, John D. McCarthy, and Mayer N. Zald. New York: Cambridge University Press, 1996.

Gates, Paul W. *Land and Law in California.* Ames: Iowa State University Press, 1991.

Gavett, Thomas W. *Development of the Labor Movement in Milwaukee.* Madison: University of Wisconsin Press, 1965.

Gibson, Mary S. *A Record of Twenty-five Years of the California Federation of Women's Clubs.* California Federation of Women's Clubs, 1927.

Giddings, Paula. *When and Where I Enter: The Impact of Black Women on Race and Sex in America.* New York: Bantam, 1984.

Goodwyn, Lawrence. *The Populist Moment: A Short History of the Agrarian Revolt in America.* New York: Oxford University Press, 1978.

Gordon, Robert W. "Legal Thought and Legal Practice in the Age of American Enterprise, 1870–1920." In *Professions and Professional Ideologies in America,* ed. Gerald L. Geison. Chapel Hill: University of North Carolina Press, 1983.

Gosnell, Harold F. *Machine Politics: Chicago Model.* Chicago: University of Chicago Press, 1937.

Graebner, William. "Federalism in the Progressive Era: A Structural Interpretation of Reform." *Journal of American History* 64, no. 2 (1977): 331–57.

Granger, Mrs. A. O. "The Work of the General Federation of Women's Clubs against Child Labor." *Annals of the American Academy of Political and Social Science* 25 (May 1905): 102–7.

Grant, H. Roger. *Self-Help in the 1890s Depression.* Ames: Iowa State University Press, 1983.

Gray, Virginia. "Innovation in the States: A Diffusion Study." *American Political Science Review* 67, no. 4 (1973): 1174–85.

———. "Rejoinder to 'Comment' by Jack L. Walker." *American Political Science Review* 67, no. 4 (1973): 1192–93.

Greene, Julia. "'The Strike at the Ballot Box': The American Federation of Labor's Entrance into Election Politics, 1906–1909." *Labor History* 32, no. 2 (1991): 165–91.

Griffiths, David Burke. "Populism in the Far West, 1890–1900." Ph.D. diss., University of Washington, 1967.

Hannan, Michael T., and John Freeman. *Organizational Ecology.* Cambridge, Mass.: Harvard University Press, 1989.

———. "Where Do Organizational Forms Come From?" *Sociological Forum* 1, no. 1 (1986): 50–72.

Hansen, John Mark. "Choosing Sides: The Creation of an Agricultural Policy Network in Congress, 1919–1932." *Studies in American Political Development* 2 (1987): 183–229.

———. *Gaining Access: Congress and the Farm Lobby, 1919–1981.* Chicago: University of Chicago Press, 1991.

Hanson, Russell L. *The Democratic Imagination in America: Conversations with Our Past.* Princeton, N.J.: Princeton University Press, 1985.

Harper, Ida Husted. *The History of Woman Suffrage, 1900–1920.* Vol. 6. New York: J. J. Little and Ives, 1922.

Hart, Vivien. "Feminism and Bureaucracy: The Minimum Wage Experiment in the District of Columbia." *Journal of American Studies* 26, no. 1 (1992): 1–22.

Hartz, Louis. *The Liberal Tradition in America: An Interpretation of American Political Thought since the Revolution.* New York: Harcourt Brace Jovanovich, 1955.

Hattam, Victoria C. *Labor Visions and State Power: The Origins of Business Unionism in the United States.* Princeton, N.J.: Princeton University Press, 1993.

Hawley, Ellis. *The New Deal and the Problem of Monopoly.* Princeton, N.J.: Princeton University Press, 1966.

Hechter, Michael. *Principles of Group Solidarity.* Berkeley and Los Angeles: University of California Press, 1987.

Heckelman, Jac. C. "The Effect of the Secret Ballot on Voter Turnout Rates." *Public Choice* 82 (1995): 107–24.

Heidenheimer, Arnold J. "Education and Social Security Entitlements in Europe and America." In *The Development of Welfare States in Europe and America,* ed. Peter Flora and Arnold J. Heidenheimer. New Brunswick, N.J.: Transaction, 1981.

Heider, Fritz. *The Psychology of Interpersonal Relations.* New York: Wiley, 1958.

Heinz, John P., Edward O. Laumann, Robert L. Nelson, and Robert H. Salisbury. *The Hollow Core: Private Interests in National Policy Making.* Cambridge, Mass.: Harvard University Press, 1993.

Hennings, Robert E. *James D. Phelan and the Wilson Progressives of California.* New York: Garland, 1985.

Hernes, Helga Maria. *Welfare State and Woman Power: Essays in State Feminism.* Oslo: Norwegian University Press, 1987.

Herrick, Genevieve Forbes, and John Origen Herrick. *The Life of William Jennings Bryan.* Chicago: Buxton, 1925.

Herring, Pendleton. *Group Representation before Congress.* New York: Russell and Russell, 1929.

Hichborn, Franklin. *Story of the Session of the California Legislature of 1909.* San Francisco: Press of the James H. Barry Co., 1909.

———. *Story of the Session of the California Legislature of 1911.* San Francisco: Press of the James H. Barry Co., 1911.

———. *Story of the Session of the California Legislature of 1913.* San Francisco: Press of the James H. Barry Co., 1913.

Hicks, John D. "The Legacy of Populism in the Western Middle West." *Agricultural History* 23, no. 4 (1949): 231.

Higham, John. *Strangers in the Land: Patterns of American Nativism, 1860–1925.* 2d ed. New Brunswick, N.J.: Rutgers University Press, 1988.

Hillman, Arthur. "The Unemployed Citizens' League of Seattle." *University of Washington Publications in the Social Sciences* 5, no. 3 (1934): 181–270.

Hirschman, Albert O. *The Passions and the Interests: Political Arguments for Capitalism before Its Triumph.* Princeton, N.J.: Princeton University Press, 1977.

Hochstein, Irma. *A Progressive Primer*. Madison: Wisconsin Women's Progressive Association, 1922.

Hofstadter, Richard. *The Age of Reform*. New York: Vintage, 1955.

———. *The Idea of a Party System: The Rise of Legitimate Opposition in the United States, 1780–1840*. Berkeley and Los Angeles: University of California Press, 1969.

Holmes, William F. "Populism: In Search of Context." *Agricultural History* 64, no. 4 (1990): 26–58.

Horowitz, Ruth L. *Political Ideologies of Organized Labor: The New Deal Era*. New Brunswick, N.J.: Transaction, 1978.

Houghton, N. D. "Arizona's Experience with the Initiative and Referendum." *New Mexico Historical Review* 29, no. 3 (1954): 183–209.

Howe, Frederick C. *Wisconsin: An Experiment in Democracy*. New York: Charles Scribner's Sons, 1912.

Hundley, Norris C., Jr. "Katherine Philips Edson and the Fight for the California Minimum Wage." *Pacific Historical Review* 29 (1960): 271–85.

Hunt, Lynn. *Politics, Culture, and Class in the French Revolution*. Berkeley and Los Angeles: University of California Press, 1984.

Huntington, Samuel. *Political Order in Changing Societies*. New Haven, Conn.: Yale University Press, 1968.

Immergut, Ellen M. "The Rules of the Game: The Logic of Health Policy-Making in France, Switzerland, and Sweden." In *Structuring Politics: Historical Institutionalism in Comparative Analysis*, ed. Kathleen Thelen, Sven Steinmo, and Frank Longstreth. New York: Cambridge University Press, 1992.

Jepperson, Ronald L. "Institutions, Institutional Effects, and Institutionalism." In *The New Institutionalism in Organizational Analysis*, ed. Walter W. Powell and Paul J. DiMaggio. Chicago: University of Chicago Press, 1991.

Johansen, Dorothy O. "A Working Hypothesis for the Study of Migrations." *Pacific Historical Review* 36 (1967): 1–12.

Johnson, Claudius O. "The Adoption of the Initiative and Referendum in Washington." *Pacific Northwest Quarterly* 35, no. 4 (1944): 291–304.

Johnson, Warren B. "Muckraking in the Northwest: Joe Smith and Seattle Reform." *Pacific Historical Review* 40 (1971): 478–500.

Josephson, Matthew. *The Politicos, 1865–1896*. New York: Harcourt, Brace and World, 1938.

Kane, R. James. "Populism, Progressivism, and Pure Food." *Agricultural History* 38, no. 3 (1964): 161–66.

Kanter, Rosabeth Moss. *Commitment and Community: Communes and Utopias in Sociological Perspective*. Cambridge, Mass: Harvard University Press, 1972.

Karl, Barry. *The Uneasy State: The United States from 1915 to 1945*. Chicago: University of Chicago Press, 1983.

Karson, Marc. *American Labor Unions and Politics, 1900–1918*. Carbondale: Southern Illinois University Press, 1958.

Katz, Sherry. "Frances Nacke Noel and 'Sister Movements': Socialism, Feminism, and Trade Unionism in Los Angeles, 1909–1916." *California History* 67, no. 3 (1988): 180–90.

Kazin, Michael. "Barons of Labor: The San Francisco Building Trades, 1896–1922." Ph.D. diss., Stanford University, 1982.

———. *Barons of Labor: The San Francisco Building Trades and Union Power in the Progressive Era.* Urbana. University of Illinois Press, 1987.

———. *The Populist Persuasion: An American History.* New York: Basic Books, 1995.

Keller, Morton. *Affairs of State: Public Life in Late Nineteenth-Century America.* Cambridge, Mass.: Harvard University Press, Belknap Press, 1977.

———. *Regulating a New Economy: Public Policy and Economic Change in America, 1900–1933.* Cambridge, Mass.: Harvard University Press, 1990.

Kennan, Kossuth Kent. "The Wisconsin Income Tax." *Annals of the American Academy of Political and Social Science* 58 (March 1915): 65–76.

Kerber, Linda K. *Women of the Republic: Intellect and Ideology in Revolutionary America.* Chapel Hill: University of North Carolina Press, 1980.

Kerr, K. Austin. "Organizing for Reform: The Anti-Saloon League and Innovation in Politics." *American Quarterly* 32, no. 1 (1980): 37–53.

Kettleborough, Charles. "Direct Primaries." *Annals of the American Academy of Political and Social Science* 106 (March 1923): 11–17.

Key, V. O. *American State Politics.* New York: Knopf, 1956.

———. *Southern Politics in State and Nation.* New York: Knopf, 1949.

———. "A Theory of Critical Elections." *Journal of Politics* 17, no. 3 (1955).

Key, V. O., and Winston W. Crouch. *The Initiative and the Referendum in California.* Berkeley and Los Angeles: University of California Press, 1939.

Kile, Orville Merton. *The Farm Bureau Movement.* New York: Macmillan, 1921.

———. *The Farm Bureau through Three Decades.* Baltimore: Waverly Press, 1948.

Kingdon, John W. *Agendas, Alternatives, and Public Policies.* Boston: Little, Brown, 1984.

Kirkpatrick, Jeanne Jordon. *Dismantling the Parties: Reflections on Party Reform and Party Decomposition.* Washington, D.C.: American Enterprise Institute, 1978.

Kizer, Benjamin H. "May Arkwright Hutton." *Pacific Northwest Quarterly* 57, no. 2 (1966): 49–56.

Kleppner, Paul. *Continuity and Change in Electoral Politics, 1893–1928.* New York: Greenwood Press, 1987.

———. *The Third Electoral System, 1853–1892: Parties, Voters, and Political Cultures.* Chapel Hill: University of North Carolina Press, 1979.

———. "Voters and Parties in the Western States, 1876–1900." *Western Historical Quarterly* 14, no. 1 (1983): 49–68.

———. *Who Voted? The Dynamics of Electoral Turnout, 1870–1980.* New York: Praeger, 1982.

Kloppenberg, James T. *Uncertain Victory: Social Democracy and Progressivism in European and American Thought, 1870–1920.* New York: Oxford University Press, 1986.

Knoke, David. "The Spread of Municipal Reform: Temporal, Spatial, and Social Dynamics." *American Journal of Sociology* 87, no. 6 (1982): 1314–39.

Kolko, Gabriel. *The Triumph of Conservatism: A Reinterpretation of American History.* New York: Free Press, 1963.

Kraditor, Aileen. *The Ideas of the Woman Suffrage Movement, 1899–1929.* Garden City, N.Y.: Anchor/Doubleday, 1971.

Krasner, Stephen D. "Approaches to the State: Alternative Conceptions and Historical Dynamics." *Comparative Politics* 16, no. 2 (1984): 223–46.

Kriesi, Hanspeter, Ruud Koopmans, Jan Willem Duyvendak, and Marco G. Giugni. "New Social Movements and Political Opportunities in Western Europe." *European Journal of Political Research* 22 (1992): 219–44.

Kuhn, Thomas. *The Essential Tension: Selected Studies in Scientific Tradition and Change.* Chicago: University of Chicago Press, 1977.

Ladd-Taylor, Molly. *Raising a Baby the Government Way: Mothers' Letters to the Children's Bureau, 1915–1932.* New Brunswick, N.J.: Rutgers University Press, 1986.

Larsen, Grace. "A Progressive in Agriculture: Harris Weinstock." *Agricultural History* 32, no. 3 (1958): 187–95.

Larson, T. A. "The Woman Suffrage Movement in Washington." *Pacific Northwest Quarterly* 67, no. 2 (1976): 49–62.

Larson, Robert W. "Populism in the Mountain West: A Mainstream Movement." *Western Historical Quarterly* 13, no. 2 (1982): 143–64.

Laumann, Edward O., and David Knoke. *The Organizational State: Social Choice in National Policy Domains.* Madison: University of Wisconsin Press, 1987.

Layton, Edwin. "The Better American Federation: A Case Study of Superpatriotism." *Pacific Historical Review* 30 (1961): 137–47.

Leff, Mark H. "Consensus for Reform: The Mothers' Pension Movement in the Progressive Era." *Social Service Review* 47, no. 3 (1973): 397–417.

Leffler, George Leland. "Wisconsin Industry and the Wisconsin Tax System." 2d ed. *Bulletin of the University of Wisconsin Bureau of Business and Economic Research* 3 (1931): 1–124.

Leiby, James. "State Welfare Administration in California, 1879–1929." *Pacific Historical Review* 41 (1972): 169–87.

Lescohier, Don D., and Florence Peterson. *The Alleviation of Unemployment in Wisconsin.* Madison: Industrial Commission of Wisconsin, 1931.

Levine, David. "The Transformation of Interests and the State." In *Changes in the State: Causes and Consequences,* ed. Edward S. Greenberg and Thomas F. Mayer. Newbury Park, Calif.: Sage, 1990.

Levine, Susan. "Labor's True Woman: Domesticity and Equal Rights in the Knights of Labor." *Journal of American History* 70, no. 2 (1983): 323–39.

Loewy, Jean. "Katherine Philips Edson and the California Suffragette Movement, 1919–1920." *California Historical Society Quarterly* 47, no. 4 (1968): 343–50.

Logan, Edward B. "Lobbying." *Annals of the American Academy of Political and Social Science,* supplement to vol. 144 (September 1929): 1–91.

Lorwin, Lewis L. *The American Federation of Labor: History, Policies, and Prospects.* Washington, D.C.: Brookings Institution, 1933.

Lothrop, Gloria Ricci. "Strength Made Stronger: The Role of Women in Southern California Philanthropy." *Southern California Quarterly* 71, nos. 2–3 (1989): 143–94.

Lovejoy, Allen Fraser. *La Follette and the Establishment of the Direct Primary in Wisconsin, 1890–1904.* New Haven, Conn.: Yale University Press, 1941.

Lower, Richard Coke. *A Bloc of One: The Political Career of Hiram W. Johnson.* Stanford, Calif.: Stanford University Press, 1993.

Lowi, Theodore J. *The End of Liberalism: The Second Republic of the United States.* 2d ed. New York: Norton, 1979.

Lowrie, S. Gale. "The Wisconsin Plan for the Initiative and Referendum." *Annals of the American Academy of Political and Social Science* 43 (September 1912): 179–90.

Lunardini, Christine A. *From Equal Suffrage to Equal Rights: Alice Paul and the National Woman's Party, 1910–1928.* New York: New York University Press, 1986.

Lundberg, Emma O. "Aid to Mothers with Dependent Children." *Annals of the American Academy of Political and Social Science* 98 (November 1921): 97–104.

Lustig, R. Jeffrey. *Corporate Liberalism: The Origins of Modern American Political Theory, 1890–1920.* Berkeley and Los Angeles: University of California Press, 1982.

Lyons, Louis S, ed. *Who's Who among the Women of California.* San Francisco: Security Publishing Co., 1922.

MacArthur, Walter. *Trade Union Epigrams: Some Reasons for the Faith That Is within Us.* Washington, D.C.: American Federation of Labor, 1904.

MacKay, Kenneth Campbell, *The Progressive Movement of 1924.* New York: Columbia University Press, 1947.

Madison, James. "No. 10." *The Federalist Papers.* New York: New American Library, 1961.

Maier, Charles S. "'Fictitious Bonds . . . of Wealth and Law': On the Theory and Practice of Interest Representation." In *Organizing Interests in Western Europe: Pluralism, Corporatism, and the Transformation of Politics,* ed. Suzanne Berger. New York: Cambridge University Press, 1981.

Mansbridge, Jane J. "A Deliberative Theory of Interest Representation." In *The Politics of Interest,* ed. Mark P. Petracca. Boulder, Colo.: Westview Press, 1992.

March, James G., and Johan P. Olsen. *Rediscovering Institutions: The Organizational Basis of Politics.* New York: Free Press, 1989.

Marcus, Robert D. *Grand Old Party: Political Structure in the Gilded Age, 1880–1896.* New York: Oxford University Press, 1971.

Margulies, Herbert F. *The Decline of the Progressive Movement in Wisconsin, 1890–1920.* Madison, Wis.: State Historical Society of Wisconsin, 1968.

———. "The La Follette–Philipp Alliance of 1918." *Wisconsin Magazine of History* 38, no. 4 (1955): 248–49.

Marks, Gary. *Unions in Politics: Britain, Germany, and the United States in the Nineteenth and Early Twentieth Centuries.* Princeton, N.J.: Princeton University Press, 1989.

Marti, Donald B. "Answering the Agrarian Question: Socialists, Farmers, and Algie Martin Simons." *Agricultural History* 65, no. 3 (1991): 53–69.

———. "Sisters of the Grange: Rural Feminism in the Late Nineteenth Century." *Agricultural History* 58, no. 3 (1984): 247–61.

Martin, Theodora Penny. *The Sound of Our Own Voices: Women's Study Clubs, 1860–1910.* Boston: Beacon, 1987.

Mason, Mary Ann. "Neither Friends Nor Foes: Organized Labor and the California Progressives." In *California Progressivism Revisited,* ed. William Deverell and Tom Sitton. Berkeley and Los Angeles: University of California Press, 1994.

Mathews, Shailer, ed. *The Woman Citizen's Library.* Vol. 12, *The Woman Citizen and the Home.* Chicago: Civics Society, 1914.

Matthews, Lillian R. "Women in Trade Unions in San Francisco." *University of California Publications in Economics* 3, no. 1 (1913): 1–100.

Maxwell, Robert S. *La Follette and the Rise of the Progressives in Wisconsin.* Madison: State Historical Society of Wisconsin, 1956.

Mayhew, David. *Placing Parties in American Politics: Organization, Electoral Settings, and Government Activity in the Twentieth Century.* Princeton, N.J.: Princeton University Press, 1986.

McAdam, Doug. *Political Process and the Development of Black Insurgency, 1930–70.* Chicago: University of Chicago Press, 1982.

———. "Tactical Innovation and the Pace of Insurgency." *American Sociological Review* 48 (1983): 735–54.

McBride, Genevieve G. "Theodora Youmans and the Wisconsin Woman Movement." *Wisconsin Magazine of History* 71, no. 4 (1988): 243–75.

McCarthy, Kathleen. *Noblesse Oblige: Charity and Cultural Philanthropy in Chicago, 1849–1929.* Chicago: University of Chicago Press, 1982.

———. *Women's Culture: American Philanthropy and Art, 1830–1930.* Chicago: University of Chicago Press, 1991.

McConnell, Grant. *The Decline of Agrarian Democracy.* Berkeley and Los Angeles: University of California Press, 1953.

———. *Private Power and American Democracy.* New York: Knopf, 1966.

McCormick, Richard L. *The Party Period and Public Policy: American Politics from the Age of Jackson to the Progressive Era.* New York: Oxford University Press, 1986.

———. *The Second American Party System: Party Formation in the Jacksonian Era.* Chapel Hill: University of North Carolina Press, 1966.

McCune, Wesley. *The Farm Bloc.* Garden City, N.Y.: Doubleday, Doran, 1943.

McDonagh, Eileen. "The 'Welfare Rights State' and the 'Civil Rights State': Policy Paradox and State Building in the Progressive Era." *Studies in American Political Development* 7 (1993): 225–74.

McFarland, Andrew S. "Interest Groups and Theories of Power in America." *British Journal of Political Science* 17 (April 1987): 129–47.

McGerr, Michael E. *The Decline of Popular Politics: The American North, 1865–1928.* New York: Oxford University Press, 1986.

McNall, Scott G. *The Road to Rebellion: Class Formation and Kansas Populism, 1865–1900.* Chicago: University of Chicago Press, 1988.

McSeveney, Samuel T. *The Politics of Depression: Political Behavior in the Northeast, 1893–1896.* New York: Oxford University Press, 1972.

McVoy, Edgar C. "Patterns of Diffusion in the United States." *American Sociological Review* 5 (1940): 219–27.

Merriam, Charles Edward. "Nominating Systems." *Annals of the American Academy of Political and Social Science* 106 (March 1923): 1–10.

Merriam, Charles Edward, and Louise Overacker. *Primary Elections.* Chicago: University of Chicago Press, 1928.

Merton, Robert K. *Social Theory and Social Structure.* Glencoe, Ill.: Free Press, 1957.

Meyer, David S. *A Winter of Discontent: The Nuclear Freeze and American Politics.* New York: Praeger, 1990.

Meyer, David S., and Nancy Whittier. "Social Movement Spillover." *Social Problems* 41, no. 2 (1994): 277–98.

Meyer, John, and Brian Rowan. "Institutionalized Organizations: Formal Structure as Myth and Ceremony." *American Journal of Sociology* 83 (1977): 340–63.

Michels, Robert. *Political Parties: A Sociological Study of the Oligarchical Tendencies of Modern Democracy.* New York: Free Press, 1962.

Mills, C. Wright. *The Power Elite.* New York: Oxford University Press, 1956.

———. *The Sociological Imagination.* New York: Oxford University Press, 1959.

Mink, Gwendolyn. *Old Labor and New Immigrants in American Political Development: Union, Party, and State, 1875–1920.* Ithaca, N.Y.: Cornell University Press, 1986.

Mitchell, Theodore. *Political Education in the Southern Farmers' Alliance, 1887–1900.* Madison: University of Wisconsin Press, 1987.

Moe, Terry M. *The Organization of Interests: Incentives and the Internal Dynamics of Political Interest Groups.* Chicago: University of Chicago Press, 1980.

Montgomery, David. *The Fall of the House of Labor: The Workplace, the State, and American Labor Activism, 1865–1925.* New York: Cambridge University Press, 1987.

Morone, James A. *The Democratic Wish: Popular Participation and the Limits of American Government.* New York: Basic Books, 1990.

Morris, Aldon D., and Carol McClurg Mueller, eds. *Frontiers in Social Movement Theory.* New Haven, Conn.: Yale University Press, 1992.

Moss, David A. "Kindling a Flame under Federalism: Progressive Reformers, Corporate Elites, and the Phosphorus Match Campaign of 1909–1912." *Business History Review* 68 (1994): 244–75.

Mowry, George E. *The California Progressives.* 1951. Reprint, Chicago: Quadrangle Books, 1963.

Moynihan, Ruth Barnes. *Rebel for Rights: Abigail Scott Duniway.* New Haven, Conn.: Yale University Press, 1983.

Muncy, Robyn. *Creating a Female Dominion in American Reform, 1890–1935.* New York: Oxford University Press, 1991.

Munro, William Bennett. *The Initiative, Referendum, and Recall.* New York: D. Appleton and Co., 1916.

Murray, Keith Alexander. "Republican Party Politics in Washington during the Progressive Era." Ph.D. diss., University of Washington, 1946.

Nash, Gerald D. "The Influence of Labor on State Policy, 1860–1920: The Experience of California." *California Historical Society Quarterly* 42, no. 3 (1963): 241–57.

Nash, Roderick. "Victor L. Berger: Making Marx Respectable." *Wisconsin Magazine of History* 47, no. 4 (1964): 301–8.

Nathan, Maud. *The Story of an Epoch-Making Movement.* Garden City, N.J.: Doubleday, Page and Co., 1926.

Nelson, Barbara J. "The Origins of the Two-Channel Welfare State: Workmen's Compensation and Mothers' Aid." In *Women, the State, and Welfare,* ed. Linda Gordon. Madison: University of Wisconsin Press, 1990.

Nelson, Daniel. *Unemployment Insurance: The American Experience, 1915–1935.* Madison: University of Wisconsin Press, 1969.

Neu, Charles E. "Olympia Brown and the Woman's Suffrage Movement." *Wisconsin Magazine of History* 43, no. 4 (1960): 277–87.

Neylan, John Francis. "California's State Budget." *Annals of the American Academy of Political and Social Science* 62 (November 1915): 69–72.

Nordin, D. Sven. *Rich Harvest: A History of the Grange, 1867–1900.* Jackson: University Press of Mississippi, 1974.

Norris, George W. "Why I Believe in the Direct Primary." *Annals of the American Academy of Political and Social Science* 106 (March 1923): 22–39.

North, Douglass C. *Institutions, Institutional Change, and Economic Performance.* New York: Cambridge University Press, 1990.

———. *Structure and Change in Economic History.* New York: Norton, 1981.

Nye, Ronald L. "Federal vs. State Agricultural Research Policy: The Case of California's Tulare Experiment Station, 1888–1909." *Agricultural History* 57, no. 4 (1983): 436–49.

Nye, Russel B. *Midwestern Progressive Politics: A Historical Study of Its Origins and Development, 1870–1950.* East Lansing: Michigan State University Press, 1951.

Oberdeck, Kathryn J. "'Not Pink Teas': The Seattle Working-Class Women's Movement, 1905–1918." *Labor History* 32, no. 2 (1991): 193–230.

Oberholtzer, Ellis Paxson. *The Referendum in America.* New York: Charles Scribner's Sons, 1912.

O'Connor, Harvey. *Revolution in Seattle: A Memoir.* New York: Monthly Review Press, 1964.

Odegard, Peter H. *Pressure Politics: The Story of the Anti-Saloon League.* New York: Columbia University Press, 1928.

Oestreicher, Richard. "Urban Working-Class Political Behavior and Theories of American Electoral Politics, 1870–1940." *Journal of American History* 74, no. 4 (1988): 1257–86.

Ogburn, William F. *Progress and Uniformity in Child-Labor Legislation: A Study in Statistical Measurement.* 1912. Reprint, New York: AMS Press, 1968.

Olin, Spencer C., Jr. *California Politics, 1846–1920: The Emerging Corporate State.* San Francisco: Boyd and Fraser, 1981.

Olson, Frederick I. "The Socialist Party and the Union in Milwaukee, 1900–1912." *Wisconsin Magazine of History* 44, no. 2 (1960–61): 110–16.

Olson, Mancur. *The Logic of Collective Action.* Cambridge, Mass.: Harvard University Press, 1967.

O'Neill, William L. *Everyone Was Brave: A History of Feminism in America.* Chicago: Quadrangle Books, 1969.

Orloff, Ann Shola. "The Political Origins of America's Belated Welfare State." In *The Politics of Social Policy in the United States,* ed. Margaret Weir, Ann Shola Orloff, and Theda Skocpol. Princeton, N.J.: Princeton University Press, 1988.

Orloff, Ann Shola, and Theda Skocpol. "Why Not Equal Protection? Explaining the Politics of Public Social Spending in Britain, 1900–1911, and the United States, 1880s–1920." *American Sociological Review* 49 (1984): 726–50.

Orren, Karen. *Belated Feudalism: Labor, the Law, and Liberal Development in the United States.* New York: Cambridge University Press, 1991.

———. "Organized Labor and the Invention of Modern Liberalism in the United States." *Studies in American Political Development* 2 (1987): 317–36.

Orren, Karen, and Stephen Skowronek. "Beyond the Iconography of Order: Notes for a 'New Institutionalism.'" In *The Dynamics of American Politics,* ed. Lawrence C. Dodd and Calvin Jillson. Boulder, Colo.: Westview Press, 1994.

Ostler, Jeffrey. *Prairie Populism: The Fate of Agrarian Radicalism in Kansas, Nebraska, and Iowa, 1880–1892.* Lawrence: University Press of Kansas, 1993.

Ostrander, Gilman M. *The Prohibition Movement in California, 1848–1933.* University of California Publications in History, 57, 1957.

Owens, John R., Edmond Costantini, and Louis F. Weschler. *California Politics and Parties.* London: Macmillan, 1970.

Ozanne, Robert W. *The Labor Movement in Wisconsin: A History.* Madison, Wis.: State Historical Society of Wisconsin, 1984.

Park, Maud Wood. *Front Door Lobby.* Boston: Beacon, 1960.

Pavalko, Eliza K. "State Timing of Policy Adoption: Workmen's Compensation in the United States, 1909–29." *American Journal of Sociology* 95, no. 3 (1989): 592–615.

Perrow, Charles. "A Society of Organizations." *Theory and Society* 20 (1991): 725–62.

Perry, Lewis. *Radical Abolitionism: Anarchy and the Government of God in Antislavery Thought.* Ithaca, N.Y.: Cornell University Press, 1973.

Perry, Louis B., and Richard S. Perry. *A History of the Los Angeles Labor Move-*

ment, 1911–1941. Berkeley and Los Angeles: University of California Press, 1963.

Petracca, Mark P., "The Rediscovery of Interest Group Politics." In *The Politics of Interests: Interest Groups Transformed,* ed. Petracca. Boulder, Colo.: Westview Press, 1992.

Phelan, Raymond Vincent. "The Financial History of Wisconsin." *Bulletin of the University of Wisconsin,* 193. Economics and Political Science Series, 2, no. 2. Madison: University of Wisconsin Press, 1908.

Phelps, Edith M., ed. *Selected Articles on the Initiative and Referendum.* New York: H. W. Wilson, 1914.

Pisani, Donald J. "Land Monopoly in Nineteenth-Century California." *Agricultural History* 65, no. 4 (1991): 15–37.

Pitchell, Robert J. "The Electoral System and Voting Behavior: The Case of California's Cross-Filing." *Western Political Quarterly* 12, no. 2 (1959): 459–84.

Pitkin, Hanna Fenichel. *The Concept of Representation.* Berkeley and Los Angeles: University of California Press, 1967.

Piven, Frances Fox, and Richard A. Cloward. *Poor People's Movements: Why They Succeed, How They Fail.* New York: Vintage, 1979.

———. *Regulating the Poor: The Functions of Public Welfare.* New York: Vintage, 1971.

Poggi, Gianfranco. *The State: Its Nature, Development, and Prospects.* Stanford, Calif.: Stanford University Press, 1990.

Platt, Chester C. *What La Follette's State Is Doing: Some Battles Waged for More Freedom.* Batavia, N.Y.: Batavia Times Press, 1924.

Polanyi, Karl. *The Great Transformation.* Boston: Beacon, 1977.

Pollack, Norman. *The Just Polity: Populism, Law, and Human Welfare.* Urbana: University of Illinois Press, 1987.

———. *The Populist Response to Industrial America: Midwestern Populist Thought.* New York: Norton, 1962.

Porter, Susan L. "Benevolent Women at Work: Cultural Exchange in Female Charitable Institutions, 1800–1850." Paper presented at the annual meeting of the Social Science History Association, Chicago, 1989.

Posner, Russell M. "The Progressive Voters League, 1923–26." *California Historical Society Quarterly* 36, no. 3 (1957): 251–61.

Powell, Thomas Reed. "Umpiring the Federal System, 1922–24." *Political Science Quarterly* 40, no. 1 (1925): 101–26.

Powell, Walter W. "Expanding the Scope of Institutional Analysis." In *The New Institutionalism in Organizational Analysis,* ed. Walter W. Powell and Paul J. DiMaggio. Chicago: University of Chicago Press, 1991.

Powell, Walter W., and Paul J. DiMaggio, eds. *The New Institutionalism in Organizational Analysis.* Chicago: University of Chicago Press, 1991.

Prescott, Gerald L. "Farm Gentry vs. the Grangers: Conflict in Rural America." *California Historical Quarterly* 56, no. 4 (1977–78): 328–45.

———. "Gentlemen Farmers in the Gilded Age." *Wisconsin Magazine of History,* 55, no. 3 (1972): 197–212.

————. "Wisconsin Farm Leaders in the Gilded Age." *Agricultural History* 44, no. 2 (1970): 183–200.

Putnam, Jackson K. "The Persistence of Progressivism in the 1920s: The Case of California." *Pacific Historical Review* 35 (1966): 395–411.

Quadagno, Jill. *The Transformation of Old Age Security: Class and Politics in the American Welfare State.* Chicago: University of Chicago Press, 1988.

Raftery, Judith. "Los Angeles Clubwomen and Progressive Reform." In *California Progressivism Revisited,* ed. William Deverell and Tom Sitton. Berkeley and Los Angeles: University of California Press, 1994.

Rankin, George William. *William Dempster Hoard.* Fort Atkinson, Wis.: W. D. Hoard and Sons, 1925.

Ranney, Austin. *Curing the Mischief of Faction: Party Reform in America.* Berkeley and Los Angeles: University of California Press, 1975.

————. "United States of America." In *Referendums: A Comparative Study of Practice and Theory,* ed. David Butler and Austin Ranney. Washington, D.C.: American Interprise Institute, 1978.

Rappard, William E. "The Initiative, Referendum, and Recall in Switzerland." *Annals of the American Academy of Political and Social Science* 43 (September 1912): 100–45.

Reese, William J. *Power and the Promise of School Reform: Grass-roots Movements during the Progressive Era.* Boston: Routledge and Kegan Paul, 1986.

Reid, John Philip. *The Concept of Representation in the Age of the American Revolution.* Chicago: University of Chicago Press, 1989.

Reynolds, Lisa. "Reassessing the Impact of Progressive Era Ballot Reform." Ph.D. diss., University of California at San Diego, 1995.

Rice, Stuart A. *Farmers and Workers in American Politics.* New York: Columbia University Press, 1924.

Robertson, David Brian. "The Bias of American Federalism: The Limits of Welfare-State Development in the Progressive Era." *Journal of Policy History* 1, no. 3 (1989): 261–91.

————. "The Return to History and the New Institutionalism in American Political Science." *Social Science History* 17, no. 1 (1993): 1–36.

Rodgers, Daniel T. *Contested Truths: Keywords in American Politics since Independence.* New York: Basic Books, 1987.

————. "In Search of Progressivism." *Reviews in American History* 10, no. 4 (1982): 117.

Rogin, Michael Paul. "Progressivism and the California Electorate." *Journal of American History* 55, no. 2 (1968): 297–314.

————. "Voluntarism: The Political Functions of an Antipolitical Doctrine." *Industrial and Labor Relations Review* 15, no. 4 (1962): 521–35.

Rogin, Michael P., and John L. Shover. *Political Change in California: Critical Elections and Social Movements, 1890–1966.* Westport, Conn.: Greenwood Press, 1970.

Rouse, Jacqueline A. "Atlanta's African-American Women's Attack on Segregation, 1900–1920." In *Gender, Class, Race, and Reform in the Progressive Era,* ed. Noralee Frankel and Nancy S. Dye. Lexington: University Press of Kentucky, 1991.

Ruddy, Ella Giles, ed. *The Mother of Clubs, Caroline M. Seymour Severance: An Estimate and Appreciation.* Los Angeles: Baumgardt Publishing, 1906.

Ruggie, Mary. *The State and Working Women: A Comparative Study of Britain and Sweden.* Princeton, N.J.: Princeton University Press, 1984.

Ryan, Mary P. *Women in Public: Between Banners and Ballots, 1825–1880.* Baltimore: Johns Hopkins University Press, 1990.

Saloutos, Theodore. "The Wisconsin Society of Equity." *Agricultural History* 14, no. 2 (1940): 78–95.

Saloutos, Theodore, and John D. Hicks. *Agricultural Discontent in the Middle West, 1900–1939.* Madison: University of Wisconsin Press, 1951.

Saltvig, Robert Donald. "The Progressive Movement in Washington." Ph.D. diss., University of Washington, 1966.

Sanders, Elizabeth. "Farmers and the State in the Progressive Era." In *Changes in the State: Causes and Consequences,* ed. Edward S. Greenberg and Thomas F. Mayer. Newbury Park, Calif.: Sage, 1990.

———. "Industrial Concentration, Sectional Competition, and Antitrust Politics in America, 1880–1980." *Studies in American Political Development* 1 (1986): 142–214.

Sapiro, Virginia. "The Gender Basis of American Social Policy." *Political Science Quarterly* 101, no. 2 (1986): 221–38.

Saxton, Alexander. *The Indispensable Enemy: Labor and the Anti-Chinese Movement in California.* Berkeley and Los Angeles: University of California Press, 1971.

———. *The Rise and Fall of the White Republic: Class Politics and Mass Culture in Nineteenth-Century America.* New York: Verso, 1990.

Schaffer, Ronald. "The Problem of Consciousness in the Woman Suffrage Movement: A California Perspective." *Pacific Historical Review* 45 (1976): 469–93.

Scheiber, Harry N. "Federalism and the American Economic Order, 1789–1910." *Law and Society Review* 10, no. 1 (1975): 57–118.

Scheinberg, Stephen J. "Theodore Roosevelt and the A. F. of L.'s Entry into Politics, 1906–1908." *Labor History* 3, no. 2 (1962): 131–37.

Schiesl, Martin J. *The Politics of Efficiency: Municipal Administration and Reform in America, 1880–1920.* Berkeley and Los Angeles: University of California Press, 1977.

Schmidt, Gertrude. "History of Labor Legislation in Wisconsin." Ph.D. diss., University of Wisconsin, 1933.

Schmidt, Louis Bernard. "The Role and Techniques of Agrarian Pressure Groups." *Agricultural History* 30, no. 2 (1956): 49–58.

Schwantes, Carlos A. *Coxey's Army: An American Odyssey.* Lincoln: University of Nebraska Press, 1985.

———. "Farmer-Labor Insurgency in Washington State: William Bouck, the Grange, and the Western Progressive Farmers." *Pacific Northwest Quarterly* 76, no. 1 (1985): 2–11.

———. "The Ordeal of William Morley Bouck, 1918–1919: Limits to the Federal Suppression of Agrarian Dissidents." *Agricultural History* 59, no. 3 (1985): 417–28.

———. *Radical Heritage: Labor, Socialism, and Reform in Washington and British Columbia, 1885–1917*. Seattle: University of Washington Press, 1979.

Scott, Anne Firor. *Natural Allies: Women's Associations in American History*. Urbana: University of Illinois Press, 1991.

Scott, Donald M. *From Office to Profession: The New England Ministry, 1750–1850*. Philadelphia: University of Pennsylvania Press, 1978.

Scott, James C. *Domination and the Arts of Resistance*. New Haven, Conn.: Yale University Press, 1990.

Scott, Roy V. *The Agrarian Movement in Illinois, 1880–1896*. Urbana: University of Illinois Press, 1962.

Seftel, Howard. "Government Regulation and the Rise of the California Fruit Industry: The Entrepreneurial Attack on Fruit Pests, 1880–1920." *Business History Review* 59 (1985): 402.

Sewell, William H., Jr. "A Theory of Structure: Duality, Agency, and Transformation." *American Journal of Sociology* 98, no. 1 (1992): 1–29.

Shafer, Byron E., ed. *The End of Realignment? Interpreting American Political Eras*. Madison: University of Wisconsin Press, 1991.

Shaffer, Ralph Edward. "Radicalism in California, 1869–1929." Ph.D. diss., University of California at Berkeley, 1962.

Shefter, Martin. *Political Parties and the State: The American Historical Experience*. Princeton, N.J.: Princeton University Press, 1994.

———. "Regional Receptivity to Reform: the Legacy of the Progressive Era." *Political Science Quarterly* 98, no. 3 (1983): 459–83.

———. "Trade Unions and Political Machines: The Organization and Disorganization of the American Working Class in the Late Nineteenth Century." In *Working-Class Formation: Nineteenth-Century Patterns in Western Europe and the United States*, ed. Ira Katznelson and Aristide R. Zolberg. Princeton, N.J.: Princeton University Press, 1986.

Shepsle, Kenneth A., and Barry R. Weingast. "Structure-Induced Equilibrium and Legislative Choice." *Public Choice* 37 (1981): 503–19.

Silbey, Joel H. *The American Political Nation, 1838–1893*. Stanford, Calif.: Stanford University Press, 1991.

———. "The Rise and Fall of American Political Parties, 1790–1990." In *The Parties Respond: Changes in the American Party System*, ed. L. Sandy Maisel. Boulder, Colo.: Westview Press, 1990.

Simmel, Georg. *On Individuality and Social Forms: Selected Essays*. Ed. Donald Levine. Chicago: University of Chicago Press, 1971.

Simpson, Anna Pratt. *Problems Women Solved. Being the Story of the Woman's*

Board of the Panama-Pacific International Exposition. What Vision, Enthusiasm, Work, and Co-operation Accomplished. San Francisco: Woman's Board, 1915.

————. "Story of the Associated Charities since the Fire of 1906." Reprinted from the San Francisco *Call.* N.p.: n. p., 1909.

Sklar, Kathryn Kish. "Hull House in the 1890s: A Community of Women Reformers." *Signs* 10 (1985): 658–77.

Sklar, Martin J. *The Corporate Reconstruction of American Capitalism, 1890–1916: The Market, the Law, and Politics.* New York: Cambridge University Press, 1988.

Skocpol, Theda. *Protecting Soldiers and Mothers: The Political Origins of Social Policy in the United States.* Cambridge, Mass.: Harvard University Press, Belknap Press, 1992.

Skocpol, Theda, and Kenneth Finegold. "State Capacity and Economic Intervention in the Early New Deal." *Political Science Quarterly* 97, no. 2 (1982): 255–78.

Skowronek, Stephen. *Building a New American State: The Expansion of National Administrative Capacities, 1877–1920.* New York: Cambridge University Press, 1982.

Slingerland, William H. *Child Welfare Work in California: A Study of Agencies and Institutions.* New York: Russell Sage, 1915.

Smith, Rogers M. "Beyond Tocqueville, Myrdal, and Hartz." *American Political Science Review* 87, no. 3 (1992): 549–66.

————. "If Politics Matters: Implications for a 'New Institutionalism.'" In *Studies in American Political Development* 6 (1992): 12–30.

Smith-Rosenberg, Carroll. *Disorderly Conduct: Visions of Gender in Victorian America.* New York: Oxford University Press, 1985.

Snow, David A., E. Burke Rochford Jr., Steven K. Worden, and Robert D. Benford. "Frame Alignment Processes, Micromobilization, and Movement Participation." *American Sociological Review* 51 (1986): 464–81.

Solomons, Selina. *How We Won the Vote in California.* San Francisco: New Woman Publishing Co., [1912?].

Somers, Margaret R. "Narrativity, Narrative Identity, and Social Action: Rethinking English Working-Class Formation." *Social Science History* 16, no. 4 (1992): 591–630.

Sorauf, Frank J. "Extra-legal Political Parties in Wisconsin." *American Political Science Review* 48, no. 3 (1954): 692–704.

Spencer, Mrs. Dorcas James. *A History of the Woman's Christian Temperance Union of Northern and Central California.* Oakland, Calif.: West Coast Printing Co., n.d.

Starr, Kevin. *Inventing the Dream: California through the Progressive Era.* New York: Oxford University Press, 1985.

Starr, Raymond. "Philanthropy in San Diego, 1900–1929." *Southern California Quarterly* 71, nos. 2–3 (1989): 227–73.

Stedman, Murray S., Jr., and Susan W. Stedman. *Discontent at the Polls: A Study of Farmer and Labor Parties, 1827–1948.* New York: Columbia University Press, 1950.

Stimson, Grace Heilman. *Rise of the Labor Movement in Los Angeles.* Berkeley and Los Angeles: University of California Press, 1955.

Stinchcombe, Arthur L. *Information and Organizations.* Berkeley and Los Angeles: University of California Press, 1990.

———. "Social Structure and Organizations." In *Handbook of Organizations,* ed. James G. March. Chicago: Rand-McNally, 1965.

———. *Theoretical Methods in Social History.* New York: Academic Press, 1978.

Sundquist, James L. *Dynamics of the Party System: Alignment and Realignment of Political Parties in the United States.* Washington, D.C.: Brookings Institution, 1973.

Swidler, Ann. "Culture in Action: Symbols and Strategies." *American Sociological Review* 51 (1986): 273–86.

Taft, Philip. *Labor Politics American Style: The California State Federation of Labor.* Cambridge, Mass.: Harvard University Press, 1968.

———. *Organized Labor in American History.* New York: Harper and Row, 1964.

Tarrow, Sidney. *Power in Movement.* New York: Cambridge University Press, 1994.

———. *Struggle, Politics, and Reform: Collective Action, Social Movements, and Cycles of Protest.* Ithaca, N.Y.: Cornell University Center for International Studies, 1989.

Taylor, Verta. "Social Movement Continuity: The Women's Movement in Abeyance." *American Sociological Review* 54 (1989): 761–75.

Thelen, David P. *The New Citizenship: Origins of Progressivism in Wisconsin, 1885–1900.* Columbia: University of Missouri Press, 1972.

———. *Paths of Resistance: Tradition and Dignity in Industrializing Missouri.* New York: Oxford University Press, 1986.

———. *Robert M. La Follette and the Insurgent Spirit.* Madison: University of Wisconsin Press, 1985.

Thelen, Kathleen, and Sven Steinmo. "Historical Institutionalism in Comparative Politics." In *Structuring Politics: Historical Institutionalism in Comparative Analysis,* ed. Steinmo, Thelen, and Frank Longstreth. New York: Cambridge University Press, 1992.

Thomas, George M., John W. Meyer, Francisco O. Ramirez, and John Boli. *Institutional Structure: Constituting State, Society, and the Individual.* Beverly Hills, Calif.: Sage, 1987.

Thompson, James. *Organizations in Action.* New York: McGraw-Hill, 1967.

Thompson, Margaret Susan. *The "Spider Web": Congress and Lobbying in the Age of Grant.* Ithaca, N.Y.: Cornell University Press, 1985.

Tilly, Charles. *The Contentious French.* Cambridge, Mass.: Harvard University Press, 1986.

————. "Contentious Repertoires in Great Britain, 1758–1834." *Social Science History* 17, no. 2 (1993): 253–81.

————. *From Mobilization to Revolution.* Englewood Cliffs, N.J.: Prentice-Hall, 1978.

————. "Reflections on the History of European State-Making." In *The Formation of National States in Western Europe,* ed. Charles Tilly. Princeton, N.J.: Princeton University Press, 1975.

Tocqueville, Alexis de. *Democracy in America.* Ed. J. P. Mayer. Trans. George Lawrence. New York: Anchor Books, 1969.

————. *The Old Regime and the French Revolution.* Trans. Stuart Gilbert. New York: Anchor Books, 1955.

Tomlins, Christopher L. *The State and the Unions: Labor Relations, Law, and the Organized Labor Movement in America, 1880–1960.* New York: Cambridge University Press, 1985.

Tontz, Robert L. "Memberships of General Farmers' Organizations, United States, 1874–1960." *Agricultural History* 38, no. 3 (1964): 143–56.

Tripp, Joseph F. "An Instance of Labor and Business Cooperation: Workmen's Compensation in Washington State (1911)." *Labor History* 17, no. 4 (1976): 530–50.

————. "Progressive Labor Laws in Washington State (1900–1924)." Ph.D. diss., University of Washington, 1973.

————. "Toward an Efficient and Moral Society: Washington State Minimum-Wage Law, 1913–1925." *Pacific Northwest Quarterly* 67, no. 3 (1976): 97–112.

"Trouble in the Coal Mines, 1889: Documents of an Incident at Newcastle, W.T." *Pacific Northwest Quarterly* 37, no. 3 (1946): 231–57.

Truman, David B. *The Governmental Process: Political Interests and Public Opinion.* 2d ed. Berkeley, Calif.: Institute of Governmental Studies, 1993.

Tucker, William P. "Populism Up-to-Date: The Story of the Farmers' Union." *Agricultural History* 21, no. 4 (1947): 198–208.

Ulman, Lloyd. *The Rise of the National Trade Union: The Development and Significance of Its Structure, Governing Institutions, and Economic Policies.* Cambridge, Mass.: Harvard University Press, 1955.

Valelly, Richard M. *Radicalism in the States: The Minnesota Farmer-Labor Party and the American Political Economy.* Chicago: University of Chicago Press, 1989.

Van Voris, Jacqueline. *Carrie Chapman Catt: A Public Life.* New York: Feminist Press at the City University of New York, 1987.

Vaughn, William Preston. *The Antimasonic Party in the United States, 1826–1843.* Lexington: University Press of Kentucky, 1983.

Vincent, Leopold. *The Alliance and Labor Songster: A Collection of Labor and Comic Songs, for the use of Alliances, Grange Debating Clubs and Political Gatherings.* Indianapolis: Vincent Bros., 1891. Reprint, New York: Arno Press, 1975.

Voss, Kim. "The Collapse of a Social Movement: The Interplay of Mobilizing Structures, Framing, and Political Opportunities in the Knights of Labor." In *Comparative Perspectives on Social Movements: Opportunities, Mobilizing Structures, and Cultural Framings,* ed. Doug McAdam, John D. McCarthy, and Mayer N. Zald. New York: Cambridge University Press, 1996.

———. *The Making of American Exceptionalism: The Knights of Labor and Class Formation in the Nineteenth Century.* Ithaca, N.Y.: Cornell University Press, 1994.

Wachman, Marvin. *History of the Social-Democratic Party of Milwaukee, 1897–1910.* Urbana: University of Illinois Press, 1945.

Walker, Jack L. "The Diffusion of Innovations among the American States." *American Political Science Review* 63, no. 3 (1969): 880–69.

Walters, Ronald G. *The Antislavery Appeal: American Abolitionism after 1830.* Baltimore: Johns Hopkins University Press, 1977.

Walton, John. *Western Times and Water Wars: State, Culture, and Rebellion in California.* Berkeley and Los Angeles: University of California Press, 1991.

Ward, James A. "Power and Accountability on the Pennsylvania Railroad, 1846–1878." *Business History Review* 49 (1975): 37–59.

Ware, Susan. *Beyond Suffrage: Women in the New Deal.* Cambridge, Mass.: Harvard University Press, 1981.

Warner, Donald F. "The Farmers' Alliance and the Farmers' Union: An American-Canadian Parallelism." *Agricultural History* 23, no. 1 (1949): 9–19.

Warren, Charles. "The Progressiveness of the United States Supreme Court." *Columbia Law Review* 13, no. 4 (1913): 294–313.

Watson, Frank Dekker. *The Charity Organization Movement in the United States: A Study in American Philanthropy.* New York: Macmillan, 1922.

Weber, Max. *Economy and Society.* Ed. and trans. Guenther Roth and Claus Wittich. Berkeley and Los Angeles: University of California Press, 1978.

Weinstein, James. *The Corporate Ideal in the Liberal State, 1900–1918.* Boston: Beacon, 1968.

Westney, D. Eleanor. *Imitation and Innovation: The Transfer of Western Organizational Patterns to Meiji Japan.* Cambridge, Mass.: Harvard University Press, 1987.

Wiebe, Robert H. *Businessmen and Reform: A Study of the Progressive Movement.* 1962. Reprint, Chicago: Quadrangle Books, 1968.

———. *The Search for Order, 1877–1920.* New York: Hill and Wang, 1967.

———. *Self-Rule: A Cultural History of American Democracy.* Chicago: University of Chicago Press, 1995.

Wildavsky, Aaron. "Choosing Preferences by Constructing Institutions: A Cultural Theory of Preference Formation." *American Political Science Review* 81, no. 1 (1987): 1–21.

Wilensky, Harold. *The Welfare State and Equality: Structural and Ideological Roots of Public Expenditures.* Berkeley and Los Angeles: University of California Press, 1975.

Wilentz, Sean. "Against Exceptionalism: Class Consciousness and the American Labor Movement." *International Labor and Working Class History* 26 (fall 1984): 1–24.

———. *Chants Democratic: New York City and the Rise of the American Working Class, 1788–1850*. New York: Oxford University Press, 1984.

Williams, R. Hal. *The Democratic Party and California Politics, 1880–1896*. Stanford, Calif.: Stanford University Press, 1973.

Williamson, Mrs. M. Burton. "Ladies' Clubs and Societies in Los Angeles in 1892." Reported for the Historical Society of Southern California. 1892. Reprint, Los Angeles: Misses Lillian A. and Estella M. Williamson, 1925.

Williamson, Oliver. *The Economic Institutions of Capitalism*. New York: Free Press, 1985.

Wilson, Margaret Gibbons. *The American Woman in Transition: The Urban Influence, 1870–1920*. Westport, Conn.: Greenwood Press, 1979.

Winter, Alice Ames. *The Business of Being a Clubwoman*. New York: Century Co., 1925.

Wisler, Dominique, and Marco G. Giugni. "Institutional Selectivity and Social Movements." *Sociological Perspectives* 39, no. 1 (1996): 85–109.

Wismer, Otto G. "Legal Aid Organizations: 'Lobbyists for the Poor.'" *Annals of the American Academy of Political and Social Science* 136 (March 1928): 172–76.

Witte, Edwin E. "A Law Making Laboratory." *State Government* 3, no. 1 (1930): 3–11.

Wood, Mary I. *The History of the General Federation of Women's Clubs: For the First Twenty-Two Years of Its Organization*. New York: General Federation of Women's Clubs, 1912.

Wood, Samuel Edgerton. "The California State Commission of Immigration and Housing: A Study of Administrative Organization and the Growth of Function." Ph.D. diss., University of California at Berkeley, 1942.

Wooddy, Carroll H. "Populism in Washington: A Study of the Legislature of 1897." *Washington Historical Quarterly* 21, no. 2 (1930): 103–19.

Wyman, Roger E. "Middle-Class Voters and Progressive Reform: The Conflict of Class and Culture." *American Political Science Review* 68, no. 2 (1974): 488–50.

Yearley, C. K. *The Money Machines: The Breakdown and Reform of Governmental and Party Finance in the North, 1860–1920*. Albany: State University of New York Press, 1970.

Yoder, Fred R. "The Farmers' Alliance in Washington—Prelude to Populism." *Research Studies of the State College of Washington* 16, nos. 3–4 (September–December 1948): 123–78.

Young, Arthur N. *The Single Tax Movement in the United States*. Princeton, N.J.: Princeton University Press, 1916.

Zillner, Raymond T. "State Laws: Survival of the Unfit." *University of Pennsylvania Law Review* 62 (1914): 509–24.

Zimmerman, Joan G. "The Jurisprudence of Equality: The Women's Minimum Wage, the First Equal Rights Amendment, and *Adkins v. Children's Hospital, 1905–1923." Journal of American History* 78, no. 1 (1991): 188–225.

Zucker, Lynne G. "Where Do Institutional Patterns Come From? Organizations as Actors in Social Systems." In *Institutional Patterns and Organizations: Culture and Environment,* ed. Zucker. Cambridge, Mass.: Ballinger, 1988.

Zunz, Olivier. *Making America Corporate, 1870–1920.* Chicago: University of Chicago Press, 1990.

Index

abeyance structures, 71, 290, 292
accountability of elected officials, 38, 39, 41–42, 80, 101, 113, 117, 120, 277, 279, 297, 315; as enforced in California, 124–26, 134–36, 252; as enforced in Washington, 132; as enforced in Wisconsin, 117–18, 136, 173, 282, 361n.74; increased by erosion of party control, 276, 319; laws obstructing, 373n.94; techniques for enforcing, 125, 134, 135, 168–77, 217, 293, 303–4. *See also* friends-and-enemies strategy; good man policy; monitoring; questioning and pledging system; roll-call vote tabulation
advertising methods, 218, 320; as used by women's associations, 186, 217
African-Americans, 93
agrarian associations, 5, 43; in California, 152–55, 156–59, 165–66, 168–72, 174–75, 182, 252–53; diffusion of, 155; and legislative lobbying, 170–71, 303–4, 308; membership, 147, 153; national political influence, 303, 355n.109; as political challengers, 93, 145, 150, 167, 222, 237; regional variations in, 149, 153, 167, 176, 367n.12; ties to state agencies, 146, 160–61, 164, 166, 172–80; use of fraternal model, 146, 148, 152–56, 168–69, 200; in Washington, 155–59, 164–65, 175–77, 181, 261–63; in Wisconsin, 151, 163–64, 173–74, 181, 244–45, 282–83, 403n.137. *See also* American Farm Bureau Federation; American Society of Equity; Farmers Alliance; Farmers' Union
agrarian interests, 175–76; and agrarian de-

mocracy, 147, 169; identified with national interest, 146–48; regional conflicts over, 176–77; and socialists, 370n.61
Agricultural Adjustment Administration, 5
Agricultural Bloc, 29, 168, 183, 297, 304. *See also* Farm Bloc
agricultural experiment stations, 5, 178; federal funding of, 312; metaphor of, 65; ties to agrarian associations, 174–75, 374n.131; in Wisconsin, 245, 387n.39
agricultural laborers, organization of, 372n.86
agricultural productivity, and employment, 151, 163, 245
Alcohol Education Act (Washington), 215
Aldrich, John H., 3
Alford, Robert, 10, 55
All-American Farmer-Labor Cooperative Congress, 163, 299, 318; delegates to, 399n.84. *See also* farmer-labor alliance
Alley, Brother O. F., 222
alternative models, 11, 144, 323; evidence of, 60; institutionalization of, 58. *See also* organizational repertoires
ambition theory, of political careers, 338n.81, 370n.59
American Association for Labor Legislation, 137, 311, 388n.75, 402n.114, 403n.127
American Farm Bureau Federation, 5, 168; alliances with party politicians, 373n.102; in California, 163, 165–66, 252; and cooperative marketing, 372n.83; membership, 94, 147; as national lobby, 303
American Federation of Labor (AFL), 5,

437

agrarian democracy, 146–48, 171; and theory of representation, 170. *See also* group interest; partial interest; privileged class

special legislation, California laws against, 120

spectacular politics, 22, 24, 27, 384n.158

Spencer, Herbert, 48

spiritualists, 187, 216

Spokane Chamber of Commerce, 264

Spokane Trades Council, 110, 366n.166

Sprague, Rev. Lila F., 208

Stanton, Elizabeth Cady, 189

state agencies, 292; agrarian associations and, 146, 160–61, 164, 172–75, 177–81, 239, 244–45, 372n.86; and articulation of group interests, 173, 279, 291; autonomy of, 385n.1; in California, 126, 166, 172, 174–75, 254, 257–58, 279, 363n.10; as campaign promises, 276, 297, 306, 320, 398n.76; capture by, 181; centralization of, 273, 323; and expertise, 239; funding of, 247; organized labor and, 130, 137, 243–44, 263–65; and postwar retrenchment, 277, 280, 283–85, 292, 295–96; voluntary associations and, 236, 249, 257–58, 265, 269–70; in Washington, 130, 228, 261, 263–65, 268–69, 280; in Wisconsin, 137, 164, 242–50, 279; women's associations and, 185, 194, 207, 219–24, 254, 264–65, 309; and women's careers, 254–55

state capacity, 27

state expansion, 239, 316–17; agrarian opposition to, 175, 179–80, 261–62; and group interests, 279; led by women's associations, 185–86, 194–95, 219–24, 228–31, 253–54; and organized labor, 257; and taxation, 252–53, 266, 284

State Industrial Commission, plan for, 138

state marketing boards, 162, 247, 282

state polities: institutionalization of, 239–42, 269–72; typology of, 240, 242

states' rights, and woman suffrage movement, 86

State Taxpayers League (California), 285

Stephens, William D., 285

Stinchcombe, Arthur, 323

Stone, Lucy, 89, 187

strikes, 108, 111, 274–75

subjective models, 48. *See also* cognitive models

suffrage: educational, 58, 382n.118; home protection, 191; municipal, 87; school, 209. *See also* voting; woman suffrage

Sundquist, James, 400n.90

Sunkist, 166

Sunshine Society, 277

suspended sentence, as regulatory mechanism, 284

Sutro, Adolph, 157

Taft, Philip, 362n.85

Taft, William Howard, 265

Tammany Hall, 232

Taubeneck, Herman, 159

taxation, 240–42; and agrarian associations, 93, 151, 165, 175, 178–80, 235, 266; in California, 151, 178–80, 250, 252, 279, 284–86; and increased public spending, 236, 240, 284–86; in Washington, 165, 175, 235, 261–62; in Wisconsin, 374n.135. *See also* income tax

temperance, 43, 74, 220; and antipartisanship, 267; in California, 179, 192, 215; and organized labor, 142; regional variation in support of, 293; in Washington, 142, 215, 267, 393n.122; in Wisconsin, 225; *See also* political corruption, and liquor interests; prohibition

third-party politics, 25, 117, 77, 297–99; and agrarian associations, 156–61; approximated by electoral blocs, 304–5; in California, 120–21, 138–39; and organized labor, 101, 103, 104, 113, 114, 130–31, 281; in Washington, 130–31, 261, 271, 289; in Wisconsin, 113, 114–17, 137, 181. *See also* Anti-Masonic Party; farmer-labor alliance; Greenback-Labor Party; Nonpartisan League; People's Party; Progressive Party; Social Democratic Party; Socialist Labor Party; Union Labor Party, Workingmen's Party; party model

ticket splitting, 27, 297

Tilden, Samuel, 24